POPULATION ECONOMICS

POPULATION ECONOMICS

Selected Essays of JOSEPH J. SPENGLER

Compiled by Robert S. Smith, Frank T. de Vyver, and William R. Allen

Duke University Press · Durham, North Carolina · 1972

© 1972, Duke University Press

LCC card number 78-17209

ISBN 0-8223-0286-1

HB
871
S652

PRINTED IN THE UNITED STATES OF AMERICA
BY KINGSPORT PRESS, INC.

Foreword

Friends of Joseph J. Spengler—including students, colleagues, and other professional associates—have long wanted republication of an appropriate collection of his essays. The initiative in arranging this book was taken primarily by the late Robert S. Smith, Frank T. de Vyver, and William R. Allen.

During his remarkable career as a scholar, spanning a period of more than forty years, Professor Spengler was on the faculties of Ohio State University and the University of Arizona before permanently joining Duke University in 1934. He has carried the title of James B. Duke Professor since 1955. Among the most honored of economists, Professor Spengler has been President of the American Economic Association, the Southern Economic Association, and the Population Association of America, and he has been Vice President of the American Economic Association and the Economic History Association.

His enormous outpouring of published research has reflected an extraordinary catholicity of interests, extending beyond economics into sociology, history, and political science. Within his widesweeping scholarly output, three subject areas have bulked large: population, history of economic theory, and economic development. The papers of this volume represent all three areas, oriented throughout toward analysis of population and including studies of the history of population theory and of applications of such theory to issues of development.

The essays in this collection appeared in publications which follow a diversity of editorial practice. Rather than attempt to impose on their styles what would be at best a superficial consistency, they are reprinted in essentially their original form. The compilers thank the publishers and journals named below for permission to reprint these collected essays.

Canadian Political Science Association and University of Toronto Press for "Malthus's Total Population Theory: A Restatement and Reappraisal" from *Canadian Journal of Economics and Political Science,* 11, Copyright 1945.

Harvard University Press for "Pareto on Population" from *The Quarterly Journal of Economics,* 58, 59, Copyright 1944 by the President and Fellows of Harvard College.

The London School of Economics and Political Science for "Marshall on the Population Question" from *Population Studies,* 8, Copyright 1955.

Southern Economic Association and University of North Carolina for "Aspects of the Economics of Population Growth" and "Was Malthus Right?" from *Southern Economic Journal,* 14, 23, Copyright 1947, 1948 and 1966.

"Journalfranz" Arnulf Liebing, oHG, 87 Würzburg, Germany for "Some Economic Aspects of the Subsidization by the State of the Formation of 'Human Capital'" and "Limitational Factors in Population Theory: A Note" from *Kyklos*, 4, 7, Copyright 1950 and 1954.

Societa Italiana di Sociologia for "Measures of Population Maladjustment" from *Proceedings of the XIVth International Congress of Sociology*, 3, Copyright 1951.

Scientia for "Welfare Economics and the Problem of Overpopulation" from *Scientia*, 89, Copyright 1954.

Population Reference Bureau for "The Aesthetics of Population" from *Population Bulletin*, 13, Copyright 1957.

University of Chicago Press for "Capital Requirements and Population Growth in Underdeveloped Countries: Their Interrelations" and "Population Change: Cause, Effect, Indicator" from *Economic Development and Cultural Change*, 4, 9, Copyright 1956 and 1961.

American Economic Association for "The Population Obstacle to Economic Betterment," "The Population Problem: Dimensions, Potentialities, Limitations" and "The Economist and the Population Question" from *American Economic Review*, 41, 46, 56, Copyright 1951, 1956 and 1966.

American Philosophical Society for "Economic Factors in the Development of Densely Populated Areas" from *Proceedings of the American Philosophical Society*, 95, Copyright 1951.

American Association for the Advancement of Science for "Population and World Economic Development" from *Science*, 131, Copyright 1960.

FRANK T. DE VYVER

WILLIAM R. ALLEN

Contents

HISTORY OF THOUGHT

Malthus's Total Population Theory: A Restatement and Reappraisal[1]

Commentators on Malthus's population theory have generally based their remarks upon the *Essay,* particularly upon his observation that "population invariably increases where the means of subsistence increase, unless prevented by some very powerful and obvious checks" which are resolvable into "moral restraint, vice, and misery."[2] They have overlooked important passages in the *Essay,* having to do with the circumstances on which depend the increase and the *availability* of subsistence, and, therefore, the growth of population.[3] They have overlooked his extended consideration of the question of population in the *Principles* where his primary concern was the increase of the supplies on which population growth depends.[4] They

1. Our references are generally to first (1798), second (1803), and last (sixth, 1826) editions of the *Essay on the Principle of Population.* We have used the 1926 reprint of the first edition and the edition published, with introduction by G. T. Bettany, in 1890 (London), as a re-edition of the sixth. When the last edition differs from the second, the difference is noted; and when otherwise advisable, reference is made to both editions. Our references are to the second edition of the *Principles of Political Economy* (London, 1836; reprinted in 1936) except when the second edition differs significantly from the first (1820), which is rarely for the purposes of the present study. Use has been made of several of Malthus's pamphlets, cited in the text; of articles by Malthus in the *Edinburgh Review* (July, 1808, vol. VII, pp. 336–55; July, 1821, vol. XXXV, pp. 362–77) and in the *Quarterly Review* (January, 1824, vol. XXIV, pp. 297–334); of an article attributed to Malthus (*Edinburgh Review,* Aug., 1810, vol. XVI, pp. 464–76); of G. W. Zinke, "Six Letters from Malthus to Pierre Prevost" (*Journal of Economic History,* vol. II, 1942, pp. 174–89); of Malthus's letters (1829) to N. W. Senior, printed in the latter's *Two Lectures on Population* (London, 1829); and of *A Summary View of the Principle of Population* (London, 1830), an abridgment of the article on population done by Malthus, apparently in late 1822, for the 1824 Supplement to the *Encyclopaedia Britannica.* Malthus's opinions, expressed in *A Summary View,* are the same as those expressed in the last editions of the *Essay* and the *Principles.* Aspects of Malthus's work have been well treated by, among others, J. Bonar, *Malthus and His Work* (London, 1924), and J. H. Hollander, in his introduction to David Ricardo's *Notes on Malthus* (Baltimore, 1928), edited by Hollander and T. E. Gregory. The population situation in England in Malthus's lifetime has been treated by T. H. Marshall in "The Population Problem during the Industrial Revolution" (*Economic History* [Supplement to *Economic Journal*], vol. I, 1929, pp. 429–56) and "The Population of England and Wales from the Industrial Revolution to the World War" (*Economic History Review,* vol. V, 1935, pp. 65–78); M. C. Buer, *Health, Wealth, and Population, 1760–1815* (London, 1926); G. T. Griffith, *Population Problems of the Age of Malthus* (London, 1926).

2. *Essay,* p. 14; cf. 1st ed., pp. 140–1.

3. E.g., his qualifying footnote (*Essay,* p. 14, also p. 295; first added in the 1817 edition): "It should be observed that, by an increase in the means of subsistence, is here meant such an increase as will enable the mass of the society to command more food. An increase might certainly take place, which in the actual state of a particular society would not be distributed to the lower classes, and consequently would give no stimulus to population."

4. In the *Essay,* well described by Bonar (*Malthus,* p. 5) as an inquiry "into the nature and causes of poverty," Malthus "endeavoured to trace the causes which practically keep down the population of a country to the level of its actual supplies"; while in the *Principles* his object was "to shew what are the causes which influence these supplies, or call the powers of production forth into the shape of increasing wealth." See *ibid.,* p. 309; 1st ed., p. 345.

have, therefore, missed his *total* population theory, and the manner in which it developed.

It is our purpose, in this essay, to discover the *whole* of Malthus's population theory, and to indicate, in some measure, the views of earlier and contemporary writers regarding elements of which this theory is composed.[5] In section I we discuss Malthus's theory of economic progress and the "effectual demand" for labour, as it relates to the population question. While this discussion is based upon the *Principles* much more than upon the *Essay* and other writings, it is evident, as we state in the conclusion, that Malthus's theory of demand probably evolved out of his consideration of the population question. In section II, we examine Malthus's treatment of industrialization, in which he apparently found a workable solution to both the problem of economic progress and the question of population. In section III we examine his views on luxury, on the exportation of "work," and on the encouragement of population growth, together with his conception of optimum population and his supposed role as a counter-revolutionary. Consideration of these topics serves to illuminate his social philosophy and to bring into sharper focus aspects of his theory treated in sections I and II.

I

It is in Malthus's *Principles* that we find most fully developed the thesis that the progress of population in number and well-being depends upon the maintenance and expansion of the "effectual demand" for labour.[6] True, a number of writers anticipated Malthus in making population growth dependent upon the state of employment, but none developed, as he did, the importance and pre-conditions of an "effective demand" for labour. In several papers, written in 1751–60, Benjamin Franklin reasons that population growth depends upon employment, "room," the ease with which families may be supported, and habits of consumption.[7] His arguments, advanced in support of freedom on the part of the American colonists, to expand

---

5. In the second edition (preface) Malthus states that he deduced the main argument of the first essay from the writings of Hume, Wallace, Adam Smith, and R. Price. The writings of Condorcet and Godwin, of course, gave form and direction to his argument. He both rejected and adopted views set forth in William Paley's widely read *Principles of Moral and Political Philosophy* (London, 1785). Among the writers who saw that poverty arises from "a too rapid increase of population" Malthus numbered Plato, Aristotle, Montesquieu, Benjamin Franklin, James Steuart, Arthur Young, Joseph Townsend, and some of the Physiocrats. The editions of the *Essay* of most significance are the first, the second, and the fifth. He gave final form to most of what he had to say in the fifth (1817). Our references, of course, are usually to the sixth which, for the purpose of the present discussion, is virtually identical with the fifth.

6. This thesis is set forth most fully in the last chapter of the *Principles* where he treats of "the immediate causes of the progress of wealth"; it appears in substantially the same form in the 1836 as in the 1820 edition.

7. On Franklin's views see my "Malthusianism in Eighteenth Century America" (*American Economic Review*, vol. XXV, 1935, pp. 691–8). Franklin's *Observations . . . etc.*, written in 1751 and published in 1755, were printed in Burke's *Annual Register* (London) in 1760. Franklin's recommendation that Canada be annexed by Britain, a recommendation based in part upon

geographically and industrially, were echoed by several English writers. "So that one of our Countrymen established in *America*, finds full Employment for several Hands here; and as full Employment will always draw people, it plainly follows from thence, that our Settlements abroad must increase the Number of People at home."[8] Arthur Young asked: "Is it not evident that demand for hands, that is employment, must regulate the numbers of the people?"[9] Steuart declared that mankind "must ever be, in proportion to the food produced"; but he added that "provided there be a demand for man, whatever use he be put to, the species will multiply" as long as "food is to be found."[10] Adam Smith observed that marriage and multiplication are encouraged when the demand for labour "is continually increasing."[11] Howlett, in a criticism of Price's view that England had suffered a decline in population, mentions "room," urban markets for agricultural products, and the prospect of employment, as conducive to population growth.[12] From his "fundamental proposition" Paley deduced, among other things, that: "Employment affects population 'directly,' as it affords the only medium of distribution, by which individuals can obtain from the common stock a supply for the wants of their families: it affects population 'indirectly,' as it augments the stock itself of provision, in the only way by which the production of it can be effectually encouraged, by furnishing purchasers."[13]

his population thesis, was followed. Malthus refers to Franklin in the second and later editions of the *Essay* (i, i). Malthus got from a pamphlet by Styles and cited by Price evidence that the American population was doubling in twenty-five years (*Essay*, 1st ed., pp. 105, 185). Adam Smith, too, stated that population doubled in twenty to twenty-five years in the British colonies in North America. See *Wealth of Nations* (Cannan edition, Modern Library), pp. 70, 392.

8. John Campbell, *The Present State of Europe* (London, 1753, 4th ed.), p. 508. Arthur Young cites this passage with approval in his *Political Arithmetic* (London, 1774), pp. 107–9. A similar argument appeared in *An Account of the European Settlements in America* (London, 1758), vol. II, pp. 293ff., attributed to Edmund Burke. Adam Smith (*Wealth of Nations*, p. 416) observed that the discovery of America opened new markets, intensified divisions of labour and improvements, and augmented wealth and income; it must, therefore, on his principles, have facilitated population growth in Europe and England.

9. *Political Arithmetic*, p. 86; also pp. 61–2, 68–9, 91, 107ff., 319–20. Franklin is cited on p. 68. Young took exception to James Steuart's making population depend immediately upon the quantity of food instead of upon employment which gives man the "value of food." Malthus later criticized opinions such as Young's "Increase your people as much as you please, food will increase with them" (*ibid.*, p. 69).

10. *An Inquiry into the Principles of Political Economy* (1767) (*Works*, London, 1805, vol. I, pp. 31, 49; also pp. 30, 49, 73, 191, 193). On p. 154 he speaks of "the *effectual* demand . . . which makes the husbandman labour . . . ." His italics.

11. *Wealth of Nations*, p. 80, also pp. 68–9, 79, 81.

12. John Howlett, *Examination of Dr. Price's Essays on the Population of England and Wales*, etc. (1781). See J. Bonar, *Theories of Population from Raleigh to Arthur Young* (New York, 1931), pp. 210–11; C. E. Stangeland, *Pre-Malthusian Doctrines of Population* (New York, 1904), p. 348; sec. III (iv) of this article.

13. *Principles of Moral and Political Philosophy*, p. 453. His fundamental proposition was (p. 443): "Wherever the commerce between the sexes is regulated by marriage, and a provision for that mode of subsistence, to which each class of the community is accustomed, can be procured with ease and certainty, there the number of the people will increase; and the rapidity, as well as the extent of the increase will be proportioned to the degree in which the causes exist."

Malthus's thesis appears in the *Essay,* especially in the later editions, but does not stand out; because he was not there greatly concerned, as in the *Principles,* with what makes for progress in "supplies." Nor is it evident, in the *Essay,* by what writers, if any, he was influenced with respect to the effect of the state of employment upon population growth. His thesis appears to be vaguely foreshadowed in the first edition; and in the second, a number of its elements are discussed. In the fifth edition, finally, he achieved a greater integration of his earlier and narrower treatment of demographic matter with his developed analysis of the dependence of population growth upon employment, and with his discussion of the circumstances upon which progress in wealth and employment rests. Yet his *total* population theory is hardly to be gleaned from the *Essay* alone; it must be discovered in both the *Essay* and the *Principles.*

Malthus's primary concern in the last chapter of the *Principles* is "the progress of Wealth" and what conditions this progress. It is taken for granted that what makes for progress in wealth makes for progress in number and well-being. This is not quite his view in the first and second editions of the *Essay* where he makes the progress of the "labouring poor" (i.e., the vast majority) in number and well-being depend predominantly upon "the increase of the funds destined for the maintenance of labour" – i.e., upon the food supply made available to the masses; and where he points out that these funds do not tend to keep pace with wealth[14] as defined by Adam Smith. In the fifth edition, however, he writes: "A rapid increase of wealth indeed, whether it consists principally in additions to the means of subsistence or to the stock of conveniences and comforts, will always *ceteris paribus,* have a favourable effect on the poor." But he adds that it will have this effect only if "individual prudence" is joined with the skill and industry that produce wealth.[15]

In the first *Essay,* in reply to Godwin, Malthus commented briefly on the demand for labour, and justified expenditure by the wealthy, but he gave no prominence to the demand factor and its determinants.[16] The frugal man,

14. 1st ed., chap. XVI; 2d ed., III. vii. He repeats the proposition that the funds for the maintenance of labour do not bear a fixed relation to wealth and capital in the last edition (III. xiii) and in the *Principles* (2d ed., pp. 234–5). See also below, sections II and III. Adam Smith had said that it is not the actual greatness of national wealth (i.e., "revenue" and "stock") "but its continual increase, which occasions a rise in the wages of labour"; that "the progressive state is the best for the labouring poor"; and that wages are low in a stationary state and inadequate in a declining state. The "demand for labour, according as it happens to be increasing, stationary, or declining" requires an "increasing, stationary, or declining population" (*Wealth of Nations,* pp. 69, 71, 73, 81, 85). With this statement Malthus would agree in so far as the "demand for labour" is resolvable into "funds . . . for the maintenance of labour." See note 27, below.

15. 5th ed., III, xiii, last paragraph; 6th ed., *ibid.*

16. In his essay, "Of Avarice and Profusion," William Godwin sought to refute the "currently established" maxim that "it is the duty of the rich man to live up to his fortune," and to demonstrate that the "profuse" man injures the mass of mankind in much greater measure than does

he declared after Adam Smith, saves from his income to add to his capital; and this he uses to maintain "productive labour," or to lend to others "who will probably employ it in this way." Godwin's "avaricious man," on the contrary, "locks up his wealth in a chest, and sets in motion no labour of any kind, either productive or unproductive"; he "locks up the power of producing" wealth and denies to workers a market for their labour.[17] Malthus remarked also that whereas several centuries earlier there was "much less labour in England, in proportion to the population," and more "dependence," there was now more work and less dependence because the introduction of manufactures had enabled the poor "to give something in exchange for the provisions of the great Lords, instead of being dependent upon their bounty."[18] He indicated, moreover, that an "increasing demand for labour," together with an "increasing produce," ameliorates the condition of the labourer and thus encourages marriage.[19]

"What is mainly necessary to a rapid increase of population, is a great and continued demand for labour," he wrote in 1820.[20] If the demand for labour is not sufficient to convert "supplies" into consumable provisions[21] and

---

the "avaricious" man. The avaricious man lives a life of self-denial; he does not burden the labouring poor, and yet he does not lock up physical goods against use by his contemporaries. The many wants of the profuse man, on the contrary, but increase the burden of work upon the poor and deprive them of the leisure and means necessary to "intellectual cultivation"; whence, whoever invents a new dish or creates a new luxury, adds to the hardship and drudgery of the lower orders but not to their wages and comfort. See *The Enquirer* (Philadelphia, 1797), pp. 135–48; also *Enquiry Concerning Political Justice* (Philadelphia, 1796), vol. II, bk. VIII, chap. II, pp. 316ff.

17. *Essay,* 1st ed., pp. 282–5, 295–8. Even supposing production were not checked, how could the unemployed establish title to "a proper share of the food and raiment produced by the society?" (*ibid.,* pp. 298–300). See also sec. III (iii) of this article.

18. *Ibid.,* pp. 293–4. This statement was obviously inspired by Godwin's comment (*Enquirer,* p. 140) that several centuries earlier, when there "was little of manufacture," the great proprietors could not, together with their families, consume all the foodstuffs to which they had title.

19. *Essay,* 1st ed., p. 119. Wages are made to depend, in the first edition, upon the ratio of workers to "the fund appropriated to the maintenance of labour, . . . the aggregate quantity of food possessed by the owners of land beyond their own consumption" (*ibid.,* pp. 205, 305–6). It followed that population pressure was the real cause of low wages (*ibid.,* pp. 30–6, 82–3); that it was better to increase agricultural than non-agricultural production (e.g., 324–6); that an increase in the ratio of proprietors to labourers would benefit the latter and facilitate population growth (*ibid.,* pp. 344–5). He was still thinking predominantly, as did so many eighteenth-century writers (e.g., see my *French Predecessors of Malthus,* Durham, 1942) in terms of an essentially cereal or provision standard of life.

20. *Principles,* 1st ed., p. 261. In the second edition, p. 234, he writes "essentially necessary"; see also *ibid.,* p. 224.

21. The term "wage goods," as used by modern writers, does not quite represent Malthus's later view inasmuch as he looked upon provisions as the limitational factor (see note 26, below). Following F. M. Eden, Malthus supposed that in a labourer's family of average size two-fifths of the expenditures went for bread or meal, one for meat and dairy products and potatoes, and two for house-rent, fuel, soap, candles, tea, sugar, and clothing. It followed that the price of corn, while it exerted a powerful influence upon the price of labour, did not regulate it "wholly"; and that corn and labour rarely kept "an even pace together." See *Observations on the Effects*

channel these goods to the labouring masses, the growth of the latter in number and well-being is retarded.[22] Accordingly, assuming that subsistence is obtainable, the measure of population is the quantity of employment. For employment regulates "the wages of labour, on which the power of the lower classes of people to procure food depends; and according as the employment of the country is increasing, whether slowly or rapidly, these wages will be such, as either to check or encourage early marriages; such as to enable a labourer to support only two or three, or as many as five or six children."[23]

The continuation of an effective demand for labour is necessary, in the short as well as in the long run, to the continuation of population growth, well-being and nuptiality fluctuating with the short-run demand for labour. Population growth oscillates because a population cannot immediately adjust the supply of labour to oscillations in the demand for it. "But though the progress of population is mainly regulated by the effective demand for labour, it is obvious that the number of people cannot conform itself immediately to the state of this demand. Some time is required to bring more labour into the market when it is wanted; and some time to check the supply when it is flowing in with too great rapidity."[24] When the demand for labour declines sharply, population growth falls off even though provisions are plentiful, because marriages are less frequent when the prospect of employment is poor. "If the general demand for labour fail, particularly if the failure be sudden, the labouring classes will be wretched in the midst of cheapness; if the demand for labour be considerable, they will be comparatively rich in the midst of dearness."[25]

---

of the Corn Laws (1814), edited by J. H. Hollander (Baltimore, 1932), pp. 9–11, 15, 20; also *Inquiry into the Nature and Progress of Rent* (1815), edited by J. H. Hollander (Baltimore, 1903), pp. 39–42.

22. "An increase in the means of subsistence . . . which in the actual state of a particular society would not be distributed to the lower classes, . . . would give no stimulus to population" (*Essay*, p. 14. n. added in 1817; also p. 295, cf. 2d ed., p. 421). See also below on family earnings.

23. *Essay*, p. 426; 2d ed., p. 471. See also *Essay*, pp. 93–4. 127. 138–9. 172; 2d ed., pp. 119–20, 162. 178. 221.

24. *Essay*, p. 331; also pp. 428–9 (2d ed., p. 471). On oscillation of population growth see sec. III (iii) of this article. In a small country, with little variety of employment and a snug fit of population to available employment, nuptiality is more sensitive to conditions of employment than where numbers are great and the employment situation is obscure (*Essay*, pp. 144–6; 2d ed., pp. 186–8).

25. *Principles*, pp. 436–7; also p. 437n. (not in 1st ed.) where he says that when there is no demand for labour, "charity" is their only source of food. See also *Essay*, pp. 331, 429; 2d ed., pp. 471–2; *Quarterly Review*, 1824, pp. 326–7. Malthus's concern above is with the decline in the demand for labour that developed upon the termination of the Napoleonic wars. See *Principles*, II. i, 10; J. J. O'Leary, "Malthus's General Theory of Employment and the Post-Napoleonic Depressions" (*Journal of Economic History*, vol. III, 1943, pp. 185–200). See sec. III (iii) of this article, on public works and emigration. Malthus's attitude toward manufacturing was conditioned in part by his belief that employment therein was uncertain and unstable (*Essay*, pp. 420–3; 2d ed., III, vii).

A country's population may fall far short of its capacity to support numbers at the same time that it is redundant in relation to employment opportunities. For while the potential population capacity of a country is fixed by its resources,[26] the progress of a country's population in number and well-being depends upon the growth of the "effectual demand" for labour. If this demand does not continue to increase, the population will not be actuated to increase,[27] and cannot increase, whatever be the country's resource equipment. This demand "is proportioned to the rate of increase in the quantity and value of those funds, whether arising from capital or revenue, which are actually employed in the maintenance of labour."[28] If, for any reason, these funds do not increase and flow to labour, the demand for labour will be checked,[29] even though there "be a great deficiency of population compared with the territory and powers of the country"; and while "it might be very desirable that it should be greater," efforts to encourage the growth of the population will prove futile until an effectual demand for labour develops and wages rise in consequence. Until such demand develops, labour and

26. He uses the term "resources" at times; e.g., see *Essay*, pp. 547–50 (written in 1807). The *limitational* group of resources, however, appears to be food; for he nowhere suggests that some lack other than food fixes the potential maximum. Furthermore, he described "want of food" as the "ultimate check" and as the "most efficient cause of the three immediate checks"; and an "increase in the means of subsistence" as the "only true criterion of a real and permanent increase in the population." See *Essay*, pp. 7. 288. 294; 2d ed., pp. 336. 340. 347. He nowhere observed that what constitutes the *limitational* resource, or group of resources, depends upon the consumption habits of the population, presumably because he supposed this limitational resource to be food. He anticipated that the situation of the labouring classes would improve, if they exercised moral restraint, even though subsistence had come nearly to a stand (Senior, *Two Lectures on Population*, p. 71).

27. "When the demand for labour is either stationary, or increasing very slowly, people not seeing any employment open by which they can support a family, or the wages of common labour being inadequate to this purpose, will of course be deterred from marrying. But if a demand for labour continue increasing with some rapidity, although the supply of food be uncertain, on account of variable seasons and a dependence on other countries, the population will evidently go on, till it is positively checked by famine or the diseases arising from severe want." See *Essay*, p. 429; 2d ed., pp. 471–2. Cf. Adam Smith, note 14 above.

28. *Principles*, p. 234. "These funds consist principally in the necessaries of life, or in the means of commanding the food, clothing, lodging, and firing of the labouring classes of society" (*ibid.*, p. 234); "luxuries" are not included in the "funds . . . for . . . ordinary labour" (*ibid.*, p. 365). This statement does not appear in the first edition (cf. pp. 261. 418–19) where he sometimes uses the term "resources" as he uses the term "funds etc." in the second (cf. 1st ed., p. 246 with 2d ed., p. 223). He had already employed the concept of "funds" (which, as Taussig observes [*Wages and Capital*, New York, 1898. p. 160], he apparently derived from Adam Smith [*Wealth of Nations*, bk. 1. cap. viii]) in the *Essay* (1st ed., p. 305; 2d ed., p. 420). Adam Smith (*ibid.*, p. 421) had made employment depend upon a society's "whole capital." See also note 21 above.

29. Elsewhere (*Quarterly Review*, 1824. pp. 326–7) he said that if the elasticity of demand for produce were less than unity, an increase in the supply of the funds destined for the maintenance of labour would be accompanied by a diminution in the quantity of labour employed. He was thinking in terms of the demand for labour and had in mind a situation in which the demand for produce was slack and the money price of labour apparently was high and sticky in relation to the money price of corn (cf. below, note 48). See also *Principles*, pp. 231–3.

population will be redundant in relation to demand, however deficient they may be in relation to resources.[30]

But supposing that an effective demand for labour continues, how far will population growth proceed in a country? The answer, Malthus's discussion suggests, depends ultimately upon the habits of consumption of the population and upon the skill and industry with which they develop and utilize their resource equipment.[31] Population will come to a stand when cultivation has been pushed to the point where "the labour of a man upon the last land taken into cultivation will scarcely do more than support such a family as is necessary to maintain a stationary population," and when, in consequence, profits sink "to the lowest rate required to maintain the actual capital."[32] Habits of consumption being given, how far cultivation can be pushed depends upon its efficiency. How low wages may fall, and therefore how far cultivation may be pushed, depend upon the habits of the lower classes, or upon "the amount of those necessaries and conveniences, without which they would not consent to keep up their numbers to the required point."[33] He pointed out that population growth never dropped precipitately, but tapered off gradually, the falling off in the rate of increase in the funds destined for labour generating the necessary habits and feelings.[34]

It is worth noting that when Malthus states that population is regulated by wages,[35] he does not mean wage rates; he means family earnings and the purchasing power of the masses. It is the "average earnings of the families of the labouring classes throughout the year on which the encouragement to

30. *Principles*, II, i, 10, pp. 414–15, 424. See also *Essay*, pp. 96, 367–8, 428–30; 2d ed., pp. 122, 472. Malthus reasoned in like manner with respect to capital whose law of increase he compared to that of population. If an effectual demand for capital is lacking, and in consequence the rate of return on it is too low, saving from revenue to add to capital will merely aggravate the distress of the capitalists just as an increase of births augments misery and mortality when an effective demand for labour is lacking (*Principles*, pp. 404, 414–15, 433–5).

31. On the effect of trading relations, here supposed given, see below, sections II and III (ii). The increase of the funds destined for the maintenance of labour depends "upon the degree of industry, intelligence and activity" with which a country's physical powers of production are called forth (*Edinburgh Review*, 1810, p. 467).

32. *Essay*, pp. 400, 420, 428; *Principles*, pp. 281–2, also pp. 114–15, 158–9, 275–6, 278–9, 297–8. Under these circumstances, rent too would come to a stand (*ibid.*, I, iii, pp. 140–3, 146, 154, 160–1, 199, 211). On Malthus's views on rent see Bonar, *Malthus*, pp. 237ff.; Hollander, *Notes*, pp. xxxiv–lxvii. Between interest of landlord and that of state Malthus found the "strictest union" at least so long as a country did not import food; but between other classes (e.g., labour, capitalists) and the state there existed no such close identity of interest (*ibid.*, pp. lxiff.; *Principles*, p. 206). See also sec. III (iii) of this article.

33. *Essay*, pp. 400, 428; *Principles*, I, iv, 2, pp. 224–6, also p. 279. See his discussion of the forces that might bring population growth in Ireland to a stop (*Edinburgh Review*, 1808, pp. 343, 353). Also *Essay*, 2d ed., p. 427, where he refers to Steuart's statement (*Works*, vol. I, chap. XVIII) of the limit to population growth in a commercial state.

34. E.g., see *Edinburgh Review*, 1808, p. 345.

35. Population is "regulated by the real wages of labour" and comes to "a stand when the necessaries which these wages . . . command [are] not sufficient, under the actual habits of the people, to encourage an increase of numbers" (*Essay*, p. 400, not in 2d ed.; also pp. 420, 428; also *Summary View*, pp. 35, 64).

marriage, and the power of supporting children, will depend, and not merely the wages of day-labour estimated in food."[36] The highest rate of population growth, therefore, did not necessarily coincide with the highest real wage rate;[37] in fact "some increase of prices generally accompanies the most effective demand for produce and population."[38] For when prices (including that of "corn") rise, or are rising somewhat, in relation to the money wage rate, there is "fuller employment" (including "task work" and other employment for women and children[39]): and both the money and the real income of the family rise. When, on the contrary, the price of "corn" falls in relation to the money wage rate and employment diminishes, the "command of the labouring classes over the necessaries of life" declines, and with it the stimulus to population growth.[40]

It was commonly assumed, said Malthus, that progress in wealth, and therefore in number and well-being, necessarily accompanies population growth, saving, the introduction of labour-saving inventions, and soil fertility.

This assumption was invalid, he reasoned; it took for granted both that mankind produce and consume at the maximum possible rate, and that every increment in productive power generates an offsetting increment of consumption.

Progress in wealth, without which a continuing increase in numbers cannot take place, is not begotten of the hard pressure of numbers upon subsistence, or of "want alone." Neither "encouragements to population," nor even the "natural tendency of population to increase beyond the funds for its maintenance," furnishes an "effective stimulus" to the continued increase of wealth. If the desire of the labouring classes for "necessaries and con-

---

36. *Essay*, p. 427; also pp. 426–8; not in 2d ed. See also *Edinburgh Review*, 1821, p. 373.

37. The standard of life, differences in which also account for differences in the effect of given real wage rates, is here implicitly supposed constant (*Essay*, p. 428).

38. *Principles*, p. 240, also p. 252; also p. 387, where he suggests that when prices fall, wages lag, and consequently, production and employment decline. An influx of money, occasioned by a favourable balance of trade, Paley had said, encourages population growth: indirectly, by stimulating employment; directly, but only for a time, by increasing money wages faster than the price of provisions (*Principles of Moral and Political Philosophy*, pp. 462–5).

39. Of the extension of the practice of task work, with its long hours and low rates of pay, Malthus disapproved; it was prejudicial to health and happiness, even though it provided temporary relief in times of scarcity. See *Inquiry*, p. 40n.; and cf. *Principles*, p. 279.

40. *Essay*, pp. 426–8; *Principles*, i, iv, 3, 5, pp. 232–4, 239–40, 258–60. Population grew at a higher rate in 1790–1811 than in 1735–55; corn wages were lower in 1790–1811 than in the earlier period but, because of fuller employment and greater parish allowances, the real income of the lower classes was greater. See *Essay*, p. 428; also *Principles*, i. iv, 4–5, and p. 234. When prices are rising, entrepreneurial prospects improve, together with the demand for labour. E.g., see Zinke, "Six Letters from Malthus to Pierre Prevost," pp. 185–7. Malthus attributed the lack of demand for labour and capital at the close of the Napoleonic wars to a diminution of "home revenues" aggravated by "contraction of the currency"; but he rejected proposals to issue paper money, saying that what was wanted was higher prices and lower wages in terms of bullion (*Principles*, i, ii, 10, pp. 416, 424–6, 430–2).

veniences" were a sufficient stimulus to production, Europe would be peopled to the limit of "its power to produce," and the earth would probably contain "at the very least, ten times as many inhabitants as are supported on its surface at present"; and yet, "almost universally," the wealth of states "is very far short of their powers of production." The desire of the labourer for goods and services will avail towards their production only if there is a "reciprocal demand" for his labour. This demand he cannot provide himself; it is forthcoming only when the employers of labour can dispose of its product at a profit. "An increase of population, when an additional quantity of labour is not required, will soon be checked by want of employment and the scanty support of those employed, and will not furnish the required stimulus to an increase of wealth proportioned to the power of production."[41] Here, by his emphasis upon the importance of demand, Malthus is setting limits to the capacity of the principle of population to generate progress, limits not so clearly indicated in the *Essay*.[42]

Of saving he wrote in like vein, even though he esteemed the eighteenth-century virtues, frugality and thrift, and accepted the current opinion that growth of capital depends primarily, not upon science and technology, but upon accumulation which, like labour, is accompanied by "spiritual anguish."[43] Wealth can be increased only through the "conversion of revenue into capital."[44] But saving from revenue "to add to capital" can augment capital and thus facilitate population growth only on condition that it does not diminish the "effectual demand" for commodities and labour. Suppose the productive power of farmers and manufacturers to grow as the result of an increase in the output per worker. If each group is disposed to consume the added increment of output of the other, all will be well. But if one or both parties "were disposed to save largely, with a view of bettering their condition, and providing for their families in future, the state of things would be very different." The demand for labour would diminish; for the manufacturer, "owing to the parsimony of the farmers and the want of demand for manufactures," would be unable to absorb the additional output of the far-

41. *Principles*, II. i, 2. especially p. 313.

42. See sec. III of this article.

43. C. E. Ayres, *The Theory of Economic Progress* (Chapel Hill, 1944), pp. 52–61. The progress of a country in capital equipment, population, and/or well-being, Malthus observed as had Adam Smith (*Wealth of Nations*, p. 464), depends upon "the produce of a country" exceeding "the consumption of those employed in its production" (*Principles*, p. 41).

44. *Principles*, p. 314. Malthus criticized (*ibid.*, p. 314n.) Lauderdale (*Nature and Origin of Public Wealth*, Edinburgh, 1804) for going "much too far in deprecating capital accumulation." Lauderdale (*ibid.*, pp. 339–42) cites Malthus (*Essay*, 2d ed., pp. 9–10) and declares that the distribution of wealth to which the preventive check is to be traced, "in a great degree determines the progress of population throughout the world." Lauderdale quoted with approval (pp. 247–8) Quesnay's attack upon hoarding and emphasis upon consumption, in which view Hollander (*Notes*, p. lxxix) finds the beginning of the doctrine against which Say's law was directed. In his *Letters to Malthus* ([1821], London, 1936) Say did not examine critically Malthus's views on population as enunciated in the *Principles*.

mer; while the farmer, because of the inability of the manufacturer to buy, would lack a market for his added output. Hence Malthus concluded that the adoption of too "parsimonious habits" might be accompanied "by a marked depression of wealth and population."[45]

The "laws that regulate the increase of capital" resemble those which regulate the increase of population. When there is an "effectual demand for commodities . . . a demand by those who are able and willing to pay an adequate price for them" — and in consequence wages and profits are high enough, population and capital tend to increase; if such demand is lacking, they do not increase. Malthus inferred, therefore, that a population might be "greatly redundant, compared with the demand for it and the actual means of supporting it, although it might most properly be considered as deficient, and greatly deficient, compared with the extent of territory, and the powers of such territory to produce additional means of subsistence." In like manner capital might be redundant in relation to a country's demand for it at the same time that such country was under-equipped with capital. In the former situation the encouragement of births would not finally add to population, while in the latter case saving from revenue would add little to the capital supply.[46]

Malthus dealt with soil fertility and invention much as he had dealt with saving; but he emphasized in greater measure the psychological barriers to the expansion of demand upon which he had touched in his discussion of savings. He emphasized, in keeping with his conception of human behavior tendencies,[47] that the demand for income in terms of effort is such as to yield a backward falling supply curve for effort.[48] "An efficient taste for luxuries and conveniences, . . . such . . . as will properly stimulate industry, . . . is a plant of slow growth"; for the "luxury of indolence" tends always to swamp the luxury of goods.[49] It may be true, Malthus states, that those who

45. *Principles*, II, i, 3, pp. 320–6; cf. *Essay*, pp. 94–6, 127; 2d ed. pp. 120–2, 162.

46. *Ibid.*, pp. 328, 326–30, 414–15; also *Essay*, pp. 430–1 (2d ed., pp. 473–4) and sec. III (iv) of this article.

47. See sec. III of this article.

48. Cf. L. Robbins, "On the Elasticity of Demand for Income in Terms of Effort" (*Economica*, vol. X, 1930, pp. 123–9); J. R. Hicks, *Value and Capital* (London, 1939), pp. 36–7; P. H. Douglas, *The Theory of Wages* (New York, 1934), chap. XII. Malthus did not apply this type of analysis in his discussion of saving. See also note 29, above.

49. *Principles*, pp. 320–2, 402–4. The "general desire of mankind to better their condition, and make provision for a family" re-enforced and intensified the limit imposed on the demand for luxuries and conveniences by the "luxury of indolence" (*ibid.*, p. 402). Edward Gibbon, having noted that luxury prompts the landowner to improve his estate and distributes to non-landowners that which they otherwise would not receive, declared that "in the present imperfect condition of society, luxury, though it may proceed from vice or folly, seems to be the only means that can correct the unequal distribution of property" (*The Decline and Fall of the Roman Empire*, Modern Library Edition, vol. I, p. 48). Wallace considered simplicity of tastes most favourable to propagation when lands were evenly divided. Yet he supposed that when many or most men have more land than they need to maintain themselves, they "must be lazy and indolent" and less populous than they would be if arts and manufactures were introduced

possess "fixed monied revenues, obtained by inheritance, or with little or no trouble," stand ready to spend such income and thereby create employment for the labour and capital that satisfies the resulting demand. "But where the amount of the revenues of a country depend[s], in a considerable degree, upon the exertion of labour, activity and attention, there must be something in the commodities to be obtained sufficiently desirable to balance this exertion, or the exertion will cease . . . . Most men place some limits, however variable, to the quantity of conveniences and luxuries which they will labour for."[50] For example, unless cultivators have a taste for conveniences and luxuries which they wish to satisfy out of greater profits, they tend to employ less labour in cultivation when output per unit of labour input increases; and under similar circumstances receivers of profits and rents behave in like manner. The disposition of workers to offer their services is similarly conditioned.[51] Love of indolence, therefore, operates to check progress in wealth, numbers, and well-being.[52] For this reason, in part, Malthus came to look with greater favour upon industrialization, which tends to expand tastes and move the curve of supply of effort downward and to the right.

---

among them, their tastes were refined, their wants were increased, and their desires were excited by alluring objects: "this awakens ambition, kindles emulation, quickens industry, and engages men to labour, that they may procure the tempting objects they desire"; and it facilitates progress in wealth and number (*A Dissertation on the Numbers of Mankind in Ancient and Modern Times*, Edinburgh, 1753, pp. 27–9); but see sec. III (i)–(iii) of this article. See also C. Montesquieu, *De l'esprit des lois* (1748), XXIII, xv, IV, iv.

50. *Principles*, p. 355.

51. *Ibid.*, pp. 320–1. This thesis is well developed in the *Essay*. "If the labourer can obtain the full support of himself and family by two or three days labour," he will usually prefer leisure rather than work the remainder of the week "to furnish himself with conveniences and comforts" (*Essay*, pp. 424–5). In the first edition (pp. 77–8) Malthus suggests that an increase in money wages alone would cause workers to fancy themselves richer and therefore to reduce the number of hours of labour they stood ready to supply.

52. E.g., see *Principles*, pp. 337, 340; *Essay*, pp. 424–5. Adam Smith did not estimate the demand for income in terms of effort as did Malthus. "The desire of food is limited in every man by the narrow capacity of the human stomach; but the desire of the conveniences and ornaments of building, dress, equipage, and household furniture seems to have no limit or certain boundary" (*Wealth of Nations*, p. 164). Plenty did not cause men, as a rule, to relax their industry. "Some workmen, indeed, when they can earn in four days what will maintain them through the week, will be idle the other three. This, however, is by no means the case with the greater part. Workmen, on the contrary, when they are liberally paid by the piece, are very apt to over-work themselves . . ." (*ibid.*, p. 81, also pp. 82–3). Steuart (*Works*, vol. I, p. 193) had remarked that "the most delicate liver in Paris will not put more of the earth's productions into his belly, than another"; but he added that "there are no bounds to the consumption of *work*." Steuart believed, however, that where men are lazy, or tastes and manners are simple, cultivation tends to be restrained and with it multiplication; he considered such nations "in a *moral incapacity* of multiplying" (*ibid.*, pp. 38–40, 44, 47, 157). Human happiness, observed Hume, consists in "action, pleasure, indolence." When the "mechanical arts" are undeveloped, there is left to men only indolence, and it loses much of its relish because it does not succeed to labour. Where there is no taste and no demand for "superfluities, men sink into indolence, lose all enjoyment of life, and are useless to the public." See "Of Luxury" (*Essays Moral, Political, and Literary*, edited by T. H. Green and T. H. Grose, New York, 1898, vol. I, pp. 300–3). Hume later entitled this essay, "Of Refinement in the Arts."

In view of the shape of the supply curve of effort, a continued increase of wealth and population is not necessarily assured when the soil is fertile and production is easy; these conditions, in fact, may permit and foster indolence and so check progress in number and well-being. Fertility of the soil conduces to production only if there is an effective demand for work and product, for income in terms of effort; only if the owners of land are incited by the prospect of conveniences and luxuries to evoke its productive powers, and the labouring classes are pressed by "the want of necessaries" to create conveniences and luxuries.[53] If these conditions do not prevail, labourers will be disposed to put forth only enough effort to win an easy subsistence; landowners, content with little luxury other than retainers, will call forth small agricultural output; and few persons will engage in the production of conveniences and necessities. Whence there may at once be overpopulation in relation to the demand for labour and underpopulation in relation to resources. These unpropitious circumstances are found when, as under feudalism, the ownership of land is concentrated in the hands of the few, and "caprice and indolence . . . prevent many from cultivating their lands." He pointed, by way of extreme illustration, to Ireland and New Spain. "The power of supporting [or "employing"] labour may exist to a much greater extent than the will . . . . The necessity on the part of labourers of employing only a small portion of time in producing food does not always occasion the employment of a greater portion of time in procuring conveniences and luxuries . . . . The deficiency of wealth in a fertile country may be more owing to want of demand than to want of capital . . . . The fertility of soil alone is not an adequate stimulus to the permanent increase of wealth."[54]

Malthus approved all saving of labour and inventions because "their tendency is to increase the gross produce and to make room for a larger population and a larger capital."[55] But of the introduction of labour-saving inventions, which are "the natural consequence of improvement and civilization," he wrote as of the fertility of land.

53. Among the three causes of rent Malthus numbered "that quality peculiar to the necessaries of life of being able, *when properly distributed,* to create their own demand, or to raise up . . . demanders in proportion to . . . necessaries produced." See *Principles,* 1st ed., pp. 139–40, 541; 2d ed., p. 140; *Inquiry,* p. 18; Hollander, *Notes,* pp. xlviff.; my italics. While an increase in raw produce alone cannot occasion a proportionate increase in population, Malthus noted, it should be recollected that land produces besides food the materials for clothing, lodging, and firing—the means, in short, by which people are brought into being and supported. Land thus differs from every other kind of machine. See *Principles,* 1st ed., pp. 141–2; 2d ed., p. 142. Malthus's discussion here is not well integrated with that in the text above.

54. *Principles,* II, i, 4, especially pp. 344, 351, 331–5, 342–3, also *Essay,* e.g., I, ix (in 2d ed.). Cf. Malthus's views (e.g., *Principles,* pp. 342–3) with those of Cantillon and Garnier (in *French Predecessors,* chap. IV). Hume ("Of Commerce," *Essays,* vol. I, pp. 298–9) remarked that favourable agricultural conditions sometimes make for poverty. In Ireland, Malthus observed (*Edinburgh Review,* 1808, p. 341), indolence and holidays restricted the supply of labour and thus prevented wage rates from falling as much as they otherwise would; in this instance the effect was beneficial.

55. *Principles,* p. 370, note on Ricardo's treatment of "gross and net revenue." See also Hollander, *Notes,* pp. xcii–xcvi.

The pre-eminent advantages derived from the substitution of machinery for manual labour, depend upon the extension of the market for the commodities produced, and the increased stimulus given to consumption; . . . without this extension of market and increase of consumption, they must be in a considerable degree diminished. Like the fertility of land, the invention of good machinery confers a prodigious power of production. But neither of these great powers can be called fully into action, if the situation and circumstances, or the habits and tastes of the society prevent the opening of a sufficient market, and an adequate increase of consumption.[56]

Unless the power to produce is united in proper proportion with the "means of distribution," Malthus concluded, it will not beget wealth and population.

The powers of production, to whatever extent they may exist, are not alone sufficient to secure the creation of a proportionate degree of wealth. Something else seems to be necessary in order to call these powers fully into action. This is an effectual and unchecked demand for all that is produced. And what appears to contribute most to the attainment of this object, is, such a distribution of produce, and such an adaptation of this produce to the wants of those who are to consume it, as constantly to increase the exchangeable value of the whole mass.[57]

Of this thesis Malthus had found support in the increase of the English population in 1800–10, which he attributed to a greatly increased demand for labour, combined with increased powers of production in both agriculture and manufactures. "What has taken place is a striking illustration of the principle of population, and a proof that in spite of great towns, manufacturing occupations, and the gradually-acquired habits of an opulent and luxuriant people, if the resources of a country will admit of rapid increase, and if these resources are so advantageously distributed as to occasion a constantly-increasing demand for labour, the population will not fail to keep pace with them."[58] Production and general wealth, "like particular portions of it," always proceed in the wake of "effectual demand," — savings generally issuing out of the "increase in the value of the national revenue" without diminishing demand and consumption; and population follows. But when the

56. *Principles*, II, i, 5, p. 360; also 355–7.

57. *Principles*, II, i, 6, p. 361. Distribution, as Malthus used the term, adapts products, "in quantity and quality, to the actual tastes and wants of the consumers, and creates new tastes and wants by means of greater facilities of intercourse" (*ibid.*, p. 371; not in 1st ed.). Paley (*Principles of Moral and Political Philosophy*, pp. 451ff.) had described "distribution" as "of equal consequence with the production" of provision. On the idea of distribution see E. Cannan, *History of the Theories of Production and Distribution*, 3rd ed., London, 1924, chaps. VI–VIII. Malthus's thesis, stated above, appears in the *Essay*, pp. 93ff., 127, 138–9; 2d ed., pp. 119ff., 162, 178. Malthus criticized both Sismondi's reply to the *Essay* and his assertion that the "free-contract" wages system was responsible for unemployment, poverty, and population pressure (*Principles*, p. 366n.; Zinke, "Six Letters from Malthus to Pierre Prevost," pp. 182ff.).

58. *Essay*, p. 244, 5th ed., II, pp. 103–4.

"two grand elements of wealth," production and distribution, are not conjoined in proper proportions, and distribution cannot therefore satisfactorily circulate produce and give adequate value to it, they do not carry riches and population "to the utmost limits" of the available resources; they "produce only, after the lapse of many thousand years, the scanty riches and scanty population, which are at present scattered over the face of the globe."[59]

In the *Principles,* as in the *Essay,* Malthus described as "most important" with respect to progress in wealth and numbers those elements "which come under the head of politics and morals": e.g., security of property which depends upon the "political constitution of a country," upon its laws, and upon their administration; "those habits" which make for "regular exertions" and "general rectitude of character."[60] But he devoted most attention to conditions which join the will with the power to consume and generate a demand to evoke and offset the power to produce, and which favour "that increase of value which depends upon distribution." These conditions are three in number: division of landed property; internal and external commerce; maintenance of "an adequate proportion" of society in personal services and situations enabling them "to make a demand for material products without contributing directly to their supply."[61]

Writing, as he did, at a time when the feudal land economy still blanketed much of the world, Malthus stressed the fact that the non-division of land was retarding progress in number and well-being. Only if land is sufficiently subdivided to permit an effective demand for produce and labour can wealth and population increase appreciably. Laws and customs which perpetuate, as they did in Europe during feudal times, "a most unequal and vicious division of landed property," retard the growth of wealth and cause countries to "remain for ages very scantily peopled, in spite of the principle of population." This is especially true of inland countries unfavourably situated for foreign and domestic commerce. Great proprietors, as Adam Smith observed, are commonly bad cultivators. Furthermore, even if they are animated by a passion for the consumption of manufactures, they are too few in number to supply a demand sufficient to actuate the production of "any important mass" of manufactured products. "The excessive wealth of the few is in no respect equivalent, with regard to effectual demand, to the more moderate wealth of the many." Natural resources will not be fully exploited, and manufacturing will not flourish, so long as immense landed properties are not broken down and there has not been created "a greater number of demanders in the middle ranks of life who [are] able and willing to purchase the results of productive labour." The judicious division of landed property

59. *Principles,* p. 371, also pp. 363–7, 415, 424. Cf. *Essay,* pp. 95, 428; *Summary View,* pp. 6, 18, 27, 37–40.
60. *Principles,* pp. 309–10; also note 86 below.
61. *Ibid.,* p. 372.

was essential, therefore, to the maintenance and augmentation of the "exchangeable value" of wealth, to the stimulation of production, and to the increase of the population in number and well-being.[62]

To commerce Malthus now attached much greater importance than in his early writings. Internal and external commerce—the "exchange of what is wanted less for what is wanted more"—distributes the produce of a country in a manner consonant with the wants and tastes of the population and thereby increases the "exchangeable value of our possessions, our means of enjoyment, and our wealth." It facilitates the "formation of those wants and tastes, and that desire to consume, which are absolutely necessary to keep up the market prices of commodities, and prevent the fall of profits." It serves to join the will to employ with the ability to employ, and thus to set labour in motion in so far as the available "funds for the maintenance of labour" permit. It operates, in short, to supply that "effectual demand," lack of which occasions stagnation. But since exchange is mediated by money, commerce will help keep labour employed only if the prices of commodities sufficiently exceed the price of the labour embodied therein to allow adequate profits to producers; and this condition is more likely to be met when money wages and prices are stable or rising than when they are falling.[63]

In every society there must be "a considerable class of persons who have both the will and power to *consume more material wealth* than they produce."[64] For in every society there are many who produce more material

62. *Principles*, II, i, 7; *Essay*, pp. 93ff., 127, 134ff. (2d ed., pp. 119ff., 162, 172ff.); also *Principles* (p. 154; cf. p. 199) where he states that improperly conceived taxes upon the produce of land check cultivation and bring population to a premature stop. Although Malthus observed, as had Adam Smith (*Wealth of Nations*, p. 392), that primogeniture checks cultivation (*Essay*, p. 286; 1st ed., p. 344), and that in America "easy division of landed property" had facilitated cultivation and population growth (*Principles*, p. 373), he opposed extreme subdivision, because it prevented efficient cultivation, discouraged "prudence in marriage," and undermined civil liberty. Unlike Ricardo (*Notes*, p. 211), he was alarmed lest the French law of succession bring about a minute subdivision of agricultural property, and, within a century, visit "extraordinary poverty and distress" upon the French people and destroy their republican form of government. See *Principles*, pp. 375–9; *Essay*, pp. 204, 210, 214, 511. On later interpretations of the effect of this law see my *France Faces Depopulation* (Durham, 1938), pp. 146–56. In the British Empire primogeniture and entail did not prevent the breaking up of landed property; and their usual effects were offset by the fact that England was industrially developed and possessed a great consuming middle class. Furthermore, in England the landed aristocracy counterbalanced the mercantile class, thus making the constitution more secure; while the opportunity "to contend in wealth with the great landlords" stimulated merchants and manufacturers to exercise their skills. See *Principles*, pp. 379–81. Paley (*Principles of Moral and Political Philosophy*, pp. 450–1, 474–5) had described "the right of *common*" and "*manorial* claims" as condemning the land "to perpetual sterility," and tithes as retarding cultivation, and all these conditions as unfavourable to population growth.

63. *Principles*, II, i, 8, especially pp. 384–8, 393–7, also pp. 240, 403. Earlier (p. 324n.) Malthus states that economists "from the fear of appearing to attach too much importance to money, have perhaps been too apt to throw it out of their consideration in their reasonings." On Malthus's role in the development of the theory of trade see J. Viner, *Studies in the Theory of International Trade* (New York, 1937); Hollander, *Notes*, pp. c–cvi.

64. *Principles*, p. 400, my italics.

wealth than they consume. Those engaged in the production of the "neces-saries of life," or funds for the maintenance of labour, produce a "neat surplus above what is required for the maintenance of the persons so em-ployed."[65] Those engaged in other lines of material production likewise produce more than they consume. Accordingly, unless there exist persons who can and will absorb these material surpluses, "effectual demand" will be deficient, producers will no longer create a great deal more than they consume, and wealth and population will cease to grow long before they reach the limit "which bounds the power of maintaining population." More specifically, the master producers and capitalists, their workmen, and the landlords cannot together supply a demand sufficient "to keep up and in-crease the value of that which is produced." The first may have the power, but they lack the will. The workmen may have the will, but they lack the power; for their employers cannot pay them enough to supply this power and at the same time realize the profit necessary to induce undertaking and production. Landlords are too few in number. The deficiency in consump-tion must be made up, therefore, by Adam Smith's "unproductive labour-ers,"[66] by that "body of persons engaged in personal services of various kinds"; these (i.e., menials, soldiers, statesmen, judges and lawyers, physi-cians, clergy, and teachers, etc.) provide necessary services and "call forth those exertions which are required to give full play to [the] physical re-sources" of a country.

The specific use of a body of unproductive consumers, is to give en-couragement to wealth by maintaining such a balance between produce and consumption as will give the greatest exchangeable value to the re-sults of the national industry. If such consumers were to predominate, the comparatively small quantity of material products brought to market would keep down the value of the whole produce, from the deficiency of quantity, If, on the other hand, the productive classes were in excess, the value of the whole produce would fall from excess of supply. There is therefore a certain proportion between the two which will yield the great-est value, and command for a continuance the greatest quantity of labour.[67]

Malthus laid down several qualifications with respect to the manner in

65. *Ibid.*, p. 234. It was frequently noted that agriculturalists produce a surplus above their own maintenance for which they must find vent, and upon which depends the size of the non-agricultural population. E.g., see Hume, "Of Commerce" in *Essays,* vol. I, p. 289; Steuart, *Works,* vol. I, pp. 40, 46, 117; Adam Smith, *Wealth of Nations,* bk. III, cap. i, iv; my *French Predecessors.*

66. Malthus included under "productive" labour, that which is "directly productive of material wealth"; and under "personal services," that which does not directly create material wealth, and which Adam Smith called "unproductive" (*Principles,* pp. 35, 49; cf. 1st ed., pp. 30ff.).

67. *Principles,* II, i, 9, especially pp. 412–13, 404–12. Malthus noted that since menials are complements to unproductive forms of wealth such as houses, the demand for the latter depends in part upon the availability of the former (*ibid.*, pp. 408–9).

which "unproductive consumers" were to be employed and paid. The number of menials must not be disproportionately large in relation to the "neat revenue" of the society; because if too many persons are so employed the augmentation of subsistence and wealth is checked. Furthermore, while it is possible to spend the whole of the "neat surplus" upon menials, soldiers, sailors, and other suppliers of personal service, it is preferable that part of this surplus be used to maintain those engaged in the production of conveniences and luxuries. For the latter form of employment provides a more stable source of income and a greater "stimulus to production" and cultivation "in modern states" than does diversion of the whole "neat revenue" to the sustenance of menials, soldiers, and sailors. But not all that can be spent will be spent upon "material luxuries and conveniences" because, the demand for these soon abating, the "owners of land and capital would have very slender motives to employ them in the most productive manner." Hence some of the "neat surplus" must be spent for personal services; and the "most effective encouragement even to the production of necessaries" results when the two "stimulants," material luxuries and conveniences and personal services, operate "under the most favorable proportions."[68] In so far as practicable, those engaged in personal services should be "paid voluntarily by individuals," for then they are "most likely to be useful in exciting industry, and . . . least likely to be prejudicial by interfering with the costs of production"; and while it is desirable and necessary that some be paid out of public revenues, it is important that these not be supported through "injudicious" taxation which is a deterrent to progress.[69]

To summarize: Malthus always looked upon the available and accessible means of subsistence as setting the upper limit to population growth and capacity, and upon "the increase of the means of subsistence" as the "only true criterion of a real and permanent increase in the population of any country," the "habits of living" being given.[70] The food supply became the sole and sufficient limiting agency, however, only when the population of a country had been carried to the maximum of whose support that country was capable, "habits of living" and external trading relations being given. Until this point was reached population growth was conditioned by the amount of employment available and in prospect: for upon employment depended the stimulus to agricultural production, access, on the part of the masses, to the means of subsistence, and their disposition to marry. If, for any reason, employment failed to expand, population failed to grow, whatever the food producing potentialities of a country. Population growth, therefore, depended upon the growth in the "effective demand" for labour, by which actual and prospective employment was fixed; it did not depend

68. *Ibid.,* 1, iv, 3, pp. 234–6, 239; cf. *Essay,* pp. 416–17.
69. *Principles,* II, i, 9. especially pp. 404–13.
70. *Essay,* pp. 294–5.

upon the mere power to produce, for the power to produce did not necessarily generate an offsetting power to consume, and did not, therefore, necessarily bring into being a corresponding and growing "effective demand" for labour. Such a demand, in fact, tended to be realized only when proper moral and political conditions prevailed, when the social structure was elastic, when agricultural land holdings were adequately broken up, when commerce was active, when there were enough persons willing and able to consume more material wealth than they produced, and when human wants were multiplying sufficiently to overcome the inelasticity of the demand for goods and services in terms of effort.

As we state in the conclusion, Malthus apparently came to recognize the importance of the role of the effectual demand for labour in consequence of his initial concern with the checks to population growth, and with the less immediate origins of some of these checks. For this reason too he considered the long-run as well as the short-run determinants of the effectual demand for labour and population. These considerations, in turn, led him to note the importance of industrialization as a means of dissolving obstacles to the expansion of the demand for labour and to the progress of population in number and well-being. This we examine in section II.

II

Industrialization has commonly been advanced by twentieth-century economists as the means whereby population pressure may eventually be reduced in areas which at present are relatively overpopulated. For industrialization, it is supposed, provides employment for the excess agrarian population, supplies purchasing power wherewith deficiencies in the domestic food supply may be made up, and brings about urbanization and the adoption of a cultural pattern suited eventually to bring population growth to a stand. For much the same reasons Malthus too favoured industrialization: a nation's economy should be sufficiently industrialized to establish a working balance between its agricultural and its non-agricultural branches, but not so industrialized as to make it partly dependent upon foreign sources for foodstuffs and therefore insecure with respect to provision.[71] In such an economy, Malthus's argument suggests, an adequate "effectual demand" for labour tends to be maintained, and the inhabitants tend to utilize their resources effectively and to make provision for growth in number and well-being at the same time that they acquire habits of work and consumption appropriate to guard the nation against the evils of undue multiplication.

In the First Essay Malthus did not fully appreciate the significance of industrialization, in part because he was impressed by the seeming impor-

71. On this last point, see sec. III, (i) and (ii) of this article.

tance of subsistence and concerned lest English economic policies restrain agricultural progress. He carried these views over into the second edition in which, none the less, especially in his discussion of the checks, he dwelt upon the importance of industrialization. His final and more integrated views appear already in the fifth edition, which reflects his consideration of the problems subsequently treated in the *Principles*. To the end he stressed the primacy of agriculture in economic expansion, and the principle that food must precede population.[72]

In the first edition, in criticism of Adam Smith's view that an increase in national wealth necessarily redounds to the advantage of the common man, Malthus states that "every accession to the food of a country" immediately benefits the whole society in greater measure than a corresponding accession to manufactures; that "ornamental luxuries" add little to "the mass of happiness"; that the expansion of manufactures had enticed labour from agriculture and checked the augmentation of the food supply; and that foreign commerce can contribute little to the maintenance of labour. In Europe, urban industry had been unduly encouraged and the "natural order of things" had been inverted, agricultural expansion having been founded upon the surplus capital of manufactures instead of manufactures upon the surplus capital of agriculture; had the natural order been followed, Europe would have "been much more populous, . . . and yet not more incumbered by its population."[73] He proposed, as a means of aiding the poor, premiums for turning up fresh land and "all possible encouragements held out to agriculture above manufactures."[74]

In the second edition Malthus was much more friendly to industry.[75] He observed that although "agriculture cannot flourish without a vent for its commodities," which may be furnished by commerce and manufactures, it is the "disposable produce" of agriculture which sets, or at least should set, the limits to the development of commerce and manufactures within a country. For if these two branches of the economy are overdeveloped, and the population of a state comes to subsist in part upon imported provision, it is "exposed to all the accidents of time and chance." When things are "left to take their natural course, . . . the commercial part of the society"

72. E.g., *Essay*, III, xiv; 2d ed., III, xi; also Bonar's comments, *Malthus*, pp. 136 ff. On agriculture see *ibid.*, 1st ed., chaps. XVI–XVII and pp. 95–7; 2d ed., III, vii–x; 5th ed., III, viii–xiii. Our discussion is based largely on his final views.

73. *Essay*, 1st ed., chaps. XVI–XVII, especially pp. 301–2, 308–10, 312–15, 320–6, 329, 332–7, 344; cf. Adam Smith, *Wealth of Nations*, pp. 391ff. Malthus apparently was not too friendly to industry (*Essay*, 1st ed., p. 293); but he considered it as reasonable to expect to prevent a "mistress from growing old by never exposing her to the sun or air" as to expect to prevent the development of manufactures and luxury in new countries (*ibid.*, pp. 343–4).

74. *Ibid.*, pp. 96–7, 300–1.

75. He now looked upon "commerce and manufactures" as "the most distinguishing characteristics of civilization, the most obvious and striking marks of the improvement of society, and calculated to enlarge our enjoyments, and add to the sum of human happiness. No great surplus produce of agriculture could exist without them . . ." (*Essay*, 2d ed., pp. 467–8, n.).

does not tend to increase "beyond the surplus produce of the cultivators." But — and here his discussion relates primarily to England — things had not been left to take their natural course in England. Commerce and manufactures had been stimulated, and agriculture checked, by the navigation acts and colonial trade monopolies; hence "the body politick" was in a somewhat diseased state, and threatened with a scarcity of provision. For this reason, and because adequacy of the food supply was "a matter of the very highest importance," Malthus concluded that agriculture must be restored to its proper proportions, and that a bounty would be justified if necessary to re-establish balance.[76] In his discussion of great landed areas, such as Siberia, and of countries with little manufacturing and commerce, however, he dwelt upon the need to develop these branches of the economy, if agriculture was to expand and population to grow as it might and ought.[77]

A number of reasons apparently acted in combination to lead Malthus to attach greater importance, in his later writings, to manufactures and commerce. First, his consideration of the role of private property and of the views of the Physiocrats and others led him to note that the agriculturalist must have a vent for the surplus which, under a system of private property, he normally produces, and which he would exchange for non-agricultural goods and services and for the contributions of the state.[78] Although in theory all effort might be directed into agriculture until it was fully developed, in practice, with men constituted as they are and with society founded (as it must be) upon private property, agriculture cannot expand in the absence of a growing demand for its products. Second, "the condition of the lower classes certainly does not depend exclusively upon the increase of funds for the maintenance of labour, or the means of supporting more labourers." For while the growth of population depends principally upon the increase of the food supply, the lower classes "cannot be considered as in a good state" unless they enjoy, in addition to "strict necessaries" and food, "some conveniences and even luxuries." And they cannot command these conveniences and luxuries unless, instead of allowing their numbers to keep pace with the means of subsistence (i.e., "means of supporting more labourers"), they exercise prudential restraint. Nor are they likely to "acquire a decided taste for conveniences and comforts" and, therefore, a strong disposition to practise moral restraint, until conveniences and comforts have "become plentiful compared with food, which they never do till food has become in some degree scarce," as in economies that are not pre-

76. *Essay*, 2d ed., pp. 422, 426–9, 436–40, 450–1, 465–6; also sec. III (ii) of this article. Malthus's concern at the supposed neglect of agriculture is remindful of the Physiocrats. He was careful to point out, however, that in the absence of moral restraint, no measures could make the food supply keep pace with an unchecked population (*ibid.*, pp. 467–9; also 1st ed., pp. 27–9, 346–7, where he is more pessimistic than in the second).

77. *Essay*, 2d ed., pp. 120ff., 162, 193–4, 205–6, 221–2.

78. E.g., *Essay*, p. 369; 2d ed., pp. 433–9.

dominantly agricultural.[79] Third, in so far as the well-being of the lower classes depends upon non-agricultural goods and services, Malthus's reasoning suggests, it is in order to encourage their production, for "the powers of the earth in the production of food have narrower limits than the skill and tastes of mankind in giving value to raw materials."[80]

The condition of the labouring classes in an agricultural country may be good, but it is not likely to be good, even though there the evils attendant upon urban employments are necessarily at a minimum. It will be good if, even though the price of manufactures expressed in corn is high, corn wages suffice to provide workers with both food and an adequate residuum of purchasing power with which to obtain the relatively expensive conveniences and luxuries — relatively expensive because they are imported, or produced at high cost by undeveloped domestic industries. Such a favourable situation was enjoyed by labour in America. The "condition of the labouring classes must be the worst possible," however, if "the wages of labour estimated in food are low" and, because the country lacks manufactures, the prices of manufactures, in terms of food, are high, as they must inevitably be. This unfortunate condition, moreover, will tend to persist. For the labouring classes will not have the opportunity to acquire "the custom of enjoying conveniences and comforts" and hence will not develop "those habits of prudential restraint" which operate to push wages above the subsistence level; and the owners of landed property, or those who determine the uses to which it is put, will not be actuated to employ it in a manner suited to evoke large yields.[81]

It was not the predominance of agriculture as such which accounted for

79. *Essay*, III. xiii, pp. 416. 419. 424–5. Here Malthus is taking exception to Adam Smith's (*Wealth of Nations*, bk. I. cap. viii) manner of reasoning that every increase in wealth makes for the improvement of the condition of the lower classes. In the second edition (pp. 420–9. 435; cf. 1st ed., pp. 305–21) Malthus said: "The comforts of the labouring poor must necessarily depend upon the funds destined for the maintenance of labour; and will generally be in proportion to the rapidity of their increase." These funds do not tend to keep pace with wealth. If wealth increases at the expense of agriculture, workers tend to suffer a decrease in real wages, and some of their number are shunted into relatively unhealthful urban occupations. "Unless the increase of the riches of a country from manufactures give the lower classes of the society, on an average, a decidedly greater command over the necessaries and conveniences of life, it will not appear that their condition is improved." In the last editions he states that although an increase of wealth "does not imply a proportionate increase of the funds for the maintenance of labour, yet it brings with it advantages to the lower classes of society which may fully counterbalance the disadvantages with which it is attended" (*Essay*, p. 425).

80. *Essay*, p. 419. Malthus's point here is that the supply of food is less elastic (cf. p. 310 in 1st ed.) than that of non-agricultural products; but he remarks (*Essay*, p. 424: not in 2d ed.) that, with the labourer converting less of his wages into food, "he will not indeed have the same power of maintaining a large family; but with a small family he may be better lodged and clothed, and better able to command the decencies and comforts of life." Cf. Senior, *Two Lectures on Population*, p. 71. See above, note 21. for composition of worker's budget.

81. *Essay*, III. viii, especially pp. 360–8; also *Principles*, pp. 364–5. This argument does not appear in first and second editions, but there (1st ed., pp. 293–4: 2d ed., pp. 221–2. 438. 593) Malthus notes the evils peculiar to a feudal agricultural economy and indicates that agriculture, to be prosperous, must have vent for its products.

the tendency, in agricultural systems, of the growth of capital and the demand for labour to suffer a "premature check," and of the progress of the population in number and well-being thereby to be retarded. This tendency originated in the "vices of the government and the structure of society, which prevents its full and fair development" of agriculture. He pointed to America as "perhaps the only modern instance of the fair operation of the agricultural system,"[82] and to the feudal system of land tenure, together with the complex of tastes and practices joined thereto, as the social arrangement most unfavourable to the progress of agriculture and the improvement of the condition of the labouring masses. The "remains" of this system continued to impede cultivation "in every country of Europe, and in most of its colonies in other parts of the world"; at the same time they did not "proportionably" encourage commerce and manufactures. Under the feudal system there was no mass demand for agricultural products, no disposition on the part of the land-owning class to maximize agricultural production, and no body of satisfiable but unsated wants to prompt members of all classes to exert themselves. It operated, therefore, to check the augmentation of "the surplus produce of the cultivators [which], taken in its most enlarged sense measures and limits the growth of that part of the society which is not employed upon the land; . . . [of] the number of manufacturers, of merchants, of proprietors, and of persons engaged in the various civil and military professions . . . ." And, because it operated to check the augmentation of surplus produce, it restrained the progress of population in number and well-being.[83]

When, for whatever cause, land was undivided, and there existed little or no commerce and manufactures to supply a market for the surplus produce of agriculture, to stimulate its extension and improvement, and to provide all classes with incentives to work, population growth came to a premature stop, and the masses languished in indolence and misery. "If in the best cultivated and most populous countries of Europe the present divisions of land and farms had taken place, and had not been followed by the introduction of commerce and manufactures, population would long since have come to a stand from the total want of motive to further cultivation, and the consequent want of demand for labour."[84]

82. *Essay*, pp. 364. 368: also *Principles*, p. 373. where he notes the stimulus to American agriculture supplied by "foreign commerce" and the "easy division of landed property."

83. *Essay*, pp. 173. 368-9. 423-5: 2d ed., pp. 221-2: *Principles*, pp. 374-5. Griffith (*Population Problems of the Age of Malthus*, pp. 255-6) attributed the fact, that before the Industrial Revolution the English population was practically stationary, to the localized character of markets and demands and to "the general water-tight structure of society." Before 1860 American pro-slavery writers defended the slave economy on the ground, among others, that, being less elastic than free-labour economies. it was more immune to population pressure. See my "Population Theory in the Ante-Bellum South" (*Journal of Southern History*, vol. II, 1936. pp. 360ff.); "Malthusianism and the Debate on Slavery" (*South Atlantic Quarterly*, vol. XXXIV, 1935. pp. 170ff.).

84. *Essay*, I, ix, p. 95 (not in 2d ed.). Excessive soil fertility merely aggravated the difficulty described. For similar opinions, see 2d ed., pp. 120-1. 162. and note 88, below.

Malthus pointed, by way of illustration, to Poland, Russia, Siberia, and Turkey where, "under the agricultural system, the condition of the lower classes . . . is very wretched." In Poland, for example, misery was widespread, not because the country was agricultural, but because landed property was not divided, the inhabitants were in a servile situation, and consequently, urban industry was without encouragement.

> While the land is cultivated by boors, the produce of whose exertions belongs entirely to their masters, and the whole society consists mainly of these degraded beings and the lords and owners of great tracts of territory, there will evidently be no class of persons possessed of the means either of furnishing an adequate demand at home for the surplus produce of the soil, or of accumulating fresh capital and increasing the demand for labour. In this miserable state of things, the best remedy would unquestionably be the introduction of manufactures and commerce; because the introduction of manufactures and commerce could alone liberate the mass of people from slavery and give the necessary stimulus to industry and accumulation.

He adds that if the Polish people were already free and industrious and the land was easily divisible and alienable, Poland might still for many years exchange raw products for the finer manufactures of foreign countries; but that under these circumstances, "the condition of the people would more resemble that of the inhabitants of the United States of America than of the inhabitants of the unimproved countries of Europe."[85]

Undoubtedly Malthus was led, by his study of the checks to population, to recognize the importance of industrialization and the expansibility of employment. Already in the 1803 edition, in consequence of his analysis of population growth in economies founded upon slavery, or upon concentrated ownership of property in land,[86] he observed that "the distribution of the means of subsistence" is as essential to the growth of population as is their production; that their distribution is necessary to evoke their production; and that their distribution is contingent upon there being an effectual demand for labour to distribute these means to the masses.[87] In the ancient world, so long as landed property was divided into small shares, this "division itself" provided "distribution." But when the system of small property gave place to one of inequality and concentration, distribution had to be

85. *Essay*, p. 368, also pp. 93ff., 173, 424–5; 2d ed., pp. 120ff., 221–2; *Principles*, II, i, 4, on Ireland and New Spain.

86. Malthus noted, of course, such impediments to agriculture and population as bad government, tyranny, insecurity of person and property, lack of habits of industry, and localized institutional obstacles to effective cultivation. See *Essay*, pp. 72, 80, 83, 89, 100, 104–5, 148–9, 158, 428; 2d ed., pp. 92, 103, 106, 113–14, 126, 132, 190–1, 204–5; citations in Bonar, *Malthus*, pp. 78–9, 196, 198. See note 60 and text.

87. *Essay*, pp. 80, 93–4, 138–9, 150, 156, 159, 172; 2d ed., pp. 103, 119–20, 178, 193, 202, 205–6, 221.

provided in other ways.[88] This the Romans had failed to do. Instead of setting the landless free citizens to work in agriculture and manufactures, they had filled these employments with slaves, thereby denying work and support (other than gratuities) to the free population. For this reason, and because Italian agriculture was permitted to decay, the free population had declined.[89]

Defective distribution operated also in the modern world to put the population under a "moral impossibility of increasing,"[90] when, though a plentiful subsistence might be procured with facility, conditions were not favourable to the division and improvement of land, and few or no manufactures existed. In these circumstances there was little demand for labour at a wage sufficient to provide support for a family; for there was little employment to be had off the farms, while farmers, able to provide their own subsistence, were without the prospect of manufactured goods to excite them to overcome their "natural indolence" and engage labour to produce an agricultural surplus. What is wanted in these countries, in order to increase population, Malthus declared, is not mere immigration, or a direct encouragement to procreation, "but the creation of an effectual demand for the produce of the soil, by promoting the means of distribution. This can only be effected by the introduction of manufactures, and by inspiring the cultivator with a taste for them, and thus enlarging the internal market."[91]

In light of his analysis, Malthus concluded that wealth had increased, and with it the number and well-being of the population, as the feudal system had given way, a mercantile and manufacturing middle class supplied with capital had come into being, a taste for material conveniences and luxuries had developed, a mass demand for goods and services and therefore for labour had evolved, and agriculture had received the stimulus of an expanding market.

> If a taste for idle retainers, and a profusion of menial servants, had continued among the great landholders of Europe from the feudal times to the present, the wealth of its different kingdoms would have been very

88. "In countries where . . . land is divided into very large shares; . . . arts and manufactures are absolutely necessary to the existence of any considerable population. Without them modern Europe would be unpeopled" (*Essay*, p. 127; 2d ed., p. 162). Cf. Hume, *Essays*, vol. I, p. 412, whom Malthus cites in the preceding paragraph. See also Wallace, note 49 above.

89. *Essay*, pp. 127, 134–9; 2d ed., pp. 162, 172–9. Malthus's emphasis is upon the defective distributive system which accompanied slavery in Rome rather than upon the acknowledged unfavourableness of slavery to propagation. Steuart (*Works*, vol. I, pp. 50, 52) had contended that so long as the wants of men were few, slavery was necessary to agricultural progress and multiplication. "Men were then forced to labour because they were slaves to others; men are now forced to labour because they are slaves to their own wants." Cf. Herrenschwand's analysis, summarized in my *French Predecessors*, pp. 291ff.

90. Malthus here cites Steuart, *Works*, vol. I, pp. 38–40, 154–6. See note 52 above.

91. *Essay*, pp. 93–6; 2d ed., pp. 119–22. Because it is "most difficult" to change long-existing habits, Malthus added, the importation of industry and industrial workers may be advisable in these circumstances (*Essay*, p. 98; 2d ed., p. 124).

different from what it is now. . . . The growing taste of our ancestors for material conveniences and luxuries, instead of personal services, was the main cause of the change. While the latter continue to be the predominant taste, few comparatively will be living on the profits of capital. The great mass of society will be divided chiefly into two classes, the rich and the poor, one of which will be in a state of abject dependence upon the other. But a taste for material objects, however frivolous, almost always requires for its gratification the accumulation of capital, and the existence of a much greater number of manufacturers, merchants, wholesale dealers, and retail dealers. The face of society is thus wholly changed. A middle class of persons, living upon the profits of stock, rises into wealth and consequence; and an increasing accumulation of capital, almost exclusively derived from the industry of the mercantile and manufacturing classes, affects to a considerable extent the division and alienation of those immense landed properties, which, if the fashion of personal services had continued, might have remained to this time nearly in their former state, and have prevented the increase of wealth on the land, as well as elsewhere.[92]

In the feudal times . . . the landlords could in no other way spend their incomes than by maintaining a great number of idle followers; and it was by the growth of capital in all the employments to which it is directed, that the pernicious power of the landlords was destroyed, and their dependent followers were turned into merchants, manufacturers, tradesmen, farmers, and independent labourers — a change of prodigious advantage to the great body of society, including the labouring classes.[93]

Malthus concluded, furthermore, that a country is best off when it unites "great landed resources with a prosperous state of commerce and manufactures," and is free, therefore, of the evils peculiar either to a commercial or to an agricultural economy.[94] Such a country is free of the evils of feudalism; it is free of dependence, for markets and foodstuffs and raw materials, upon foreign countries; it is free to distribute its capital between agricultural and non-agricultural enterprise, to equalize profits in both branches, and to preserve economic balance between them; and it is more than compensated for the evils ("diminished power of supporting children"; increased employment in "occupations less favourable to health, and more exposed to fluctuations of demand and unsteadiness of wages") attendant upon industrialization.

Under these circumstances, it is scarcely possible that it should ever experience that premature stagnation in the demand for labour, and the produce of the soil, which at times has marked the history of most of the

92. *Principles*, pp. 42–3, also pp. 115–16, 350n.; *Essay*, pp. 367–70, and pp. 145–6 (2d ed., pp. 187–8), where he compares the composition of employment in Norway with that in England.
93. *Essay*, pp. 423–4; also pp. 534–5 (2d ed., p. 593).
94. *Essay*, III, ix; 2d ed., pp. 425–7, 467–9n.; also sec. III (ii) of this article. The security of a nation's capital, Adam Smith wrote (*Wealth of Nations*, p. 395), is contingent on its being invested in part in domestic agriculture.

nations of Europe. In a country in which manufactures and commerce flourish, the produce of the soil will always find a ready market at home; and such a market is peculiarly favorable to the progressive increase of capital. But the progressive increase of capital, and particularly of the quantity and value of the funds for the maintenance of labour, is the great cause of a demand for labour, and of good corn wages, while the high relative price of corn, occasioned by the improved machinery and extended capital employed in manufactures, together with the prosperity of foreign commerce, enables the labourer to exchange any given portion of his earnings in corn for a large proportion both of domestic and foreign conveniences and luxuries.

Even when the demand for labour begins to slacken, and corn wages to fall, and the increase of labour to be checked, "the high relative value of corn" wages keeps up "comparatively the condition of the labouring classes"; they cannot be reduced to the miserable state of agricultural countries where the demand for labour is stationary and wages supply only necessities.[95]

In sum, a population seldom can be well off and increasing until considerable progress has been made in industrialization. For industrialization is an important component of the complex of elements favourable to an effective and expanding demand for labour, and to the increase of "supplies" generally. It acts as a solvent upon inelastic feudal structures. It helps to offset the check to the demand for luxuries and conveniences arising from the "general desire of mankind to better their condition, and make provision for a family." It inspires people with wants "calculated to excite their exertions in the production of wealth," and, therefore, overcomes in part the "luxury of indolence," always a weighty obstacle to progress in wealth, number, and well-being.[96] Manufactures and commerce

infuse fresh life and activity into all classes of the state, afford opportunities for the inferior orders to rise by personal merit and exertion, and stimulate the higher orders to depend for distinction upon other grounds than mere rank and riches. They excite invention, encourage science and the useful arts, spread intelligence and spirit, inspire a taste for conveniences and comforts among the labouring classes; and, above all, give a new and happier structure to society, by increasing the proportion of the middle classes, that body on which the liberty, public spirit, and good government of every country must mainly depend.[97]

While Malthus's analysis here runs in terms of commerce and manufactures, he foresaw, as had Petty in some measure as early as 1691, that with economic progress the working population moves "from agriculture to

95. *Essay*, III. x, xiii, especially pp. 379. 372–3. 378–82. 387. 423–5.
96. *Principles*, pp. 402–3.
97. *Observations*, pp. 24–5.

manufacture, and from manufacture to commerce and services."[98] Were the powers of production in a rich and well-peopled country trebled, he supposed by way of illustration, the potentially available output would be called forth only on condition that it could be distributed. And it would be distributed, he argues in substance, only on condition that intelligent members in lower occupational classes were moved upward, and, if necessary, new occupations and situations were created.[99] At the time Malthus was writing, expansion of employment in manufactures and commerce and, in a lesser measure, in the professions and services, gave promise of bringing about sufficient distribution to release the growing powers of production.

Industrialization, Malthus's argument runs, also makes for the growth and spread of habits suited to prevent undue natural increase and so to guard the economic and social gains of the poor, — of habits, the lack of which unleashes population pressure and visits poverty upon populations, whatever be their "supplies."[100] A "permanent and general improvement in the condition of the poor" is contingent upon the generation of "prudential habits" among the lower classes; it cannot be effected "without an increase in the preventive check." Nothing is more likely to generate prudential habits than civil liberty; and nothing is more calculated to induce deferment of marriage without endangering virtue than the diffusion of luxury, of a taste for the comforts and conveniences of life, among the mass of the people.[101] But civil liberty flourishes, as a rule, where the growth of commerce and manufactures has brought feudalism to term;[102] and a taste for conveniences and comforts tends to become diffused where industrialization provides both these classes of goods and services and the opportunity, on the part of the labourer, to purchase them with that portion of his income not absorbed by food and other necessaries.[103]

98. See C. Clark, *The Conditions of Economic Progress* (London, 1940), p. 176. Clark substantiates this thesis stated several years earlier by A. G. B. Fisher (e.g., "The Economic Implications of Material Progress," *International Labor Review*, vol. XXXII, 1935, pp. 5ff.).

99. *Principles*, 1st ed., pp. 482–3 (not in 2d ed.). The substance of this argument, however, appears in the second edition. See also O. Pancoast, "Malthus versus Ricardo . . ." (*Political Science Quarterly*, vol. LVIII, 1943, pp. 47–66).

100. "The condition of the labouring classes of society must evidently depend . . . partly, on the habits of the people in respect to their food, clothing, and lodging"; upon the amount of necessaries and conveniences "without which they would not consent to keep up their numbers" (*Principles*, I, iv, 2, p. 224). See also *Essay*, pp. 536–7; 2d ed., pp. 595–6.

101. *Essay*, IV, xiii, pp. 534–5, also pp. 367, 471, 479–80, 491; *Principles*, pp. 226–7.

102. E.g., see *Essay*, pp. 368, 378–9, 424–5; 1st ed., pp. 123n., 293–4; *Principles*, II, especially vii–viii. Adam Smith (*Wealth of Nations*, p. 385) had said: "Commerce and manufactures gradually introduced order and good government, and with them, the liberty and security of individuals." Hume, Adam Smith believed, was the first writer to note this. See Hume's essays, "Of Commerce" and "Of Luxury," in *Essays*.

103. *Principles*, I, iv, 2, pp. 224–5; *Essay*, pp. 378–9, 424–5. He noted, however, that in some Scottish parishes the introduction of manufactures had made possible the employment of very young children with the result that both marriages and child mortality had increased (*ibid.*, p. 251; 2d ed., p. 324). Malthus, of course, looked with disapproval upon the indiscriminate employment of children (*Essay*, p. 530; 2d ed., p. 586).

Industrialization is favourable also to the generation of habits of industry and prudential restraint, in that it tends to push up the relative price of food and to reduce the relative price of the remaining elements in the worker's budget.[104] "The desirable thing, with a view to the happiness of the common people, seems to be that their habitual food should be dear, and their wages regulated by it."[105] For then habits of industry and prudence tend to prevail, and the overall purchasing power of the worker's wages is favourable. If the labourer can satisfy his food requirements with little effort, he tends to prefer leisure to giving up additional time in exchange for conveniences and comforts; and he acquires neither a higher standard of life nor habits of industry. If, on the contrary, the price of food is relatively high, and the labourer finds it necessary to devote the "main part" of his time to procuring food, his behaviour undergoes modification. He develops habits of industry and, as a rule, acquires "a decided taste for the conveniences and comforts of life"; for since he already has given up most of his time in exchange for food, he "seldom" grudges working his "remaining time, which is but inconsiderable compared with the commodities it will purchase." With the progress of a country in wealth, industry, and cultivation, the cost and price of corn rise in relation to the cost and price of other goods. Hence, while the labourer's "power of maintaining a large family" declines, his opportunity and desire to "command" decencies, comforts, and better lodging and clothing increase, and his disposition to unite "individual prudence" with skill and industry acquires strength.[106]

Industrialization operates in still another manner to strengthen the overall inclination to exercise prudential restraint; because it serves, as has already been noted, to increase the relative number in the middle part of society.[107] For an increase in the relative number in the middle part of society, and a decrease in the relative number in the inferior part of society, is "most favourable to virtuous and industrious habits, . . . to the growth of all kinds of

104. *Essay*, iii, viii, pp. 364–7, also p. 379.

105. *Ibid.*, p. 515, also p. 379; 2d ed., p. 579. Here Malthus has in mind that if the price of food is high, and money wages and the supply of labour are largely regulated by it, the overall condition of the common people must improve for reasons indicated in the text. Malthus did not, however, say wages are regulated by the price of corn, or of food. He observed, rather, that they are influenced by the prices of both food and the other elements included in the worker's budget, and by changes in his habits of consumption (*Observations*, pp. 9–12, 15, 20; *Principles*, pp. 218ff., 225–9). In another connection he said that a high price for raw produce signified a favourable state of economic affairs (*Inquiry*, pp. 39–42; Hollander, *Notes*, pp. xliiiff.); and even in the *Principles* (2d ed., pp. 184–9) he indicated that when a country was prosperous the price of its raw produce tended to be high.

106. *Essay*, pp. 364–7, 379, 423–5. Malthus's attitude toward the repeal of the corn laws may have been somewhat influenced by the above considerations, since repeal would lower the prices of corn and labour (*Principles*, p. 105). Were the ports opened to grain, the stimulus to population arising from the cheapness of grain would probably depress real wages in England (*Observations*, p. 26). His argument is similar to that he advanced against a cheapened diet (*Essay*, pp. 515–16).

107. E.g., see *Essay*, pp. 423–5; *Principles*, pp. 373–6.

talents," to the improvement of the prospects of the lower classes, and to the diffusion and animation of the desire to better one's condition.[108]

Malthus did not emphasize the retention of a taste for conveniences and luxuries. For, following Hume in part, he supposed that a nation, like an individual, having acquired a given scale of living, would not easily relinquish it. When a nation has acquired the "tastes necessary to give value to a great quantity of labour not employed upon actual necessaries . . . a considerable resistance will be made to any essential fall in its value."[109] In the first as well as in later editions of the *Essay* he indicated that he believed it very difficult to reduce a standard of living that had been acquired.[110]

Malthus's heightened approval of industrialism and commerce brought his opinions more into line with those of Hume and others, who, however, were less concerned with the population problem. Where manufactures and "mechanic arts" do not flourish, Hume declared, agriculturalists are without markets and, therefore, without temptation "to encrease their skill and industry. . . . A habit of indolence naturally prevails." And much land remains uncultivated. Whence commerce and awakened wants are necessary to rouse men and release the forces of production.[111] Men multiply when agriculture prospers, Steuart observed; and agriculture prospers most when wants are many and complex, there is vent for its products, and agriculturalists feel need for non-agricultural goods.[112] Adam Smith traced the dissolution of the comparatively static feudal economy and the expansion of agriculture to the rise of commerce and manufactures and the development of the town economy.[113] Young emphasized the dependence of prosperity in agriculture upon the adequacy of outlets for its products, and the dependence of population growth upon the state of agriculture and employment generally.[114] Paley wrote that "The business of one half of mankind is to set the other half at work; that is, to provide articles, which, by tempting the desires, may stimulate the industry, and call forth the activity of those, upon the exertion of whose industry, and the application of whose faculties, the production of human provision depends."[115] These writers, in short, found in an expanding market for agricultural products a stimulus to agriculture and to the production of provision, on which population growth depends;

108. *Essay*, IV, xiii, pp. 534–6, also p. 543; 2d ed., pp. 594–5, 603–4; cf. 1st ed., pp. 367–9. Industrialization intensified somewhat the operation of the positive checks because urban and manufacturing employments were less healthful than rural employments, and probably would always remain so (*Essay*, pp. 420–1, 538; cf. 2d., pp. 422, 597).

109. *Principles*, pp. 355–6.

110. *Essay*, p. 294; 1st ed., p. 132.

111. "Of Commerce" (*Essays*, vol. I, pp. 289–90, 293, 296).

112. *Works*, vol. I, chaps. v–viii, xviii, pp. 177, 203–4, 210–12.

113. *Wealth of Nations*, bk. III. Cf. Steuart's account (*Works*, vol. I, chap. x) of the decline of the feudal economy.

114. *Political Arithmetic*, chap. I, sec. vii.

115. *Principles of Moral and Political Philosophy*, p. 456. See also E. Burke, *Works* (London, 1803), vol. I, pp. 203–4, vol. V, pp. 290–2.

but they did not apparently seek in industrialization the source of a cultural barrier to undue multiplication.

III

In this section, consisting of five parts, we examine: (i) Malthus's views on "luxury"; (ii) his appraisal of the frequently expressed "export of work" argument; (iii) in what sense his doctrine was counter-revolutionary; (iv) his stand on measures to encourage marriage and natality; and (v) his position on optimum population.

(i) Luxury

Luxury has ever been the subject of controversy, and in the course of this controversy many arguments have been advanced both against and in support of luxury. Some of these, present in the writings of his day, and relating to the population problem, were touched upon by Malthus,[116] and will be considered here.

(1) Young expressed an ancient opinion when he wrote that "on the soft beds of luxury most kingdoms have expired";[117] and so did those who supposed luxury to be a deterrent to marriage and the dispostion to procreate.[118] Malthus did not say much of the possible evil effects of luxury, in part because he considered the deterring influence exercised upon marriage by luxury to be necessary and salutary, and in part because he supposed that luxury would not unduly check population growth so long as it did not operate to restrict the augmentation of the food supply.[119] He did not approve of luxury when compounded with vice,[120] nor of great luxury on the part of the opulent few at the expense of the labouring majority. He apparently

116. For an account of some of these arguments, see my *French Predecessors of Malthus;* E. A. J. Johnson, *Predecessors of Adam Smith* (New York, 1937); H. Baudrillart, *Histoire du luxe* (Paris, 1878–80); F. B. Kaye, introduction and notes to *The Fable of the Bees . . . Bernard Mandeville* (Oxford, 1924).

117. E. Young, *The Centaur, not Fabulous* (1755) (Philadelphia, 1795), p. 47.

118. Thus Paley, *Principles of Moral and Political Philosophy,* p. 444, having noted that "habitual superfluities become actual wants: opinion and fashion convert articles of ornament and luxury into necessaries," added that, "in the present relaxed state of morals and discipline," men will not "enter into marriages which degrade their condition, reduce their mode of living, deprive them of the accommodations to which they have been accustomed, or even of those ornaments or appendages of rank and station, which they have been taught to regard as belonging to their birth, or class, or profession, or place in society." See also Wallace, *Dissertation,* pp. 19, 26ff., 160.

119. E.g., see *Essay,* pp. 429–31, on the causes of depopulation; and p. 11, where he says that, given access to the means of subsistence, population tends to increase "even in the most vicious societies." Cf. the views of Baron Grimm (*French Predecessors,* pp. 236ff.) and Paley (*Principles of Moral and Political Philosophy,* pp. 445–6).

120. *Essay,* pp. 9–10, 134–7, 171; 1st ed., p. 100; 2d ed., p. 467n. "The vices of mankind are active and able ministers of depopulation" (1st ed., p. 139).

agreed with those who supposed that a "prodigious quantity of human exertion wasted upon trivial, useless, and sometimes pernicious objects . . . might be wholly saved or more effectively employed," but he rejected the egalitarian correctives usually proposed.[121]

In 1803 Malthus observed that luxury, "when it falls short of actual vice," stimulates agriculture, commerce, and manufactures, but he added that "there seems to be a point, beyond which it must necessarily become prejudicial to a state, and bring with it the seeds of weakness and decay." He did not refer, as did Paley, to the tendency of luxury to diminish the "frequency of marriage among the poor," or to its supposed enervating effects. Rather, luxury becomes "prejudicial" when those employed "in preparing or procuring luxuries" become too numerous in relation to "the funds which are to support them"; when "it is pushed so far as to trench on the funds necessary for its support, and to become an impediment instead of an encouragement to agriculture"; when, because too few people are employed in agriculture, food imports become necessary. For he did not believe that those engaged outside agriculture "can be sufficiently secure of this food, if they depend for it principally on other countries." No large nation, become dependent in part upon foreign food supplies, had continued "with undiminished vigour," nor would England, or any other large nation, prove an exception to this rule in the future. Whence he inferred that English agriculture, which, he believed, had suffered in consequence of undue stimulation of commerce and manufactures, needed to be encouraged and developed so it could supply the nation's food requirements. This thesis appears in modified form in the fifth and later editions where he emphasizes the superiority of the agricultural-commercial system over both the agricultural and commercial systems.[122]

(2) Goods and services, Richard Cantillon had observed, vary in respect to their coefficients of production; they may embody much land and little labour, or much labour and little land. If they embody relatively large amounts of land, the labour requirement of an economy will be less than if they embody relatively large amounts of labour; and if the labour requirement is less, either wages will be lower, or (annual wages being assumed constant) employment will be less, or both wages and employment will be less, than if the labour requirement is great. Population, the scale of living being given, will vary with the labour requirement. And the labour requirement will depend upon the "Taste, Humours and Manner of Living of the Proprietors of Land," who, as the principal property owners and leading consumers in an economy, largely determine the volume of goods and services

121. *Essay*, III, iii, p. 318; not in early editions.

122. *Essay*, 2d ed., pp. 467–9n., 592–4n. See also sec. II and sec. III (ii) of this article. Steuart (*Works*, vol. I, p. 117) had said: "That number of husbandmen, therefore, is the best, which can provide food for all the state; and that number of inhabitants is the best, which is compatible with the full employment of every one of them."

called for, and the extent to which these goods and services will consist predominantly of labour rather than of land. Upon the tastes of the proprietors, therefore, depend the means allotted for the support of population and, consequently, population growth itself. If, for example, proprietors prefer horses to goods and services composed largely of labour, numbers will be less, for there will not be so much subsistence for their support, and its relative price may be higher.[123]

Of the writers with whose views on population Malthus was acquainted, none emphasized the point that it is through the media of coefficients of production that tastes influence both the demand for labour and the wage level; but several touched upon whether or not population growth is checked when resources are utilized in the production of goods and services other than subsistence. Thus Hume observed that were the land of a convent bestowed upon a nobleman, not many more citizens would be furnished; that the conversion of fertile land into vineyards checked population growth; and that "great equality of fortune" was favourable to propagation.[124] And Wallace, an exponent of the virtues of small landownership and simplicity of tastes, declared that, so long as the earth is not fully cultivated, the employment of men upon "works of ornament" and many other non-agricultural tasks instead of upon "multiplying food," operates to restrain world population growth.[125] Mirabeau when still a disciple of Cantillon, contended, among other things, that one horse, *ceteris paribus*, displaced four men.[126] Steuart remarked that numbers become greater when a people live on a cereal rather than on an animal food diet; but he denied Mirabeau's thesis that, in France, the "unnecessary consumption of the earth's productions" and the use of land for gardens, highways, etc., reduced the food supply available to man

123. "The more Horses there are in a state the less food will remain for the People." On Cantillon's theory see my *French Predecessors*, chap. IV, and A. Landry's historical and analytical essay, "Une théorie, négligée. De l'influence de la direction de la demande sur la productivité du travail, les salaires et la population" (*Revue d'économie politique*, vol. XXIV, 1910, pp. 314, 364, 747, 773); also Douglas, *Theory of Wages*, pp. 266-7. Cantillon glimpsed but did not develop the point that since non-proprietors also are consumers, the number of non-proprietors depends in part upon the tastes of non-proprietors and the extent to which they prefer goods and services consisting predominantly of labour; or the corollary that the level of wages, if not fixed by a constant scale of living, depends in part upon the tastes of non-proprietors. Eubulus, said V. Pareto (*Cours d'économie politique*, Lausanne, 1896-7, vol. I, p. 139), criticized those who nourished beasts for pleasure rather than children.

124. "Of the Populousness of Ancient Nations" (*Essays*, vol. I, pp. 395-6, 397-8, 430).

125. *Dissertation*, pp. 17, 20-30. He admitted, however, that where the "lands are very unequally divided . . . that country must be thinly peopled, unless elegance is studied, and proper encouragement given to the arts which conduce to it." *Ibid.*, pp. 17-18. Wallace did not assert, however, that the production of ornaments should be delayed until the earth was fully cultivated (*ibid.*, p. 21).

126. At this time (1756) Mirabeau had not yet joined the Physiocrats who reasoned that, in France at that time, luxury which eventuated in a demand for subsistence was more favourable to agriculture and population growth than was decorative luxury. See my *French Predecessors*, pp. 131, 182, 185ff. Malthus referred to Mirabeau's observation that revenue was the source of population (*Essay*, p. 433; 2d ed., p. 477).

and thus "hurt population." For France was not fully cultivated; and so long as a state was not fully cultivated, men did not want for subsistence, and an increase in the demand for agricultural products, whatever their destination, served to stimulate agriculture and therefore to favour population growth.[127]

Although Paley did not assign to landed proprietors the important role allowed them by Cantillon, he did indicate that both the amount of subsistence and the volume of employment were conditioned by tastes. He noted that the adoption of an animal food diet by the English had restrained their population growth, inasmuch as a country could not support so many people on an animal food as on a cereal diet; and he observed that manufactures and commerce might divert resources from the production of subsistence. But he did not believe that the development of commerce and manufactures had checked population, saying, on the contrary, that it had favoured propagation; for it had augmented employment and, by expanding the demand for agricultural produce, had absorbed and distributed the surplus production of agriculture and stimulated its increase. Some branches of commerce and manufactures, he noted, however, promoted employment, and therefore population, in greater measure than others; namely, those which embodied relatively large amounts of labour and relatively small amounts of land suited for the cultivation of subsistence. Whence he concluded that a nation would reach "its proper extent of population" only if its soil were "applied solely to the raising of provision" for its inhabitants, and if its commerce and manufactures were devoted primarily to the creation and sale of labour-embodying wrought goods.[128]

Malthus did not treat of the "horses versus men" thesis as such, nor did he evaluate the views expressed on this matter by his predecessors, or consider Cantillon's analysis of the demand for labour. But he gave expression to this thesis in the First Essay, only to reject it, and the inferences drawn from it, in later editions. In the 1798 edition he observed, apparently following Paley in part, that a country would not support as many inhabitants on a meat as on a corn diet; and that the new system of grazing, under which cattle were fattened on good land instead of on waste land as formerly, "together with the great number of horses at present kept for pleasure," were the "chief causes, that have prevented the quantity of human food . . . from keeping pace with the increased fertility of the soil." He added that the English population would experience greater growth were these two condi-

127. *Works*, vol. I, pp. 156–7, 189–99.
128. *Principles of Moral and Political Philosophy*, pp. 446, 449–50, 455–9. Those branches of "manufactory . . . are, in their nature, the most beneficial, in which the price of the wrought article exceeds in the highest proportion that of the raw material: for this excess measures the quantity of employment" (*ibid.*, p. 459). See also sec. III (ii) of this article. Paley did not consider "mechanical contrivances, which abridge labour," to be detrimental to population, inasmuch as they did not diminish "the quantity of employment" (*ibid.*, pp. 470–2).

tions modified, but he did not recommend such modification.[129] Furthermore, he esteemed the production of food above that of luxuries, because it contributed more to the "mass of happiness in the society"; and he expressed alarm that manufactures were expanding at the expense of agriculture and diverting resources from farming. But he considered impractical proposals to shunt into agriculture either the idle rich, or those employed in "the labours of luxuries."[130]

In the second and later editions of the *Essay* Malthus modified his earlier evaluation of the "horses versus men" thesis. He admitted that the shunting of resources from the production of subsistence for men to other uses tended to make the population of a country, or its actual capacity to support numbers, less than it otherwise would be; but he rejected the inferences that were commonly drawn from this fact, and pointed out that under a system of private property it was impossible to produce as large a volume of foodstuffs as the land, in conjunction with a nation's labour power, was capable of producing.

The lot of the lower classes would not be better were no foodstuffs and no resources diverted to non-food uses; in fact, such diversion in good times served to cushion the population against failing crops and bad times. The "real effect" of "waste among the rich," of "land remaining uncultivated," of keeping horses "for pleasure," "is merely to narrow the limit of the actual population; but they have little or no influence on what may be called the average pressure of distress on the poorer members of society."[131] These circumstances serve, as does "the consumption of grain in distilleries" in China, to prevent the arrival of population at the "utmost limits of subsistence" and to provide a disposable reserve in bad times.

> On the supposition that the food consumed in this manner may be withdrawn, on the occasion of a scarcity, and be applied to the relief of the poor, they operate certainly, as far as they go, like granaries, which are only opened at the time that they are most wanted, and must therefore tend rather to benefit than to injure the lower classes of society.[132]

> China, without her distilleries, would certainly be more populous; but on a failure of the seasons, would have still less resource than she has at present; and, as far as the magnitude of the cause would operate, would

129. *Essay,* 1st ed., pp. 76, 308–10, 314–21, 329. The new system of grazing, made profitable by the increased price of meat, he traced to "the present great demand for butchers meat of the best quality." *Ibid.,* pp. 316–19.

130. *Ibid.,* pp. 289–92, 298–9. Because the rich were few in number, their assistance would be "comparatively trifling"; and because of the principle of population, want would still exceed supply even if the creators of luxuries turned to the production of necessaries. Here Malthus is replying to Godwin (*Enquirer,* pp. 139–40).

131. *Essay,* III, xiv, p. 435; 2d ed., p. 477. Wretchedness, Malthus pointed out elsewhere, was the lot of a large proportion of the population in China where "no arable land lies fallow" and where relatively little labour and few vegetable and animal products were diverted to non-food uses. *Essay,* I, xii, pp. 116–17; 2d ed., pp. 148–9.

132. *Essay,* III, xiv, p. 435; 2d ed., p. 478.

in consequence be more subject to famines, and those famines would be more severe.[133]

Malthus reasoned in like manner that a relatively expensive diet tended to cushion the impact of "scarcity."

When the common people of a country live principally upon the dearest grain, as they do in England on wheat, they have great resources in a scarcity [in the form of cheaper but nourishing food] . . . ; but when their habitual food is the lowest in this scale, they appear to be absolutely without resource, except in the bark of trees, like the poor Swedes; and a great portion of them must necessarily be starved.[134]

Already in the First Essay he had observed, following comment upon population pressure in China, "It is probable that the very frugal manner in which the Gentoos are in the habit of living, contributes in some degree to the famines of Indostan."[135] Malthus therefore opposed, as had Necker by implication, the substitution, in times other than of scarcity, of cheap for relatively expensive diets; he looked upon cheap foods merely as means of easing the impact of occasional scarcity and distress.[136]

To those who would do away with horses and cattle and substitute spade culture, Malthus replied that such a policy would reduce agricultural output, the demand for labour, and population. English soil could not produce much without dressing, and the best dressing was provided by cattle.[137] Horses were necessary to transport produce and manure; without their help in the fields it would be impossible to cultivate effectively land of poor quality.[138]

To those who inferred from "the appearance of uncultivated heaths" that the "internal economy" of a country was necessarily unsound, Malthus replied that it did not and could not pay to dress and cultivate all land, poor, middling, and good alike: — this would constitute a "palpable misdirection and waste both of individual and national resources." For since the supply of soil dressing was almost always limited, and the supply of labour was sometimes limited, the maximization of agricultural production was con-

133. *Essay*, i, xii, p. 126; 2d ed., p. 161. Pro-slavery writers in America defended the loose slave economy and the associated wasteful consumption on the ground that it permitted retrenchment when times were hard. See references in note 83 in sec. ii of this article.

134. *Essay*, iv, xi, p. 514; 2d ed., pp. 577–8.

135. *Ibid.*, p. 131.

136. *Essay*, iv, xi, pp. 514–16; 2d ed., pp. 577–80. See also his discussion of the population-increasing effect of the introduction of the cheap potato diet into Ireland (*Essay*, pp. 259–60, 365–7; 2d ed., pp. 334–5, 579–81; *Principles*, pp. 211, 345ff.; *Edinburgh Review*, 1808, pp. 339–40, 344). Adam Smith (*Wealth of Nations*, pp. 160–1) was more enthusiastic than Malthus about the potato.

137. *Essay*, iii, ii, p. 311, also pp. 435–8; 2d ed., pp. 371, 466–9; 1st ed., p. 187. Malthus here is emphasizing the difficulties in the way of increasing the supply of subsistence and the impossibility, in a country like England, of living by vegetable cultivation alone.

138. *Principles*, i, iv, 3, pp. 237–8; 1st ed., p. 263.

tingent upon putting these productive agents where they would do the most good.[139]

Under the system of private property – which Malthus supposed would always prevail – "the practical limits of population . . . must be always very far short of the utmost power of the earth to produce food"; because land is cultivated only up to the point where "the last employed labourers" can produce enough to replace themselves (i.e., support a wife and rear two children). "And it is happy for mankind that such are the laws of nature." For under this arrangement the excess produce (above maintenance) of the cultivating class serves to support the non-cultivating population whose efforts supply the non-food components of the family budget; and a supra-subsistence scale of living is attainable by most. Were the system of private property, and the limit set by it to population growth, removed, incessant labour and degradation would soon become the lot of most if not all.

> But what statesman or rational government could propose that all animal food should be prohibited, that no horses should be used for business or pleasure, that all the people should live upon potatoes, and that the whole industry of the nation should be exerted in the production of them, except what was required for the mere necessaries of clothing and houses? Could such a revolution be effected, would it be desirable? particularly as in a few years, notwithstanding all these exertions, want, with less resource than ever, would inevitably recur.[140]

(3) The production and consumption of luxuries and conveniences, as was shown in part in sections I and II, served three major purposes, in Malthus's opinion. They overcame indolence and called forth effort in general;[141] they stimulated agriculture by providing a market for its products, and helped to sustain an effective demand for labour; and they operated to establish a suitable barrier in the way of too great population growth. But luxuries

139. *Essay*, III, xiv, pp. 435–8; 2d ed., pp. 466–9, 478–82. Malthus pointed to the "barren heaths" of China and to the error of the French in cultivating too much poor land.

140. *Essay*, III, vi, p. 346, x, pp. 382–4; 2d ed., pp. 414–15. Chap. x, in its final form, first appeared in the fifth edition (1817). In chap. VI, on the poor laws, Malthus's object is to show that the abolition of private property would greatly worsen the material lot of most men. See sec. III (iii) of this article.

141. It is their "passions" that cause men to labour, Hume had said; it is the "spirit of avarice and industry, art and luxury" that actuates men to work effectively; it is their "desires and wants" that determine how many hands the "proprietors and labourers" of land will employ. It is foreign commerce, which presents the more opulent with undreamed-of objects of luxury, that "rouses men from their indolence" and raises in the better-to-do "a desire of a more splendid way of life than what their ancestors enjoyed." See "Of Commerce" (*Essays*, vol. I, pp. 289–90, 293, 296). Mandeville and others, before Hume, had emphasized the role of the passions (Kaye, *The Fable of the Bees . . . by Bernard Mandeville*, vol. I, Introduction, parts IV–V). Malthus would not have approved Mandeville's view that national wealth consists in "a Multitude of laborious Poor" (*ibid.*, vol. I, p. 287); and he did not approve Mandeville's "system of morals" (*Essay*, p. 553n.); but he made use of the notion of "passions" (see note 180 below, and text).

and conveniences could not serve these three purposes unless the taste and demand for them were widely diffused through the population; then only would the vast majority acquire habits of industry and be able to provide a necessary mass demand. Malthus, therefore, differed from such writers as Paley, who believed that the vast majority should toil incessantly and live frugally "in order to minister to the excessive luxuries" of the opulent few.[142]

> It is by no means necessary that the rich should be excessively luxurious, in order to support the manufactures of a country; or that the poor should be deprived of all luxuries, in order to make them sufficiently numerous. The best, and in every point of view the most advantageous manufactures in this country, are those which are consumed by the great body of the people. The manufactures which are confined exclusively to the rich are not only trivial, on account of the comparative smallness of their quantity, but are further liable to the great disadvantage of producing much occasional misery among these employed in them, from changes of fashion. It is the diffusion of luxury therefore among the mass of the people, and not an excess of it in a few, that seems to be most advantageous, both with regard to national wealth and national happiness.[143]

He differed from Paley, furthermore, in that he considered the widespread diffusion of a taste for luxuries among the mass of people to be the condition best calculated to actuate restriction of number. For if it be allowed that "some powerful check to population must prevail," and that "a taste for the comforts and conveniences of life will prevent people from marrying, under the certainty of being deprived of these advantages," then it must be allowed that the extension of this taste is both "little prejudicial to the happiness and virtue of society" and well suited to raise "that standard of wretchedness" or point below which the lower classes "will not continue to marry and propagate their species."[144] Finally, it is among peoples through whom a taste for luxuries and decencies has become diffused, that the master-springs of industry, the hope of betterment and the fear of want, exercise the most salutary influence.[145]

142. "The condition most favourable to population is that of a laborious, frugal people, ministering to the demands of an opulent, luxurious nation; because this situation, whilst it leaves them every advantage of luxury, exempts them from the evils which naturally accompany its admission into any country." Under these circumstances much employment is provided by luxury manufacture; yet, since the vast majority are without a taste for these luxuries, they are not under pressure to support this taste by refraining from the "formation of families." See Paley, *Principles of Moral and Political Philosophy*, pp. 446–8.

143. *Essay*, IV, xiii, pp. 534–5; 2d ed., pp. 592–3; *Principles*, pp. 373ff., where this view is developed more fully; also sec. I–II of this article. Hume had said that everyone should enjoy "all the necessaries and many of the conveniences of life." See "Of Commerce" (*Essays*, vol. I, pp. 296–7).

144. *Essay*, IV, ix, p. 498, xiii, pp. 534n., 535; 2d ed., pp. 557, 593–4. See also *Essay*, pp. 471, 491; 2d ed., pp. 524, 545; *Principles*, I, iv, 2; Senior, *Two Lectures on Population*, pp. 85–6. Malthus may have got his "standard of wretchedness" (*Essay*, p. 498) from Paley who said (see Malthus, *ibid.*, p. 534n.) that mankind will "breed up to a certain point of distress." See 2d ed., pp. 557, 592n.

145. *Essay*, III, xiv, pp. 431–2, IV, xiii, pp. 535–6; 2d ed., pp. 475, 594–5, and notes, pp. 592, 593.

(ii) *Exportation of Work*

Long before Malthus wrote, English mercantilists were contending that the greater the exports, and the smaller the imports, the greater was the employment of English labour.[146] It followed that insomuch as population growth depended upon employment, it found a stimulus in an excess of exports over imports. Steuart, who looked upon employment as the primary stimulus to multiplication,[147] declared:

> If the value of the matter imported be greater than the value of what is exported, the country gains. If a greater value of labour be imported, than exported, the country loses. Why? Because in the first case, strangers must have paid, *in matter,* the surplus of labour exported; and, in the second case, because the country must have paid to strangers, *in matter,* the surplus of labour imported.
>
> It is therefore a general maxim, to discourage the importation of work, and to encourage the exportation of it.[148]

Yet he apparently did not look with great favour upon a people's carrying "their numbers far beyond the proportion of their own growth" and becoming dependent, in part, upon potentially transient foreign sources for provisions.[149] Wallace remarked that a given country could, by exchanging goods and services for foodstuffs, support more people than the produce of its lands could subsist; but he added that such commerce, by diverting labour from agriculture, tended to diminish the number of mankind in the world as a whole.[150] Paley described the exchange of domestic wrought goods for foreign raw produce as conducive to the augmentation of employment and population, and the exchange of domestic raw produce for foreign wrought goods as "unfavourable to population, because it leaves no . . . demand for employment"; and he characterized the exportation of corn, except by new countries or in years of great plenty, as "noxious to population," or as indicative of "a defect of population."[151]

Malthus did not specifically evaluate the "export of work" thesis, as formulated by its exponents. He admitted, of course, that a nation might add to its food supply by importation. But, in 1803, he rejected a Smithian variant of this thesis, and warned against England's becoming dependent upon foreign-produced foodstuffs. A nation which exchanges wrought goods

146. Viner, *Studies in the Theory of International Trade,* pp. 51ff.; Johnson, *Predecessors of Adam Smith,* chap. xv.
147. *Works,* vol. I, p. 191.
148. *Ibid,* vol. II, p. 2 (italics in text). Arthur Young (*Political essays,* 1772, p. 538; cited by Viner, *Studies in the Theory of International Trade,* p. 54) stated that a favourable balance of trade suggested that foreigners "employ more of our poor than we do of theirs." Cantillon, by whom Steuart was influenced, had indicated that a country could increase its population by exchanging products embodying labour for agricultural products, but he did not recommend a state's becoming dependent upon foreign-produced foodstuffs (*French Predecessors,* pp. 118ff., 124ff.).
149. *Works,* vol. I, pp. 117, 158-9, 212-14; vol. II, pp. 6-8.
150. *Dissertation,* pp. 18, 21-3, 148.
151. *Principles of Moral and Political Philosophy,* pp. 458-9, 469-70.

for rude produce, said Adam Smith, "exports what can subsist and accomodate but a very few, and imports the subsistence and accomodation of a great number."[152] To such exportation Malthus took exception. He pointed to the relatively great "clear national profit" yielded by the exportation of raw produce; to the fact that a nation must produce more than enough food in good years if it is to have enough in bad years; and to the industrial disadvantage of high wages which tend to accompany a domestic scarcity of provision. And he remarked, much as in the first edition, that a country which, for a time, "exported its raw produce, would be able" in the end "to subsist and accomodate a much greater population than" a country which relied appreciably upon imported raw produce. He therefore opposed a large country's becoming dependent upon foreign-produced provision.[153]

Malthus's principal concern remained the difficulty of making the food supply keep pace with a continually growing population, and the necessity of rendering this food supply secure.[154] In the 1817 and 1826 editions, however, his main thesis was that a nation, particularly if it was large, could not safely and judiciously exchange labour embodied in commerce and manufactures for foreign-produced foodstuffs, and thus support a part of its population at the expense of foreign-owned food funds. For it could not safely be supposed that a country with a "commercial system"—i.e., an economy founded predominantly upon manufacturing and foreign commerce—could export a continually expanding volume of manufactures, receiving in exchange a correspondingly expanding volume of food and raw materials, and so support a continually expanding population at a level of living consistent with the "existing habits of the people"; this supposition held true at best only so long as those in control of the foreign sources of food and raw materials were both willing and able to go on increasing their exports of these commodities to importing "commercial" countries.

A number of circumstances may operate individually or jointly to cause a "commercial" country to suffer difficulty in the procuring of subsistence even "while the means of raising food in the surrounding countries may still be comparatively abundant." The absolute and/or comparative advantages of an exporting country, which depend on "capital and skill," and the present possession of commercial channels, "cannot in their nature be permanent"

152. Adam Smith, *Wealth of Nations,* vol. IV, ix, p. 642.
153. It was worse for a country like England to become slightly dependent upon foreign sources than for small countries like Holland and Hamburg to become largely dependent. England "is in a much more precarious situation with regard to the constancy of its supplies, than such states as draw almost the whole of their provisions from other countries." *Essay,* 2d ed., p. 425. For reply to Adam Smith, not included in 1817 revision, see *ibid.,* pp. 448–51, and for general view, pp. 426, 429, 437–8, 467–9n. See for his similar but less developed position, 1st ed., pp. 311–13, 322–6, 336–7.
154. No policy, of course, could obviate the need to exercise moral restraint (e.g., *Essay,* 2d ed., pp. 467–9). On the differences between Malthus and Ricardo regarding criteria of national well-being and effects of trade, see Hollander, *Notes,* pp. xxxixff., xliii, xcixff.

and secure against the competition of other producing areas. Moreover, the countries which supply food and raw materials may, in the course of their "natural progress," also come to supply their own requirement of manufactures. Furthermore, an exporting commercial country may, while it still retains its comparative advantage in production and exportation, glut its foreign markets, suffer an adverse turn in the terms of trade, and depress the profitability of its own manufacturing industries. Finally, if the customer countries which furnish raw materials and food are, "from indolence and want of accumulation," not progressive, they will fail to provide an *expanding* market or to constitute an *expanding* source of supplies. The situation of a food-importing country is, therefore, somewhat precarious at best; "it could not longer exist" if food and raw materials were denied to it, and it would begin to decline if its commercial transactions furnished it with a diminishing volume of food imports. "Though it be most readily admitted that, in a large landed nation, the evils which belong to the manufacturing and commercial system are much more than counterbalanced by its advantages, as long as it is supported by agriculture, yet, in reference to the effect of the excess which is not so supported, it may fairly be doubted whether the evils do not decidedly predominate."[155]

Malthus's attitude toward import restrictions and export bounties derived from his belief that a nation should provide its own foodstuffs in adequate quantity.[156] It would not do for Europe to become dependent upon America for "corn," giving manufactures in exchange; for when "America began to withdraw its corn from Europe and the agricultural exertions of Europe were inadequate to make up for this deficiency, it would certainly be felt that the temporary advantages of a greater degree of wealth and population (supposing them to have been really attained) had been very dearly purchased by a long period of retrograde movements and misery."[157] It was advantageous, on balance, to facilitate population growth through the development of an agricultural-commercial system that furnished adequate foodstuffs from domestic sources. But it was not advantageous to found the support of part of the population upon imported

155. *Essay*, III, ix, xii, p. 409; also *Observations*, pp. 22–4, 28–9. Malthus did not expect "perfect freedom of trade" ever to be realized (*Essay*, p. 415; cf. 2d ed., p. 466). He did not dwell upon the possible ill effects of naval or other forms of blockade except to suggest that a commanding navy gives an importing country surer access to foreign supplies (*Essay*, 2d ed., pp. 425, 468n.; 1st ed., p. 311).

156. *Essay*, III, x–xii; 2d ed., III, vii–x; *Principles*, p. 427; Bonar, *Malthus*, pp. 217–29, 245–52. In his *Observations*, etc. (1814) Malthus, having considered the supposed advantages and disadvantages of export bounties and import restrictions, expressed himself in favour of a constant protective import duty on corn, and of continuation of the "old bounty" with a view to relieving a "glut" (*ibid.*, p. 34). British agriculture could not, in the face of foreign competition, grow enough corn to support the increasing population, Malthus noted, but he did not stress so much as later the risk of making a considerable part of the population dependent upon foreign supplies (*ibid.*, pp. 16–24, 28–9).

157. *Essay*, pp. 403–4; 2d ed., pp. 446–7.

corn, purchased at the expense of industrial and urban evils and a present and future precariousness of the food supply. "I should have no hesitation in considering such wealth and population as much too dearly purchased. The happiness of a society is, after all, the legitimate end even of its wealth, power, and population."[158] While Malthus did not continue to favour export bounties on corn,[159] his concern over the security of the food supply, together with his scepticism regarding the adequacy of foreign trade as a guard against "scarcity," led him to conclude that large countries, capable of producing a sufficient and not too variable supply of corn, might with advantage impose restrictions upon the importation of corn. Such a system of restrictions, provided that it allowed for the importation of corn in years of scarcity, would prevent the evils peculiar to a "commercial system," and, by assuring an adequate domestic food supply, would render a country secure in the possession of such improvements in manufactures as it developed.[160] Malthus's conclusion therefore resembled that of the nineteenth-century German writers who favoured measures to make that nation self-sufficient in terms of provision.

(iii) Was Malthusianism Counter-revolutionary?

Malthus's population theory, as set down in the *Essay*, has commonly been looked upon, by both right wing and left wing writers, as part of the counter-revolutionary answer to the rational movement which culminated in the French Revolution.[161] It was so viewed by Godwin. Marx, having declared that the principle of population "was greeted with jubilation by the English oligarchy as the great destroyer of all hankerings after human development," sought to refute it.[162] Godwin and William Thompson had already made the attempt, as had Proudhon and others. So varied a group of writers as Henry George, August Bebel, and G. B. Shaw, were to respond in like manner. In early nineteenth-century France certain Catholic writers discovered in Malthus support for their social philosophy, while

158. *Essay*, III, xii, p. 409; also III, ix, pp. 376ff. on the decline of Venice and other places. Malthus was not familiar with the population and economic theories of G. Ortes which reflected the situation of which Malthus wrote.

159. He wrote approvingly of bounties in the second edition of the *Essay* (pp. 451, 465–6), in view of the then state of English agriculture.

160. *Essay*, III, xi–xii, especially pp. 400–4, 412–15.

161. "The Age of Reason ended in the French Revolution. The Age of Stupidity began with Malthus." See J. R. Commons, *Institutional Economics* (New York, 1934), p. 244. "Malthus's book was anti-jacobin, expressly written to refute the equalitarian Utopia." Élie Halévy, *The Growth of Philosophic Radicalism*, translated by Mary Morris (London, 1928), p. 205. "Malthus was steeped in an inveterate Toryism as to social and economic organization." Hollander, *Notes*, p. xxiv, also p. xcvii. On replies to Malthus, see Bonar, *Malthus*, bk. IV.

162. *Capital* (Chicago, 1906), vol. I, p. 676n. See also S. M. Levin, "Marx versus Malthus" (Papers of the *Michigan Academy of Science, Arts, and Letters*, vol. XXII, 1936, pp. 243ff.). Pareto (*Cours d'économie politique*, pp. 118–19) had contended that Malthus's philosophy weakened the argument against revolutionary change.

liberal economists found in the *Essay* a complete answer to the arguments of the exponents of revolution.[163] In England and in America his work met a similar reception.[164] In fact, not until the twentieth century and the widespread diffusion of contraceptive practice, did the Malthusian argument against social revolution cease to be urged.

Three doctrines, or sets of beliefs, were converging in the latter part of the eighteenth century, and Malthus's *Essay* is a product of this convergence. It had been noted that man was making progress, technological and social; and that, since progress is cultural in character and culture is cumulative, progress must, *ceteris paribus,* be cumulating and unending. Of this view Godwin and Condorcet were enthusiastic exponents.[165] Secondly the common man, once looked upon as a creature of little dignity placed in the world for the service of the master classes, was coming into his own. A beneficiary, primary and secondary, of the redistribution of economic and political power under way, he was held in greater esteem than formerly; his wants, rights, and potentialities were receiving more attention than ever, and they would receive even greater attention as the democratic movement, and the values it stood for, gained in scope. It had been remarked, thirdly, that man does not live in a *boundless* physical, social, and psychological universe; that limitations are imposed upon his behaviour, and upon the outcome of this behaviour, by this circumscribed physical milieu, by his restricted physiological and psychological makeup, and by the social and institutional controls which issue out of these physical and personal conditions. Efforts to resolve and synthesize acceptably these three somewhat inconsistent sets of beliefs were brought to a head by the French Revolution and the principles it posed, and by consideration of proposals for the relief of the poor made as a result of the economic crisis occasioned in England by war with France and by bad harvests.[166]

The social philosophies of those who, before Malthus, concerned themselves with aspects of the problem to whose solution he addressed himself, were compounded in varying proportions of the three sets of beliefs which converged in Malthus's *Essay*. At one extreme is Hobbes who, supposing limited that for which men strive, and practically unbounded the appetites which actuate men to strive, concluded that men could live together in peace only if there was "a common power to keep them all in awe" and establish

163. See my "French Population Theory since 1800" (*Journal of Political Economy,* vol. XLIV, 1936, pp. 585ff., 743ff.).

164. See my "Population Doctrines in the United States" (*Journal of Political Economy,* vol. XLI, 1933, pp. 433ff., 639ff.). Cursory examination of English materials supports the above opinion.

165. E.g., see J. B. Bury, *The Idea of Progress* (London, 1924); Halévy, *The Growth of Philosophic Radicalism;* my *French Predecessors.* On differences between views of Godwin and Condorcet, see note 172 and text.

166. On these precipitating circumstances see Halévy, *The Growth of Philosophic Radicalism,* pp. 230ff.; Bonar, *Malthus,* pp. 27–31.

a maintainable balance between want and want-satisfaction.[167] Wallace, though not a disciple of Hobbes, reasoned in a like manner when he concluded that man's passions must eventually "involve . . . in universal confusion" even those living under the most perfect of governments. For under such governments "the inconveniences of having a family" would be removed, and the limited "earth would at last be overstocked" with inhabitants, with the result that force and fraud, war, cruel and unnatural customs, inequality, and other impediments to human happiness and population growth would be restored.[168] So also reasoned Townsend when, premising that fear of want impels men to work and that population growth is desirable only insofar as it is the consequence of industry and frugality, he condemned both communism and the poor laws.[169] Hobbes, Wallace, and Townsend, in short, supposed that progress, however great, would never free men of the necessity of resolving, albeit most imperfectly, the problems arising out of the pressure of unrestrained appetites against limited resources, or establish among men an essential identity of interests.

At the other extreme are Locke and, more particularly, Godwin and Condorcet. For Locke postulated a natural identity of interests, a state of nature that was peaceful and virtuous, a theory of nature essentially optimistic, and a comparatively easy solution—peaceful competition and exchange—for the problem of distribution and order Hobbes saw issuing out of scarcity.[170] Godwin, believing that self-love is incompatible with virtue, that a fusion of interests is attainable, that benevolence may be substituted for self-love as the primary motive to action, that labour could be changed "from a burthen into an amusement," and that progress, which is cumulative in character, was being retarded by the existing institutional framework of society, found in the abolition of this framework the key to the augmentation of human happiness. He proposed substituting for the system of property a system of equality, and for the existing institution of marriage—a "system of fraud" and the "worst of monopolies"—a system of free and flexible unions, it being "a question of no importance" in a "state of equality . . . to know who is the parent of each individual child"; and he looked forward to a time when every "species of public institution, may be laid

---

167. *Leviathan,* vol. I, xiii.

168. *Various Prospects of Mankind, Nature, and Providence* (London, 1761), pp. 113–25. Earlier he had said that "had it not been for the errors and vices of mankind, and the defects of government and education, the earth . . . perhaps might have been overstocked, many ages ago"; but he added that, with conditions as they were, there was no reason to fear that the earth would be fully cultivated, or that every country would be "plentifully stored with inhabitants." See *Dissertation,* pp. 13, 149.

169. *A Dissertation on the Poor Laws* (London, 1786). See Halévy, *The Growth of Philosophic Radicalism,* pp. 228–30.

170. On Hobbes and Locke, see T. Parsons, *The Structure of Social Action* (New York, 1937), pp. 87–106; Halévy, *The Growth of Philosophic Radicalism.* Locke's competitive solution was adopted by Adam Smith, Ricardo, and others.

aside as unnecessary.""¹⁷¹ Among the objections to the establishment and perpetuation of a system of equality considered by Godwin was that arising from the "principle of population" and developed by Wallace in 1761. To this Godwin replied that "myriads of centuries" might pass before the "habitable globe," as yet only one-fourth cultivated and badly at that, would be fully stocked; and that "when the earth shall refuse itself to a more extended population," men, their minds having established empire over matter, "will probably cease to propagate."¹⁷² Condorcet, in contradistinction to Godwin, emphasized the cumulative and progressive character of cultural and institutional change, suggesting that, if population pressure ever threatened, mankind would subject it to rational control.¹⁷³ Godwin and Condorcet, in short, discovering in mental, moral, and cultural progress an easy means of escape from the limitations recognized by Hobbes and stressed by Wallace, were not alarmed lest the democratic scheme of values be threatened by the free play of men's passions in a circumscribed universe.

While the form which Malthus's reply to Godwin took was largely determined by the latter's argument, its substance reflected Malthus's conception of the ends of man, his estimate of man's behaviour tendencies, and his expectations regarding cultural progress. That Malthus subscribed to the democratic scheme of values, is evident in his views on education, on the extension of the right of suffrage,¹⁷⁴ and on the happiness of men. Accepting, as he did, the Christian view, which "places our present as well as our future happiness in the exercise of those virtues which tend to fit us for a state of superior enjoyment," and the principle of utility, in his opinion the surest natural "criterion of moral rules," and deeming good that which makes for virtue and happiness, he urged men to subject their passions to the guidance of reason and so avoid pain and evil, or having suffered these, to profit thereby and direct themselves back into the path of virtue.¹⁷⁵ Evidently, therefore, Malthus differed from Godwin and Condorcet regarding values and ends, democratic and otherwise, in terms of detail far more than in terms of generality.

But Malthus did not believe these values and ends so easy of realization

---

171. *Political Justice*, vol. I, pp. 125–8, 330–42, vol. II, pp. 152–4, 170–1, 350ff., 361ff., 367–75. There is, Godwin believed, a natural tendency in men toward justice which, if allowed to develop, fuses the interests of men. On this point see Halévy, *The Growth of Philosophic Radicalism*, pp. 193ff.

172. *Political Justice*, vol. II, bk. VIII, chap. IX, Godwin, referring to Condorcet's work on progress, said that Condorcet rested his hopes upon the "growing perfectibility of art" instead of "upon the immediate and unavoidable operation of an improved intellect," as did Godwin. *Ibid.*, p. 377n. See note 182 below.

173. On Condorcet's views, see my *French Predecessors*, pp. 259–63.

174. Halévy, *The Growth of Philosophic Radicalism*, p. 244.

175. *Essay*, pp. 10n., 440–1, 446, 448–9, 455, 543–4, 567–8; 2d ed., pp. 484–5, 490–1, 494–5, 502–3; 1st ed., chaps. XVIII–XIX; *Summary View*, pp. 76–7; Zinke, "Six Letters from Malthus to Pierre Prevost," p. 183; Bonar, *Malthus*, bk. III.

as did Godwin and Condorcet, and he considered it better that men be alert to the difficulties that might beset their ventures than that they remain ignorant.[176] While he anticipated a "brilliant career of physical discovery," and "confidently" hoped that in consequence mankind would progress in virtue and happiness "to no unimportant extent,"[177] he looked upon resources as fixed by the niggardliness of nature far more than by the state of the industrial arts; and he always remained less optimistic than Godwin and Condorcet with respect to the prospective rate of technological progress and its effect upon production, particularly in agriculture where the augmentation of output on land under tillage and at the extensive margin was attended with much and increasing difficulty.[178] He pointed, moreover, to the limitedness of space, which would restrict increase as surely as would lack of food.[179]

Of greater practical importance, in Malthus's opinion, than the inability of progressing technology to overcome the limits to the augmentation of production set by a comparatively fixed physical milieu, were the obstacles interposed, in the way of the improvement of the human lot, by man's passions, of which that between the sexes was but one. For, while the human passions are either necessary to human welfare, or capable of being made conducive thereto, and, in accordance with the apparent intent of the Creator, should be directed to this purpose,[180] they cannot be subjected completely to appropriate discipline by human reason and institutions, and,

176. *Essay*, pp. 567–8 (1807). In this respect, and in his philosophy generally, Malthus reflected in some measure the philosophical "optimism" of the eighteenth century, with its emphasis upon the reality and the necessity of evils. See A. O. Lovejoy, *The Great Chain of Being* (Cambridge, 1936), chap. VII. Against this gloomy necessitarianism the philosophers of progress revolted; and in this revolt Malthus, despite his strictures upon the philosophy of indefinite progress, played no small part, being in some measure (see Bonar, *Malthus*, pp. 376ff.) under the influence of the same ideas as affected Godwin and Condorcet.

177. *Essay*, pp. 543–4.

178. This is evident in his emphasis upon the two ratios (e.g., *ibid.*, I, i and p. 551); in his estimate (1817) that England might support two or three times as many people at a somewhat improved scale of living; and in his supposition that in America, which might support fifty times its then (1817) population, the rate of growth would fall appreciably and labourers would "in time be much less liberally rewarded" (*ibid.*, pp. 292–4, 360, 461, 551). Only in newly settled areas (*ibid.*, pp. 285ff., 329–31, 439), and for a limited time, could food and numbers increase rapidly (cf. Adam Smith, *Wealth of Nations*, pp. 532ff.). In the 1803 *Essay* (pp. 7, 473 and note), Malthus, who had merely implied a law of diminishing returns in agriculture in the 1798 edition, expressed such a law, and declared contrary to fact James Anderson's position that a law of increasing returns prevailed in intensive cultivation. See J. H. Hollander's introduction to Malthus's *Inquiry into the Nature and Progress of Rent* (1815) (Baltimore, 1903). In the Encyclopedia article (*Summary View*, pp. 4–6, 26–7, 31, 34), Malthus emphasized the "diminishing and limited power of increasing the produce of the soil," observing that the forces of improvement ("division of labour," "invention of machinery," "accumulation of capital") are less efficient in increasing food than in augmenting conveniences and luxuries.

179. *Summary View*, p. 5; *Principles*, pp. 208–9. See also Ricardo's comment upon Malthus's observation that the Creator did not ordain "unlimited facility of producing food" inasmuch as space was limited (*ibid.*, p. 209; Hollander, *Notes*, pp. 108–10).

180. *Essay*, pp. 444–8, 452–5 (also in 2d ed.); also Bonar, *Malthus*, pp. 324–35. Here Malthus follows Paley (*Natural Theology* [1802], Albany, 1803, chap. xxvi, pp. 344–45), who

therefore, because of their over-pursuit and misdirection, produce pain and evil as well as happiness and welfare.[181] In short, because he attached greater weight than did Godwin to the impelling power of the "corporeal propensities" and lesser weight to the ordering power of "reason," Malthus was forced to substitute for Godwin's expectation of indefinite improvement in human affairs the expectation of only limited improvement,[182] and for Godwin's proposal that institutions be removed, the counter-recommendation that institutional restrictions and self-control be strengthened through appropriate education.[183]

The passion between the sexes, out of which issued the principle of population, was good and necessary in Malthus's scheme, for he looked upon this principle as "best suited to the nature and situation of man"[184] and as the main motive behind social progress.[185] Hence, whereas earlier writers had been content to recount almost every supposed advantage of population growth except that which Marlowe put in the mouth of Mephistophilis, Malthus pointed to both the necessary and the salutary character of the tendency of numbers to increase faster than supplies, emphasizing, however, its influence upon man's individual motivation rather than its possible effect upon the division of labour. For man is unsuited to profit by unearned leisure, indolent and torpid by nature, "inert, sluggish, and averse from

---

referred (*ibid.*, p. 340) to Malthus's first essay; and who looked upon vice and misery as consequences, in part, of the excessive pursuit and the misdirected use of the passions, and who emphasized the need for their subjection to reason and self-government aided by religion. On the doctrine of passions see Kaye, *The Fable of the Bees . . . by Bernard Mandeville*, Introduction; Halévy, *The Growth of Philosophic Radicalism*, vol. I, i; J. Laird, *Hume's Philosophy of Human Nature* (London, 1932), chap. VII. See note 141 above.

181. *Essay*, IV, i; also pp. 10n., 551–2.

182. *Essay*, 1st ed., chap. XIII; also *Edinburgh Review* (1810), pp. 472, 475. Of Godwin's remark that the passion between the sexes might be extinguished, Malthus said: "Men in the decline of life have, in all ages, declaimed against a passion which they have ceased to feel" (*Essay*, 1st ed., pp. 210–11). On the Malthusian versus the anti-Malthusian view of progress, see Halévy, *The Growth of Philosophic Radicalism*, pp. 242–4, 275–6, 363ff.

183. On the important role of education in the later utilitarian scheme, see Halévy, *The Growth of Philosophic Radicalism*, pp. 20ff., 282ff. Malthus's faith in education, while not so marked as that of Helvetius, was great. See *Essay*, pp. 439–43, 531–40 (in 2d ed.). In 1807, having indicated that he had not intended by his opinions to alarm the prejudices of the poor, he said: "We have only to proceed in improving our civil polity, conferring the benefits of education upon all, and removing every obstacle to the general extension of all those privileges and advantages which may be enjoyed in common" (*ibid.*, p. 565).

184. *Principles*, p. 208.

185. "The principle of population, therefore, appears as the essential motive force behind social progress." See E. F. Penrose, *Population Theories and their Application* (Stanford, 1934), p. 24. Here (*Essay*, pp. 446–7) Malthus is thinking in terms of man's supposed psychological nature. Elsewhere (see secs. 1 and 11 of this article) Malthus noticed other determinants of progress when he observed that extreme misery checks progress, and that bad government and watertight institutional structures bring the growth of wealth and population to a premature stop. T. H. Marshall (*Economic History Review*, 1935, p. 76), having noted that population "must be regarded as a cause and not merely as an effect," concluded that in England "the rapid growth of the population may have been on the whole a stimulus to economic progress, but it was at times a cause of friction and distress."

labour, unless compelled by necessity." The principle of population—its effort "to increase with greater rapidity than its supplies"—provides this necessity. It excites man to action, "to further the gracious designs of Providence," and, operating in conjunction with the pressure of his wants, awakens his mind and sharpens his faculties. It presses man to extend cultivation and fulfil the "end of nature," namely, the peopling of the earth. It overcomes that *vis inertiae,* which, as Nieboer has remarked, has played so great a part in the history of mankind.[186] In fact, were control of numbers easy, population would not "reach its natural and proper extent," a "necessary stimulus to industry" would be removed, and the improvement of man's mundane lot would be retarded.[187] For this reason, far more than because of any immediate theological prejudice,[188] he approved only of "moral restraint," at which he had at least hinted in the First Essay, as a preventive check; he ignored the question of post-marital control; and he opposed the practice of contraception.[189]

It was essential, however, that the passion between the sexes be subjected to proper restraint; for the principle of population could not, if its multiplicative effects were insufficiently contained, efficiently generate social progress. When the pressure of numbers became so great as virtually to universalize misery and poverty and to check capital formation, stimulants to industry were dulled, and despotism and ignorance, so fatal to the improvement of the standard of living, tended to flourish.[190] When, on the contrary, men were alert to the imminence of intensified population pressure and to the evils that accompanied it, they tended to develop habits of prudence, thrift, and industry, and in consequence, to conduct themselves in a manner conducive to progress in well-being.

Institutions and customs, Malthus's argument runs in substance, develop largely out of the underlying nature of man and his physical environment. If they are both to survive and to contribute to man's welfare, they must

186. *Slavery as an Industrial System* (The Hague, 1910), p. 414. While Paley looked upon the principle of population as good, he nonetheless described the *vis inertiae* as making for tranquility and order (*Natural Theology,* pp. 340–1, 344–5).

187. *Essay,* pp. 445–52, 545–7, 572; 1st ed., pp. 354, 358–66, 370–1; *Principles,* pp. 208–9; also sec. III (iv) and (v) of this article.

188. This distinction is not important, for his interpretation of the role of the principle of population had a theological basis.

189. *Essay,* IV, i–ii, pp. 9, 301, 559–61, 572; 1st ed., p. 340; Penrose, *Population Theories and their Application,* pp. 21–30; S. M. Levin, "Malthus' Conception of the Checks to Population" (*Human Biology,* vol. X, 1938, pp. 214–34). Malthus referred to prolongation of lactation, considered by Petty to be a hindrance to speedy propagation (cited by R. R. Kuczynski, in L. Hogben, *Political Arithmetic* [New York, 1938], p. 293), but did not suggest it, as did certain nineteenth-century writers, as an effective preventive check, either because he considered it *per se* ineffective (*Essay,* pp. 23, 81), or because he considered it too powerful and otherwise unsanctionable.

190. *Essay,* pp. 431–2, 434–5, 471–3, 498; also in 2d ed. "Even poverty itself, . . . the great spur to industry, when it has once passed certain limits, almost ceases to operate"; and hopeless indigence "destroys all vigorous exertion." *Essay,* p. 432.

consist with his nature and impose direction and restraint upon his passions. And they must be consonant with the principle of population, serving at the same time to promote industry and thrift and to favour the more salutary and less objectionable of the checks whose function it is to repress the superior power of population.[191] Malthus, therefore, found untenable both Godwin's conception of the nature of man and his complete oversight of the regulatory function of existing institutions. The socio-economic organization of mankind could not be built around the principle of benevolence;[192] it had to be founded upon self-love, upon the "principle of self-interest" and those institutions which gave expression to this principle — namely, marriage and the family, private property and inheritance, and a form of government calculated to preserve these institutions. It was to this principle and to these institutions that men owed whatever progress they had made and whatever capacity they had shown for curbing the principle of population.[193] These institutions served to channelize properly the passions of men, to make each person of discretionary age and status dependent predominantly upon himself, and to visit upon each the fruits, good or bad, of his behaviour and practice.[194] Where these circumstances prevailed, the "master spring of industry, the desire of bettering our condition," together with the fear of making it worse, had freest play, and man was most prone, *ceteris paribus*, to practice prudential restraint;[195] there too and there alone competition and competitive individualism could flourish without degenerating into war.[196]

191. *Essay,* III, i–iii, also pp. 21, 24, 571–3; *Summary View,* pp. 35–6, 41–2, 72. Although men tend to blame their troubles upon institutions, the effects of institutions are "superficial" in comparison with the effects of "those deeper-seated causes of evil which result from the laws of nature and the passions of mankind." *Essay,* pp. 307–8, 457–8; also in 2d ed. On the checks, the conception of which Malthus got (*Essay,* 1st ed., pp. 339ff.) from a consideration of Price's untenable conclusion, see Levin, cited in note 189 above.

192. *Essay,* III, ii, p. 317, also p. 573; 2d ed., pp. 378–9. In the Encyclopedia article, Malthus states that the alternatives are Godwin's system of common property and that of private property, of which the latter is by far the more productive and the more conducive to the generation of desirable habits and moral qualities; and that popular education cannot fit men for a system of common property. See *Summary View,* pp. 35–7, 72–4; Bonar, *Malthus,* pp. 76–7.

193. *Essay,* III, ii–iii, p. 543; 2d ed., pp. 366ff., 604; 1st ed., pp. 286ff.; *Principles,* pp. 208–9. The passion of self-love, however, if "pushed to excess" becomes the vice of selfishness (*Essay,* p. 554n.). That egoism is the predominating, if not the exclusive, inclination of human nature, was commonly accepted in the eighteenth century (Halévy, *The Growth of Philosophic Radicalism,* p. 14).

194. He attributed the improved condition of the lower classes in France after the revolution to the diminished proportion of births which he traced to the fact that everyone now depended "more upon himself and less upon others." *Essay,* p. 361; this was written in 1817. See note 62 in sec. 1 of this article.

195. *Essay,* pp. 347, 529, 535, 539, 543; in 2d ed. "The desire of bettering our condition, and the fear of making it worse, . . . is the *vis medicatrix reipublicae* in politics, and is continually counteracting the disorders arising from narrow institutions" (*ibid.,* p. 347). Cf. also Bonar, *Malthus,* pp. 120–2.

196. Parsons, *The Structure of Social Action,* p. 106.

Were existing institutions abolished and a system of equality established in their place, man would no longer feel those "stimulants to exertion which can alone" overcome his natural indolence and prompt him to cultivate the earth and fabricate the conveniences and comforts necessary to his happiness. This argument Malthus considered decisive. But he added a second and supposedly as decisive argument, which followed from the tendency of the human race to increase faster than the means of subsistence. In a system of equality no one is or feels himself to be under constraint not to marry; nor is marriage in any wise rationed; nor is the tendency to multiply too rapidly restricted by those means "which result from the laws of private property, and the moral obligation imposed on every man by the commands of God and nature to support his own children." It followed, Malthus concluded, either that this tendency must be restrained by means "infinitely more cruel," or that a system of equality must, soon after having been established, terminate in poverty and misery.[197] He rejected as unworkable, therefore, the systems of Godwin, Condorcet, Owen, and the Spenceans, together with Raynal's view that man had a right to subsistence and Paine's opinion that man's want of happiness originated in his governmental institutions.[198]

Suppose a state of equality were established, free of all those institutions to which many attributed man's want of happiness. Could such a state persist, Malthus asked, in the face of the fact that it did not consist with the laws of nature and the passions of men? His answer was in the negative. Upon the establishment of such a state of equality, numbers would grow until want again made itself generally felt and the spirit of benevolence gave place once more to "self-love." Thereupon private property and marriage would be restored and with them inequality; all without property would be under the necessity of working; and numbers would be restrained by the checks growing out of the re-established parental responsibility for offspring. Attempts to set up systems of equality, therefore, were doomed to failure; because they generated population pressure which, in turn, brought about the return of the institutions of property and family and the restoration of inequality and of a society divided into classes. Even so, attempts to establish a system of equality could visit much misery upon men before such a system finally gave way to a set of institutions consistent with the laws of nature and the passions of men.[199]

197. *Essay*, III, iii, pp. 320, 323, also, pp. 49n., 479. Although chap. III in bk. III was not added until 1817, the substance of the above argument appears in both the first and second editions.

198. *Essay*, III, i–iii, IV, vi, pp. 475–7; Malthus expressed substantially the same opinion in the first and second editions.

199. *Essay*, III, ii–iii. Hume, noting that property was inconsistent with both "profuse abundance" and extreme scarcity, associated its origin with relative scarcity. See Commons, *Institutional Economics*, pp. 140ff.; Laird, *Hume's Philosophy of Human Nature*, pp. 227ff.

Malthus's several views on charity and public relief have the appearance of inconsistency; in his opinion, however, they were consistent, one with another, and with his conception of man's proclivities. When a prosperity-inducing stimulus to wealth and population is suddenly removed, and as a result, "produce" and "consumption" get out of balance, it is better to employ those thrown out of work by the decline in the demand for labour than to expose them to the "bad moral effects of idleness" and the "evil habits" which come with extended dependence upon alms. The employment provided, however, should be of the sort whose results "do not come for sale into the market," or "interfere with existing capitals," and thus worsen the actual state of affairs; it should add to consumption without adding to the output of immediately salable produce. Employment on public works of all kinds—e.g., the making and repairing of roads, bridges, railways, canals, etc.—and on the improvement of the land met this requirement, in Malthus's opinion.[200] Even so there was some danger that the provision of such employment through the expenditure of revenues raised by taxation or public subscription might "have the effect of concealing too much the failure of the national demand for labour, and prevent the population from gradually accommodating itself to a reduced demand."[201]

Malthus observed also that, under circumstances such as Great Britain then (1816–17) found itself—a sharply contracted demand for labour and much unemployment—"emigration is most useful as a temporary relief," serving to shorten the interval required by a population to "conform itself to the state of demand for labour." Emigration would not, however, provide permanent relief of population pressure.[202]

Because Malthus was a utilitarian he could not subscribe to the doctrine

200. *Essay*, pp. 352–3; *Principles*, II, i, 10, pp. 429–30. These views were first published in the 1817 *Essay* and the 1820 *Principles*. Malthus is dealing here with the problem of post-war unemployment—an extreme instance of the oscillatory nature of population growth; of the tendency of numbers, in response to the stimulus of increased employment, to grow temporarily beyond the capacity of the labour market to absorb them. See *Essay*, pp. 11–14, 141, 411, 481–2; *Principles*, pp. 279–80, 416–17, 435–6. In the First Essay (pp. 30–5), Malthus, already alert to the time factor, commented upon the oscillatory character of population growth, saying that this vibration had escaped notice because the histories of mankind "are histories only of the upper classes." Steuart (*Works*, vol. I, p. 193) remarked that agricultural production and therefore population growth oscillate; he proposed that, when the demand for labour falls short of the supply, balance be restored by diminishing hands through their employment as soldiers, in colonies, and on public works (*ibid.*, p. 310). Condorcet was somewhat aware of this oscillation, Malthus (*Essay*, 1st ed., p. 152) noted.

201. *Principles*, pp. 429–30. Malthus opposed proposals to supply the deficiency in demand for labour through an issue of paper money (*ibid.*, pp. 431–2), or through a reduction in taxes (*Essay*, pp. 354–5); he supposed, rather, that a public works programme would divert purchasing power to those employed thereon and so spread unemployment "over a larger surface" (*ibid.*, pp. 353–4).

202. *Essay*, III, iv, pp. 331–2 (1817), 573–4; also Bonar, *Malthus*, pp. 195–9, for Malthus's evidence before the Emigration Committee in 1827. "A certain degree of emigration is . . . favourable to the population of the mother country," he remarked (*Essay*, p. 287; 2d ed., p. 340), as had Franklin and others (see notes 7–8 and text in sec. 1 of this article).

of natural rights, or admit that the indigent had a natural right to relief as some writers maintained;[203] because he supposed the principal cause of poverty to be undue population growth, he entertained no hope of permanent relief from redivision of wealth and similar measures,[204] and because he believed that man should depend upon "his own exertions, his own industry and foresight," he approved of work-relief only under the conditions indicated and of charity only when men were the victims of "unmerited calamities."[205] Were the idle and the negligent assured public support, the tendency on the part of men to exert themselves in order to better their condition and win security would be weakened, and population growth would be unduly stimulated.[206] The English poor laws operated to generate idleness and dissipation and "to create the poor which they maintain," to lower wages, to divert resources from the more industrious to the less valuable members of society, and to diminish the general resources of a country; therefore they defeated their benevolent purpose.[207] The determination of the proper rate of population growth, Malthus implied, should be left to the price of labour, which, if "left to find its natural level . . . expresses clearly the wants of

203. *Summary View*, pp. 71–4; *Essay*, pp. 552–8; also pp. 475–7, for criticism of views of Paine and Raynal on rights, pp. 541–2, where he denies right of the poor to demand employment and maintenance; also 2d ed., pp. 531, for the famous feast passage expunged from later editions. Malthus looked upon man's rights as not unconditional (Halévy, *The Growth of Philosophic Radicalism*, pp. 242ff.). On Malthus's idea of utility, which he may have gotten from Paley, see *Essay*, pp. 500–1, and Bonar, *Malthus*, pp. 39, 213, 331–3, 346–8. The principle of utility, which Bentham and others apparently took from Hume (Halévy, *The Growth of Philosophic Radicalism*, pp. 11ff.), was employed by Burke to attack the theory of the Rights of Man (*ibid.*, pp. 156–7). From Burke Malthus may have learned the suitability of this principle to the defence of necessary institutions.

204. *Essay*, pp. 541–2, 580, 582–3; also sec. III (v) of this article. "No desire, however great, of increasing our subsistence can keep us out of the reach of the most miserable poverty, if we do not, at the same time, exercise the more efficient power we possess of restraining the progress of population by prudential habits." Senior, *Two Lectures on Population*, p. 70, also p. 84. The poor alone are "the arbiters of their own destiny" (*Principles*, p. 279).

205. *Essay*, IV, x, especially pp. 503–4; also chaps. XI–XIII. Most of the cited material appeared in the second edition. In his unpublished *The Crisis* he had advocated outdoor relief and commended Pitt's proposal to accord special relief to fathers of more than three children (Halévy, *The Growth of Philosophic Radicalism*, p. 235). Malthus opposed public housing, the use of cash reserve subsidies to encourage deferment of marriage, more than limited application of the cow system, and assured assistance for the aged and for widows and orphans. See *Essay*, III, i, IV, xi; pp. 556–64; Zinke, "Six Letters from Malthus to Pierre Prevost," p. 184.

206. *Essay*, III, i, pp. 299ff.; 1st ed., pp. 149ff. Here Malthus is criticizing Condorcet.

207. *Principles*, pp. 72–3; *Essay*, III, v–vii, pp. 342ff.; IV, ix, p. 493; most of this material is also in the second edition. Elsewhere he expressed "doubt of the effect of our poor laws in encouraging an increase of population. Their direct effects are certainly to do this"; but their indirect effects upon housing may counterbalance their direct effects (Zinke, "Six Letters from Malthus to Pierre Prevost," p. 184). Young (*Political Arithmetic*, pp. 93ff.) had said that the poor law, by causing the supply of cottages to be restricted, checked marriage and population (cf. Malthus, *Essay*, p. 532). Griffith (*Population Problems of the Age of Malthus*, chap. VI, pp. 165, 169) concludes that the effect of the poor laws upon marriage and natural increase was slight, but Marshall ("The Population Problem during the Industrial Revolution," *Economic History*, pp. 431ff.) believes that only by a comparative study of local figures may the Malthusian view, if invalid, be disproved.

society respecting population";[208] and each should be made to depend upon his own resources and efforts for the support of himself and his family. Malthus therefore advocated that the poor laws be gradually abolished; that each be made solely responsible for the support of himself and his family; that by means of a suitable educational programme, such as Adam Smith had proposed, the poor be acquainted with the true cause of their poverty and with the necessity of practising moral restraint; and that maximum possible effect be given to "the desire of bettering our condition, . . . the true mode of improving the state of the lower classes."[209]

Malthus was a counter-revolutionary in that he opposed certain principles associated with the French Revolution and condemned revolution in general. He was a conservative in that he attached great weight to the essentially constant, and less weight to the essentially variable, elements in nature, man, and social relations; in that he stressed the regulatory function of institutions in general, and not only opposed but also considered very improbable any important change in the fundamental institutional and social structure of English society; and in that he held, and believed it necessary to hold, the individual almost completely responsible for his actions and for his failure to act. He was a conservative too in that, while he advocated the education of the masses, he did not suppose man to be so plastic as Helvetius had assumed, and therefore readily transformable, by law and training, into a virtuous being. He was a conservative, finally, in that he could find no grounds for easy optimism and an easy harmonizing of interests: man's road had been hard and it would probably continue hard. But he was not a counter-revolutionary in that he opposed all changes in government and in institutional structure; for he estimated their value in terms of their utility and not in terms of their mere preservation. Hence his opposition, for example, to feudalism. Neither did he oppose improvement of the condition of the common man. This he always sought, and this, together with the strengthening of democratic values, the implementation

---

208. *Essay,* III, v, pp. 339–40, also pp. 172, 506 (also in 2d ed.); *Principles,* pp. 72–3.

209. *Essay,* IV, iii, vi–ix, xii; most of this material is already in the second edition; see also 1st ed., chap. v. Hume (*Essays,* vol. I, p. 439) had said that the parish-rates tended to produce "idleness, debauchery, and a continual decay" even as had the ancient Roman *sportula.* Charity, wrote Steuart (*Works,* vol. I, pp. 118–23, 210–11) with especial reference to Spain, because it gives food, stimulates multiplication that is not of advantage to society; it does not cure misery. Adam Smith (*Wealth of Nations,* pp. 135ff.) declared that the poor laws obstructed "the circulation of labour." Townsend, looking upon the poor laws as the beginning of communism, condemned them on the same ground he condemned communism (see note 169 and text above). Although Malthus did not at first know Townsend's work, he was criticizing, in his discussion of Condorcet, what appears to be the latter's reply to Townsend (Halévy, *The Growth of Philosophic Radicalism,* pp. 228–30; also Malthus's comments on Townsend, *Essay,* pp. 502, 506–8). Already in the late seventeenth century, at which time a large population was considered desirable because it meant a large labour supply, the poor law was condemned on the ground that it reduced the available supply of labour. See T. E. Gregory, "The Economics of Employment in England, 1660–1713" (*Economica,* vol. I, 1921, pp. 37, 40, 41).

of his doctrines was intended to accomplish. He supplied, in the form of his concept of effective demand (which implicitly denied a natural identity of the interests of men), an instrument of analysis conducive to the amelioration of the condition of the common man, the full potentialities of which were not grasped until a century after his death.[210]

(iv) Pro-marriage and Pro-natality Measures

Many writers, in the eighteenth and preceding centuries, had advocated the adoption, by the state, of measures intended to multiply marriage and to stimulate natality.[211] Moreover, the second half of the eighteenth century had witnessed, in England, both controversy over whether the ancient or the modern nations were the more populous, and expression of apprehension at the seeming non-growth of the English population.

Malthus took the side of Hume against Wallace on the question of the comparative populousness of ancient and modern nations,[212] and the side of those who said that England's population had grown since the revolution (1688),[213] inasmuch as he believed that the means of subsistence had increased, and in consequence, population. Furthermore, he opposed both measures designed directly to encourage marriage and natality, and institutional arrangements which, though not established for this purpose, tended to exercise the same effect; because he supposed that, when food was avail-

210. See J. J. O'Leary, "Malthus and Keynes" (*Journal of Political Economy*, vol. L, 1942, pp. 901–19). Malthus was not a reactionary, concludes Bonar (*Malthus*, pp. 298–9, 336), and "would have been much amazed to hear that his doctrines were . . . a vindication of things as they are."

211. E.g., see Stangeland, *Pre-Malthusian Doctrines of Population;* E. A. J. Johnson, *Predecessors of Adam Smith;* A. Small, *The Cameralists* (Chicago, 1909); my *French Predecessors*.

212. Wallace had said that ancient nations were more populous in his *A Dissertation on the Numbers of Mankind in Ancient and Modern Times* (1753); Hume had said the modern nations were more populous ("Of the Populousness of Ancient Nations," *Essays*, vol. I, pp. 381–442). See Malthus, *Essay*, pp. 59ff., pp. 136ff., 158; 1st ed., pp. 55–9. This controversy engaged the attention of many eighteenth-century writers.

213. Price had said that England's population had decreased since 1688; and John Brown in *An Estimate of the Manners and Principles of the Times* (London, 1757), pp. 186ff. had found "great Reason to believe . . . the Nation is less populous than it was fifty years ago," inasmuch as "Vanity and Effeminacy" had lessened the "Desire of Marriage," and "Intemperance and Disease" had increased mortality and occasioned, "among the *lower Ranks* . . . in some Degree an Impotence of Propagation." That Price was mistaken and that England's population had increased had been asserted by Young (*Political Arithmetic*, pp. 64ff., 96ff., 322ff.), by Wales (1781), and by Howlett (*Examination of Dr. Price's Essays on the Population of England and Wales*, etc.) who supposed a one-third increase since 1688. In the first *Essay* (pp. 314–15) Malthus supposed that the truth "lies between" the estimates of Price and Howlett. On Malthus's later views see *Essay*, II, viii–ix, and p. 428; *Principles*, I, iv, 5. Concerning population growth in eighteenth-century England, see Griffith, *Population Problems of the Age of Malthus*, chap. I; Marshall, "The Population Problem during the Industrial Revolution"; Buer, *Health, Wealth and Population;* E. C. K. Gonner "The Population of England in the Eighteenth Century" (*Journal of the Royal Statistical Society*, vol. LXXVI, 1913, pp. 261–303). On the views of Price, Howlett, and others see *ibid.;* also Bonar, *Theories*, chap. VII, and *Malthus*, pp. 108–9, 171–9.

able and accessible to the masses, men needed no additional stimulus to multiply, and because he disapproved certain of the objectives of the populationists. He did not, of course, oppose economic improvements which, by making for the increase of wealth and employment, operated also to increase numbers.[214]

The disposition on the part of men to marry and multiply, Malthus always supposed, is sufficiently strong to provide whatever numbers the prevailing prices of labour, the habits of consumption of the population, and the resources and available food supply of a country call for.[215] It would suffice to do this if the produce of the earth were unlimited; it has sufficed and does suffice to do this in the face of many obstacles;[216] it suffices, and often more than suffices, to do this when, as is almost always the case, a population's economic universe is limited, its food supply is susceptible of only slow augmentation, and it can obtain little relief through emigration or through importation of provision.[217] It is futile, therefore, to encourage early marriage, to disgrace celibacy, or otherwise to force natality and population growth. For when the available food supply and resources can accommodate only a given rate of growth, an increase in natality above the level required to supply this rate merely brings about an offsetting increase in mortality,[218] and it may produce a state of misery unfavourable to the augmentation of production, and, therefore, to population growth.[219] A nation can no more load population upon its agricultural resources beyond their capacity to

214. See sec. III (v) of this article, on optimum population. He did not generally evaluate the theses of populationist writers; but he criticized Montesquieu and Süssmilch for advocating encouragement to marriage (*Essay*, pp. 181–2), and Young for supporting the cow system and a potato diet (*ibid.*, IV, xi); and he approved the views of Townsend and the French Committee of Mendicity (see my *French Predecessors*, pp. 307ff.) on the poor laws (*Essay*, pp. 485, 506ff., in 2d ed.). Of earlier populationist doctrine he wrote: "In the earlier ages of the world, when war was the great business of mankind, . . . legislators and statesmen . . . encouraged an increase of people in every possible way." Popular religions had supported this view. The consequent rapid procreation had conduced to incessant war and so to the perpetuation of these pronatalist moral sentiments. The Christian religion, however, had subordinated marriage to higher duties and had imposed on man the obligation not to marry until he could support his children; it thus operated to prevent a redundancy of population and resultant offensive war, and to bring about widely diffused well-being which made for effective defence against aggression. *Essay*, pp. 453–5 (in 2d ed.); also 5th edition (preface), where he comments on the demand, now (1817) at an end, for men, occasioned by the Napoleonic wars.

215. *Essay*, pp. 156, 227, 339–40, 363, 377–8, 433–4, 547–8, 578–9; Senior, *Two Lectures on Population*, pp. 61–4; Bonar, *Malthus*, pp. 114–16, 329. Prudence would never win "too great a mastery over the natural passions and affections." See *Edinburgh Review*, 1810, pp. 472, 475.

216. *Essay*, II, xiii, also pp. 429–30; also in 2d ed.

217. *Ibid.*, pp. 324, 438–9 (in 2d ed.). Malthus was not disposed, as were some of the perfectibilians, to look upon the source of provision as an almost inexhaustible widow's cruse (2 Kings 4.4).

218. *Ibid.*, pp. 181, 432–5, 547–51; also bks. I–II; also Bonar, *Malthus*, pp. 139–42. A similar argument appears in Steuart, *Works*, vol. I, pp. 104–7, 207–9; cf. Adam Smith, *Wealth of Nations*, p. 79.

219. *Essay*, pp. 431–5.

support than a grazier can crowd stock upon his pastures beyond their capacity to subsist.[220]

If numbers fail to increase, or if they decline, Malthus's argument continues, it is not for want of a disposition on the part of men to marry and multiply; it is for want of food.[221] The underlying causes of the non-growth or decline of population must be sought, therefore, in the conditions which prevent the augmentation of the food supply or its being made available to the lower classes.[222] Efforts to stimulate natality, as distinguished from successful efforts to augment the food supply, are doomed to failure. For this reason, and because they tended to worsen the condition of the lower classes, Malthus opposed encouragements to natality, the poor laws, and all other arrangements that transferred from the individual to the community responsibility for the support of his offspring. But he did not oppose allowances for children above six and he did not condemn measures such as Colbert's, because these schemes for relief, while they provided help to occasional very large families, did not encourage marriage.[223]

Malthus did approve, however, as was shown earlier, of changes in the economic structure of society which, while consistent with the sentiments and passions of men and conducive to the improvement of the state of the lower classes, served to augment the output of goods and services, to increase the effective demand for labour, and to facilitate population growth. For he looked upon population growth, if it took place under proper conditions, as good, and upon the usual pro-natality measures as bad, not because they might induce an increase in births, but because they could not evoke both an increase in births *and* the other conditions prerequisite to the support and happiness of the population.[224]

Malthus was always at pains to show that population normally tends to increase when the food supply accessible to the masses expands; for much of his social theory rested upon this assumption. He denied that "the passion between the sexes, or the natural prolifickness of women, diminishes in the progress of society."[225] And while he admitted of a "very few in-

---

220. *Ibid.*, pp. 360–1, 546–7.
221. "There never has been, nor probably ever will be, any other cause than want of food, which makes the population of a country permanently decline," *Ibid.*, p. 429.
222. *Ibid.*, e.g., pp. 136, 138–9, 428–30.
223. *Ibid.*, pp. 453–5, 536–7; also IV, xi. Malthus criticized Pitt's poor bill on the ground that it might tend to increase population (*ibid.*, 1st ed., pp. 94–5, 134–5).
224. Even Paley, a populationist, emphasized only indirect stimulants such as encouragement of agriculture and employment (*Moral Philosophy*, pp. 472–4).
225. *Essay*, p. 575 (1817); *Summary View*, pp. 58–62. Had he pursued his line of thought regarding the effect of European contact upon natives (*Essay*, pp. 36–7; cf. also p. 46), or the desire-weakening effect of overindulgence, and licentiousness (e.g., *Essay*, pp. 56, 103, 139n., 171–2), he might have hit upon John Rae's theory of the decline in the "effective desire of offspring." Because he was intent upon demonstrating the existence of the principle of population, he overlooked this possibility. See also Levin's discussion, "Malthus' Conception of the Checks to Population" (*Human Biology*, vol. X. pp. 230ff.).

stances, such as the negroes in the West Indies, and one or two others, where population does not keep up to the level of the means of subsistence," he insisted upon their unimportance and unrepresentativeness.[226] "Under every form of government, however unjust and tyrannical, in every climate of the known world, however apparently unfavourable to health, it has been found that population, almost with the sole exception above alluded to, has been able to keep itself up to the level of the means of subsistence."[227] Had Malthus assigned considerable weight to checks of the sort he here has in mind, or had he anticipated the subsequent widespread diffusion of effective contraceptive practices, he would not only have had to modify his evaluation of measures intended to encourage marriage and natality; he would also have had to reformulate his theory of social progress.

(v) *Optimum Population*

Although the notion of an optimum population is not recent, it was not until the nineteenth century that this concept was rather carefully formulated in terms of per-capita income, or per-capita welfare.[228] Many pre-nineteenth century writers observed that power, national strength, happiness, etc., are conditioned by population density and population growth. These writers differed, however, with respect to what they wanted maximized, for they differed in social philosophy and value attitudes; and while every social philosophy and set of value attitudes emphasizes a maximum of some sort, not all emphasize the same maximum. These writers differed, therefore, regarding what constitutes an optimum population. Some of the mercantilists, for example, favoured population densities and growth rates suited to maximize national power. Others favoured a population condition designed to maximize the income of the dominant minority. Still others favoured a population situation somewhat consistent with the welfare of the common man. In general, late eighteenth-century writers, who attached importance to the happiness of the many, and who shared the new emphasis upon the dignity of the human personality and the right of the common man to participate significantly in the fruits of economic and political progress,

226. *Essay,* 3rd ed., vol. I, I, ii, p. 28. In the fifth and sixth editions he wrote "some instances" and described them as "extreme cases." Slaves in the West Indies would be able "by procreation fully to supply the effective demand for labour," were their condition raised to that of the masses in the "worst governed countries of the world" (*Essay,* p. 569 [1807], also p. 137). He supposed that "depravity of morals" checked marriage "at least among the upper classes" in ancient Rome, but he attributed the lack of population growth in the other classes to slavery and other institutions unfavourable to industry (*ibid.,* I, xiv).

227. *Essay,* p. 569. The word "almost" was not included in this passage when it first appeared in 1807.

228. See A. B. Wolfe, "The Optimum Size of Population," in L. I. Dublin, *Population Problems* (New York, 1926); L. Robbins, "The Optimum Theory of Population," in *London Essays in Economics in Honour of E. Cannan* (London, 1927); S. S. Cohn, *Die Theorie des Bevolkerungsoptimums* (Marburg, 1934); my "Pareto on Population, II" Section VII, *Quarterly Journal of Economics,* November, 1944).

had begun to think in terms of population densities and growth rates consistent with the improvement of the economic lot of the lower classes; and in their writings are foreshadowed the later income and welfare optimum concepts. These eighteenth-century foreshadowings of the optimum concept, unlike the late nineteenth- and twentieth-century notion, ran in essentially static rather than in dynamic terms. Furthermore, the late eighteenth-century writers, unlike those of earlier periods, did not suppose that population growth could be stepped up or down in accordance with the requirements of their optima; for it had come generally to be accepted that population growth adjusts itself to the food supply and the prevailing patterns of consumption.

Malthus, as has already been indicated, looked upon the principle of population as good and necessary to social progress, and he stressed the advantages associated with population growth. A country's power to increase its resources and defend its possessions depends upon its having a population that is efficient—i.e., almost "constantly employed." It is the Creator's intention that the earth be replenished. There is nothing "more desirable than the most rapid increase of population, unaccompanied by vice and misery."[229] "There is not a truer criterion of the happiness and innocence of a people than the rapidity of their increase."[230] Malthus did not, however, educe an argument for population growth from the principle of division of labour, presumably because he took this for granted, preferring instead to consider barriers to the extension of specialization.[231]

At the same time Malthus was interested primarily in the prevention of poverty, in the amelioration of the condition of the underlying population, and in democratic values generally. Hence, while he favoured the growth of population, he insisted upon its being "healthy, virtuous, and happy"; and he declared himself "an enemy to vice and misery, and consequently to that unfavourable proportion between population and food, which produces these evils."[232] He did not admit the opinion that numbers should be sufficiently great to make manpower continually available to recruiting sergeants and employers at very low wages; for then the lower classes could experience neither the personal respectability nor the improved economic situation that might otherwise be theirs, and war, because of the redundancy of population, would be more probable.[233] "The wealth and power of nations," Malthus wrote, in consistence with his utilitarian philosophy, "are,

229. *Essay,* pp. 546–50 (1817); also p. 460.

230. *Essay,* 1st ed., p. 108, also p. 137.

231. The checks in operation, he implied, reflect in some measure the prevailing division of labour (*Essay,* p. 176).

232. *Essay,* pp. 546, 547.

233. *Essay,* pp. 453–4, 461–2, 546, 549, 565, 582–3. The same view appears in the second edition. On military aspects of population growth, see also *Edinburgh Review,* 1808, pp. 350–1, 1810, pp. 474–5. He declared himself "an enemy to large standing armies" (*Essay,* p. 473; 2d ed., p. 526).

after all, only desirable as they contribute to happiness."[234] And nations are "happy according to the liberality with which" the food they can produce or acquire "is divided, or the quantity which a day's labour will purchase."[235] Hence he said that the object of those who would better the condition of the lower classes "must be . . . to enable the labourer to command a larger share of the necessaries and comforts of life."[236] And he pointed to the undesirability as well as to the practical and institutional impossibility of utilizing land and resources in such manner as to carry population to a theoretical maximum.[237]

In his treatment of the significance of low mortality, and of the superiority of death-control to birth-increase as a means of augmenting population, Malthus anticipated modern writers. Death-control necessarily presupposed birth-control; it could not be realized in the absence of the latter. A diminished proportion of births, he said, means reduced mortality, a saving of that which otherwise would be expended upon those who die prematurely, and a population composed more largely of adults and therefore more efficient and productive. Hence he advocated "such a price of labour, combined with such habits" as would reduce natality and mortality and eventuate in an efficient population.[238] He pointed to low mortality, furthermore, as an index of civilization and happiness. "A decrease of mortality at all ages is what we ought chiefly to aim at; and as the best criterion of happiness and good government, instead of the largeness of the proportion of births, which was the usual mode of judging, I have proposed the smallness of the proportion dying under the age of puberty."[239] This end—a necessary result of a diminished proportion of births—was to be sought, not through the practice of birth control which Malthus condemned, but through the practice of moral restraint.[240]

It is evident, in view of what has been said, that Malthus did not conceive of an income optimum, or maximum per capita income, population. He favoured both numbers and the abolition of poverty. He insisted upon uniting in a compatible manner "the two grand *desiderata,* a great actual population, and a state of society, in which abject poverty and dependence are comparatively but little known."[241] He had in mind a society in which

234. *Essay,* p. 516 (in 2d ed,); Zinke, "Six Letters from Malthus to Pierre Prevost," p. 183.

235. *Essay,* p. 295; 1st ed., p. 136. In *Principles* (pp. 33-4) he said that "the people will be rich or poor, according to the abundance or scarcity with which they are supplied," in comparison with their population, with "wealth" (i.e., "material objects, necessary, useful, or agreeable to man").

236. *Essay,* pp. 459, 535 (in 2d ed.). This was his object (*Edinburgh Review,* 1821, p. 374).

237. See sec. III (i) (2) of this article.

238. *Essay,* pp. 181, 533-4, 537, 566 and note.

239. *Essay,* p. 549; first published in 1807.

240. *Ibid.,* pp. 559-61, 572. On this point see also Norman Himes, Appendix A in the reprint of Francis Place's *Illustrations and Proofs of the Principle of Population* (London, 1930); and Penrose, *Population Theories and their Application,* pp. 28-30.

241. *Essay,* p. 460; in 2d ed.

the vast majority could enjoy an income sufficient to provide some conveniences and comforts, and as many could marry as the resources of a country and an economic system founded upon private property and individual responsibility would permit. It was his wish apparently that the principle of population continue to challenge men, but under such circumstances that they might meet this challenge effectively.[242] Specifically, he conceived of a society whose members would consider themselves duty-bound not to marry and have families until they could support them, and in which women could "look forward with just confidence to marriage at twenty-seven or twenty-eight."[243] Accordingly, since he supposed that prior to marriage moral restraint would rule, and presumably that after marriage neither moral restraint nor contraception would be practised, he had also to suppose that under normal conditions population would grow, and that, if welfare were not to be endangered, the supply of food and other goods would at least keep pace with population growth. But he blunted these suppositions by making marriage contingent upon the ability of those marrying to support their families, and by thus making the age at which men and women might actually marry with propriety conditional upon the augmentability of the food supply.[244] In theory, therefore, he made sufficient provision, in his "ideal" society, for the exorcising of the devil he had raised, and for the avoidance of the evils associated with a too great ratio of population to resources.

Malthus did not concern himself with what many present-day writers consider to be the real Devil of Population—a continuing deficiency of births. This possible source of underpopulation did not alarm him since he assumed that, given sufficient industry and sufficient emphasis upon agriculture, there would be no persisting deficiency of births or population.[245]

242. "I have always considered the principle of population as a law peculiarly suited to a state of discipline and trial" and as confirming the scriptural view of man's state on earth (*Essay*, p. 585; published in 1817). A. J. Toynbee (*A Study of History*, London, 1939, vol. IV, pp. 207ff.), in his discussion of the Solonian solution of the Hellenic population problem, provides us with a kind of illustration of what might be called the demographic "challenge and response" theory implicit in Malthus's writings. Malthus did not note this outcome, commenting only upon Solon's sanctioning of child exposure (*Essay*, pp. 128–9).

243. *Essay*, pp. 451–2, 493–5; 2d ed., pp. 497–9, 549, 552–3; Penrose, *Population Theories and their Application*, pp. 27–8. Malthus condemned as unjust and immoral positive laws limiting the age of marriage; it was up to the individual to decide whether he was in a position to marry or not (*Essay*, p. 357; published in 1817). Malthus's view regarding moral restraint and deferment of marriage was substantially the same as the medieval view that a man should not marry until he had a living. Malthus observed that in America the rigours of existence tended to eliminate the physically unfit (*ibid.*, p. 24), but he ignored questions relating to selection and eugenic values, adverting, in his treatment of the views of Plato and Aristotle (*ibid.*, I, xiii), only to the quantitative problem. He did not anticipate the argument Galton was later to direct, on grounds of selection, against the mischievous results of "prudential" postponement of marriage (*Inquiries into Human Faculty and its Development*, Everyman ed., pp. 207ff.).

244. *Essay*, pp. 3–4, 285–8, 439; in 2d ed. He noted that the age at marriage cannot be so low in old and settled as in new countries.

245. *Ibid.*, pp. 461–4; sec. III (iv) in this article.

He recognized, however, that a country, even though overpopulated in relation to the available food supply, might nonetheless be very much under-populated in relation to its resources, because these resources were being improperly developed and utilized. The remedy, in these circumstances, was not the encouragement of marriage and natality, but the augmentation of productive power and employment.

In sum, it may be said that while Malthus did not have in mind the modern population optimum, he did have in mind optimum densities and optimum growth rates. These depended upon circumstances. They were intended to be consistent with his underlying philosophy. They were sometimes ex-ceeded, and sometimes fallen short of. They were, if not consonant with the maximization of welfare in the modern meaning of the term, in keeping with his notions of welfare and his anticipations regarding the future.

Conclusion

Malthus lived in what, for a section of the European sphere, was the latter part of a period of transition; in a period when the industrial revolu-tion was still transforming the productive basis of society from one in which land predominated to one in which the instruments of industry and com-merce would predominate; in a period when the comparatively unlimited demand of the masses was beginning to outstrip the limited demand of the opulent few; in a period when the feudal polity and economy was being dissolved and converted into a polity that was more democratic, and an economy that was more non-agricultural, urban and free-enterprise, in character. In this new scheme of things the common man was far more im-portant than in the erstwhile pattern of society. Upon his efforts depended the output of goods and services, upon his purse depended the opportunity to sell, and upon his soldierly skill depended the national security; he was, therefore, invested with more dignity and significance than in times past. Malthus, in his demographic and economic analysis, in his condemnation of feudal values, in his opposition to sumptuary and other controls upon the common man's right to consume, and in his emphasis upon the fact that the wants of the labouring many are far more important than those of the strategically situated few, recognized the new and growing role of the common man and gave expression to it.

Malthus's demographic and economic doctrines were influenced in their development, of course, by the climate of opinion in which he found him-self, and by the views of those who preceded him or were contemporary with him. For example, his moral philosophy, as Bonar observed, "starts from a teleology. Nature makes nothing in vain."[246] Nature affords manifold evidence of the existence and the "goodness" of the Deity Who is anterior

246. *Malthus*, p. 319.

to her, and Whose instrument she is; her contrivances, even when they appear to produce evil, are directed to beneficial purposes, and, on the whole, allow more pleasure than is necessary to the fulfilment of the purposes of Nature and the Deity.[247] Malthus's teleological interpretation of the role of the "principle of population" reflects this philosophy. From the theodicy of the eighteenth-century as well as from contemporary moral and economic philosophy came the real cost elements in Malthus's theory of production. From his teleological conception of the principle of population and from his real cost theory of production flowed his defence, if not the emotional basis of this defence, of state, family, and property. In his rejection of the principle of the natural identity of interests, except insofar as landlord and state were concerned, originated in part at least his refusal to admit that a large country might, with safety, import provision and enjoy, in this respect, the advantage of international division of labour.

Far more striking is the seeming fact that Malthus's fundamental economic and demographic doctrine evolved almost naturally and necessarily out of the principles laid down and the problems recognized in the First Essay. There he showed that the "principle of population" — so named but differently analysed by Godwin — arising out of the passion between the sexes, is at once the main generator of social progress and the sufficient source of the institutions of state, family, and private property. This principle is necessary to force man out of his torpor. Yet, if it is allowed too free play in a circumscribed Nahrungsspielraum, it inevitably produces widespread and at times almost universal misery. Whence its operation must be restrained. And it can be restrained, consistently with the precepts of virtue and morality and the surety of human happiness, only under a regime of individual responsibility founded upon private property and the family and guarded by the state; — under a regime which, were it temporarily abolished, would of necessity be restored. It follows, from the necessity and inevitability of private property, that the population of a country cannot permanently be forced above the level consonant with the system of private property.

Malthus's consideration of the checks which hold down the inhabitants of a country to the number that it can subsist led him to conclude that numbers are regulated by subsistence. It also led him to observe that in many, if not in most countries, there were fewer inhabitants than these countries were capable of supporting in comfort, and that despite their comparative fewness, many of these inhabitants were living in poverty. His attention was directed, therefore, to the obstacles to the increase of subsistence, to which both the fewness and the misery of the inhabitants were to be traced, — to the impediments, in short, to the salutary operation of the principle of

247. This view, which is so evident in Malthus's works, is well expressed by Paley in both his *Moral Philosophy* and his *Natural Theology*.

population. These impediments, he found, assumed various forms: bad government, insecurity of property, concentration of the ownership of land, slavery, and so on. Yet, they were reducible to a common denominator, lack of an effective demand for labour. Between the resources (or "supplies"), actual and potential, of countries, and their inhabitants, stood institutional barriers which prevented these resources from supporting as great a demand for labour as they were capable of supporting, and from calling forth as great a growth of numbers as the principle of population could supply in consistence with human happiness and the preservation of the institutions of the family and private property. It was in consequence of his analysis of the checks to the growth of population and to the augmentation of "supplies," in short, and not to the influence of the Physiocrats and others who recognized the importance of consumption and glimpsed the circuit flow inherent in economies, that Malthus discovered the importance of the effective demand for labour, to the treatment of which the second part of the *Principles* was devoted.[248]

Malthus's analysis of the circumstances which governed the effective demand for labour directed his attention to the importance of what we have called industrialization. For he was concerned not so much with temporary interruptions of the economic circuit flow as with the conditions that regulated the expansion through time of the total effective demand for labour; and he thought not so much in terms of employment maxima and minima, as of a given time, as in terms of population maxima and minima. He found in industrialization, therefore, and in the associated development of what Fisher and Clark have called "tertiary" employments, the means of providing an effective and expanding demand for labour, and, consequently, for population. He found in industrialization, furthermore, the most satisfactory means of denying too free a play to the principle of population. For industrialization made for the development of civil liberty, for the diffusion of a taste for comforts and luxuries, and for the generation of habits of industry and prudence. It tended, therefore, to give effect to the principle of population and to insure population growth in consistence with the intent of the Creator and the happiness of men,[249] and yet to contain population growth sufficiently to guard this happiness.

---

248. It is not our intention to deny the existence of striking parallelisms between the doctrine of Lord Keynes, for example, which embodies elements found also in Malthus's theories, and the doctrine of Quesnay: viz., emphasis upon consumption, treatment of circuit flow, widespread popularity and appeal, etc. It is our intention rather to indicate that Malthus's analysis of the role of demand and consumption originated largely in his study of the operation of the principle of population.

249. It must be kept in mind that Malthus did not sanction contraception or anticipate the vital revolution it has brought about.

Pareto on Population

Summary

I. Economic movements and population movements: personal capital; emigration and migration; non-economic factors; the time factor; primitive cultures and the ancient world. — II. Wealth per capita and population: time and space; secular increase; class rates of mortality and natality; social and political institutions. — III. Determinants of population growth: the genesic forces; the non-genesic forces; residues. — IV. Malthus' theories. — V. Demographic trends: long-run influences; the future. — VI. Opinion, law, and population movements. — VII. Optima: indices; ophelimity and utility; group differences; individual vs. collective point of view; population growth. — VIII. Heterogeneity and selection: income distribution; natality and mortality; eugenic selection; residues; class circulation. — IX. Conclusion: points emphasized or passed over.

Population problems and questions occupy an important place in Pareto's principal economic writings. His treatment of "les capitaux personnels" comprises one-fifth of Volume I of his *Cours,* and that of "population" constitutes about one-tenth of his *Manuel.* Elsewhere in these two works he discusses aspects of social mobility and social selection. While considerable portions of his *Systèmes Socialistes* and of his *Trattato di Sociologia Generale* are devoted to social mobility and social selection, not much attention is given, in these works, to questions usually included under the head of population. Much, however, of what is contained in these works bears indirectly upon the population problem. Pareto dealt with aspects of the population problem in several articles.[1]

1. A bibliography of Pareto's writings appears in the Giornale degli economisti, LXIV, 1924, pp. 144–153, and in G. H. Bousquet, Vilfredo Pareto, sa vie et son oeuvre, Paris, 1928. G. Pirou outlines Pareto's economic writings in Théories de l'équilibre économique. L. Walras & V. Pareto, Paris, 1938. F. Borkenau discusses his sociology critically in Pareto, New York, 1936. Talcott Parsons presents a penetrating and constructive appraisal of Pareto's sociological work in his The Structure of Social Action, New York, 1937.

In this paper we shall refer to the Cours d'économie politique, 2 Vols., (Lausanne, 1896–97) as C; to the Manuel d'économie politique (Milan, 1906; Paris, 1909, 1927) as M; to Les systèmes socialistes, 2 Vols., (Paris, 1902–03) as S; and to the Trattato (Florence, 1916, 1923; Paris, 1917) as T. References to the Manuel are to the 1909 French edition. References to Les systèmes socialistes are to the 1926 French edition which, except for minor corrections, does not differ from the 1902–03 edition. References to the Trattato are to the splendid four-volume English translation, edited by Arthur Livingston under the title, The Mind and Society (New York, 1935). We have included no references to Pareto's Fatti e teorie (Florence, 1920) which does not deal with population; or to his Transformazione della democrazia (Milan, 1921) in which he mistakenly predicted that in Italy, upon the dissolution then in process of the Italian democratic state, political power would pass to the trade unions. References to the Cours and the Trattato are generally by paragraph; to Les systèmes and the Manuel, by page. Where reference is by page, the page number is preceded by p. or pp.; where by paragraph, only the number of the paragraph is given.

This paper is divided into nine sections: (1) economic movements and population movements; (2) wealth per capita and population; (3) determinants of population growth; (4) Malthus' theories; (5) demographic trends; (6) opinion, law, and population movements; (7) optima; (8) heterogeneity and selection; (9) conclusion.

I. Economic Movements and Population Movements

In the *Cours* Pareto devoted considerable attention to the relation between economic movements and population movements, for he was concerned to discover whether the formation of "personal capital" — i.e. population — proceeds, as does the formation of non-personal capital, in accordance with the principles which make for the maximization of ophelimity. In the *Manuel*, where his approach is less subjective than in the *Cours*, he touches only indirectly upon this question. In the *Trattato*, where he distinguishes between the determinants of economic equilibrium and the determinants of social equilibrium, he does not reexamine the relationship between the formation of personal capital and the maximization of ophelimity. While he finally concludes, in the *Cours*, that the principles which regulate the accumulation and disposition of non-personal capital exercise considerable empire over "personal capital," he does not distinguish clearly enough between the economic and the non-economic determinants of population growth, nor does he inquire at any length into the role of the non-economic determinants.[2] What he means by economic movements and conditions, however, is essentially implicit in his analysis, as reported in this section.[3]

Pareto formulated his question regarding the relation between population growth and ophelimity and then tested it empirically by comparing economic and demographic movements. If the movement of population "does not depend upon economic conditions, the formation of personal capital escapes entirely the general law" in accordance with which savings flow into the most necessary categories of capital and so "procure the maximum of ophelimity"; and this maximum can be achieved only by bringing into play other forces (e.g. through law or persuasion) which induce men to increase or diminish births in proper measure. If, however,

2. However, see Sections III–V, below.

3. Pareto was never an economic determinist. Economic determinism, he indicated, was correct in recognizing the interdependence of economic and non-economic factors, but it erred in treating this relation as one of unilateral cause and effect. See T, 829–830; S, I, introduction and Chaps. I–II. See T, 828, for his analogous criticism of "social Darwinism"; also M, pp. 96–97. In the Trattato, Pareto distinguished carefully between economic action, which is essentially logical and rational, and non-economic action, which does not meet these requirements (see Parsons, op. cit., pp. 190–192, 232, 264–268, 295–296). But he did not attempt to recast his discussion of population growth and its determinants in terms of the analytical elements developed in the Trattato. See Section IX of this paper.

the movement of the population depends, *at least in part*, upon economic conditions, then personal capital reenters, at least in part, into the category of capital, the transformation of which, under the operation of economic forces, takes place in a manner to assure the maximum of ophelimity.[4]

He concluded, since the evidence supported the latter view, that

personal capital thus enters into the category of those [capitals] whose transformation is made, at least in part, under the action of the forces which assure the maximum of ophelimity.[5]

He did not conclude, however, that the formation of population proceeded in a manner to maximize ophelimity; the actual outcome depended also upon the effect of the non-economic determinants of population movements, together with the "modifications" they occasioned in the "equilibrium which gives the maximum of ophelimity."[6]

Three sets of observations were employed by Pareto to support his inference that population movements depend upon economic movements. All vital indices move in sympathy with economic fluctuations. Personal capital has a cost of production; therefore its supply is sensitive to circumstances affecting this cost. Finally, certain customs which affect population movements are conditioned by economic factors.

Mortality varied with changing economic circumstances, but in lesser measure than nuptiality and natality.[7] While mortality was higher as a rule in the lower than in the upper classes, and while specific death rates moved inversely (he cited English data) with indices of prosperity, only among the poorer classes was mortality especially sensitive to economic turns for the better or for the worse; for among the poor the number of marginal persons with marginal vitality and marginal susceptibility to ailments was relatively large.[8] Sometimes the salutary effect of an improvement in economic conditions was masked, when the consequent increase in natality

---

4. C, 171.

5. C, 182. This conclusion, he said (C, 183), had been reached by Adam Smith (Wealth of Nations, I, 8), De Molinari (Notions fondamentales d'économie politique, 1891, p. 99), and others who inferred that the supply of men is conditioned predominantly by the demand for them.

6. C, 171–172. The maximization of ophelimity requires, among other things, the equalization at the margin of the net returns on various capitals (C, 132–145, 619, 729). The conditions for the maximization of ophelimity are given in the first part of the Cours and in Chaps. 3, 6, and appendix of the Manuel. See also Section VII of this paper.

7. One must employ, to measure fluctuations and changes in economic circumstances, an economic index truly representative of the economy of an epoch or country. Thus the movement of the price of grain may accurately reflect variations in the economic state of an agricultural country or period, but it will not truly represent that of a commercial and industrial country or epoch. See C, 176, 236; M, pp. 396–397; also T, 2279–2282, 2293. Pareto cites A. Marshall, Principles, I, pp. 243–244 (see pp. 189–190 of 8th ed.). Graphic comparisons are most suited to discover a relation, if one exists, between population and economic movements, inasmuch as demographic variables respond slowly and gradually to economic changes (M, pp. 397–398).

8. In his discussion of the distribution of population along the income curve Pareto observed that mortality was especially high among those at or in the neighborhood of the bare

produced a sufficient increase in infant mortality, and therefore in general mortality, to counterbalance the decline in adult mortality which usually accompanied such an improvement.[9]

Both natality and nuptiality rates, especially the latter, were very sensitive to economic fluctuations, Pareto found. In a number of countries (England, Belgium, Prussia, Austria, Sweden, and Finland), particularly in their rural areas, nuptiality had fluctuated with the price of grain (he cites Bela Weisz's studies); in the Netherlands, before 1835 (he cites Quetelet), nuptiality, natality, and mortality had varied with harvest yields.[10] In England, during the first two-thirds of the nineteenth century, nuptiality had varied inversely with the price of grain, and directly with the goodness of the harvest; but with the progress of industrialization and the increase of urban wages, this relationship had changed: now low grain prices, which affected the rural population adversely, no longer simultaneously stimulated urban nuptiality. Hence a fall in grain prices, which depressed the rural marriage rate, now tended to depress the national marriage rate.[11] From a comparison, for England (1860–1890), of exports, imports, bank clearings, and grain prices with nuptiality, natality, and mortality, Pareto inferred that marriages and (less pronouncedly) births moved with exports. "The maximum number of marriages corresponds pretty near to the maximum of commercial prosperity. The maximum number of births takes place only some years afterward, as is natural."[12] In other countries nuptiality and natality likewise had risen and fallen with economic conditions;[13] and "very pronounced waves" in population movements "correspond with economic tides." Thus, in the prosperous early 1870's the marriage rate had moved to a peak in the countries enjoying prosperity, but not in Ireland, which lay outside the European economic current;[14] while in Italy, upon the termination of prosperity in 1887, nuptiality and natality had fallen appreciably, and mortality had risen slightly.[15] The facts presented — and they can be multiplied, Pareto declares — indicate,

---

subsistence level; this category of society in fact served as "an organ of excretion" through which the weak and the degenerate passed into oblivion (C, 1027–1028); (M, pp. 385–386). See Section VIII of this paper.

9. M, pp. 397–398; C, 235–241, and I, pp. 81–83, on mortality among insured persons.

10. C, I, pp. 91, 131. Pareto describes Quetelet's works as models of "method . . . in the social sciences (C, I, p. 92n.)." Referring to a statement in Montesquieu (Lettres persanes, Letter 122) to the effect that misery, famine, and disease cut down many children, Pareto observed that this does not happen in countries, such as Switzerland, where the government seeks to guard the welfare of the people (C, I, p. 92n.).

11. C, 176; also 184, where Pareto reports a similar relationship between economic and population movements in France. Pareto cites Marshall's Principles (1st ed., pp. 243–245; see 8th ed., pp. 189–190) on England.

12. C, I, pp. 90–91; also M, pp. 396–397.

13. M, pp. 396–398.

14. C, 232.

15. C, I, pp. 91, 133; also ibid., p. 92, for statement that nuptiality and natality fell in an Italian wine-exporting province when wine exports declined.

with a probability in the neighborhood of certainty, that movements in the transformation of personal capital are in part dependent on the economic movement.[16]

Pareto cautioned, however, that he had not shown the "explicit dependence" of population movements on the economic situation, "but merely their dependence on variations in it." Let the economic situation be characterized by a function F of any number of variables that are functions of the time, t. Then "the numbers of marriages, births, and to a certain extent also deaths, are a function of df/dt; but we have not shown that such numbers are explicit functions of F." Mortality rates are explicit functions of F; but changes in births and marriages depending explicitly upon F are "masked by changes in tastes and habits which depend upon a difference in well-being."[17] Later he observed that nuptiality, natality, and mortality are reciprocally interrelated. Thus when economic conditions improve, nuptiality and natality increase, but the increase in natality is due largely, as Cauderlier has shown, to the increase in nuptiality; infant mortality increases with natality and may therefore push up crude mortality, even though specific death rates fall.[18]

Since "personal capital" has its cost of production, just as other forms of capital do, and since the conversion of savings into "personal capital" affects well-being, the movement of population is necessarily associated with economic fluctuations and trends. "Like all capital, man has a certain cost of production." This cost "depends upon the manner of living, upon the *standard of life*" and, in some degree, upon the level of infant mortality.[19] Personal capital absorbs savings which might otherwise be put to different use; it therefore affects the rate of wealth accumulation and the level of well-being. "France concentrates her savings to the augmentation of the well-being of her population, and Germany, to the augmentation of her population and to emigration."[20]

While Pareto touched upon emigration in this and several other connections, he said little of migration. In ancient times emigration was an efficacious remedy for population pressure. In modern times it was much less efficacious, for it carried out of the country of emigration all the capital embodied in emigrants in the form of "personal capital," together with such

16. C, 179; also 174. He repeats this statement in T, p. 42n.
17. C, I, p. 93n.; also T, p. 42n.
18. M, pp. 395–398. On Cauderlier see my France Faces Depopulation, Durham, 1938.
19. M, pp. 406–407; C, 181, 255; also "La mortalità infantile e il costo dell'uomo adulto," Giornale degli economisti, ser. 2, VII, 1893, pp. 451–456. Since many who are saved in infancy die before reaching adulthood, Pareto noted, the reduction of infant mortality does not cut the cost of production of personal capital as much as is sometimes implied.
20. C, 254. H. Bowen ("Capital in Relation to Optimum Population," Social Forces, XV, 1937, pp. 346–350) has treated carefully the relation between population growth, on the one hand, and capital formation and current consumption, on the other. He does not comment on Pareto's analysis.

mobile capital as the emigrants took with them; hence it sometimes intensified the repressive checks. In the 1880's alone, emigration had removed over four billion francs of capital from Germany.[21] The population of cities was recruited largely from rural areas, where selection was rigorous, and where the élites of the future were formed.[22] The movement of population from rural into urban areas was intensified by the fact that the savings and tax revenues furnished by rural populations were spent in urban centers, and that urban housing was subsidized; in consequence agriculture lacked capital and production was retarded.[23]

Further analysis of the circumstances by which procreation is influenced, and of those by which it is not influenced appreciably, strengthened Pareto's conclusion that population growth is regulated preponderantly by "the influence of economic conditions, . . . whether upon individuals in particular, or in forming the customs to which the masses submit."[24] Certain non-economic factors — religion, legislation, opinions, and beliefs — exercise little, if any, independent effect upon numbers.[25] The motives (he cites De Molinari) which underlie the rate at which children (i.e. "personal capital") are produced are conditioned in large measure by the relation obtaining between the cost of producing children and the economic and other advantages derivable from them.[26] Thus, in a slave régime the production of population is governed solely by the economic motive, while in a free economy it is conditioned also by other interests and sentiments.[27] In a free economy, children cannot be raised to adulthood, unless wealth is available to be transformed into "personal capital"; and they will be produced only insofar as the population wishes to make this use of its wealth.[28] Consequently, the economic motive becomes subjective, and usually operates in such wise that the individual is only vaguely conscious of the forces actuating him;[29] for few men resolve their problems rationally, the vast

21. Pareto characterized as too low Engel's estimate of 3,162½ marks as the average capital value of an emigrant as of 1891. See C, 231, 249, 254; M, p. 413; also "Il costo di produzione dell'uomo e il valore economico degli emigranti," Giornale degli economisti, ser. 2, XXX, 1905, pp. 322–27. Pareto also observed that emigration could affect the age composition of a nation's population adversely and so reduce its productive power (C, 159–160, 231).

22. C, 252; S, I, p. 33.

23. C, 250; M, p. 470.

24. C, 259.

25. C, 259, 261, 264–265; M, pp. 418–420; also Section VI, below.

26. C, 255–257. On De Molinari's views see my France Faces Depopulation.

27. C, 257–258.

28. C, 258. In return for the cost of producing children parents gain "satisfaction of the genesic instinct, the moral satisfaction which children give, and finally the economic profit which the most numerous classes of society draw from them." In parts of Sicily, where children were employed in the sulfur mines and their earnings went to the parents, child-raising had become an industry. See C, 256.

29. Earlier (C, 171) he remarked that too much importance had been attached to the question: Do economic facts so influence the human mind that the individual acts consciously and volitionally (e.g. voluntarily defers marriage or limits births), or do they affect man in such manner that he acts unconsciously and instinctively?

majority being content to accept the solutions furnished by custom. But "custom itself is formed under the empire of economic agents and of others which act upon society."[30] Pareto concluded, therefore, that the "economic factor exercises a very considerable influence" upon numbers, and that in a given society population movements vary with economic movements:

> Economic conditions act upon men, according to the tastes of the latter, and give birth to phenomena of ophelimity. . . . These conditions also have biological effects. . . . The absolute lack of aliments surely kills men, whatever be their tastes and habits. . . . Paludal miasmas augment mortality. . . . A certain degree of ease is favorable to human longevity. It is only by means of heavy expenditures that one can drain marshes, supply cities with drinkable water, and take, in general, the measures necessary to prevent epidemics.[31]

Population does not grow in a manner completely consistent with the maximization of ophelimity, however, for some factors run counter to the economic:

> The heedlessness and prejudices, which, at times, oppose themselves in part to the action of the economic factors, augment and render more intense the ills of the population.[32]

But even if the formation of "personal capital" were subject solely to economic forces, an optimum adjustment would result and persist only if men were able, when making their decisions, to allow for the time factor. For, since there is a 15–20 year interval between the birth of a child and the time when it becomes a producer, children born of marriages and pregnancies taking place in times of prosperity and good employment may arrive on the labor market in times of crisis and unemployment. Thus parents occupy a position analogous to that of producers who, seeing that in a given time period consumption has increased from (say) 100 to 110, infer that it will increase beyond 110, and consequently expand output still further and so occasion a crisis of production. "The maximum of ophelimity will be obtained only if men are sage and prudent enough not to forget the periodicity of economic crises."[33]

Pareto found evidence of the influence of economic circumstances upon

30. C, 258. This comment resembles Marshall's: "Thus economic causes play a part in governing the growth of population . . . their influence on the numbers of the population as a whole is largely indirect; and is exerted by way of the ethical, social and domestic habits of life. For these habits are themselves influenced by economic causes deeply, though slowly, and in ways some of which are difficult to trace, and impossible to predict." Principles, 8th ed., IV, vi, 8.

31. C, 239; also 266.

32. C, 266.

33. C, 267; see also Section VII of this paper. The situation of parents is analogous to that of the dog in the dog-master "courbes de poursuite" problem employed in 41 (also, M, p. 289) to illustrate producer behavior. Cf. Rosenstein-Rodan's "The Role of Time in Economic Theory," Economica, n.s., I, 1934, pp. 91ff.

population in the literature dealing with primitive cultures and in the writings of the ancients. There he discovered support for his supposition that when subsistence is hard to obtain, infants and the aged are most likely to suffer. In many primitive societies, modern and ancient, the unproductive aged were destroyed.[34] In fact, not until labor had become productive enough to permit society to support the aged and the infirm did their lot become at all secure. Largely because of economic circumstances, he implies, the Chinese practiced infanticide, the Polynesians exposed children, and the ancients sanctioned abortion and child exposure; and principally because of economic progress these acts have become uncommon:

> Abortion, infanticide, [and] exposure of infants were formerly allowed by law and even by morality (la morale). The accumulation of capital has produced civilization and permitted [men] to protect the feeble.[35]

Pareto marshalled many quotations from ancient political and belletristic writers which reveal the presence, in Greek and Roman communities, of "malthusian" attitudes, and indicate the, at least partial, subordination of reproductive behavior to economic motives.[36] Opinions of Aristotle and others to the effect that numbers must be curbed are noted, together with Hesiod's observation that the fertility of slaves must be restrained. References to child exposure are reported; and the economically actuated fact that while female infants were more likely than male infants to be exposed, female exposed infants were more likely to be rescued than male exposed infants, inasmuch as female infants could be raised as prostitutes. "It is impossible to express more clearly the motive of utility," Pareto commented regarding a statement attributed to Pseudo-Aristotle to the effect that men produce children, not only to serve nature, but also to provide security in old age.

A character in a pastoral of Longus is reported as declaring that he does not want to rear a daughter in poverty, and another as remarking that three children are enough: "In these two citations, the 'malthusian' motives appear naïvely and clearly," Pareto observes; and he adds, "it is only with economic progress that certain men possessing enough capital cease to transform their savings into personal capital in [the form of] their children."[37]

34. C, 244, 247. He cites from Strabo the Cean law of Iulis requiring those who had completed the sixtieth year to drink of the hemlock "in order that there be sufficient nourishment for the others." He adds: "it is impossible to express the economic motive more clearly." See C, I, p. 115n.

35. C, 245, also 244, 246, 248.

36. Pareto cites or quotes from (among others) Aristotle, Plato, Strabo, Demosthenes, Longus, Plutarch, Hesiod, Sophocles, Euripides, Tacitus, Pliny, Polybius, Juvenal. The present, he later wrote, enables us to understand the past (T, 348).

37. Pareto refers here to a criticism directed by Eubulus against those who provided nourishment for beasts of pleasure, instead of for children. See comparable statements in my French Predecessors of Malthus, Durham, 1942, Chaps. 3–4; also Malthus' comment on this type of argument, Essay (Everyman's Library), II, pp. 146ff.

He describes the sentiment of the lower classes, who are reported by Plutarch as not wanting children for fear they will become veritable slaves,[38] as superior to that of present-day parents who bring children into the world without thought of their future; and he finds in a statement (by the elder Pliny) of the advantages of not having heirs an "economic" explanation of the spread of the preventive check among the Roman upper classes.[39]

Economic circumstances were largely responsible for the decline in the rate of natural increase in ancient Rome during the empire period, Pareto concluded; whence he inferred that the Roman populationist legislation had not been suited to counter the forces making for depopulation. Had the decline in the rate of natural increase been limited to the aristocracy, Pareto commented, it would not have been so serious, since the upper classes are always replenished from the lower ranks of society; but the decline appears to have been general. He cited with apparent approval the observation of Polybius that the operation of the preventive check had become widespread in the Greece of his day, and noted that in Rome under the Empire a similar situation had developed.[40] But Pareto pointed out, with respect to Rome, that the "primary cause" of its depopulation did not consist, as modern moralists were wont to preach, in the "decadence of the spirit of the family"; it was compounded, instead, of war, pillage, destruction, and the "oppression of the people."

Pareto placed especial emphasis upon mobile capital in his account of depopulation in ancient times. The growth of population depends upon the availability of mobile capital. Its waste in the Europe of his day was retarding population growth; its destruction in Roman times had been a "principal cause" of depopulation. Then mobile capital was destroyed by war and pillage, which also cut down population directly; it was consumed by the payment of tribute to the barbarians; it was absorbed by outlays for the entertainment of the populace and the construction of monuments; it was eaten up by the heavy taxes and other burdens imposed upon the wealthy. Similar phenomena were becoming manifest in modern Europe.[41]

38. For analogous statements by Southern pro-slavery writers, see my "Population Theory in the Ante-Bellum South," Journal of Southern History II, 1936, pp. 360–389.

39. On the ancient writers see C, 245–246.

40. Polybius said that men, actuated by avarice and love of pomp and luxury, avoided marriage, or, if they married, produced few or no children. As A. B. Wolfe notes, this explanation is inadequate ("The Economics of Population in Ancient Greece," in Facts and Factors in Economic History, Cambridge, 1932, pp. 33ff.). If one may judge from Pareto's account of Roman population movements, he too considered it inadequate.

41. C, 246, 262, and I, pp. 140–142; S, I, p. 170; also Sections II, VI, below. The capital-destroying phenomena which accompany modern economic crises, Pareto said, resemble, in their effects and on a small scale, those experienced in Roman times. "In our epoch," he added, excessive expenditures by the states "prevent the inhabitants of the European continent from being more numerous and more prosperous"; and "if a socialist organization came to destroy the movable capital of our societies," we should "again see phenomena as intense as those produced in ancient times." See C, I, pp. 140, 142; also Section VIII of this paper for his account, in the Trattato, of the decline of Rome.

II. Wealth Per Capita and Population

Wealth per capita, in Pareto's opinion, is one of the four most important determinants of the character of any society.[42] Upon the increase of wealth (or income) per head, and not upon the redistribution of wealth (or income), depends the degree of inequality and the level of minimal incomes.[43] Upon the level of wealth per head, in particular upon that part employed as capital, depends the level of civilization and material well-being. Civilization is "a capitalisation"; it "retrogrades with capitalisation."[44] The behavior of demographic variables, therefore, depends in some measure, directly and indirectly, upon the level of per capita wealth.

The relationship between wealth and demographic variables is not always the same in space as in time, for the presence in space of offsetting elements may counterbalance variations in per capita wealth. Thus, although man multiplies, as do all forms of life, more or less in accordance with the favorableness of living conditions, and the density of population tends to vary with the fertility of the soil, the population density of areas does not always vary with the actual or potential wealth of such areas.[45] Population density is a function of many variables, of which wealth is but one; it will vary with the latter only insofar as variations in wealth are not compensated by variations in other variables. Accordingly, since the variables other than wealth differ less within given countries than between countries, density is more closely associated with wealth in given countries than from country to country.[46]

The demographic effects of a secular increase in wealth per capita differ somewhat from those which accompany the upswing of the trade cycle. As economic conditions improve with the upturn of trade, nuptiality and, consequently, natality increase, while mortality tends to fall, at least in the misery-ridden classes. A long-run increase in per capita wealth, such as was experienced in the nineteenth century, tends to be accompanied by a de-

---

42. M, p. 425; S, I, p. 41; see also Section VIII of this paper. In the preceding section we were concerned primarily with Pareto's treatment of the effects upon population movements of economic fluctuations; in this section we are concerned with the level of wealth per capita, with changes in this level, and with the longer-run consequences of such changes.

43. In other words, only if wealth (or income) increases more rapidly than population will inequality diminish; redistribution schemes can accomplish nothing. See his discussion of his income curve and of the distribution of wealth and income, C, 962–965; M, pp. 385, 392–393, 424–425. For an appraisal of Pareto's thesis by C. Bresciani-Turroni see Econometrica, VII, pp. 107–133.

44. "La question sociale," Scientia, XXXI, 1922, pp. 45–46; also M, pp. 424–425. I.e., civilization rises and falls with the increase and decrease of "capital."

45. In rural areas density is influenced by soil conditions in greater measure than in industrial and commercial regions, where livelihoods are less dependent upon telluric and geographic circumstances (M, p. 393).

46. M, pp. 393–394. Pareto notes, too, that population density reacts upon economic conditions, but does not develop this point (M, p. 393). Where population is dense, crime is less frequent in rural areas, more frequent in urban areas (M, pp. 400–401).

cline in nuptiality, natality, infant mortality, general mortality, and natural increase. Although the decline in natural increase is associated with the increase in wealth and the increased habituation of men to a more comfortable existence, it is not necessarily the consequence of the increase in per capita wealth; for per capita wealth is "in part, at least, an index" of the economic, social, moral, and political state of a people, and may have advanced in consequence of some of the changes which have depressed natality. The decline in natural increase tends to reenforce itself by facilitating the increase of per capita wealth.[47]

While mortality varies inversely with wealth and with wealth by class,[48] and while natality generally is lower among the rich than among the poor, there is not a fixed relationship between the rate of natural increase by class or society and its wealth.[49] Rates of increase, by class and society, are "closely bound to the economic and moral benefits that transformations of other capital into personal capital procure," and "these benefits depend naturally upon the tastes and habits of the individuals" under consideration.[50]

Changes in the level of wealth affect the characteristics, customs, laws, and political constitutions of peoples, and, Pareto's discussion suggests, thus indirectly influence demographic variables. Only wealthy peoples can afford to care for all their aged, invalided, and young members, and to make of women non-producing parasitic objects of luxury. In the wake of wealth come "feminism" and augmented "depravity" among women, and an easing of the rigors of natural selection. When wealth and capital become abundant, less evil attaches to the destruction of wealth; for this reason, and because of the concomitant development of humanitarianism, criminals tend to be pampered and laws against debtors are relaxed. As the supply of capital increases, the power and the privileges of the capitalist class decline, while those of the laboring classes expand: littérateurs who fawned upon the rich now flatter the common people. Democratic and socialist sentiments and movements flourish.[51] The dominant classes (i.e. the bourgeoisie and ruling

47. M, pp. 395–396, 398–399, 406–407.

48. Infant mortality is lower among the well-to-do than among the poor; it is lower, in general, when economic circumstances permit satisfactory child care. Overall mortality is lower when the availability of resources permits the suppression of preventable diseases (e.g. smallpox, scarlet fever, diphtheria, typhoid fever, marsh fever). Pareto noted, too, that low mortality tends to be associated with low natality for two reasons: (a) because low natality is accompanied by low infant mortality; (b) because low natality, by facilitating the accumulation of wealth, favors conditions conducive to low mortality. See M, pp. 394–396; C, 235–241.

49. M, pp. 394, 396; S, II, pp. 141–147.

50. C, 185.

51. Pareto's political ideal was always liberalism. He reacted strongly, however, against democracy as he saw it in action, and particularly against politicians as he became convinced that what remained of the liberal state would be superseded by a Byzantine structure. Borkenau describes the Trattato as "simply a political manifesto in scientific disguise." See Borkenau, op. cit., p. 169; also Chaps. 1, 8–10. We have not attempted to outline or appraise Pareto's political theories as such, references thereto being restricted to matter bearing upon social change and demographic fluctuations.

groups) lose taste for the use of force, by which in the long run social forms are determined; and social questions are settled at the polls through majority vote and frequently in favor of the poorer classes. The role of the politician increases in importance.[52] These conditions to which the increase of wealth per head gives rise cannot continue, however; they eventually bring about the destruction of wealth and therefore of themselves. Democracy "is its own grave-digger; it destroys that which gave birth to it." Burdensome taxes, governmental waste, socialist measures, protectionism (which is the "social-ism . . . of our governing classes"), and similar policies, which come into existence with democracy or are intensified by it, consume wealth and check capital formation,[53] and consequently retard the growth of population. These wealth-destroying forces had so far been counterbalanced, Pareto wrote, by technological progress and (in France) by the thrift of the people; but, his argument suggests, they will grow in intensity until they in turn bring to a temporary end the conditions of their existence.[54] For in social phenomena rhythmical movement rules; action begets reaction and reaction begets action. While he does not specifically say so, Pareto's analysis implies that demographic movements fluctuate in sympathy with these rhythmical movements in the formation of wealth.

III. Determinants of Population Growth

In consistence with his fundamental theory that economic movements may be described in terms of "tastes" and "obstacles,"[55] Pareto defined the movement of population as the resultant of the combined influence of two sets of forces: (*a*) the genesic; and (*b*) the non-genesic, which includes, among others, the economic forces which affect population growth immediately or "through the intermediation of other forces."[56] Hypothetically, one may suppose either that obstacles do not exist or that they do exist. If no obstacles exist, the genesic force, acting alone, carries "to its maximum the increase of population." The ensemble of non-genesic forces

52. M, pp. 102–103, 399–406, 487, 496; C, 1029; S, I, pp. 62–75, II, pp. 139ff.; "La question sociale," Scientia, XXXI, 1922, pp. 45–46. Also Section VIII of this paper.

53. Sometimes non-rich peoples copy certain practices in effect among rich peoples (M, p. 406). On these effects of wealth and democracy see M, pp. 404–406, 416–417, 516–517; C, I, pp. 140–142; "La question sociale," loc. cit.; "Protectionisme et communisme," Journal des économistes, ser. 5, XXI, 1895, pp. 33–35; Pareto's introduction to Karl Marx, Le Capital, Paris, 1893, pp. xi–xiv, lxvi–lxvii; also Section VI, below.

54. M, pp. 404–405; C, I, p. 143.

55. "The economic system is made up of certain molecules set in motion by tastes and subject to ties (checks) in the form of obstacles to the acquisition of economic values. The social system is much more complicated, . . . made up of certain molecules harbouring residues, derivations, interests, and proclivities, and which perform, subject to numerous ties, logical and non-logical actions." See T, 2079.

56. C, 186. "The increase of the population results from the opposition which exists between the generative force and the obstacles that it may encounter" (M, p. 408).

may operate either (a) to push the rate of increase to the limit fixed by the genesic force;[57] or (b) to contain the increase of population within limits that would be exceeded by the genesic force acting alone. Case (a) is exemplified when a horticulturalist, having developed a new and appreciated variety of plant, pushes its rate of multiplication to the limit set by the genesic force peculiar to the species; case (b) is exemplified when a horticulturalist, engaged in raising an old variety and actuated by fear of overproduction, curbs its rate of increase.[58] Examples of cases (a) and (b) are to be found also in human populations, or in subdivisions of such populations. For example, workers who derive advantage from the labor of their children tend to procreate as many as the laws of reproduction permit, whereas other workers, lacking means or outlets for the employment of their offspring, delay founding families. Again, after great wars, or after notable improvements in economic conditions, numbers increase significantly.[59]

As a rule, the hypothesis that the genesic force alone regulates numbers is contrary to the facts; for *"there exist forces which act in a sense contrary to the genesic force, to limit the increase of population."*[60] If the genesic force, acting by itself, can augment population from 100 to 120 within a given time period, and yet in this same period population actually increases only from 100 to 110, then one must conclude that the nongenesic forces are acting to reconduct the population from the 100→ 120 line of increase to the 100→ 110 line.[61] The variation in the number of marriages and births, which occasions such a decline in the rate of population growth, cannot be the result of a concomitant variation in the genesic force; for there is no compelling physiological evidence to the effect that such a variation in genesic force could occur. An enfeeblement of the genesic faculties, such as Herbert Spencer supposes,[62] can produce only "very slow effects, after some centuries"; it cannot, therefore, account for such notable variations in natality as take place within intervals of a few years. Moreover, even if Spencer's theory were valid and applicable, it would not follow that the genesic force encounters no non-genesic obstacles.[63] More

57. When this happens, the economic forces usually prove very important.

58. C, 186–188. He cites as a further illustration of case (a) the production of ostriches in the colony of Good Hope, whose number was increased, because their production was lucrative, from 80 in 1865 to 152,415 in 1888. Here "the economic motive has pushed the multiplication of ostriches nearly to the limit of the genesic forces"; but the time will come when the economic motive will operate to limit their production (C, 188).

59. C, 188. He presented data for the Duchy of Wurtemberg, which reveal a decrease from 445 thousands in 1622 to 97 in 1635, and an increase to 479 by 1759.

60. C, 192. His italics. See also M, pp. 408–409.

61. We have paraphrased Pareto's diagrammatic illustration (C, 191–192).

62. Here Pareto is referring to Spencer's "law of population based upon the opposition between individuation and genesis" and his thesis that natural fecundity is declining. See Spencer, Principles of Biology, II, New York, 1867.

63. C, 192, 194. Pareto denies, not the possible validity of Spencer's thesis, but only its adequacy as an explanation of demographic changes ascribed by him (Pareto) to the action of non-genesic forces (C, 192).

important still, those living species which in bygone times survived the rude ordeals of the struggle for existence must have had in reserve a considerable genesic force, which served promptly to repair the accidental losses suffered by the species; in fact, were a species to multiply at the rate of which men or elephants are genesically capable, eventually "not only means of subsistence but space would be lacking."[64]

Even if it be granted, in consistence with Spencer's thesis, that the genesic force formerly was more powerful, it remains true that "we observe in our own epoch increases which could not have existed in the past and which could not continue in the future."[65] Had the world's population numbered 50 millions at the beginning of the Christian era, and had it increased continuously at the rate observed in Norway in 1865–1880, it would have totaled 489×10^{16} by 1891. Were the combined population of England, Norway, and Germany — 73 millions in 1880 — to continue to increase at the rate then prevailing in Germany, in 1,200 years it would total 1,707 followed by eleven zeros — more than one person per square kilometer throughout the world. "That is absurd. It is therefore evident that the population of the three countries considered cannot continue to increase indefinitely at the present rate."[66] England's population, had it continually increased at the post-1860 rate, would have grown from two millions in 1086 to 84 billions in 1886. Since it had not so grown, it followed either that the genesic force had changed, and this explanation was not adequate,[67] or that non-genesic obstacles had held numbers below the level to which the genesic forces, acting alone and unimpeded, would have carried them. Whence Pareto concluded that late nineteenth-century rates of increase had not prevailed in the past, and could not persist in the future; and that, since the genesic force could not adapt itself with sufficient rapidity to changing circumstances, non-genesic forces (or obstacles) would repress the effect of the genesic force in the future, as they had repressed it in the past.[68] He indicated, too, that the rate of expansion of the European economy was falling, and that therefore population could not grow so rapidly in the future as in the recent past.[69]

Pareto divided the obstacles to population growth into two classes: (*a*) the "preventive," which act up to the moment of birth, and (*b*) the "re-

---

64. C, 193.
65. C, 194.
66. C, 196–197; M, p. 409. Calculations such as these, Pareto wrote, do not correspond with reality; they are intended to show that reality is different. He criticized Euler, who had supposed that men could increase 1/16, or 1/144, annually for long periods, and had then inferred that it was ridiculous to say that one man could not people the earth in a short time; such reasoning (says Pareto) does not show that one cannot use mathematics in social science; it shows that one must start with valid premises (C, 197n.).
67. To suppose such changes in the genesic force as were possible, would not avert the issue; it would merely defer its coming to a head. (C, 211.)
68. C, 198; M, pp. 409–410. See Section IV below.
69. See below, Section V.

pressive," which act after birth.[70] The preventive obstacles he subdivided into (1) those which diminish the number of unions and (2) those which limit the number of births, whatever be the number of unions. In some "modern civilized peoples" the number of marriages had diminished without a compensating increase in illegitimate fertility manifesting itself.[71] Unions were fewer when celibacy, polygamy, polyandry, or (usually) concubinage was practiced.[72] Among the birth-limiting preventive checks he included, with others, birth control, abortion, incontinence (e.g. prostitution), "great intellectual activity," and deferment of marriage[73] (which becomes moral restraint if attended by rigorous chastity). Among the repressive obstacles he included whatever augments mortality: deaths due directly to deficiency in alimentation (misery, famine), or indirectly to diseases caused by misery or by absence (because of cost or ignorance) of hygienic measures; deaths from violence, infanticide, murder, and war.[74] The nineteenth century had witnessed, in civilized lands, an increase in the "intensity of the preventive obstacle," and a decrease in that of the repressive obstacles.[75]

Lack of subsistence operates directly and indirectly to curb population growth, Pareto concluded in the light of his theory of income distribution.[76] Lack of subsistence strikes directly at the lowest — "wolf point"[77] — income class, serving principally to augment mortality: even before men are at the starvation level, want aggravates the death-dealing effects of diseases; and when men lack "the most indispensable aliments," any economic turn for the worse smites with "maximum intensity."[78]

70. The classification is that of Malthus; the terminology, that of P. Rossi (see M, p. 411; C, 216).

71. M, p. 412; C, 226. In Bavaria and Wurtemberg, however, when restrictions upon marriage were removed, the relative number of illegitimate births declined (C, 261).

72. M, p. 412; C, 262.

73. M, pp. 412–413; C, 238. It is not certain that intellectual activity runs counter to reproduction, he noted (M, pp. 412–413). Cp. R. Pearl, The Biology of Population Growth, New York, 1925, pp. 202–204.

74. M, p. 413. Sometimes emigration, when it carried out capital, impoverished countries and thus intensified the repressive obstacle (M, p. 413).

75. C, I, pp. 84–86, 230, 235. In Norway, England, and other countries, the frequency of marriage had fallen, and the age at marriage had risen. In France voluntary limitation of births had increased. See C, 228, 234. Pareto pointed to the high natality of the French population of Algeria and Canada as evidence of the fact that natality was low in France because of economic motivation, and not because of a weakening of the genesic force (C, 228).

76. See Section VIII of this paper. Pareto preferred Say's expression "means of existence" to Malthus' "means of subsistence." Malthus' term is too particularized; it should include at the minimum, in addition to aliments, clothing, lodging, and fuel, all of which vary with race and clime. See C, 205; M, p. 411.

77. H. T. Davis, in his discussion of Pareto's income curve, aptly labels the minimum existence value "the wolf point." See his The Analysis of Economic Time Series, Bloomington, 1941, pp. 405, 415ff.

78. C, 205, 1027–1028; M, pp. 386, 410. Death from starvation is rare in civilized societies, but death from inanition (e.g. from pellagra) occurs (C, 205n.). Furthermore, mortality is indirectly sensitive to the availability of economic resources (C, 239).

Lack of subsistence affects population growth in the higher income groups indirectly. The form of the curve of income distribution remains substantially unchanged, whether the average income is high or low, each class descending when the lowest is eliminated: accordingly, when lack of subsistence cuts directly into the lowest income class, it also operates indirectly to worsen the absolute lot of higher classes or strata.[79] The "lack of subsistence felt directly by the inferior ranks" therefore indirectly impels members of the middle income groups to remain single, to defer marriage, or to limit family size; it affects in like manner the members of the highest income classes, who also are afflicted by "the very powerful phenomenon of the decadence of the élites, which causes all elect races to disappear more or less rapidly."[80] Pareto therefore rejected J. S. Mill's thesis[81] that, unless an entire generation can, by a stroke, be habituated to comfort, measures intended to aid the working class can accomplish nothing. Mill's thesis is valid only on condition that population pressure is always at a maximum; but this condition is not characteristic of most civilized peoples, who enjoy a certain margin above subsistence, and can therefore enlarge this margin as conditions improve.[82]

Economic motives, which have their origin in the fear that the means of existence may be insufficient, vary with class and time. When primogeniture regulated inheritance, younger sons often did not marry. In France the small peasant proprietors now limited the number of their children to avoid subdividing their property and prejudicing the economic future of their children; yet prior to the French Revolution, when landed property was redistributed, their rustic forbears multiplied without restraint. The peasant population was being adjusted to "the proportion which in the actual economic state must exist between personal and landed capital"; but, were a new system of cultivation to render the subdivision of existing heritages economically advantageous, "the motive which, among small proprietors, actually limits population, would disappear and the population would increase," The bourgeois in like manner adapted the size of his family to his means and his needs. The wealthy behaved similarly; actuated by fear that their children, if too numerous, might fall in social status, they restricted their number to

the demand for personnel to direct social enterprises. If the French wealthy class had for its sons a market similar to that which, up to the present, the

79. "If the workers disappeared, the proprietors of the shops where these workers worked, and those who, in the professions called liberal, drew their profit from these proprietors, [would] fall into poverty." See M., p. 410; also p. 393, C, 1008.

80. M, pp. 384, 410–411; S, I, pp. 28ff.; T, 2053; also C, 1027. Pareto inferred from the tendency of aristocracies to die out that "great wealth does not seem to be a condition favorable to the development of the race"; but he added that this tendency did not prevent population from increasing (C, 205).

81. Principles of Political Economy, Book II, Chap. XIII, 4.

82. C, 181; S, II, p. 243.

English aristocracy has had for its younger sons, the obstacle to the augmentation of [this class of] the population would at least be removed.[83]

The checks to population growth are interrelated; they are among the interdependent elements upon which demographic equilibrium depends. When births and deaths have become equilibrated, a variation in one direction immediately gives rise to a variation in the opposite direction; and while the original equilibrium may not always be completely restored, it is susceptible only of very gradual modification, because of the complex mutual interrelations of the determinants (e.g. checks, economic conditions, etc.) of demographic equilibrium.[84] For example, with economic conditions constant, an increase in births begets an offsetting increase in deaths; whence economic conditions, which are related to natality and mortality levels,[85] undergo change, and in turn react upon mortality and natality; and so on. When, because economic circumstances are hard, infant mortality is high, a repressive obstacle is taking "the place of the preventive obstacle."[86] The preventive and repressive obstacles, in brief, are not independent entities; they are variables mutually interrelated with all the other variables that determine population equilibrium.[87]

The same circumstances which make it difficult to modify demographic equilibrium serve to restore and maintain it. After wars and epidemics, marriages and births increase in number, repair losses, and speedily restore population to its former level. Emigration tends to stimulate marriages and

83. C, 184; M, pp. 410–411. Elsewhere he observed (C, 1006) that because of the smallness of family size in the French upper classes, members of the poor classes had a better chance in France than in England to move upward. He quoted with approval a statement to the effect that democracies tolerated imperialism and colonial expansion because they provided a dignified means of livelihood to many who might otherwise join with the industrial proletariat (T, 2320n.).

84. In a comment on the theory of balance of species and individuals in nature, Pareto states that the vital equilibrium is dynamic, not static; some species are disappearing, others are increasing; the milieu within which living beings are situated may be modified by them; and so on (C, 627 and n.).

85. Age composition changes with modification of gross and net natural increase; and because of changes in age composition, the productive power of the population changes (M, pp. 413–414). In his Cours Pareto noted the economic importance of age composition, pointing out that in a stationary population, based on prevailing mortality, there were about as many persons under as over thirty years, while in populations increasing as was the Prussian, about half were under twenty-five. In a stationary population, he estimated, 42 per cent of the males were in the age group 20–50; in a population growing one per cent a year, only 40.5 per cent were in this age group. In France the average age of the population had risen, in part, because of the decline in natality. See C, I, pp. 77–80, 86.

86. C, 241, 235. The repressive obstacle operates not only because preventive obstacles are inactive; it is also brought into play when, as in Italy, resources are not employed effectively to restrain preventable diseases (C, 240).

87. C, 225; M, p. 414, also pp. 153ff. It is not the function of economic science to indicate by what means population growth should be restrained; this is the task of philosophy, physiology, and related sciences. Economics is concerned with the laws of the transformation of savings into capital (C, 227; T, 2316n. 2). However, Pareto's comments at times implied disapproval of rabbit-like fertility.

births, while an augmentation of births and marriages may be compensated by increases in deaths and emigration. Policies and practices intended to reduce numbers may modify the *moeurs,* thereby changing the population equilibrium itself, and so produce an effect other than that intended. Thus, emigration may intensify imprudence and consequently increase natality and population; recourse to abortion, infanticide, and child-exposure may have a similar effect.[88] War does not issue out of population pressure; nor does it serve as a repressive obstacle which eases such pressure, for it destroys more wealth than men.[89] When, for any reason, the "standard of life" falls (or rises), pari passu with the deterioration (or amelioration) of economic circumstances, natural increase and numbers may remain unchanged, but the conditions of demographic equilibrium have changed.[90]

Pareto did not reformulate his account of the formation of population or personal capital in terms of the concept of residues which he developed in the *Trattato,* but he several times referred to effects of changes in residue composition. He attributed the decline in natality in Gascony to the diminution in intensity of Class II residues and to the increase in intensity of Class I residues; for when Class II residues diminish in intensity, economic interests and immediately personal concerns become ascendant.[91] He did not at this point distinguish between the mode of operation of tastes and that of residues; but elsewhere he said that while human beings act in an essentially logical manner when satisfying presumably given tastes by overcoming "obstacles to the acquisition of economic values," they do not act in an analogous manner when manifesting residues. "Residues are not, like tastes, merely sources of conduct; they function through the whole course of the conduct developing from the source." The behavior to which they give rise is not logical in the sense that economic action is logical; it serves, moreover, to modify the tastes referred to above.[92] From the *Trattato,* therefore, there emerges an implied account of population formation in which the economic and logical elements occupy a lesser role than in the *Cours* and the *Manuel.*

Pareto made occasional use of the residue concept in treating of other types of population movements. He accounted, in large part, for the change in the character and the eventual decline of Rome in terms of the continuing immigration of individuals harboring different residues than the Latin and Italic peoples.[93] He did not develop, as he might have, the effect of changes

88. M, pp. 414–415.
89. C, 188, 242, also I, p. 140n. War flows out of the "competition of directing classes, who wish to augment the number of their subjects, and above all, of their taxpayers." See C, 242.
90. C, 181.
91. T, 2527n.
92. T, 2079–2080, 2097, 2141–2143; Parsons, op. cit., pp. 293–298, 454–460, 705–707. Also Sections VIII and IX of this paper.
93. T, 1840, 2360–2365, 2546, 2549.

in the residue composition of the dominant class upon population policies and theories.[94] He noted that social classes may differ in residue composition, but he did not account for differential natality in these terms.[95] He observed that class circulation and residue composition undergo change, oscillatory and otherwise, but he did not attempt to connect these changes with changes in population growth and natality.

IV. Malthus' Theories

Malthus' work, confused, imprecise, and error-ridden,[96] consists of four distinct parts, Pareto declared: (1) a false polemical part, in which he makes man's economic and social condition depend solely upon his reproductive behavior; (2) an irrelevant "sermon" on chastity, in which "moral restraint" is advanced as the solution of the "social question"; (3) a descriptive, historical part, in which Malthus seeks to demonstrate the existence, and to describe the effects, of the checks; and (4) the scientific part, in which he tries to show that, since the generative force is so powerful, it must be and is contained by other forces.[97]

The essential and scientific part of Malthus' work consisted in his distinction between *virtual* (virtuel) and *real* (réel)[98] rates of increase, and in his recognition of the role of the non-genesic factors. By *virtual* rate of increase Pareto means the rate (say, three per cent per year) at which an animal or human population would grow, if only the genesic force were at work; and by *real* rate he means the rate at which the same population grows under the combined influence of the genesic and the non-genesic factors. While the *real* and *virtual* rates for a given species may coincide for short periods, such coincidence cannot last long, and the *real* rate must fall below the *virtual* rate. Malthus' rate of doubling each twenty-five years represented the *virtual* rate fixed by the genesic force alone, whereas his arithmetical progression, determined by the arithmetical progression in the food supply, represented the *real* rate. Malthus' arithmetical progression exaggerated the *real* rate, however; for while a population could double in twenty-five

94. T, 2178–79; but see his explanation of the success of the "historical school" of political economy (T, 2020).

95. On inter-class differences in residue composition see T, 1043–1047, 2178–2179; on differential natality, S, II, pp. 142–143.

96. Malthus' errors exemplify what happens when "one confounds theory with practice, scientific research with moral preaching" (M, p. 420).

97. M, pp. 420–422.

98. On the distinction between *virtual* and *real* movements, see M, p. 154; C, 199; S, I, pp. 80–82; T, 129–140, 2097. *Real* movements are those necessary to the realization of equilibrium. *Virtual* movements are somewhat analogous to potential movements; they would take place in the absence of the equilibrating forces. See M, p. 154.

years, given appropriate conditions, it could not continue indefinitely to increase in arithmetical progression each quarter-century.[99]

The *virtual* rate of increase of which a human population is capable has not been determined—it may have been approximated in Java, where the population long grew at a rate nearly sufficient to double it every twenty-five years—nor is this rate of importance.[100] But it is of importance that the *real* rate varies with time and place, and that the *real* rates which have prevailed in the late nineteenth century cannot continue in effect indefinitely.[101] Were the population of England and Wales to continue increasing at the 1801–1891 rate, 658 years later there would be an inhabitant per square meter. However great economic progress might be, men could not live so tightly packed together; hence the 1801–1891 rate could not continue indefinitely. Pareto added that there were signs that the rate was already slackening.[102] Two decades later he presented evidence proving that in England and Wales "population is no longer following the law observable for the years 1801–1891, and that it is increasing at a slower rate."[103] He noted also that the rate of increase was falling in Germany (notably "in the large cities where wealth has appreciably increased"), for which country there were no grounds in 1895 for determining empirically the prospective trend, and in Norway.[104]

Pareto admitted the validity, in a general sense, of the thesis (advanced principally by the sociologists) that both numbers and individual well-being might increase, if resources were better organized. Such would be the experience of any country, were conditions destructive of wealth to disappear. As Martello (a socialist critic of Malthus) had observed, were it not for protectionism, heavy expenditures upon armaments, and the "malversations of politicians," Europe could support a much larger population at a higher level of well-being. The experience of England, in fact, supported Martello's

99. C, 199–200. Pareto charged Messedaglia with not distinguishing sharply between virtual and actual movements, when he substituted for Malthus' geometrical progression the progression 1, 2, 4, 6, 8, 10. . . . This progression did not express what Messedaglia sought to express; so Pareto gave mathematical formulation to what Messedaglia intended to say (C, 204).

100. C, 213.

101. C, 211–215; M, pp. 409–410.

102. C, 196, 211. He indicated (C, 229) the need of curve-fitting to determine true growth trends.

103. T, p. 42n. In his Cours (211) he fitted a curve to the population returns for England and Wales in 1801–1891, and determined the law of growth. By 1891 the estimated population, which for prior census years had usually fallen slightly below the corresponding observed population, exceeded the observed figure by 1.9 per cent; in 1910 the estimated figure exceeded the observed figure by 5.6 per cent (see T, p. 42; C, 211). Pareto reports his prediction, which was prepared in 1895 and ran counter "to the views of ethical sociologists . . . and of sentimental anti-Malthusians," as an example "of forecasts based on the scientific laws of political economy and sociology (to the exclusion of sentiment)." See T, p. 40.

104. T, pp. 40–41.

thesis, for there, contrary to Malthus' forecasts, population had grown rapidly, but less rapidly than wealth, and individual well-being had increased; and the experience of Sicily might be similar, had the island a "passably honest administration."[105] It did not follow from the above thesis, however, that population growth is not limited by economic forces; for even though it be granted that resources can be used effectively enough to permit, for a time, the *real* rate of increase to approximate the *virtual* rate, so high a *real* rate cannot persist, and the two rates must eventually diverge.[106]

Malthus' fundamental error, whence flowed both his incorrect description of the relation between numbers and prosperity and his inaccurate forecast of the future, consisted in his emphasizing one determinant of prosperity to the exclusion of other equally indispensable determinants, and in his disregarding the relations of mutual interdependence between the several determinants of prosperity, and between numbers and other conditions. It was essential to the maintenance of prosperity, for example, not only (*a*) that population not increase too rapidly, but also (*b*) that there exist a social organization suited to guard private property and prevent despoliation of the people,[107] and (*c*) that wealth not be destroyed or employed uselessly. Hence the state of well-being could not be associated exclusively with the state of determinant (*a*), with the state of (*b*), or with the state of (*c*). Malthus had reasoned correctly, when he established the indispensability of condition (*a*), but he had inferred invalidly when he implied that the state of well-being was independent of conditions (*b*) and (*c*).[108] Because of this fundamental error, Malthus did not foresee that the level of well-being in England would rise appreciably at the same time that the population was increasing markedly;[109] and he was deceived into predicting that in France the equal division of inheritance would discourage prudence and eventually visit upon that country both extreme equality and misery.[110]

Malthus' reasoning played into the hands of the socialists. For economic science diverges in one direction or the other, according as one supposes, with Malthus, that population presses fatally and inexorably upon subsistence to the limit set by famine and misery, or with some of his critics, that

105. C, 206–207, 212, 221; M, p. 421.

106. C, 206. This "disagreeable truth" was usually concealed by socialists, intent upon not weakening their propaganda; but it was admitted by Marlo (i.e., Winkelbach), who asserted that misery could not be averted, unless excessive increase of population was avoided (C, 206).

107. In the Manuel (pp. 431–442) he observed that whereas in the past the upper classes as a rule had used political power "to despoil the poor classes," now in certain democracies "a diametrically opposite phenomenon" was commencing.

108. C, 222. He refers to Martello's observation that excess population is an effect, not a cause, of lack of well-being (C, 223).

109. C, 221.

110. C, 224. Such ideas found ready currency among fox-hunting gentlemen, Pareto notes (ibid.), and were employed by governments to oppress the people. See Malthus' forecast in his Principles of Political Economy, 2d ed., p. 377.

there exists a supra-subsistence margin, at least among civilized peoples, below which numbers do not generally push the level of living.[111] Malthus proceeded from the former proposition — "the equivalent of the iron law[112] of Lassalle" — to the conclusion that limitation of births constituted the only means of improving the human lot; whence it followed that the condition of a people — their happiness and their sufferings — was virtually independent of the type of social organization they had and of the character of the government under which they lived.[113] Because he reasoned in this manner, and because he expressed himself unscientifically, Malthus facilitated misinterpretation of his central thesis, and provided the socialists, against whom his Essay was directed, with a powerful argument for socialism. When Malthus assumed that, as a rule, population is pressing hard upon subsistence, and that therefore "each diminution of the preventive obstacle must *necessarily* be compensated by a *rigorously* equal increase of the repressive obstacle,"[114] he exposed himself to easy refutation, since numbers do not usually press so hard upon subsistence; while the ease with which this view could be refuted tended to make Malthus' critics forget that his theory was basically "true," and that population does exercise "a certain pressure upon subsistence" and thereby produces important effects.[115] When Malthus evaluated the "right" of an individual to nourishment, he abandoned the domain of economic science, and he overlooked the fact that many "parasites" (e.g. "pirates," "politicians"), of those activities society had no need, nonetheless obtained subsistence from society.[116] More important still, Malthus had overlooked that, if it is true that man's lot is independent of the form of social organization under which he lives,

> there no longer is cause to fear a socialist experiment. Since the organization of society is of no moment, it is at least proper to make a trial of a new organization.

111. C, 217.

112. The "iron law" of wages, Pareto stated elsewhere (S, II, pp. 241–247), rests upon a false principle from which erroneous conclusions are drawn. There is no simple relation between wages and the cost of producing men; statistical data reveal improvement of the worker's lot.

113. C, 220; also M, pp. 406–407.

114. Pareto cited, as did many critics of Malthus, the famous passage in the second edition of the Essay (IV, vi, p. 531) which was not included in later editions: "A man who is born into a world already possessed, if he cannot get subsistence from his parents, on whom he has a just demand, and if the society do not want his labor, has no claim of *right* to the smallest portion of food, and, in fact, has no business to be where he is. At nature's mighty feast there is no vacant cover for him. . . ." Of this passage Pareto said that one could not accumulate more "errors of method" in so few words, and that, while the passage was later suppressed, its sense was retained in later editions (C, 219). Bonar (Malthus and His Work, New York, 1924, p. 307) writes of this passage: "It contains, however, at least two positions that were never retracted: — that the poor cannot claim relief as a right, but only as a favour, and that poor relief can only raise one man by depressing another."

115. C, 218–219; M, pp. 420ff.

116. C, 219.

In fact, in these circumstances, one must admit that the thesis of the socialists may be partly valid. If, on the contrary, man's lot is not independent of the form of social organization, and it is probable that a change in social organization will occasion much loss and little gain, there is reason to fear the introduction of such a new form as socialism.[117]

For many of the criticisms directed against Malthus Pareto had only contempt. These criticisms — some of which were made in bad faith — were irrelevant or untenable. To the assertion that Malthus' theory runs counter to Christian doctrine Pareto replied that "there is not in all Christian doctrine a word which permits one to suppose that man must abandon himself without restraint to his genesic passions; instead, as St. Paul's writings reveal, man must curb his passions." Objection to Malthus' doctrine usually resolves itself into objection to "moral restraint," a problem that lies "entirely outside the domain of economic science," whose function it is to infer consequences from facts, not to give counsel or to lay down precept. Criticisms of the two progressions generally reveal complete ignorance of the subject treated, for they describe, not how population does in fact grow, but how it tends to grow under given conditions.[118]

V. Demographic Trends

As we have already shown, Pareto noted the sensitivity of demographic indices to short-run economic fluctuations. He touched also upon the long-run trend in population growth, upon its determinants and upon its effects. In the *Cours* he observed: (a) that spatial and other limitations to economic expansion, inherent in all economies, already were decelerating population growth; and (b) that as men became conscious of these barriers, they tended to introduce restrictive arrangements, which served only to constrict the initial limits.[119] The abnormally high rates at which numbers had been growing for two-thirds of a century among civilized peoples could not persist; for wealth could not continue to increase as it had and thus continue to make possible a volume of savings sufficient to augment "personal capital" at the rates then prevailing. New discoveries and progress, moreover, could give only a

117. C, 220.

118. C, 201–203. When generalizations are laid down in social sciences, critics tend to direct rhetorical polemics at details, rather than to examine scientifically the underlying principles (C, 201). Pareto compares the controversy over the two progressions with the discussion of astronomy in Galileo's time: were the anti-malthusians astronomers, they would fail to see that the movement of a planet is composed of two movements, one tangential and the other toward the center of attraction (C, 202–203). Here Pareto praises J. Garnier's Du principe de population. On Garnier see my "French Population Theory since 1800," Journal of Political Economy, XLIV, 1936, pp. 588ff.

119. When he wrote the Cours Pareto was not yet making use of "a general theory positing an undulatory form for social phenomena" (T, p. 1667n.). Later he mentions the "great law of rhythm" which "dominates all social phenomena." See S, I, p. 30; M, p. 529; cp, C, 692.

transient impulse to the increase of wealth and population.[120] Inflection of the trajectories representing the movement of population and wealth therefore was inevitable.

Changes in direction of the movement of population and wealth would give rise to forces similar to the forces of inertia considered by mechanics. For populations feel "vividly the pressure that economic conditions exercise in order to modify" prevailing trajectories:

> Individuals wish to continue to reproduce themselves as their parents reproduced themselves, and they blame the social organization, if their sons do not find the work they desire.

They seek escape, therefore, in restrictive arrangements, which serve only to aggravate the limitations to expansion against which they would rebel. In England, the intensification of the economic obstacles to population growth was responsible in large measure for the "recrudescence of protectionism" and for the "development of socialism." But "these pretended remedies are more suited to make the evil worse than to cure it."[121]

In the *Manuel* Pareto merely observed that society was reintroducing the "rigid organizations" whose destruction a century earlier had made possible the industrial and demographic growth experienced in the nineteenth century.[122] In the *Trattato* he presented further evidence to the effect that the curves of population were falling, and that the adjustment of the growth rates of population and wealth to limitations upon expansion was giving rise to artificial restrictive arrangements.[123] A period of stagnation analogous to those experienced in the past was impending, and this was part of the undulatory scheme of things, "the fluctuations [of social phenomena] revealing

120. C, 471. He emphasized, not the secular trend in the standard of living, but limitations to the expansion of wealth and production. Population could no more increase in uninterrupted geometrical progression than could a quantum of capital. While he believed that there would be "considerable" saving even at a zero rate of interest, he criticized the prediction of Leroy-Beaulieu that the interest rate would continue to fall (M, pp. 448–449; C, 387, 435, 469–473); but he did not account until later (see below, n. 125) for the failure of the interest rate to fall to zero. He did not refer to Leroy-Beaulieu's thesis (see my France Faces Depopulation, 1938, pp. 168–169) that a falling interest rate would stimulate natality.

121. C, 471, 211n. Pareto always adhered to his view that "collectivism" checks economic progress (T, 2553, 2607ff.), but he subsequently modified his appraisal of protectionism to take into account its effects upon inter-class circulation (T, 2208ff.). See Section VIII of this paper.

122. The high rate of industrial progress (to which must be attributed, in part, "the extraordinary increase of wealth and population of civilized states in this century") was falling markedly; while restrictive measures of every sort, which had their origin in "non-logical," rather than in rational, economic behavior, were multiplying and putting an ever larger part of the economy in a strait-jacket. See M, pp. 410, 503–505; also C, 998n.

123. T, pp. 40–42. The facts, he said, corroborated the "soundness" of the conclusion he had expressed in the Cours (211n.). "Socialism has progressed in England. . . ." See T, 77. The United States, "which has grown up on immigration and owes its present prosperity to immigration," was setting up barriers against immigration; "other countries, Australia among them, are doing the same." See T, 2553.

and representing the various forces that affect the social aggregate as a whole."[124]

The curves of accumulating wealth for families, communities, nations—all humanity—instead of showing the regular increase that a uniform rate of interest would yield, are undulatory lines fluctuating about an average medium curve. . . . Just as certainly there is a curve of increase for the given family, community, or race, though with periods of decrease.

The duration of the periods is long for the human race as a whole, less long for nations, fairly short for communities, very brief for families.[125]

The rate of population growth, Pareto's analysis implied, would fall off in consequence of the increasing supersession of "individualism" by "collectivism." "Crystallization" was "setting in, precisely as happened in the case of Rome," and men were praising the very Byzantine institutions which a century earlier they had condemned.[126] Under the coming collectivism, the rigidified institutions of the state would utilize, at first with success, the materials assembled by private initiative during the preceding period of freedom, when wealth and numbers had grown so remarkably; but, as in times past, the "increasing damage resulting from the crystallization of society" would pave the "way for decadence, which only a revival of flexibility and freedom of private enterprise can change into progress." Then, and then only within limits, Pareto's argument suggests, would the rate of growth of wealth and numbers rise.[127]

Pareto's argument is not clear regarding the future of population growth. Presumably he meant something like the following: circumstances independent of man fix the absolute upper limit to the productive capacity of an economy, and this in turn fixes the upper limit to numbers, the per capita demand on productive capacity being given. Upon the manner in which resources are used depends the extent to which actual and realized productive capacity approaches the theoretical upper limit. The curve of total production and of population is essentially S-shaped, increasing at a decreasing rate beyond the point of inflection. The form of the curve, however, is not so regular as that of a logistic curve, and the rate of increase does not taper off in an orderly fashion. Instead, as the economy crystallizes, the rates of growth of total production and of numbers fall toward, and possibly

124. T, 1718, 2293, 2316, 2319.
125. T, 2316. Pareto attributed to "successive destructions of wealth" the failure of interest rates to fall to zero and the non-realization of such accumulations of wealth as "would result from real interest rates." See T, pp. 1664–1666, and note, p. 1665, where Pareto comments on his failure to resolve, in the Cours, the mystery of compound interest.
126. T, 2553, 2612. "Liberty" (in J. S. Mill's sense of the term) was equally doomed to decline, because it is contrary to the motives and aspirations of the coming ruling class—the masses (T, 298).
127. T, 2553 and notes; also notes to 2550, 2610–2611. On undulations see also Section VIII of this paper.

below zero. But an economy will not remain permanently crystallized; class-circulation and other forces eventually shatter the crystalline encasement. Then productivity, and with it numbers, surge upward, until again checked by the natural limits to expansion and by the growing strength of the forces of crystallization inherent in economic and social systems. Presumably, since productivity and numbers now approximate much more closely to the upper limits set by nature than they did in the late eighteenth century, and since consciousness of these limits in itself accentuates the crystallizing tendencies, sustained upsurges such as the nineteenth century witnessed are less likely to occur: the amplitude of cycles, as measured in terms of growth of production and numbers, will be narrower than in the past.

Pareto's analysis differs from present-day theories which treat the decline in population growth as an important check to economic activity and expansion.[128] In his scheme, population growth is essentially a resultant, even though it is one of the interdependent variables comprising the social system; its fluctuations are reciprocally interconnected with the undulatory elements in the social aggregate as a whole.

VI. Opinion, Law, and Population Movements

Pareto did not believe that population movements are much influenced by law or by subjective attitudes and opinions regarding such movements. He did not even include law among the determinants of social equilibrium;[129] while in his earlier works he sometimes described theories as mere verbal justifications of facts.[130] He looked upon law and opinion as more or less epiphenomenal in character — as reflecting or manifesting the more fundamental elements by which human conduct, a considerable part of which is illogical, is shaped.[131]

128. A. H. Hansen, American Economic Review, XXIX, 1939, pp. 1–15; A. R. Sweezy, Quarterly Journal of Economics, LV, 1940, pp. 64–79; P. M. Sweezy, The Theory of Capitalist Development, New York, 1942, pp. 222–226; and the writer's "Population Movements, Employment, and Income," Southern Economic Journal, V, 1938, pp. 129–157. Pareto apparently did not grasp Marx's population theories; he in no sense anticipated the investment theory of Lord Keynes and his predecessors.

129. T, 2060. See N. S. Timasheff, "Law in Pareto's Sociology," American Journal of Sociology, XLVI, 1940, pp. 139–149.

130. M, p. 433; also pp. 415–416, 432. In the Trattato (149–150; see also Parsons, op. cit., pp. 187, 190ff.) Pareto distinguished carefully between the *objective* aspect and the *subjective* aspect of social phenomena, and described as *logical* actions those which conjoined means to ends from the standpoint of both the subjective doer and the adequately informed outside observer. Political economy deals largely with "logical actions" (T, 152). "In ordinary logic," he pointed out (T, 514), "the conclusion follows from the premises. In the logic of sentiment the premises follow from the conclusion."

131. This thesis, foreshadowed in his earlier writings, is developed fully, but with qualification, in the Trattato. See Section VIII below. Pareto did not deny importance to ideas. See T. Parsons, "The Role of Ideas in Social Action," American Sociological Review, III, 1938, pp. 663–664.

"The question of the growth of population and of obstacles" thereto is one of those with which men appear unable to concern themselves dispassionately, economic and other factors operating in combination to shape opinions on this matter. For the ratio of numbers to wealth is among the most powerful of social facts, impinging upon many interests and affecting various motives. Frequently spokesmen for a given class support policies at variance with its basic interests, either because they are not aware of these interests, or because other elements, inconsistent with these interests, shape their attitudes. Such discrepancy between subjective attitude and objective interest, however, if expressed only in terms of belief, law, or opinion, exercises little if any influence upon population movements, for these are regulated by other circumstances. Seemingly, opinion is conditioned by the population situation: when the population of France was growing, savants and statesmen preached Malthusianism; when it became stationary, they called for increase.[132]

In consistence with his view that class interests are not in harmony,[133] Pareto pointed out that population growth affects differently the interests of the several classes composing society, operating directly to alter the comparative numerical size of these classes, and indirectly to redistribute power. Thus great population growth is to the interest of the wealthy and of the political oligarchies, assuming the distribution of power to be unaffected thereby, because when labor is abundant it may be purchased on terms favorable to employers, and when subjects are numerous, the power of the politically dominant class is great; for opposite reasons it is to the interest of the masses that they restrict their numbers. If, however, the distribution of power does not remain constant in the face of population growth, the effect of population growth upon the respective interests of the well-situated minority and of the mass of poor may be otherwise. Suppose that population growth alters the probability of revolution. Suppose that revolution can be accomplished with greater ease when the masses are misery-ridden, and that population growth makes for misery. Then the leaders of the masses may properly urge them to multiply and augment their misery,[134] while the spokesmen for the dominant classes may with propriety preach family limitation and so try to avert population pressure which threatens their security. If, on the contrary, revolution is more likely to take place when the poor are enjoying comfort — and this supposition is more nearly in accord with the facts[135] — the dominant classes, provided that they are actuated solely by the economic motive, will seek to check

132. M, pp. 415–420.

133. This view runs through his works; e.g. see S, II, Chap. 12.

134. Some Italian syndicalists argued that family size should not be limited, inasmuch as a high birth rate would depress wages and hasten the revolution. See R. Michels, Revue d'économie politique, XXVII, 1913, pp. 614–616, 624–625.

135. M, pp. 401–404. Cp. L. P. Edwards, The Natural History of Revolution, Chicago, 1927, pp. 33ff. Pareto believed that "socialist sentiments augment as the result of a long period

the spread of comfort, while the leaders of the poor will fight for its diffusion.[136]

The population doctrines and policies advanced by spokesmen for given social classes, however, often run counter, just as does the procreative behavior of some members of these classes, to the true interests of the classes in question. For this several circumstances are responsible. Neither spokesmen for a given class nor all its members are completely aware of the true interests of the class to which they belong. Long-run advantage is sacrificed to short-run advantage. Non-economic motives (e.g. ethical, metaphysical, aesthetic, etc.) issue in behavior at variance with economic interest. Thus, in Pareto's day, members of the upper classes stood for contradictory policies and practices; many opposed birth-control on religious, ascetic, or hypocritical grounds,[137] while others (nationalists and conservatives) favored the enactment of populationist measures; yet others sanctioned birth-control as a means of conserving the family patrimony. Generally, blindness to their real interests, together with ethical motives and physiological decadence, was preparing the ruin of the upper classes.

Contradictory policies and practices were pursued also in the lower classes. The leaders of the poorer classes — "in a word the members of the new *élite* who are preparing to dispossess those of the ancient élite" — supposed at times that misery, at other times that comfort, conduces to revolution; for this reason some favored population restriction, while others (e.g. the radical-socialists in France), unaware that populationist legislation would destroy the basis of their power, supported such legislation. The poor themselves, because of their desire for the earnings of child-labor, or because of imprudence, often were very prolific. Moreover, the desire of the poor for present material and sexual satisfactions pressed even those of their leaders who were aware of the need for population restriction to ignore the population question and to promise instead that, when capitalism had been destroyed and the "golden age" established, "all these wants, all these desires" could be "satisfied unreservedly."[138]

Equally contradictory were the population policies of politicians. They

---

of peace and of the growth of wealth," whereas counter-sentiments tend to become weaker. See M, p. 401; S, I, pp. 62–75.

136. M, pp. 416–417.

137. For the opponents of birth control, for sex reformers, and for anti-libertarians generally, Pareto, who by temperament and practice apparently was a sybarite (Borkenau, op. cit., p. 15), manifested distaste. See T, 1344–1345, 1352; S, I, pp. 96–97; Le mythe vertuiste et la littérature immorale, Paris, 1911, pp. 20–22. Birth control, he said, was viewed by its opponents as a worse crime than blasphemy or treason (T, 1126–1127, 1345). He enumerated St. Jerome's qualms regarding pregnancy and commended his writings to the opponents of birth control as in need of expurgation (T, 1370).

138. M, pp. 416–419. Some (among the people) went so far as to maintain that satisfaction of the sexual instinct must be subject to no restriction; or that, because of the decline in natural fecundity allegedly attendant upon increase in intellectual activity, there was nothing to fear from unrestrained satisfaction of sexual desires.

were always avid for subjects to despoil,[139] and therefore usually pretended that Malthusianism was against the interests of public and country;[140] yet they supported policies that checked rather than stimulated population growth. They piled up governmental expenditures and swelled the tax burden; they wasted resources on military expansion and colonial expeditions; they imposed tariffs,[141] thereby destroying wealth and increasing the cost of living. In general, they ignored the fact "that the best way to favor the reproduction of men, as that of animals, is to assure them a certain degree of well-being."[142]

Law, religion, and moral preachings exercise little if any influence upon population movements, Pareto concluded; they can do little more than sanction what the *moeurs* (which rest in considerable measure upon economic facts) support,[143] or what is consistent with the prevailing residues or sentiments.[144] Roman populationist legislation accomplished nothing; Colbert's measures failed, as did those enacted during the French Revolution; late nineteenth-century French legislation had been equally ineffective, in part presumably because protectionism, militarism, and socialism were consuming French capital.[145] The reproductive response of a people to increases in wealth depends upon their tastes and habits, upon the standard of life. Accordingly, such increases in wealth and well-being as would stimulate slaves or Hindus to multiply, or as had caused medieval populations to grow, were not sufficient to impel the French and other western peoples to augment in number.[146]

VII. Optima

The population of an area may be described as at an optimum level when the value of some index of human activity or condition, which varies with

139. "Politicians desire to have the maximum of taxpayers to skin, and it is truly amusing to hear them lament over the much too slow increase of their subjects" (C, 209, n.). In the past only honest men like Voltaire and Montesquieu had criticized those who said that the multiplication of subjects is the Prince's chief interest. See C, 209; T, 1499.

140. Politicians plumped for Malthusianism when they feared proletarians were increasing too rapidly (T, 1499).

141. Later he observed (T, 2208) that protectionism might stimulate class-circulation sufficiently to offset the direct economic effects of tariffs. See below, Section VIII.

142. C, I, pp. 140n., 143n., 143–144. The vices and the prejudices of the directing classes and of the people were primarily responsible for the destruction of wealth (C, 552).

143. C, 245, 259–262, 580; S, II, p. 10. Economic resources can be used, however, to reduce preventable mortality (C, 241–242).

144. T, 1499. In his earlier works he had noted the importance of sentiments; in the Trattato he reduced much of his analysis to terms of interests and residues. See below, Section VIII.

145. C, 264–265; S, I, p. 82. Such legislative non-accomplishment "may indeed be, in part, the effect of future socialist laws" (C, 264).

146. C, I, p. 143n. Elsewhere (C, 561, 567, notes) he criticizes De Laveleye for proposing that the French people, in order that they may increase, adopt the Javanese form of social

numbers, stands at maximum. Some indices stand at maximum when a population is small, others when it is large; hence what constitutes an optimum number is conditioned by the index being maximized—a military maximum calls for a larger population than does a per-capita-output optimum. Furthermore, the population that maximizes a given index from the standpoint of any one class may be greater or less than that which maximizes the same or a similar index from the standpoint of some other class: the population consistent with a maximum wage level is smaller than that consistent with a maximum rent level. Again, what constitutes the *present* optimum number for any class and index is conditioned by the comparative weights assigned *present* and *future* circumstances. Finally, both the *rate* of population growth and the distribution of this growth among classes, as distinguished from mere size of population, may affect the values of certain indices. There is, therefore, no one optimum, even though, within limits, as numbers rise above the zero level, all indices may increase in value; for when population reaches given levels some indices begin to fall in value, whereas others continue to increase. Moreover, as non-demographic circumstances change, the functional relationship between numbers and given indices changes.

Pareto analyzed at length the indices of ophelimity and utility which may be maximized, but he did not examine in detail the functional relations between population density and growth, on the one hand, and these indices on the other. In the main he discussed inter-group conflicts in interest with respect to numbers, and divergences in the movement of the several indices in relation to that of population factors.

In the *Cours*, in which his chief concern was with ophelimity or individual satisfaction, he touched upon the relation between numbers and both ophelimity and utility.[147] He identified four distinct population maxima: (*a*) of ophelimity, or individual satisfaction; (*b*) of utility for the human species, or for one of its determinate parts; (*c*) of the number of individuals composing a nation; (*d*) of the military and expansionist force of a nation, which depends

---

organization. A Frenchman is not content with a daily fistful of rice. Moreover, the civilization produced by the Javanese *dessa*, or by the Russian *mir*, has not attained the level of the Graeco-Roman or modern western worlds, where private property has prevailed. Elsewhere (S, II, pp. 10, 35) Pareto described the populationist proposals of Plato and Morelly as superior to those of the French and other populationists, who advocated that men multiply without limit but said nothing of providing subsistence.

147. Ophelimity refers to individual pleasure or satisfaction; it describes a subjective property of a thing, dependent upon both the thing and the individual, in virtue of which the need or desire of this individual is satisfied. Utility refers to what is "useful"; it designates any property of a thing favorable to the development and prosperity of an individual, race, species, or other group. (See C, 5–10, 181; also T, 1918.) Pareto later showed (e.g., M, pp. 547ff.) the theory of equilibrium to be independent of concepts of ophelimity, utility, etc.; but, as Hicks observes (Value and Capital, London, 1939, p. 19), he did not completely give up the use of these concepts.

on both the quantity and the quality of the population.[148] One may infer from his general discussion that while each of these indices increases, within limits, as population increases, the population total which maximizes some one of these indices will be greater or less than the total which maximizes some other of these indices; e.g. the population consistent with the maximization of ophelimity is smaller than that consistent with the maximization of the military and expansionist force of a nation. One may infer also that the actual population total will not tend to fall much short of the smallest of these maxima, or to exceed the greatest.

The population consistent with the maximization of ophelimity does not coincide, as a rule, with that consistent with the maximization of one of the measures of utility. Ophelimity may run counter to utility; "the hedonistic maximum of the individual, to that of a nation or species";[149] while the utility of the individual may not coincide with that of the species. Preservation of the race or species in number, or its augmentation, may call for greater fertility than is consistent with the maximum of ophelimity of individuals; and it may give utility to practices (e.g. protection of the young) which do not posses utility from the individual point of view. Greater fertility than is consistent with the maximization of the ophelimities of individuals is required to insure the maintenance, or improvement, of the quality of the race; for when gross fertility is relatively great, selective mortality more effectively eliminates the unfit (i.e. the less fit deviates from the average type).[150]

The population which maximizes ophelimity for the members of one group frequently differs from that which makes for a maximum of ophelimity for members of other groups. The "maximum of ophelimity of the directing classes" is usually at variance with that of the working classes; and it rarely coincides "with the maximum of *utility* for the nation, or of the human race." In like manner, the maximum of ophelimity for any other one class, considered in isolation, tends to differ from that of other classes and from that of utility for other groups.[151] "The ophelimity of parents is not identical with

148. C, 209.

149. C, 173, 208; also C, I, p. 141n. Elsewhere (C, 628) he states that ophelimity and utility for an individual do not coincide when the individual cannot foresee the consequences of his actions, or when he cannot accurately compare the future with the present.

150. C, 627–629; M, pp. 63, 424, 425. The discrepancy between the fertility levels consistent, respectively, with the maximization of individual ophelimity and with the improvement of the race is very great when the individual is not susceptible of inheritable modifications; then selection must operate by destroying large numbers of relatively unfit and so occasion much suffering (C, 629). Elsewhere (M, p. 425) he observes that a proper balance must be struck between the utility of the species and that of the individual, but he does not suggest a common denominator or set of weights to accomplish this. (However, see T, pp. 1466–1470, notes.)

151. C, I, p. 141n.; M, pp. 416–419, 501–503, 666. Elsewhere (C, 209n.) he observes that "the politicians want the largest possible number of taxpayers to despoil"; and he notes the similarity between this view and that of rulers as reflected in the writings of the Mercantilists.

that of children," for it is the parents, and not the child, who choose to transform savings into personal capital; whence it is "the egoism of the parents, putting in the world more children than they can conveniently nourish, which is the cause of a great part of the miseries of humanity."[152]

In the *Trattato* Pareto inquired at length into the nature of utility and into the relations between various species of utility, but he barely touched upon the relation between utility and numbers. He distinguished between ophelimity and utility, and between the individual and the collectivity point of view. Ophelimity *for* a collectivity is at a maximum when further change, while it serves to augment the ophelimity of some individuals, diminishes that of others. It therefore is analogous to, but not necessarily identical with, given individual maxima. There can be no maximum of ophelimity *of* a collectivity, because the ophelimities of individuals are heterogeneous and not addable. In the realm of utility, Pareto, as a sociologist, distinguished between utility to the individual and utility to the community or collectivity, and between the maximum of utility *for* the community and the maximum of utility *of* the community. The maximum of utility *for* a community is essentially a sum arrived at after heterogeneous utilities have been reduced to terms of a common denominator. The maximum of utility *of* a community presupposes an end which the collectivity as a unity ought to pursue.[153]

Pareto built no optimum theory of population on any of these species of utility or ophelimity. A population factor — density, size, rate of growth — is at the optimum when some index which is conditioned by the population factor is at a maximum. Pareto's analysis reveals that the various indices of ophelimity and utility do not continuously vary together and in the same direction as some other "independent" variable (e.g. population factor) changes. Thus, what constitutes a population of proper size, or a rate of population growth of proper magnitude, depends upon what index of utility (or ophelimity) is to be maximized. Maximization of the utility *of* the community in terms of prestige and military power calls for as large a population as is attainable short of impoverishing the community. Maximization of utility *for* the community calls for a much smaller population and a lower growth rate, for now sacrifices must be balanced against the profits accruing from prestige and military power. When proletarians "refuse to have children because children merely increase the power and profits of the ruling classes, they are dealing with a problem of maximum utility *for* the com-

152. C, 268. Hence parents must be charged with the tutelage of their offspring. Elsewhere (C, 567n.) he says it "is not the task of economics" to say whether it is better for men to multiply like rabbits, as do the Javanese, or to carry their "aspirations further," as do the English.

153. Parsons concludes: "This basis of unity Pareto finds in the last analysis to lie in the necessary existence of an 'end the society pursues.' That is, the ultimate ends of individual action systems are integrated to form a single *common system of ultimate ends,* which is the culminating element of unity holding the whole structure together." See op. cit., p. 249, his italics; also pp. 241–249 on Pareto's "social utility." See Pareto, T, 2110–2143, 2271, 2408n.; cp. M, pp. 501–503.

munity." The counter-arguments of the ruling classes usually run in terms of the maximum *of* the community, even though they are commonly disguised in terms of the maximum for the community.[154]

Pareto's discussion of the relation between numbers and population growth, on the one hand, and indices of ophelimity and utility, on the other, indicates that while he did not suppose population to move in a manner consistent with the maximization of any one of these indices, he did believe that the equilibrating forces within society served to limit the extent to which population movements could cause the indices of ophelimity and of utility for the individual and the community to deviate from their maximal values. That equilibrium which gives the maximum of ophelimity is not attained, because population movements depend upon non-economic as well as upon economic conditions;[155] but it will be approached, inasmuch as population growth is determined so largely by economic conditions,[156] and as there is a limit to the extent to which imperfections of foresight and knowledge can cause numbers to exceed, or fall short of, the level consistent with the maximization of ophelimity or utility from the individual point of view.[157] There appears to be a limit also to the extent to which the distribution of residues can deviate from that which is consistent with the maximization of utility.[158] One may infer from Pareto's discussion that so long as an increase in numbers tends to increase the value of each of the indices of ophelimity and utility, numbers tend to grow; but that when further increases in number decrease some indices, while increasing others, resistance to growth begins to augment.[159]

VIII. Heterogeneity And Selection

In the *Manuel,* in which as in the *Cours* he was primarily concerned with the problem of economic equilibrium, Pareto declared that the character

154. Earlier (M, pp. 17–19, 475–476) Pareto observed that man is a *homo ethicus* as well as a *homo oeconomicus;* whence particular interests tend to be hidden in the form of the general interest.

155. C, 172, 268. "Free competition assures the maximum of ophelimity" on condition that "each individual is free to choose, between two courses, which he prefers"; this maximum "is obtained only when the production of men is proportioned to the need for personal capital" in the same manner as the production of locomotives is proportioned to the need for them (C, 268, also 473, 729). See also next note.

156. C, 182; and T, 152, where economic action is described as largely logical; see also Sections I and III of this paper. "In so far as he acts logically, every individual tries to secure a maximum of individual utility." See T, 2131, 2122; also 2118–2119, where he says that individual utility is sacrificed to collective utility, as a rule, in virtue of non-logical impulses, and 2143, where he states that the form of society is not determined solely by logical thinking.

157. C, 41, 172–173, 267–268, 628–629.

158. T, 2316, 2418, 2429.

159. A. M. Carr-Saunders had something of this sort in mind when he wrote that the desirable density of population tends to be approximated. See The Population Problem, Oxford, 1922, pp. 230, 236, 292.

of a society is determined principally by four species of facts: heterogeneity and hierarchy, natural and social selection, the succession of aristocracies, and per capita wealth.[160] His discussion of social physiology in the *Cours* is in similar vein. In the *Trattato*, in which he was concerned with social equilibrium, Pareto treated at length of heterogeneity, inter-class circulation, and selection; but he made no use of his well-known curve of income distribution and did not discuss natural selection.[161]

Society, he always supposed, is "a hierarchically organized heterogeneous mass"; it is at all times dominated and governed by an *élite*, or aristocratic minority, composed predominantly of superior individuals well endowed with qualities that assure power.[162] He looked upon society, furthermore, much as if it consisted of an underlying immobile and relatively changeless human mass surmounted by a mobile and changeful human super structure; for he viewed social change as largely the product of the inter-class circulation of individuals, and historical oscillation as largely the result of the replacement of one aristocracy or superstructure by another.

From his analysis of income distribution Pareto drew inferences concerning the organization of society and the qualitative composition of its personnel; for he supposed that the distribution of human qualities and differences which presumably underlie income distribution also determine in significant degree the organization and the power relationships of society. The form of the curve of income distribution,[163] as developed by Pareto, "is the result of all the forces that act upon society"; it does not vary greatly in space, in time, or with social organization, and it does not descrive the binomial distribution. It reflects the "nature" of men, the distribution of the ensemble of qualities favorable to the acquisition and retention of wealth; "it probably depends upon the distribution of the physiological and psycho-

---

160. M, p. 425. The concept of hierarchy may be employed in two ways: it may be used to describe the unequal manner in which power, or control, is distributed among the individuals composing any social organization, such as a corporation, a society, or a state; it may be used to describe the fact that men, when rated in terms of some index of quality or capacity, differ markedly, a few ranking high, and many ranking low. The condition of hierarchy, in the former sense, originates in the nature of social organization; in the latter sense, in the nature of man. It is with hierarchy in the latter sense that Pareto is primarily concerned.

161. In the Trattato, in which he developed views foreshadowed in the Manuel and the Systèmes Socialistes, he refers only once, but with approval, to the income curve (T, p. 43); he emphasized the limitations to social Darwinism (T, pp. 828, 1770, 2142).

162. M, pp. 422–423, 380; S, I, p. 28. Pareto claims to use the term aristocracy in the etymological sense of "better." In his earlier works he draws upon O. Ammon, M. R. Benini, J. Novicow, V. de Lapouge, and others. Livingston points out (T, p. 1477, n.) that Pareto fails to acknowledge his indebtedness to J. Bentham, G. Mosca, J. G. Frazer, and others.

163. The income curve is skewed toward the large values of income, its variation from the modal income value toward inframodal values being limited by the fact that those who receive less than the minimum required to live must disappear (M, pp. 384–385). While the curve for all incomes may be expressed as a straight line, that for incomes from labor is concave, that for incomes from mobile capital, convex (C, pp. 958–959).

logical characters (caractères) of men,"[164] and perhaps also upon the manner in which capital is combined with men. Disposing men according to any particular aptitude or talent will yield a similar distribution: the facts of heterogeneity and hierarchy are independent of the index employed to grade men. "The classes called *superior* are also generally the most wealthy." It follows, from the dependence of the distribution of income upon the "nature" of men, that inequality is susceptible of appreciable reduction, and economic organization of significant modification, only in proportion as the "natures" of men are susceptible of alteration.[165]

The position of individuals on the income curve is subject to change, and the average level of income may rise or fall, but the form of the curve is comparatively constant. The colt becomes a horse, and movements occur within each, but the form of the animal persists. An income class increases in absolute magnitude when births exceed deaths within this class, or when more individuals move into this income class from neighboring classes than pass out of it into neighboring classes; it decreases in magnitude when movements of an opposite character occur. If, however, the magnitude of a given class changes, and that of other classes does not change correspondingly, repercussions set in until the magnitude of the class in question once again is in proper relation with those of other classes. If, for example, deaths exceed births in a given class, this deficit tends to be compensated by the movement of wealth and by the immigration into this class of individuals from neighboring classes. Where, as in France, family size in the wealthy classes is relatively small, and barriers to circulation do not exist, the poorer classes have relatively better opportunity for advancement, and the rate of inter-class circulation is greater, than in countries where family size among the wealthy is relatively large.[166]

164. C, pp. 957, 960, 962, 994, 1008, 1012; M, pp. 384–385; S, I, pp. 26–28, 161–164. Pareto admitted that the part of his curve relating to incomes at or very near the bare subsistence level was hypothetical, and suggested that in ancient times, when famines were frequent, the *relative* number of incomes in the neighborhood of bare subsistence was greater than in modern times (M, pp. 384–386). Critical evaluation of this curve does not fall within the scope of this paper. For an appraisal of Pareto's assertion that the form of his curve is stable, see C. Bresciani-Turroni, Econometrica, VII, 1939, pp. 107–133. For a general account and good bibliography see H. T. Davis, The Theory of Econometrics, Bloomington, 1941, Chap. 2. Davis (ibid., pp. 201ff.) suggests that political stability comes to an end when what he calls the "concentration ratio" rises above, or falls below, stipulated critical values; Pareto did not pursue this tack. (See next note.) For a critical appraisal of the views of Pareto and others on the relation between ability and income, see H. Staehle, "Ability, Wages, and Income," Review of Economic Statistics, XXV, 1943, pp. 77–87.

165. C, pp. 1008–1012; M, pp. 388–389; S, I, p. 28, also II, pp. 160–173; "La question sociale," loc. cit., p. 44. He observed (ibid., pp. 44–45) that inequality is not permanently determined by purely economic influences; it is modified, periodically, by the intervention of other factors, principally armed force, and now perhaps by political action. He supposed, presumably, that the factors which make for inequality always operate to restore it, even though it may be temporarily reduced. See also S, I. pp. 161–164, where he traces the supposed effects of collectivism on income levels and distribution.

166. C, pp. 1002–1006.

Intra-society heterogeneity was frequently denied. For this, said Pareto, several circumstances were responsible: egalitarian prejudices, which attributed inter-individual differences to differences in environment; the pretensions of authors (e.g. Lombroso)[167] to greater precision than the facts warranted; the disposition of writers (e.g. Lapouge) to infer conclusions and formulate policies at variance with both theory and reality. It did not follow, for example, from some men's possessing certain qualities in greater measure than other men, that there existed a class (or race) "absolutely *better*" than the rest of the population, or that the *better* "must" govern the others.[168]

In one of his earlier works Pareto considered selection of three sorts: control of the maladapted, amelioration of the race, and vertical social mobility. Concerning the first he observed that the sentiment of justice, which protects society against its maladapted members, was being superseded by the sentiment of pity; whence the controls which make for social stability were growing weaker. Neither education of the maladapted nor threatening them with the consequences of their actions was an adequate means of control; while suppression of the maladapted, although in itself efficacious, was not practicable, because it led to frightful abuses and ran counter to the socially indispensable sentiments of altruism and pity. He did not resolve this problem, but he did imply that the force of the sentiment of pity needed to be diminished if adequate control of the maladapted were to be achieved.[169]

Most important of the selective agents upon which the quality of the race depends are natality and mortality, particularly the latter. Natural selection varies in intensity and character with income class. There is no eugenic selection among those whose incomes are at or near the bare subsistence level, and fall below it when individual or collective circumstances worsen; for here intense poverty and its concomitants eliminate good and bad elements alike. In the class next above, consisting of persons with incomes slightly above bare subsistence, "selection operates with maximum intensity"; for here the incomes received, while sufficient to preserve the "better elements," are not adequate to save all, the weaker elements being eliminated in large measure through high infant mortality, passage into the bare subsistence group, and the ravages of alcoholism, tuberculosis, etc.[170] Here are hammered out new aristocracies to replace those which degenerate; whence it is important for the future of a collectivity that selection remain

167. He commented critically on Lombroso's work in two notes in Giornale degli economisti, ser. 2, XIII, 1896, pp. 449–454, XIV, 1897, pp. 502–506.

168. C, pp. 993–996, 1000. One may say only that some races possess in higher degree than others qualities suited to enable them to prosper in given places and climates (997). Nationalistics prejudices favored the doctrine of inter-society heterogeneity (993).

169. S, II, pp. 133–139, 146–152. See below on eugenics.

170. Alcoholism in part offsets the tendency of income increases to relax selection.

rigorous in this class. In the higher income classes, which include the aristocracies, selection is not intense, because incomes are great enough to preserve relatively large numbers of feeble, incapable, or vicious individuals who would be destroyed if situated in very low income classes. The consequent accumulation of inferior elements in the upper and aristocratic classes is a principal cause of their tendency to decay and disappear; and when it is accompanied by an accumulation of superior elements in the lower classes, social instability and revolution usually ensue.[171]

Pareto admitted the possibility of dysgenic selection, but rejected the proposals of the eugenists. A society might deteriorate in quality, and in consequence social equilibrium might be upset if, with the progress of civilization, too many subjects of choice (i.e. individuals in whom life activity is most intense) were siphoned out of the inferior classes at the same time that diminution in the intensity of natural selection in these classes was serving to reduce the potential supply of choice subjects. Presumably enough subjects of choice were being furnished to the upper classes and cities, which both attracted and consumed them, by rural populations and also in some places (England, America) by laboring classes. Whether in time supply would fall short was not discoverable from available statistical data.[172] But if it did, a solution was not to be found in the "new 'eugenic' logic." The evidence did not support the eugenist view that dysgenic selection had destroyed ancient Rome, or their supposition that the prevailing aristocracy produced more persons of native intelligence than did the working classes. Furthermore, eugenics could never accomplish its purpose — sacrificing the ophelimity of the individual to the utility of the species — because, since man's nature was not susceptible of radical change, his behavior would continue to be conditioned by considerations of individual ophelimity and utility, as well as by those of utility of the species; and were force employed to overcome the nature of man and put eugenic measures into effect, the evil results would outweigh the benefits. From denying liberty to men afflicted with certain diseases it was but a step to denying liberty to men who entertained certain opinions, while from the establishment of state monopolies and the closed shop it was not many steps to the restriction of reproduction to the eugenic few and to the transformation of men into sheep. In the eugenist's scheme "the choice of the 'eugenic' and the care of the propagation of the race" were handed over to

171. M, pp. 385–388, 429; C, pp. 1027–1029; S, I, pp. 28–33, II, pp. 139–141, 147. Pareto approved the theory of selection of Pfeffer, who believed that it operated by destroying the worst. He criticized Pfeffer's supposition that the numbers of individuals in the various living species are in stable equilibrium, saying that while the various forms of life are in equilibrium, it is dynamic rather than static in character. See C, p. 627.

172. C, 1029–1031; S, I, pp. 32–33. Pareto refers to the studies of Ammon, Jacoby, and Topinard, who claimed that dolichocephals, persons of activity and intelligence, tall blonds, and short brunettes were attracted on balance to designated cities (C, 1030n.). Pareto appears not to have kept abreast of studies in human heredity.

the politicians composing the State.[173] This scheme Pareto rejected on grounds of both efficacy and sentiment. He supposed, as did De Molinari, with many of whose opinions he was in accord, that amelioration of the race must be sought through individual morality: were men prudent and fore-sighted, they would procreate no more children than they could rear satis-factorily; and they would avoid procreation, if they were afflicted with hereditary defects.[174]

Pareto discussed social selection in his earlier works, but much less fully than in the *Trattato*. Two opposed sets of forces, one making for stability and the other for mutability and selection, were operative in collectivities. Sometimes one, sometimes the other, was ascendant, the opposition between the two usually assuming the form of a struggle between the older and the newer (or incipient) aristocracies. Mutability and selection originated in the desire and capacity of some men for advancement in the social hierarchy; they flourished when circumstances were favorable, as, for example, when prices were rising. Stability originated in both the institutions of private property and inheritance and the desire of the well-situated groups and aristocracies to perpetuate existing social arrangements of especial advantage to themselves. The maximization of utility is contin-gent, Pareto's analysis suggests, upon the striking of a proper balance be-tween the forces favorable to stability and those favorable to social circula-tion and change. In the absence of such balance, disadvantage outweighs advantage. For example, when the dominant groups and aristocracies froze existing societal forms and arrangements, and thereby unduly checked societal circulation and the ascent of superior individuals located in the lower ranks, the dominant classes tended in time to become enfeebled, because of the lack of sufficient able recruits; and, upon circumstances becoming propitious for change, they tended to be overthrown or displaced by the superior elements accumulating in the lower ranks.[175]

In the *Trattato* Pareto inquired at length into the roles of heterogeneity and the inter-class movement of individuals, employing, as a key to un-dulatory and other forms of group behavior, the concept of *residue*. Analy-sis of non-logical action, in especial of "derivatives" or "non-logico-experimental" theories,[176] revealed, besides factual data, certain variable and contingent elements, i.e. *derivatives,* and a residuary, substantial and essentially constant element or nucleus, the *residue*. The residues, which

173. C, 998–1001. Pareto occasionally described politicians in terms remindful of an ornithol-ogist's account of the cow bird. Were physicians appointed to pass on eligibility to marry and then to fall under the control of political rings, the latter would enjoy veritable gold mines (S, II, pp. 157–158).

174. S, II, pp. 156, 158–160.

175. M, pp. 398, 425–432; S, I, pp. 28–56, 171–172.

176. For the meaning assigned to "derivative" see T, 847, 855, 862, 868, 1397, and p. 1916; also Livingston's note to 868. On the difference between "logico-experimental" and "non-logico-experimental" see 13–14, 16 and pp. 1921–1930; also below, note 182.

correspond to "non-logical conduct," are not sentiments or instincts; they "are the manifestation of sentiments and instincts just as the rising of mercury in a thermometer is a manifestation of the rise in temperature."[177] Residues fall into six classes, each containing several genera and species: Class I, corresponding to the instinct for combinations, which is (among other things) the progressive element in human society; Class II, the persistence of aggregates (of sentiments), or the conservative force in society; Class III, need of expressing sentiments by external acts; Class IV, residues connected with sociality (e.g. uniformity, self-sacrifice, hierarchy); Class V, integrity of the individual and his appurtenances; Class VI, the sex residue.[178] Of these six classes of residues, I and II are by far the most important in Pareto's scheme, the second conducing to idealistic and related forms of behavior, and the first fostering the pursuit of less idealistic and more materialistic objectives.

While residues vary in intensity with the underlying sentiments to which they correspond,[179] and while they may change in response to altered circumstances or as the result of imitation,[180] the substance of a class of residues, in its bearing upon human conduct, changes slowly and, as a rule, relatively little, modifications in some genera and species tending to compensate modifications in others;[181] only in the longer run may significant changes occur. (It is because the residues are so stable that Pareto is compelled to seek in inter-class circulation an adequate explanation of social oscillation.) Residues are interdependent: directly, in so far as they accentu-

177. T, 798–800, 850, 875, and 868, where residue is defined. The precise meaning of the term residue is not explicitly indicated by Pareto: e.g. see 850–851, on relation of residue to instinct; 1845 on relation of heredity and environment to sentiment; 306ff., 850, 1690, on fact that residues have no objective existence. Parsons concludes, after thorough analysis, that in the early and analytical part of the Trattato residue means proposition, while in the applied part, following the classification of residues, they are treated as "concrete tendencies of action." However, neither the residues nor the sentiments which they reflect correspond to the instincts of psychology, Parsons finds. He substitutes the concept "value attitude" for Pareto's term "sentiment," which includes both "value attitude" and a psychological element; the residue then becomes "an expression of the value attitudes underlying it," and therefore in some instances an ideal end. See Parsons, op.cit., especially pp. 215, 218, 224–228, 267–268, 278n., 296–297.

Derivations serve principally to indicate the forces determining social equilibrium (T, 1397, 1403); they partially correspond to, or manifest, sentiments: directly, "sentiments that correspond to the residues in which they originate"; indirectly, sentiments to which correspond "residues [e.g. Class III] that serve for purposes of derivation." Derivations reflect man's feeling of need of logic; they clothe with logical or pseudo-logical reasoning the sentiments they manifest. See T, 798–802, 850, 1397, 1403, 1416, 1688, 1690, 1829, 1871, 2081. Derivations are divisible into four classes: assertion; authority; accord with sentiments, interest, etc,; verbal proofs (1419ff.). See below, note 182.

178. T, Chaps. 6–8, especially 888–889, 991, 1089–1091, 1113, 1207–1208, 1216, 1324, 1396n.

179. T, 1740–1743.

180. T, 2003; on the propagation of derivations see 2004.

181. T, 1699–1700, 1716, 1718, 1720, 1827–1828, 2552.

ate or weaken one another; indirectly, in so far as they support or offset one another and so determine social equilibrium.[182]

Residues—in especial, the relative proportions of Classes I and II in the several social strata—, social heterogeneity, and inter-class circulation, together with interests[183] and underlying economic conditions, are the most important of the interdependent and interacting elements which determine the form and equilibrium of a social system,[184] and which account for the oscillations and longer-run trends in such a system and its parts.[185] So important, in fact, are the proportions in which residues function in the various social strata, "especially the proportions of Class I and Class II residues in the ruling and subject classes, respectively," that one may obtain a "rough outline" of historical and social developments by "centering the main attention on these proportions, other circumstances of importance being considered in subordination to them."[186]

Social utility depends upon the ratio of I to II in the ruling class and in the

182. T, 1736, 2080, 2088–2089. Whereas residues exert a powerful influence on derivations, the latter, except for their sometime accentuation of underlying sentiments, persist just so long as the associated residues persist; changes in derivations therefore are confined to form. See T, 1397, 1416, 1733, 1735, 1746, 1766–1767, 1770–1772, 1827, 1829, 1832, 1842–1843, 1860, 2146, 2206–2207, 2340, 2343. In "logico-experimental" (T, 13–14) science, when an assertion is refuted, the act of asserting ends, because the derivation (or doctrine) has no strong sentiments (or residues) to support it. In "matters involving sentiment and non-logical conduct," on the contrary, opposition to or refutation of a derivation (or doctrine) will not deprive it of vitality so long as the underlying sentiments remain unweakened. See T, 1397, 1416, 1826, 1834, and pp. 1921ff.; also Parsons, op. cit., pp. 224ff., 296ff. on ends and science in Pareto.

183. Interests, which reflect underlying sentiments, just as do residues, and which fall largely within the economic sphere, spur individuals and groups to acquire material goods and instruments of power. The sentiments underlying interests resemble the sentiments to which Class V residues correspond; they enjoy freest play when Class I residues are ascendant. The relative importance of interests is greater among modern than among ancient peoples. Since, as the economic determinists recognized, interests are of great importance in determining social equilibrium, Pareto considered them apart from the residues. See T, 1207, 2009–2010, 2206, 2286, 2289.

184. Extending his concept of economic system, Pareto described a social system as made up of molecules "harboring residues, derivations, interests, and proclivities" which "perform, subject to numerous ties, logical and non-logical actions." See T, 2079, "Sentiments *depend* on economic conditions, just as economic conditions *depend* on sentiments; . . . there are similar correlations among the other elements" which determine the state of equilibrium (T, 2097). On social equilibrium and its determinants see also T, 1690, 2060, 2068, 2070, 2091–2099, 2141, 2146, 2206–2207, 2552–2553.

185. Oscillations are interdependent, as are the elements in which they occur (T, 2329, 2338, 2344ff., 2552ff.).

186. T, p. 1921: also 2413–2415. Hereafter the capitalized Roman numerals will represent the corresponding class of residues. Emphasis upon the ratio of I to II was warranted by their absolute importance, by the relation of I and II to interests, and by the relation between II and genera in other classes (e.g. IV and V). Pareto cautions that mere possession of I and II is not enough; proper use must be made of them. See T, 2415; also 1693–1694 on static and dynamic analysis of residue composition, and "rhythmical movement . . . in all social phenomena."

subject class.[187] In general, when I and II are not in balance in a society as a whole, it will be defective either in innovation and desire to adventure, or in stability and the perseverance and steadfastness necessary to carry out schemes; and these defects will tend to be reflected, and perhaps magnified, in the upper class. For each class there is a "most suitable" ratio: in subordinates and the masses Class II, which contributes persistence and firmness of resolve, and so conduces to the proper use of innovations, must predominate; among leaders and the *élite* Class I, which gives rise to innovation, must predominate, with the proviso, however, that Class II must be present in the governing class in sufficient measure to insure social stability.[188]

Back of Pareto's emphasis upon the relative importance of the ratio of I to II in the ruling and the subject classes, respectively, and of inter-class circulation,[189] lies his supposition that the ratio of I to II, especially in the upper class, is very sensitive to "class-circulation," the most dynamic of the determinants of social form and equilibrium. His line of reasoning, often implicit rather than explicit, suggests that residue composition in general, however important in itself, is not the really significant variable. First, since "classes of residues change but slightly or not at all,"[190] at least in short periods, one can attribute inter-society differences in form and performance to inter-society differences in residue composition,[191] but one cannot attribute shorter run oscillations, in so far as they are imputable to residue changes, to shorter run oscillations in residue intensity and composition in general. The variations in residue composition and in the intensity of II in total populations, traced by Pareto, together with his accounts of the effects of these variations, relate to longer run periods.[192] Second, while migration may alter the residue composition of a society, as it did in Rome, where the population, especially the lower classes, was transformed by the inflow from abroad, particularly from the East, of streams of individuals differing somewhat in residue composition from the Roman and Italic stock, an important part of the total effect may be exercised upon and through the upper class;[193] in fact, it often is impossible "clearly to distinguish the

187. Here Pareto is concerned with residue composition; below he is concerned also with the *quality* of the membership of the several classes.

188. T, 2184, 2227, 2254, 2419, 2424, 2427, 2429, 2513: on *élite*, see below.

189. I usually use the term "inter-class" rather than "class" before the term circulation, because the former suggests more firmly than the latter movement from class to class, and from sub-class to sub-class (e.g. from non-governing *élite* to governing *élite*).

190. T, 1720, 2417.

191. As Pareto did: e.g., T, 1720–1721, 2419–2432, 2444, 2476.

192. See his accounts of such variations and their effects in Athens, Rome, and medieval and modern Europe (e.g., T, 2343–2389). He comments several times on long-run changes: I have increased relative to II (2329, 2392); V relative to IV (1716), partly as a result of socialism (1858).

193. T, 1840, 2360, 2546, 2549. The *route* of migration, however, had exercised much less influence upon civilization than Demolins has supposed, Pareto implied (T, 1730).

respective share that belongs to proportions of residues and to phenomena of class circulation."[194]

If it be granted that, while residues are important in shaping society, observed dynamics of social change cannot be adequately accounted for in terms of variation in residue composition in general, a more significant source of variation must be sought. Pareto's theory of "class-circulation," together with his conception of the role of the *élite,* supplied this significant source of variation. In all societies, power, initiative, and decision-making are largely vested in a small fraction of the population which, because it is so small absolutely and in relation to the remainder of the population, is especially sensitive to the accumulation in, or admission to, its ranks of small increments of population differing in quality or in residue composition from its initial membership. This small fraction, corresponding to the highest class (or classes) and called the *élite,* includes primarily individuals ranking highest in each branch of activity, and secondarily inferior individuals whose qualifications do not suit them for continued membership in the *élite.*[195] The *élite* is made up of two components: the governing *élite,* comprising high ranking governing and military personnel, and the non-governing *élite,* consisting of the remainder; it includes the aristocrats, whether or not they occupy important places in the governing class. The numerically large portion of the population not part of the *élite* and corresponding to the lower classes constitutes the *non-élite.*[196]

Because of its relative and absolute smallness, the *élite,* governing and non-governing, is numerically sensitive to the influx of small increments of population from the *non-élite.* Assume that of one hundred units of population ninety-four are in the *non-élite,* and three each in the governing and non-governing components of the *élite:* then the movement of one ninety-fourth of the *non-élite* into the *élite* will increase the latter by one-sixth; if the increments are evenly divided between the two components of the *élite,* each will increase by one-sixth; and if the increment moves initially into the non-governing *élite* and later passes over into the governing *élite,* it will increase the latter by one-third. Since the residues, especially I in relation to II, are not evenly distributed, or of equal intensities in the several strata of society,[197] the movement of our hypothetical one unit, assuming

194. T, 2417.

195. Pareto does not always distinguish sharply between (i) *élite* in the sense of the class of individuals who, in virtue of their qualities, rank high in the several branches of human activity; and (ii) *élite* in the sense of those who, irrespective of their qualities, happen to occupy dominant positions in these several branches. Generally, in his treatment of "class-circulation," he writes as if he conceives of *élite* in sense (i), inasmuch as the strategically situated class (or classes), whose composition is changing, does not include all elements definable as *élite* in sense (i) and therefore is changing for this reason as well as because the ratio of I to II is undergoing modification. See also note 200 below.

196. T, 2026–2034, 2051–2052.

197. T, 2041–2045. Generally, Class II residues predominate in the several classes (e.g. farmers, workers, poorly educated) making up the *non-élite* or masses. Class I residues usually

it to differ in residue composition from the *élite*, will significantly alter the residue composition — particularly the ratio of I to II — of the *élite*. Accordingly, because the form of a society, together with the manner in which power is used and the purposes to which it is put, depends so largely upon the residue composition of the *élite*, these three conditions change *pari passu* with modifications in the residue composition of the *élite;* whence Pareto considered inter-class circulation to be the major source of societal undulations. Thus a relative increase in I intensifies the innovating capacities of the *élite*, removes restrictions on the play of the interests, and diminishes the capacity of the governing *élite* to preserve social stability and maintain itself in power. A relative increase in II strengthens the conserving and stabilizing powers of the *élite* but, if it proceeds too far, it eventually reduces the innovating capacity of the *élite* to the point where either the society in question or the existing social equilibrium is endangered.[198]

While inter-class circulation issues ultimately from the constant upward pressure of elements in the numerically large lower classes, it varies in intensity and character. As a rule "in the higher stratum of society Class II residues generally lose strength" until they are restored through gradual infiltration or revolutionary upsurges from the masses who are rich in II.[199] When decadent elements are permitted, for any reason, to accumulate in the *élite*, its capacity to fulfill its functions is reduced; and its vulnerability[200] to pressures, which is aggravated also by the accumulation of superior elements in the lower classes, is increased. When wealth can readily be amassed, inter-class circulation is great, and the ascent into the upper classes of bearers of Class I residues, who are adept at amassing and/or creating

---

predominate in the non-governing *élite*, particularly among speculators, plutocrats, and employers; they may or may not predominate in the governing *élite*. See T, 1723-1727, 2187, 2367, 2484.

198. Inter-class circulation and its effects are treated in T, 2025-2059, and in chapters 13-14; see e.g. 2178-2179, 2221, 2254-2259, 2267, 2274-2275, 2429, 2478-2482, 2484. Pareto sketches a lion-fox-lion succession of power holders. After power has been seized by the lions who, because they are rich in II, are equal to the task of seizing power and assuming authority, power tends to pass to the foxes who, in virtue of their richness in I, are skilled at retaining power, once obtained, through cunning and other forms of non-violence. The foxes, however, tend to admit foxes rather than lions to the ruling class. Furthermore, when the foxes are in power, the situation is favorable to the ascent of bearers of I into the non-governing *élite*. In consequence the *élite* becomes ridden with foxes who have neither capacity nor appetite for standing up against the lions accumulating in the *non-élite*. As a result the situation again becomes favorable to seizure of power by the lions, who in turn lose it again to the foxes. See T, 2178-2179, 2227, 2484, and 2480, nn. 1 and 4. See Parsons, op. cit., pp. 278ff., for a careful account of Pareto's cycle of social change.

199. E.g., see T, 2048, 2227, 2367.

200. T, 2054-2059. At all times the *élite*, in particular the governing portion, admission into which is more susceptible to the influence of circumstances unrelated to competence than is admission into the non-governing *élite*, contains individuals whose competence does not give them claim to the label of *élite*. See T, 2035-2040, 2052-2055.

wealth, is intensified; furthermore, since the ascent of bearers of I tends for a time to multiply wealth-amassing opportunities, class-circulation continues at a high rate until counter-forces, usually associated with the resulting modification of the *élite* and with changing circumstances, develop.[201] War favors the ascent of bearers of II under some, but not under all, conditions.[202] Immigration tends to be accompanied by the ascent of bearers of II when it introduces large numbers of bearers of II into the masses and so augments the relative strength of II, always great, in the lower classes. Legal and other obstacles may slow down inter-class circulation,[203] but they do not prevent it entirely; furthermore, the occasional consequent failure on the part of the *élite* to recruit its strength from below may bring about its destruction and a resulting intensification of circulation. Generally, while "class-circulation" varies with circumstances, it is always present; and while it may produce counter-movements and even conditions unfavorable to circulation,[204] it always revives and persists as a major source of societal fluctuation.

IX. Conclusion

We shall not attempt an appraisal of Pareto's contributions to population theory, nor an account of the possible origins of his theories, nor a summary of the materials already treated, nor a criticism of his abuse of democratic values and institutions. Instead, we shall indicate important points emphasized or passed over by him.

In many respects Pareto's greatest contribution to population thought is his conception of both the economic system and the social system as systems of interdependent variables, of which the population factor (or factors) is one, and his recognition of the fact that these systems are subject to undula-

201. T, 2221, 2225, 2286–2290, 2300, 2309–2314, 2546–2550, 2608. Protectionism and analogous policies sometimes favored the creation of wealth, because they facilitated the ascent of bearers of Class I residues (T, 2208–2236, 2310–2314). Marie Kolabinska undertook to verify Pareto's "theory of the circulation of the *élite*," as outlined by him in his *Manuel* and his *Systèmes Socialistes*; she does not make use of his concept of residue. She concluded, among other things, that in times of trouble men of courage and warlike qualities ascend; that in France wealth came to replace force as the primary determinant of ascension; that the French Revolution originated in the stoppage of class-circulation, which caused superior elements to accumulate in the lower classes while the quality of the upper classes was deteriorating. See *La circulation des élites en France*, Lausanne, 1912, pp. 27, 41–42, 55, 103, 110–111, 120–121. Pareto several times refers to this study in the *Trattato*. Pareto considered his own theory of social heterogeneity and circulation to be a particular case of the general theory outlined by G. Sensini in his "Teorai dell' equilibrio di composizione delle classi sociali," *Rivista italiana di sociologia*, XVII, 1913, pp. 556–617. See T, 2025, n. 4.

202. T, 2223–2226.

203. T, 2490–2513, 2546–2550.

204. On social crystallization and the factors which eventually shatter it, see T, 2546–2550, 2607–2610.

tory movements, which also are interdependent. Given this approach, the unilateral causation theories which still permeate thinking on population fall into their proper places. More important still, it becomes apparent that there exists, not just one population movement, but a number, not all of which he treats, which should make up the body proper of population study.

Because he started with an interdependence approach, and for other reasons, Pareto was able to introduce greater precision than had prevailed in the controversy precipitated by Malthus' Essay. He was able, through his ever-present distinction between *real* and *virtual* movements, to give satisfactory meaning to Malthus' progressions. Pareto was able, further, through his curve-fittings and rate extrapolations, to discover both the growing divergence between the *real* and the *virtual* movements of population and the limits to population totals, and to make inferences concerning the social and economic effects of this divergence. And he could say, in light of his income-curve analysis, that progress need not be saltatory, as J. S. Mill would have it, to push up the standard of life permanently. Because he looked upon population factors and population determinants as components of a system of interdependent variables, Pareto viewed each of these determinants (e.g. the checks) as reciprocally interconnected with every other determinant and hence limited in its capacity to influence population movements;[205] he could therefore conceive of population problems in terms either of partial or general equilibria. In part because of this approach, Pareto attached less importance to the dynamic effects of the movement of population totals than do contemporary writers.

Pareto's theory of "class-circulation" is important for several reasons.[206] It emphasizes the importance of social, economic, and political circulation and selection, elements which have largely escaped the attention of modern economics. Second, Pareto's theory, while open to exception, serves to focus attention on two facts which commonly tend to be ignored: (*a*) the importance of the strategically situated decision- and rule-making minority in the formation of social form and policy; (*b*) the sensitivity of this minority to numerical and qualitative change, and the consequent susceptibility of a social system to change.[207] The importance of this minority, differently defined, has been made plain recently by Toynbee.[208] Pareto, unfortunately, did not integrate his treatment of differential fertility and natural increase with that of the *élite* and class-circulation.

Although Pareto did not discuss optimum population theory as such, he

205. Pre-nineteenth-century writers, concerned with balance in nature or with the chain of being, had a primitive grasp of the modern interdependent system of Pareto.

206. Social mobility in its various forms has been treated by many writers. See P. A. Sorokin, Social Mobility, New York, 1927.

207. It is because of the importance of this minority that its age composition is of significance. See my "Some Effects of Change in the Age Composition of the Labor Force," Southern Economic Journal, VIII, 1941, pp. 157–175.

208. A Study of History, London, V (1939), pp. 20ff.

did make two indirect contributions to this matter. First, because he postulated inter-class disharmony, instead of (with Marshall) inter-class harmony, he brought out the fact that a population situation which maximizes a utility or ophelimity index from the standpoint of one social group will not usually maximize it from the standpoint of some other group. He brought out also that what constitutes an optimum population situation turns on the nature of the index for which a maximum is being sought; for maximizing some indices calls for greater populations than maximizing others. His analysis suggests, however, that in proportion as "a single integrated system of ultimate ends" becomes common to the members of a society,[209] and other indices of utility and ophelimity become subordinated thereto, a single overriding or maximum optimum emerges. Second, Pareto's analysis suggests that, even though the population optima which coincide with index maxima differ, if the maxima for a number of indices are in the same general population neighborhood, the combined pull of the elements represented by these indices will restrain in large measure tendencies on the part of the population to move from this neighborhood.

Pareto's emphasis upon the role, in human affairs, of individuals and of characteristics embodied in individuals, together with his neglect of the role of institutional, physical and spatial configurations, prevented his making as full or accurate application of his income-curve type of analysis as appears possible. He interpreted this curve to reflect the distribution, in societies, of ensembles of traits that have to do with the acquisition and retention of wealth. Likewise, in his discussion of hierarchy and heterogeneity, he thought almost wholly in terms of the distribution of characteristics embodied in individuals; he did not recognize adequately that, since human groupings and associations are by nature ordered, even as is the arrangement of seats in a theatre, the behavior to which collections of individual traits may give rise is necessarily circumscribed by this ordering of associations. In other words, Pareto did not recognize clearly that the distribution of income is conditioned, not only by the distribution of human traits, but also by the spatial and hierarchical configurations, inherent in all human groupings and associations, within which human traits seek and give expression.[210] For example, Pareto did not discover that his type of curve constitutes a good index of urbanization and reveals a high degree of stability in urbano-spatial configurations.[211] Had he done so, he might have proceeded to discover the industrio-spatial configurations which underlie the urbano-

209. See reference to Parsons, p. 112.
210. There may be a marshal's baton in every private's knapsack, but in the nature of things few can ever be provided with opportunity to use it.
211. See H. W. Singer, "The 'Courbe Des Populations': A Parallel to Pareto's Law," *Economic Journal*, XLVI, 1936, pp. 254–263; also R. Gibrat, Les inégalités économiques, Paris, 1931, pp. 250ff., and G. K. Zipf, National Unity and Disunity, Bloomington, 1941, Chaps. 1–2.

spatial configurations, and have inferred from these and from the manner in which human associations (e.g. corporations, armies, colleges, churches) must of necessity be organized and structured, that even though men were equal in native abilities, income and power would none the less be unevenly divided. He would have discovered, in short, that income and power distributions are functions of both the distribution of traits and the configurational patterns inherent in organizational and spatial structures. He would then have both modified and strengthened his theories concerning the constants in human affairs; for he would have added to individual behavioral constants the configurational dispositional constants, and he would have altered somewhat his theory of revolution.[212]

In the *Cours* and the *Manuel* Pareto concerned himself primarily with the economic determinants of population growth, and therefore made it appear that population movements were governed predominantly by economic factors. In the *Trattato* Pareto analyzed the non-economic and non-logical elements in human behavior, but he did not integrate his treatment of these elements with that of population growth, either directly by restating his theory of procreative motivation or indirectly by tracing out the effect of class-circulation upon population growth via the medium of wealth accumulation. As Parsons has shown, Pareto distinguished an intermediate means-end sector from the ultimate ends and values sector, and suggested a version of the sociologistic theorem which Parsons restates as follows:

> The actions of the members of a society are to a significant degree oriented to a single integrated system of ultimate ends common to these members. More generally the value element in the form both of ultimate ends and of value attitudes is in a significant degree common to the members of the society. This fact is one of the essential conditions of the equilibrium of social systems.[213]

Pareto's earlier account of the determinants of population growth ran largely in terms of the economic, as distinguished from the technological and political, components of the intermediate means-end sector. Had he reexamined the question of population growth in the *Trattato*, he would have had to consider it, not in terms of a system of interdependent economic variables, but in terms of an all-inclusive system of variables, some elements in which permit logical action, while others, because of their unscientific or non-scientific character, cannot give rise to completely logical action. Population movements and growth, if analyzed in terms of the all-inclusive social system, would be found to be less intimately connected with economic movements than Pareto's analysis (Sections I–IV of this paper) in terms of

212. The writer treats these points in a paper planned for publication.
213. Parsons, op. cit., p. 707.

an interdependent economic system has suggested. First, human conduct itself would appear to be shaped in a much larger measure by non-economic elements. Second, the economic movements which influence population movements would be found to depend in considerable measure upon non-economic elements. It is to be supposed, therefore, that had Pareto re-examined the population problem in terms of his sociology, he would have appreciably modified his interpretation of population movements.

In his earlier writings Pareto attributed little influence to efforts to regulate population growth other than those calculated to remove impediments to production and accumulation of wealth. His sociological analysis suggests, however, that efforts calculated to modify suitably the ultimate end and value system of a people, if successful, would tend to render the social milieu more favorable to population growth; it suggests also that the probable effects of economic stimulants to population growth are relatively limited.

Marshall on the Population Question

> *"Simplicity is the most deceitful mistress that ever betrayed man."* — Henry Adams in *The Education . . .* , chap. 30.

Although "Marshall's conception of economic change as 'organic growth'"[1] occupies an important place in his *Principles* and several other of his writings, it has received little attention at the hands of his critics and expositors. These usually have been concerned with Marshall's treatment of questions of value and distribution and so have examined his discussions of returns, wage movements, etc., primarily from this point of view. There is in Marshall also a kind of long-run theory of economic development, in which the movement of population plays an important part. It is with Marshall's treatment of the population question rather than with his discussion of economic development that the present paper is concerned, though some account of the latter is necessarily included. His handling of these matters, largely historical in character, is as much sociological as it is economic, which may account for its neglect by commentators.[2]

Marshall's active lifetime, roughly 1870–1920, witnessed marked demographic and economic change. The English death rate fell from 22.2 in 1868–72 to 19 in 1888–92 and 13.7 in 1918–22; the birth rates for the corresponding periods were 35.3, 30.9, and 20.9. The English rate of natural increase, after rising slightly in 1870–80, fell slowly from 14.1 in 1878–82 to 11 in 1908–12 and 7.2 in 1918–22. Corresponding data for Scotland are roughly similar to the English. English infant mortality rose slightly from 149 in 1870–80 to 153 in 1891–1900, then fell to 85 in 1918–22. English male life expectancy at birth rose from 41.35 in 1871–80 to 44.13 in 1891–

---

1. See G. F. Shove, "The Place of Marshall's *Principles* in the Development of Economic Theory," *Economic Journal,* vol. LII, 1942, p. 312. Marshall contemplated but never completed an extensive work on economic history.

2. Our treatment is based primarily upon the following works, which will be represented by the initials in parentheses: *Principles of Economics* (PE), 8th edition, London, 1920; *Industry and Trade* (IT), London, 1919; A. C. Pigou, ed., *Memorials of Alfred Marshall* (M), London, 1925; J. M. Keynes, ed., *Official Papers of Alfred Marshall* (OP), London, 1926. Early editions of the *Principles* are referred to, as are early editions of *The Economics of Industry,* London, 1879–1881, only when his earlier analysis differs significantly from his later analysis. Some of his papers, the titles of all of which appear in a descriptive list appended to J. M. Keynes's classic biographical memoir ("Alfred Marshall, 1842–1924," *Economic Journal,* vol. XXXIV, 1924, pp. 311–83), which are not reprinted in the *Memorials,* are made use of. As C. W. Guillebaud observes ("The Evolution of Marshall's *Principles of Economics,*" *Economic Journal,* vol. LII, 1942, p. 330), "all Marshall's chief contributions to economics as a science are to be found already stated in the 1890 Edition." The lengthy chapter XIII at the end of book VI, "Progress in Relation to Standards of Life," was added in the Fifth Edition (1907). In the preface to this edition he states that it "deals with the forces of progress" and that "the central idea in a volume on the Foundations of economics. . . must be that of living force and movement." In his preface to the Sixth Edition (1910) Marshall indicated that (to quote Guillebaud, *op. cit.,* pp. 339–40) "increasing stress had been laid in successive editions on the probable long-run importance of diminishing returns in the case of land."

1900 and 55.62 in 1920–22. There was considerable net emigration from Britain throughout this period, net emigrants in 1871–1921 constituting about 14.4% of the recorded natural increase; but her population rose from 26.1 million in 1871 to 37 in 1901 and 42.8 in 1921. The period 1870–1913 also saw an unprecedentedly large amount of capital exported, about two-fifths of all savings moving abroad, with the result that accumulated British investment abroad approximated four-ninths of that at home in 1914.[3] The terms of trade, though fluctuating somewhat, improved between the 1850's and 1911–13, particularly between 1882 and 1900.[4] Real income per occupied person increased about 68% between the 1860's and 1913, while real income per head rose about 88% in 1870–1913.[5] The proportion foodstuffs comprised of net imports rose greatly after the repeal of the Corn Laws in 1846, continuing to rise until the 1880's when a plateau was reached.[6] Total overseas trade continued to increase relatively to income until 1910–13.[7]

This paper consists of four sections. In the first we pass briefly in review the state of population theory as it stood when Marshall began to write, together with the opinions of his contemporaries. In the second section we consider Marshall's treatment of factor formation and the laws of returns; in the third his analysis of the growth of living standards and their influence upon population growth; and in the fourth, his treatment of miscellaneous demographic topics.

I. The Views of Marshall's Predecessors and Contemporaries

The views of Marshall's predecessors and contemporaries respecting the population question may be assembled under three sub-headings: (1) laws of returns and related issues; (2) population elasticity and its determinants;

3. See A. K. Cairncross, *Home and Foreign Investment* 1870–1913, Cambridge, 1953, p. 4; J. H. Lenfant, "Great Britain's Capital Formation 1865–1914," *Economica*, vol. XVIII, 1951, pp. 151–68; A. H. Imlah, "British Balance of Payments and Export of Capital, 1816–1913," *Economic History Review*, vol. V, 1952 pp. 208–39. Cairncross notes that it was the reduction in the price of imports that transformed the standard of living, domestic capital per head increasing relatively little. See *op. cit.*, p. 7; also the much higher rate of capital formation reported by E. H. Phelps Brown and S. J. Handfield-Jones, "The Climacteric of the 1890's: A Study in the Expanding Economy," *Oxford Economic Papers*, vol. IV, 1952, p. 284.

4. *Ibid.*, pp. 268–70; W. W. Rostow, *The Process of Economic Growth*, New York, 1952, pp. 194, 273 ff., chap. 9; Colin Clark, *Conditions of Economic Progress*, 1st edition, London, 1940, pp. 452 ff.

5. See Clark, *op. cit.*, p. 83; A. R. Prest, "National Income of the United Kingdom," *Economic Journal*, vol. LVIII, 1948, pp. 58–59.

6. See Werner Schlote, *British Overseas Trade from 1700 to the 1930's*, Oxford, 1952. pp. 54–55, 59ff. "It appears that home production of foodstuffs reached a level in the 1850's which was seldom surpassed," and which, if defined to consist only of cereals and tubers, declined. *Ibid.*, p. 59.

7. *Ibid.*, p. 49.

(3) miscellaneous matters. It will be assumed that Mill's *Principles* represent Ricardian political economy, particularly with regard to (1) and (2), as it stood in the 1860's when Marshall undertook its study and began the transformation of Ricardo's theory of price as expounded by Mill into his own *Principles*.[8]

The Law of Returns and Related Issues

J. S. Mill was much less optimistic concerning the likelihood that population growth would be accompanied by increasing returns than had been Senior and others who set great store by the extension of division of labour and/or the continuation of technical progress.[9] Concerning agriculture he

8. See Shove, *op. cit.,* pp. 294ff.

9. Prior to Senior's time the classical economists held in general that agriculture was subject to diminishing incremental returns, the effects of extending cultivation to poorer soils more than counterbalancing improvements in agriculture, with the result that returns per head tended to fall as population grew. Meanwhile returns in manufactures tended to be constant *ceteris paribus,* or, allowing for inventions and improvements, to increase somewhat; though, as E. Cannan observed (*Review of Economic Theory,* London, 1929, pp. 122–23), the role of accumulating knowledge was neglected (even by N. S. Senior) before J. S. Mill's time. Rising average returns in manufactures were not likely, however, to overbalance falling returns in agriculture, since the weight of the latter tended to increase at the expense of the weight of the former.

While Richard Jones (*Essay on the Distribution of Wealth and on the Sources of Taxation,* London, 1831, pp. 244–76) believed the efficiency of agriculture not so prone to decrease as opinion had it, and increase in the efficiency of manufacturing labour probably adequate to offset any decline in efficiency in agriculture; and while T. Chalmers denied that the extension of cultivation always implied diminishing returns in agriculture at the extensive margin; it was Senior who first protested effectively against the then current gloomy view. See E. Cannan, *A History of the Theories of Production and Distribution in English Political Economy,* London, 1893, 1917, chap. v, sects. 4–5. For, while he held that (*ceteris paribus*) additional labour when applied in manufactures is *more,* when employed in agriculture is *less,* "efficient in proportion," he added that returns in agriculture would not fall in the event of adequate increases in agricultural skill and/or improvements in land tenure. He admitted, however, that these increases could not continue to be adequate if population continued to grow. Even then there was no occasion for alarm, if a country had access to food imports, since they could be paid for with manufactures produced under conditions of increasing return. "Every increase in the number of manufacturing labourers is accompanied . . . by an increased productive power," since improvements in machinery and increased division of labour accompanied "every increase in the quantity manufactured." Hence "the only check by which we can predict that the progress of our manufactures will in time be retarded, is the increasing difficulty of importing materials and food. If the importation of raw produce could keep pace with the power of working it up, there would be no limit to the increase of wealth and population." See *Political Economy* (1836), London, 1850, pp. 26ff., 81–86. And this check was not likely to operate if food imports continued to be available and, despite the apprehensions of economists like Torrens (see note 14 below), on terms satisfactory to Britain. Given "unrestricted commerce" with the world, he saw "no definite term to the course of prosperity before us. I see no cause that, for ages to come, need check the progress of our wealth and our population. I see no reason why England . . . should not contain a much larger population with still greater moral and physical advantages." See his *Three Lectures on the Transmission of the Precious Metals from Country to Country and the Mercantile Theory of Wealth,* London, 1828, p. 96. Marian Bowley accredits Senior with having "very nearly discovered the optimum theory of population," since he believed that in most countries wealth per head would be greater if population were smaller, and that it "would increase more rapidly if population increased less

observed that "after a certain, and not very advanced, stage in the progress of agriculture; . . . every increase of produce is obtained by a more than proportional increase in the application of labour to the land." But he indicated that this tendency might be held in check by large-scale improvements in agriculture and by "the progress of civilisation" generally.[10]

While he admitted that, as Senior had declared, it was "probable and usual" for increased manufacturing production to take "place at a smaller cost," this was "not a necessary consequence."

As manufactures, however, depend for their materials either upon agriculture, or mining, or the spontaneous produce of the earth, manufacturing industry is subject, in respect of one of its essentials, to the same law as agriculture. But the crude material generally forms so small a portion of the total cost, that any tendency which may exist to a progressive increase in that single item, is much over-balanced by the diminution continually taking place in all the other elements; to which diminution it is impossible at present to assign any limit.[11]

Mill did not, however, attach so much importance to falling costs for manufactures as had Senior because he did not find in "the importation of food from abroad" any more than in emigration a solution for a situation in which, the growth of numbers having outstripped "the progress of improvement" in a country, its land was unable "to meet additional demands except on more onerous conditions." Emigration was not likely to be great enough in volume to afford permanent relief in such situations. Importation could not offer much relief since population growth in the small number of progressive wheat-exporting countries would prevent their producing much of an export surplus, whilst in other countries wheat production would be checked by lack of capital and by habits unsuited to exertion.[12] Although he

---

rapidly." See her *Nassau Senior and Classical Economics*, New York, 1949, pp. 125–26.

For the views of writers less guarded than Senior in their expressions of faith in the continuing operation of overall increasing returns see, e.g., Samuel Read, *Political Economy, An Inquiry into the Natural Grounds of Right to Vendible Property or Wealth*, Edinburgh, 1829, book 1, chap. 10, sect 4; G. P. Scrope, *Principles of Political Economy*, London, 1833, chap. 11; Thomas Hodgskin, *Popular Political Economy*, London, 1827, pp. 59, 85–6; T. R. Edmonds, *An Enquiry into the Principles of Population*, London, 1832, p. 63; Piercy Ravenstone, *A Few Doubts as to the Correctness of Some Opinions generally Entertained on the subjects of Population and Political Economy*, London, 1821, pp. 119, 186; Joseph Lowe, *The Present State of England*, London, 1822, pp. 220–21. Even Ricardo, said Marshall (PE, p. 814), recognised increasing as well as dimishing return though, for purposes of convenience in exposition, when analysing value-determination, he provisionally assumed that all commodities "obeyed the law of constant return."

10. *Principles of Political Economy* (Ashley ed.), pp. 177, 179, 183, 703ff.

11. *Principles of Political Economy* (Ashley, ed.), p. 703.

12. *Ibid.*, pp. 189–90, 193–96. He rejected the view that it was unsafe for a country to become dependent upon food imports. See *ibid.*, pp. 920–21. He noted also that if maize were accepted as a substitute for wheat, it would "require some generations for population . . . to overtake this great accession to the facilities of its support," *Ibid.*, pp. 196–97. Mill com-

did not believe that the repeal of the Corn Laws would of itself make labourers much better off, he based his argument primarily upon the supposition that the habits of the working class would not be permanently affected thereby rather than upon the belief that the volume of imports would be small.[13] Mill recognised that the cost of food imports might rise, but he did not emphasize a prospective worsening of the terms of trade as had Torrens.[14] Neither did he stress, as did Jevons, the prospect of rising mineral costs as minerals approached exhaustion.[15]

Mill expressed himself in favour of the maintenance of a population of optimum size, but he defined it as being of a magnitude that became virtually unchanging and impervious to internal and external change after a population had attained the degree of density found in the countries most populous in the mid-nineteenth century.

> After a degree of density has been attained, sufficient to allow the
> principal benefits of combination of labour, all further increase tends in
> itself to mischief, so far as regards the average condition of the people;
> but the progress of improvement has a counteracting operation, and allows
> of increased numbers without any deterioration, and even consistently

---

mented on the large volume of spontaneous emigration out of Ireland, but questioned whether it would continue in sufficient volume. *Ibid.*, pp. 197–98, 974–75. Actually Ireland's population declined one-fifth in 1841–54, and one-third in 1841–70; while the Irish birth rate, comparable to the English in the 1840's descended to the level of the French by the 1860's and thereafter moved similarly until the 1890's. The potato failure may have acted analogously to "a great change" of the sort essential to reduce fertility (*ibid.*, p. 348; see note 13 below), but Mill did not so interpret it. However, on p. 384 he comes close to doing so, for there he indicates that the cheapening of transport may make emigration an effective source of relief. This was written in 1865.

13. *Ibid.*, p. 348, also 719. By the 1860's two-fifths of Britain's wheat came from abroad. The French Revolution altered French habits and so brought about a lasting improvement of the majority. *Ibid.*, p. 349. Mill's statement, that "it is questionable if all the mechanical inventions yet made have lightened the day's toil of any human being," is based on the premise that only if "the increase of mankind shall be under the deliberate guidance of judicious foresight," can scientific discoveries, inventions, etc., elevate "the universal lot." *Ibid.*, p. 751.

14. *Ibid.*, pp. 736–39. R. Torrens believed that "in the progress of wealth and population, the exchangeable value of wrought goods, as compared with raw produce would gradually fall. . . . The increasing value of raw produce must gradually check its exportation, and the falling value of wrought goods progressively prevent their importation. . . . But centuries must roll away before the full peopling of the world interposes difficulties in the way of England's exchanging her cheap manufactured goods for cheap agricultural produce of less advanced countries." See *Essay on the Production of Wealth*, London, 1821, pp. 96, 98, 288–89.

15. *Op. cit.*, p. 477. Mill did not consider this contingency "as probable." See *ibid.* While W. S. Jevons did not consider the population problem "a part of the direct problem of Economy" (*The Theory of Political Economy*, 2nd. ed., London, 1871, pp. 254–55) he forecast (*The Coal Question*, London, 1865) a rise in the price of coal incidental to the working out of more accessible coal seams long before the stock of coal was exhausted three or more centuries hence, with the result that British industry would be adversely affected since there were no available commercial substitutes for coal. Possible exhaustion of British coal had been alluded to at least as early as 1789. See H. S. Jevons, *The British Coal Trade*, London, 1915, chaps. 26–27, on anticipated British population growth, coal consumption, and coal exports; also T. E. Thorpe, *Coal—Its History and Uses*, London, 1878.

with a higher average of comfort. . . . The density of population necessary to enable mankind to obtain, in the greatest degree, all the advantages both of cooperation and of social intercourse, has, in all the most populous countries, been attained.[16]

Henry Fawcett and J. E. Cairnes continued in the Mill tradition, but with some modification. Fawcett, impressed by the cheapening of transport, observed that wheat, its production stimulated by English capital and English emigrants, would continue to be available to Britain's growing population at satisfactory prices from abroad;[17] and that emigration now could be of sufficient volume, as the post-1848 experience of Ireland showed, to produce so great a rise in wages "that a permanent effect is produced on the social conditions of the people." The "day when the earth shall become" too densely populated for emigration any longer to be a remedy for overpopulation was "too remote" to be an occasion of concern. The "stationary state" was less probable now than formerly.[18] Cairnes was less optimistic than Fawcett. Though the extension of division of labour and the use of machinery tended to cause the cost of manufactures—especially that of the less coarse ones—to fall as population grew, the welfare of the growing working class tended to be adversely affected by this growth, since the cost of "labourers' commodities" tended to rise and the ratio of the "wages-fund" to a country's stock of capital tended to fall. The permanent improvement of the labourer's condition turned on his limiting his numbers, but he would not so act as long as he remained a mere hired employee. His status in industry must therefore be changed, so that he would acquire prudence

16. *Ibid.*, pp. 191-92, 750. My interpretation, if correct, suggests that, although improvements may operate to increase average income, they do not increase the size of a country's population with which is associated the maximum income attainable with any one of the prospectively realisable states of the arts. Mill notes (pp. 750-51) the evils associated with crowding and the destruction of the beauties of the countryside. Marshall referred to this discussion.

17. *Manual of Political Economy*, London, 1863, pp. 89-96, 324, 474. Meat and dairy products, not being very transportable, would rise in relative price (p. 95). Frozen meat did not begin to be shipped from Australia and the Western Hemisphere until the late 1870's, modern refrigeration not having been invented until 1861.

18. *Ibid.*, pp. 159-60, 249-50, 474-75. Australia could "maintain in comfort a population of 100,000,000." *Ibid.*, p. 160. The price of manufactures need not rise and might fall whilst "agricultural improvements" would continue to be important. *Ibid.*, pp. 324ff. See also his *Free Trade and Protection*, London, 1882, p. 131, where he said emigration might raise English wages to the Australian level. Whereas some of Fawcett's contemporaries gave qualified support to the view that emigration benefited the workers (e.g., J. A., Hobson, *Problems of Poverty*, London, 1896; William Farr, *Vital Statistics*, London, 1885; J. G. Godard, *Poverty: Its Genesis and Exodus*, London, 1892), others ranging from critics of the classicists (e.g., T. E. C. Leslie, "Political Economy and Emigration," *Frazier's Magazine*, vol. LXXVII, 1868, pp. 611-17) to writers of socialist persuasion rejected some of the pro-emigration arguments as founded upon untenable assumptions or upon principles of the classical economists. My attention has been drawn to a number of papers dealing with emigration and immigration by a reading of Professor Thornton Steele's Master's Thesis (Duke University, 1940), *British Population Theory, 1870-1914: A Survey*. Cp. R. D. Collison Black, "The Classical Economists and the Irish Problem," *Oxford Economic Papers*, vol. V, 1953, pp. 26-40.

and a better understanding of the wages problem. Cooperation – the "contribution by many workmen of their savings toward a common fund they employ as capital and cooperate in turning to profit" – constituted the means thereto, "the sole path by which the labouring classes . . . can emerge from their condition of mere hand-to-mouth living."[19]

Toward the close of the nineteenth century "a reaction . . . set in against the exaggerated views of Mill . . . and the importance of the real teaching of Malthus" was in danger "of being neglected."[20] Emigration (which fluctuated with business conditions)[21] was supposedly reducing the impact of natural increase;[22] food imports, which furnished about four-fifths of the wheat consumed in Britain in 1885–1900, were preventing the incidence of diminishing return in agriculture;[23] the birth rate had fallen steadily since 1876; and men were becoming more optimistic concerning the possible productive contributions of division of labour, technical progress, etc.[24]

19. *Some Leading Principles of Political Economy Newly Expounded*, New York, 1874, pp. 118, 132–35, 278–85, 287–89, 291–94. See also *The Character and Logical Method of Political Economy*, London, 1858, 1875, pp. 149–82, 207–13, for his criticism of the argument of G. K. Rickards (*Population and Capital*, London, 1854) and others that Malthus's theory was refuted by the fact that subsistence had grown faster than population in parts of the world. J. S. Mill, too, emphasised the importance of cooperation as a means to the improvement of the material and moral conditions of the labouring classes, but he tied it less closely to the population question. See *Principles*, book IV, chap. 7, pars. 4–7.

20. J. S. Nicholson, *Principles of Political Economy*, vol. I, London, 1893, p. 187.

21. See Robert Giffen, "Emigration and Immigration in the Year 1880," *Journal of the Royal Statistical Society*, vol. XLIV, 1881, pp. 99–100; W. A. Carrothers, *Emmigration from the British Isles*, London, 1929, *passim*; H. Jerome, *Migration and Business Cycles*, New York, 1926; Julius Isaac, *Economics of Migration*, London, 1947; I. Ferenczi, *International Migrations*, vols. I, II, New York, 1929, 1931.

22. Actually only from 3 to 20 per cent, per decade of the natural increase was removed in 1871–1911, despite the absence of serious barriers to immigration, the intermittent eagerness of dominions and colonies for immigrants, and the existence in Britain of a considerable opinion (including that of trade union leaders prior to the 1880's) and some arrangements favourable to emigration as a means of alleviating population pressure and unemployment. Of course some writers feared that the lands available for settlement would soon be filled up (e.g., see William Ogle, "On Marriage-Rates and Marriage-Ages, with Special Reference to the Growth of the Population," and the discussion, *Journal of the Royal Statistical Society*, vol. LIII, 1890, pp. 244–87).

23. However, Robert Giffen and Sir William Crookes (in 1898) feared that population growth in the grain-exporting countries would greatly reduce the surplus available for export. See R. Giffen, *Economic Inquiries and Studies*, London, 1904, pp. 382ff., II, 14–17, 35–38, 46, 230, 340–44; J. S. Davis, "The Spectre of Dearth of Food; History's Answer to Sir William Crookes," in *Facts and Factors in Economic History*, Cambridge, 1932, pp. 733–54.

24. During the last 30 years of Marshall's active lifetime, arguments were advanced in support of restrictive and selective control of immigration into Britain and into the colonies and dominions. The subject was discussed primarily in non-economic terms, however. H. Sidgwick, while generally in favour of the free admission of aliens, held that a government should be free to regulate their coming if it affected adversely "the internal cohesion" or the level of civilisation of a nation (*The Elements of Politics* [1891], London, 1929, pp. 309–10). Herbert Samuel, having refuted several crude economic fallacies relating to immigration, advocated exclusion of the unfit only ("Immigration," *Economic Journal*, vol. XV, 1905, pp. 15–37). Edwin Cannan favoured the exclusion of immigrants who did not regulate their fertility; but he indicated that newly arrived immigrants tended to be complementary to, rather than competi-

Henry Sidgwick was the first British economist to treat of the laws of return in a way making possible formulation of a dynamic optimum theory.[25]

The degree of density of population, beyond which returns in terms of output (or the economy) as a whole begin to fall,[26]

varies with the development of the industrial arts, and the accumulation of capital: it tends to be continually advanced by the progress of Invention, provided that, through the accumulation of capital, the improvement of processes which Invention renders possible is actually realised. . . . In a thinly-peopled country we have to note a tendency to increasing returns; every additional labourer tends to make labour on the average more productive, since he enables the whole body of labourers to realise more fully the advantages of cooperation. And this tendency to increasing returns continues to operate, in all branches of industry except agriculture and mining, without any known limit from density of population, except such as arise from sanitary considerations. The closer human beings live to one another, the greater tends to be the *quantum* of utility derived from a given *quantum* of labour in conveyance and communication; the greater, therefore, tends to be the development of cooperation by exchange; and as the scale on which each particular branch of manufactures may be profitably organised becomes thus proportionally larger, the production itself tends correspondingly to become more economical.[27]

From the fact that labour and capital produced less in Britain than in countries settled by Englishmen, Sidgwick inferred "that the growth of our population has passed the point at which the average efficiency of labour tends to be decreased by any addition to its quantity, other things remaining the same, even though capital has been accumulated to the proportional extent.[28] But "other things did not remain the same." The "arts of industry" were improving, the most important among them at the time being "the system of Cooperation through Exchange with less densely populated countries"; and the industrial progress associated with these improvements was counteracting any tendency to diminishing return. Accordingly, supposing foreign trade to go on, it could be said that "the population of the whole region with which England trades cannot be said to have reached the

---

tive with, the resident population; and he believed it probable that immigrants were more rigorously selected than were natives. (*Wealth*, London, 1914, 1928, pp. 270, 285–87.)

25. "With a little judicious editing," wrote Lionel Robbins, "a strong case could be made out for the claim of Sidgwick to be the real parent of the modern theory." This parentage Robbins assigns to Cannan. See "The Optimum Theory of Population," in T. E. Gregory and H. Dalton, eds., *London Essays in Economics*, London, 1927, pp. 113, 114. See also S. S. Cohn, *Die Theorie des Bevölkerungsoptimums*, Marburg, 1934, pp. 15ff.

26. The degree at which returns in extractive industries begin to fall is lower. See *Principles of Political Economy*, New York (1883), 1887, p. 144.

27. *Ibid.*, p. 144; also pp. 104–107 on the gains in the productiveness of labour arising from "association and cooperation." On diminishing returns in agriculture see book II, chap. 7.

28. *Ibid.*, pp. 144–45, also 146, 147.

point at which returns diminish," and that "the possibilities of England's obtaining additional subsistence by trade have only a remote and indefinite limit."[29] Whether "Invention" (which embraced "all improvements in the general organisation of industry, and upon which depended the extent of the "field for the employment of capital")[30] would proceed at a more or less rapid rate in the future than in the past was not foreseeable, though it was probable that inventions would be more capital-saving in the future than in the past, thereby presumably reducing somewhat the capital requirements of increasing return.[31]

Sidgwick did not unqualifiedly endorse policies making for the maximization of average productivity as an end, since what was endorseable turned more on what ultimate ends were sought. In his *Methods of Ethics*[32] he observed that, if Utilitarianism prescribed "happiness on the whole," even though achieving this end involved a decrease in average happiness, then

> the point up to which, on Utilitarian principles, population ought to be allowed to increase, is not that at which average happiness is the greatest possible, but that at which the product formed by multiplying the number of persons living into the amount of average happiness reaches a maximum.

Again, in his *Elements of Politics,* he described as "objectionable" measures tending to restrict the growth of population

> so far as they tend to check the expansion of civilised humanity: assuming that the increase of the amount of human life in the world, under its present conditions of existence in civilised countries, is a good and not an evil; except so far as increase of numbers tends to be accompanied by increase of disease, or even of physical discomfort not involving disease. If this assumption be granted, we may clearly regard as a benefit to humanity the stimulus to population which organised emigration and colonisation would tend to give — accompanied as it would be with a tendency to improve the average condition of human beings in the colony and the mother country taken together.[33]

Sidgwick's recognition that what constituted an optimum population turned on the ends sought as well as upon the circumstances affecting

29. *Ibid.,* p. 146. *In Elements of Politics* (1891), London, 1919, chap. 18, sect. 6, he states that governments may eventually have to restrict population growth.

30. Compare F. W. Taussig, "Capital, Interest, and Diminishing Returns," *Quarterly Journal of Economics,* vol. XXII, 1908, pp. 354–63.

31. *Op. cit.,* pp. 151–152. Though the effects of foreign investment produced through the medium of foreign trade are noted, attention is not given to the extent to which the operation of overall increasing return in a country like England turns on its capital contribution to the larger international economic community of which it is a part. See *ibid.,* pp. 157–58.

32. 1st ed., 1874, 4th ed., London, 1890, book IV, chap. i, par. 2.

33. 4th ed., pp. 317–18 (pp. 315–22 in the 4th edition are substantially as they were in the 1st ed.) The last sentence implies that, as he had said in the *Principles,* average productivity was still responding positively to population growth in the overall relevant community. Sidgwick also discusses the role of government respecting migration and colonisation.

material output was approved by F. Y. Edgeworth who stated that the degree of populousness "prescribed by the exigencies of military and commercial rivalry" probably exceeded that dictated by utilitarianism even as the latter exceeded that urged by Mill.[34] He had earlier, in his *Mathematical Psychics*,[35] observed that "there may be a plurality of values for the sought number of population, corresponding alternately to utilitarian and pessimistic arrangement," and touched upon divers circumstances by which the optimum magnitude and population policy might be affected. He agreed with Sidgwick's definition of the end of political action as being the maximization of "the *quantum* of happiness" rather than with J. S. Mill's view of it as the achievement of "the greatest average well-being."[36]

Edwin Cannan is usually accredited with having been the first writer to define in dynamic terms what later came to be called the "optimum population," to state explicitly what was meant by overpopulation and underpopulation, to reject the sharp distinction (held to by at least four generations of economists) between agriculture and manufactures, to argue sophisticatedly that population growth had increased output per head in the nineteenth century whatever might happen in the twentieth, and to note the variedness and the susceptibility to change of the circumstances whereupon depended the optimum number of people that could be supported in a country at any time.[37] In 1888 Cannan, having noted that the productiveness of industry is affected by the growth of knowledge, useful material objects, and inter-individual cooperation, said it was also affected by variations in population.

> At any given time the population which can exist on a given extent of land, consistently with the attainment of the greatest productiveness of industry possible at that time, is definite. . . . A large population is necessary for

34. See *Papers Relating to Political Economy*, London, 1925, vol. III, pp. 19–20; the comments are made in a review of Sidgwick's *Elements of Politics* (1st ed.).

35. London, 1881, pp. 68–76, 79, 122, 125.

36. *Papers*, vol. I, p. 72. The paper on "Laws of Increasing and Diminishing Returns," *ibid.*, pp. 61–99, is not concerned with the population problem. Elsewhere he comments, seemingly with approval, upon Marshall's evaluation of population growth (*ibid.*, vol. III, pp. 14–15, in review of the *Principles*, 1st ed.) and notes (p. 221) that Mombert's theory of population may be regarded "as coincident" with Marshall's.

37. It was, of course, argued in the late nineteenth and early twentieth centuries that the food supply and produced income had outstripped population, or that a larger population would be advantageous under existing conditions, but these arguments were loose inductions from the supposed course of events, and not founded upon a carefully formulated economic rationale; e.g., see William Farr, *Vital Statistics*, London, 1885, pp. 14–15; J. E. T. Rogers, *A Manual of Political Economy*, 2nd ed., Oxford, 1869, *passim*. In works concerned with the dangers of continuing population growth, as well as in some of those critical of Malthus, attention is not given to the nature of the response of total output to population growth; e.g., see George Drysdale, *The Elements of Social Science*, London, 1854 and later editions; Bonamy Price, *Chapters on Political Economy*, London, 1878; J. A. Hobson, *Problems of Poverty*, London, 1896; M. Crackenthorpe, *Population and Progress*, London, 1907; William Smart, *Studies in Economics*, London, 1895; A. W. Flux, *Economic Principles*, London, 1904; S. and B. Webb, *Industrial Democracy*, London, 1902; S. J. Chapman, *Political Economy*, London, 1912.

the proper division of employments and for carrying out great works. . . . Hitherto in the world's history it is probable that increase of population has generally, if not always, increased or rather assisted to increase the productiveness of industry. . . . It is always by acting on agriculture and a few kindred branches of industry that variations of population affect the productiveness of all industry. . . . The existence of overpopulation or underpopulation is not susceptible of exact demonstration.[38]

In 1903 he observed that the point of "maximum productiveness," at which "the returns to industry cease increasing and begin to diminish . . . is constantly being shifted by the progress of knowledge and other circumstances, and that the shifting is generally in the direction of increasing the population which is consistent with the maximum productiveness possible at that time."[39] In 1914 he elaborated his earlier views and rejected the sharp distinction between agriculture and manufactures, still present in his earlier writings.

The advantages of producing a large aggregate quantity, and therefore the advantages of a large population to produce and consume the large quantity, are more obvious in manufacture than in agriculture. . . . In both agriculture and manufacture returns increase up to a point and beyond that they diminish. If we start from what I have called the point of maximum return, we can say of manufacture as well as of agriculture that returns diminish as we move in either direction from that point. . . . Just as there is a point of maximum return in each industry, so there must be in all industries taken together. If population is not large enough to bring all industry up to this point, returns will be less than they might be, and the remedy is increase of population; if, on the other hand, population is so great that the point has been passed, returns are again less than they might be, and the remedy is decrease of population.

It is very important not to fall into the error of supposing that the point of maximum return remains permanently fixed, either for particular industries or for industry taken as a whole. . . . [It] is perpetually being altered by the progress of knowledge and other changes. . . . These changes shifted the point of maximum return, pushing it farther along in the direction favourable to large population.[40]

Cannan's approach seems to have exercised little influence upon English thought concerning the population question before the 1920's. It was ignored by Marshall, and appreciation of its significance probably remained confined to the London School of Economics.[41] For example, J. S. Nicholson indicated that an increase of population might "involve a diminishing return

38. *Elementary Political Economy*, London, 1888, part I, sect. 7.
39. *Theories of Production and Distribution*, chap. 9, sect. 4.
40. *Wealth*, London, 1914, 1916, chap. 4; in the 3rd ed. (1928) the term "optimum" is used and an additional section is added, but otherwise the treatment is as in the 1st ed.
41. See Robbins, *op. cit.*, pp. 115–17, and p. 118 where Wicksell is said to be (perhaps) the first to use the term "optimum population." However, in 1906 G. U. Yule used the concept, "the 'optimum,' or best possible number," to describe the normal population or labour-supply

to its general productive power," but he little more than noticed that increase of population might have an opposite effect, perhaps because he felt that economists mistakenly attributed to division of labour and largeness of scale of production effects properly attributable to inventions unconnected therewith.[42] W. H. Beveridge, subsequently a critic of the concept of optimum, at first was content to note the absence of classical "over-population."[43] Whereas Pigou ignored the optimum, P. H. Wicksteed, having distinguished between industries of increasing and decreasing return, indicated that if all relevant agencies including population increased in the same proportion output per head would increase, but he did not translate his discussion into terms of the optimum.[44] J. M. Robertson confined his discussion largely to weaknesses of the anti-Malthusian position.[45]

Population Elasticity and Its Determinants

In his discussion of the manner in which population responds to an increase in subsistence J. S. Mill observed that

the conduct of human creatures is more or less influenced by foresight of consequences, and by impulses superior to mere animal instincts: and they do not, therefore, propagate like swine, but are capable, though in very unequal degrees, of being withheld by prudence, or by social affections, from giving existence to beings born only to misery and premature death. In proportion as mankind rise above the condition of the beasts, population is restrained by the fear of want rather than by want itself. . . . Among the middle classes, in many individual instances, there is an additional restraint exercised from the desire of doing more than maintaining their circumstances – of improving them; but such a desire is rarely found, or rarely has that effect, in the labouring classes.[46]

---

magnitude. When the actual population was in excess of the optimum, natality fell below its normal level and remained there until the actual population approximated the optimum; and when the actual population fell short of the optimum, natality moved above its normal and remained there until the actual population again approximated the optimum. An oscillation of natality about its norm was set up by the 15–20 year lag between a worker's birth and his entry into the labour market. While Yule's optimum was an increasing magnitude, it did not describe what Cannan had in mind. See "On the Changes in the Marriage and Birth Rates in England and Wales during the past Half Century; with an Inquiry as to their Probable Causes." *Journal of the Royal Statistical Society,* vol. LXIX, 1906, p. 131. In the discussion, *ibid.,* pp. 133–47, Yule's optimum is not considered.

42. *Op. cit.,* vol. I, pp. 172–174, 343. He considered it probable that during the next century "the progress of invention" might be "more marked in the acquisition of raw produce than in its manufacture." *Ibid.,* p. 173. Of Mill's forecast of the future of the labouring classes he said that "general estimates of the future are extremely hazardous." *Ibid.,* vol. III (1901), p. 171.

43. *Unemployment,* London, 1908, 1912, pp. 6–7, 70, 217. In the 1930 edition the concept of optimum is criticised.

44. See A. C. Pigou, *Wealth and Welfare,* London, 1912, part I, chaps. 2, 4; P. H. Wicksteed, *The Common Sense of Political Economy* (1910), L. Robbins, ed., London, 1933, book II, chap. 5, esp. pp. 527–32, 548–49.

45. *The Economics of Progress,* London, 1918, chaps. 7–8.

46. *Principles,* pp. 158–59. Senior was more optimistic, saying that in all ranks above the lowest "men of more enterprise are induced to postpone marriage . . . also by the hope that . . .

But he did not, as did many of his contemporaries[47] suppose the power of the preventive check was increasing sufficiently to make it probable that, at least in the Western European sphere of civilisation, capital would more and more outstrip labour and the means of existence would more and more outdistance population, with the result that real wages, average income, and the standard of living would continue to rise.

But whatever be the causes by which population is anywhere limited to a comparatively slow rate of increase, an acceleration of the rate very speedily follows any diminution of the motives to restraint. It is but rarely that improvements in the condition of the labouring classes do anything more than give a temporary margin, speedily filled up by an increase of their numbers.[48]

The condition of the labouring classes would improve only if their "in-

they may rise. . . . As they mount, the horizon of their ambition keeps receding." The luxuries of one generation become the decencies or necessities of the next. See N. S. Senior, *Two Lectures on Population*, London, 1829, pp. 27, 34–35.

47. A variety of reasons were advanced by both critics and followers of Malthus why it was to be expected empirically that preventive checks would increase sufficiently in power to permit real wages and the average level of living to rise through time. Economic progress and the increase in civilisation continually pushed up the standard of living, and the habits of men were continually adjusted to this rise. Men both feared a decline in their levels of living and aspired to elevate them, and this aspiration was reinforced in the lower classes when the rates of natural increase in the upper classes were relatively low, and resulted in gaps in the upper portion of the social pyramid. The birth-depressing influence of urbanisation was stressed much more than in France where lack of prudence and of foresight were associated with an urban proletariat. Various factors which supposedly operated to reduce fecundity were noticed: e.g., inbreeding, changes in diet, increases in mental exertion, etc. As a rule, authors failed to convert their analyses into terms of process and so were unable to show why it was to be expected that the checks would necessarily continue to be sufficiently operative. The Neo-Malthusians, both before and after 1850, believed it impossible for men to control their numbers adequately unless assisted by suitable contraceptive devices. For detailed accounts of pre-1860 theories of checks see Kenneth Smith, *The Malthusian Controversy*, London, 1951; D. M. Harrison's doctoral dissertation, *A Survey of English Population Theory:* 1800–1860 (1941; in Duke University Library); also N. E. Himes, *Medical History of Contraception*, Baltimore, 1936.

Of Mill's contemporaries only Herbert Spencer sought to discover a necessarily self-adjusting principle of population and rejected as incomplete theories which did not incorporate such a principle. He asserted that the power to maintain life, which varied directly with the development of the nervous system, was antagonistic to the power to propagate the species. Excess fertility produced population pressure, and this in turn stimulated improvements and intensified the need for skill, intelligence, self-control, and education, and put the mentally sluggish at increasing disadvantage. In consequence, man's nervous centres tended to become enlarged, his power to maintain life tended to increase, and his power to reproduce to diminish. The evolutionary process initiated by excess fertility would persist until the power to maintain life and the power to reproduce were in equilibrium and mortality and fertility were in balance at a low level. Then excess fertility and population pressure would have come to an end. This theory, first developed in 1852, is more fully developed in his *Principles of Human Biology*, New York, 1867, vol. II, pp. 406–10, 479–508.

48. *Op. cit.*, p. 161. On the degree of dependence of the movement of wages upon that of the capital/population ratio, see book IV, chap. 3; also book IV, chap. 6, on when the stationary state was "not in itself undesirable." It was essential, if man were to profit by improvements, scientific discoveries, and capital accumulation, that the "increase of mankind . . . be under the deliberate guidance of judicious foresight." *Ibid.*, p. 751.

tellectual and moral culture" improved, or they so used "favourable circumstances" as to raise their "habitual standard," the level below which they would not multiply.[49] This was most likely to happen when, as during the French Revolution, a great improvement took place in a very short time interval, enabling the workers to change their habits and raise their standards and those of their children before population growth had removed this possibility.

To produce permanent advantage, the temporary cause operating upon them must be sufficient to make a great change in their condition – a change such as will be felt for many years, notwithstanding any stimulus which it may give during one generation to the increase of people. When, indeed, the improvement is of this signal character, and a generation grows up which has always been used to an improved scale of comfort, the habits of the new generation in respect to population become formed upon a higher minimum, and the improvement in their condition becomes permanent.[50]

This type of argument, an analogue of which finds expression to-day,[51] though not noticed by Cairnes, was apparently considered valid by Fawcett.[52] It was rejected by Bagehot (who exercised considerable influence upon Marshall) and endorsed by J. N. Keynes. Bagehot believed that "a really thrifty people used to self-denial" would profit "exceedingly by a series of small improvements" devoting their fruits to "happiness" rather than to "numbers"; whereas "an easy-going enjoying nation" would not use the fruits of "any boon of plenty, however great or sudden," to raise their average level of living.[53] Keynes pointed to the great permanent increase produced in the level of real wages by the Black Death, saying it

49. *Ibid.*, p. 161.

50. *Ibid.*, pp. 348–49. See on the impact of the French Revolution, pp. 292–95, 371, 380ff.; on improvement in England in 1715–65, p. 349n.; also pp. 383–84, 719ff. J. R. McCulloch, in an unsigned article ("Dr. Chalmers on Political Economy," *Edinburgh Review*, vol. LVI (no. III), 1832, p. 55) had already indicated that, because 16–18 years intervened between the birth of an individual and his entry into the labour market, an increase in the demand for labour and hence an increase in wages tended to result in the acquisition by workers' families of higher standards, since the increase in wages could not for years (if ever) evoke an increase in the supply of labour sufficient to press wages back to the initial level. It was possible also for the standard of living to be reduced by a decline in the demand for labour, its supply remaining constant, if the resulting fall in wages caused workers to lower their opinions respecting what was necessary for their comfortable subsistence. This argument is more fully developed in McCulloch's *Principles of Political Economy*, Edinburgh, 1842, 1864, part III, chap. 2, and preface to 1842 edition. Cf. Yule, cited in note 41 above; also M. Longfeld, *Lectures on Political Economy*, Dublin, 1834, pp. 202–04, 263–66.

51. It is commonly held to-day that very heavy and sustained investment must be made in under-developed countries with high natality if they are to be enabled to break through the Malthusian barrier to progress. Cf. H. Leibenstein, *A Theory of Economic-Demographic Development*, Princeton, 1954.

52. See note 18 and text above.

53. Walter Bagehot, *Economic Studies*, 1879, essay on "Malthus," in *Works* (ed. F. Morgan), Hartford, 1889, vol. V, p. 397.

supported the "conclusion that if a general rise in wages is to be rendered permanent, it must be able to exert an influence upon the labourer's standard of comfort before an increase in population has had time to bring about a reaction."[54]

Economists generally found a barrier to excessive multiplication in the presence of a habitual standard of living, desire for the preservation and/or the improvement of which inspired men to subject their increase to judicious restraint.[55] According to Fawcett there was wanting in the labouring classes that prudence which guarded the customary standards of the middle and upper classes.[56] Cairnes wondered if "even a very great change in the habits of the labouring classes would suffice" so long as the worker remained "a mere receiver of wages."[57] In 1870 F. Jenkin said that since "the feelings of men," their "expectation of comfort," determined "the cost of production of labour [which] determines wages," increase in this expectation and hence in population limitation would elevate wages.[58] W. Cunningham indicated that the "amount of population which can be supported at any one place and time," given the current limit of its productive power, depended on the "standard of adequate support" prevailing, a standard which might rise as a result of material progress.[59] Nicholson considered "improved education" essential, along with elevation of the worker's "standard of comfort," to the permanent advance of wages.[60] These writers, and others of similar persuasion, did not, however, sequester and describe the sequence of steps, or the socio-economic processes, underlying the expansion of the minimum standard of comfort.

54. *The Scope and Method of Political Economy*, London, 1891, chap. 9, sect. 2.

55. Writing in 1884, Wicksteed (*op. cit.* vol. II, p. 706) observed that "Economists of the most widely divergent schools" held that "the only means (always under existing conditions) by which wages could be permanently raised would be a collective refusal on the part of the working classes to live and propagate on the terms at present granted, i.e. a raising of the standard of minimum comfort." Wicksteed himself believed that "the supply of raw human material is determined largely . . . by non-economic considerations"; but, like Jevons, he considered "the whole question of the ultimate supply of human effort . . . beyond the limits of economic inquiry." *Ibid.*, vol. I, pp. 336–37.

56. *Manual*, p. 157; also his treatment of pauperism and poor relief in *Essays and Lectures on Social and Political Subjects*, London, 1872, pp. 84, 102–103. That poor relief had a beneficial effect upon the behaviour of the poor was urged by W. L. Sargant, *Essays of a Birmingham Manufacturer*, London, 1872, vol. IV, pp. 69–317. The Irish experience had much earlier caused James Mill and others to modify their views concerning the impact of poor laws upon population growth (R. D. C. Black, *op. cit.*, pp. 36–38).

57. *Political Economy*, p. 281, also note 19 above and text. Matthew Arnold too stressed the need for a re-definition of the object of living. See *Culture and Anarchy*, London (1869), New York, 1925, pp. 196–97; cp. John Ruskin, *Unto this Last and other Essays* (1862), Everyman ed., New York, pp. 185–191.

58. *Papers Literary, Scientific, &c*, vol. II, London, 1887, London School of Economics reprint, 1931, pp. 93–106, esp. 100–101; also 130. Compare Duke of Argyll's account (*The Unseen Foundations of Society*, London, 1893, p. 491) of the restraints on population growth arising from an increase in the "standard of life."

59. "On the Statement of the Malthusian Principle," *Macmillan's Magazine*, vol. XLIX, 1883, pp. 81–86. See also Sidgwick, *Principles*, pp. 149–50.

60. *Principles*, vol. I, pp. 193–94, 333–40.

Miscellaneous Matters

Under this heading we shall touch upon reactions to the decline in the birth rate, reactions that did not become pronounced until the turn of the century when more refined statistical methods suggested the advent of a stationary population.[61] Thereafter alarm was frequently expressed lest the birth rate continue to fall and depress the rate of increase to the level obtaining in neighbouring France,[62] and this alarm was intensified when it was observed that the rate of increase was lower in the upper than in the lower socio-economic categories of the population.[63] As a result of the discussions carried on in the *London Times* and elsewhere a National Birth Rate Commission was established in 1913, and it made a report in 1916 and again, after having been reconstituted, in 1920.[64]

Among the circumstances described as responsible for the decline in the birth rate were the increase in the standard of comfort and the desire for luxury; the slackening of religious restraints; the decline in the asset value of children occasioned by the prolongation of their education; increased knowledge of contraception, attributable to urbanisation and the earlier influence of the Bradlaugh-Besant trial in 1877; the impact of changing economic conditions; and increased thrift. Comparative highness of fertility was no longer found especially associated with agricultural activity or with particular industrial activities. Marriage rates and birth rates were found to fluctuate with variations in the degree of economic prosperity and availability of employment. It was noted that although the crude birth rate had fallen since 1876, corrected indices of natality did not begin to fall until in the 1880's.[65]

61. See E. Cannan's forecasts, made in 1895 and 1901, and republished in *Economic Scares,* London, 1933, pp. 108–35.

62. See E. Castlelot, "Stationary Population in France," *Economic Journal*, vol. XIV, 1904, pp. 244–61; J. H. Schooling, "The Natural Increase of Three Populations," *Contemporary Review*, vol. LXXXI, 1902, pp. 227–41; A. Newsholme, *The Declining Birth Rate*, New York, 1911, p. 54; G. T. Bisset-Smith, "The Census; Population and Progress," *Westminster Review*, vol. CLXXIII, 1910, pp. 601–16. See also William Farr, "On Some Doctrines of Population," *Journal of the Royal Statistical Society*, vol. XL, 1877, pp. 576–77.

63. See S. and B. Webb, *Industrial Democracy*, pp. 638–42; S. Webb, "Physical Degeneracy or Race Suicide," *London Times*, Oct. 11, 1906; Crackenthorpe, *op. cit.*, pp. 84–86. But cf. Sidney Low, "Is Our Civilization Dying?" *Fortnightly Review*, vol. XCIX, 1913, pp. 628–39; also Newsholme and Stevenson, cited in note 65 below.

64. *Problems of Population and Parenthood*, London, 1920.

65. See Newsholme, *op. cit.*, chap. 4; Yule, *op. cit.*; Himes, *op. cit.*, pp. 244–45. Newsholme and T. H. C. Stevenson, "The Decline of Human Fertility in the United Kingdom and other Countries as shown by Corrected Birth Rates," *Journal of the Royal Statistical Society*, vol. LXIX, 1906, pp. 34–87 and discussion, pp. 133–47; Marcus Carlyle, "The Birth Rate (1905)," *Westminster Review*, vol. CLXIV, 1905, pp. 278–301; G. B. Lissenden, "Race Suicide, the Reply of the Masses," *ibid.*, vol. CLXXII, 1909, pp. 270–72. See also Crackenthorpe, *op. cit.*, and C. V. Drysdale, *Can Everybody Be Fed? A Reply to Prince Kropotkin*, London, 1913. Crackenthorpe and Drysdale both emphasised the fact that parents should produce no more children than could be satisfactorily supported. There was no recognition of the possible impact of the late nineteenth century decline in the rate of economic advance to which E. H. Phelps Brown and others have called attention; but see PE, p. 190 (p. 239 in 1st ed.). See note 3 above.

II. Laws of Returns; Formation of Non-Human Agents of Production

Marshall's discussions of these two subjects are here bracketed together because he dealt with both when treating of the possible consequences of continuing population growth.[66] While his treatment of the laws of return was nearly as well developed in the first as in the eighth edition, his account of long-run supply of labour and capital underwent greater elaboration in later editions.[67]

Marshall's various discussions suggest that he had in mind six or seven analytically distinct though somewhat interconnected forces which made for increases in income per head, of which population growth,[68] when it so operated, was but one. (i) Population growth, in so far as it stimulates or makes possible the general development of industry, gives rise to certain inventions (together with their application) and to various economies consequent upon improvements in the organisation of expanding economic activities, and these in turn bring about increases in output per head. Increases are brought about also by (ii) increases in wealth or capital per head; by (iii) inventions which, coming into being and use independently of the stimulus of population growth, may be called autonomous; and by (iv) improvements in the terms on which imports are to be had. Increases

66. While Marshall touched upon the rent-increasing influence of population growth (e.g., in PE pp. 156, 632ff., 687), his treatment of rent does not fall within the boundaries of the present paper. See F. W. Ogilvie, "Marshall on Rent," *Economic Journal*, vol. XL, 1930, pp. 1–24, and M. T. Hollond's reply, *ibid.*, pp. 369–83; also R. Opie, "Marshall's Time Analysis," *ibid.*, vol. XLI, 1931, pp. 199–215, and G. J. Stigler, *Production and Distribution Theories*, New York, 1941, pp. 87–97.

67. In the preface to the sixth edition (1910) which is very nearly identical with the fifth (1907), the seventh (1916), and the eighth (1920) editions, Marshall noted that while up to then cheap transport had "almost suspended the tendency to Diminishing Return," continuing population growth might again push upward the return to land and its value. "Increasing stress has been laid in successive editions up to the present on these facts." While increasing return was treated more fully in the eighth than in the first edition, it is plainly treated in the first, book IV, chaps. 3 and 13 assuming virtually final form in the first, and much of book V, chaps. 12, 13 and 15 appearing there. Treatment of the importance of cheap transport was substantially the same in the first as in the eighth editions. The third and fourth editions approximated the final edition in respect of returns more closely than did the first, and the discussion assumed virtually final form in the fifth. In *The Pure Theory of Domestic Value*, written about 1873 and printed in 1879, he admitted that agriculture might be subject (given sufficient time for change) to increasing as well as to diminishing return, and asserted that economies in production usually attended an "increase in the total amount of a commodity manufactured" whether it was produced by many or few firms, sub-division of processes, education and economy of technical skill, and the multiplication and intercommunication of ideas acting in combination to reduce costs (*ibid.*, pp. 6, 7–10, 16–17). Compare *Principles*, 8th ed., book IV, chap. 3, book V, chap. 12). See also his *Economics of Industry* (1879), pp. 27ff. (1881), pp. 22–26, 57. Changes in Marshall's treatment of the supply of capital and labour are noted when significant and relevant.

68. Here the term population growth is intended primarily to signify increase in the overall density of the population; it is not particularly intended to signify a process which operates to increase the rate of investment and so possibly makes for fuller employment.

result also from (v) improvements in the health, vigour, education, and efficiency of the labour force, improvements which have their origin primarily in the general betterment of the conditions under which workers live and bring up their children and secondarily in such economically rational investment as is made in individual training, etc.[69] (vi) Output per head tends to be higher when the manner in which an economy is organised is relatively favourable to the selection of men with business genius.[70] (vii) There are other savings, organisational in character, consequent upon the growth of an economy in magnitude, of the sort included under (i) but not occasioned by population growth and not otherwise included above.[71]

Some branches of an economy being subject to what Marshall called "increasing return," others to "diminishing return," and yet others to "constant return" (i.e., a state of balance between "the actions of laws of increasing and diminishing return"), an economy was describable as subject to "increasing return" when the industries subject thereto outweighed in importance those subject to "diminishing return."[72]

Increasing return has its origin in the tendency of "external economies" and (to some extent) "internal economies" to increase as the "aggregate volume of production" increases. A condition of increasing return obtains in an economy as a whole, or in one of its branches, when "an increase of labour and capital leads generally to improved organisation, which increases the efficiency of the work of labour and capital"; and it manifests itself in the fact that "the output of a certain amount of labour and capital," or the quantity of product associated with a given "quantity of effort and sacrifice," rises as more labour and capital are used and a greater output is produced.

> We say broadly that while the part which nature plays in production shows a tendency to diminishing return, the part which man plays shows a tendency to increasing return. . . . Therefore in those industries which are not engaged in raising raw produce an increase of labour and capital generally gives a return increased more than in proportion; and further this improved organisation tends to diminish or even to override any increased resistance which Nature may offer to raising increased amounts of raw produce.

69. On (v) see PE, pp. 510, 561–69, 693–95; pp. 681ff., on the shift from "investment as material capital to investment as personal capital"; and pp. 216, 561–65, on the tendency for underinvestment in training to be occasioned by the fact that the marginal private benefit of such investment usually fell short of its marginal social benefit. On (ii) and (iii) see book IV, chap. 13 and pp. 460, 541ff.; on (iv) see pp. 674–75; on (i), book IV, chap. 13, book VI, chap. 12. The continuing impact of science, to which Marshall attached great weight, is included above under that of invention. In *Economics of Industry*, 2nd ed., p. 57, division of labour is stressed.

70. E.g., see IT, pp. 153ff.; PE, 686n., 745, and on innovator types, 597ff., 663ff.

71. Income per head is also affected by the length of the working week, and by yet other circumstances, but these are not here considered.

72. Through the use of excise taxes on increasing-cost and subsidies on decreasing-cost industries the relative weight of industries of increasing return could be somewhat increased. See PE, book V, chap. 13; also Appendix H.

In general, the economies underlying tendencies to increasing return arise out of increased knowledge, greater specialisation of labour and machinery and activities, better localisation of industry, the increasing scale of industry, more economic use of factors and materials, better and more time-saving communication, more efficient marketing, and other improvements in organisation, all of which may be associated with increases in the aggregate volume of production in some if not in all industries.[73]

Evidently, therefore, increasing return may be consequent upon population growth, or it may be consequent upon changes which take place independently of population growth, or it may be both. Marshall does not, however, separate the two sources out sharply, perhaps because he was concerned with the movement of average income rather than with the specific influence of population growth, and also because he looked upon the movement of population as interacting with other agents participating in economic development in the manner of participants in an organic growth process.[74]

Continuing population growth tends to have an adverse effect upon individual well-being, Marshall reasoned, when a country's supply of land is so limited that the supply of the products of land is highly inelastic to labour and capital inputs, and the alternative of relatively cheap raw-produce imports is not available. So long as a country's land supply remains adequate, or as its population, though short of land, can exchange manufactured goods and services on suitable terms for raw produce imported from abroad, population growth not only is not likely to depress income per head but may even be accompanied by increases in average well-being, provided that the evils associated with urban crowding are avoided. When so reasoning, Marshall seems usually to have had in mind the concrete case of Britain, to whose ability to import raw produce on satisfactory terms he adverted a number of times.

The contributions of extractive industries other than agriculture were noticed but not stressed by Marshall. He merely stated that fish constitute an important source of food and that some if not all fisheries are subject to diminishing return.[75] He observed that the important thing about mineral extraction was not so much the operation ("other things being equal") of

73. See PE, esp. pp. 318–21, also book IV, chaps. 8–11, e.g., pp. 286ff., 396ff., 457ff.; also IT, pp. 187ff., and, on science, p. 133. See PE, 1st ed., book IV, chaps. 13, 7–11. Marshall cited with approval C. J. Bullock's, "The Variation of Productive Forces," *Quarterly Journal of Economics*, vol. XVI, 1902, pp. 473ff., which, however, does not treat of the population question. For a critical appraisal of Marshall's treatment of returns see Stigler, *op. cit.*, pp. 68–83. Marshall makes no reference to such writers as Julius Wolf (*Die Volkswirtschaft der Gegenwart und Zukunft*, Leipzig, 1912) who emphasized limitations to technical progress itself.

74. See Shove, *op. cit.*, p. 312; "Mechanical and Biological Analogies in Economics," in M, pp. 312–18; also PE, 1st ed., pp. 71, 301, 6th ed., preface.

75. River fisheries were subject to diminishing incremental return to additional applications of capital and labour. Sea-fisheries were subject to diminishing return according to some opinions, and not subject thereto according to other opinions. "The question is important, for

diminishing returns in mining as the fact that "nature's storehouse" was subject to eventual exhaustion.[76] While Marshall did not stress so much as had Jevons the consequences for the British economy of increases in the costs of mineral extraction which would long precede exhaustion of Britain's minerals, and while he did not observe that population growth would accelerate the upward movement of these costs and the advent of mineral exhaustion, he commented upon the fact that Britain's coal and ore supplies were being depleted,[77] and he declared it unwise for her to exchange coal for imports.[78] He may have supposed that economies attendant upon the increasing conversion of coal into electricity near the mines would counterbalance increases in costs of extraction, and that the harnessing first of water power and eventually of tidal and solar energy would offset the depletion of coal supplies.[79] Also he may not have considered the investment of labour and capital in mineral production to be relatively large enough to enable rising costs to occasion as much trouble in the relatively near future as Jevons had anticipated.[80]

Describing land as something whose fundamental attribute "is its extension" and as an agent which "has an 'inherent' income of heat and light and air and rain, which man cannot greatly affect," Marshall stressed the fact

---

the future population of the world will be appreciably affected as regards both quantity and quality, by the available supply of fish." See PE, p. 166, or 1st ed., p. 218. When discussing the fishing industry Marshall did not distinguish sharply between a diminution in returns attributable to a change in factoral proportion and a diminution attributable to a contraction of the size of fish populations. See H. S. Gordon, "On a Misinterpretation of the Law of Diminishing Returns in Marshall's *Principles*," *Canadian Journal of Economics and Political Science*, vol. xviii, 1952, pp. 96–98.

76. PE, pp. 166–67; IT, pp. 188–89.

77. See his "Memorandum on the Fiscal Policy of International Trade (1903)," OP, pp. 365–420 esp. pars. 20, 64, 70, 80–82. A century or two hence Britain could no longer raise all her people out of extreme poverty in the absence of external help. See *ibid.*, par. 20. However, in *The Economics of Industry*, 2nd ed., p. 26, he anticipated the replacement of coal by "the forces of the air and water," together with power storage and transmission.

78. IT, p. 628. "The position which Britain will hold in the world some centuries hence will depend largely on the care with which she has husbanded her stores of it; any generation which exports it, in order to pay for those manufactures in the production of which Britain should hold her own, will inflict an injury on coming generations." *Ibid.*, n. A country lacking mineral oil "must always jealously guard her supplies of coal for use at sea." M, p. 364.

79. IT, pp. 162, 788–90; M, p. 137–39, 364, note 76 above. In his paper (published in 1879) on the role of water, he indicated the contribution that water power had made and could make to the nation's energy supply, and he emphasised the economic and the sociological significance of inland waters and (above all) the sea as means of intranational and international communication; but he did not deal with the growing industrial, municipal, and related uses of water. See M, pp. 134–41.

80. In 1901 about 5.8 per cent. of the British labour force was engaged in mining; in 1841, about 3; and in 1911, about 6.6. See Colin Clark, *op. cit.*, 1st ed., London, 1940, p. 187; and, for recent internationally comparative figures, *ibid.*, 2nd ed., pp. 398–99. In the United States in 1900 minerals other than gold comprised, in value terms, about 3 per cent. of the gross national product whereas agricultural and forestry products (about 90 per cent. of which were consumed domestically) comprised 23 per cent. See The President's Materials Policy Commission, *Resources for Freedom*, Washington, 1952, vol. 1, p. 7, vol. 11, pp. 176, 180.

that, from the point of view of a nation as a whole, its stock of land was fixed and hence not susceptible, as were implements and other agents of production, of great if not unrestricted increase.[81]

It followed that when, as in an old country, all cultivated land had been brought into use, its people "can cultivate its land more intensively, but it cannot get any more." Such intensification of cultivation, in turn, was subject, in the absence of improvements in the arts of agriculture, to diminishing incremental returns to labour and/or capital as the ratio of labour and/or capital to the land increased (as it almost invariably would in an old country) beyond the point where the marginal productivity of land stood at zero. Under these conditions

> the application of increased capital and labour to land will add a less than proportionate amount to the produce raised, unless there be meanwhile an increase in the skill of the individual cultivator. Secondly, whatever may be the future developments of the arts of agriculture, a continued increase in the application of capital and labour to land must ultimately result in a diminution of the extra produce which can be obtained by a given extra amount of capital and labour.[82]

Population growth was not always accompanied by diminishing average returns to labour and/or capital applied to land, since improvements in the agricultural arts, together with various other agencies of increasing return, sometimes operated, even in old countries, to raise the level of returns to applications of labour and capital to land.

> Even in agriculture the law of increasing return is constantly contending with that of diminishing return, and many of the lands which were neglected at first give a generous response to careful cultivation; and meanwhile the development of roads and railroads, and the growth of varied markets and varied industries render possible innumerable econ-

81. PE, pp. 145, 169–70, 422n., 534–36, 629. Marshall therefore criticised American and other economists who, reasoning on the basis of a new country much of whose land remained uncultivated, disregarded the significance of the fixity of the stock of land and exaggerated the importance of land's situational advantages (which also were largely beyond man's control). See PE, pp. 170–71, 629.

82. PE, p. 153 (p. 203 in 1st ed.), also p. 150. See also pp. 151 and 172 on historical evidence of man's response to diminishing returns; p. 155 on Arkansas experimental data; pp. 407–10 where the problem of factoral proportion, as distinguished from that of diminishing returns in land, is treated; and pp. 150–51, 156, 651ff. (also IT, pp. 189–90n.), on the tendency of returns to labour and/or capital to rise when too little labour and/or capital is being applied to a given amount of land.

83. PE, p. 670 (p. 714 in 1st ed.). Elsewhere (p. 651) he said that "man's part in agriculture conforms to the law of increasing return" just as does man's part in manufacture. Similarities and dissimilarities are touched upon in *ibid.*, pp. 651–55. While Marshall believed Henry Carey's argument, that cultivation proceeded from the poorer to the better soils, to be "based largely on facts relating to warm countries" whose oppressive climate presently made their efficient cultivation impossible, he admitted that "many of those lands which are the least fertile when cultivation is merely extensive, become among the most fertile when cultivation

omies in production. Thus the tendencies to increasing and diminishing return appear pretty well balanced, sometimes the one, sometimes the other being the stronger.[83]

Increases in returns in agriculture flowed out of changes in both the immediately agricultural milieu and the adjoining non-agricultural milieu which accompanied the growth of population, changes which ranged from improvements in education, medicine and communication to improvements in markets and in the composition of agricultural production.[84]

Given that a nation's raw produce was forthcoming, either domestically or from abroad, under conditions of constant or not very rapidly falling return, it stood to benefit from population growth, since the operation of increasing returns (consequent upon population growth) in manufacture, transport and other branches of activity (wherein raw materials counted for little and human agents and capital for much) would more than offset some diminution in returns in agriculture and thus yield increasing returns in terms of output as a whole.

Taking account of the fact that an increasing density of population generally brings with it access to new social enjoyments we may give a rather broad scope to this statement and say: An increase of population accompanied by an equal increase in the material sources of enjoyment and aids to production is likely to lead to a more than proportionate income of enjoyment of all kinds; provided firstly, an adequate supply of raw produce can be obtained without great difficulty, and secondly there is no such overcrowding as causes physical and moral vigour to be impaired by the want of fresh air and light and of healthy and joyous recreation for the young.[85]

It was necessary, in other words, that the formation of capital (i.e., "material aids to production") proceed at least as rapidly as that of population, that there be access to sufficient supplies of raw material and produce, that these supplies be obtainable on satisfactory terms, and that the evils of over-

---

is intensive," and pointed, by way of example, to marsh, pasture, and similar lands which had been converted to the cultivation of grains, root crops, etc. See PE, pp. 157–59, 164–65. The growth of population and wealth thus tended to "make the poorer soils gain in value on the richer," particularly when the former were as well endowed as the latter with light, heat, and air. See PE, p. 162.

84. PE, pp. 165–66. Ricardo had erred in not allowing "enough for the increase of strength that comes from organisation" and in supposing that "the lands which were first chosen, should turn out always to be those which ultimately come to be regarded as the most fertile." See *ibid.*, pp. 164, 165; also preceding note. It was essential, Marshall's argument ran, to look at the response of a whole region to an increase in population, since this was undergoing reorganisation, rather than only at the immediate response of a field to more inputs. See *ibid.*, pp. 165–66.

85. PE, p. 321 (pp. 379–80 in 1st ed.). Given also what we have called autonomous invention (cp. Marshall's "substantive" invention, *ibid.*, p. 460), the case would be stronger, since both capital and invention are complementary to labour (*ibid.*, pp. 542, 665ff.), and serve to raise wages as well as income per head.

crowding be avoided through a suitable distribution of economic activities and population. Then, and only then, was population growth likely to be accompanied by rising wages, rising income per head, and increased satisfaction issuing out of increasing return in terms of output as a whole.

Wealth per head had been growing since the seventeenth century and was likely to continue to grow, since man's capacity for deferred gratification had grown; he had gradually become "more willing to sacrifice ease or other enjoyment in order to obtain them in the future." As a result of his improved "'telescopic' faculty" man

> is more prudent, and has more self-control, and is therefore more inclined to estimate at a high rate future ills and benefits—these terms being used broadly to include the highest and lowest affections of the human mind. He is more unselfish, and therefore more inclined to work and save in order to secure a future provision for his family; and there are already faint signs of a brighter time to come, in which there will be a general willingness to work and save in order to increase the stores of public wealth and of public opportunities for leading a higher life.[86]

It was not likely, Marshall's sociological analysis suggests, that men, having acquired this improved estimate of the future and the thriftiness that goes along with it, would easily relinquish their savings habits. It was essential, however, that there be security, that wealth not be consumed by great wars, and that an end be made to the "'Achilles' heel' of Britain's industries," the restriction of output by British workers; otherwise the "middle and upper classes," in whose hands the task of capital formation lay for the greater part, would not provide the required capital.[87] In fact, "if the motives and op-

86. PE, p. 680 (not in 1st ed.; in 4th ed., pp. 679–80). See also, on the slow development of thriftiness, PE, pp. 224–30 (289–96 in 1st ed.). Marshall considered family affection a chief motive to saving (PE, pp. 228–29), but he did not, as did J. A. Schumpeter (*Business Cycles,* New York, 1939, pp. 699, 1035–36), therefore infer that with the spread of childlessness and very small families much of the drive toward saving would be eliminated.

87. IT, pp. 641n., 648–50; PE, pp. 236, 320. Given "anti-social contrivances for stinting output," capital would emigrate to places where a better return was to be had. See PE, pp. 699–700. Lower rates of return would result in lower rates of saving, since, as a rule, "the higher the rate of interest the greater the saving." *Ibid.,* p. 234. While Marshall noted that the shift "from investment as material capital to investment as personal capital" was reducing the relative scarcity of "trained ability" and so reducing its relative but not its absolute earnings, he did not weigh the impact of this effect upon saving. *Ibid.,* pp. 681–82. Elsewhere Marshall observed (in 1887) "that the great economic feature of this age, more important than every other fact put together, is that the amount of capital is increasing many times as fast as that of population"; and he did "not see any necessity at all why interest should be more than 2 per cent. a century hence." See OP, p. 49. He did not analyse the impact of the heavy outflow of capital upon the developing economies, nor inquire into the comparative advantage to Britain of home and foreign investment under various conditions. However, see *Money, Credit and Commerce,* London 1923, pp. 135–37; also pp. 202–03, where he notes that emigration from old to new countries expands the market for the products of old countries, but disregards the complementary relation existing between the emigration of capital and that of men. He does not refer to the estimates of Flux (1907) or C. K. Hobson (1914) though he does touch upon aspects of Giffen's.

portunities for the accumulation of private capital in Britain were considerably reduced," the supply of material appliances might be so reduced that income per head would fall.[88] Marshall supposed, however, that "as a matter of fact an increase of population is likely to continue to be accompanied by a more than proportionate increase of the material aids to production."[89]

So far as raw produce was concerned, an old country almost certainly must, if her numbers continued to grow, become increasingly dependent upon external sources, since "improved knowledge and methods" could not continue to contend successfully "against Nature's resistance to the demands made on her by an increasing population."[90] Britain had long since found recourse necessary to the importation of produce, the British worker not having derived much advantage from the industrial revolution until the removal of trade barriers and the improvement of transport had cheapened his food and freed him of the burden of rising food costs. It was the availability abroad of agricultural products at prices sufficiently low and sufficiently stable, together with the operation of increasing returns in transport and communication generally, that had enabled the growing British population to derive advantage from the operation of increasing return in manufactures and other activities and to experience a great improvement in real income after the repeal of the Corn Laws.[91]

> In the present age, the opening out of new countries, aided by low transport charges on land and sea, has almost suspended the tendency to Diminishing Return, in that sense in which the term was used by Malthus and Ricardo. . . . And yet, if the growth of population should continue for very long even at a quarter of its present rate, the aggregate rental values of land for all its uses . . . may again exceed the aggregate of in-

88. IT, p. 649. Marshall's argument resembles somewhat that of K. E. Boulding, "The Fruits of Progress and the Dynamics of Distribution," *American Economic Review*, vol. XLIII (2), May, 1953, pp. 482–83.

89. PE, p. 321 (p. 380 in 1st ed.). He anticipated no dearth of demand for capital; for on all sides there are "openings . . . all of which will tend to change the character of our social and industrial life, and . . . enable us to turn to account vast stores of capital in providing new gratifications and new ways of economising effort by expending it in anticipation of distant wants." He saw no capital-full stationary state in the offing. See *ibid.*, p. 223, and note indicating how much capital would be required merely "to enable a large part of the population to live in towns and yet to be free from many of the present evils of town life."

90. While he believed that the rate of invention would continue for several centuries as in the first two decades of the twentieth century, he indicated that he could not forecast whether returns in agriculture would rise, fall, or remain constant. See IT, pp. 159, 189; also PE, p. 138, on the importance of knowledge as an agent of production.

91. PE, pp. 321–22, 671–75, 691–93; IT, pp. 649–50n., 749–62. See Colin Clark, *op. cit.*, 1st ed., p. 256, on operation of diminishing return before the repeal of the Corn Laws. "Probably more than three-fourths of the whole benefit she has derived from the progress of manufactures during the nineteenth century has been through its indirect influences in lowering the cost of transport of men and goods, of water and light, of electricity and news: for the dominant economic fact of our own age is the development not of the manufacturing, but of the transport industries. . . . It is they also which have done by far the most towards increasing England's wealth." PE, pp. 674–75 (pp. 718–19 in 1st ed.).

come derived from all other forms of material property; even though that may then embody twenty times as much labour as now.[92]

But would food and raw materials continue to be available on satisfactory terms? Were Torrens's fears to be realised sooner than he anticipated? While Marshall sometimes expressed optimism,[93] he observed that if this influx was checked by the trade regulations of other countries, or should heavy military and naval expenditures have to be made to guard this influx, much of the advantage Britain "derives from the action of the law of increasing return" would be lost.[94] It was likely that the terms of trade would turn against Britain in time, as the result of the rise of competitor countries exporting products similar to those exported by Britain, of the development of manufactures in countries that formerly imported them from Britain, and of the operation of diminishing returns in food and raw-material exporting countries as their domestic requirements increased. He pointed to the case of Germany and America, to the rise of Japan, to other potentially industrial powers, and to the fact that it was much easier to introduce manufacturing processes developed abroad than to pioneer them as Britian had.[95] It was essential, therefore, that Britain overcome her self-complacency and guard herself against foreign competition by maintaining her position as an industrial leader.

> Britain can obtain her necessary supplies of food and material only by continued leadership in those industries which make large use of the most expensive mechanical appliances: that is in those industries which have the greatest need of the bold, judicious, unfettered undertaking of grave risks under difficult and ever-changing conditions.[96]

Concerning the available supply of food and raw materials, Marshall regarded the "future of England with grave anxiety" though he saw no "pros-

92. PE, preface, pp. xv–xvi (also in preface to 6th ed.); also p. 679 on the increase in aggregate rent already experienced. Adam Smith, Malthus, Ricardo, and J. S. Mill were pessimistic in part because they did not foresee these changes. See *ibid.*, pp. 177. 180; M, p. 316; OP, "Fiscal Policy . . . .," pp. 402–03.

93. E.g., see PE, p. 166 (pp. 217–18 in 1st ed.), where he says: "In spite of the law of diminishing return, the pressure of population on the means of subsistence may be restrained for a long time to come by the opening up of new fields of supply, by the cheapening of railway and steamship communication, and by the growth of organisation and knowledge."

94. PE, pp. 321–22. The dangers attendant upon a population's becoming significantly dependent upon raw produce of foreign provenience, emphasised by Malthus (*Essay . . . on Population,* book III. 9), had been stressed by a number of German economists (e.g., see Lujo Brentano's analysis of the problem in his *Die Schrecken des überwiegenden Industriestaats,* Berlin, 1902). England was not in a position to take reprisals against foreign tariffs and other adverse measures, being more dependent than ever upon "external supplies of food and materials" which could best be obtained under conditions of free trade. See IT, p. 650; OP, pp. 408–12; Marshall's letter to the secretary of the Unionist Free Food League, *The Times,* Nov. 23, 1903.

95. See PE, pp. 674–75; OP, pp. 397–99, 401–404; IT, book I, chaps. 7–8. Around the mid-nineteenth century Britain had encountered little competition in foreign markets (*Money, Credit and Commerce,* pp. 119–20).

96. IT, pp. 647ff., OP, pp. 404–06.

pect of any immediate danger."[97] Writing of Mill's chapter on the "Influence of the Progress of Industry and Population, on Rents, Profits and Wages,"[98] Marshall declared:

> A century hence the substance of that chapter may seem more modern than it does to-day; for at the present rate of growth the whole world will be fully peopled ere many generations are passed. But just at present the acreage of fertile land, from which the nations of Western Europe can conveniently draw their supplies of raw produce, is increasing much faster than the population; and in this bright interval the outlines of the influence of progress on distribution and exchange are freed from that particular black shadow.[99]

For when most of the raw-material exporting countries had acquired enough capital both to develop "their abundant resources" and to set up steel and other industries; when they had experienced great increase in population and hence in domestic raw-material requirements; and when, therefore, but few sellers with "surplus raw products" remained; then these sellers would possess "an unassailable monopoly" which would enable them to impose extremely onerous trading terms upon countries as densely peopled as England.[100] Presumably, even in the absence of the establishment of such monopoly England's situation would worsen, since the terms of trade tended to turn against rich countries whose import requirements were expanding; while younger nations, as they became more densely peopled and developed efficient internal transport systems, tended to become skilled in certain manufactures, to export these, and even to import raw materials.[101]

In view of the fact that resources were limited and that, for this and other reasons, undue multiplication would affect the welfare of some individuals adversely, it was essential that premature and improvident marriage be avoided and that a growth of population so rapid as to be "an evil" be averted. Presumably both these undesirable outcomes would be avoided

97. OP, p. 402.

98. See J. S. Mill, *Principles*, book IV, chap. 3. Marshall considered this "the most advanced and modern part" of Mill's work. See M, p. 316.

99. M, p. 316; see also OP, pp. 383ff., 401ff.

100. OP, pp. 401–02. His discussion of the possibility of air conditioning in the tropics suggests that he may have regarded these also as an important potential though transient source of raw materials. See IT, p. 162.

101. *Money, Credit and Commerce*, pp. 112, 125, 163–64, 168–69. Marshall (perhaps under the influence of German economists who expected foreign trade to diminish in importance) anticipated the opinion of Colin Clark and others that the demand for the product of tertiary industries rises faster in a progressive economy than that for the output of primary and secondary industries; and so he expected that the advent of an adverse turn in the terms of trade would be retarded but not prevented by the tendency of Englishmen to spend an increasing proportion of their income on services. See OP, p.407, also PE, p. 276. After World War I, J. M. Keynes stressed the importance of this adverse turn in the terms of trade for Britain and Europe in *The Economic Consequences of the Peace*, New York, 1920, chap. 2, and found therein evidence of overpopulation, evidence which was challenged by Sir William Beveridge. On the controversy and the literature, see Rostow, *op. cit.*, pp. 184–88. See also our earlier reference to Torrens, one of the first to develop the Marshall-Keynes type of argument.

if everyone acted on the principle that "just as a man who has borrowed money is bound to pay it back with interest, so is a man bound to give his children an education better and more thorough than he himself received," together with a "lot in life, happier and better than his own." For then "society" could see "that no child grows up in ignorance," the requirements of bodily nurture would be met within the family, population would be "retained within due limits," and the labour market would no longer be crowded with unskilled job-seekers. "Such a state of society . . . would then, if once attained, be ever maintained."[102] He did not, however, approve "the rather violent checks to population which have recently appeared in some strata of some Anglo-Saxon peoples," checks which he attributed in part to selfishness;[103] and, though he "strongly supported Malthusian doctrines, he disappointed orthodox Malthusians by saying nothing in favour of limitation of births."[104]

Though Marshall recognised that a country's population might be too large or too small, he made no use of the concept of an optimum. Presumably, had he done so, he would have concluded that experienced technological and other changes had tended to modify the optimum magnitude, even though he might have supposed that, under sufficiently less dynamic conditions, the optimum magnitude would have tended to remain constant. He indicated that wealth per head would grow faster if population grew more slowly, but he did not advocate slower growth on this ground. While he did not say that income per head ought to increase as rapidly as possible, he did say that it was not sufficient merely for it to rise; it was essential also that the evils of urban overcrowding be avoided, and that there be sufficient room, fresh air, light, access to beautiful scenery and space for recreation, and so on. The solution for overcrowding consisted primarily, however, in the achievement of a suitable distribution of population in space rather than in a limitation of its overall size.[105] Presumably, Marshall did not find the optimum concept sufficiently determinable and conduct-affecting to be useful. He apparently believed some population growth to be good, as a rule, and he seems to have looked upon a population's growth as being in large measure a resultant, along with the behaviour of its economy, of its underlying habits, customs, institutions, ethical standards, and moral values.[106]

102. M, pp. 114–18. This was written in 1873. See also PE, pp. 166, 202–03, 320, 691–92, and discussion in next section.

103. M, pp. 459–60; written in 1909.

104. M, p. 501; this is a summary of a lecture given in *The Malthusian*, Oct., 1885. The reporter understood Marshall to say "that it would be a calamity if we English, by limiting our numbers, allowed foreigners to have a larger share than ourselves in peopling the world; and there was no need to fear the effects of our prospective increase at home."

105. PE, pp. 88, 107, 166, 199–200, 203, 321, 659; M, pp. 142–51, on housing the London poor, published in 1884.

106. Commenting on the slow growth of the French population, he said that he did "not regard a moderate retardation of the growth of population as a great social and industrial evil

III. Population Growth, Living Standards, Etc.

While Marshall made relatively little reference to the works of demographers[107] he did present some statistical information on the progress of population growth, always in Book IV, Chapter 4, which underwent little change in post-1890 editions. In the first edition the movement of the British population in 1086–1700 is tabulated, and this table appears as late as in the sixth edition, but not in the eighth. A table summarizing the growth of the English population by decade, between 1700 and 1881–1901, appears in all editions. In the first edition marriage, birth, death, natural increase, annual increase, nuptiality, infant mortality, and illegitimacy rates are presented for European countries and Massachusetts. In the fourth edition changes between 1865–83 and 1887–91 in marriage rates, natality, mortality, and actual and natural annual rates of increase are reported; and it is noted, among other things, that "the marriage rate, the birth rate and the death rate are diminishing in almost every country" even though the age at marriage has been falling in many of these countries.[108] This information is no longer presented in tabular form in the sixth or the eighth editions, but these do include a table on the movement of English urban and rural natality (not included in the first or the fourth editions).

Describing man as both the "chief means" and the "ultimate aim" of the production of wealth, and believing that poverty, together with its cumulative and degrading effects, could be abolished, Marshall found it necessary to deal at length with man's propensity to multiply, to the lack of restraint of which it had been customary since Malthus's time to trace mass poverty.[109] The opinions of men concerning population had varied through time, reflecting in part variation in the current effective demand for manpower.

---

in itself"; but he noted that it might be an effect of "national decadence" produced in part by such French institutions as the law of equal inheritance, the dowry system, the seniority system in governmental employment, and so on, all of which made for avoidance of risk, of creative and energy-requiring enterprise, and so on. M, pp. 459–61. See also IT, pp. 114ff.; and discussion of the genesis of standards in the next section.

107. He refers to Bertillon, Bodio and Rawson in the first edition; to Hooker, Booth, Cannan (on Malthus), Körösi, Levasseur, and Ravenstein in the eighth edition; to Darwin, Farr, Galton, Leroy-Beaulieu, and Ogle in both. There is no reference to the writings of authors such as Newsholme, Stevenson, Yule, and so on, or to Cannan's forecasts.

108. PE, 4th ed., 1898, pp. 269–70; it is noted (*ibid.*) that high mortality and high natality are usually associated. See also PE, 8th ed., pp. 191–92; 1st ed., p. 241.

109. PE, pp. 2–3, 35, 173. Marshall, as Pigou reports (in *Alfred Marshall and Current Thought*, London, 1953, p. 65; also M, p. 37), was "a mixture of philanthropist and scientist." Poverty was largely responsible for the existence of "the Residuum" which was made up predominantly of unemployables; and it contributed to the under-development of the faculties of the "vast numbers" composing the group just above "the Residuum." Yet, given changed activities which would give rise to new wants, membership in both these groups could be reduced; in fact it was declining under the impact of economic progress. See PE, pp. 2–3, 89–90, 714–15. Also OP, p. 205; also note 161 and text below. Cp. Marshall's treatment with V. Pareto's (e.g., *Manuel d'économie politique*, Paris, 1909, pp. 386, 393).

In his *Essay* Malthus (who was responding to unacceptable ideological and adverse economic events) correctly demonstrated that the growth of numbers would have been very great in the absence of diverse checks; but, failing to foresee the great increase in the access England and other old countries would have to "the products of the richest lands of the earth at comparatively small cost," he exaggerated the inability of a "very thickly peopled" territory to obtain raw produce and materials. But even so, unless there was an increase in the checks on population growth "in force" around 1900, it would "be impossible for the habits of comfort prevailing in Western Europe to spread themselves over the whole world and maintain themselves for many hundred years."[110] It was on somewhat different grounds, however, that Marshall advocated what amounts to moral restraint. For while he believed that "the State gains much from large families of healthy children," he supposed that since many parents could better rear children under small-family conditions, they ought to preserve such conditions. If children were brought up under conditions conducive to strength and vigour, "the increase of numbers will not for a long time to come cause a diminution of the average real income of the people."[111]

Marshall's treatment of the checks may be divided into (i) that pertaining to the socio-economic and other conditions underlying the behaviour of mortality and natality, and (ii) that pertaining to mortality and natality as such. (i) Whereas among animals natural increase was governed entirely by present conditions, among men it was affected by regard for (and hence forecasts of) the future, by traditions of the past, and by the pressure society exercised "on the individual by religious, moral and legal sanctions, sometimes with the object of quickening, and sometimes with that of retarding, the growth of population." In every grade of society the birth rate was much influenced by "custom and opinion" (themselves "the outcome of the experience of past generations"), but not so much by "deliberate calculations of the future." He believed with Levasseur that economic conditions and natality were not directly but indirectly inter-connected, "through the mutual influence of the two on manners and the habit of life." Mortality and nuptiality too were indirectly affected by economic conditions.

110. PE, pp. 173–80. With population increasing 8 per 1,000 a year, with the equivalent of about 30 million square miles of "fairly fertile land" in the world, and allowing for "great improvements in the arts of agriculture, . . . the pressure of population on the means of subsistence may be held in check for about two hundred years, but not longer." For by 2,090 the world's population would approximate six billions, or about 200 per square mile of fairly fertile land. *Ibid.,* p. 180n. (not in 1st ed., but in 4th, p. 257).

111. PE, pp. 202–203. "It seems *prima facie* advisable that people should not bring children into the world till they can see their way to giving them at least as good an education both physical and mental as they themselves had; and that it is best to marry moderately early provided there is sufficient self-control to keep the family within requisite bounds without transgressing moral laws." *Ibid.,* 202 (p. 258 in 1st ed.) See M, pp. 116–17, and note 102 and text above; also Marshall's lecture on Henry George's economic ideas, *Bristol Times and Mirror,* March 6, 1883; also *Economics of Industry,* 2nd ed., p. 32.

Thus economic causes play a part in governing the growth of population as a whole as well as the supply of labour in any particular grade. But their influence on the numbers of the population as a whole is largely indirect; and is exerted by way of the ethical, social and domestic habits of life. For the habits are themselves influenced by economic causes deeply, though slowly, and in ways some of which are difficult to trace, and impossible to predict.[112]

Among economic conditions which affected population growth was what Mombert was later to call *"Nahrungsspielraum,"*[113] whereon depended, directly and indirectly, nature's demand for population.[114] This condition had been made much more favourable to population growth initially by the industrial revolution[115] and subsequently by improvements in transport and trade which brought cheap wheat to England from abroad.[116] In consequence population growth was no longer checked, as in the early nineteenth century, "by the difficulty of obtaining raw produce," but by the difficulty of obtaining "gratifications which contributed but little to the maintenance of life and efficiency."[117] Food was no longer the limitational factor, though it might again be "when the wheatfields of the world were worked at their full power."[118]

Turning now to (ii) mortality and natality we find Marshall attributing the steady decline in mortality to the increased application of cumulating medical and related scientific knowledge and to the growth of wealth and the easing of both want of food and urban overcrowding.[119] Legitimate natal-

112. PE, pp. 218 (p. 298 in 4th ed.; cp. pp. 278–83 in 1st ed.), 173, 572; also M, pp. 460–61 and PE, p. 185n. (where the findings of Levasseur and Le Play respecting the impact of French inheritance law are considered). Marshall believed that inheritance laws could significantly influence the course of a nation's development. See PE, pp. 740, 742; IT, pp. 113–115. Pareto treats the influence of economic conditions on population growth in a manner somewhat similar to that of Marshall. See my "Pareto on Population," *Quarterly Journal of Economics,* vol. LVIII, 1944, pp. 577–78.

113. See Paul Mombert, *Bevölkerungslehre,* Jena, 1929, *passim;* see part I, p. 272.

114. "The produce which Nature returns to the work of man is here effective demand for population." See PE, p. 178.

115. This revolution, towards the end of the eighteenth century, "broke up the old traditions of industry," stimulated "an increase of population for which no provision had been made beyond standing room in factories and workshops," and "set free competition . . . loose," producing both increased efficiency and great evils. See PE, pp. 11, 747–48.

116. PE, pp. xv, 177, 180, 672ff., 691ff. (p. 45 in 1st ed.) where he observes that despite these improvements "even now, if wealth were distributed equally, the total production of the country would only suffice to provide necessaries and the more urgent comforts for the people, and that as things are, many have barely the necessaries of life." See also *Economics of Industry,* 2nd ed., p. 31.

117. PE, pp. 166, 530, 690–91.

118. PE, p. 692, also 166. Compare Jevons who argued in effect that coal had replaced corn as a primary if not the major population-limiting factor, and that the limitational role of coal would be increasingly felt as its cost of extraction rose under the double impact of increasing coal consumption and decreasing coal resources. See *The Coal Question,* 3rd ed., London, 1906, chap. 9; the same chapter is found in the 2nd ed., 1866.

119. PE, pp. 50, 188–89, 195–96, 198, 200, 203.

ity (which usually comprised over nine-tenths of all natality) depending predominantly upon how many married and at what age,[120] Marshall dealt largely with the circumstances affecting these determinants.[121] Age at marriage tended to be lower in warm climates; it varied, climate being given, with "the ease with which young people can establish themselves, and support a family according to the standard of comfort" prevailing among their friends and acquaintances and characteristic of their station in life. It was relatively high in some groups (e.g., the middle classes, the well-to-do, peasant proprietors, persons engaged in "high mental work") and in places where institutional or customary hindrances to early marriage existed (e.g., in mediaeval and some contemporary communities); it was relatively low in other groups (e.g., artisans, persons making little provision for the future, and, above all, unskilled labourers and American farmers) and in places (e.g., towns) where few or no institutional hindrances to early marriage existed. Marriage rates fluctuated with economic conditions, varying inversely with the price of wheat so long as the working classes spent half or more of their income on bread, and now that bread absorbed less than one-fourth of working-class income, with the level of "commercial prosperity."[122]

Just as increases in the price of labour usually evoked effort in the short run and always produced more vigour and efficiency in the somewhat longer run,[123] so did they tend to stimulate natality and augment the supply of labour in the long run, unless, as was possible, a "permanent increase in prosperity" served eventually to diminish natality more than mortality.[124]

120. Marshall noted (in PE), as had Galton, that marital selection sometimes made for comparative infecundity in the families of English peers (p. 183) and that fecundity tended to be diminished by "severe mental strain" and "luxurious habits of living" (p. 185); but he did not accept Spencer's view that "reproductive power" was less in civilized than in barbarous races, or Doubleday's view that want stimulated fecundity (184n.). But in the 4th ed., p. 261n., Miss J. L. Brownell's study of American data prompted Marshall to write that "on the whole the facts seem to support Herbert Spencer's position."

121. He refers to the practice of family limitation as common among peasant proprietors (PE, p. 183; 1st ed., p. 232) and "in some strata of some Anglo-Saxon peoples" (M, p. 460).

122. On marriage see PE, pp. 180–83, 186–92, 684–85. Marshall indicated that while urban fertility was below rural fertility in England, both urban and rural fertility fell at about the same rate in 1870–1902 (PE, p. 184). He noted that since informal unions tended to become legalized, average age at legal marriage somewhat exceeded average age at de facto marriage.

123. PE, pp. 195–96, 217–18, 510, 532, 562–63, 693–95. Even as the effects of poverty were cumulative and self-perpetuating so were the effects of increases in the incomes of workers. Ibid., pp. 248, 562–63, 569. Smith, Ricardo, Malthus, and Mill had overlooked something that the American economists emphasized, namely, the tendency of high wages to increase the efficiency of workers and their descendants. Ibid., pp. 508, 510, 550n. Because the marginal private benefit of investment in the instruction of children and training of workers fell short of its marginal social benefit, investment in instruction and training was not carried far enough, particularly in the lower ranks of society. Ibid., pp. 207ff., 211, 216–17, 561–66. "The main concern of economics," Marshall said in the sixth edition (p. ix), is "with human beings."

124. PE, p. 529 (p. 600 in 4th ed.; not in 1st ed.). However, the aggregate effect of a wage increase was an increase in the supply of labour, Marshall apparently believed, since the re-

There existing for "each grade of work" (or trade) "a certain consumption which is strictly necessary for efficiency," together with "conventional necessaries" and "habitual comforts," — that is, "a supply-price" —

> the question how closely the supply of labour responds to the demand for it, is in great measure resolved into the question how great a part of the present consumption of the people at large consists of necessaries, strictly so called, for the life and efficiency of young and old; how much consists of conventional necessaries which theoretically could be dispensed with, but practically would be preferred by the majority of the people to some of those things that were really necessary for efficiency; and how much is really superfluous regarded as a means towards production, though of course part of it may be of supreme importance regarded as an end in itself.[125]

As matters stood in most parts of the world, the standard of living was very low and increases in the earnings of workers tended quickly to increase their numbers and restore their wages nearly to previously existing levels.

> Over a great part of the world wages are governed, nearly after the so-called iron or brazen law, which ties them close to the cost of rearing and sustaining a rather inefficient class of labourers. . . .[126]
>
> It remains true that, taking man as he is, and has been hitherto, in the western world the earnings that are got by efficient labour are not much above the lowest that are needed to cover the expenses of rearing and training efficient workers, and of sustaining and bringing into activity their full energies.[127]

Marshall was not pessimistic, however, with respect to the Western world, for he believed that with the rise of the free enterprise system there had been associated the development of capacity for forethought, together with various qualities, values, and activities which were freeing man and would keep him free from the trap in which Malthus had found him enmeshed. He did not espouse Mill's thesis that only large improvements in

---

sulting increase in efficiency and decrease in mortality would more than offset any decline in natality attributable to the wage increase. *Ibid.,* pp. 529, 532.

125. PE, p. 530 (p. 601 in 4th ed.; not in 1st ed., but see pp. 555–56), also pp. 68–69, 572, 691. Presumably, since "the fluidity of labour is sufficient to make it true that the wages of labour of the same industrial grade or rank tend to equality in different occupations throughout the same western country," the standard of living and the supply price of labour tended to equality within each such grade or rank. *Ibid.,* p. 539; also pp. 218–19n., 547.

126. PE, pp. 530–31 (p. 602 in 4th ed.); also pp. 505–06n., 508–09, 690–91, 826. In the first edition only Ricardo's version is treated. See also *Economics of Industry,* 2nd ed., pp. 28, 29, 102–03, 129–31.

127. PE, p. 531 (p. 602 in 4th ed.; not in 1st ed.). "But in fact it is probable that not one-tenth of the present populations of the world have the mental and moral faculties, the intelligence, and the self-control that are required for [manufactures]: perhaps not one-half could be made to do the work well by steady training for two generations." PE, pp. 205–06 (p. 262 in 1st ed.).

the condition of the labouring classes were likely to prove permanent.[128] Instead he reasoned that economic evolution must necessarily proceed gradually. "Progress must be slow." *Natura non facit saltum.*[129] For while man was pliable and his nature was subject to modification, his habits changed very gradually and his nature improved slowly, and their rates of change set limits to the rate at which man's institutions could undergo enduring change.[130]

It was because many kinds of change, for the better as well as for the worse, produced cumulative effects in man and in his culture that small changes, especially if repeated, could in time bring about significant modifications in what men did. Thus improvements in earnings or in environment tended to augment the productivity of the currently affected generation and to elevate the level of life from which the next generation would take off; deterioration of earnings or environment had an opposite effect. Furthermore, "when the effects of a cause, though small at any one time, are constantly working in the same direction, their influence is much greater than at first sight appears possible."[131] Given this cumulative tendency and the fact that in the Western world there were operative various causes which acted to initiate upward movements in the standard of living, it was probable that this standard would continue to rise.[132]

Marshall distinguished three standards. (*a*) A minimum efficiency standard embraced only that which was physiologically or conventionally essential to the efficiency of a member of some grade of labour, together with his family.[133] (*b*) A "standard of comfort" embraced "conventional necessaries,"

128. See his references to the Black Death, etc., in PE, pp. 174–75, 186–87. In IT, pp. 705–08, the contribution of the Black Death to the breaking up of the structure of mediaeval society is noticed, but not Mill's thesis.

129. Darwin had endorsed this canon of natural history (enunciated as early as 1613), in *The Origin of Species* (chap. 6); though Marshall always used it as a maxim, he did not insert it into book IV, chap. 8, until after the 4th ed. See PE, pp. 248–49; 6th ed., p. VII, where he says that "Economic evolution is gradual. Its progress is sometimes arrested or reversed by political catastrophes: but its forward movements are never sudden; for even in the Western world and in Japan it is based on habit, partly conscious, partly unconscious."

130. PE, pp. 205–06, 218, 224–25, 248–49, 720–21, 751–52, 762–64. This view is present in the 1st ed.

131. PE, p. 728 (p. 16 in 1st ed.), also pp. 248–49, 559–60, 562; also IT, pp. 197–200, 797–98; also *The Pure Theory of Foreign Trade* (1879), sect. 7. "In sociology as well as in biology we are learning to watch the accumulated effects of forces, which, though weak at first, get greater strength from the growth of their own effects; and the universal form, of which every such fact is a special embodiment, is Taylor's theorem." See PE, p. 844 (p. 742 in 1st ed.).

132. He observed that wants increased and activities changed with the progress of civilization and invention; that tastes tended to change with the passage of time; that even in a stationary economy the standard of living could change as a result of non-economic causes; that ideals changed for non-economic as well as economic reasons; that the habit of discounting the future at a low rate, a habit "at once a chief product and a chief cause of civilization," tended to develop in modern industrial nations among whose peoples "self-reliance, independence, deliberate choice and forethought" flourished. See PE, pp. 5, 86–89, 94, 197–98, 216–17, 542, 577. The disposition to change was greater than formerly (*ibid.*, p. 213).

that is, "gratifications which contributed but little to the maintenance of life and efficiency," together with "that which was necessary for life and efficiency." (*c*) The term "standard of life" referred to

> the standard of activities adjusted to wants. Thus a rise in the standard of life implies an increase of intelligence and energy and self-respect; leading to more care and judgment in expenditure, and to an avoidance of food and drink that gratify the appetite but afford no strength, and of ways of living that are unwholesome physically and morally. A rise in the standard of life for the whole population will much increase the national dividend, and the share which accrues to each grade and to each trade.[134]

A mere increase in wants would not make for a rise in wages unless it operated directly to diminish the supply of labour, or indirectly to increase "activities" and otherwise raise the "standard of life." A rise in the "standard of comfort" would probably increase wages both by making the labour supply less than it otherwise would have been and by elevating the "standard of life" and opening the "way to new and higher activities" and an improved "condition of the people." Most to be desired was an improvement in the "standard of life," for after it had exerted its full effect on the efficiency of the workers, "their increased energy, intelligence and force of character would enable them" to do more in a lesser amount of time and hence produce a larger amount of income and wealth per head.[135]

Marshall's discussion of the several standards reflects his underlying view that what is of greatest significance is not wants but activities, not the goods and services men may seek but the uses they make of their time and resources. On these uses ultimately depended the extent to which societies would progress as well as remain free of the evils of overpopulation.

> While wants are the rulers of life among the lower animals, it is to changes in the forms of efforts and activities that we must turn when in search for the keynotes of the history of mankind. . . . It is, again, the desire for the exercise and development of activities, spreading through every rank of society, which leads . . . to the pursuit of science, . . . art. . . . Although it is man's wants in the earliest stages of his development that give rise to his activities, yet afterwards each new step upwards is to be regarded as the development of new activities giving rise to new wants, rather than of new wants giving rise to new activities. . . . If either, more than the other, may claim to be the interpreter of the history of man . . .

133. PE, pp. 68–70, 529–31. With Talcott Parsons (*The Structure of Social Action*, New York, 1937, pp. 139–40) we may reduce the wants listed by Marshall into three categories: biological needs; non-biological needs whose satisfaction makes for increase in strength, efficiency, etc.; gross, artificial wants whose satisfaction does not augment strength, efficiency, etc. See PE, pp. 67–70, 87–89, 689.

134. PE, pp. 689–91 (not in 1st ed.; pp. 777–78 in 4th ed.), also pp. 504, 529–30. The "standard of life" obviously included children.

135. PE, pp. 689–94. The British trade unions originally had been almost as much concerned to improve the "standard of life" as to secure wage increases (*ibid.*, pp. 703–04).

it is the science of activities and not that of wants. . . . The true key-note of economic progress is the development of new activities rather than of new wants.[136]

Marshall's account of the role of activities[137] in socio-economic evolution implies that wants are not independent, constant, or the sole objects of activities; that they undergo change in number and content; and that therefore their satisfaction is not subject to maximization.[138]

Marshall's emphasis upon activities makes it difficult to specify the objects of economic and related behaviour. Activities had as their immediate objects both further activities and the satisfaction of supposedly essential wants. Activities also had more ultimate objects. These objects, it seems valid to infer from his discussion, included the exercise and development of man's faculties and qualities, the improvement of his "standard of life," the enrichment of life, and the carrying forward of evolution itself. The goodness of employments, of modes of poor relief, of systems of economic organization, and so on, turned significantly upon the degree to which they furthered these ends.[139] Had Marshall sought to define an optimum population, he would have had to formulate it in terms of activities and their objectives. He could not have expressed himself merely in terms of a point of maximum returns. It is for this reason presumably that he gave no attention to the optimum concept, that he remained content to suppose a satisfactory solu-

136. PE, pp. 85, 88–90, 689. The discussion of wants and activities does not appear in the 1st ed.; it appears in the 4th ed., pp. 160–65, 777, which differs little from the 3rd. Marshall, of course, rejected the view of Jevons and Banfield that the theory of consumption constituted the scientific basis of economics, and the argument of Banfield that satisfaction of a lower want creates "a desire of a higher character." It was more accurate to say with McCulloch that "gratification of a want is merely a step to some new pursuit," to engagement in some new undertaking (PE, p. 90). Parsons treats at some length of Marshall's analysis of the roles of wants and activities. See *op. cit.*, chap. 4, pp. 452–54, 702–04.

137. According to Parsons (*op. cit.*, p. 703): "Both the wants adjusted to activities and the modes of activity themselves are to be regarded . . . as manifestations of a single, relatively well-integrated system of value attitudes. . . . Along with increasing rationality and the accumulation of empirical knowledge, the development of this value system becomes to him the primary moving force of social evolution."

138. But see PE, book v, chap. 13, where Marshall deals with maximization in essentially static terms. As Parsons has indicated, the presupposition of maximization, that ends are given and that resources are rationally directed to their satisfaction, no longer holds when ends are modified by the process of their attainment. See *op. cit.*, pp. 132–33, 702–03.

139. "Man's character has been moulded by his every-day work" (PE, p. 1). "Work in its best sense, the healthy energetic exercise of faculties, is the aim of life, is life itself" (M, p. 115, also pp. 310, 367). The "most economic use of man as an agent of production is wasteful if he is not himself developed by it." See PE, p. 265; also pp. 247–48. The schoolmaster's main duty "is to educate character, faculties and activities" (PE, p. 718). On the superiority of the free enterprise system to collectivistic systems with respect to the development of faculties, qualities, etc., see sect. IV below, PE, pp. 5–6, 246–48, 263, 309–10, 502, 713, 750–52; M, pp. 279–83; also Parsons, *op. cit.*, pp. 135, 143, 151–55, 158. On the question of poor relief see below, notes 162–163 and text. Marshall attached more weight to the formative influence of nature than did Marx when he asserted (in the preface to his *Critique of Political Economy*)

tion to the population problem would be realized under a progressive free-enterprise system.[140]

IV. Natural Selection, Competition, Migration, Location, Poverty

Marshall, much under the influence of Darwin,[141] Spencer, and others, devoted considerable attention to the selective processes operative in societies, among them economic competition, differential natural increase, and differential migration. The struggle for group survival functioned in a most salutary way when the impact of the struggle among individuals was sufficiently cushioned by inter-individual forms of mutual as well as of unilateral forms of aid whilst remaining guarded against extremer forms of parasitism. Concerning inter-racial competition he remarked that

> the struggle for existence causes in the long run those races of men to survive in which the individual is most willing to sacrifice himself for the benefit of those around him; and which are consequently the best adapted collectively to make use of their environment. . . . But on the whole, and subject to grave exceptions, those races survive and predominate in which the best qualities are most strongly developed.[142]

Concerning inter-individual and inter-group relations under so minute a division of labour as prevailed in the Western world Marshall was careful to indicate that although the pursuit of individual interest tended to contribute markedly to the benefit of mankind, this tendency was subject to notable exceptions (e.g., underinvestment in personal capital; underemphasis on the development of "the religious, the moral, the intellectual and the artistic faculties on which the progress of industry depends" as well as on the genesis and the role of the "well-ordered state"; underestimation of the degree to which contemporary industrial organization was susceptible of

---

that "the social existence" of men "determines their consciousness"; for Marshall observed that "man is himself largely formed by his surroundings, in which nature plays a great part" (PE, p. 139).

140. Parsons also subscribes to this conclusion. See *op. cit.*, pp. 159–60. Cp. my "Welfare Economics and the Problem of Overpopulation," *Scientia*, 1954.

141. See esp. *The Descent of Man*, 1871, chap. 5, where the selective influence of mortality, natality, and migration are treated.

142. PE, pp. 243–44 (pp. 303–04 in 1st ed.); IT, pp. 176–77. Marshall subsequently (IT, p. 681) described as "brilliant" Kropotkin's *Mutual Aid, a Factor of Evolution*, London, 1902. While Marshall slightly anticipated later views respecting the profit-guarding influence of differentiation, he did not note the competition-cushioning influence of division of labour remarked by Durkheim (see Parsons, *op. cit.*, p. 322). See PE, pp. 287, 458.

improvement).[143] Yet he found the effects of competition generally good,[144] and he noted that economic progress was relatively greatest in those branches of industry and in those countries where "natural selection" was most free to bring to the front persons especially capable of undertaking, organizing, and managing, and where individuals of very high ability had ready access to the upper ranks of the middle class.[145]

Reproductive selection, Marshall's analysis suggests, was producing three adverse effects. First, it was somewhat dysgenic in character, and could be improved by the "application of the principles of Eugenics."[146] Second, anticipating Pigou's succinct observation that "environments, in short, as well as people, have children,"[147] Marshall recognized that progress would be greater or less according as more or less children were born into better rather than into worse home environments, particularly since environmental influences were cumulative in character.[148] Third, he no more than implied, however, that if natural increase were relatively high among the unskilled and others, the demand for whose services was falling relatively to that for labour services in general,[149] and if, as was the case, given grades of labour tended to be recruited in large measure from the children of parents belonging thereto, the distribution of workers among occupations would become less satisfactory.[150]

Of the aspects of migration upon which Marshall touched, its selective effects received most attention. For migration, which tended to develop

143. PE, pp. 5–6, 9–10, 245–48, 561ff.; also M, pp. 237–40, 281–82. See also IT, p. 161, on the role of idealism, etc., in economic development, and pp. 174–77, on the role of "natural selection." On the place of egoism, altruism, and individual ethical responsibility in Marshall's system see Parsons, *op. cit.*, pp. 160–64.

144. "The action of competition, and the survival in the struggle for existence of those who know best how to extract the greatest benefits for themselves from the environment, tend in the long run to put the building of factories and steam-engines into the hands of those who will be ready and able to incur every expense which will add more than it costs to their value as productive agents." PE, p. 561 (pp. 589–90 in 1st ed.), also pp. 241–43.

145. PE, pp. 686n., 719, 745–46; also IT, pp. 141ff., 153ff., 358ff.; M, pp. 266–67, 282–83, 367, also 327–29. The same views appear in the 1st ed.

146. PE, pp. 201–03, 247–49. Marshall apparently did not subscribe to the view that medical progress was unduly reducing the selective influence of mortality (PE, pp. 200, 202, notes). The reference to eugenics is not in the 1st and 4th editions, but the essence of the argument is; it is in the 6th edition.

147. *Wealth and Welfare*, p. 59.

148. PE, pp. 2–3, 202, 207, 561–65, 569, 714–15, 720–21, 749. Much of this is in 1st ed. See also *Economics of Industry,* 2nd ed., pp. 102–03, 105–07, 130–31.

149. "Mere manual skill is losing importance relatively to general intelligence and vigour of character" whilst trained faculties "are ever rising in importance." See PE, pp. 206, 209, also pp. 212, 261, 716; but see pp. 258–59 on increases in mobility. These views appear in the 1st ed. See also *Economics of Industry,* 2nd ed., p. 57.

150. PE, pp. 181–85 on differential natality; also pp. 217–19, 258–60, 541, 571–73, 716–18; M, pp. 116–17. These views are in 1st ed. Adjustment was hindered by the fact that whereas methods of industry changed rapidly, the skill of a worker needed to be used for 40–50 years after he had acquired it (PE, p. 721). But see p. 716 where it is indicated that the relative number of unskilled had fallen and that of skilled had risen in the nineteenth century.

when the migrant could improve his situation sufficiently to compensate him for the hardships involved, tended to select and remove superior persons and persons of productive age.[151] The strong and the adventure-seeking tended to move from old countries to their colonies and to new countries.[152] From England's rural areas to her large towns and cities moved "the most enterprising, the most highly gifted, those with the highest *physique* and the strongest characters . . . there to find scope for their abilities."[153] From the South of England to the North "the strongest labourers" constantly migrated in the nineteenth century.[154] England owed the character of her population in part to selective migration, having been peopled "by the strongest members of the strongest races of northern Europe," by successive waves of the most daring and self-reliant migrants; and the seriousness of this character was subsequently "intensified" by French, Flemish, and other artisans and manufacturers who sought "safe asylum from religious persecution."[155] Migration tended to benefit the immigrant-receiving territory, for it sometimes brought in new knowledge and it relieved this territory of a part of the cost of equipping itself with population;[156] it tended to free the migrant of old and ineffective ways of doing things, to give urge to his creativity, and to enable him, if he had skill and energy, to rise to important positions; and it facilitated "the mixture of races."[157]

While Marshall listed a number of circumstances by which the location of

151. PE, pp. 68–69n., 151, 197, 199, 200, 279, 429–30. A small volume of internal migration served to prevent marked interregional wage differences within countries (*Money, Credit and Commerce*, pp. 7–8).

152. PE, p. 197; IT, pp. 142–46, 148–50. He noted (IT, pp. 149, 430 notes) that the cheapening of transport had reduced the cost of transoceanic migration, but did not say how much its selectivity had been diminished as a result.

153. PE, p. 199 (in 1st ed., M, 253–54). As a result improvements in agriculture came slowly. "For the most enterprising agriculturalists drift towards the town; those who stay behind live more or less isolated lives; and, as a result of natural selection and education, their minds have always been more staid than those of townsmen, and less ready to suggest or even to follow new paths." *Ibid.*, p. 649; also p. 654n., where he refers to "the great evil of the continued flow of the ablest and the bravest lads to the towns" where living conditions were not so conducive to good health. See also M, p. 147. Townward migration, which had been hindered in the Middle Ages by the rigidity of the mediaeval economy and in the century preceding 1760 by the slowness with which manufactures developed, flourished after 1760 with the acceleration of the development of manufactures. See PE, pp. 185–89, 199, also p. 11. Concerning the influence of invention on urbanward migration in the nineteenth century, see M, pp. 142–43.

154. PE, pp. 68–69n. (not in 1st ed.).

155. PE, pp. 740, 743–44 (in 1st ed.); IT, pp. 700–01, 708.

156. PE, pp. 269–70, 743–44 (in 1st ed.). After the early nineteenth century, immigrants rarely brought highly specialized skills with them; instead they fell in "with the industrial methods of their new home." See *Money, Credit and Commerce*, p. 8 and note. The capital-saving influence of immigration was not stressed by Marshall. See PE, pp. 564–65n.

157. PE, p. 197 and note (in 1st ed.); IT, pp. 147–50. Compare Colin Clark, *op. cit.*, 2nd ed., pp. 206–07, 245. In IT (p. 146), Marshall observed that the diversity of industrial aptitude of America's immigrant population had facilitated both invention and contentment with the use of semi-automatic machinery, whilst the diversity of its racial background, by preventing any group from becoming ascendant, had made for homogeneity in matters of consumption and hence for "an unrivalled market for standardized products."

economic activities and hence of population was affected,[158] his main concern was the avoidance of urban overcrowding with its denial of adequate air, light, repose out of doors, healthy recreation, and so on.[159] Accordingly, he favoured the decentralization of industry and population, in so far as practicable, to the suburbs, the smaller towns, and the new Garden cities;[160] for such movements would tend to improve the "standard of life."

The problem of poverty had replaced that of pauperism which had "reached its maximum" in the first third of the nineteenth century even as newer theories concerning its treatment had replaced those current in Malthus's day; and it was to be expected that the problem of poverty, being "a mere passing evil in the progress of man upwards," would itself disappear in time.[161] The object of measures for the relief of the poor was in so far as possible to improve the situation and "standard of life" of the poor, to increase their earning power and that of their descendants,[162] and to set in motion a cumulative upward movement. Generous and even lavish governmental aid was indicated, together with suitable sanitary, public health, educational, and worker-training measures.[163] It was no longer supposed as a century earlier, that intelligently conceived measures would stimulate natality on the balance or consume capital and depress wages.[164]

V. Conclusion

Marshall's views represent both a continuation of and a break with those of his predecessors, some but not all of which can be noticed in this incomplete summary. His treatment of the laws of returns as of the population-

158. Among the circumstances affecting the location of particular industries he emphasized "physical conditions" and the "character of the people, and . . . their social and political institutions." See PE, pp. 268–72; also IT, pp. 283–88. The development of steam power had fostered the concentration of manufacturing industries in the towns and cities (M, p. 142). See also PE, pp. 273–74.

159. PE, pp. 166, 203, 321, 659; M, pp. 143, 144, 149. These views are in the 1st ed.

160. PE, pp. 199–200. Marshall's paper (done in 1884) on housing the London poor gave impetus to the Garden City movement which got underway subsequently (M, p. 142). He indicated that a considerable fraction of the London labour force could carry on their work elsewhere (M, p. 146).

161. OP, pp. 199, 244–45; PE, p. 3. Early nineteenth century economic dogmas remained current in Poor Law literature, Marshall declared in 1893 (OP, p. 225). See his criticisms of eighteenth century settlement laws and poor relief measures (PE, pp. 177–78, 188–89, 226; OP, pp. 200–201).

162. OP, pp. 224–25, 227, 239–40, 248, 261. Intelligent concern for the poor had greatly increased, while changes in socio-economic organization had made necessary changes in the methods of dealing with the poor. (OP, pp. 237, 246–47). In *Economics of Industry*, 2nd ed., pp. 32–35, outdoor relief is criticized and Octavia Hill's rules are approved.

163. PE, pp. 715–19 (in 5th and later eds.); OP, pp. 200–204; M, pp. 386–87.

164. In 1897 he expressed concern, however, lest overkindness "to the children of the pauper class, relatively to those of the self-respecting poor, would directly frustrate nature's rule that the better strains of the population shall have a better chance of moving upwards and multiplying than the inferior strains have." (M, p. 403.)

limiting role of produce and raw materials is essentially in the classical tradition, serving as a bridge to the subsequent treatment of returns by Allyn Young, G. T. Jones, and Colin Clark. Emphasis upon the role of natural selection is pronounced in Marshall, as it was among many late nineteenth century writers under the influence of Darwin. What amounts to "standard of living" plays a role in Marshall's account of the long-run supply of labour similar to that which it played in the classical writers. Marshall breaks with the classical writers, however, when he introduces his new concept of a "standard of life" and therewith somewhat redefines the office of living standards and their influence upon earnings and the response of population and labour supply to increases in earnings. Marshall's neglect of the then newly developing concept of optimum population probably issued out of his definition of the ends of life in terms of this "standard of life" and out of his redefining the role of "activities" in consistence with this standard. In consequence he appears to neglect or underestimate the hidden costs of population growth; and he cannot embrace an approach such as Cannan's. Marshall gave relatively little attention to the dynamic aspects of the behaviour of living standards, a matter stressed by Mill and others, in part because he thought that the Western free-enterprise system was solving the population problem, and in part because he conceived of most if not all change in terms of the cumulation of small effects, themselves sometimes of increasing absolute magnitude. The relation supposedly obtaining between systems of poor relief and population growth is redefined in modern terms. While the evils of urban overcrowding are noted and protested against, no elaborate theory of optimizing population distribution is attempted, emphasis being placed primarily upon the need for decentralization and suburbanization. Far less importance is attached to the effects exercised upon population growth by changes in the price structure than to the effects produced by changes in income and in non-economic determinants of natality.

THEORY

Aspects of the Economics of Population Growth

> Man's industrial activities are merely a highly specialized . . . form of the general biological struggle for existence. . . . Dissipation must in some way be balanced if the regime is to continue.[1]

Malthus, in his famous essay on population, dealt primarily with the reproductive response of man to an increase in the supply of things available for his support and with the reaction of man as a producer and capital-former to an increase in his numbers.[2] Malthus's account of man's reproductive response to his changing situation has proved inadequate, at least in respect to a considerable portion of mankind. His apprehensions regarding the probable effect of increasing numbers upon aggregate and per capita production have not been realized in culturally advanced states. In recent years, therefore, there has developed a disposition on the part of contemporary social scientists, particularly on the part of those who look upon themselves as "population experts," to underrate Malthus's very real contributions to the setting and the formation of "population theory."

Although this disposition to misunderstand Malthus is not important in itself, it becomes significant in so far as its untenable presuppositions become the basis of population policies. On such a basis rest most of the criticisms of the income- or welfare-optimum theories as well as a part of the theoretical under-structure of contemporary programs whose purpose is the stimulation of population growth. On this basis also rests the belief that industrial development alone can overcome the niggardliness of nature, dissolve the perversity of man, and drive a stake through the heart of the Malthusian vampire.

It is not our purpose in this essay specifically to appraise the policies to which we have referred. It is our purpose rather to state carefully some of the elements of what may be called the economics of population growth. In Section I of this paper we develop the theory of interfactor substitutability and examine its determinants. In Section II we apply this theory to the population problem under essentially constant conditions, and inquire into the circumstances regulating the substitutability of labor (or population) for the resources with which it is cooperant. In Section III the principle of convertibility, together with its relation to the principle of substitutability, is analyzed. In Section IV we examine the dynamic influences to which the principles of substitutability and convertibility are exposed, while in Section V we consider the constraints to which these dynamic influences are subject. In Section VI certain relevant aspects of the optimum theory are tersely

1. A. J. Lotka, *Elements of Physical Biology*, p. 208.
2. See my "Malthus's Total Population Theory: A Restatement and Reappraisal," *Canadian Journal of Economics and Political Science*, XI, 1945, pp. 83, 234.

treated. In Sections VII–VIII we present data which are intended to suggest the demographic situation of the world and to provide realistic illumination of the principles discussed in the preceding sections. Sections I–IV comprise Part I; Sections V–VIII constitute Part II.

I

In this section we shall describe two concepts of elasticity of substitution, of which we make use in subsequent sections. Let us suppose a closed economy in which only two homogeneous agents of production are used, a variable agent P whose supply is increasing relative to that of an agent R whose supply may be defined as relatively or absolutely fixed. Other relevant circumstances that may affect the comparative productivity of the two agents of production — e.g., patterns of tastes, methods of production, organization of productive agents, etc. — remain constant. Let P_{m1} and P_{m2} represent, in our closed economy, the respective marginal products of P when n and $n + 1$ units of P are being combined, under optimum conditions of productive organization, with a fixed quantity k of agent R. Let P_{a1} and P_{a2} be the corresponding average products of P, and R_{m1} and R_{m2}, the corresponding marginal products of R. Let T_1 and T_2 represent the total net product of goods and services when n and $n + 1$ units, respectively, of P are combined with the fixed quantity k of agent R. Let S_{p1}, S_{p2}, S_{r1}, and S_{r2} represent the fraction of T imputable to P and R, respectively, when n and $n + 1$ units of P are combined with quantity k of R.

It will be supposed for the present that under the conditions laid down the production function of our economy is essentially linear and homogeneous: if the quantities of P and R that are being combined in our closed economy are each increased by a given fraction f, total net product T will also be increased by f. In reality, of course, this supposition does not hold for each small fractional increase of agents P and R, since productive services and technological processes are not infinitely divisible. Yet we shall suppose it to hold essentially, nonetheless, since, if we postulate a sufficiently large (though absolutely small) fractional increase f in the utilized quantities of agents P and R, T will increase in like measure.

Let σ (or σ_{pr}) represent the elasticity of substitution of variable agent P for fixed agent R, as defined by Allen, following Hicks and Robinson.[3] In

3. For convenience we write σ instead of σ_{pr}, since our discussion usually runs in terms of the substitution of varied agent P for fixed agent R. If P is fixed and R is varied, we write σ_{rp}. For like reason we write S instead of S_{pr} to represent Machlup's concept when P is varied. The concept of elasticity of substitution was developed originally by Hicks and Robinson to deal with problems in the field of the theory of distribution. Moreover, as originally formulated, it

terms of our particularized symbols, σ, which was originally employed to describe variation along a constant product curve, approximates $\dfrac{1}{n} \div \dfrac{dr}{r}$ when: $\dfrac{1}{n}$ is small, $r = \dfrac{R_{m1}}{P_{m1}}$, and $dr = \dfrac{R_{m2}}{P_{m2}} - \dfrac{R_{m1}}{P_{m1}}$. Then, as a rule,

$$\sigma = \frac{R_{m1}P_{m2}}{n(P_{m1}R_{m2} - P_{m2}R_{m1})}. \tag{1}$$

Equation (1) may be expressed in more general terms. Let x represent the varying quantity of the variable agent P that is being combined, in the economy, with the fixed quantity k of the invariable agent R. Let $f(x) = $ the average product P_a of P. Then $xf(x) = xP_a = $ total net product $T; f(x) + xf'(x) = P_m$, the marginal product of P; $x[f(x) + xf'(x)] = xP_m(= S_pT)$, the imputed product of agent P; $\dfrac{d}{dx}(P_a) = f'(x); \dfrac{d}{dx}(P_m) = 2f'(x) + xf''(x)$. The imputed product of the fixed agent R is $T - xP_m$ which equals $xf(x) - x[f(x) + xf'(x)]$. This reduces to $-x^2f'(x)$; and R_m, the marginal product of the fixed agent R, becomes $\dfrac{-x^2f'(x)}{k}$. The equation $\sigma = \left[d\left(\dfrac{x}{k}\right) \div \dfrac{x}{k}\right] \div \left[d\left(\dfrac{R_m}{P_m}\right) \div \dfrac{R_m}{P_m}\right]$ is reducible

---

was expressed in terms of the technical substitutability of one factor of production for another under given conditions of production. It did not take into account the indirect substitution of factors for one another through the medium of commodity substitution; nor apparently did it take explicitly into account the substitution of some given factor for another through the introduction of a method of production making relatively greater use of this given factor. In our discussion of the elasticity of substitution in the economy as a whole, we do not refer to the elasticity of demand for product as a whole since this is infinite; but in our treatment of the changes in industrial composition which may accompany population growth, we must take into account the accompanying changes in demand since these, together with the elasticity of technical substitution within given industries, govern changes in industrial composition.

In this paper we are concerned with the bearing of substitutability upon per capita output, and only incidentally with the possible effects of population growth upon the distribution of income. It is assumed that, given correct factor pricing, the division of income may reflect either (*a*) the productivities of the several factors and the distribution of their ownership, or (*b*) condition (*a*), together with such institutional arrangements as have been introduced to modify the force of (*a*). In the real world, of course, division of income is under the government of both condition (*b*) and the circumstances that make for factor immobility and the incorrect factor pricing.

On the elasticity of substitution see J. R. Hicks, *The Theory of Wages*, chap. vi and pp. 241–47, and "Distribution and Economic Progress: A Revised Version," *Review of Economic Studies*, IV, 1936, pp. 1–12; Joan Robinson, "The Classification of Inventions," *Review of Economic Studies*, V, 1938, pp. 139–42; and *The Economics of Imperfect Competition*, pp. 256ff., 330n.; R. G. D. Allen, *Mathematical Analysis For Economists*, pp. 340ff.; Fritz Machlup, "The Commonsense of the Elasticity of Substitution," *Review of Economic Studies*, II, 1935, pp. 202ff.; A. C. Pigou, "The Elasticity of Substitution," *Economic Journal*, XLIV, 1934, pp. 232–41. R. F. Kahn and D. G. Champernowne, "Elasticity of Substitution," *ibid.*, XLV, 1935, pp. 242–58; and a number of notes by P. M. Sweezy, A. P. Lerner, R. F. Kahn and J. R. Hicks, *Review of Economic Studies*, I, 1933, pp. 67–80, and by M. Friedman, J. Robinson, A. Lerner, and F. Machlup, *ibid.*, III, 1936, pp. 147–52.

to

$$\sigma = \frac{P_m d(P_a)}{P_a d(P_m)} .^4$$

(2)

Thus σ = the marginal product of the variable agent P times the rate of change (fall) in the average product of P divided by the average product of P times the rate of change (fall) in the marginal product of P.

So long as $\sigma > 1$, the quantity $\frac{xP_m}{kR_m}$ increases with the increase in x/k (that is, the amount x of the variable agent P which is being combined with the fixed amount k of the invariable agent R). When $\sigma = 1$, the quantity $\frac{xP_m}{kR_m}$ remains unchanged as x/k increases; while when $\sigma < 1$, the quantity $\frac{xP_m}{kR_m}$ diminishes with the increase in x/k. As we shall indicate later, the rate of decline in the average product P_a is lower in the first than in the second case, and lower in the second than in the third case. What has been said is represented graphically in Figure I. The logarithmic values of x/k and $\frac{P_m}{R_m}$ are represented along the abscissa and the ordinate, respectively. The diagonal line (1) describes a situation in which $\sigma = 1$, for at all points along this line the logarithm of the number $\frac{P_m}{R_m}$ plus the logarithm of the number x/k equals a constant value c (= log 3). Line (2), lying below the diagonal, describes a situation in which $\sigma < 1$, for the sum of the logarithms of the numbers x/k and $\frac{P_m}{R_m}$ diminishes as x/k increases. When the sum of the logarithms of the numbers x/k and $\frac{P_m}{R_m}$ increases with the increase in x/k, as in the situation described by line (3), $\sigma > 1$.

The fraction S_p of the total net product T that is imputable to P remains constant so long as $\sigma = 1$; it declines when $\sigma < 1$, and it increases when $\sigma > 1$. Accordingly, if the only force operating to increase the aggregate

4. $\sigma = \left[d\left(\frac{x}{k}\right) \div \frac{x}{k} \right] \div \frac{dr}{r}$, when $r = R_m \div P_m$ and $dr = d(R_m \div P_m)$.

Hence

$$\sigma = \left[d\left(\frac{x}{k}\right) \div \frac{x}{k} \right] \div \left[d\left(\frac{-x^2 f'(x)}{f(x) + x f'(x)}\right) \div \left(\frac{-x^2 f'(x)}{f(x) + x f' x}\right) \right].$$

This becomes, when $k = 1$,

$$\sigma = \frac{[f(x) + x f'(x)] f'(x)}{f(x)[2 f'(x) + x f''(x)]} .$$

(3)

net product T is the increase in x/k, and if the division of net product is governed solely by the marginal productivity principle,[5] one may infer from the change in S_p whether $\sigma \gtreqless 1$. If, under these same circumstances, it is possible to determine P_a, P_m, and the rates of change (i.e., $\frac{d}{dx}[P_a]$ and $\frac{d}{dx}[P_m]$) in P_a and P_m, the precise value of σ may be arrived at. When product-affecting forces (e.g., changes in productive techniques, in productive organizations, in patterns of consumption, etc.) other than increases in x/k are at work at the same time that x/k is growing, changes in the mar-

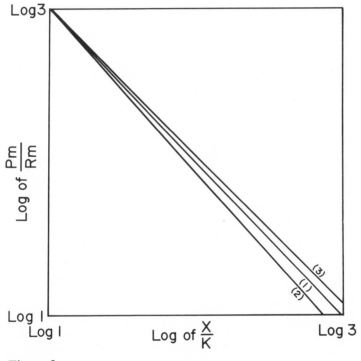

Figure I

ginal substitutability of P for R reflect the influence of these other forces as well as that of increases in x/k; hence the value of σ as such can be determined, given the other relevant data, only in so far as indices of these other product-affecting forces are at hand.[6]

5. That is, with $T = xP_m + kR_m$, xP_m and kR_m, respectively, flow to P and R.
6. In manufacturing in the United States in 1899–1922 the ratio of fixed capital to labor rose from 1.0 to 2.7; yet the fraction of the product distributed to capital and presumably imputable to capital remained practically constant at 0.25. Had there been no significant

The σ concept, since it had to do with the substitution of one agent for another along a constant product curve, related only to the elasticity of the direct technical substitutability of one agent for another; it did not take into account the indirect substitution of one factor for another through the medium of commodity substitution.[7] For purposes of the present discussion it probably is permissible, so long as the necessary *ceteris paribus* conditions are observed and the variable agent is labor and (therefore) a consuming unit, to conceive of the whole economy as a firm and to describe the change in the marginal substitutability of P for R in terms of σ. It is possible also to take both technical and commodity substitution into account by defining the elasticity of substitution S (or S_{pr}) of a variable agent P for a fixed agent R as Machlup has defined it. In our simpler terms[8]

$$S = \frac{P_{m2} - (n[P_{m1} - P_{m2}])}{nP_{m1}} \div \frac{P_{m2}}{nP_{a1}}. \tag{4}$$

This equation reduces to

$$S = \frac{P_{a1}\{P_{m2} - (n[P_{m1} - P_{m2}])\}}{P_{m1}P_{m2}}. \tag{5}$$

When, given an increase of n to $n + 1$ in the ratio of P to R (hereinafter called P/R), the amount of net product imputable to the varied agent P increases at the same rate as does total net product T_1, $S = 1$. When this amount increases at a lesser rate than T_1, $S < 1$, and when at a greater rate, $S > 1$; if it does not increase because $P_{m2} = 0$, $S = 0$.

Equations (4) and (5) may be expressed in more general terms.[9] Equation (4) may be restated

$$S = \frac{d(xP_m)}{xP_m} \div \frac{d(xP_a)}{(xP_a)}. \tag{6}$$

This equation reduces to equation (7) which may replace equation (5):

---

technological changes, innovations, etc., in this period, it could be inferred that the elasticity of substitution of capital for labor had continued at unity. But there were improvements of various sorts. Hence the constancy of the share of the product going to capital must be attributed in part to these improvements which prevented the decline in the elasticity of substitution of capital for labor that otherwise would have taken place. See Paul H. Douglas, *The Theory of Wages*, esp. chap. 5; also David McC. Wright, "Limits to the Use of Capital," *Quarterly Journal of Economics*, LVIII, 1944, pp. 331–58. See also note 21 below.

7. This point is discussed again below. Hicks has proposed that the combined elasticity of the technical and the commodity substitutability of one factor for another be defined as "the arithmetical sum of the elasticity of commodity substitution and . . . elasticity of technical substitution." See his "Distribution and Economic Progress," *loc. cit.*, pp. 8, 10, and p. 8, note on formula for commodity elasticity of substitution between factors.

8. See first paragraph in this section.

9. For meaning of terms see the paragraph above in which equation (2) is developed.

$$S = \frac{P_a d(xP_m)}{P_m d(xP_a)} \cdot {}^{10}$$

(7)

Thus S = the average product of the variable agent P times the rate of change in the imputed product of the variable agent divided by the marginal product of the variable agent times the rate of change in the total net product.

Although S and σ are equal only when $S = \sigma = 1$ and when (because $P_m = 0$) $S = \sigma = 0$, they vary in the same direction. When $S < 1$, $\sigma < 1$; and when $S > 0$, $\sigma > 0$. The possible maximum values for S and σ differ. When a small increment in the variable agent P is accompanied by no decrease in the marginal product of P, we have infinite elasticity of substitution of the variable for the fixed agent and $\sigma = \infty$. The maximum value of S, on the contrary, is governed, *ceteris paribus*, by the ratio of P_m to R_m, being high when this ratio is low and low when this ratio is high. In the limiting case in which the whole of the net product T is imputable to P, the maximum value of $S = 1$. Illustrative values based on equation (5) for S are given in columns 2 and 3 of Table I; corresponding values for σ are given in the last column.

Table I. Illustrative Cases.*

| Cases | Marginal values | | Average | σ |
	Pm	Rm	Pa	
I: $Pm_1 = .1$	$Pm_1 = .10000$	$Rm_1 = .90000$	$Pa_1 = 1.00000$	—
(a) $S = 10$	$Pm_2 = .10000$	$Rm_2 = .90000$	$Pa_2 = .991089$	∞
(b) $S = 1$	$Pm_2 = .09911$	$Rm_2 = .90089$	$Pa_2 = .991080$	1
(c) $S = 0$	$Pm_2 = 0$	$Rm_2 = 1.00000$	$Pa_2 = .990099$	0
II: $Pm_1 = .5$	$Pm_1 = .50000$	$Rm_1 = .50000$	$Pa_1 = 1.00000$	—
(a) $S = 2$	$Pm_2 = .50000$	$Rm_2 = .50000$	$Pa_2 = .99505$	∞
(b) $S = 1$	$Pm_2 = .49751$	$Rm_2 = .50249$	$Pa_2 = .99500$	1
(c) $S = 0$	$Pm_2 = 0$	$Rm_2 = 1.00000$	$Pa_2 = .99010$	0
III: $Pm_1 = .9$	$Pm_1 = .9000$	$Rm_1 = .1000$	$Pa_1 = 1.000000$	—
(a) $S = 1.11$	$Pm_2 = .9000$	$Rm_2 = .1000$	$Pa_2 = .999010$	∞
(b) $S = 1$	$Pm_2 = .8991$	$Rm_2 = .1009$	$Pa_2 = .999001$	1
(c) $S = 0$	$Pm_2 = 0$	$Rm_2 = 1.0000$	$Pa_2 = .990099$	0

*The values in these cases are based upon the assumption that the values for Pm and Pa approach equality as the amount of P combined with R approaches zero.

Since S and σ vary in the same direction, each concept of elasticity of substitution may be utilized for the purposes of this essay. As a rule we shall use S, since it explicitly takes commodity as well as technical substi-

10. That is,

$$S = \frac{f(x)\,[f(x) + 3xf'(x) + x^2 f''(x)]}{(f(x) + xf'(x))^2}.$$

(8)

Although the denominator reads $(P_m)^2$ since $P_m = d(xP_a)$, the second element in the denominator of equation (7) is represented as $d(xP_a)$, or the rate of change in the aggregate net product $T(= xP_a)$.

tution into account. When, however, it is more convenient to use σ, it will be employed.

(i) The magnitude of the average product P_a of the variable agent P depends, *ceteris paribus*, upon the magnitude of P_m, the marginal product of P, and upon the elasticity of substitution S by which the rate of decline in P_m is conditioned.[11]

(ii) The incremental rate of decline in the average product P_a is conditioned by the incremental rate of decline in the marginal product P_m, and this rate is conditioned in turn by S and by the incremental rate of change in S.[12] When (with other conditions constant) S equals and continues at some given value (say 1), the average product P_a declines as x/k increases, at the rate corresponding to the given value of S. If $d(S)$ is negative and S is declining, then, as x/k increases, P_a declines at a rate increasingly higher than that ruling in the previous case. If, on the contrary, with P_m and P_a diminishing, $d(S)$ becomes positive and S increases, P_a continues to decline but at a lower rate than would have ruled if S had remained constant.[13]

In column 4 of Table I illustrative values for particular cases are presented to show that the mean rate of decline $\dfrac{P_{a1} - P_{a2}}{P_{a1}}$ in the average product P_{a1} varies inversely with S,[14] other conditions being given. For example, in Case I with $R_{m1}/P_{m1} = 9$, the rate of decline in P_{a1} is .008911 when $S = 10$, and .00892 when $S = 1$.[15]

11. From equation (7) it follows that

$$P_a = \frac{S(P_m)^2}{d(xP_m)}; \text{ and that } Pm = \frac{P_a d(xP_m)}{Sd(xP_a)}.$$

12. This follows from the equations in the preceding footnote.

13. It follows from equation (2) that

$$P_a = \frac{P_m d(P_a)}{\sigma d(P_m)}, \text{ and that } P_m = \frac{\sigma P_a d(P_m)}{d(P_a)}.$$

Whence it is evident that the incremental rate of change in P_a is conditioned by the incremental rate of change in P_m which rate in turn is conditioned by σ and the rate of change in σ. For, *ceteris paribus*, the greater is the value of σ, the lower is the rate of decline in P_m; and the lower the rate of decline in P_m, the lower is the rate of fall in P_a. If $d(\sigma)$ is negative, and σ is declining, the rate of decline in P_a increases in accordance with the magnitude of $d(\sigma)$. If $d(\sigma)$ is positive, and σ is increasing, the rate of fall in P_a declines in accordance with the magnitude of $d(\sigma)$.

14. This is to be expected, of course, since the rate of decline in P_a is conditioned by the rate of decline in P_m, which depends in turn upon the substitutability of P for R. Consider the special case in which P_a and P approach equality as the amount of P combined with R approaches zero. Under these conditions the mean rate of decline in P_a equals the mean rate of decline in P_m if the elasticity of the average curve is constant. If the elasticity of the average curve is increasing, the mean rate of decline in P_a is less than that in P_m; while if the elasticity of the average curve is falling, the mean rate of decline in P_a exceeds that in P_m. The elasticity e of the average curve and changes in e are conditioned, respectively, by S and changes in S. For since $e = f(x)/-xf'(x) = P_a/-xd(P_a)$, it follows from the first equation in footnote 11 above that $e = S(P_m)^2/-xd(xP_m)d(P_a)$.

15. From equation (4) it may be inferred that the rate of decline $\dfrac{P_{a1} - P_{a2}}{P_{a1}}$ in the average product P_{a1} varies inversely with S. For the greater the magnitude of P_{a2}, the smaller is the decline

The rate of decline in the average product varies inversely with the ratio P_m/R_m, other conditions remaining constant. Let $S = 1$ and let $P_m + R_m = 1$. Then, since the change in average product consequent upon increase Δx in x depends upon the magnitude of P_m, and since prior to the addition of Δx, P_m was defined as equal to $1 - R_m$, the rate of fall in P_a is conditioned by P_m/R_m.[16] Illustrative figures are given in Table II. Thus, if $P_{m1} = 0.01$ and (therefore) $P_{m1}/R_{m1} = 0.0101$, $\dfrac{P_{a1} - P_{a2}}{P_{a1}}$ approximates 0.9803 per cent; while if $P_{m1} = 0.99$ and $P_{m1}/R_{m1} = 99$, $\dfrac{P_{a1} - P_{a2}}{P_{a1}}$ approximates 0.01 per cent. What has been said in this paragraph involves no modification of the previous argument, however. For, given the ratio x/k of P to R and given that other conditions remain constant, the magnitude of P_m/R_m and the rates of fall in P_m/R_m and (therefore in) P_a are governed by the elasticity of substitution S.[17] The higher the value of S and the lower its rate of fall (if any), the lower

Table II

Element	Values						
P_{m1}	.0100	.100	.250	.5000	.7500	.9000	.990
$\dfrac{P_{m1}}{R_{m1}}$	.0101	.111	.333	1.0000	3.0000	9.0000	99.000
$\dfrac{P_{a1} - P_{a2}}{P_{a1}}$*	.9803	.892	.744	.4975	.2494	.0999	.010

*In per cent.

will be the rate of fall in P_m, P_m/R_m, and P_a, associated with given increases in the ratio x/k of P to R; while the lower the value of S and the greater its rate of fall, the higher will be the rate of fall in P_m, P_m/R_m, and P_a associated with increases in x/k.

(iii) Inasmuch as the purpose of this section is facilitation of the subsequent discussion of the population problem, it will be assumed that as the amount x of P increases relatively to the fixed amount k of R, average prod-

---

$\dfrac{P_{a1} - P_{a2}}{P_{a1}}$ in P_{a1}; and the greater is S, the greater is P_{a2}, since

$$P_{a2} = \frac{n}{n + 1}\left(\frac{SP_{m1}P_{m2}}{P_{m2} - n[P_{m1} - P_{m2}]}\right) + \frac{P_{m2}}{n + 1}.$$

16. If $S = 1$ and $P_{m1} = 1 - R_{m1}$, it follows from the equation for P_{a2} given in footnote 15 that P_{a2} varies directly with P_{m1}/R_{m1}. Whence, since $\dfrac{P_{a1} - P_{a2}}{P_{a1}}$ varies inversely with P_{a2}, and P_{a2} varies directly with P_{m1}/R_{m1}, $\dfrac{P_{a1} - P_{a2}}{P_{a1}}$ varies inversely with P_{m1}/R_{m1}.

17. Or by σ if this concept is preferred.

uct P_a passes from a stage in which P_a and P_m are increasing and $P_a < P_m$ through a point where $P_a = P_m$ into a stage where P_a and P_m are decreasing and $P_a > P_m$. In Figure II we present three marginal and three corresponding average curves to illustrate the behavior of P_a and P_m under stipulated conditions; in Table III we give selected values from Figure II. Consideration of the behavior of P_a and P_m in Figure II will indicate that the rate of

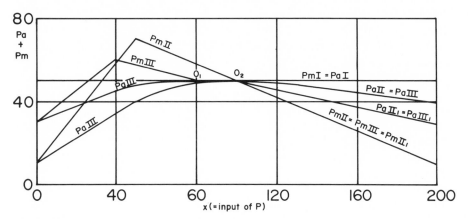

Figure II

Table III. Selected Values from Figure II.

Population = x	Yields per unit input of population				
	Marginal $PmII$	Average $PaII$	Marginal $PmIII$	Average $PaIII$	Average $PaII_1 = PaIII_1$
40	58	34	60	45	—
50	70	40	57.5	47.75	—
60	66	44.67	55	66	—
80	58	49.00	50	58	—
100	50	50.00	50	50	50*
110	46	49.82	46	49.82	48
150	30	46.67	30	46.67	40
170	22	44.24	22	44.24	36
200	10	40.00	10	40.00	30

*Since the origin of $PaII_1 = PaIII_1$ is at $x_0 = 0$, the x and y values are: 0, 50; 10, 48; 50, 40; 70, 36; 100, 30.

fall in P_a after the optimum point for P (where $P_a = P_m$)[18] is conditioned, *ceteris paribus,* by the relative magnitude of the preoptimum stage in which P_a and P_m are increasing and $P_a < P_m$.

18. By optimum point for P we mean the point where the average product P_a of P is at a maximum. This point is of much more importance for population analysis than for the usual

The curves in Figure II represent varying conditions. The curve $PmI = PaI$ describes the polar case in which $S = 1$ and $\sigma = \infty$, the substitutability of P for R being perfect with $P_m = P_a$ for all values of x. Curve $PmII$ rises to a peak of 70 at $x = 50$ and then falls at a constant incremental rate to 10 at $x = 200$; it passes through the corresponding average curve $PaII$ at the optimum point 0_2 where $x = 100$. $PmIII$ rises to a peak of 60 at $x = 40$, then falls at a constant incremental rate until at 0_1 (where $x = 80$) it meets its corresponding average curve $PaIII$. Between 0_1 and 0_2 (i.e., between $x = 80$ and $x = 100$) $PmIII$ and $PaIII$ are equal; but beyond $x = 100$, $PmIII$ falls below $PaIII$, $PmIII$ coinciding with $PmII$ and $PaIII$ with $PaII$.[19] $PaII$ is at a maximum in the optimum range lying between $x = 80$ and $x = 100$. If we assume that the optimum point where $Pa = Pm$ lies in the neighborhood of $x = 0$, and if accordingly we reduce $x = 100$ to $x = 0$ and make this (i.e., 0_2) the point of origin, the formula for $PmII = PmIII$ becomes $y = 50 - .4x$, and the formula for the corresponding average curve $PaII_1 = PaIII_1$ becomes $y = 50 - .2x$. The difference between $PaII = PaIII$ and $PaII_1 = PaIII_1$ increases with the increase in the relative magnitude of that portion of x which lies to the right of the optimum point O_2 where the average and the marginal values are equal. In short, the greater the ratio of the quantity x (of the variable agent P) being used under postoptimum conditions (e.g., between $x = 100$ and $x = 200$) to the quantity being used under preoptimum (e.g., between $x = 0$ and $x = 100$) conditions, the lower *ceteris paribus* is average product P_a.[20]

---

treatment of the laws of return; for this point marks what will be called the population optimum (see Section VI).

It will be argued below that there is a limit to the substitutability of P for R; in like manner it must be argued that there is a limit to the substitutability of R for P. Accordingly, for some very low value for x/k total net product $T = 0$; for a high value for x/k, P_m becomes zero; and for a much higher value for x/k, T again becomes zero. See F. H. Knight, *Risk, Uncertainty, and Profit*, pp. 98–104. The curves in Figure II do not conform rigorously to the principle that $T = 0$ when x/k is very small but positive.

19. The argument that $PmIII$ remains constant between $x = 80$ and $x = 100$ is not tenable under the conditions postulated in Figure II, since infinite elasticity of substitution is not a permissible assumption even within a short range. Nor is the polar case $PmI = PaI$ tenable. $PmIII$ will remain constant between $x = 80$ and $x = 100$ if the quantity of R being combined with P is increased at the same rate as P between the points $x = 80$ and $x = 100$. See note 28 below where use is made of this feature of Figure II.

20. Let $x_0 = $ the optimum quantity of variable agent P (e.g., 100 at O_2 in Figure II); $x = $ the aggregate amount of P being used; $x_e = x - x_0 = $ amount of P being used in excess of optimum amount; $A_o = $ optimum (i.e., maximum) value of average function (e.g., of $PaII$); $Ax = $ value of same function (e.g., $PaII$) at x; $A_e = $ value of same function if it has origin at $x_o = O$ (e.g., $PaII_1$ with origin at O_2). Then

$$Ax = \frac{x_oA_o + (x - x_o)A_e}{x}.$$

If there were no initial stage of increasing returns such as the postulating of an optimum population implies, Ax would be identical with Ae, and the magnitude of A_e as represented by $PaII_1$

In our discussion of the elasticity of substitution no attention has been devoted to the fact that since the substitutability of one factor for another is limited, the elasticity of substitution S (or σ) must inevitably decline and eventually become zero if x (the amount of P combined with k of R) continues to increase. Some production functions rest upon the assumption that σ ($= S = 1$) continues unchanged at the level of unity however much P increases relatively to R. The production function $T = bR^{1-c}P^c$, where b is a constant and c is the fraction (S_p) imputable to P, is a case in point.[21] It is supposed that P is continuously substitutable for R and that therefore P_m, although declining, will not fall to zero.[22] So great a degree of divisibility in the fixed agent R and so continuous a variation in the proportionality of R to P is not tenable.[23] We shall suppose that even though a production function may imply an elasticity of substitution of unity or slightly higher for some range of values of x, it is nevertheless to be inferred that if x is continually increased, the elasticity of substitution will finally fall to zero and the marginal product of the variable agent will become zero.

It has been assumed thus far that since no product-increasing forces other than the increase in x are at work, P_a must fall when x passes the value at which $P_a = P_m$. If, however, other product-increasing forces are working to raise P_a, then the increase in quantity x of P beyond the optimum amount operates to make the increase in P_a less than it would be were x constant. The repressive effect of the increase in P will depend upon S, P_m/R_m, and the extent to which x exceeds its optimum value. In terms of curve $PaII$ in Figure II, these three circumstances govern the (negative) elasticity of $PaII$ while the forces operating to increase average product elevate the level of $PaII$; the path which P_a traces is fixed by the sum of the two opposing forces. The product-increasing forces are not sufficiently strong, however, to counterbalance the downward pressure exerted upon P_m by a continuing increase in x; for, given a finite economic universe, the product-increasing forces themselves are subject to limitations arising out of the finitude of the economic universe.

---

would be governed solely by the movement of the corresponding marginal curve $PmII_1$ with origin at $x_o = 0$. But given an initial stage of increasing returns, the value of Ax is governed both by that of A_e and that of A_o, which exceeds that of A_e at $x_e > 0$.

21. This function Professor Douglas (see note 6 above) has used in many of his studies in manufacturing. In the United States the exponent for capital (i.e., R in the above equation) Douglas found to be 0.25; that for labor (i.e., P in the above equation), 0.75. Higher exponents for capital were found in Australia and New Zealand. See Douglas, "Professor Cassel on the Statistical Determination of Marginal Productivity," *Canadian Journal of Economics and Political Science,* IV, 1938, pp. 22–33. For criticisms see H. Mendershausen, "On the Significance of Professor Douglas' Production Function," *Econometrica,* VI, 1938, pp. 143–53, and M. W. Reder, "An Alternative Interpretation of the Cobb-Douglas Function," *Econometrica,* XI, 1943, pp. 259–64.

22. Other cases in point are $T = ax/x^n$ when $n < 1$ and a is a constant; and $T = P_m(1 - r^x)/(1 - r)$ when r is the ratio between successive marginal products.

23. See note 18 above; also George J. Stigler, *The Theory of Price,* chap. 8.

II

In this section we express the effect of population growth under given conditions in terms of the principle of substitutability developed in the preceding section. For the sake of convenience we shall let P represent the variable population (or labor) factor; R, the comparatively invariable resources factor; and P_m, R_m, P_a, and R_a, the marginal and average products, respectively, of P and R. The other conditions postulated follow:

(i) the economy is closed;

(ii) the state of the arts, innovation, and product-influencing organization is constant;

(iii) individual preference scales continue unchanged;

(iv) the population factor P is homogeneous;

(v) the resources factor R is homogeneous;

(vi) the age composition of the population is stable;[24]

(vii) the number of persons employed constitutes a constant fraction of the population of working age;[25]

(viii) the relative amount of "disguised unemployment" continues unchanged.[26]

To these conditions yet another must be added:

(ix) that the income-increasing forces postulated by the optimum theory have been exhausted, and that population has grown to the upper limit of the optimum range (if there be such a range).

The income-optimum population theory supposes that, as the population composing an economy increases in number, per capita output rises until the attainable maximum permitted by prevailing nondemographic circumstances is reached.[27] When this maximum is exceeded, further population

24. Whence the population of working age constitutes an unchanging fraction of the total population; and each age-group component of the population of working age forms a constant fraction of the population of working age. On the influence of changes in age composition see my "Population Movements, Employment, and Income," *Southern Economic Journal*, V, 1938, pp. 142–48; "Some Effects of Changes in the Age Composition of the Labor Force," *ibid.*, VIII, 1941, pp. 157ff.; and "Population Trends and the Future Demand for Teachers," *Social Forces*, XIX, 1941, pp. 465ff.

25. For the present, therefore, we ignore the possible effects of changes in the rate of population growth upon the level of employment.

26. Unemployment may range between 100 per cent when no one is employed and zero per cent when everyone is so employed that, given his training and inclinations and a fixed period of time for making adjustments, he could not produce enough more in any other line or place of employment to induce his shifting or being shifted thereto. All productive agents in an economy are in zero-unemployment equilibrium when what has just been said of labor holds for all agents. Other conditions being given, what constitutes zero-unemployment equilibrium is a function of the time interval allowed for making shifts and adjustments. See Joan Robinson, *Essays in the Theory of Employment*, pp. 82ff., and C. D. Long, "The Concept of Unemployment," *Quarterly Journal of Economics*, LVII, 1942, pp. 6–25; also my "Population Trends . . . ," *loc. cit.*, pp. 130–34. See also note 50 below.

27. The increase in per capita output is attributable to increasing division of labor, improved organization, fuller exploitation of "lumpy" factors, and increasing returns to scale. The above

growth is accompanied by a decline in per capita output unless there exists a *reserve* supply of *idle* resources for combination with further increments of population; after this reserve has been put into use and it is no longer possible to equip additional increments of population so well as the population already in existence, per capita output must decline.[28]

Given the nine conditions listed above, per capita output must fall if population continues to grow while the resource supply remains constant, or if, the optimum point having been passed, the population grows faster than the resource supply. For the only product-increasing force supposedly operative is the increase in population.

The rate of decline in per capita output P_a will depend upon the degree to which labor (i.e., population)[29] is substitutable,[30] throughout the *whole* economy, for the resources with which it is used jointly in productive processes. If an additional increment of population[31] cannot be used jointly with the resources available and in use, and cannot, therefore, add anything[32] to aggregate output, the rate of decline in per capita output is, *ceteris paribus*, at a maximum. If, on the contrary, population is a perfect substitute for resources, and marginal product P_m does not diminish, the rate of decline in per capita output P_a is at a minimum under the circumstances given. Since, as a rule, population is imperfectly substitutable for resources, per capita output falls as population increases (given the above nine conditions), but not so rapidly as it would fall if the marginal substitutability of population for resources approximated zero.

discussion has to do with the population optimum measured in terms of per capita income (= output); it does not have to do with optima measured in terms of other indices. See Section VI.

28. Output is governed not by resources which are idle and in reserve but by resources which are joined with population in productive activity. A reserve supply of resources may, under the conditions given, delay the advent of a decline in per capita output originating in population growth; but it cannot augment per capita output.

In terms of Figure II, O_2 marks the maximum per capita output figure when production conditions are as described by PmII, and the optimum population coincides with $x = 100$. Curve PmIII may be said to describe a situation in which a reserve supply of idle resources exists. Per capita output is at a maximum when population = $x = 80$; it does not fall until $x = 100$ because as P increases from $x = 80$ to $x = 100$ the quantity of R is augmented at the same rate from an idle reserve of R and the ratio P/R is constant. When population has grown to $x = 100$ and there remains no further reserve stock of R to equip additions to P, P/R increases and P_a falls. Within the range $x = 80$ and $x = 100$ constant returns to scale rule, given that P and R increase at the same rate with other conditions constant.

29. Hereinafter we shall sometimes use the term labor instead of the term population; for, although the two terms are not interchangeable, any finding for "labor" is readily convertible into terms of population, given conditions (vi) and (vii) described above.

30. The principle of convertibility is ignored here; it is discussed below.

31. The phrase "additional increment of population" is intended to refer to any situation in which population grows faster than resources.

32. It is assumed that the increment of population cannot be used in complete isolation from resources. (This assumption, although unnecessary, makes for greater ease of expression.) It is always assumed that sufficient time has elapsed, following the addition of an increment of population, to permit as much reorganization of production and as much adjustment of the economy to the increment of population as conditions of production and consumption permit.

The substitution of population for resources consequent upon an increase in the ratio P/R will be governed by the responses, respectively, of producers and of consumers to the addition of an increment of labor to the stock of labor and resources already in use. When producers are primarily and immediately responsible for the absorption of the increment of labor, the substitution process is predominantly technical in character. Such will be the case if producers in a given industry, since they now can obtain labor at a lower relative price, combine a larger quantity of it with the cooperating resources employed in that industry. When, on the contrary, the addition of an increment of labor to the quantity of labor already in use in the economy operates primarily to reduce the relative production costs and selling prices of goods and services in the fabrication of which the labor factor is comparatively important, there will be an increase in the relative amount produced and consumed of such goods and services; or, because of the change in the cost and price structure, there may now be produced for the first time goods and services in which the labor factor bulks relatively large, and the production of which has not heretofore been undertaken because of the relatively high cost of labor. Here we have commodity-substitution rather than technical substitution; for the additional increment of labor is absorbed primarily through the substitution, in the consumption and utilization budgets of the population composing the economy, of certain kinds (i.e., comparatively labor-absorbing) of goods and services for other kinds (i.e., comparatively non-labor-absorbing) of goods and services. The substitution that takes place consequent upon an increase in P/R will usually consist in a combination of technical and commodity substitution, with sometimes one form and sometimes the other predominating.

We may think of the unspecialized and (more or less) "original" agents of production as situated at one pole, of final consumer services as situated at the other, and of producers and consumers as the instruments by which undifferentiated productive powers are transformed into specialized consumer services. Thus:

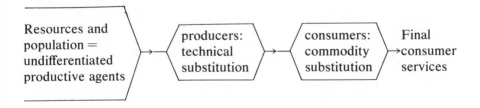

The arrows indicate the direction of the substitution process. The two intermediate hexagons indicate that we must search in the patterns, respectively, of producer and consumer behavior, for the elements which either restrict or facilitate the processes of substitution.

In light of the analysis presented in Section I and given the nine conditions laid down in this section, it follows that the decline in per capita output consequent upon an increase in the ratio of population to resources will be governed by three circumstances; (a) the elasticity of substitution of labor for the resources with which it is jointly used in productive processes throughout the economy; (b) the ratio of the marginal product of labor to that of resources (P_m/R_m) prevailing at the time population increases; and (c) the extent to which the population of the economy already has grown beyond the optimum number at which per capita output is at a maximum. The influence of circumstance (b) is conditioned by circumstance (a), since (*ceteris paribus*) changes in P_m/R_m are conditioned by the past and the present magnitude of the elasticity of substitution. The importance of circumstance (c) also turns on the magnitude of S. If some of the nine conditions laid down above are relaxed and to the increase of quantity of P other product-augmenting forces are added, these forces may (*within limits*) either decelerate the rate of fall in P_a consequent upon population growth or more than offset the income-depressing influence of population growth; but they will not be capable of continually offsetting a continuing increase in population in a finite economic universe.

III

In this section, we show that: (a) since resources are composed in part of population, their quantity may be augmented by converting population into resources; (b) that the convertibility of population into resources in the economy as a whole is conditioned by P_m/R_m and by the industrial composition of the economy; and (c) that the rate of decline in this convertibility is conditioned by the elasticity of substitution of labor for resources in the economy as a whole.[33]

Given an economy in purely competitive equilibrium, the fraction of a representative unit of resources that may be derived from population through conversion is fixed by the fraction of its price (= cost = value) that is imputable ultimately to labor (or population). Suppose a representa-

---

33. Conversion of population into resources is desirable within limits because population and resources cooperate in production; it is possible in so far as resources are composed in part of labor (or population). Conversion would not be possible if all productive agents cooperant with labor were nonsusceptible of economic modification by man and were used only in their pristine state. But this is not the case. Virtually all production is joint, and virtually every productive agent which is used jointly with labor is analyzable into terms of the labor and resources which have cooperated in the creation of this agent. (Of course an agent by which economic production is conditioned is significant for the present discussion only if and when it is economically scarce and therefore capable of having something imputed to it.)

tive unit of resources G_1[34] is produced under conditions such that 0.9 of its price (= cost) is imputable ultimately to labor and 0.1 to resources. Suppose that the corresponding proportions for resources G_2 and G_3 are, respectively, 0.75 and 0.25, and 0.1 and 0.9; and that still other proportions rule for resources $G_4 \cdots G_n$. Evidently, given that other things are equal, in an economy marked by population growth the supply of G_1 may be augmented with greater ease than that of G_2 and with much greater ease than that of G_3. In general, the larger the fraction of a resource that is imputable to labor, the greater is the ease, *ceteris paribus,* with which labor can be converted into this resource and with which the supply of this resource can be made to keep pace with the growth of population.

The fraction of a resource G_1 that is imputable to labor and therefore derivable from labor P[35] is governed by two circumstances: (*a*) the ratio P_m/R_m ruling in the economy; and (*b*) the ratio of labor P to resources R in the industry that produces G_1.[36] The rate of decline in this fraction is conditioned by the elasticity of technical substitution of labor for resources in the industry (or industries) responsible for the production of G_1 and by the elasticity of demand for G_1.[37] The elasticity of the demand for G_1 depends, in turn, upon the elasticity of technical substitution between G_1 and the agents with which it cooperates in the productive process and upon the elasticity of the demand for the goods in the production of which G_1 cooperates.

The fraction of the aggregate resource equipment of an economy that is imputable to labor and therefore derivable from labor will be high in proportion as this aggregate consists largely of individual types of resources predominantly imputable to labor and therefore derivable from labor. Accordingly, if the population of an economy is growing in relation to its resources, this population can ease its adjustment to the decline in the population : resources ratio by modifying its preference scales and increasing its relative consumption of goods in the production of which resources that consist largely of labor are relatively important.

34. It must be remembered that we are here concerned with resources, not with goods in general.

35. In this section we continue the assumptions regarding conditions of production that were set down in Section II. For purposes of the immediate discussion, however, we suppose resources R to differ with respect to the degree to which they consist of labor. In Section IV we deal in detail with the matter of heterogeneity of resources.

36. Let q_p and q_r be the number of units, respectively, of P and R being used in the production of G_1; P_m and R_m, the marginal products in the economy as a whole per unit of P and R, respectively; and s_p, the share of a representative unit of G_1 that is imputable to P. Then $s_p = q_p P_m/(q_p P_m + q_r R_m)$.

37. When the elasticity of technical substitution of labor for resources is high in an industry, the rate of fall in marginal physical productivity of labor is low. When this elasticity is greater than the elasticity of demand for the finished product, the ratio of labor to capital increases more than when this elasticity of substitution equals or is less than the elasticity of demand. See Joan Robinson, *Economics of Imperfect Competition,* pp. 258–60; also Kahn, *Review of Economic Studies,* I, 1933, pp. 75ff.

In an economy marked by population growth it is technically easier, other conditions being given, to augment the supply of resources when the fraction of resources imputable to labor is high than when it is low; but, since other conditions do not remain equal, this technical ease tends to be counterbalanced by other circumstances. First, the population of an economy with a low resources : population ratio is not very free to shift its consumption to goods in the production of which resources consisting predominantly of labor are relatively important.[38] Second, the augmentability of any specific resource G_1 is conditioned also by the degree of availability of the productive agents other than labor of which G_1 is composed. Third, since the augmentability of resources in general is conditioned by the rate of saving (= investment) which in turn is governed by (among other things) the magnitude of per capita output (= income)P_a and sometimes by the rate of return on investment (= savings), it is difficult to elevate the resources : population ratio when this ratio is relatively low and the population is increasing. Given that other things are equal, P_a will be higher when the rate of population growth is low than when it is high,[39] while the rate of return on savings will be higher when population grows rapidly than when it grows slowly. Since the former force is the stronger,[40] resource formation per capita will be greater (other things equal)[41] when population is growing slowly than when it is growing rapidly.[42]

38. See Sections V, VII–VIII.

39. It is assumed that population exceeds the optimum number.

40. If we suppose the supply of savings to be positively correlated with the rate of return up to a given point and negatively correlated with it beyond this point, we must conclude that when population growth pushes the rate of return above this critical level, the rate of saving will fall. Here, for the sake of simplicity, we shall assume the correlation to be positive throughout. Since the psychic disposition to save at any given rate of interest is influenced, *ceteris paribus*, by the extent of the saver's property holding, and since this holding is likely to be low when the resources : population ratio is low, the correlation between rate of return and rate of saving is more likely to be positive at all relevant levels when the resources : population ratio is low than when it is high. Moreover, secular changes may shift the interest-savings function rightward and downward.

41. Per capita income being given, the rate of saving is conditioned not only by the rate of return on savings but also by other circumstances which influence saving and spending habits both in the shorter and in the longer run. Among these circumstances must be included the effect exercised upon the individual's pattern of values and his attitude toward the future by the magnitude of his family. This effect may strengthen the will to save of an individual with family; but whether it increases this individual's absolute amount of saving depends on whether it increases his capacity to save (which is governed by both his will to save and his earning power) sufficiently more than to offset those increases in expenditure which necessarily accompany increase in family size. In the United States the relation between family size and the propensity to save is an inverse one; and there is little reason to suppose that the relation elsewhere is substantially different. See F. Lorimer and H. Roback, "Economics of the Family Relative to Number of Children," *Milbank Memorial Fund Quarterly*, XVIII, 1940, pp. 19ff.; M. V. Jones, "Secular Trends and Idle Resources," *The Journal of Business*, XVII, No. 4, Part 2, pp. 35ff.; also Eric Schiff, "Family Size and Residential Construction," *American Economic Review*, XXXVI, 1946, pp. 97–112.

42. Here we are not concerned with the thesis that population growth increases both the average propensity to consume and the average propensity to invest, thus generating income

The convertibility of population into resources, it is evident, is governed largely, given an initial population : resources ratio, by S, the elasticity of substitution of labor for resources throughout the economy as a whole. For S reflects the influence of both commodity substitution and technical substitution, and it conditions the movement of P_m/R_m. Recourse to convertibility would be impossible if S were zero; it would be unnecessary if S were perfect. In general, convertibility is positively correlated with S and subject to the same limitations as is substitutability.[43]

In this as in the preceding sections our discussion has been couched in terms of a situation in which population has grown beyond the optimum and is growing more rapidly than the supply of resources. Our conclusions are easily adapted, however, to a situation in which population is growing less rapidly than the resources with which it cooperates in production. In such a situation population growth operates to decelerate the rate at which the resources : population ratio can rise, thus depressing present and future per capita income. For productive power which might otherwise be transmuted into per capita income-raising productive resources is absorbed by the reproduction and rearing of *additional* increments of population and by the equipping of these increments with consumers' and producers' capital. Moreover, the rate at which depletable and nonreplaceable resources are exhausted is stepped up.[44]

IV

The discussion in the preceding sections has been based upon the nine conditions stipulated in Section II. In this section we shall consider in Parts

---

and savings and making both per capita income and the rate of resource formation higher than they otherwise would be.

This thesis is of limited applicability, even on the assumption that there is a persisting tendency to the underutilization of productive agents, for which population growth may constitute a significant counterforce. For, since an economy is an essentially finite universe, the capacity of population growth to stimulate investment and savings must necessarily diminish as the limits of this universe are approached; and long before these limits are reached the adverse effects of a high population : resources ratio will swamp any such positive influence as population growth may exercise upon savings via the medium of investment.

The problems confronting an economy are functions of (among other things) population growth. Consequently, somewhat different policies are called for when the growth rate is low than when it is high. These policies cannot, however, imply that population growth is good or bad; such an evaluation must rest upon other foundations. On aspects of this problem see M. V. Jones, *op. cit.*; W. Fellner, *Monetary Policies and Full Employment;* A. R. Sweezy, "Population Growth and Investment Opportunity," *Quarterly Journal of Economics,* LV, 1940, pp. 64–79; George Terborgh, *The Bogey of Economic Maturity,* especially chaps. 2–6; also my "Population and Per Capita Income," *Annals of the American Academy of Political and Social Science,* CCXXXVII, 1945, pp. 188–90.

43. See Section V below.

44. See H. Bowen, "Capital in Relation to Population," *Social Forces,* XV, 1937, pp. 346–50. Nineteenth century economists were alert to this effect of population growth upon

(a)–(e) the effects attendant upon relaxation of any one of the first five of these conditions. We shall not examine in detail the effects attendant upon a decrease in P/R, since these effects are, in general, the reverse of those attendant upon an increase in P/R.

(a) Suppose that we remove condition (v) and assume resources to be heterogeneous. If we merely postulate them to be qualitatively heterogeneous and assume further that the utilization of resources proceeds on the whole from superior to inferior grades, we get a faster decline in P_a than we would get if resources were qualitatively homogeneous; and this proposition holds whether there be one or several kinds of heterogeneous resources.

Of the circumstances which distinguish types of resources used jointly with labor, the most important for the present discussion is variation in augmentability through time. This variation in augmentability is traceable to variation in the augmentability through time of some or all of the elements of which the resources consist.[45] Resources may be analyzed into terms of their "original" elements, or they may be analyzed into terms of their less "original" elements (e.g., labor, land, natural resources, man-made equipment). In either case it is the augmentability of the elements composing a given kind of resource that regulates its augmentability.[46]

For the present it suffices for us to group resources R (i.e., the instruments used jointly with labor in economic production) in five classes ($R_1, R_2, \cdots R_5$), ranging from the least augmentable to the most augmentable: (1) depletable and nonreplaceable natural resources; (2) nondepletable natural resources whose supply is essentially fixed; (3) land, expressed in terms of terrestrial space in which agricultural and other economic activities may and can be carried on; (4) natural resources which are replaceable and augmentable; and (5) equipment—i.e., machinery, buildings, etc. Since the number of kinds of resources in this world is much greater than five, and since nearly all kinds of resources vary in quality, the components of any one of these five classes will differ in kind and quality and yet resemble one another rather closely in direct augmentability.

Of the first (R_1) of these five classes of resources the absolute supply is a diminishing quantity; and its increasing relative scarcity can be offset only in so far as population or resources $R_2 - R_4$ can be substituted for it (R_1).

---

capital formation; e.g., see my "Pareto on Population," *Quarterly Journal of Economics,* LVIII, 1944, pp. 576ff. See Section VII below.

45. It is necessary to stress augmentability through time. If the supply of a resource for use is increased temporarily but at the expense of the supply available for use at a later period, there is no long-run increase in supply; there is merely an acceleration of the rate of depletion.

46. In so far as the place of a given kind of resource may be taken by a substitute, the supply of the former is indirectly augmentable through substitution. Here, however, our concern is with direct augmentability, since indirect augmentability is reducible ultimately to terms of direct augmentability of the substitute.

While the absolute physical supply of R_2 is a fixed quantity, its economic supply may be increased within limits by substituting for it population or resources R_1 and $R_3 - R_5$. The supply of land R_3 as defined is comparatively fixed; but the physical supply of land as a situs for most economic activities that are nonagricultural in character may be increased by changing the pattern of industrial location and shifting other land to this use, while the supply of agricultural land may be maintained and even increased somewhat in effective quantity by recovering land theretofore inutile, by preventing erosion, etc., and by preserving and/or increasing the fertility of the soil.[47] Within limits also the supply of R_3 may be increased indirectly by substituting for it labor and R_5. The supply of R_4[48] is directly augmentable, but only within limits, since its physical supply is conditioned by that of R_1 and R_3 in particular; it is susceptible also of some indirect increase through substitution. In an economy whose population is increasing, R_5 is the most (directly) augmentable of the five classes of resources $R_1 - R_5$, for R_5 consists in greater measure than the other four of population which by definition is a growing factor; R_5 also appears to be more augmentable indirectly than the other four, since population appears to be more substitutable for R_5 than for $R_1 - R_4$. The physical augmentability of R_5 appears to be limited principally by R_1.

Since both convertibility and substitutability not only diminish but are also subject to limitations, the combined augmentability of classes $R_1 - R_5$ is limited. The *indirect* augmentability (through substitution) of each of these five classes is limited both because the substitutability of population and the other four classes of resources for the class in question is a diminishing quantity and because the supply of the substitutes is ultimately limited. The *direct* physical augmentability of each of these five classes of resources is restrained both by (1) the tendency of the substitutability of any one factor for any other to fall, and by (2) the comparative fixity of supply of some of the constituent elements of some of the resources, which restricts convertibility.[49]

(b) If we relax condition (iv) and suppose the population factor to be heterogeneous, we encounter effects analogous to those which attended the relaxation of condition (v). Suppose population P to consist of five categories $P_1 - P_5$ ranging from highest to lowest in terms of capacity for production. If $P_4 - P_5$ increase relatively more rapidly than $P_1 - P_2$, the

47. In effect this is accomplished by converting into land, labor, and/or some of the other four resources (particularly R_1 and some of both R_4 and R_5).

48. In this class fall most products of organic growth as distinguished from minerals which fall largely in R_1 and nonmineral power resources which fall in R_2.

49. When productive factors are heterogeneous and in effect multiple, direct substitution and conversion may have to give place to indirect and roundabout conversion and substitution. For example, it may be less economical to accomplish a given purpose by using factors 1 and 2 in appropriate combination than by combining factors 1 and 3 to produce 4, which is then combined with 2 to achieve the purpose in question.

rate of decline in P_a will be greater than it would be if the population were homogeneous or if the rates of increase of all categories were the same. The greater the substitutability of members of inferior categories (say $P_4 - P_5$) for members of superior categories (say $P_1 - P_2$), the less will be the tendency for a relatively greater increase on the part of these inferior categories to increase the rate of decline in P_a above what it would be given a homogeneous population P.[50]

Because, in the shorter run, the overriding relation between any two categories of population is one of complementarity rather than one of substitutability, the tendency for a relatively greater increase on the part of inferior categories to push the rate of decline in P_a above what this rate would be, given a homogeneous population (or one in which all components are increasing at the same rate), is more pronounced in the shorter run than it would be if the overriding relation were one of substitutability. For example, if P_5 increases appreciably relative to P_1 when the dominant short-run relation between them is one of complementarity, the productivity per unit of P_5 eventually will fall appreciably, whatever be the over-all population : resources ratio; whence P_a (which in this case is a weighted average of the corresponding rates of the component categories of population P) declines faster than it would if P_5 were a substitute for P_1 or for $P_2 - P_4$. But substitutability, like complementarity, is a function of time: given time for adjustment and the condition that other things remain equal, substitutability, increases while complementarity diminishes with time. Accordingly, in the longer run (to continue our example) the substitutability of P_5 for $P_1 - P_4$ and/or for R increases (within limits) above what it was for the given population : resources ratio, and the initially depressive influence of the relative increase in P_5 is somewhat reduced.

50. Differential natural increase may augment the cost of distributing labor among employments according to the marginal principle and may intensify the tendency to disguised unemployment, particularly when the over-all ratio of population to resources is relatively high. Suppose a number of employments $E_1 - E_{10}$ are recruited predominantly from population category P_4. Then, if persons attached to E_1 increase faster than do those attached to $E_2 - E_{10}$, and if the elasticity of demand for the products of E_1 is not enough in excess of that for the products of $E_2 - E_{10}$ to maintain the marginal productivity of labor in E_1 at the level ruling in $E_2 - E_{10}$, we have disguised unemployment in E_1. This disguised unemployment may be corrected, *ceteris paribus*, by transferring P_4 members from E_1 to $E_2 - E_{10}$, or by adding the whole of new and as yet occupationally undifferentiated increments of P_4 to the numbers employed in $E_2 - E_{10}$ until the marginal productivity of P_4 relative to that of other productive agents is the same in all ten employments.

As a rule disguised unemployment is greater in agriculture than in other employments since usually the rate of natural increase is higher in the agricultural population than in most segments of the nonagricultural population.

The disposition of the units of any given kind of productive agent among employments is governed by the action of entrepreneurs and also, in the case of labor, by the action of the labor factors. Accordingly, since nonhuman productive agents have no control over their disposition, and since presumably entrepreneurs are better judges on the whole than are the units of labor regarding where these units are relatively most productive, disguised unemployment of labor tends to be greater than does disguised unemployment of other agents of production. See note 26 above.

Since technological progress presumably is contingent upon there being an adequate relative supply of population categories P_1 and P_2, relatively slow growth on the part of P_1 and P_2 operates, *ceteris paribus*, to slow down the rate of technological progress. And since both substitutability and complementarity between population categories are conditioned by the state of technology, these relations are affected by changes in the relative rates of growth of P_1 and P_2. Whence, if it may be assumed that substitutability rather than complementarity is fostered by technological change whose primary purpose is cost reduction, it may be inferred that a decline in the relative magnitude of categories P_1 and P_2 slows down the forces making for substitutability.[51]

(*c*) When the population : resources ratio in an economy changes, the industrial composition of that economy also tends to change. For example, if this ratio increases, the relative price of labor falls and the forces of technical and commodity substitution are set in motion. Relatively resources-using industries the demand for whose products is elastic tend to contract while relatively labor-using industries the demand for whose product is elastic tend to expand.[52] In general, labor will flow into industries in which the elasticity of technical substitution of labor for resources is high and/or the demand for whose product is elastic; and resources will flow into industries in which the elasticity of demand for the product exceeds the elasticity of technical substitution of labor for resources.[53] These changes are consistent with condition (iii) that individual preference scales stay put.

It is possible, in theory, if condition (iii) is relaxed, for an economy to increase its real income, given some population : resources ratio, by making appropriate adjustments in the preference scales of the individuals composing its population. Demand functions must be adjusted upward for goods consisting largely of relatively abundant productive agents and downward for goods consisting largely of relatively scarce productive agents. If labor is the relatively abundant factor, per capita output (= income) can be increased by the introduction of changes in tastes which cause the demand function for relatively labor-using goods to rise and that for relatively resources-using goods to fall. The change in tastes must continue the force of commodity substitution in the direction which it takes when, in the absence of such a change, the relative price of labor falls. In general, therefore, the

51. *Ceteris paribus*, technological change designed to reduce cost will tend to make for economy in the use of productive agents the outlay for which bulks large in aggregate cost and to stimulate the use of relatively inexpensive productive agents. Within the latter class fall productive agents which, because they are complements and their relative number has increased, have become relatively plentiful and cheap. See note 61 below.

52. The change in the industrial composition of the economy consequent upon an increase in the population : resources ratio reflects, besides the combined influence of technical and commodity substitution, the effect of any change in income distribution occasioned by the fall in the relative price of labor and the increase in the relative price of resources.

53. E.g., see Robinson, *Economics of Imperfect Competition*, pp. 258ff.; Hicks, *Theory of Wages*, pp. 242–46.

income-depressing effect of population growth can be reduced in so far as the substitutability of labor for resources, together with its elasticity, can be increased through the modification of the tastes of the population in favor of relatively labor-using products and services.[54]

(d) Relaxation of condition (i) that the economy is closed may permit the substitution ratio between population P and resources R to be improved in one or both of two ways: (a) through net emigration; (b) through the establishment of trade with other economies. If there is a net emigration[55] of population, particularly (when the population is heterogeneous) of the inferior elements, per capita output P_a rises;[56] for, because of the increase in the ratio of resources to population, the substitutability of labor for resources rises.[57]

The establishment of trade permits labor to emigrate by proxy in the shape of exports which consist in relatively large proportion of the labor (or kinds of labor) with which the populous economy is relatively well supplied.[58] In exchange for these exports this economy receives imports which consist largely of those resources with which it is poorly endowed.[59] Trade thus serves to increase the substitutability of labor for resources and, therefore, to augment per capita output. This substitutability declines, however, as

54. It has long been noted that the productivity of labor is conditioned by the pattern of tastes. See A. Landry, "Une théorie négligée. De l'influence de la direction de la demande, sur la productivité du travail, les salaires et la population," *Revue d'économie politique*, XXIV, 1910, pp. 314, 364, 747, 773; also my *French Predecessors of Malthus*, chap. iv. In the text above this argument is generalized and it is shown that per capita output is conditioned, *ceteris paribus*, by the communal pattern of tastes. See also (i) in Section V below.

55. Here we abstract from the fact that emigration may reduce the relative amount of employment (e.g., see J. Robinson, *Essays* pp. 75–77); or that, under certain circumstances, it may shift unemployment to other economies (see my *France Faces Depopulation*, pp. 201ff.).

56. It will be recalled that the actual population is assumed to exceed the optimum in number. If there is a net emigration of superior elements (say P_1 and P_2), P_a may fall despite the decline in P/R. Likewise, even though the aggregate population exceeds the optimum, a net immigration of superior elements may increase per capita output; it may also, if the influx of superior immigrants produces a change in the state of the arts, increase the magnitude of the optimum. E.g., see A. Plummer, "The Theory of Population: Some Questions of Quantity and Quality," *Journal of Political Economy*, XL, 1932, pp. 617–37.

57. Even if emigration does restore some given more favorable population : resources ratio that once existed in a given country, it will not restore the same economic conditions and income level as were formerly associated with this population : resources ratio. For, in the interval separating the initial period and the period of restoration, the habits of consumption and the methods of production must have changed in consequence of the initial increase in the population : resources ratio. E.g., see A. Marshall, *Principles of Economics*, pp. 807ff.; E. Rothbarth, "Causes of the Superior Efficiency of U.S.A. Industry as Compared with British Industry," *Economic Journal*, LVI, 1946, pp. 388–90.

58. As B. Ohlin notes (*Interregional and International Trade*, p. 42) M. Longfield (*Lectures on Political Economy*, p. 239) looked upon commerce as a substitute for emigration. James Steuart and other eighteenth-century writers seem to have drawn the same inference. These early writers did not clearly indicate, however, that trade, being only an imperfect substitute for migration, cannot increase *over-all* average income as much as can migration; or that trade almost always tends to raise per capita output in all participating areas whereas migration may affect it adversely in countries of immigration.

59. The entertainment of foreign travelers by relatively populous countries also facilitates the exchange of relatively labor-using for relatively non-labor-using products.

the population of the exporting economy increases (with other conditions remaining the same) both because per capita physical output in the exporting industries tends to decline and because the terms of trade worsen.[60]

(*e*) Relaxation of condition (iv) and allowance for change in the state of the arts, organization, the innovation call for no modification of the analysis of this and the preceding section. While an improvement in this state may, under certain conditions, adversely affect the situation of labor, and while it may diminish the elasticity of technical substitution of labor for resources, it increases output per unit input of labor and (sometimes) output per unit input of resources;[61] whence it operates to increase per capita output (= income). The extent to which such an improvement serves to increase per capita output depends, not upon whether the improvement is capital- or labor-saving, but upon the relative amount of productive power that is released,[62] and upon the length of the period during which this release persists.[63] If the improvement reduces resource input per unit of output, or if it brings into the orbit of economic utilizability agents which theretofore have lain outside this orbit, it operates, *ceteris paribus*, to bring about a more sustained increase in output than it does if it serves merely or primarily to increase the present rate of use of resources whose supply is both depletable and nonreplaceable (i.e., R_1 and, in some measure, R_3) and thus to diminish the supply that will be available at some future date.

V

Dynamic forces may at times counterbalance the tendency of the substitutability of population for resources to decline as population increases.

60. The less elastic the foreign demand (in real terms) for exports, the greater will be the tendency of the terms of trade to worsen.

61. M. V. Jones (*op. cit.,* pp. 20–34; see also Fellner, *op. cit.,* pp. 79ff.) presents data which suggest that capital input per unit of output has not risen and may have fallen. Labor input per unit of output has fallen for, as G. F. Bloom shows ("Note on Hicks's Theory of Invention," *American Economic Review,* XXXVI, 1946, pp. 83ff.), labor-saving inventions predominate and will predominate so long as the outlay for labor forms a large fraction of total expense. See also G. T. Jones, *Increasing Return.* Concerning the influence of invention upon the relative and the absolute share of income going to labor, see Bloom, *op. cit.,* pp. 93ff.; J. Robinson, *Essays,* pp. 129–36, and "The Classification of Inventions," *loc. cit.,* pp. 139ff. See also A. C. Pigou, *The Economics of Welfare,* pp. 671–80. Whereas the elasticity of substitution may be altered by inventions, it is merely determined (in part) by those adaptations of technique to circumstances which are implicit in the given body of technical knowledge (see Robinson, *Essays,* pp. 134–35n.).

62. Rothbarth (*op. cit.,* pp. 385ff.) attributes much of the comparatively high efficiency of American industry to the relative plentifulness of land and the relative scarcity of labor which characterized the American economy in the last century. These conditions stimulated the introduction of labor-saving equipment and gave rise to a social structure which "has put purchasing power in the hands of those who are ready to buy large quantities of standardised goods" which are easily supplied through efficient mass-production methods.

63. We suppose that the effect of the improvement is not counterbalanced by reduction in the fullness with which productive agents are used, or by a decline in the propensity to form capital. Moreover, since we have postulated a competitive economy, we may not suppose that the introduction of the improvement destroys barriers to the competitive allocation and use

But these forces are subject to limitations of two sorts: (*a*) those which, being institutional and/or habitual in character, are somewhat susceptible of being removed; (*b*) those which, arising out of the finitude of the components of a circumscribed universe, or out of the comparative constancy of some of the elements which shape social organization and patterns of individual behavior, are not removable.

Were it not for these limitations, it would be possible in very large measure to offset the output-depressing influences of population growth by a combination of (i) modification of consumption patterns, (ii) diminution of the input of productive agents per unit of output, and (iii) augmentation of the supply of utilizable resources. But man's capacity to make these changes is limited. Hence the augmentability of population in a given area, and at a given level of living, is quite restricted.

(i) A modification of consumption patterns produces an increase in real income if from a given quantity of labor and resources a larger quantity of real income is obtained than before these patterns were modified.[64] This increase results because (*a*) labor input is reduced and/or (*b*) less scarce productive agents are substituted for more scarce productive agents. In the present instance, where our concern is principally with the economizing of scarce resources through their replacement by labor which is plentiful, it is (*b*) that is most important — (*b*) in the form of the substitution of less resource-absorbing goods and services for those which are more resource-absorbing. The factors which limit the modifiability of consumption patterns are physiological, psychological, and social in character. For illustrative purposes we turn to food consumption which is especially subject to these limitations.

Within limits many may utilize either *primary* or *derived* food units to supply his needs: he may use *primary* or *derived* calories to meet his energy requirements, and *primary* or *derived* units to satisfy his other food wants.[65]

---

of productive agents and thus serves also indirectly to increase per capita output. (In the real world inventions, etc., play an important part in preserving competition).

64. A consumption pattern is modified when, because of a change in tastes (i.e., in indifference maps) with other determinants of demand remaining the same, the demand function for a given category of goods (or services) shifts. See note 73.

65. A *primary* food unit is one drawn from foodstuffs raised immediately upon land (e.g., vegetables, fruits) or in water (plant organisms); a *derived* food unit is one drawn from foodstuffs, raised only mediately upon land or in water, that is, from foodstuffs (e.g., fish, meat, dairy products) into which *primary* food units have been converted. The terms *primary* or *original* have usually been applied only to calories (see John Lindberg, *Social Research*, XII, 1945, pp. 181–204; Food and Agricultural Organization of the United Nations, *World Food Survey*, Washington, 1946, pp. 19ff.). The nomenclature suggested above is preferable on grounds of generality. On the conversion ratio between primary and animal-food calories, by type, see R. D. Jennings, *Feed Consumption by Livestock 1940–41*, USDA Circular No. 670, 1943, esp. p. 44. On the land, labor, and other resource costs of calories and nutrients, by food type, see R. P. Christenson's (mimeographed, USDA) *Using Resources to Meet Food Needs* (1943). On nutrient costs see G. J. Stigler, *Journal of Farm Economics*, XXVII, 1945, pp. 303–14.

If, like Nebuchadnezzar, man lived upon primary calories alone, he would require to satisfy his food needs only about one-seventh as much land and resources as if he lived upon derived calories alone.[66] But for agronomic and physiological reasons man cannot live upon primary calories alone. (*a*) The maintenance (to say nothing of the increase) of soil fertility and crop yields and the prevention of erosion make necessary the devotion of a considerable amount of agricultural land to the production of animal food.[67] (*b*) When a nation derives too small a fraction of its calorie consumption from animal products, vitamin and other nutrient deficiencies develop. In practice this fraction (which probably needs to be at least 20 per cent)[68] must be large enough to provide both absolute requirements and a margin of safety against carelessness in food consumption. For the ordinary consumer is less skilled than the expert nutritionist in drawing energy, vitamins, and mineral requirements from foodstuffs.[69]

A 2,800 calorie intake per day, of which 25–35 per cent are of animal origin, represents 7,000–8,680 primary calories; a 2,400 daily intake under

66. Lindberg (*op. cit.*, p. 185) estimates that a completely animal-food diet of 3,000 (derived) calories represents an original input of 21,000 *primary* calories. The ratio of derived to primary calories varies with the composition of the animal-product diet under consideration; it may be less than or more than 1 : 7 (*World Food Survey*, p. 19, n.). See also A. J. Lotka on food chains in *Elements of Physical Biology*, chap. 14.

67. E.g., see Lindberg, *op. cit.*, pp. 185–86, 196–200. In Europe agricultural output per acre is generally higher where the production of animal products is important than where this is not the case.

68. H. R. Tolley states: "When a nation derives 80 or 90 per cent of its calorie requirements from cereals and potatoes, there is a strong presumption that mineral and vitamin deficiencies are widespread. On the other hand, when 35–50 per cent of all calories come from animal products, such deficiencies are not likely to be widespread among all groups and classes." See Tolley's essay in T. W. Schultz, *Food for the World*, p. 164. M. K. Bennett states: "One can probably say conservatively that national diets composed more than 70 per cent of cereal-potato calories are very likely to be qualitatively inadequate, in some degree or other damaging to the human organism." Yet five-sevenths of the world's population live on such diets. See "International Contrasts in Food Consumption," *Geographical Review*, XXXI, 1941, pp. 372, 375. A "restricted emergency" diet prepared by H. K. Stiebling and M. M. Ward stipulates (on the assumption that one-third of the fats are of animal and fish origin) that 25 per cent of the calories be of animal and fish origin and 48 per cent of cereal-potato origin. Corresponding percentages for an "adequate diet at minimum cost" are 37 and 38. See *Diets at Four Levels of Nutritive Content and Cost*, USDA Circular No. 296, 1933, pp. 3, 28, 37. While it is sometimes said that about one-half "of the protein in a diet should be of animal origin" (see *Final Report of the Mixed Committee of the League of Nations on the Relation of Nutrition to Health, Agriculture and Economic Policy*, p. 60), H. C. Sherman states "that the old habit of specifying some fixed proportion of animal protein in setting a protein standard for dietaries or food supplies is now superfluous" (see USDA Miscellaneous Publication No. 546, *Principles of Nutrition and Nutritive Value of Food*, p. 12).

69. E.g., in Japan, where only 10–15 per cent of the calories available for consumption come from livestock products (see Tolley, *op. cit.*, p. 165), malnutrition originated in the dietetic habits of the people as well as in the absolute restrictedness of the food supply (see E. F. Penrose, *Population Theories and Their Application*, pp. 125ff.). Even in the United States where more than 35 per cent of the calories available originated in livestock products in the 1930's the average American dietary was short of calcium and riboflavin and, at times, of other nutrients (Sherman, *op. cit.*, pp. 21, 36–38). See Section VII below.

the same conditions, 6,000–7,440 primary calories.[70] These primary calorie requirements must be increased by 20–30 per cent to allow for seed, waste, loss, and feed for animals (e.g., draft) not used primarily as food sources.[71]

Consumers, if left free to choose, are not likely to substitute primary for derived calories, even when such substitution is physiologically feasible. Consumption vectors do not point in this direction. The importance of derived calories in dietaries is positively associated with the level of per capita income and the evidence suggests that income elasticity of demand is greater for derived than for primary calories.[72] When, upon the advent of adverse economic circumstances, consumers substitute primary for derived calories, they do this because their incomes have fallen and/or the price of primary calories has declined relatively to that of derived calories. If these changes were also accompanied by an appropriate modification of tastes, primary would be substituted for derived calories in greater measure. But habit and social practice stand in the way of such modification. Presumably it could be brought about through the use of force and propaganda.[73]

The food supplies accessible abroad to food-importing nations are limited for two reasons. The domestic requirements of food-exporting countries rise as their living standards improve. Opulent nations are not disposed to modify their tastes in order that more calories may be made available to food-importing nations.

While the limits to the modifiability of tastes for nonfood products are socio-psychological rather than physiological in character, these limits are not easily raised. When population growth depresses per capita income and the relative price of labor, resource-absorbing products are replaced in part by labor-absorbing products. But this income-increasing substitution is effected *within* the existing framework of tastes, which continues essentially unchanged. Moreover, it does not appear that autonomous changes in tastes are much more likely to be labor-favoring than resource-favoring,

70. The Food and Nutrition Board of the National Research Council in 1943 recommended 2,730 calories for the then American population. Recommended allowances for adult males ranged from 2,500 for the sedentary to 4,500 for the very active; for adult females, from 2,100 for the sedentary to 3,000 for the very active. See *ibid.*, pp. 6–7, 36; National Research Council Circular 122, *Recommended Dietary Allowances*, 1945, p. 10.

71. Although Richter's figures suggest a 23 per cent allowance, a "some 30 percent" figure is indicated (Lindberg, *op. cit.*, p. 188).

72. E.g., see R. G. D. Allen and A. L. Bowley, *Family Expenditure*, pp. 45–47; H. Staehle, *Quarterly Journal of Economics*, LIV, 1940, pp. 217–31; N. L. Gold and M. Enslow, *ibid.*, LVII, 1943, pp. 596–629. Also C. E. V. Leser, *Review of Economic Studies*, IX, 1941, pp. 40–58.

73. The initial effect of such involuntary modification would be the descent of affected persons to a lower plane of satisfaction. If in time, however, they became adjusted and developed a greater liking for what they were "induced" to consume, they might find themselves able to satisfy both their former and additional wants, and their incomes would be higher. Note the apparent effect of the food stamp plan (J. D. Coppock, *American Economic Review*, XXXV, 1945, pp. 99ff.), or the alacrity with which the female, though protesting against the ukases of the overlords of fashion, adjusts the length and grip of her skirt to their unwelcome obsolescence-accelerating dictates.

even when population pressure prevails. Force and propaganda can, in some degree, substitute labor-favoring for resource-favoring tastes.

Limitations upon the modifiability of consumer tastes curb the consumption-modifying power of international trade. (*a*) If a populous country which is short of capital tries to ease this shortage by borrowing abroad, it must closely supervise the use of the borrowed foreign exchange; otherwise some of the borrowed funds will be exchanged for goods which do not add to or free domestic productive power.[74] (*b*) If a populous country is dependent upon foreign sources for some of its foodstuffs and raw materials, exchanging labor-absorbing goods therefor, its ability to import these commodities is conditioned, *ceteris paribus,* by foreign consumption patterns over which, as a rule, it can exercise little dominion.[75]

Consumers are more free, in theory, to augment their real incomes by changing their tastes when their incomes are high than when they are low. Accordingly, since relatively high incomes are associated with relatively high resource : population ratios, consumers are free to change their tastes when they are under little demographic compulsion to do so.[76] For when incomes are high, the attainable substitution possibilities open to consumers are greater in number and in degree than when incomes are low.[77] Thus, a high-income consumer can substitute primary for derived calories in a variety of ways whereas a low-income consumer has left few if any opportunities to substitute primary for derived calories. Consequently, even

74. Since a large fraction (say one-half) of a nation's capital equipment consists of immovable assets, a nation's power of adding to its capital stock by borrowing abroad is limited; it can import for this purpose only movable assets and consumables which release domestic productive power for the purpose of making immovable assets. See N. S. Buchanan, *International Investment and Domestic Welfare,* pp. 17–19, 110–16. In prewar England the marginal propensity to import was 15 per cent, and part of these imports were consumables. See W. H. Beveridge, *Full Employment in a Free Society,* p. 358.

75. In the past 150 years most international trade has been carried on by countries the economic condition of whose population improved greatly despite marked population growth. Available studies do not deal directly with the effect of population growth upon the nature, direction, and terms of trade. Although the growth in industrial countries of export balances in manufactures has been more than offset by the growth of import balances of primary products, the relative extent to which manufactures are exchanged for food and raw materials has not changed, international trade in food continues less important than that in manufactures or in raw materials, and the terms of trade are more favorable to industrial countries in this than in the 19th century. See F. Hilgerdt, *Industrialization and Foreign Trade,* p. 100; A. O. Hirschman, *Quarterly Journal of Economics,* LVII, 1943, pp. 574–75, 590; C. Clark, *Conditions of Economic Progress,* chap. 14, also p. 249. E. Staley, *World Economic Development,* chap. 8. Britain's present trade problem illustrates the dangers to which a nation greatly dependent upon trade because of past population growth is exposed in an industrializing world (G. D. A. MacDougall, *Economic Journal,* LVII, 1947, pp. 78–83).

76. "For unto everyone that hath shall be given, . . . ; but from him that hath not . . . shall be taken away," Matthew, XXV, 29.

77. We are not here concerned with the question: is the price elasticity of demand greater at high than at low income levels? E.g., see N. L. Gold *et al., op. cit.,* pp. 599ff. This question relates to movements along demand functions, not to shifts of demand functions. The answer that it evokes is conditioned by the manner in which "commodity" is defined, for the degree of elasticity is positively associated with the specificity and restrictedness of the "commodity."

though a combination of force and propaganda were employed in a low-income country to augment real income by compelling a change in tastes, the potential effect of this combination would be limited.[78]

(ii) Diminution of the input of productive agents per unit of output serves both to release the economized agents for other purposes and to extend the period during which nonreproducible and depletable resources continue to be available. The factors making for diminution of input are subject to several forms of constraint, however. (a) The introduction of a factor-saving industrial process may be accompanied by direct and indirect changes which bring other limitations into play. For example, the development of iron-ore-saving steels has accelerated the exhaustion of nickel and chrome reserves; and the introduction of time-saving jet engines has stepped up the use of scarce cobalt and columbium. More generally, because of the interconnectedness of events, the effectuation of a saving in the use of any resource f_1 produces changes in the use rates of one or more of the other resources $f_2, f_3, \cdots f_n$, some of which, if they are relatively restricted in supply,[79] now become limitational elements.

(b) Even though the introduction of a factor-saving process does not bring other limitational elements into being, such a process cannot prevent the ultimate exhaustion of the economized resources, or defer indefinitely the advent of a time when the direct and the indirect cost of supplying the economized resources begins to rise. For the activity of the *world*[80] economy is

78. As per worker remuneration rises relatively to the price of the use of resources, the substitution effect conduces to a relatively greater increase in the utilization of resource-absorbing than of labor-absorbing goods and services. If this effect is not more than counterbalanced by consequences attendant upon an increase in per capita income, the utilization of resource-absorbing goods will expand relatively to that of labor-absorbing goods in countries marked by a favorable resource : population ratio and a rising per capita income. On similar grounds it may be argued that a decrease in per capita income originating in increased population pressure would produce an opposite effect.

A vailable statistics do not fully illuminate the preceding argument. At first, as per capita income rises, the relative number of persons employed in secondary occupations (mining, building, manufacturing) increases while that in primary occupations (agriculture, forestry, fishing) falls; but eventually, with per capita income continuing to increase, the relative number in tertiary occupations (commerce, transport, services) rises. (See Clark, *Conditions*, chap. 5, and *The Economics of 1960*, chap. 3; M. K. Bennett, *Quarterly Journal of Economics*, LI, 1937, pp. 317–336; F. Hilgerdt, *op. cit.*, pp. 26–27.) Whether this underlying consumption trend makes for increased equipment per worker is not clear. A study of Gastonia, N.C., suggests, however, that average investment per worker is higher in trade and service ($6,902) and the professions ($4,984) than in manufacturing ($4.289); it is highest in transportation and public utilities. If these averages are representative, and if allowance is made for the relatively greater amount of investment embodied in professional than in nonprofessional persons, the effects described are being realized. On investment per job see the U. S. Chamber of Commerce study, *Investment per Job*, 1945; also C. A. Bliss, *The Structure of Manufacturing Production*, pp. 106, 109–10; S. Fabricant, *Employment in Manufacturing, 1899–1939*, p. 257; National Resources Committee, *The Structure of the American Economy*, Part I, pp. 63, 374–77.

79. This principle is somewhat analogous to the Sprengel-Liebig "law of the minimum" which relates the productivity of a field directly to that necessary constituent of the soil which is present in the smallest relative amount.

80. It is assumed that the *world* economy, as distinguished from any particular *state* economy, is essentially an isolated system.

subject to what may be called the law of increasing economic entropy: economic activity consists of (what are in practical effect) irreversible processes which in the aggregate dissipate the *potential* utility embodied in the stock of resources, actual and potential,[81] existent in the world. A particular part of the world may draw upon the resources of another part, a salvage rate (e.g., of copper) may be stepped up, and so on. But use imposes its tax upon the utility embodied in the resources utilized, and economic entropy increases in the world as a whole, for a portion of this utility is dissipated and becomes economically irrecoverable.[82]

(iii) Augmentation of the supply of utilizable[83] resources may add to present and/or future productive power. This process of augmentation, so important in the past century, is restricted directly by the fixity of the supply of that which is potentially transformable into utilizable resources, and indirectly by the relative limitedness of the supplies of resources complementary to the resource whose supply is augmented.[84] The newly added resources are subject also to what we have called the principle of increasing economic entropy.

It is sometimes implied that technological progress, which is principally responsible for both diminution in resource input and increase in utilizable resource supply, may continue to offset both population growth and the production of income-depressing effects by what we have called increasing economic entropy. For it is assumed that technological progress is at an accelerating rate.[85] To this assumption exception must be taken in respect to the possibilities of technological progress suited to reduce the relative

81. Since what is a resource depends upon (*a*) man's wants and (*b*) the technological knowledge which governs his capacity to utilize the things about him, the stock of *actual* resources may be added to through changes in tastes and accretions to technological knowledge. The principle of increasing entropy stated above rests upon the postulate, therefore, that in the course of time actualization of potential resources does not counterbalance the resource-destroying transformation of the supply of actual resources theretofore in existence.

82. Cf. Lotka's treatment of energy transformation and irreversibility, *op. cit.,* especially chaps. 2–3, 24–25. Underlying what we have called economic entropy is the second law of thermodynamics, according to which the entropy of the universe tends toward a maximum whose attainment entails the "death" of the universe. If, however, we substitute a statistical approach for that of pure thermodynamics, states Frank, we may assume that in time a less frequent state such as that of the present will again occur. See Philipp Frank, *Foundations of Physics,* International Encyclopedia of Unified Science, Vol. I, No. 7, pp. 19–27. Such a recurrence, of course, is too removed to be of any significance for the present discussion.

83. Until a resource is utilized, augmentation of its supply cannot increase present income even though it may increase future income. For example, if in the existing state of technology a worker can utilize q resources, the addition of Δq to his equipment cannot increase his present productivity even though it may insure that at some future date his equipment does not fall below q. (Psychological factors supposedly are constant.)

84. See note 79 and text above.

85. Professor Hart, whose studies in the field of cultural growth have been notably careful and informing, suggests as an hypothesis: "Throughout the entire sweep of history and prehistory, the power of human beings to achieve their basic purposes has been increasing at accelerating speed, with local and temporary stagnations and setbacks. This long-run acceleration has taken place through series of logistic and Gompertz surges, having higher and higher rates of increase." See Hornell Hart, *American Sociological Review,* XI, 1946, p. 281; also

scarcity of resources. The nonaugmentability of the stock of resources, actual and potential, imposes a constraint which becomes greater as this stock diminishes. Moreover, the application of an invention may be limited by the lack of factors essential to its implementation and embodiment, or by man's inability to make and apply necessary complementary inventions. Finally, since the capacity of any specific kind of invention to accomplish a purpose is limited, accomplishment of this purpose in higher and higher measure calls for more and more powerful kinds of appropriate inventions, and these will not be continually forthcoming if restraints are imposed by the finiteness and/or the nature of the physical world, or by the direction taken by cultural progress.[86]

In this section we have indicated the nature of the circumstances which limit the capacity of dynamic forces to counterbalance the tendency of the

---

American Journal of Sociology, L, pp. 349–50, where it is suggested that the conformity of social trends to logistic curves may imply a rational rather than a merely empirical principle. See also Hart, *ibid.,* LII, 1946, pp. 112–22.

86. To illustrate. Suppose the steam locomotive is newly invented, and that it is possible through the gradual perfection of this invention to achieve a maximum speed k. This achievement is possible because the distinctive element in the new invention may be combined with other elements. Let p represent the proportion of possibilities achieved and q the proportion yet to be achieved, subject to the restriction that $p + q = 1$. Let us assume that the "number of pregnant contacts at any given time," and, therefore, the increment of speed added by the improvement of the locomotive through these contacts, are proportional to pq, the magnitude of the increment rising to a maximum at $p = q = \frac{1}{2}$ and thereafter declining in the same manner as it had increased. If we plot the values of the increments proportional to pq we get the first derivative of a logistic curve. If we cumulate (integrate) the increments we get a logistic curve whose upper limit is k. If man would exceed speed k he must make a new kind of invention, the automobile, which, when perfected, will permit a maximum speed m. If man would exceed speed m he must develop a yet different invention, the airplane, capable, upon being perfected, of speed n. This man has done. He has made analogous improvements in the range of projectiles and in the destructiveness of explosives. (His discovery of ways of transmuting elements — until recently he could only rearrange elements in chemical combinations — gives him control over phenomena formerly beyond his control and thus lays the groundwork for many particular paths of invention.) See Hart, *American Sociological Review,* XI, pp. 282, 285, 289.

Our thesis is this. If man would exceed the maximum level of accomplishment realizable within the framework of any given invention (the summation of the increments in the capacity of which generates something like a logistic curve), he must develop a new kind of invention. Moreover, since in many fields of activity current performance is close to the maximum realizable within the present inventive framework, the need of new kinds of inventions is actual and not merely potential. Only in some fields does there remain much room for improvement within the present framework. For example, attained locomotive speed is near the attainable maximum k, while airplane speed, though farther removed from its maximum n, probably soon will approximate it. Accordingly, if speed n is to be exceeded, a new type of invention is called for. It does not follow, however, that, because man's inventiveness has enabled him to achieve higher and higher maxima in certain fields such as speed, it will continue to do this in these fields, or that his accomplishments will be correspondingly great in other fields. In many fields, it is to be presumed, he will encounter insurmountable limitational elements; in some fields he appears to have encountered them already. Whence one may not infer universal technological acceleration from particular time-bound instances of such acceleration.

substitutability of population for resources to decline as population increases. In Section VI the optimum is considered; in VII–VIII data which in some measure confirm our theoretical arguments are presented.

VI

When a population situated in a given territory endowed with given resources is *just* large enough, under the circumstances[87] stipulated, to permit the maximization of over-all per capita output (= income), that population is of optimum size. This optimum is called the per capita output (or income) optimum. It is a function of (a) the quantity and quality of the resource equipment of the territory under consideration, and (b) the conditions governing the division of labor, the economies of scale, and the rates at which producing units can be operated. If (a) is not a constraining force, the magnitude of the optimum is governed by (b). If, on the contrary, (a) exercises constraint before the income-generating forces included under (b) have been maximized, the optimum will be of such magnitude that the marginal income-restricting force of (a) just balances the marginal income-augmenting force of (b).

There are other population optima than the income optimum. For any value index that varies with population density may be maximized. It is probable, however, that maximum values for many indices of well-being—e.g., expectation of life at some stipulated age, state of health, per capita welfare—will be associated with maximum or near maximum values for per capita income. For example, "if countries are considered as units, there is almost a logistic relationship between per capita income and mortality," mortality responding only slightly to income changes in countries with very low or with very high incomes. In like manner expectation of life at birth, while positively correlated with per capita income, becomes relatively insensitive to income changes in countries with very high or very low incomes.[88] Empirical analysis will probably demonstrate that between per capita income and other indices of welfare which have upper and lower limits, an essentially logistic relationship exists. If this kind of relationship obtains, something like maximum values for other indices will be found in a region or state whose population is of income optimum size.[89]

The per capita income optimum is not easy to determine with precision,

87. Let these conditions be (i) to (viii) as formulated in Section II, it being understood also that condition (viii) implies the optimum distribution of economic activities in the given territory. If one or more of these conditions is modified, the magnitude of the optimum population may be increased or decreased. For an excellent discussion of the theory of the optimum see M. Gottlieb, *Journal of Political Economy*, LIII, 1945, pp. 289–316.

88. See *Population Index*, XIII, 1947, p. 103.

89. Let *a* be the actual population, *o* be the income optimum, and *m* the attainable maximum value for some composite and overriding index of per capita "welfare" which the pop-

nor is it highly stable. It is not easy to determine precisely because the necessary data are lacking. Even so, it probably can be determined for most countries with a relatively small margin of error. The optimum is not highly stable because its determinants in the realms of consumption and production tend to change when the economy is dynamic. But it is not probable that these dynamic changes greatly increase or decrease the magnitude of the income optimum.

A per capita output optimum population is not the same thing as a military optimum population. The former, since territory and other conditions are given, is a function of numbers; the latter is a function of both numbers and territory, particularly in an atomic age when territorial depth and industrial scatter are important. An income optimum may, however, be reconciled with a military optimum. Let the income optimum of a population situated in territory t be n. Let the military optimum require at least $10t$ of territory and $12n$ of population. Then, if the two optima may be assumed to be essentially independent of each other, the military optimum consistent with the economic optimum is $12n$ of population on $12t$ of territory, each of the quality of the original t.[90] Other noneconomic optima may be reconciled in like manner with the income optimum.

While a fairly satisfactory income optimum may be achieved by a relatively small population on a relatively small territory, it is doubtful if, under present conditions, a military optimum can be achieved in a territory much smaller than that of the United States. If this be true, most modern states can achieve something like military security short of membership in an efficient world state only by organizing integrated regional blocs with adequate bases.[91]

Per capita output is at a maximum when a population is of optimum size because then the forces making for the augmentation of per capita output are

---

ulation, given its current scheme of values, desires to maximize. Then if, even though $a \leqq o$, m is realized, the population will gain nothing at present by making $a = o$. Only if m depends in part upon resources and the population desires to have m persist into the future, is there a case for making a as small as is consistent with the realization of m. If a logistic or Gompertz or similar kind of relationship obtains between per capita income and the value index which the community is bent upon maximizing, the income optimum may no longer coincide with the magnitude of population making for the maximization of this value index. Under these conditions, therefore, the income optimum should be replaced by an optimum expressed in terms of the preferred value index.

90. The above argument suggests that the military optimum is independent of the income optimum. This is not true. Military strength depends, *ceteris paribus*, upon the fraction of a nation's population available for military service and the production of the sinews of war. The higher output per worker, the higher will this fraction be. It is possible, therefore, for the more productive of two populations of the same size and age-sex composition, to provide twice as many persons for military and related activity as the other can.

91. Hart's studies suggest that the respective areas dominated by national (or quasi-national) states are bound to grow and the number of states to decline. The above argument, if valid, is consistent with Hart's projection. See Hornell Hart, *Can World Government Be Predicted by Mathematics?*, pp. 12ff.

at a maximum for the postulated conditions (see Figure 2 in Part 1). Therefore, as population increases from a suboptimum to an optimum number, *ceteris paribus*, per capita output rises.[92] Per capita output increases under these conditions because of a combination of circumstances: (*a*) smaller and less efficient producing units give place to larger and more efficient producing units in some or all fields of economic activity; (*b*) a better interunit fit is made possible; and (*c*), effects (*a*) and (*b*) are not wholly offset by adverse changes consequent upon increases in the rates at which resources are used.

Columns A–G in Table IV are designed to illustrate what has just been said. It is supposed that 10 distinct products numbered 1–10 (col. A) are being produced in an economy;[93] that each of these products is being consumed at the same rate (col. C); that, in the existing state of the arts and division of labor, the optimum rate of output for a plant of optimum size in each of the 10 industries is that reported in column B.[94] Under these circumstances there will be required for each optimum plant producing product 1, one-half an optimum plant producing product 2, and so on as reported in column D. Accordingly, if a perfect interplant fit is to be achieved – that is, if in each of the 10 lines of production only plants of optimum size operating at optimum capacity are to be used – the number of plants required will be as reported in column E.[95] Whence, if it be assumed that output per worker in each line of production is 10, and that workers constitute 0.4 of the population, the optimum number of workers will be 27,720,000 while the optimum number of population will be 69,300,000, subject to the postulate that effects under (*c*) do not render the optimum smaller.[96]

92. In Figure II of this essay it is assumed that per capita output rises smoothly and continuously. In reality, however, under the conditions assumed and under any at all probable conditions, the upward movement will be jerky rather than smooth because improvement in interfirm coordination and fit will be jerky.

93. By product is meant any commodity or service supplied by private or by public enterprise and into the composition of which labor and/or resources enter. Consumer goods are not distinguished from producer goods since productive agents, being mobile, will be used as demands dictate.

94. A plant is of optimum size when its operation at optimum scale permits the realization of the lowest attainable cost per unit of output. For convenience output per worker under optimum conditions of plant operation is assumed to be 10 in each of the 10 industries. If a smaller and less efficient size of plant were employed, cost per unit would be higher and output per worker would be lower.

For the sake of simplicity it is assumed that the plant optima reported in column B are plant optima in terms of the economy as a whole; that whatever elements enter into the determination of optima thus conceived have been taken into account; and that, if plant optima are in any wise interdependent, this interdependence has been allowed for. On some of the factors which determine optimum size for producing and/or distributing units, see E. A. G. Robinson, *The Structure of Competitive Industry*, chaps. 2–5, 7, 9; also my note, *Southern Economic Journal*, VII, 1941, pp. 399ff.

95. The L.C.D. of the denominators of the fractions in column D is 27,720.

96. In the absence of adverse effects under (*c*), a multiple of 69.3 millions would also be an optimum. The larger the optimum, however, the higher is the rate of increase in economic entropy (see Section V).

Table IV

| Specific product | Plant optimum (000) | Relative demand | Relative numbers of plants needed (C × 1/B) | Optimum need | | | Plants Required | |
A	B	C	D	Plants E	Product (000) F	Workers[a] (000) G	H[b]	I[c]
1	1	1	1	27,720	27,720	2,772	12	72
2	2	1	$1/_2$	13,860	27,720	2,772	6	36
3	3	1	$1/_3$	9,240	27,720	2,772	4	24
4	5	1	$1/_5$	5,544	27,720	2,772	$2^2/_5$	$14^2/_5$
5	7	1	$1/_7$	3,960	27,720	2,772	$1^5/_7$	$10^2/_7$
6	8	1	$1/_8$	3,465	27,720	2,772	$1^1/_2$	9
7	9	1	$1/_9$	3,080	27,720	2,772	$1^1/_3$	8
8	10	1	$1/_{10}$	2,772	27,720	2,772	$1^1/_5$	$7^1/_5$
9	11	1	$1/_{11}$	2,520	27,720	2,772	$1^1/_{11}$	$6^6/_{11}$
10	12	1	$1/_{12}$	2,310	27,720	2,772	1	6
Total	—	—	—	74,471	277,200	27,720	—	—

[a] Output per worker = 10.
[b] Column H based upon assumption there are 12,000 workers.
[c] Column I based upon assumption there are 72,000 workers.

Further consideration of Table IV leads to a number of conclusions, given *ceteris paribus*. First, the smaller the plant optimum in terms of output and/or workers, the smaller will be the optimum population.[97] If we assume for each product a plant optimum of 1,000 instead of the optima reported in column B, worker and population optima become, respectively, 1,000 and 2,500. If we assume an output per worker[98] of 100 instead of 10, the worker optimum (col. G, last line) becomes 2,772,000. Second, the smaller the deviation of the relative demand for specific commodities from the average demand for all commodities, the smaller, as a rule, will be the worker and population optima.[99] Third, the smaller the dispersion of plant optima about the average of all plant optima (cols. B and D), the smaller commonly will the population optimum be.[100] Fourth, the fewer the kinds of commodities wanted, the smaller will be the worker and population optima.[101]

If the actual population increases beyond 69.3 millions, per capita output will fall slightly because of the worsening of the inter-production-unit fit. It will also fall if output per worker in some of the extractive industries begins either to diminish, or to diminish in greater measure, because of increased pressure at the intensive and/or extensive margins. Worsening of the fit is a less important source of decline than increased pressure in the extractive industries.

The method of arriving at an optimum already described tends to under-emphasize the role of diminishing returns in the extractive industries and to overlook the fact that a much smaller approximate optimum exists. Let us turn to columns A–C and H–I in Table IV. Given 12,000 workers and the conditions of columns A–C, the number of plants required in each of the 10 industries is that reported in column H. The resulting condition of plant utilization in industries 4–8 is unsatisfactory and not easily remedied. If the number of workers is increased to 72,000, with the other conditions

97. This statement holds, of course, whether there be only one plant optimum (say 1,000 units of output), or several (say 1, 7, and 10 thousands) that give the same results.

98. This statement implicitly assumes that the plant optimum is independent of the output per worker. This assumption may or may not be valid. Production within a plant is a complex process involving a greater or a lesser number of stages. An increase in the output per worker in any given stage is equivalent to an increase in the over-all output of finished product per worker in the plant; yet an increase in the output per worker in some stage may (e.g., by raising the L.C.M. of the outputs by stage) increase rather than decrease the size of the optimum plant in terms of both aggregate output and number of workers.

99. E.g., if the relative demands reported in column C are not always 1 but 1, 2, 4, 1⅓, 8, 6, 14, 18, 4, 10, the worker and the population optima become 94.71 and 236.775 millions, respectively.

100. This will not be true under all conditions; e.g., if the relative value for each of products 2–10 in column C is the reciprocal of the corresponding value in column B.

101. The L.C.D. of the denominators of the fractions in column D will tend to be smaller; the total number of plants (col. E, last line) will be smaller. If only product 1 were required, the population optimum would be 250, and per capita consumption would be 4. Under the conditions of production and consumption of Table IV, per capita consumption of each of the 10 products is 0.4; of all 10 together, 4.

unchanged, the number of plants required in each industry is that reported in column I. In but four industries (4-5, 8-9) is demand not a multiple of the plant optimum. In three of these (4-5, 8) the demand can be met by operating each plant $\frac{1}{35}$ beyond optimum capacity; in industry 9 each plant must be operated $\frac{1}{11}$ beyond capacity. If plant marginal cost curves are highly elastic in each industry, and if the demand for each of the 10 products is highly elastic, output per worker will continue to approximate 10. For, given elastic cost curves, output per worker falls little when optimum capacity is exceeded; while, given elastic demand curves, some of the estimated supra-capacity demand in industries 4-5 and 8-9 will shift to industries 1-3, 6-7, and 10 where the cost curve remains relatively lower and probably more elastic.

Our second method of arriving at an optimum population has given us nearly as good a result in terms of inter-production-unit fit for a worker population of 72,000 as we got for one of 27,720,000. The more elastic the cost and demand curves in the industries composing the economy, the less will be the advantage of the larger population.[102] In no realistic case which allows for economic fluctuation and dynamic change can the advantage of the larger over the smaller population be appreciable on grounds of fit. Accordingly, since present and future pressure upon resources in the extraactive industries is bound to be much less with the smaller than with the larger population, it is the smaller rather than the larger which constitutes the true long-run income optimum population.

While the augmentation of international trade serves (within limits) to increase per capita output, it may or may not alter a country's income optimum. (i) It will increase or decrease the optimum accordingly as it increases or decreases the magnitude of the population required for a perfect interproduction-unit fit. (ii) It may increase or decrease the optimum, in the future if not in the present, accordingly as it eases or intensifies the pressure of population upon resources, and particularly as it decelerates or accelerates the rate of increase in economic entropy.

The augmentation of a country's international trade may, if it gives rise to population growth and an increase in the dependence of that country upon foreign sources for foodstuffs and raw materials, increase the potential insecurity of that country's resource base. For, as industrialization progresses and income rises in the countries of provenance, their demands for their own raw materials and (in greater measure) foodstuffs (or food-producing resources)[103] will expand, and their export "surpluses" will shrink.[104]

102. The conditions which we noted above as making for a smaller optimum population are equally applicable in the present case.

103. In 1937 the percentages of world production, by type, consumed outside the country of production were: foodstuffs, 16.6; raw materials and semifinished goods, 56.8; manufactured goods, 11.7; all products, 19.2. Computed from Clark, *Conditions*, p. 457.

104. In 1937 industrial countries absorbed about three-fifths of the imports of foodstuffs and raw materials and finished goods, with most of the two former classes coming from non-

This shrinkage will probably be felt more keenly in the food[105] than in the raw material categories.[106]

Our analysis suggests that income optima are smaller than is usually supposed.[107] If this analysis and our argument regarding the military optimum be valid, it follows that military strength should be sought through blocs, bases, and alliances rather than through populationist policies which can contribute little for 15 or more years.

VII

Because the circumstances governing industrialization and production are complex,[108] our short account of the augmentability of resources and of the substitutability of labor for resources in (*a*) agriculture and (*b*) nonagriculture is incomplete.[109]

(*a*) Evidence of various sorts suggests how the substitutability of labor for agricultural resources declines as the population : resources ratio rises. (i) Clark presents data for 20 countries and 9 divisions of American states. Let y = output per male worker in agriculture; x = density expressed as the number of male workers per 1,000 hectares (= 2,471 acres) of farm land.

---

industrial countries. See League of Nations, *The Network of World Trade*, pp. 17-18, 22-24.

105. Of the continents only Europe, which has imported one-fourth of its food consumption (dry basis), will be adversely affected; only 6 per cent of world food consumption enters intercontinental trade (F. A. Pearson and F. A. Harper, *The World's Hunger*, pp. 9-11).

106. A small number of countries account for most of the exports and the imports of specific commodities. See *Network*, pp. 7, 30-36; Hilgerdt, *op. cit.*, pp. 56, 100.

107. Professor John Jewkes, having observed that if Britain's population were smaller, her least efficient firms could be closed, declared: "It is difficult to think of any one important industry or public service which could not seize upon the full economies of large scale production with (say) a market of 20 million persons in an area as small as that of Great Britain. On the other side the cost of congestion in our main centres of population in the way of traffic delay and time spent in reaching and returning from work must be considerable" (*Manchester School of Economic and Social Studies*, X, 1939, p. 110). Since economies of scale, after they have been developed by larger firms, may be introduced by smaller firms (Rothbarth, *op. cit.*, pp. 389-90), a population that has diminished in size will retain many of the economies of scale which emerged originally because the population was larger.

108. See Rothbarth (*op cit.*, pp. 383-90) and L. Rostas (*Economic Journal*, LIII, 1943, pp. 39ff., and Royal Economic Society Memorandum 107, 1946).

109. In this section the relationship of agriculture to nonagriculture is largely disregarded. Yet income per capita, by country or region, is positively correlated with the smallness of the per cent of all workers engaged in agriculture (for 35 countries the Spearman rank coefficient of correlation is +0.878 with a probable error of ±.027). This relationship has its origin in part in two circumstances. First, since output per worker usually is lower in agriculture than in industry (Clark, *Conditions*, p. 342), over-all average income is low in proportion as the relative number of agricultural workers is high. Second, output per worker in agriculture is higher, as a rule, and output per acre tends to be somewhat higher, in industrial than in nonindustrial countries. The rank coefficient (based on 22 countries for which Clark gives data) of correlation between smallness of per cent of workers in agriculture and output per agricultural worker is +0.714 (P.E. = ±.074), and between smallness of this percentage and output per hectare is +0.193 (P.E. = ±.095). See also Hilgerdt, *op. cit.*, p. 38.

Then $y = \dfrac{A}{x^n}$ where $n = \frac{1}{2}$, and A is a constant with a value (in this case) of about 4,200 I.U.[110] "Production per head tends to vary inversely with the square of the density." The marginal product of labor is $\dfrac{A}{2x^n}$; that of a unit (1,000 hectares) of land is $\dfrac{Ax^n}{2}$. The elasticity of technical substitution, σ, of labor for land is one, the substitutability of labor for land falling at the same rate as that at which labor (x) increases.

Clark's formula is not wholly adequate. First, the value of σ is not as the formula implies, independent of the magnitude of x. σ cannot remain equal to one; it must fall and eventually descend to zero. The formula implies that not until $x = 17,640,000$, and there are 7,139 male workers per acre, does the marginal product of labor fall to 0.5 I.U. Yet, long before this, the marginal product would have fallen to zero, and earlier still it would not have sufficed for the support of a worker.[111] Second, the formula does not take into account international differences in raw data, in quality of land and climate and workers, and in type of equipment and methods used.[112] For this reason actual average product frequently exceeds theoretically expected product in advanced countries, and falls below it in backward countries.

(ii) W. E. Moore overcame some of these shortcomings by converting land into terms of relatively homogeneous "arable equivalents," and output into terms of relatively homogeneous "crop units."[113] Even so, because many international differences persist, output per worker is not highly correlated, by country, with land per worker, nor is output per hectare highly correlated with number of workers per hectare.[114]

110. I.U. are International Units of Value. Rank correlation between x and y for 24 countries is $+0.756\pm.062$ (data from Clark, *Conditions*, p. 244; *Economics*, pp. 34–39).

111. In China, J. L. Buck's data suggest, the marginal product of labor becomes zero when the input of labor per acre exceeds 0.25 man (*Land Utilization in China*, chap. 9, Tables 9–12, 16). In densely peopled lands where labor is cheap it tends to be used unproductively (e.g., see *ibid.*; H. G. Moulton, *Japan*, pp. 398–99; Lau Shaw's novel, *Rickshaw Boy*). In proportion as an economy is mobile, factor movement is free, and distribution is on a marginal productivity basis, the population of an occupational area tends to become stationary when the worker's marginal product in such area approximates his direct and indirect reproduction cost. See note 147 below.

112. On the effects of climate see E. Huntington, *Principles of Economic Geography*, and *Annals of the American Academy of Political and Social Science*, CLXLVIII, 1938, pp. 77ff. If modern systematic agriculture were introduced throughout Europe, present regional differences in yields would be reduced but not eliminated (E. Dániel, *Review of Economic Studies*, XII, 1944-45, pp. 31–49).

113. *Economic Demography of Eastern and Southern Europe*, esp. pp. 35, 197ff. On W. Staniewicz's method of reducing heterogeneous land to units of plowland see C. L. Stewart, *Land Policy Review*, VII, 1944, pp. 15ff., and *Illinois Farm Economics*, No. 127ff., 1945-46, pp. 313ff.

114. If all conditions other than the number of workers per hectare were constant, we should expect: (*a*) a high positive correlation between output per worker and land per worker; (*b*) a high negative correlation between output per hectare and land per worker; and (*c*) a high negative correlation between output per worker and output per hectare. The expected relation-

The countries of Europe fall roughly into three groups, with the members of each group lying about a distinct regression line. Let y = average output per person dependent upon agriculture, and x = number of persons dependent upon agriculture per square kilometer of "arable-equivalent" agricultural land. For the high output-per-worker group (1), which includes seven countries (Denmark, England and Wales, Scotland, Netherlands, Belgium, Germany, and Switzerland), $y = 152.8 - 0.65476x$. For the nine-country (France, Sweden, Austria, Luxemburg, Norway, North Ireland, Latvia, Czechoslovakia, and Ireland) intermediate group (2), $y = 79.1 - 0.3977x$. For the low output-per-worker group (3), which includes 13 countries (Estonia, Spain, Hungary, Lithuania, Italy, Finland, Portugal, Roumania, Greece, Poland, Bulgaria, Yugoslavia, and Albania), $y = 42.03 - 0.2102x$.[115]

The marginal values corresponding to these average y-values are: (1) $y_m = 152.8 - 1.30952x$; (2) $y_m = 79.1 - 0.7954x$; and (3) $y_m = 42.03 - 0.4204x$. The elasticity of technical substitution σ is below one-half for all positive values of x, diminishing as x increases; at $x = 50$ it approximates one-third in all three cases.[116] The marginal product, therefore, must descend to zero, in case (1) when x approximates 117, and in cases (2) and (3) when x approximates 100.

The data suggest that, given agricultural conditions such as prevailed in prewar Europe, the marginal product of agricultural workers approximates zero when the number of persons dependent upon agriculture rises above 100–120 per square kilometer (247 acres). In view of the fewness of observations and of other data limitations, this finding is merely approximate. Nonetheless, it suggests that the substitutability of labor for land is limited and diminishing, and that marginal product must eventually fall to zero if the worker : land ratio is continually increased.[117]

---

ships are not found, however, because sometimes a relative shortage of land is offset in part by superior methods of cultivation, and because in general conditions other than the worker : land ratio vary from country to country. For 29 European countries for which Moore gives data the Spearman rank coefficient of correlation for the three indicated relationships are: (a) +.498 ±.098; (b) −.057 ±.131; and (c) +.806 ±.106. These correlations are determined for persons dependent upon agriculture. The same finding obtains for males engaged in agriculture, since the rank correlation between yield per male engaged in agriculture and yield per person dependent on agriculture is +.978 ±.006.

115. The standard error of estimate σy_s, together with the number of countries within ±1 σy_s, is 17.67 and 5 for group (1). The corresponding figures for group (2) are 5.08 and 5; for (3), 4.6 and 10. The sigma representing the standard of error of estimate should not be confused with the sigma representing the elasticity of technical substitution. Of the total variance in y (= average output), the fraction attributable to variation in x (= worker : land ratio) is about one-half in case (1) and about three-quarters in cases (2) and (3). The number of cases in each group is very small.

116. When the average value $y = a - bx$, $\sigma = (a - 2bx)/2(a - bx)$. That is, σ = the marginal product divided by two times the average product. See Section I.

117. In but four of the 29 countries was the number of persons dependent upon agriculture at or above 100: Switzerland, 107.1; Ireland, 102.5; Yugoslavia, 100.1; Albania, 176.4. The ability of densely populated countries in Western Europe to escape this pressure, together

(iii) From American data presented by J. D. Black one may draw a conclusion similar to that derived from Moore's European data. Black reports, largely as of 1929 for nine geographic divisions and a number of individual states, net farm income and equipment (i.e., land [by type] in farms, together with the value of land, farm buildings, and capital goods) per agricultural worker. Account may therefore be taken of variations in the quality of the land and in the amounts of capital used jointly with land, or as a substitute for it.[118] Let y = net income per agricultural worker and x = the number of agricultural workers per \$10,000 of agricultural property. For the nine divisions and the country as a whole $y = 1,409 - 1.991x$; $\sigma y_s =$ 169, and five of ten units lie within $\pm 1\sigma y_s$. When the three western divisions are excluded, $y = 1142 - 1.33x$, with $\sigma y_s = 65$, and five of seven units lying within $\pm 1 \sigma y_s$; the amount of variance explainable in terms of variation in x (worker : property ratio) rises from about seven-tenths to above eight-tenths. The corresponding marginal values are $y_m = 1,409 - 3.982x$ and $y_m = 1,142 - 2.66x$.

As in (ii) the elasticity of technical substitution σ is under one-half for all positive values of x, declining as x increases. The marginal productivity of agricultural workers must eventually descend to zero. The data suggest that when agricultural property per worker falls in the neighborhood of \$26–\$29 hundred, the product of workers at the margin is at or close to the zero level.[119] Our findings are essentially suggestive in character, since our observations are few in number.

with their high per worker yields, is attributable in part to their ability to import foodstuffs and feed. E.g., English wheat yields per acre have risen with the reduction in wheat acreage (Clark, *Conditions*, pp. 256–57).

About 35–45 per cent of the population dependent upon agriculture in Eastern and Southeastern Europe, Moore estimates (*op. cit.*, pp. 61–75), is unneeded in agriculture and adds little to aggregate output. See note 119 below.

118. Capital goods other than farm buildings are complements to farm land rather than substitutes for it. For the nine divisions the rank correlation of the per worker value of farm land with the per worker value of capital goods and farm buildings, respectively, is +.8 ±.085 and +.27 ±.22. (In parts of Europe, Moore reports [*op. cit.*, pp. 89ff.], small land holdings sometimes are overequipped with certain forms of capital.)

Although both the quality of land per worker and the associated amount of equipment are highly correlated with the amount of land per farm worker, each independently influences output per farm worker. Output per farm worker is (rank) correlated (in the nine divisions and the country as a whole) with these variables as follows: with land in farms per worker, +.85 ±.06; with value of farm land per worker, +.95 ±.02; with all agricultural property per farm worker, +.985 ±.007. Black's averages on which this analysis is based are given in *Annals of the American Academy of Political and Social Science*, CLXXXVIII, 1936. pp. 205–17; *Review of Economic Statistics*, XVIII, 1936. pp. 66–83.

119. In 1929 agricultural property per worker was at or near the \$26–29 hundred level only in the three southern divisions of states. It was below this level only in the east south central states where it averaged \$1,920 in contrast with a national average of \$6,320 and a divisional maximum of \$11,120 in the west north central states.

The census returns for 1930 tend to support the above reasoning. If in 1929 the farms grossing under \$1,000 had been withdrawn from cultivation, aggregate agricultural production

(iv) Analysis of McCormick's findings relating to farm population pressure in Wisconsin suggest that the marginal product of a unit of farm population descends in the neighborhood of zero when the number of acres per unit of farm population falls near to or below 20 acres.[120] McCormick divided Wisconsin into three somewhat homogeneous agricultural areas (I, II, and III)[121] and then estimated what would be the farm population required in a given area[122] and what would be its gross farm income (= gross output) if the land : man ratio in each of the counties in this area were raised to the level prevailing in those counties where per capita income was at or near the maximum. The basic facts are given in columns 2–8 of Table V. I_2 represents the aggregate gross income by area, given the actual farm population P_2; the corresponding average income is given in column 7. I_1 represents the estimated aggregate gross income by area, on the assumption that the farm population has been reduced from P_2 to P_1; the corresponding average income is given in column 6. In column 8 is given the

Table V

Area	Income in $(000,000)		Farm population (000)		Average income		Marginal income	
	I_1	I_2	P_1	P_2	At P_1	At P_2	$\dfrac{I_2 - I_1}{P_2 - P_1}$	Hypothetical at $(P_2 + P_1)/2$
I	76.69	77.27	270.1	314.1	$284	$246	$13.08	$13.00
II	59.59	68.07	245.6	341.3	243	199	88.35	87.00
III	23.51	28.70	139.0	203.8	169	138	72.12	72.00

Source: Derived from McCormick, *op. cit.*

would have been reduced only about 15 per cent. In that year 21.3 and 41.2 per cent, respectively, of the nation's non-part-time farms grossed under $600 and $1,000. The corresponding percentages for the south Atlantic and the east and west south central states were 29.7 and 55; 35.1 and 63.3; 29.1 and 53.6. In these three divisions were located 71 per cent of the national under-$600 farms, 75 per cent of the under-$1,000 farms, and about 71 per cent of the excess farm population. See notes 117, 122.

120. This analysis is based principally upon T. C. McCormick's Tables II, IV, and VI in the *Journal of the American Statistical Association*, XXXVIII, 1943, pp. 165–177.

121. G. Tintner's analysis of agricultural production functions indicates that the effect of an increase in the relative amount of land is conditioned by the type of product. In Iowa he found a 1 per cent increase in land was accompanied by an increase of 0.586 per cent in crops but of only 0.276 and 0.278 per cent, respectively, in beef feeders and hogs. Elasticity of output with respect to labor is greatest in dairying and hog production; with respect to both improvements and liquid assets, in the production of beef; and with respect to working assets and cash operating expense, in dairying. See *Econometrica*, XII, 1944, pp. 28–30, 33–34; cf. Clark, *Conditions*, pp. 270–71.

122. In 1930, McCormick concludes, "excess" farm population approximated 204,000, or 24 per cent of the total farm population. At that time the farm population living on non-part-time farms grossing under $1,000 approximated 142,000.

estimated marginal income per unit of farm population centered at $(P_1 + P_2)/2$. In the last column is given the marginal income per unit of farm population at $(P_1 + P_2)/2$, based upon the assumption that the marginal income curve for a given area corresponds to a linear average income curve which passes through the average income values associated in this area with populations P_1 and P_2.[123] Since the hypothetical marginal value reported in the last column corresponds very closely by region with what may be called the "observed" marginal value reported in the penultimate column, it may be inferred that the hypothetical marginal income curve describes the actual situation reasonably well and that the elasticity of technical substitution σ is below one-half and falling as farm population increases. If this inference is valid, it may also be inferred that marginal gross income (= gross output) will move in the neighborhood of zero when the number of acres per unit of farm population becomes somewhat less than 24 in area I, 25 in area II, and 21 in area III.[124]

The data presented indicate that since the elasticity of substitution of labor for resources is limited and subject to decline, the marginal productivity of agricultural labor must fall to zero unless this declensional tendency is arrested by technological improvements.

Since labor and other productive agents are not continually substitutable for cultivatable land, the population capacity of the earth is limited by: (1) the number of acres suitable (in view of their topographic, rainfall, and other limitational qualities) for food production; (2) the fraction of these acres that can be devoted to food production; (3) the quantity of primary calories consumed per capita; and (4) the output of primary calories per acre.

Of the world land area (35.7 billion acres) only about 2.6 billion, or 7 per cent, are adapted to agricultural production.[125] Six-tenths of the adaptable acres are devoted to food crops (including grain for livestock), the balance being used to grow hay, cotton, etc., or to lie fallow; by continent

123. See columns 6–7. The equations for average income (= y), by region, are: I, $y = 517 - 0.86363x$; II, $y = 355 - 0.45833x$; III, $y = 235 - 0.477x$. The corresponding marginal values for y, by region, are: $517 - 1.72726x$; $355 - 0.91666x$; $235 - 0.954x$.

124. McCormick gives several optimum ratios for each area: I, 27 and 32; II, 34 and 40; III, 31 and 45. He finds the variation in per capita income to depend much more upon variation in the man : land ratio than upon that in the value of farm land. With the value of the land and the type of farming held constant, the variance "in per capita income from county to county that may be attributed to differences in the land-man ratio and associated factors" in 0.63 in area I, 0.68 in area II, and 0.49 in area III. See op. cit., 166, 170–71. Since in 1930 about one-third of the farm population was reported as gainfully employed in agriculture, the averages given above may be converted into terms of gainfully employed agriculturalists by multiplying by 3.04. In Europe the productivity of peasant farms is at an optimum in the size-range 37.5–75 acres (Clark, Conditions, p. 271).

125. See information-packed The World's Hunger (by Pearson and Harper), p. 50. Huntington (op. cit., pp. 28–30) reports 2.24 billion acres under cultivation. E. Raisz (Atlas of Global Geography, p. 50) and J. F. Timmons (Land Policy Review, VII, 1944, p. 9) estimate the world's cultivatable acreage at four billion. Soilless culture is not a significant substitute for land culture (USDA Yearbook of Agriculture, 1943–47, pp. 289–92).

this fraction ranges from 0.38 in South America to 0.79 in Asia (see cols. 2–3 in Table VI). If this fraction were raised to 85–90 per cent, the number of acres available for food crops would approximate 2.2–2.3 billion acres;[126] but even so, the population of Asia, comprising about 53 per cent of the world total, cannot be equipped with as much as one-half crop acre per capita, while 25 years hence, the world average will probably be under 0.8.

In the prewar period per capita calorie consumption in the world approximated 2,500 with about one-half the population consuming under 2,250, two-thirds under 2,750, and one-third over 2,750. Since per capita production *in terms of primary* calories, which ranged from 10,000 or more in some parts (North America, Oceana, and a few additional countries) to 2,750 and less (in parts of Asia, Africa, and Latin America), averaged perhaps 4,200 in the world as a whole, per capita consumption *in terms of primary* calories was below 4,000.[127] This average is much below what may be considered a minimal safety diet of 3,000 calories, one-fifth of which are of animal origin, which entails the production of 6,600 primary calories. For although per capita consumption of foodstuffs on a dry basis does not vary markedly with interregional differences in income, per capita consumption of grain (directly and in the form of animal foods) and animal food is positively correlated with income (see cols. 7–10, Table VI; also Table VII). Accordingly, the smaller the fraction of total calorie intake consisting of animal foodstuffs, the larger the number of people a given area can support; thus with this fraction at one-tenth instead of at two-fifths, 112.5 per cent more people can be supported. Given the per capita grain consumption reported for Asia in Table VI (col. 8), world grain supplies could maintain some 2,831

126. In Europe, Oceana, and North America inedible farm products constituted (in value) 12 and 10 per cent, respectively, of recorded and of all (recorded plus unrecorded) farm products in 1925–34 (computed from Clark, *Conditions*, p. 249). In the United States about 85 per cent of net farm output "is destined for human food, most of which is consumed domestically" (H. Barger and H. Landsberg, *American Agriculture 1899–1939*, pp. 27, 293); about 88.5 per cent of the labor power (as of 1940) needed in agriculture was devoted (on the assumption that export allowances balance import requirements) to the production of food (O. V. Wells, *Land Policy Review*, III, 1940, p. 4); about 10 per cent of the crop acres are used in nonfood production. Individual countries, of course, may import inedibles. Thus industrial Great Britain and Japan, which used inedible farm products equal in value to one-fifth of their food consumption, imported 91 and 29 per cent of these inedibles; for nonindustrial Poland, the corresponding percentages were 4 and 13 (computed from Clark, *Conditions*, p. 249).

127. On nonfood calorie consumption see note 71 above. Given a daily per capita intake of 3,000 calories, per capita daily and annual consumption *in terms of primary* calories, when 5 per cent of the 3,000 consists of animal foodstuffs, is (in thousands) 3.9 and 1,424; when 10 per cent, 4.8 and 1,752; when 15, 5.7 and 2,081; when 20, 6.6 and 2,409; when 30, 8.4 and 3,066; when 40, 10.2 and 3,725. The calorie averages given in the text are taken or estimated from the FAO, *World Food Survey;* M. K. Bennett, "Wheat in National Diets," *Wheat Studies,* XVIII, 1941–42 and *loc. cit., Geographical Review,* XXXI, 1941, pp. 365–76; H. R. Tolley, *loc. cit.;* and V. D. Wickizer and M. K. Bennett, *The Rice Economy of Monsoon Asia.* Data for individual countries are given in Table VII below.

millions of people; the corresponding figures, given European and North American standards, respectively, are 2,127 and 902.[128]

TABLE VI.

| Continent | Acres (million) | | Acres per capita | | Food crop yield per harvested acre (lbs.)[c] | Consumption per capital | | Animal food ÷ all food[e] | |
	Agri-culture[a]	Food[b]	Agri-culture[a]	Food[b]		All food[c]	Grain[d]	Pro-duced	Con-sumed
Asia	600	476	0.52	0.41	1046	543	592	2	3
Europe	890	477	1.55	0.83	976	587	788	10	17
N. America	570	317	3.10	1.72	1058	567	1859	7	25
Africa	240	152	1.53	0.97	643	545	605	3	4
S. America	220	83	2.47	0.93	1066	552	966	9	16
Oceana	60	24	5.45	2.18	740	572	1545	14	36
World	2580	1529	1.19	0.70	1003	558	772	6	9

Source: Taken or computed from Pearson and Harper, op. cit., pp. 50, 20, 51, 12, 68, 7, 13.
[a] Acres adapted to agricultural production.
[b] Acres in food crops, including grain fed to livestock but excluding hay, fallow, cotton, etc.
[c] Weight on dry basis with water excluded.
[d] Weight on wet basis with water included.
[e] Animal food produced as per cent of all food produced and animal food consumed as per cent of all food consumed, both on dry basis.

Although the per acre yield of foodstuffs on a dry weight basis does not differ so much from continent to continent (Table VI, col. 6), the per acre yield on a value basis does, ranging from about 3.4 I.U. in Argentine to 60.8 in Holland.[129] It varies widely also in primary calories, ranging from about 2.74 millions per acre in West Europe to 0.95 millions in North America. Per acre yield of primary calories varies widely by crop: e.g. (in the United States, by thousands): Irish potatoes, 2,283; white rice, 2,134; corn (grits), 2,030; wheat, 1,132; fresh asparagus, 178.[130] In prewar Germany wheat and potatoes yielded 2.76 and 4.48 million calories, respectively, per acre; in Holland the wheat yield may have been a third higher, and the potato yield at least a sixth higher than in Germany. In prewar Japan the primary calorie yield of an acre of rice was about 4.7 million.[131]

128. Pearson and Harper, op. cit., pp. 68–69.
129. Computed from Clark, Conditions, chap. 7, p. 246. Diets in densely populated Japan, India, and China approximate 23, 22, and 16 I.U. whereas 60 is optimum (ibid., pp. 249–51; Economics, pp. 42–43).
130. See R. P. Christensen, op. cit., pp. 38–40, 50–51.
131. On European yields see A. Dániel, op. cit., pp. 50, 60. The figure for Japan is estimated from Wickizer and Bennett, op. cit., p. 319. The Japanese prewar rice yield was nearly 3–5 times that in non-Japanese parts of Asia. Cereals and potatoes "tend generally to be the cheapest" sources of calories. Wheat, or wheat in combination with another grain, is the principal source of calories for some 700 millions of people; rice, for some 950 millions, in areas where

Unless agricultural yields per acre are greatly increased throughout most of the world, there will not be sufficient agricultural production to improve food consumption and meet the needs of a growing population. With present and prospective American yields, probably 1–1.5 acres (exclusive of grazing land) will be needed to supply a combination moderate and liberal cost diet.[132] At this level of consumption, given that 90 per cent of the adaptable acres are used to raise food, the world can support only about 1.6–2.3 billion inhabitants. Given that per capita consumption be raised to the equivalent of 6,600 primary calories (i.e., a 20 per cent meat diet) in Europe, Asia, and Africa; that present consumption be continued elsewhere; and that all calories produced are consumed: then the output of primary calories must be increased about three-fifths, to 5,600 trillion. At calorie yields per acre typical of prewar Eastern Asia (which was reasonably representative of world yields), about 2.8 billion acres are needed. At West European calorie yields per acre (which corresponded to prewar German wheat yields in calories), 2,043 million acres are needed; at Netherlands wheat yields, only about 1.5 billion acres are needed. Since these estimates make no allowance for the 20–30 per cent leakage of output into seed, draft-animal feed, etc., they must be increased accordingly. If this is done, a 20 per cent meat diet can be supplied only if average world per acre yields are raised close to the Netherlands level. By 1970, however, the world's population will have risen about one-third above the 1946 level, and by the year 2,000, nearly one-half. It is evident, therefore, that only if there is a miraculous increase in output per acre can the present and the prospective population be provided with at least a minimal safety diet. It is much more likely that the present situation in which five-sevenths of the world's population gets 70 or more per cent of its calorie intake from cereals and potatoes will persist.[133]

---

rice is the cheapest food. See *ibid.*, pp. 108, 126n.; Bennett, "Wheat etc.," *loc. cit.*, pp. 53, 57, 63.

132. To provide four types of diets the following numbers of acres "exclusive of grazing land" were required on the basis of 1917–26 yields: emergency, 1.2; adequate minimum cost, 1.5; adequate moderate cost, 1.8; adequate liberal cost, 2.1 (Stiebling, *op. cit.*, p. 5). In recent years yield per acre has been about three-tenths above the 1917–26 level (J. F. Dewhurst and associates, *America's Needs and Resources*, pp. 609, 614); therefore the required acres may be reduced correspondingly. They may be reduced even more if per acre yield rises to higher levels. According to Dewhurst (*ibid.*, p. 604), however, 2.4–2.6 acres per capita are needed to provide a moderate of higher cost diet at present and (presumably) to meet our export requirements. To provide Clark's optimum diet (*Conditions*, pp. 246, 251) about one acre would suffice in Holland and Belgium; 1.85 in Germany; about 2.5 in France.

133. It is estimated that the agricultural output of India can be increased 50 per cent (FAO, *World Food Survey*, p. 20). The per capita supply of calories at retail before 1939 was about 2,021, of which not more than 200 were of animal origin. These 2,021 calories, therefore, were equivalent to about 3,200 primary calories, of which not over 3,000 were actually consumed directly or indirectly. Hence elevating per capita consumption to the 6,600 primary calories represented by a 20 per cent animal food diet calls for an increase, in terms of primary calories, of 3,600, or 120 per cent. Evidently a 50 per cent increase in India's agricultural output could at most make possible a 10 per cent animal food diet; and this possibility would be reduced by

(b) The data readily available which bear upon the relationship between output and resources per worker in nonagriculture are less satisfactory than are analogous agricultural data. Notwithstanding, these data clearly indicate that the substitutability of labor for resources is limited and diminishing.

(i) Per capita output (= income) is closely associated with the amount of energy used per worker. In the United States the total output of energy used in performing work has increased at about the same rate as the national income, "the average amount of energy used per dollar of national income" rising only "from 2.7 horsepower-hours in 1860 to 2.8 in 1940.[134] In the early 1920's, Douglas found the Spearman rank coefficient of correlation between kilowatt hours per capita and the average real wage in the United States, Canada, and seven European countries was +.58 with a standard error of ±.149.[135] Let y = income and x = energy used per breadwinner. For 28 countries for which data are available the Spearman rank coefficient of correlation is +0.78 with a probable error of ±.052.[136] The coefficient is no higher for a number of reasons, among them that employment varied, that not all energy (e.g., from work animals, photosynthesis) is included, that the efficiency with which energy is used varies, and that energy, though physically homogeneous, is economically heterogeneous, being employed in varying proportions in the more and in the less economically significant uses.[137] Even so it is evident that per capita output rises with per capita energy used, and that man can increase the latter only by drawing more energy from non-human sources. In the United States in 1929 of the energy derived from coal, petroleum, water, and human workers, only 2.4 per cent came from human workers. The corresponding percentages for certain low-income countries were: China, 73.8; India, 70.2; Yugoslavia, 39.7; Japan, 19.1.[138]

(ii) Per capita output is positively associated with equipment per worker. The rank coefficient of correlation between the per capita value of manufacturing production and the per capita value of machinery in 15 European

---

population growth which is at the rate of about one per cent, or four million, per year. In most other parts of Asia, and in parts of Africa and Latin America, similar situations are found. For a like opinion see G. C. L. Bertram, *Geographical Journal*, CVII, 1946, pp. 196–99.

134. Dewhurst, *op. cit.*, p. 784.

135. *The Theory of Wages*, p. 109.

136. The energy rates, as of 1929, are computed from T. T. Read, *American Economic Review*, XXXV, 1945, p. 144, and Colin Clark's data for 1925–34. Inspection of a scatter diagram indicates that the data do not lie closely about a single regression line, and that a fair fit appears to lie in the neighborhood of $y = 160 + 50x$.

137. E.g., see E. W. Zimmerman, *American Economic Review*, XXIV, 1934, pp. 239–49.

138. Computed from Read, *op. cit.*, p. 144. In the United States the percentages of energy output from mineral fuels and water power, work animals, and human workers, respectively, were: in 1850, 5.8, 78.8, and 15.4; in 1930, 83.7, 11.7, and 4.6; estimated for 1960, 96.3, 1.3, and 2.4 (Dewhurst, *op. cit.*, p. 787). In 1850, of the energy from sources other than work animals, about 73 per cent came from human workers; in 1930, 5.2; in 1960, 2.4. Income per capita was much higher, of course, in 1850 America than in 1929 China, in part because both the work animal and the land supply per worker were much higher.

countries about 1925 is 0.91 ± .031.[139] An increase of 100 units in national income, E. H. Stern found, called (in the present century) for an increase of about 330 units in the national capital employed in the United Kingdom and the United States, and for about 200 in South Africa.[140] Clark found a parabolic relationship between y = income and x = capital per occupied person: $\log y = 2.884 - 1.108 \log x + 0.323 (\log x)^2$.[141] This curve is based upon the income-capital relationships reported for a number of countries in 1865–1939 and for nine divisions of American states. The relationship, therefore, probably is what it is in part because of the uneven distribution of influences other than that of the capital : worker ratio.[142] Among the countries to which the parabola was fitted are the United States, Japan, Australia, Argentine, and 10 European countries, for which capital and real income per worker are given as of 1913.[143] Let y = real income and x = capital per worker; then $y = 853.3 - 0.858x$, with $\sigma y_s = 212.7$, and about one-half of the variance in y attributable to variation in x. While the corresponding computed marginal value (i.e., $y_m = 853.3 - 1.716x$) becomes zero when capital per worker falls in the neighborhood of $1,000, actual income per worker in Japan, where capital per worker averaged only $460, was $128.[144] Evidently the elasticity of technical substitution of labor for capital σ declines with the continuing increase in the worker : capital ratio, and worker marginal product approaches zero when the capital equipment per worker becomes very low.

(iii) Since the elasticity of substitution of labor for capital other than land must fall (*ceteris paribus*) to a very low level if population continues to increase relatively to capital,[145] continuous population growth is feasible only if the supply of capital (i.e., of resources other than land which was treated in subsection [a]) can be sufficiently augmented. If this cannot be done, dynamic changes in the methods of production will be offset by the effects of population growth, per capita income will fall, and eventually population growth will cease.

139. Data from Moore, *op. cit.*, p. 276.

140. *Economica*, XII, 1945, pp. 164–70.

141. *Economics*, pp. 72–74. "Capital" is defined to include dwelling-houses and useful publicly-owned assets, but to exclude land and non-income-yielding personal possessions (*ibid.*, p. 72).

142. Clark states that the rise in income in Australia in the face of an essential constancy in the capital : worker ratio runs counter to "the commonly held supposition that increases of population relative to natural resources in newly settled countries are bound to reduce the average return per unit of labour and capital" (*ibid.*, p. 74). He fails to note that the *ceteris paribus* condition did not hold in Australia; for changes were taking place in productive methods, and possibly the population was approaching more closely to the optimum number.

143. See Clark, *Conditions*, p. 389.

144. A first degree curve does not fit the 1913 data so well as would a higher degree curve. Capital does not include land (*ibid.*, p. 389).

145. As in the case of the substitutability of labor for land, what is important is not that the marginal yield must eventually fall to zero, but that it must fall so low as to make further population growth impossible.

The rate at which capital (other than land) per worker can be increased is conditioned by a number of circumstances, among them (1) the ratio of population to resources, (2) the rate at which population grows, and (3) the augmentability of available mineral and fuel supplies. (1) The per worker capital growth rate is conditioned by the population : resources ratio because the rate of capital formation per worker is conditioned by the magnitude of per worker income, which is governed by the population : resources ratio. Clark's data suggest that, if y = saving and x = real income in I.U. per occupied person by country, $y = -19 + .136x$ for incomes under 1,000 I.U.; beyond 1,000 the curve bends downward slightly, giving a lower value for the coefficient of x.[146] (2) The population growth rate, when positive, diverts to the formation and equipment of new increments of population labor and resources which might otherwise have been employed to produce consumer goods or to increase the equipment of the given working population (and their replacements).[147]

For propositions (1) and (2) we have some empirical evidence. The per capita amount of capital equipment is positively associated with per capita income, by country, presumably because continued lowness of per capita income (whatever be its causes) makes for sparseness of savings and capital formation.[148] Analysis of some data presented by Clark indicates a slight association between lowness of population growth rate and highness of

---

146. *Economics*, chap. 6 and chart facing p. 118. Although Clark's figures relate to many countries and extend over a number of decades, they are suggestive. See also *Conditions*, chap. 11, esp. p. 406, and note 151 below.

147. Let A = average direct cost of producing an adult; B = average cost incurred in producing those individuals who die before reaching maturity; C = average total cost (including indirect costs) of producing an adult worker; n = number of individuals per year who become productive workers; n' = number of individuals who attain maturity but do not become productive workers; and n'' number of individuals per year who would have attained maturity but who died before reaching a productive age (see Bowen, *op. cit.*, cited in note 44). Then

$$C = \frac{A(n + n') + Bn''}{n}.$$

Now subdivide n into n_r and n_i; n' into n'_r and n'_i; and n'' into n''_r and n''_i. The subscript r indicates that the component bearing it represents the number required for replacement purposes; and the subscript i, that part of n_1, n'_1, and n'', respectively, which contributes to the *increase* of the working population. (For the sake of simplicity it is assumed that the ratio of the replacement component to the increase component is the same in each of the three categories n, n', and n''. The total cost T_c of population growth equals R_c, the replacement cost, plus I_c, the cost of the additional increment, with $R_c = n_r C = A(n_r + n'_r) + Bn''_r$ and $I_c = n_i C = A(n_i + n'_i) + Bn''_i$). The productive effort of the labor and resources which is transformed into I_c could otherwise be transformed into additional equipment for the then supposedly constant population. The greater the ratio of I_c to T_c, the more difficult, *ceteris paribus*, is it to increase the capital : worker ratio.

For a practical illustration of the influence of population growth upon capital requirements, given a desired rate of progress, see Stern, *op. cit.*, pp. 169–70.

148. Some relevant data are given in Clark, *Economics*, pp. 73, 77, 81–87. See also E. Staley, *op. cit.*, chap. 4 and appendix.

absolute rate of growth in income, by country.[149] Some corroborative evidence is supplied also by Leon Goldenberg in a comparative study of France, Germany, and the United Kingdom.[150] The population growth rate both before 1870 and in 1870–1914 was much lower in France than in the other two countries. "Before the 1870's [France] excelled in the per capita accumulation of wealth as compared with England and Germany." Between 1870 and 1914 wages, per worker output, and the fraction of annual income saved, were somewhat lower in France than in the other two countries; nonetheless, because population growth absorbed a smaller proportion of savings in France, per capita wealth in France continued to grow and in 1914 was similar to that in Great Britain and superior to that of Germany.[151]

(3) While it may be possible to augment the *available* supply of fuel and mineral resources as population grows and/or per capita consumption rises, it is not possible in all instances to countervail what we have called the law of increasing economic entropy,—i.e., to circumvent the process of depletion by which fuel and mineral reserves are reduced. This inability is unimportant so long as fuel and mineral reserves of the first order are adequate, but it becomes important as a deterrent to income creation and capital formation when the depletion process exhausts the supply of a nonreplaceable mineral, or (what is more usual and of greater practical significance) increases the cost of extracting a mineral.[152] For then relatively more of a nation's productive power must be shunted into mineral production to ac-

149. Clark reports for 1913–30 the percentage increase in working population (let us call this x) and in potential real income per head (let us call this y) for 24 countries (*Conditions*, p. 151). The rank coefficient of correlation between y and x for the 24 countries is $-.226 \pm .114$; when Canada, Australia, U.S.A., Spain, and Japan are excluded, the correlation becomes $-.28 \pm .15$. The rank coefficient of correlation between y and the actual increments in income per head is $+.914 \pm .024$. The coefficient of correlation between x and the *increments* in per capita income is about -0.41 ± 0.20; only about one-sixth of the variance in income increment is explainable in terms of variation in x, the large balance being attributable to other circumstances. In the period 1913–30, a period marked by war and disturbance whatever influence the population growth factor may have exercised was practically swamped by other factors. See below, note 160 and text.

150. *Quarterly Journal of Economics*, LXI, 1946, pp. 40–65.

151. *Ibid.*, p. 53. "The wider dispersion of income in France was one of the factors that led to lower national savings (*ibid.*, p. 54)." During the two decades preceding 1914 about one-half of French savings, one-fourth of the British, and only about one-tenth of the German were invested abroad (*ibid.*, pp. 160–61). Goldenberg attributes this largely to the supposed fact that since France's population was growing slowly, there was less opportunity for investment and less need for savings in France than in the other two countries (pp. 61–62). See also Clark's chart facing p. 147 of *Conditions*.

152. For a description of the depletion process, see *Recent Social Trends*, I, pp. 77–85. Its effect is illustrated with respect to gasoline in a chart (see *The Lamp*, XXIX, 1947, p. 11) which indicates the estimated cumulative quantities of gasoline available in the United States from oil, natural gas, tar sands, oil shales, and (chiefly, 97 per cent) coal at the following service station prices (in trillions of barrels): up to 26¢, 0.3; up to 31¢, 3.8; over 36¢, 3.9. In Great Britain the depletion process had, by 1933–37, when about 94 per cent of the original coal reserve still remained, increased the purchasing power of coal in terms of all other goods about

complish a given objective, with the result that less is available for other purposes. Moreover, if a given mineral is no longer available and not replaceable, the composition of consumption must change, presumably to the disadvantage of consumers.

We have relatively little empirical evidence to illustrate what has been said, for mineral output per mine worker generally remains high, while countries with mineral deficiencies can make them up through importation. It must be remembered, however, that only in the second half of the nineteenth century did the modern economy become so completely founded upon minerals as it presently is and that consequently the depletion process has not long had opportunity to be operative. Already in 1937 world mineral production was seven times what it had been in 1880, while American production was nearly 12 times what it had been 57 years earlier. Moreover, since mineral production and consumption have been closely associated with industrialization, it may be assumed that mineral consumption in the future will grow nearly as fast as the output of world industry.[153] Finally, in proportion as per capita mineral consumption in the rest of the world approaches the American level, and the American level continues to rise, the

---

143 per cent above the 1833-37 level (see *Recent Social Trends*, I, p. 89, and H. W. Singer, *Review of Economic Studies*, VIII, 1941, p. 166).

The effects of the depletion process cannot be predicted with certainty or precision. Increased use of scrap metal may ease the pressure of need. Discoveries of fresh deposits and technological advances (which frequently are stimulated by rising costs) may long counterbalance the operation of diminishing returns originating in the depletion process and even, as in the United States, increase per worker output greatly. "Nevertheless, however favorable the technological situation is today, it would seem that, if one takes a long enough view, the effects of depletion must eventually be of a kind which cannot be fully offset, as they have been so frequently offset in the past, by changes in mining methods. . . . Eventually exhaustion of deposits must occur, and productivity becomes zero as the industry closes down. A more reasonable expectation is a gradual failure of technology adequately to offset the effects of depletion. But this may happen only in the very long run. . . . If a stage of falling productivity must eventually be reached, the American mineral industry is too young, or our period of study is too short, for us to observe it." For at present output per worker, despite occasional declines in the past, is close to its all-time high. See H. Barger and S. H. Schurr, *The Mining Industries, 1899-1939*, p. 254, also chap. 4 and pp. 255-65.

A statement made in 1928 by Robert A. Millikan illustrates the hazards of prophecy with respect to new supplies. "The energy available . . . through the disintegration of . . . atoms may perhaps be sufficient to keep the corner peanut and pop-corn man going, . . . but that is all" (cited in *Recent Social Trends*, I, p. 73n.). Yet, less than two decades later, it was estimated that atomic power could be produced to compete with coal at $10 per ton, and indicated that "nuclear power plants would make feasible a greater decentralization of industry" and the exploitation of "fields of application not open to other types of power-producing plants." See *Atomic Energy*, U.S. Department of State Publication 2661, 1946, pp. 125-27; also J. Marschak, *Bulletin of the Atomic Scientists*, II, 1946, pp. 8-9.

Land degradation is a form of depletion which, while it may be controlled, is diminishing the effective land supply (Bertram, *op. cit.*, pp. 202-203). Irrational exploitation of organic sources of food and materials has a like effect (*ibid.*), but can be checked through countermeasures (e.g., see the USDA 1946 Forest Service report, *Gaging the Timber Resources of the United States*).

153. Growth indexes for the world and the United States for industrial, mineral, metal, and

rate of depletion will be accelerated. In fact, had the whole world consumed minerals at the American rate in 1937, world consumption would have been about eight times what it was.[154]

The present mineral situation of the United States may serve to indicate what is in store in the future. In 1937 the United States consumed about one-half of the world output of minerals but produced only 42, 27, and 47 per cent, respectively, of the global supply of metals, of fuels, and of metals and fuels combined. It imported a fraction (often considerable) of 26 minerals and exported eight.[155] Although the commercial reserves of a number of minerals suffice to meet prospective American consumption requirements for a century or more, the reserves of many others are close to exhaustion.[156]

---

fuel production are given in Table A, based upon C. K. Leith, J. W. Furness, and C. Lewis, *World Minerals and World Peace*, Appendix A:

Table A

Year	Production						
	World				United States		
	Industrial	Metals and fuels	Metals	Fuels	Metals and fuels	Metals	Fuels
1880	18	15.2	16.4	14.8	8.8	8.9	8.8
1900	42	36.4	37.6	36.0	78.9	34.0	27.7
1929	100	100.0	100.0	100.0	100.0	100.0	100.0
1937	119	112.5	115.8	111.3	101.3	91.1	103.8

It is expected that the recent tendency for mineral consumption to lag slightly behind national income will continue into the future (see Dewhurst, *op. cit.*, pp. 593ff.).

154. In 1937 the United States with about 6 per cent of the world's population consumed about one-half of the world's mineral output (National Resources Planning Board, *Industrial Location and National Resources*, pp. 150–51). By 1960 American per capita mineral consumption may be one-fourth higher than in 1937 (estimated from Dewhurst, *op. cit.*, p. 593).

155. Production of four minerals approximately balanced consumption. See NRPB, *Industrial Location* etc., pp. 150–51, 152; C. K. Leith *et al.*, *op. cit.*, pp. 214, 221.

156. Reserves fall into two categories, the commercial, and the submarginal and highly speculative. At the 1935–39 annual consumption rate commercial nitrogen reserves will last for an indefinite period, and submarginal reserves for over 500 years. Corresponding periods for other minerals are: magnesium, indefinite and over 500; salt, indefinite and over 500; phosphate rock, 805 and over 500; potash, 117 and over 500; molybdenum, 422 and 100–500; iron ore, 111 and over 500; sulfur, 55 and over 500; fluorspar, 40 and 5–25; copper, 34 and 5–25; zinc, 19 and 5–25; petroleum, 18 and 25–100; cadmium, 16 and 5–25; gold, 14 and 5–25; lead, 12 and under 5; silver, 11 and 5–25; bauxite, 9 and 100–500; vanadium, 7 and 100–500; antimony, 4 and under 5; tungsten, 4 and 5–25; platinum, 4 and under 5; mercury, 3 and 5–25; asbestos, 3 and 5–25; manganese, 2 and 100–500; chromite, 1 and 5–25. Bituminous coal and lignite commercial reserves will last 4,300 years; anthracite, 195. Submarginal reserves of flake graphite may last 25–100 years; mica (block) and nickel, 5–25; industrial diamonds, quartz crystals, and tin, under 5. See E. W. Pehrson, "The Mineral Position of the United States and the Outlook for the Future," reprinted from *Mining and Metallurgy*, April 1945, p. 4, also p. 3. On oil see L. M. Fanning, *Our Oil Resources*, pp. 115–16, 136, 149, 159, 207. Estimates based upon sedimentary rocks suggest a 100–300 year United States oil supply.

While imported minerals may take the place of domestically exhausted minerals, they can do this only so long as foreign reserves are unexhausted and accessible; and they can do this at present terms of trade only so long as foreign consumption is not greatly stepped up.[157]

The available data suggest that the mineral situation of both the United States and the rest of the world is more likely in time to become worse than better. Population growth will accentuate this tendency as will efforts to improve living conditions in countries which are now overpopulated.[158]

Continued population growth makes more difficult the relief of population congestion in agriculture, itself in part the consequence of the general pressure of numbers upon resources. At present about 60 per cent of the world's 800 million gainfully employed are engaged in agriculture; yet today about 40 per cent and eventually 15–25 per cent of this number, if properly trained and equipped, could produce the present world agricultural output and much more in addition.[159] Reduction of the percentage of workers employed in agriculture to 30 in the Western Hemisphere and to 40 in Europe, Asia, and South Africa, Bean estimates, would increase per capita and aggregate incomes in the 20 countries concerned about $120 and $150 billion, and world income about 60 per cent. Equipping the estimated some 190 million transferring workers involved at an outlay of 1,600 I.U. (or 1925–34 dollars) per worker would cost about 310 billion I.U.'s, with the cost falling most heavily upon the countries at present least well equipped.[160] The problem of provid-

157. At present the principal minerals in which the United States is deficient are produced chiefly in less industrially advanced countries. See *The Index,* winter issue, 1946, p. 196. In 1943 world petroleum reserves sufficed for world needs for about 25 years. Yet North American coal, oil shale, and tar sands resources were deemed adequate to produce over seven trillion barrels (3,000 or more years supply); and it was estimated that 5–10 million acres of sugar cane would suffice to produce liquid fuel for 30 million prewar automobiles (Fanning, *op. cit.,* pp. 115–16, 159, 136). (Since 1920 the replacement of draft animals on the farms alone has released 25–30 million acres.)

158. The full peacetime significance of nuclear, solar, tidal, and similar power sources remains to be determined and is not here taken into account.

159. By 1960 the percentage of the United States labor force engaged in agriculture will approximate 11.5; it was 17.3 in 1940, 42.6 in 1890, and 58.9 in 1860 (Dewhurst, *op. cit.,* p. 621). This decline originates in the fact that whereas physical productivity per worker in agriculture has nearly kept abreast of that in the balance of the economy, the income elasticity of demand for agricultural products is lower. Cf. H. A. Simon, *Econometrica,* XV, 1947, pp. 31–42. The remainder of the above paragraph is based upon L. H. Bean's essay in *Studies in Wealth and Income,* VIII, Part Five, and Clark, *Economics,* pp. 28–30, 71, 73, 80–81.

160. Bean's estimates center about 1940. Clark's respective estimates (for 1945) of workers (in millions) to be transferred out of agriculture and of the prewar stock (in billion I.U.) of capital of the transferring areas are: Asia, 148.8 and 183; U.S.S.R., together with the Balkans, Hungary, and Poland, 36.9 and 112.7; Latin America, 4.2 and 61.4; rest of Europe 3.1 and 55.3. The corresponding figures for Africa are 28 and 44.8. The amount of capital required to equip the transferring workers (at 1,600 I.U. each) divided by Clark's estimate of the prewar stock of capital is as follows for the affected areas: Asia, 1.28; U.S.S.R. etc., 0.5; Latin America, 0.2; rest of Europe, 0.1; Africa, 1.4 (if Staley, [*op. cit.,* chap. 4] is correct in believing Clark's capital estimate for Asia too high, the Asia ratio will exceed 1.28).

The 1,600 I.U. estimate employed above is close to that estimated for Czechoslovakia in the 1930's by Clark. P. N. Rosenstein-Rodan estimated at £300–350 per head the cost of industrializing Eastern Europe (*Economic Journal,* LIII, 1943, pp. 210–11).

ing capital for the transfer of excess agricultural workers out of agriculture is intensified by the fact that by 1955 the world's working population will have increased about 86 millions beyond the 1945 level, with about three-fourths of this increase taking place in countries marked by agricultural overpopulation.

It is commonly held at present that industrialization can ease the poverty of those parts of the world in which the pressure of numbers upon resources is great and, by urbanizing the population and introducing the modern pattern of values, bring population growth under control in these areas. This argument presupposes, among other things: (*a*) that the supply of agricultural raw materials and foodstuffs can be increased sufficiently to meet the requirements of the much larger population which the industrialization process will bring into being before the growth of numbers is checked;[161] (*b*) that capital can and will be accumulated in sufficient quantities to permit the necessary industrialization;[162] and (*c*) that an adequate supply of the requisite minerals can be obtained. In view of the difficulties regarding the increase of resources and food supply noted in this section, it is likely that it will take most of the countries marked by population pressure many years to win relief from poverty even though their population growth rate falls to zero.[163]

VIII

The materials in this section, most of which are by country and appear in Table VII, support the argument of the preceding sections.

Although the annual population growth rate varies widely from one continent to another, ranging at present from about one-half of 1 per cent in Europe to about two in Latin America, the world growth rate has not yet changed much. It was 29.2 in 1800–50, 45.9 in 1850–1900, and 44.8 in 1900–1950; it may approximate 41–43.6 in 1950–2000. Present forecasts

161. See notes 103–06 above.

162. Judging by the experience of the past century, 5–20 per cent of a national income may be saved and invested (see Clark, *Conditions*, p. 406; Goldenberg, *op. cit.*). The proportion saved in the future will probably be less, since underlying populations are less docile than formerly, unless vigorous state intervention can augment the proportion saved without depressing aggregate income. Rosenstein-Rodan estimated the cost of industrializing Eastern and Southern Europe at £6 billion, or three times the annual income of this area (*op. cit.*, pp. 210–11); accomplishing this through domestic savings would probably take 20–25 years. S. K. Iyengar estimated that "the initial capital requirements of a 'zero' programme for India would require one-tenth of the national income for ten or more years" (*Economic Journal*, LIV, 1944, pp. 200–01). This estimate is too optimistic, for 10 per cent of the national income will serve to equip at $800 a worker only slightly over one-half the annual increment in working population, with the result that the excess workers in agriculture cannot be equipped. On China and the Far East see Staley, *op. cit.*, chap. 4.

163. Concerning other difficulties attendant upon industrialization, see Hilgerdt, *Industrialization*, chap. 4; Buchanan, *op. cit.*, and his illuminating essay in *Economic Journal*, LVI, 1946, pp. 533–53; also B. A. Rahmer, *ibid.*, p. 662.

assume a decline in the rate of increase in the closing third of this century, with rates of 29.1 in 1900–36, 44.5 in 1937–70, and 11.5 in 1970–2000. By 2000 world population, which numbered 2,251 millions in 1946 and will number about 3 billions in 1970, may number about 3.35 billions. Even at that date the (assumed) lowness of the population growth rate in large sections of the population will probably be the result of an equilibration of births and deaths at a mortality level still sufficiently high to permit appreciable increase. In view of these growth prospects, of the already widespread lack of foodstuffs, and of the imminent shortage of low-cost supplies in some mineral fields, it is likely that the exchange value of foodstuffs and minerals will rise appreciably in the present century.[164]

In terms of growth potential the countries of the world fall into three classes, according to Thompson: (I) those in which birth and death rates are largely under control; (II) those in which natality and mortality are passing under control even though mortality has fallen faster than natality; and (III) those in which neither mortality nor natality "has come under reasonably secure control." In 1935, according to Clark's figures, the number of millions and the percentage of the world's population living in each class of countries were: I, 424 and 20.2; II, 430 and 21; III, 1,230 and 58.8. The population of the I countries will reach a peak in the neighborhood of 470 millions within a decade and slowly decline after 1970 if not before. That of the II countries may slightly exceed 600 millions by 1970, and by 2000 aggregate 700 millions; that of the III countries may approximate 1.9 and 2.2 billions respectively, by 1970 and 2000.[165] The percentages of the world population in I, II, and III countries therefore will run something like this in the future: in 1955, 19.3, 21.1, and 59.6; in 1970, 15.6, 20.2, and 64.2; in 2000, 13.5, 19.5–21.1, and 65.5–66.7.

The population of class I countries is relatively wealthy, urban, non-agricultural, and healthy while that of class III countries is poverty-ridden, rural, preindustrial, and (often) sickly; that of the class II countries, by comparison, is intermediate and transitional. The *relative* order of magnitude of per capita capital equipment, Clark's very rough estimates suggest, is something like this: I, 100; II, 39; III, 11. Per capita land equipment in

---

164. The population data presented in this section are taken or estimated from F. W. Notestein's essay in T. W. Schultz, *op. cit.*, pp. 36ff.; OIR Report No. 4192, *World Population Estimates* (Department of State, 1947); W. S. Thompson, *Plenty of People*, and *Population and Peace in the Pacific*; and A. M. Carr-Saunders, *World Population*. Gross and net reproduction and expectation of life at birth values are reported periodically in *Population Index*: e.g., see XI, 1945, pp. 150ff., 249ff., XIII, 1947, 88–94; see also on China, A. J. Jaffe, *Human Biology*, XIX, 1947, pp. 6–8, and on Egypt and India, F. W. Notestein, ed., *Demographic Studies of Selected Areas of Rapid Growth*, pp. 47ff., 118–19. Iceland is included with Denmark; Luxemburg with Belgium; Albania with Yugoslavia; Cyprus with Turkey; Formosa with China; and the rest of Oceana with the rest of Africa. We use Clark's 1925–34 income estimates because they are internationally comparable and (abstracting from the effect of war) representative of international differences (cf. data in *Population Index*, XIII, 1947, pp. 100–101).

165. The margin of error in prediction probably is greater for II than for I countries, and much greater for III countries where the checks are more "Malthusian" in character.

many of the class III countries approximates the half-acre reported for Asia (Table VI, cols. 4–5); in the I and II countries it is three or more times as great. Of the occupied population in I about 22 per cent were engaged in agriculture; in II, 56.6; and in III, 74.7. Income differentials reflect these equipment and occupational differentials. In 1925–34, 58.2 per cent of the world's income went to people living in class I countries, 20.4 to II, and 21.3 to III. Per capita income in the I, II, and III countries approximated, respectively, 350, 118, and 44 I.U. Food consumption differentials reflect these income differentials (see Table VII, cols. 9–11). In all but two class I countries 20–40 per cent of the calories consumed are of animal origin; in but one is this percentage as low as 10–15. In all but the more favored South American and South African members of class II, this percentage approximates 10–15, while in the large class III countries it is close to or below 10. Whereas but two class I countries draw as much as 60–70 per cent of their calorie consumption from cereals and potatoes, many of the III countries get more than 80 per cent from this source, while all but two class II countries fall in the over-60 class.[166] Moreover, per capita total calorie consumption is somewhat lower in the III countries than in the others. It is not surprising, therefore, that expectation of life at birth is lower in the II than in the I countries, and much lower still in the III countries.[166]

What has been said is supported by the data presented on an individual country basis in Table VII.[167] The countries in which population growth is not under effective control (and which contain over one-half the world's population [cols. 1–2]) are marked by agricultural overpopulation (col. 3)

166. In the I countries expectation of life at birth is above 55, usually about 60; in II countries it is above 45. In India, Egypt, and China it is in the neighborhood of 30–32; in representative class III Latin American countries, around 37–42. Life expectation is logistically associated with income, by country (*Population Index*, XIII, pp. 100–103).

167. Explanation of Table VII and its sources: The Arabic numeral 1, 2, or 3 designates the population growth class (I, II, or III) into which the country falls (col. 1). In col. 2 population (by millions) as of 1946 is presented as given in the OIR report cited in note 164. In col. 3 is given the percentage of workers in primary occupations as estimated by Colin Clark; the italicized figures, taken from or based on Hilgerdt (*op. cit.*, pp. 26–27), are not quite comparable with Clark's for other countries. In col. 4 income per breadwinner in I.U. in 1925–34 is given as estimated by Clark, with conjectural figures italicized. In col. 5 is given the number of hectares in fields, meadow, and pasture per 100 inhabitants as of 1937; italics indicate that a country imports considerably more food than it exports. The figures are principally from German Institute for Business Research, *Weekly Report*, Feb. 9, 1939, pp. 17–18, and occasionally from the USDA's *Agricultural Production and Trade by Countries*, 1945. The index values for roughly estimated capital per worker given in col. 6 are calculated from Clark, *Economics*, p. 80. The figures on agricultural output per male farm worker (col. 7) and per hectare (col. 8) are taken or estimated principally from Clark, *ibid.*, pp. 42–43, 65, and *Conditions*, pp. 244–46. The italicized figures are rough approximations, particularly in col. 8, obtained by splicing Moore's (*op. cit.*, pp. 35, 42), and Clark's estimates. The figures in col. 9 (taken from FAO, *World Food Survey*, pp. 37–39) represent calories "as purchased" at retail level; corresponding figures for calories actually consumed will be less by the amount lost between the retail level and final consumption. Col. 10, giving the percentage calories of animal origin form of all calories available, and col. 11, giving the corresponding percentage for cereals and potatoes, are estimated from *ibid.* when not reported by Tolley (*op. cit.*, p. 165) or Bennett (*Wheat Studies*, XVIII, p. 73). I have italicized the estimates.

Table VII*

Country (1)	Population (1946) (mils.) (2)	Primary workers (%) (3)	Income per worker (1925–34) (4)	Hectares per 100 people (5)	Capital per worker (6)	Agric. yield per Male farm worker (7)	Agric. yield per Hectare (8)	Calories per head All (9)	Calories per head Animal (%) (10)	Calories per head Cereal and potato (%) (11)
1 United States	142.7	19	1381	113	429	661	16.5	3249	35–40	30–40
1 Canada	12.7	35	1337	243	353	618	21.6	3109	35–40	30–40
1 New Zealand	1.8	27	1202	481	382	2444	48.8	3281	45–50	30–40
1 Great Britain	49.7	6	1069	42	405	475	33.3	3005	40–45	30–40
1 Switzerland	4.5	21	1018	53	279	433	71.9	3049	30–40	30–40
2 Argentina	14.6	23	1000	1228	313	1233	8.6	3275	30–35	50–60
1 Australia	8.5	24	980	221	404	1524	10.7	3128	40–45	30–40
1 Netherlands	9.5	21	855	28	243	579	13.6	2958	30–40	40–50
1 Eire	3.0	53	707	157	223	292	36.2	3184	30–35	50–60
1 France	41.1	25	684	83	228	415	55.6	3012	25–30	50–60
1 Denmark	4.5	36	680	83	228	642	93.7	3249	35–40	40–50
1 Sweden	6.8	32	653	78	228	352	60.1	3052	35–40	30–40
2 Uruguay	2.3	44	650	...	313	1000	23.0	2902	35–40	50–60
1 Germany	66.5	24	646	42	223	490	79.4	2967	20–25	40–50
1 Belgium	8.7	17	600	22	206	394	151.9	2885	25–35	50–60
2 Spain	27.7	57	550	63	158	244	27	2788	10–15	60–70
3 Chile	5.5	38	550	402	...	...	...	2481	15–20	60–70
1 Norway	3.1	35	539	36	198	288	88.2	3129	35–40	40–50
1 Austria	7.1	25	511	65	...	332	78	2933	30–40	40–50
1 Czechoslovakia	12.3	27	455	55	132	287	58.8	2761	25–30	50–60

2	Brazil	47.2	75	435	31	…	…	…	2552	25–30	60–70
2	Greece	7.7	44	397	34	87	125	39.3	2523	10–15	60–70
1	Finland	3.9	51	380	90	150	182	46.9	2950	25–35	40–50
3	Philippines	18.5	75	375	25	…	64	53.8	2021	10–15	80–90
3	Mexico	23.0	68	360	435	…	…	…	1909	10–20	60–70
3	Palestine	1.9	53	360	64	123	195	44.4	2570	15–20	60–70
1	Hungary	8.9	54	359	84	113	120	104.2	2815	15–20	50–60
2	Japan	76.0	50	353	14	100	195	40.2	2268	10–15	70–80
2	Poland	22.6	62	352	75	120	…	…	2702	15–20	70–80
3	Rest of America	57.0	72	350	…	100	…	…	2200	10–20	60–80
1	Latvia	2.0	52	345	195	122	268	40.8	…	25–35	50–60
1	Italy	46.0	43	343	49	111	176	35.2	2627	10–15	60–70
1	Portugal	8.3	48	342	…	100	137	24	2461	10–15	60–70
1	Estonia	1.1	52	341	258	87	268	21.2	…	25–35	50–60
2	Yugoslavia	16.8	79	330	95	…	112	35.2	2866	10–20	70–80
3	Egypt	18.2	67	325	34	94	…	…	2199	5–10	70–80
2	U.S.S.R.	187.3	74	320	368	…	112	7.2	2827	10–15	80–90
2–3	Algiers	8.4	…	300	364	…	…	…	2236	5–15	70–80
2–3	South Africa	11.4	85	276	76	87	…	…	2300	20–25	60–70
2	Bulgaria	7.0	67	259	65	87	143	40.4	2831	10–15	70–80
2	Roumania	15.9	65	243	95	100	137	35.2	2865	10–15	80–90
1	Lithuania	2.6	65	207	155	…	192	35.2	…	15–25	60–70
3	Turkey, Syria	22.5	73	200+	47	…	81	39.6	2590	10–15	60–70
2–3	Morocco, Tunisia	13.1	…	200+	239	…	…	…	2342	5–15	70–80
3	India	414.0	62	200	47	48	127	41.7	2021	5–10	80–90
3	China, Korea	457.9	75	110	26	15	46	…	2201	1–5	80–90
3	Dutch Indies	72.0	73	200–	13	32	…	…	2040	1–5	80–90
3	Rest of Asia	124.0	72	200–	…	32	…	…	2080	5–10	80–90
3	Rest of Africa	124.0	85	200–	…	48	…	…	2300	10–15	80–90

*See note 167 for sources and explanation.

and often by a shortage of capital and agricultural land (cols. 5–6). These circumstances, in turn, make for smallness of agricultural yields (cols. 7–8) and lowness of income (col. 2). Lowness of income limits capital formation and holds down the rate at which workers can transfer from agriculture into other activities. The estimates of calories available per capita at the retail level (col. 9) indicate that consumption is low in most of the countries marked by population pressure and high fertility.[168] The smallness of the percentage of calories got from animal foods in many II and III countries, and the largeness of the percentage drawn from cereals and potatoes (cols. 10–11) indicate that no further replacement of derived by primary calories is feasible, since minimum dietary standards already are being violated.[169]

The evidence presented in Table VII and elsewhere in this paper lends no support to the easy optimism of those who see in industrialization a simple and ready solution for the overpopulation that already affects more than half the world. Countries marked by intense overpopulation must virtually raise themselves by their own bootstraps. They lack land, capital, and the opportunity to make up this lack. They can get only limited relief through trade and capital imports. In part because of the pressure of the inhabitants of these countries upon their resources, the composition of their food consumption operates to impair health and make inadvisable any further substitution of primary for derived nutrients. The salutary influence of such improvements as are effected in these countries is shortlived when the resulting decline in mortality is not adequately compensated by a decline in natality.[170]

Given present technological prospects, together with the current world income and resource situation, a speedy cessation of world population growth appears to be essential to the gradual alleviation and removal of widespread poverty. Social and economic programs which fail to take this condition into account are almost certainly doomed to fail, howsoever skillfully they may be clothed in the rhetoric of latterday sentimentalism and credulity.

168. The gross reproduction rate, which reflects growth potential better than does the net reproduction rate, in recent years was in the neighborhood of 3 in Egypt, China, and India, and above 2 in Chile and Mexico. Presumably, similar rates obtain in similar class III countries. On the Malthusian character of Chinese population growth see C. M. Chiao, W. S. Thompson, and D. T. Chen, *An Experiment in the Registration of Vital Statistics in China.*

169. E.g., see Wickizer and Bennett, *op. cit.,* pp. 129–32, and chap. 7 of the League of Nations report cited in note 68 above.

170. Let x = the annual number of births in a country, and e = the expectation of life at birth. Population tends roughly to stabilize at ex. If e increases markedly while x remains constant or declines only slightly, the magnitude of ex increases greatly. Since the expectation of life of much of the world's population is below 40, even though 70 is being closely approached in advanced lands, there is room for a great increase in ex unless x declines. If the economic and related fetters upon population growth in representative class III countries were removed, logistic upsurges might be initiated similar to that which carried the Japanese population from a long stationary 28–30 millions to a new equilibrium figure about three times as large in the 125–50 years succeeding 1850.

Some Economic Aspects of the Subsidization by the State of the Formation of "Human Capital"

In this paper the indifference curve technique is employed to discover acceptable answers to questions respecting the formation of "human capital" which heretofore have not been satisfactorily answered. In Section I, the basic problem is posed. In Section II, the indifference curve technique as utilized in this paper is described. This section may be passed over rapidly by readers familiar with the technique. In Sections III–IV, it is applied. Section V is devoted to certain underlying assumptions. Our findings, together with some of their implications for demographic policy, are summarized in Section VI.

I

By the formation of "human capital" is meant the reproduction, support, and rearing of children until they join the nation's labor force either as net additions thereto, or as replacements for individuals removed by disability, age, or death.[1] "Human capital" is formed by converting into it goods and services that flow from the productive agents composing an economy, and which otherwise might be put to different use.

The rate at which human capital is formed in an economic society may be augmented in one or more of three ways: (*a*) by reducing the per unit resource-cost[2] of producing human capital while holding sufficiently unchanged the aggregate amount of goods and services devoted to its formation;

1. The expression "human capital" (or "personal capital") is used on the ground of convenience. This term may not, with verbal and institutional propriety, be applied to human beings in a "free" society; for therein the term is reserved to nonhuman instruments employed by man. The term is properly applicable only in a "non-free" society to human beings whose status is that of slave.

2. This cost is governed *ceteris paribus* by the objective standard of living obtaining within the representative household; hence it varies with the determinants of this standard which, in the aggregate, have operated for many decades to push up its cost. This cost is governed also by circumstances which regulate the input of productive services per unit of output. Because the production of human capital has proved less amenable than that of other forms of capital to the application of improved technology and economies of scale, the unit cost of the former has not tended to fall as has the unit cost of the latter.

On the composition of the cost of human capital, see L. I. Dublin and A. J. Lotka, *The Money Value of a Man*, Ronald Press, New York, rev. ed., chap. 4. See also G. Mortara, *O Custo de Produção de Homen Adulto e Sua Variçaõ em Relaçaõ a Mortalidade*, Livraria Kosmos Editora, Rio de Janeiro, 1946. On the influence of family size upon expenditure patterns see Dublin and Lotka, *op. cit.;* F. Lorimer and H. Roback, *Economics of the Family Relative to the Number of Children*, Milbank Memorial Fund Quarterly, XIV, 1940, pp. 114ff.; Eric Schiff, *Family Size and Residential Construction*, American Economic Review, XXXVI, 1946, pp. 97–112; A. Girard, *Les conditions d'existence des familles*, Population, III, 1948, pp. 11–46, 349–360, 519–522; also Monthly Labor Review, LXVI, 1948, pp. 131ff., especially pp. 157, 179–181.

(*b*) by increasing the nation's output of goods and services while holding constant both the fraction of them devoted to the formation of human capital and the cost per unit of this capital;[3] (*c*) by diverting a larger fraction of society's goods and services to the formation of human capital, while holding constant its cost of production and the aggregate output of goods and services. Objective (*c*) may be accomplished (i) by appropriately altering the prevailing pattern of tastes (e.g., through the use of force, repression, or propaganda to stimulate natality), or (ii) by activating the latent (or potential) demand for human capital whilst keeping the pattern of tastes unchanged. Method (ii) entails either a redistribution of income,[4] or a modification of the price-structure, or a combination of these two approaches.

This paper has to do with method (ii) of achieving objective (*c*). Our discussion, therefore, is based upon the assumption that parenthood is voluntary. Adminstrative aspects of method (ii) are dealt with only incidentally.[5]

Formerly, the rate at which a nation formed human capital was left to the discretion of its individual members. Today, by contrast, this rate has become a matter of concern for national governments, particularly for those which are apprehensive lest their populations increase too slowly or not at all. In most instances this concern has led to the introduction of family allowance schemes and diverse prenatal and postnatal subventions intended to stimulate natality.[6]

The introduction of measures designed to stimulate natality has precipitated many questions regarding the comparative effects, costliness, and

3. The demographic role of the level of employment lies outside the scope of this discussion. It may be noted, however, that an increase in the relative amount of employment tends to be accompanied by an increase in the birth rate. E.g., see D. Kirk, *The Relation of Employment Levels to Births in Germany*, Milbank Memorial Fund Quarterly, XX, 1942, pp. 126–138; and compare the post-war experience of many countries. It may be noted also that subsidies and similar devices employed to stimulate the formation of human capital may help to sustain relatively high levels of employment. For these devices usually entail a redistribution of income in the direction of greater equality. And this tendency towards greater equality need not be checked in part by the rise of rents, consequent upon an increase in the relative demand for goods (e.g., foodstuffs) subject to increasing cost; for taxes may be devised to absorb and counterbalance the resulting increases in rents.

4. When advocates of measures intended to achieve objective (*c*) seek also to bring about a more equal distribution of income, they favor compound proposals which are designed to realize both objectives. Advocates of pure family-wage systems, on the contrary, are supporting a system which is regressive in character since, under this system, the cost of the subventions is predominantly incident upon those members of the nation who are wage-earners.

5. Every program designed to stimulate natality entails administrative problems peculiar to this program. It is probable, however, that in the aggregate the purely administrative cost of one type of program will not differ greatly from that of another.

6. On the development of these policies up to the outbreak of World War II, see D. V. Glass, *Population Policies and Movements in Europe*, Clarendon Press, Oxford, 1940. Developments since then have been reported in summary form in the *Monthly Labor Review* (Washington), *Population* (Paris), and the *Eugenics Review* (London). On the development of theory and practice in one country, see my *France Faces Depopulation*, 1938, and *French Predecessors of Malthus*, 1942, both published by Duke University Press, Durham.

efficacy of these measures. The following questions are typical. Do sub-ventions and allowances tend to increase the scale and/or the standard of living of the household receiving them and thus operate, in the longer run, to strengthen anti-natalist motives? Should supplements be paid in cash or in kind? If allowances are paid in cash, should the receiver be free to spend them as he chooses, or should he be required to spend them in specified ways? If specification is indicated, how detailed should it be? Can the desired degree of specificity be obtained more fully when sub-ventions are paid in cash, or when they are in the form of price-reductions? Does the use of special-purpose money facilitate the achievement of speci-ficity? In general, which type of subvention is least costly to the state, one dispensed in kind,[7] one paid in cash, one distributed in the form of privileges to buy specified goods and services at reduced prices, or one that combines these alternative forms. Answers to these questions may be obtained through the use of the indifference curve technique.[8]

II

In this section, the indifference curve technique is described, with Figure I and Table I providing illustrative materials. The values reported in Table I have been read from Figures I–II. The sets of curves presented in Figures

7. Payments in kind have been described as superior to payments in cash for a number of reasons. Payments in kind, it is said, are more adapted to the needs of children than are cash doles which, if they are to benefit children fully, must be combined with "obnoxious police control"; they are cheaper in that they may be made an integral part of a larger social policy that permits economies of scale; and they favor quality (e.g., health, well-being, etc.) in children whereas cash doles favor mere quantity inasmuch as the prospect of cash assistance induces the "least desirable" families to procreate, while subventions in kind appeal to those who are relatively more responsible socially. See A. Myrdal, *Nation and Family*, Harper & Brothers, New York, 1941, chaps. 8–9; also Glass, *op. cit.*, pp. 326ff., and J. Drouhet, *Deux modalités de la politique d'aide à la famille. Prestations in espèces et prestations en nature*, Population, III, 1948, pp. 651–660. Drouhet, after having passed in review the forms of family assistance in effect in representative countries, concludes that appraisal of the role of assistance in kind must take into account both the objectives of the assistance program and the cultural condi-tions obtaining in a country.

8. The approach employed in this paper was suggested by Coppock's studies of the use of special purpose money to augment the consumption of surplus commodities in the United States. See J. D. Coppock, *Indifference Curve Analysis Applied to the Food Stamp Plan*, American Economic Review, XXXV, 1945, pp. 99–110, and *The Food Stamp Plan*, Transactions of the American Philosophical Society, n.s., XXXVII, 1947, Part 2, pp. 131–200. See also H. M. Southworth, *The Economics of Public Measures to Subsidize Food Consumption*, Journal of Farm Economics, XXVII, 1945, pp. 38–66.

The use of the indifference curve technique has become popular since the appearance of J. R. Hicks' *Value and Capital*, Clarendon Press, Oxford, 1939. For somewhat earlier treat-ments, see L. L. Thurstone, *The Indifference Function*, Journal of Social Psychology, II, 1931, pp. 139–166, and R. G. D. Allen, *The Nature of Indifference Curves*, Review of Eco-nomic Studies, I, 1934, pp. 110–121. On the limitations of this technique, see W. A. Wallis and M. Friedman, *The Empirical Derivation of Indifference Functions*, in O. Lange et al., eds., *Studies in Mathematical Economics and Econometrics in Memory of Henry Schultz*, University of Chicago Press, 1942, pp. 175–190.

I–II are designed to illustrate the argument of this paper. While each of these two sets incorporates particular quantitative values, the conclusions drawn from them have a high degree of generality.

For purposes of our analysis, consumer goods and services are divided into two categories, X and Y, each of which within limits is substitutable for the other in the systems of living of most households. (Although goods are bundles of services and may be so treated, we usually distinguish between goods and services.) All goods and services which are complements to the formation of human capital (i.e., to the reproduction and rearing of children) are placed in category X; all other goods and services are put in category Y. A good or service is defined as a complement to the formation of human capital if, *ceteris paribus*, an increase in the reproduction and rearing of children tends (*a*) to augment the rate of consumption of this good or service, or (*b*) to be stimulated by an increase in the rate of consumption of this good or service. In category X, therefore, fall goods and services ranging from those employed in preconceptual and prenatal care to those used in the maintenance and training of children in their teens.[9] Savings (cash plus deferred claims purchased with income) are ignored, it being assumed that in each case considered the amount of purchasing power initially available per time period for consumption is both given and predestined to this use.[10]

Since, by definition, the rate at which men form human capital is positively associated with their rate of consumption of X, stimuli which augment

9. We are not explicit respecting the treatment of the influence of family size upon the leisure of parents and the response of potential parents to the prospect of this influence. The amount of time which parents devote to child-care increases with the number of children (e.g., see J. Stoetzel, *Une étude du budget-temps de la femme dans les agglomérations urbaines*, Population, III, 1948, pp. 47ff.) and represents a diversion from leisure. In so far as it is a matter of indifference to the parent whether a quantum of time is devoted to child-care or to leisure-time activity, this diversion may be ignored; but in so far as it is not a matter of indifference and does therefore influence family size among potential parents, it must be considered. Compensation for leisure unwillingly given up may be included under X and is in fact included insomuch as the subsidy program includes nurseries, etc.; to the extent that it is not included, we simply assume that the demand of potential parents for X reflects their realization that augmentation of family size (in response to the prospect of a greater supply of X) entails some sacrifice of leisure. See also next note concerning possible effect of increase in family size upon disposition to work.

10. Savings is treated, in effect, as a residual varying directly with income-minus-taxes; the alternative of including savings under Y has been rejected for the sake of simplicity.

The relation that does or can obtain between savings and reproduction is not always a simple one. Disposable income being given, the rate of savings tends to vary inversely with the income-receiver's number of dependents. But this tendency may be partly offset by two sometime facts: (*a*) the income-receiver's disposition to work hard and long may vary directly with the number of his dependents; (*b*) resources which have been diverted from consumption and impersonal-capital formation and incorporated in personal capital serve (within limits) one of the purposes of saving, namely, the provision of security in the saver's declining years. See my *Aspects of the Economics of Population Growth*, Southern Economic Journal, XIV, 1947–48, notes 41, 147; C. Clark, *The Fruits of Economic Progress*, Economia Internazionale, I, 1948, p. 243.

the latter rate also augment the former. Because we have ruled out changes in tastes (see Section I) we must assume that an increase in the rate of consumption of X may be stimulated in one or the other of two ways: (*a*) by a direct addition to a household's income; or (*b*) by a decrease in the relative price of X (expressed in terms of Y) which operates indirectly to increase the household's real income.

Households may be classified into those in which there exists a latent but as yet unactivated demand for children and those in which no such demand exists. Our assumption that an increase in the rate of consumption of X will be accompanied by an increase in the rate at which men form human capital is valid only for the former class of households. In this class, however, fall most households except those which are excluded by the age factor. The sensitivity of the members of this class to the increased availability of X varies widely, of course, the number of respondents increasing with the size of stimulus. The absence of a latent demand for children may be traced either to the value system prevailing within the household or to the advanced age of the spouses. In the former case, the remedy consists in appropriate changes in the value system. In most households containing children, more adequate provision can be made for them if the supply of X at the disposal of these households is increased; here the increase in X conduces to an improvement in the *quality* of the human capital.

Consideration of alternative stimuli (*a*) and (*b*) indicates that each is consistent with reality. Alternative (*a*) is consistent with the frequently observed inverse relationship between family size and income. This inverse relationship has its origin in inter-family variation respecting variables here impounded within *ceteris paribus;* for alternative (*a*) rests upon the postulate that everything is constant but the two relevant variables, income and rate of human capital formation. Alternative (*b*) implies that, within limits, X is an imperfect substitute for Y in the household's system of living, and that, therefore, the rate at which X is purchased rises as its price falls, the degree of rise depending upon the elasticity of demand for X. Alternative (*b*) implies that the actual quantity of Y taken will remain unchanged only if the demand for X is unitarily elastic; it will fall (rise) if the demand for X is more (less) than unitarily elastic. Under the economic conditions that usually attend the formation of human capital, an increase in its rate of formation entails a diminution in the affected household's consumption of Y.

Scale and standard of living, together with changes therein, are defined in terms of X and Y. An increase in the consumption of X per dependent child constitutes an increase in its (objective) *scale* of living; an increase in the consumption of Y per nonchild (or adult) member of the household in question constitutes an increase in the scale of living of the nonchild part of the household. An increase (decrease) in the desire for Y at the expense of X (= provision for the reproduction and rearing of children) constitutes an increase (decrease) in the (subjective) *standard* of living of adult members of the household; this means, in terms of the household head's indifference map (described below), a shift of the curves in such a manner as to generate greater purchases of Y and lesser purchases of X even though income and prices remain unchanged.[11] Since decisions regarding the purchase of X are made by the household head, no supposition is made regarding change in the standard of living of dependent children who by definition consume only X.

I_1 is an indifference curve of the head of a representative household, consisting of himself, wife, and dependent child. He receives an income per time period equivalent to 40 Y and destined for expenditure upon X and Y. As the decision-expressing purchasing agent for the household, he decides how the expended income is to be divided between X and Y. The assumption of one child is introduced so that two further assumptions respecting this household head may be taken into account. 1. The household head is supposed to have an active demand for some X and a latent demand for still more X. In his dual capacity as consumer and purchasing agent for the household, he has a given set of tastes reflected in the system of indifference curves given in Figure 1: he finds any member of a set of collections of X and Y lying on a given indifference curve to be as attractive as any other member of the same set, whilst he prefers some sets (i.e., curves) to others. (Some X is found in the collections he chooses under given circumstances, for if under no circumstances were any X included, we could not construct a system of indifference curves depicting the effect of price and/or income changes upon his consumption of X.) 2. Our household head is initially devoting to X some quantum of expenditure (measured in Y) which rate he may be required to maintain as a condition of his receiving a subsidy. Frequently a system of indifference curves is used to represent the way the consumer who does the actual consuming responds to changes in price and/or income. In this paper, however, the indifference curve system represents the responses of a household head who, while he himself actually consumes only a part of what is purchased, makes and/or executes for the household decisions respecting the division of expenditure between X and Y; therefore, we shall hereinafter employ the terms consumer and household head interchangeably.

A given indifference curve joins together those combinations of two different commodities, or categories of goods and services, which the consumer finds equally attractive. Thus, indifference curve I_1 joins together

11. A decrease or an increase in the adults' standard of living as here defined does not necessarily signify a decrease or an increase in their welfare; for the alteration of the indifference map makes simple comparison impossible. What is of import here, however, is not the significance for welfare of the change in indifference map, but the fact that although other conditions remain unchanged, the division of expenditure between X and Y is changed, and the formation of human capital is affected accordingly.

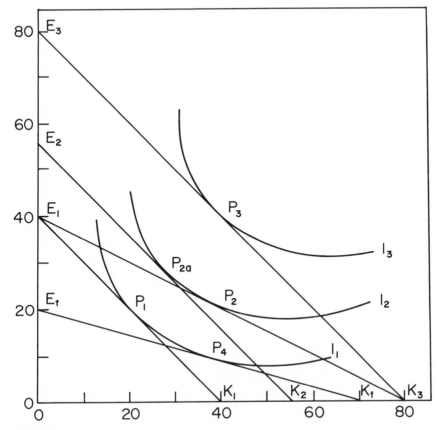

Figure I

combinations of X and Y (whose respective quantities are measured along the abscissa and the ordinate) in respect to the purchase of which the consumer is indifferent, it being immaterial to him whether he receive 20 Y and 20 X, 27 Y and 15 X, or any other combination lying on I_1. Each other indifference curve in Figure I joins together a set of equally attractive combinations of Y and X. Each combination of X and Y on I_2 is preferred by our consumer to any combination on I_1, and each combination on I_3 is preferred to any combination on I_2, and so on, with combinations on higher curves being preferred to those on lower curves. (While a higher curve is preferable to a lower curve, there is no indication respecting the *amount* of preferability; for the indifference system is a means of making an ordinal but not a cardinal comparison of alternatives.)

E_1K_1 is a price line indicating an exchange rate of 1 X @ 1 Y between X and Y; for the consumer's income is equal either to OE_1 (= 40) units of Y or to OK_1 (= 40) units of X. Other price lines in Figure I are E_2K_2 and

E_3K_3, with 1 X @ 1 Y, and E_1K_3, with 1 X @ $^1\!/_2$ Y. E_tK_t signifies that in effect 1 X @ $^2\!/_7$ Y, since the consumer, when he purchases X at a nominal price of 1 X @ $^4\!/_7$ Y, must also pay a 100 per cent unit sales tax.

If a consumer with a given income to spend is absolutely free to allocate it as he would between two kinds of goods such as X and Y, he will so distribute it as to make the marginal rate of substitution between the two coincide with the exchange ratio ruling between them. For example: given price line E_1K_1, an allocable income equal to 40 Y, and indifference curve I_1, the consumer's most preferred position is at P_1 where the marginal rate of substitution between X and Y equals the exchange ratio obtaining between them, namely, 1 X @ 1 Y, and where he purchases 20 Y and 20 X; hence, if he purchased more X and less Y, or more Y and less X, he would find himself on a lower and less attractive indifference curve.

Indifference curves may differ greatly in shape whilst possessing the necessary properties, for the difference in shape reflects the difference in the rate at which the marginal rate of substitution between X and Y changes. Thus the curves in Figure I indicate a greater substitutability of X for Y than do the curves in Figure II, and hence within limits a greater expansion of the demand for X as its price falls.

The relative orders of magnitude assigned X and Y in Figures I and II are hypothetical, having been chosen for expositive convenience. American data suggest that, with the cost of living of a 2-person family equal to 100, the respective relatives for 3-person and 4-person families are, very roughly, 117–129 and 133–154, the magnitude of the relatives varying inversely with that of the absolute level of the 2-person family.

The indifference curves in Figure I imply that since X and Y are (within limits) imperfect substitutes for each other in the household system of living, the commodity whose relative price falls will be substituted for the other, but only within the indicated limits. For example, I_1 indicates the consumer to be willing, under the stimulus of an adequate modification of the exchange ratio, to give up Y for X so long as his holding of Y exceeds 6 units, and X for Y so long as his holding of X exceeds 10 units. The amounts, 6 Y and 10 X, are minima, or *threshold* quantities, below which the consumer is unwilling to barter. Greater minima are associated with higher indifference curves (and higher incomes) in Figure I. These minima, which reflect the consumer's pattern of tastes, change as this pattern changes.[12]

The indifference map (or system of indifference curves) pictured in Figure I depicts the pattern of tastes of a typical individual (or of the household he represents) and reveals how, given this pattern, he will respond to changes

12. Thurstone (*op. cit.*) initially postulated continuous substitutability of the contrasted commodities. For he assumed an indifference curve that is asymptomatic to the coordinates — a curve of the general form $x\dfrac{k_1}{1} \cdot x\dfrac{k_2}{2} = m$, in which x_1 and x_2 are the quantities of the two commodities (i.e., *X and Y* in the text above) entering into the several equally satisfactory collec-

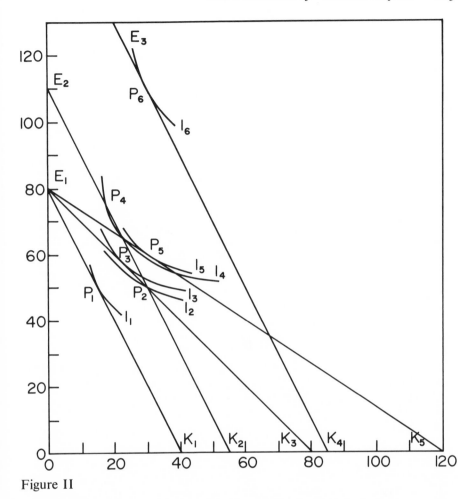

Figure II

tions lying on a given indifference curve, m is a constant designating the total amount of satisfaction represented by the indifference curve, and k_1 and k_2 are constants descriptive of the individual consumer and his preferences for commodities 1 and 2 and representing "the different rates at which satisfaction increases with increase in the amounts of" commodities 1 and 2. Thurstone arrived at the above assumed equation by postulating that the aggregate amount of satisfaction yielded by a commodity grows in accordance with Fechner's Law, with $\dfrac{ds}{dx} = \dfrac{k}{x}$, and $s = k \log x + c$, in which $s =$ satisfaction, $x =$ the amount of the commodity possessed, k is defined as above, and c is the constant of integration which here indicates the arbitrary origin or the amount of the commodity below which the owner will not barter. Empirical study revealed, however, that the indifference curves of his subject were not asymptotic to the coordinates, and that "all barter ceases entirely when the quantity of a commodity reaches a lower limit which the subject regards as a necessity." To this minimum value (which is analogous to a *threshold* quantity that must be exceeded before barter can begin) for the one commodity corresponds the *saturation value* (see Allen, *op. cit.* [1934], pp. 112, 114–115) for the other.

in income and/or the exchange ratio between X and Y. Since indifference maps tend to vary with the individual, a given change in price or in income will evoke somewhat different responses from different individuals. The aggregate response of a whole society of individuals (or households) to a given change in price or in income will be a composite of the responses of the individuals forming that society.

As was indicated in Section 1, we always assume, in the absence of any statement to the contrary, that the pattern of tastes—i.e., the indifference map—of each individual (or household) remains unchanged, and that changes in his purchases of X and Y are elicited solely by changes in his income and/or the exchange ratio between X and Y. It is not our intention to imply that a state cannot employ propaganda and/or force to produce taste changes conducive to more consumption of X and more childbearing; for this a state can do within limits. Our discussion is restricted, however, to a comparison of the effects of income and price-cut subsidies and to an appraisal of the consequences of restrictions upon the consumer's freedom to divide his expenditure between X and Y. Therefore, we always postulate fixity of the individual's indifference map or pattern of tastes.

III

In this section we apply the indifference technique described, subject to three assumptions that are modified in later sections. These assumptions are: (*a*) the consumer is free to distribute his expenditure between X and Y as he chooses; (*b*) the advent of offspring does not modify the pattern of tastes (i.e., indifference map) of the household head; (*c*) X goods and services are sufficiently divisible and variable to permit analysis of consumer behavior in indifference terms. These assumptions do not impair our principal findings, however.

Let us begin with our consumer's initial situation in Figure 1, described as Case (a_I) in Table I. Herein he divides his income (the equivalent of 40 Y) evenly between X and Y, purchasing 20 units of each at a price equal to 1 Y per unit of each.

Let us now suppose that the state desires our consumer to increase his consumption of X from the 20 units (in Case [a_I]) assumed to be approximately sufficient for the maintenance of one child to the 40 required for the support of two children.[13] The state determines to bring this about by means

13. In Figure II and the relevant cases based thereupon, maintenance cost per child is assumed to be 15 X. We could equally well assume that the state sets as its objective, not the subsidization of the whole of the X-cost of each child beyond the first, but the subsidization of a fraction (constant or increasing) of the X-cost of each child beyond the first; but for the sake of convenience we have postulated the former objective. See note 28 below.

of a subsidy, whilst allowing our consumer complete freedom to divide his expenditure between X and Y howsoever he chooses. The state may select one or the other of two courses of action (i). It may subsidize the consumer directly, thereby increasing his income and activating his latent demand for additional units of X at the market price; or (ii) it may subsidize the sellers of X, thereby inducing and enabling them to reduce the *relative* price of X by the amount of subsidy per unit of X.[14]

Of the two courses of action indicated, (ii) involves a lesser outlay by the state than does (i), given that the sellers of X reduce its price by the amount of the subsidy, or at least by a sufficiently large fraction of the subsidy. Consider the behavior of a consumer with the indifference map presented in Figure I. An income subsidy of 40 Y is necessary to move him from P_1 to P_3, induce him to increase his consumption of X from 20 to 40, and convert his situation from that of Case (a_1) to that of Case (b_1); for his income elasticity of demand for X is unitary. Twenty units of the subsidy are devoted to X and 20 are diverted to Y, the subsidy outlay per unit increase in X being 2 Y. By contrast, a subsidy of 20 Y, or 1 Y per unit increase in X, brings about a 20-unit increase in the consumption of X when the subsidy is paid to the sellers of X and causes them to cut the price of X from one to one-half Y; for within the relevant range the price elasticity of demand is unitary (see Case [c_1]). Under the given circumstances, therefore, subsidy method (ii) is only one-half as expensive as subsidy method (i).

There is a simple basic reason for the superiority of method (ii) to method (i),—for the fact that the aggregate money cost to the state of a price-cut subsidy is less than the cost of an equally effective income subsidy. An income subsidy produces only an income effect, and this may affect the consumption of X positively, negatively, or not at all; its influence in any given case will depend upon the form of the consumer's system of indifference curves. If, on the contrary, a similar subsidy is employed to reduce the price of X, a double effect is produced: (*a*) the consumer's real income rises in consequence of the fall in the price of X: (*b*) X is substituted for Y as a result of the fall in the price of X relative to that of Y. Effect (*a*), the income effect, as has been said, may or may not increase the consumption

14. We suppose that both X and Y are produced under conditions of constant cost in an economy in complete competitive equilibrium, and that, in respect of both X and Y, marginal cost = average total cost = necessary selling price in the absence of subsidy and/or taxes. In Cases (a_1–e_1) the cost of production of a unit of X equals that of a unit of Y; in Cases (a_{11}–g_{11}) the cost of production of a unit of X equals that of two units of Y. The amount of subsidy is reported by case in Table I, col. 11. When a direct income subsidy is employed, it is equal to the amount added to the initial income, and total income (in terms of Y) becomes equal to the initial income plus the subsidy. When a subsidy in the form of a price cut is employed, the total income of the household head (in terms of Y) is equal to what he and the government pay for the amounts of X and Y purchased by him (see Table I, col. 10); his subsidy is equal to the difference between this figure and his initial income. When a tax is imposed upon Y, the proceeds are deducted from the subsidy figure given to yield the net cost of the subsidy (e.g., see Case [e_1]).

of X; but effect (b), the substitution effect, will always increase the consumpion of X. Suppose the price of X is cut 50 per cent and Case (a_1) is thereby converted into Case (c_1). Of the 20-unit increase in the consumption of X, 8 result from the increase in income and 12 from the decline in the relative price of X.[15] If indifference curve I_2 were so shaped and situated as to be tangent to the relevant price line[16] at $X = 20$ or less, the income effect would be zero or negative; but the substitution effect would still be positive. In view of the composition of X and Y and their relation to one another, it does not seem likely that a substitution effect in favor of X would be more than offset by an associated negative income effect; hence we do not consider such a case.

A unit tax upon Y may be employed to reenforce a cut in the price of X and to diminish the net cost to the state of executing a subsidy program; for the imposition of a unit tax upon Y diminishes its consumption, while the proceeds from the tax constitute an offset against the state's outlay for a subsidy to sellers of X. For purposes of illustration, let us convert Case (a_1) into Case (e_1). The consumer has an initial income equivalent to 40 Y, and it is desired that he increase his consumption of X from 20 to 40 units. If a tax of 1 Y is added to the initial price of a unit of $Y (= 1 \, Y)$ and its total unit cost to the consumer is thereby increased from one to two Y, it is necessary only to reduce the price of X from one Y to four-sevenths Y instead of to one-half Y as in Case (c_1). For, since the unit tax upon Y exercises a substitution effect *against* Y, a lesser reduction in the relative price of X is required to produce a given substitution effect *in favor of* X. Given (see Case [e_1]) that a unit of X @ $^4/_7 \, Y$ and that the actual cost (= price plus tax) to the consumer of a unit of Y is 2 Y, the consumer purchases with his income (= 40 Y) 40 units of X at a cost to him of $22^6/_7 \, Y$ and $8^4/_7 \, Y$ at a cost to him of $17^1/_7 \, Y$. In this instance, the tax upon Y has operated, in conjunction with the reduction in the relative price of X, to diminish the consumption of Y by $11^3/_7$ units (cp. Cases [a_1] and [e_1]). The cost to the state of subsidizing a three-sevenths reduction in the price of 40 X is $17^1/_7 \, Y$, while the gain to the state from the tax upon Y is $8^4/_7 \, Y$. Accordingly, the net cost to the state is the difference between these two figures, namely, $8^4/_7 \, Y$; and the net cost per unit increase in the consumption of X from 20 to 40 units is $^3/_7 \, Y$. (This case is representative in one sense of a usual effect of an increase in family size, namely, that the family's consumption of Y declines.)

The assertion that method (ii) is superior to method (i), made in this and later sections, relates only to the former's greater economy as a means of bringing about an increase in the consumption of X. A consumer prefers a direct income subsidy to an indirect one in the form of a cut in the price of X, and one that he is free to divide as he chooses between X and Y to one

15. See Figure I, points P_{2a} and P_2 on I_2 and data in Cases (c_1) and (d_1).
16. In Figure I as drawn, the actual price line is E_2K_2.

that he is not free to divide. In Figure I, P_2 and P_{2a} lie on the same indifference curve I_2 and therefore are preferred in the same degree over P_1 on I_1; yet the cost in terms of Y of moving from P_1 to P_2 is 20 units, while that of moving from P_1 to P_{2a} is only 16 units. In Figure II, it costs (in terms of Y) 30 units to move from P_1 on I_1 to P_2 on I_2; but this cost would be only about 15 units if the consumer were free to spend as he chose, in which event he would ascend to that point on I_2 which indicates a collection of approximately 62 Y and $16\frac{1}{2}$ X. Accordingly, if the objective of a state subsidy be the augmentation of the individual's satisfaction as well as his rate of consumption of X, the state, as a rule, can achieve this objective more economically if it employs a direct income subsidy (i.e., method [i]), together with freedom for the consumer to divide his subsidy between X and Y as he chooses.

What has been said in the preceding paragraph may be made to bear upon the question of the comparative merits of subsidies in kind and subsidies in cash. If the objective of the subsidy be both the augmentation of the household's satisfaction and the stimulus of the formation of human capital, a given composite effect can usually be produced at lesser cost when the subsidy is in cash than when it is in kind. For every restriction upon the household head's freedom to spend as he chooses diminishes the satisfaction-providing effect of a subsidy. If, however, the objective of the subsidy be the stimulation, at minimum cost to the state, of the formation of human capital, restrictions will have to be imposed upon the household head's freedom to spend the subsidy. (Reasons for this conclusion are given in later sections of this essay.) Subsidies in kind entail greater restriction upon the use to which the household head may put the subsidy than do restrictions which merely require him to exchange the subsidy for X but do not stipulate what specific kinds of X he must buy. The household head sets great store by this freedom. For the patterns of living obtaining within households differ widely with regard to both their X and their Y components, and the head of each household will want to integrate his subsidized purchases of X with the system of living pursued by his household. The household head, therefore, will need to be relatively free respecting his expenditure of the subsidy upon X; and there will be a limit to the extent to which he finds subsidies in kind to be practicable and acceptable. It follows, therefore, that it will cost the state more to impart a given stimulus to the formation of human capital if the subsidy employed is wholly in kind than if it is in the form of special-purpose money (see Section IV) exchangeable only for X but not restricted as to type of X.

Presumably, the subsidy that imparts a given impetus to human-capital formation at the lowest cost to the state is one which combines payments in kind with subventions in the form of cash rebates (i.e., price-cuts) that must be expended upon unspecified X goods and services. For some X

goods and services are collective in character (e.g., nurseries, education, recreation, forms of medical care) while certain others are more likely to be used as intended if they are received in kind.[17]

In this section, we have demonstrated that, when the consumer is free to divide his income between X and Y as he chooses, it costs the state less to induce a given increase in the consumption of X by subsidizing the sellers of X and enabling them to reduce its price by the amount of the subsidy than by directly augmenting the income of consumers while holding the price of X constant. It has also been demonstrated that the cost to the state can be further reduced by imposing a unit tax on Y and thereby introducing a substitution effect against Y. Finally, it has been shown that a subsidy in kind is less economical than a subsidy that is partly in kind and partly in the form of special-purpose money that enables its receiver to purchase X goods and services at reduced prices.

IV

A state bent upon increasing the rate at which human capital is formed will not usually allow the household head complete freedom of choice in his expenditure of the subsidies given him. As a rule, the state will aim to maximize the stimulus imparted by a given subsidy expenditure. It will do this by making the amount of subsidy distributed to a household depend upon the number of children, actual and/or in prospect,[18] belonging to the household. It is supposed, in this section, that the state seeks to maximize the impetus its subsidy program gives to the consumption of X and therefore to the formation of human capital.

It is assumed that the state, as a means toward maximizing the influence of its subsidy program, employs a special-purpose money, or stamp-money, applicable only to the purchase of X goods and utilizable only by heads and other qualified members of households to whom it has been distributed by the state. This money may be designed in one of two possible ways to confer benefits upon its qualified recipients. (i) It may constitute a direct supplement to the recipient's income, to be utilized by him to purchase X goods and services at going market prices and thus raise his rate of consumption of X by some quantity q above an initially stipulated rate r. (ii) It may empower its possessor to purchase X goods and services at some stipulated discount[19] below going market prices and thus in effect stimulate him to raise his rate of consumption of X by some quantity q above an ini-

17. It may also be that some kinds of X which are not collective in character nonetheless can be supplied at lesser cost and perhaps at greater convenience when in kind than when obtained through the expenditure of special-purpose money.

18. The phrase *in prospect* covers relevant expenses preceding pregnancy and birth.

19. The magnitude of this discount will vary with amount of the subsidy to which a consumer is entitled. If this amount is made contingent upon the number of dependent children the con-

tially stipulated rate *r*. Each method thus provides the recipient with an increase in income subject to restrictions respecting its use: (i) consists in a direct addition to the recipient's income of special-purpose money expendable solely upon *X;* (ii) is an indirect income subsidy, conveyed in the form of special-purpose money that confers upon eligible recipients the right to purchase *X* at a stipulated discount. This stamp-money, whether type (i) or (ii), upon being received from supposedly qualified possessors by qualified sellers, is presented by the latter to agencies of the state for conversion into *de facto* lawful money (i.e., currency and demand deposits).

It will now be demonstrated that method (ii) tends in practice to be a less expensive means of importing a given stimulus to the consumption of *X* and therefore to the formation of human capital than is method (i). For purposes of illustration, we shall utilize Figure II and Cases (a_{II}–g_{II}) based thereupon (cf. Table I). We begin with a consumer in Case (a_{II}) situation, who receives an income equivalent to 80 *Y*, of which he spends 50 units upon *Y* and uses 30 to purchase 15 units of *X*, the amount required for the maintenance of his one child. It is desired that he increase his rate of purchase of *X* by 15 units, to 30 on the assumption that if he does this he will increase the number of his children from one to two. In the terms of the preceding paragraph the initial 15 *X* corresponds to *r*, the additional 15 to *q*, and the eventual 30 to *r* + *q*. The condition of the consumer's receiving a subsidy of type (i) or (ii) is that he continue in effect to purchase 15 units of *X* out of his presubsidy income of 80 *Y* and to use the entire subsidy to purchase 15 additional *X*.

Superficial analysis suggests that it costs the state as much to convert Case (a_{II}) into Case (b_{II}) by means of method (ii) as to convert Case (a_{II}) into Case (c_{II}) by means of method (i); for in both instances the consumer, in response to subsidies of like amount, moves from P_1 on I_1 to P_2 on I_2. Method (i) requires that the state give our consumer a subsidy of stamp-money equal to 30 *Y*, which he must exchange for 15 *X* in addition to the 15 he has already been purchasing. His consumption of *X* is augmented from 15 to 30 at a cost of 2 *Y* per unit increase in *X*. Method (ii) requires that the state give our consumer stamp-money equal in purchasing power to 30 *Y*, all of which must be applied to the purchase of *X*. Use of this money

---

sumer has in actuality or in immediate prospect, and if, as in the discussion that follows, the subsidy begins with the second child, is doubled when there are three, trebled when there are four, etc., the discount will vary directly with the number of children. If the cost of maintaining a child be *r*, and if a subsidy in the form of reduced prices equal to *r* be allowed for each child beyond the first, then the real price-index of *X*, after allowing for the discount conferred by the stamp-money, must vary as follows: 1 child, 100; 2 children, 50; 3 children, 33$\frac{1}{3}$; 4 children, 25; and so on. In general, if *n* be the number of children, the required price index is $1/n(100)$. For administrative purposes, method (ii) requires that distinct types of stamp-money be issued to those with 2, 3, 4, etc., children (actual or in immediate prospect), and that each type entitle the qualified possessor to the amount of discount respecting *X* allowed to a family head with the number of children indicated by the type of stamp-money he presents.

Table I. Values Taken from Figures I and II[a]

| Case | Consumer position | Consumer income in terms of Y | Price of X in terms of Y | Amount purchased | | Expenditure of consumers in terms of Y upon | | | Cost or producing[b] amount purchased of Y + X in terms of Y | Subsidy in terms of Y | Increase in consumption[c] | | Subsidy per unit increase in X (11 ÷ 13) |
| | | | | Y | X | Y | X | Y + X | | | ΔY | ΔX | |
1	2	3	4	5	6	7	8	9	10	11	12	13	14
a_I	P_1 on I_1 and E_1K_1	40	1	20	20	20	20	40	40	—	—	—	—
b_I	P_3 on I_3 and E_3K_3	80	1	40	40	40	40	80	80	40	20	20	2
c_I	P_2 on I_2 and E_1K_3	40	$\frac{1}{2}$	20	40	20	20	40	60	20	0	20	1
d_I	P_2 on I_2 and E_2K_2	56	1	28	28	28	28	56	56	16	8	8	2
e_I	P_4 on I_1 and E_1K_1	40	$4/7$[d]	$8\frac{4}{7}$	40	$17\frac{1}{7}$	$22\frac{6}{7}$	40	$48\frac{4}{7}$	$8\frac{4}{7}$[e]	$-11\frac{3}{7}$	20	$\frac{3}{7}$
a_{II}	P_1 on I_1 and E_1K_1	80	2	50	15	50	30	80	80	—	—	—	—
b_{II}	P_2 on I_2 and E_1K_3	80	1	50	30	50	30	80	110	30	0	15	2
c_{II}	P_2 on I_2 and E_2K_2	110	2	50	30	50	60	110	110	30	0	15	2
d_{II}	P_3 on I_3 and E_1K_3	80	1	57	23	57	23	80	103	23	7	8	$2\frac{7}{8}$
e_{II}	P_4 on I_1 and E_2K_2	110	2	70	20	70	40	110	110	30	20	5	6
f_{II}	P_5 on I_5 and E_1K_5	80	$2/3$	60	30	60	20	80	120	40	10	15	$2\frac{2}{3}$
g_{II}	P_6 on I_6 and E_3K_4	170	2	110	30	110	60	170	170	90	60	15	6

[a] Cases a_I–e_I are from Figure I; cases a_{II}–g_{II} are from Figure II.

[b] In Cases a_I–e_I the cost of production is: 1 X α 1 Y; 1 Y α 1 Y. – In Cases a_{II}–g_{II}: 1 X α 2 Y; 1 Y α 1 Y.

[c] The increase in consumption of X and Y is measured from Cases a_I and a_{II} respectively, columns 5 and 6.

[d] 1 X α $4/7$ of the price of Y, and $2/7$ of the cost (= price-plus-tax) to the consumer of a unit of Y.

[e] Subsidy to sellers of X (= $17\frac{1}{7}$ Y) minus proceeds from tax on Y (= $8\frac{4}{7}$ Y) equals net subsidy of $8\frac{4}{7}$ Y.

enables the consumer to purchase at 50 per cent below the going market price the X items to which it is applied, and the whole of the subsidy enables him to purchase with his own 30 Y not 15 X as in Case (a_{II}) but 30 X.[20] It thus costs the state 30 Y to reduce the price of X 50 per cent and thereby enable the consumer to increase his consumption of X from 15 to 30; the outlay by the state per unit increase in X is 2 Y just as under method (i).

Further analysis suggests, however, that *in practice* method (ii) will be less expensive, for it exposes the consumer to less pressure from his private or household pattern of tastes to violate the condition that he increase his consumption of X by the required amount[21] than does method (i). When method (i) is employed, the consumer moves from P_1 to P_2 on I_2 and price-line E_1K_2. Position P_2 is not a stable one, and the consumer will tend to move from it in proportion as he is disposed to violate the condition that he consume 30 units of X. If he were free to divide his income-plus-subsidy ($= 110$ Y) between X and Y as he chose, he would move along price-line E_2K_2 until he reached P_4 which also lies on the highest indifference curve (I_4) to which an income equivalent to 110 Y can elevate him when 1 X @ 2 Y. P_4 is a point of stable equilibrium at which he purchases 70 units of Y and only 20 units of X. Two-thirds of the subsidy ($= 30$ Y) has been diverted to the purchase of Y (see Case [e_{II}]); in fact, if the consumer were free to purchase as he chose, he would not purchase 30 X until his aggregate income approximated 170 Y (see P_6 on I_6 and E_3K_4 in Figure II, and Case [g_{II}]).

When method (ii) is employed, the consumer moves from P_1 to P_2 on I_2 and price-line E_1K_3. P_2 is not a stable position, and the consumer will move from it if he is disposed to violate the condition that he purchase 30 X at the reduced price.[22] If he were to divide his income as he chose between X and Y he would move from P_2 along E_1K_3 to P_3 on I_3, the highest indifference curve he can reach with an income equal to 80 Y and 1 X @ 1 Y. At this point, he purchases 57 Y and 23 X, using a part of his benefit from the reduction in the price of X to purchase 7 more units of Y (see Case [d_{II}]). If he were free to purchase as he chose, he would not purchase 30 units of X unless its unit price were reduced to two-thirds Y (see Case [f_{II}]).

In view of what has been said, method (ii) is more efficient and less ex-

20. In this instance, we require the consumer to behave as if his elasticity of demand for X is unity within the relevant range whereas the consumer postulated in Figure I voluntarily exhibited an elasticity of unity in his demand. If the consumer's elasticity of demand for X exceeded unity, he would increase his consumption of X by 15 in response to a less-than-50 per cent in the price of X, diverting some of his Y to the purchase of X. If the consumer looked upon X as a *negative* complement to Y, he would increase his consumption of X by 15 only if the aggregate value of his subsidy exceeded 15 $X(= 30Y)$.

21. I.e., 15 in the cases under consideration.

22. If his elasticity of demand for X were unitary through the relevant range, the consumer would voluntarily purchase 30 instead of 15 X upon the reduction of the price of X from two

pensive *in practice* than is method (i) even though in an ideal world, in which stipulated conditions were always complied with, the two methods would be alike in cost and effect. In the real world, the consumer enjoying subsidy (ii) tends to move from P_2 towards P_3, whereas the consumer enjoying subsidy (i) tends to move from P_2 towards P_4. The strength of this tendency to move is conditioned by the composition[23] of X, by the force of the moral and legal obligation[24] the consumer feels himself under to conform fully to the condition that he purchase and use 30 X in his household and in no wise secretly exchange some of his subsidy for Y, and by the degree of instability surrounding the consumer's position at P_2. Of import here is this last factor. Let us therefore compare (i) and (ii) under *ceteris paribus* conditions. P_4 lies on a higher indifference curve than does P_3. Therefore, our consumer experiences greater pressure from his pattern of tastes, under method (i) than under method (ii), to violate the condition of his receiving the subsidy and divert a part of it from the required purchase of X to the prohibited purchase of additional Y. The imposition of a tax upon Y, while it generates a substitution effect against Y and thus strengthens whichever method it is combined with, does not alter the basic fact that (ii) is inherently superior in practice to (i).

Comparison of the analysis in this section with that in the preceding section indicates that, irrespective whether (i) an income subsidy or (ii) a price-cut subsidy is employed, a given subsidy tends to produce a greater effect when the consumer is denied complete freedom of choice than when he is permitted it. Our analysis in this section leads also to a conclusion consistent with our finding in the preceding section: that in practice it is more economical for the state to subsidize the formation of human capital by reducing the price of X than by adding directly to the incomes of eligible families.

V

In this section, we examine further two assumptions underlying the preceding analysis and presentation.

(i) It has been assumed that X and Y are continuously substitutable for

---

to one Y. Such a situation was represented in Figure I. In Figure II, however, the price elasticity of demand for X is less than unitary.

23. Many goods and services (e.g., many foodstuffs, shelter, etc.) used by children and therefore describable as X are also used by adults and therefore describable as Y to the extent that adults use them. Let us call this last subcategory X_y and label all the rest of X as X_x. Accordingly, since consumers will be more disposed to violate the condition of their receiving the subsidy in respect to X_y than in respect to X_x, and since it is easier to divert X_y than X_x to adult members of the household, the overall tendency to violate the condition of nondiversion of the subsidy will vary directly with the ratio of X_y to X_x. This ease of violation might be reduced somewhat through the use of distinct kinds of stamp-money for X_y and X_x.

24. The force of this obligation to comply may be reenforced by legal and other sanctions.

one another along each indifference curve,[25] and that the curve representing the individual's demand for X is continuous. This assumption, however, is not valid, as a rule. Presumably, the demand for X will be elastic only within narrow ranges if income (in terms of Y) and number of children are held constant, while it will tend to vary in proportion to the number of children if income and price are held constant.[26] In general, the individual household head's Marshallian demand curve for X will tend to be discontinuous, or step-like, in character, the quantity taken remaining relatively constant until the price of X has fallen sufficiently to activate the consumer's latent demand for an additional child and thereby generate a large increment in his rate of purchase of X.[27] This quality of discontinuity will be accentuated, furthermore, by the condition to which the consumer must conform to be eligible to purchase X at reduced prices, namely, that he purchase a stipulated amount of X at the reduced prices, the amount depending upon or being a multiple of the number of his children, actual and in immediate prospect.

The discontinuity characteristic of individual curves of demand for X does not affect the subsidy program appreciably, since the real precondition to a consumer's receipt of a given subsidy is the number of dependent children he has in reality and/or in immediate prospect. When (as was assumed in Section III) consumers are free to divide their expenditures between X and Y as they choose, the curve representing the aggregate demand of all consumers for X will be continuous if their number, together with interindividual variation in indifference maps, is great enough. When, however, the price-cutting subsidy program assumes the form outlined in Section IV, the aggregate demand curve will not be completely continuous. Nonetheless, it will remain true *ceteris paribus* that in a society of many and diverse individuals each improvement in the terms on which X is to be had in terms of Y will induce some families to undertake to increase the number of their children, while each worsening of the terms will exercise a dampening influence upon the effective demand of families for additional X and offspring. Therefore, if the average annual number of births is too great or too small, the state may seek to diminish or to augment their number by decreasing or increasing its contribution and thereby increasing or reducing the price of

25. This continuity of substitutability is restricted to that portion of the indifference curve that lies between the threshold quantities of X and Y (see note 12 and text above).

26. The relations among commodities are more complex in reality than the above discussion suggests. Thus, if income and price are constant, an increase in the number of dependent children tends to be accompanied by a reduction in saving, a substitution of X in general for Y in general, and a substitution of some kinds of X for other kinds of X. The manner in which consumption data are reported does not permit a detailed empirical account. The available evidence is consistent with what has been said, however (e.g., see references in note 2 above).

27. The same reasoning applies if price is held constant while income is increased in terms of Y: the increase in income will not be followed by much of an increase in the purchase of X until total income has been increased enough to activate the consumer's latent demand for another child and thereby generate a large increment in his rate of purchase of X.

X to eligible households. Likewise, if the state finds some groups contributing too many or too few births, it may worsen or improve the terms under which the members of such group obtain X.[28]

(ii) It has been assumed that the advent of an additional child does not modify the consumer's indifference map. But this assumption is not wholly valid since it postulates greater rationality, foresight, and knowledge of the household's present pattern of tastes than the representative household head has. Empirical study would probably reveal that in most cases the advent of a child does modify the household head's indifference map somewhat, rendering it more favorable to the purchase of X and less favorable to that of Y; for such advent usually commits the householder to a greater diversion of expenditure from Y to X than was foreseen at the time the advent was planned.[29] Since the amount of subsidy required to impart a given stimulus to reproduction varies inversely with the lack of foresight in a population, and since the advent of a child tends to modify the indifference map in favor of X, lack of foresight may operate within limits to reduce the cost of forming human capital of given quality. The conclusions reached in this paper are not substantially affected, however, by operations of the tendency of patterns of tastes to change somewhat in favor of X.

VI

In this section, our findings are presented. Our main purpose has been to discover what types of family allowances or subsidies are most economical in terms of their effects upon the rate at which human capital is formed (i.e., the rate at which children are reproduced and reared to adulthood). We have concerned ourselves, moreover, only with methods designed rather to oper-

28. Let $1 X @ 1 Y$; let r denote the cost of maintaining a child; let q_1, q_3, and q_4 denote the contribution of the state, respectively, to the support of the second, third, and fourth children, and n the number of dependent children (actual and/or prospective). If, irrespective of its subscript, $q = r$, the contribution of the state will be $(n - 1)r$; the discount will be $I - I/n$; and the consumer will not be compelled by the advent of second and later children to diminish his consumption of Y, but will behave as if his elasticity of demand for X is unitary. If the preceding arrangement is too expensive, or produces too many births, the state's contribution may be reduced. Let $q_2 = \frac{1}{3}r$, $q_3 = \frac{2}{3}r$, and $q_4 = r$. Then the two-child family enjoys a price discount on X of one-sixth below market, the advent of the second child reducing the family's consumption of Y by $\frac{2}{3}r$. The advent of a third child increases the discount on X to one-third and further reduces the family's consumption of Y by $\frac{1}{3}r$. The advent of the fourth child causes no further reduction in the consumption of Y, the discount on X rising to one-half. If this second arrangement does not stimulate enough reproduction, the values of q_2 and q_3 may be raised. If r has been assigned a value in terms of X that is not sufficient to cover the maintenance cost of a dependent child, the value of r may be increased, accompanied if necessary by appropriate adjustments in q_2 and q_3. If some particular group is producing too many or too few births, appropriate adjustments may be made in the r and q values assigned to it. Presumably, if special r and q values are assigned to subgroups in the population (e.g., members of selected professions, or individuals whose biological heredity is rated superior), this differential treatment can best be administered through the use of distinct types of stamp-money for such subgroups.

ate within a given pattern of tastes than to change this pattern, and we have ruled out methods which seek to alter the tastes of a people through force, repression, or propaganda. We have divided all consumer goods and services into two types, X, which are complementary to the formation of human capital, and Y, which comprises all other consumer goods and services; and we have assumed that whatever causes the productive power of a nation to be shunted toward the formation of X, particularly if away from the creation of Y, is conducive to an increase in the rate at which human capital is formed.

In consistence with our previous analysis, we have defined as superior those types of subsidy which divert productive agents to the creation of X (and hence the formation of human capital) without at the same time appreciably increasing the Y income of the subsidized households, or substantially modifying their patterns of tastes. Our specific findings regarding methods of subsidy, formulated in terms of X and Y, follow:

1. If the household head is free to divide the subsidy he receives between X and Y in whatever manner he chooses, a given increase in the consumption of X can be produced more cheaply by subsidizing the sellers of X and reducing its relative price than by directly subsidizing the incomes of the purchasers of X and holding the price of X constant. In the former case, the substitution effect will certainly favor X, and the income effect may favor it, whereas, in the latter case, there is only an income effect that may favor X.

2. As a rule, a given subsidy, whether designed to increase the householder's income directly or to reduce the price at which he may purchase X, will cause a greater increase in the consumption of X when the recipient of the subsidy, as a condition of its receipt, is required to spend the subsidy upon X than when he is not so obligated.

3. If the condition described in 2. is not met and part of the subsidy is diverted from X to Y, the rate at which human capital is formed is not immediately affected adversely in terms of quantity, since receipt of the subsidy is contingent upon the recipient's having a stipulated number of children.[30] The quality of the human capital being formed tends to be adversely

29. A subsidy program could affect the cultural pattern of a people as distinguished from the living standards of individual households, and this effect in turn would further modify living standards. In the late nineteenth and the twentieth centuries a change of this sort took place, although in a manner to strengthen rather than to weaken antinatalist motives; for, as Glass (*op. cit.*, pp. 371–372) has shown, the circumstances which initiated the trend towards smaller families altered the economic and cultural pattern of the community and consequently operated with "cumulative intensity." In like fashion, an increase in the relative number of families with 2–4 children issuing out of a subsidy program would be accompanied by adjustments in the character of housing and the structure and purpose of some institutions and, in some measure (see [10] in Section VI), by a diminution in the consumption of Y; and these changes would render the community more favorable *ceteris paribus* to the formation of human capital.

30. It is implicitly assumed that the reduction of the consumption of X does not increase mortality among dependents. In the longer run, the diversion of subsidy to Y, if it raises the household's standard of living, will tend to make a given subsidy program less effective.

affected, however, for as a result of the diversion, the input of X per dependent per time period is reduced below the quantity deemed necessary.

4. A householder, when subject to the condition described in 2., will be more disposed in practice to conform to it if he receives his subsidy in the form of a reduction in the price of X than if he gets it in the form of a direct addition to his income with the price of X unchanged. In fact, if the price-elasticity of the householder's demand for X is great enough, it is unnecessary to impose the condition described, since he will automatically conform to it.

5. A subsidy in the form of X (i.e., a subsidy in kind) is a particular type of subsidy subject to the condition described in 2.; it is superior, in terms of the household head's response, to a subsidy in the form of a cut in the price of X insofar as a subsidy received in the form of X is less easily and less likely to be exchanged surreptitiously for Y than is a subsidy received in the form of stamp-money conferring the right to purchase X at a discount. If the two types of subsidy are equal, in terms of the household head's response, while the subsidy in kind permits greater economies of scale and administration, the subsidy in kind is superior in overall terms. In practice, however, a subsidy program including both types is superior to one consisting of either type alone; for the household head prefers freedom respecting his purchase of many kinds of X.[31]

6. The imposition of a tax upon Y will generate a substitution effect against Y and in favor of X, and thus reenforce the stimulation through subsidy of the consumption of X.

7. If a state seeks a given increase in the rate of human capital formation at the lowest possible cost, it will make use of a combination of price-cuts respecting X, subsidies (in kind) of X, and taxes upon Y. This is the only combination with any chance of success in a low-income state.

8. If the objective of the subsidy program is *both* to augment the rate of human capital formation by stimulating the consumption of X and to increase the welfare of the nonchild members of the household by increasing their consumption of Y and thus raising them to higher indifference levels, this double objective can be most effectively accomplished by giving the household head a direct and *adequate* income subsidy and allowing him to divide it between X and Y in whatever proportion he prefers.

9. It is not valid to argue that, because every individual prefers a cash subsidy which he may spend as he chooses to one of like magnitude which he is required to spend in certain ways, a cash subsidy is the most efficient

31. A subsidy-receiver will almost certainly prefer to have some X (say X_k) in kind because of the resulting convenience and economy. But, for reasons indicated (see note 17 and text), he prefers to be free to select other types of X (say X_f) and integrate his purchases thereof with the household's pattern of living. Even though a household head were disposed to comply fully with the nondiversionary condition (see [2.] above), he would prefer, as compensation for a given amount of human capital formation, a somewhat smaller subsidy in the form of X_k and X_f to a larger subsidy in kind only.

means of stimulating the formation of human capital. It is true that a markedly foresightless individual will greatly underestimate the X costs of offspring and will, therefore, be more stimulated to procreate by a cash subsidy which he is free to spend as he chooses than by a type of subsidy which he must take in the form of X. But it is also true that the formation of human capital calls for continuous and adequate consumption of X during the years of dependency. Hence the household head must be continuously motivated to purchase X; and this motivation is most economically supplied by a combination of subsidy in the form of X and subsidy in the form of reduced prices for X. Recourse to such a combination rather than to a cash subsidy tends to operate somewhat selectively against the relatively foresightless.

10. Given that recipients of subsidies comply with the condition specified in 2. above, a program of subsidies will not raise the *scale* of living (i.e., consumption of Y) of the subsidized households if (i) the population being homogeneous and consisting of households that respond identically to subsidies, the subsidies are not greater than necessary, or if (ii), the population being heterogeneous and consisting of households that respond differentially to subsidies, the subsidy program is made perfectly discriminatory in that no family is given a subsidy greater than necessary. Neither of these qualifications can be met, however. A population consists roughly of two groups: (*a*) families which would have produced the same or nearly the same number of children even in the absence of the subsidy program; and (*b*) families which produce some or all of their children in consequence of the subsidy program. The Y consumption of the (*a*) group will increase as a result of the subsidy program, though not by the full amount of the subsidies, for the state in effect will relieve the families of providing as much X out of their own means as they would have provided in the absence of subsidies, and a part of this saving will be spent for Y. If the subsidy falls appreciably short of the estimated average cost of producing a child, the (*b*) group will have to make up the difference — largely by diverting expenditure from Y to X, and their consumption of Y consequently will decrease. Only as the subsidy approaches the estimated average cost of a child does a tendency to divert some of the subsidy from X to Y become significantly manifest, with the strength of this tendency dependent upon the size of the subsidy and the disposition of the receiving families not to comply with the condition that the subsidy be devoted to X. The total effect of the subsidy program, particularly its net effect upon the consumption of Y, varies directly with the magnitude of the subsidy and with the ratio of the number of (*a*) to the number of (*b*) families. The effect of a subsidy program upon the *standard* of living (i.e., the relative desire for Y, *ceteris paribus*) is less easy to determine; presumably it would change, in so far as it did change because of the subsidy program, in the same direction as the *scale* of living.

11. The instrument most suited to carry out that part of the subsidy pro-

gram which cannot best be effected by means of a distribution of X in kind is a special-purpose money or stamp-money that conveys to the eligible holder either a claim to a given amount of X goods and services, or the right to purchase X at a given discount below market prices, the magnitude of the subsidy depending upon the receiver's number of children (and possibly other qualifications). The use of special-purpose money gives the recipient considerable freedom of choice respecting kinds of X while making non-compliance with the conditions of the subsidy difficult; it facilitates the combination of other socio-economic programs (e.g., the sale of "surplus" commodities) with the program of subsidies designed to augment the rate at which human capital is formed. Finally, just as the special-purpose money is differentiated according to the number of children of the recipient, so also may it be differentiated according to some other classification of the society intended to modify existing differentials in rates of natural increase (e.g., stimulate growth in professional groups, among those with "superior" biological heredity, etc.).

12. While it is not possible with the methods of analysis employed to determine the effects of the several types of subsidy upon the taste patterns of households, there seems to be no reason for supposing that, if effects upon taste patterns were taken into account, the above appraisal of the several methods would have to be modified significantly.

Measures of Population Maladjustment

Two approaches commonly are made to the measurement of population maladjustment. The one seeks answer to the question, What degree of population maladjustment obtains? The other seeks answer to the question, Is population growth operating to increase or decrease the degree of population maladjustment?

These two approaches tend to be confused. It is frequently inferred that, because a precise answer cannot be obtained to the first question, a satisfactory answer cannot be gotten to the second. In a sense, therefore, the confusion is somewhat analogous to that prevailing before the older utility economics, with its postulation of cardinally measurable utility, gave place to the newer welfare economics with its emphasis upon ordinal preference.[1] It will be argued that even though we cannot obtain a precise answer to the first question, we can satisfactorily answer the second and reach conclusions of significance for public policy should the attainment of certain values be the declared objective of public policy.

This paper consists of six sections. I is devoted to the meaning of population maladjustment and II to a review of some proposed measures of population maladjustment. III is given to a description of a measure that should prove especially sensitive to changes in the degree of population maladjustment, while IV is concerned with the influence of population growth upon progress in per capita income via the medium of capital formation. In V the significance of a country's or a region's size for the analysis of population maladjustment, a subject ignored in the first four sections, is considered. It is concluded in VI that, although ambiguities may in practice surround any index of population maladjustment, the indicators available, if employed jointly, are adequate to discover the direction of change in the degree of population maladjustment even though they may not serve to disclose empirically the degree of maladjustment actually obtaining.

I

The concept of population maladjustment presupposes that the actual population of a country may differ in size from the population which, had it been attained, would be of ideal or optimum magnitude[2] for the country in question. Let us, following Dalton,[3] make A represent the actual population,

---

1. See J. R. Hicks, *Value and Capital,* London, 1939, Part I.

2. For a recent excellent account of the optimum concept see M. Gottlieb, *The Theory of Optimum Population for a Closed Economy,* Journal of Political Economy, LIII, 1945, pp. 289–316. See also note 5 below and Gottlieb's paper cited in note 10 below.

3. See H. Dalton, *The Theory of Population,* Economica, VIII, 1928, pp. 28–50.

O the optimum population, and m the degree of maladjustment. Then

$$m = \frac{A}{O} - 1,$$

with the value of m being zero, positive, or negative according as the actual population is equal to, in excess of, or below the optimum in magnitude.

The concept of optimum population presupposes that there exist variables, the magnitude of any one of which (given that the other determinants of the variable in question are in effect held constant) varies with the magnitude of the population of a country, being a function of (among other determinants) this magnitude. Let us call this variable V and represent its average and its incremental values by V_a and V_m, respectively. Let us call the population magnitude D_p and the other determinants of the variable under consideration $D_1, D_2, \ldots, D_n$. Then the form of V in whose maximization we are interested, namely, V_a, equals $f(D_p, D_1, D_2, \ldots, D_n)$. The optimum value of the population magnitude is that value of D_p at which (given the values $D_1, D_2, \ldots, D_n$ in so far as these values are independent of the value of D_p) $V_a = V_m$, and, therefore, the value of V_a is at a maximum. A maximum value for V_a may be associated with a single value of D_p or with a range of values for D_p. In the former case we have a single population optimum, the values for the other determinants of V_a being given, while in the latter case we have a range of optimum values (i.e., an optimum range). In both cases the value of V_a will be less sensitive to changes in D_p in the neighborhood of the optimum value or range for D_p than in neighborhoods somewhat removed from the optimum. In other words, if D_p is measured along the x-axis and V_a is measured along the y-axis, then, while the increase in the value of D_p is accompanied at first by a rise and then by a fall in the value of V_a, the rate of change in the value of V_a is lowest in the neighborhood of its maximum value.

If not one maximum value but a range of quite similar values is obtained, the introduction of a time dimension may still permit the selection of a single value that is to be preferred to the others lying within the range. It will permit this when each of the values within the range takes on a unique value upon being redefined in terms of time. Consider, for example, a variable such as per capita net output or income. As A. B. Wolfe has pointed out, the desideratum is not the largest short-run per capita value but the largest comparatively *permanent* per capita value. It follows, on this definition, that the *smallest* population consistent with the maximization of per capita output or income over the very long run is the preferred optimum, since, other things equal, the smaller the population, the less rapidly will depletable and nonreplaceable resources be used up. Of course, if some other method of giving weight to the time dimension is employed, a somewhat different answer may be obtained, but even so the range of choice will be very much narrowed.

The variables whose magnitude is sensitive to changes in the magnitude of the population are many in number, with some being of considerable social significance and others of little or no importance. Among the variables usually deemed of significance are military strength, expectation of life at birth, per capita net output, per capita objective welfare, and per capita subjective welfare. Accordingly, what constitutes the optimum population magnitude turns on the variable being maximized, since the maximum point for any one variable does not coincide, in respect of size of population, with the maximum point of each other variable. Thus the military optimum will be greater than the net per capita output optimum, while the population magnitude compatible with maximum life expectancy probably both exceeds and falls short of the per capita objective welfare optimum, there apparently being a considerable range of population magnitudes within which life expectancy is insensitive to changes in population size.[4]

In this paper the only index in terms of which we shall define optimum population is net output per capita over a suitable time period. This index is preferred to one formulated in terms of per capita objective welfare, since objective welfare depends upon net output, the proportion of output devoted to consumption, and the rate of time preference assumed to rule. Net output per capita is to be preferred also to subjective welfare per capita for a number of reasons, but principally because, the distribution of output being given, subjective welfare is positively correlated with net output, probably progressing much in the manner of some root of net output. Subjective welfare is somewhat more highly correlated with net output, of course, when consumption is ordered according to scientifically established principles (in so far as such ordering is possible) than when this is not the case.[5]

For purposes of expositive simplicity it is assumed that the distribution of the net product is independent of the magnitude of the actual population

4. Health, morbidity and life expectancy are both interrelated and associated, on an individual or a geographical basis, with per capita income. The data on income and life expectancy suggest, however, that if life expectancy is measured along the *y*-axis and per capita income along the *x*-axis, the relationship between the two variables will be rather logistic in character, the response of life expectancy to changes in income being much greater at the intermediate than at the more extreme values for income.

5. On the income and the welfare population optima see E. F. Penrose, *Population Theories and Their Application with Special Reference to Japan*, Stanford, 1934, chaps. 2–3, and my *France Faces Depopulation*, Durham, 1938, pp. 273–277. On the history of the theory of the optimum see S. S. Cohn, *Die Theorie des Bevölkerungsoptimums*, Marburg, 1934. On optimum theory generally see also I. Ferenczi, *The Synthetic Optimum of Population*, Paris, 1938; R. Mukerjee, *The Political Economy of Population*, London, 1943; A. Sauvy, *Richesse et Population*, Paris, 1944; and many of the writings of C. Gini. Some of the problems involved in evaluating the significance of national income data and therefore of importance to students of optimum theory are treated by P. A. Samuelson in *Evaluation of Real National Income*, Oxford Economic Papers, II, 1950, pp. 1–29. Because the significance, in terms of the psychic or subjective welfare of the individual, of

and, in so far as our analysis requires, is unaffected by changes in the population magnitude. This assumption, while conceivable, is not very probable. For, under most institutional arrangements, income tends to be distributed somewhat more equally when the size of the population is below or in the neighborhood of the per capita net output optimum than when it is larger. The distribution of income making for the maximization of welfare is that one which, given the distribution throughout the population of both pleasure-machine capacity and the disposition to exercise effort economically, gives rise to the appropriate equilibrium between effort-oriented and welfare-oriented division of the product.[6]

A crucial question posed by the definition of m is the stability of the magnitude of O. J. S. Mill looked upon this magnitude as not likely to change. Students of economic history, on the contrary, have observed that the evolution of economic societies served to enlarge the population optimum for various countries, at least until the Industrial Revolution became far advanced. (They sometimes overlooked the significance of exchange relations and the spatial requirements of politico-economic viability to which we give attention below.) It is still often asserted that (even with exchange relations given), technological change makes for the increase of the optimum magnitude. Presumably this assertion involves confusion of the spatial with the population optimum, for there is no convincing evidence to the effect that technological change is continuing to enlarge the population optimum even though it does operate to elevate output per capita.

II

Four measures have been employed in the past to measure the degree of population maladjustment supposedly obtaining when the optimum population is defined in terms of net output per capita or a comparatively similar index: (a) the movement of per capita net output or income; (b) the index of employment; (c) the terms of international trade of the country under analysis; and (d) the state of returns. Of these measures (a) has been most frequently fallen back upon, it having been customary, ever since Malthus's day, to interpret an increase in per capita income as evidence of a decrease in population maladjustment.

---

income expressed in terms of supposedly constant or comparable dollars turns on many factors which are not caught within the statistical net, and because many of these factors probably are fairly constant from one to another region, country, or other locational situation, we must suppose that international and other interlocational differences in per capita subjective welfare must be far less pronounced than the estimated differences in real money income per capita. This conclusion is accentuated by the fact that at any given time and place the rate of saving is a positive function of the level of income.

6. In this connection see M. Friedman's comments in *Lerner on the Economics of Control*, Journal of Political Economy, LV, 1947, pp. 409–412.

Measure (*a*) is unsatisfactory for two reasons: (i) the movement of per capita income is governed by many factors, of which the population magnitude is but one; (ii) even if all relevant variables other than the population variable remain unchanged, a decline in per capita income may be compatible with a diminution in population maladjustment, while an increase in per capita income may coincide with an increase in population maladjustment. Other measures whose movements are closely associated with that of per capita output or income (e.g., composition of the diet, or composition of the budget) are objectionable on like grounds. Per capita net output (or income, since income approximates output) is preferable for most purposes of demographic analysis to indices highly correlated with income, since output (or income) figures are easier to get at and, as a rule, more sensitive to economic changes.

(i) For purposes of analysis the determinants of the level and/or the movement of per capita net output may be distributed among twenty analytically distinguishable categories. A residual category may be provided for factors which have been excluded because they appear to be relatively insignificant at present. While the magnitude of the population probably exerts some influence upon most of these categories, this influence is not significant in many instances, and per capita income can change significantly even in the absence of change in the size of the population. There follows a list of the twenty categories, together with a brief description of each and an indication of the relation of each to the population factor.

(1) Material equipment ("natural" and "man-made") *in use* per worker, the qualification "in use" guarding against the inclusion of equipment which is not augmenting the productivity of workers.

(2) Age composition of the population.

(3) Genetic composition of the population.

(4) State of health of the population.

(5) The exchange relations obtaining between a given economy and other economies (i.e., the degree of restriction to which an economy's international trade is subject).

(6) Degree of specialization and division of labor in effect.

(7) Scale of economic organization and activity prevalent. (Hereunder are included those sources of economy in operation consequent upon increase in scale which do not properly fall under [6].)

(8) The distribution of workers among occupations and the relative amount of unemployment (complete, partial, or disguised) present in the economy.

(9) State of the industrial arts.

(10) The educational, the scientific, and the related cultural equipment of the population. (Hereunder is included all basic and facilitating information—i.e., basic as distinguished from the applicable and applied knowledge

included under [9] — together with the elements that govern the accumulation and dissemination of basic knowledge. Inasmuch as institutional and other circumstances cause the level of applied knowledge to fall below the level of available knowledge, the state of the industrial arts may usually be improved somewhat even though [10] is unchanged. In the longer run, however, the progress of [9] is governed by that of [10].)

(11) Degree of cooperation and amity obtaining between the groups and classes composing the population.

(12) Flexibility of the institutional structure and the physical apparatus of the economy.

(13) Relative amount of vertical and horizontal mobility characteristic of a population, since only if there is sufficient mobility will the labor force be appropriately distributed among employments and combined with other agents of production.

(14) Internal geographical distribution of economic activities.

(15) The degree to which a population's pattern of consumption is adjusted to the pattern of resources available and designed to make effective use of those resources which are relatively plentiful.

(16) The relative magnitude of that part of the population which is adept at making entrepreneurial and innovational decisions, together with the location and the distribution of the power to make and execute such decisions.

(17) The dominant character of the politico-economic system (i.e., free-enterprise, mixed, social-democratic, or "totalitarian").

(18) Make-up of the prevailing value-system, in especial the values which animate a society's leaders and/or affect the disposition of men to put forth productive effort and behave in an economically creative manner.

(19) Effectiveness and stability of the rules, institutions, and legal arrangements designed to preserve economic, political, and civil order.

(20) The structure of that part of the institutional framework which touches immediately upon economic activities, together with the manner in which this structure functions (e.g., institutions having to do with money, banking, taxation, fiscal policy, and primary, secondary, and technical education).

(21) Residual.

Some of these categories are essentially independent of the size of the population, some are largely independent, and some are quite sensitive to changes in the size of the population, other conditions being given. Categories (2), (3), (15), (16), (17), (18), (19), and (20) appear to be essentially independent of the size of the population. Categories (5), and (14) may or may not be independent of the magnitude of the population, depending upon whether or not margins of substitution are permitted to change in response to changes in this magnitude. While categories (8), (9), (10), (11), (12), and

(13) appear to be largely independent, as a rule, of the magnitude of the population, each tends to be more favorable to the advance of per capita net output when the magnitude of the population is relatively small than when it is relatively large. Inasmuch as the state of health of a population tends to be comparatively good when per capita income is high and categories (9) and (10) are favorable, it may be said that the state of health is significantly sensitive to the magnitude of the population. Categories (6) and (7) will be conducive to the progress of per capita net output in something like a maximum degree only if the population is sufficiently great to permit maximum specialization, division of labor, and attainment of economies of scale. Category (1) is, by definition, related more closely than any other to the magnitude of the population; it is also related thereto in time since the absolute rate at which capital equipment per worker grows is significantly conditioned by the level of output per worker. In sum, in view of what has been said, the level of per capita income is free to change independently of changes in the magnitude of the population. This conclusion, of course, has had ample confirmation in the past several hundred years.[7]

It should be noted that output-estimating equations usually consist of a few elements some of which in effect are made up of a number of the variables included in the above list of twenty. For example, let Y represent national income; P, employed population; E, total energy (excluding human energy) consumed per year; L, number of livestock units; and make $Y = f(P, E, L)$. Then, as Olson has estimated, a 1 per cent change in P, with E and L remaining unchanged, is accompanied by a change of about 0.23 per cent in Y. The approximate corresponding values for E and L are 0.5 and 0.28 per cent. Olson, however, concludes that a given output-estimating equation yields good results only when it is applied to countries with appropriate culture patterns. The point here emphasized may be illustrated thusly: The capacity to accumulate and effectively utilize nonhuman energy and livestock, being a function of many of the twenty determinants listed above, the values of E and L, together with increases in these values, epitomize the values of more basic determinants. In like manner factor analysis of many cultural dimensions suited to represent the original variables.[8]

(ii) Let us return to the formula $m = (A/O) - 1$. Since A and/or O are subject to change, an increase in m may accompany a rise in per capita income

7. As yet the best estimates of the comparative movement of per capita income and output by country are those given by Colin Clark in *Conditions of Economic Progress*, London, 1940, and *The Economics of 1960*, London, 1942. See also the various numbers of the *Review of Economic Progress* (Brisbane) for the year 1949. On the relations obtaining between income and demographic variables see my *Aspects of the Economics of Population Growth*, Southern Economic Journal, XIV, 1947–48, pp. 123–147, 233–265, and relevant literature there cited.

8. See E. C. Olson, *Factors Affecting International Differences in Production*, American Economic Review, Proceedings, XXVIII, No. 2, 1948, pp. 502–522. On the findings of factor analysis applied to the study of cultural variables see R. B. Cattell, *Dimensions of Cultural Patterns*, Journal of Abnormal and Social Psychology, XLIV, 1949, pp. 443–469.

while a decrease in m may be associated with a decrease in per capita income. Inasmuch as the value for O tends to be higher in technologically more advanced than in technologically less advanced societies, marked technological progress tends to be accompanied initially by a decrease in m and an increase in per capita income if, as is usual, $A > O$ at the time such marked progress begins. After a certain stage of technological development is reached, however, further such improvements are not accompanied by a further increase in O. Accordingly, if, after this stage is reached, technological improvements continue to be made and A continues to grow, m increases (eventually if not immediately) even though per capita income rises. While it is possible that m and per capita income may decrease simultaneously, such a coincidence is not likely.

Measure (b) is not a very satisfactory index of m, since the annual level of employment, the labor force being given, is conditioned by many factors which are essentially independent of the magnitude of the population. The cyclical determinants of employment, while sometimes sensitive to variations in population growth rates, are not greatly influenced by the size of the population. The secular determinants of employment are sensitive to changes in the rate of population growth; yet whether these changes are conducive, on the balance, to unemployment (as has been asserted) is by no means clear, particularly since the influence of the rate of population growth is so largely conditioned by the prevailing institutional framework. Population pressure may, however, contribute to unemployment in two ways. First, it may (as in the Orient) cause the human agent to be undervalued and, therefore, wastefully used. Second, it may accentuate both labor immobility and inflexibility on the part of a society's economic apparatus, thus making for imperfectness of competition which, in turn, produces complete, partial, and disguised unemployment. On the whole, however, because of the plurality of the sources of unemployment, variations in the annual level of employment cannot reveal much respecting the degree of population maladjustment (i.e., the value of m) prevalent in a country.[9]

Measure (c) is ambiguous, even though it was suggested by Malthus, implied by George Tucker,[10] and made use of by J. M. Keynes when he helped to initiate the population scare of the 1920's. For while changes in

9. E.g., see B. F. Keirstead, *The Theory of Economic Change*, Toronto, 1948, chaps. 4–5, 7, 9; and my *Population and Per Capita Income*, Annals of the American Academy of Political and Social Science, CCXXXVII, 1945, pp. 189–190, and the studies there cited.

10. On the course of the terms of trade in the past see Clark, *Conditions*, chap. 14, and *The Economics of 1960*, chap. 7; also the United Nations, *Relative Prices of Exports and Imports of Under-Developed Countries*, Lake Success, 1949. This measure was employed by a mid-nineteenth century American economist Tucker in a controversy with A. H. Everett, a critic of Malthus; its significance was the basis of a controversy between Keynes and William Beveridge. On the significance of external trading relations for both the magnitude of the optimum population and its degree of stability see M. Gottlieb's excellent paper, *Optimum Population, Foreign Trade and World Economy*, Population Studies, III, 1949, pp. 151–169.

a country's (let us call it country C) terms of trade tend *ceteris paribus* to accompany an increase in a country's population, and while such changes may signify a worsening of C's population situation, these changes may be, and commonly are, partly or wholly nondemographic in origin. It is, of course, to the advantage of each country, other conditions remaining equal, to obtain the most favorable terms of trade possible. But, since other conditions cannot remain equal, this proposition must be reformulated to the effect that it is to the advantage of a country to obtain those terms of trade which will make the greatest net contribution to that country's income. It will be assumed, when such assumption facilitates analysis, that all conditions, other than those issuing out of a change in C's population size, remain unchanged.

The terms of trade of country C decline when, all other conditions (in particular, foreign demand) being given, its supply of goods for export increases because (i) its labor force increases, or (ii) its output per worker increases, or (iii) a combination of (i) and (ii) is experienced. The degree of decline, given some increase in supply consequent upon (i) and/or (ii), will be governed chiefly by (1) the arc elasticity of foreign demand for C's exports and (2) the percentage increase in these exports, with (2) dependent principally upon the fraction of these exports initially supplied by C and the elasticity of supply characteristic of these exports in those countries other than A which supplied the remainder. If only increase (ii) is operative, the decline in C's terms of trade almost certainly will be much more than offset by the increase in output per worker, and per capita income will rise, with the net advantage to C being fixed by conditions (1) and (2). If, however, only increase (i) is operative, the resulting decline in C's terms of trade signifies an increase in its degree of population maladjustment, but does not constitute a precise measure of this increase. If increases (i) and (ii) are operative, the same conclusion holds unless it can be shown that increase (ii) is a consequence of increase (i).

C's terms of trade will decline if, with the demand for the exports in question remaining substantially constant, C's competitors increase their supply of these exports. While a decline of such origin signifies a worsening of per capita income in C, it does not indicate whether or not population maladjustment has increased in C. A like conclusion holds when, as is assumed in the next paragraph, foreign demand for the exports of C and C's competitors rises and offsets or partly offsets an increase in the output of C's competitors.

When the previously postulated condition — that foreign demand for the exports in question remains unchanged — is relaxed and only increase (i) is assumed to be operative, C's terms of trade, whether or not they change, will be worse than they would have been had increase (i) not taken place. For then the increase in foreign demand (whether originating in a change in foreign tastes, labor force, or output per worker) will not render A's terms of trade as favorable as they would have been in the absence of increase (i). The same conclusion holds if increases (i) and (ii) are operative, provided that (ii) is not consequent upon (i). If only (ii) is operative, per capita income rises in C, but the changes, if any, in C's terms of trade reveal nothing respecting any possible change in C's degree of population maladjustment. It may be said, in general, that unless C's population is below the optimum in size, any increase in its numbers, whether in absolute terms or relative to the populations of the countries with which it trades, will affect its terms of trade adversely.

In view of what has been said it may be concluded that a change in C's terms of trade does not constitute a satisfactory index of change in the degree of population maladjustment, since the terms of trade are affected also by other circumstances than changes in the magnitude of C's population. If, however, these circumstances are taken into account, a decline in the terms of trade often may be interpreted to indicate an increase in the degree of population maladjustment. The long-run change in the terms of trade of Northern and Western Europe in the nineteenth century is consistent with this analysis, reflecting the influence of population growth both in Europe and in many of the regions with which Europe traded.

Measure (d) is not satisfactory. If the state of returns under consideration is that characteristic of the production of "natural resources," it is inadequate because, as is shown in Section III, account is not taken of the state of returns in other industries. If, however, the phrase "state of returns" is designed to indicate whether V_m exceeds or falls short of V_a, as described in Section I, the phrase amounts to no more than a statement of where the optimum lies; it does not facilitate the empirical determination of the degree of population maladjustment, if any.

In this section we have examined four proposed measures of population maladjustment, and have found each inadequate, under the circumstances prevailing, to reveal empirically the degree of population maladjustment m. But two of the measures may help disclose whether population growth is entailing an increase in population maladjustment. These measures are the longer-run movement of per capita output and the longer-run trend in the terms of trade. For if per capita output falls, or fails to rise as rapidly as it ought in view of experience elsewhere, and if at the same time the population is growing, it may be inferred that population growth is accentuating the degree of maladjustment already obtaining. As we have indicated, every worsening of a country's terms of trade is disadvantageous, other things equal, and population growth makes for such a worsening. Accordingly, if no compensatory advantage can be pointed to, it may be inferred that population maladjustment has increased. The converse of these two arguments is not necessarily valid, for it must first be shown that other circumstances than population growth are not accountable for the longer-run rise in income and/or the terms of trade.

III

The problem of population maladjustment within either a closed economy or one operating in accordance with given rules of international trade has a double origin: (i) the utilization of labor is itself subject to increasing returns in the sense of increasing output per composite unit of input; (ii) there exist many "natural" resources whose supply is fixed and/or depletable and for which, human labor can only be substituted imperfectly, within limits, and with increasing difficulty. If labor were the only agent of production the optimum population would be that population, given which and given the prevailing state of technology, specialization, division of labor, and inter-industry fit could be maximized, or some multiple of this population. (Some would include among the variables to be maximized the amount of mental stimulus per person, together with the pressure toward technological improvements; but we have left these out on the ground that they depend upon the location of the population, the conditions of communication, and the state of social organization, that is, upon variables not significantly under the empire of overall population density and growth.) If there were no increasing returns and only "natural" resources had to be taken into account, the smallest population capable of utilizing these resources would be the optimum since, given such population, the adverse influence of depletion would be minimized. The most useful approach to the problem of population maladjustment is one that is founded principally upon conditions (i) and (ii) described above; and it is this type of approach we shall now make.[11]

In view of what has been said, certain of the effects that may accompany the growth of population, it being assumed that conditions not affected by such growth remain unchanged, will stand out. Such effects may be grouped into three internally homogeneous categories. In (1) may be placed three

11. This type of approach is made in my paper cited in note 7 above; Gottlieb makes a somewhat similar approach in his paper cited in note 2 above, but does not lay so much stress upon inter-industry fit. On the law of increasing returns, which received emphasis at the hands of A. Marshall and which received its initial statistical treatment from G. T. Jones, see C. Clark, *Conditions*, pp. 306ff., and numbers 6–10 of the *Review of Economic Progress*, I, 1949. As we indicate later in the text above, however, care must be taken lest increases in output per composite unit of input, which are the result of technological and innovational change and not of mere increase in scale or organization, are attributed to the operation of "increasing returns." Considerable information bearing upon the incidence of economies of scale and certain related economies by industry, together with relevant bibliography, is provided by L. Rostas in *Productivity, Prices and Distribution in Selected British Industries*, Occasional Paper 11, Cambridge, 1948, and *Comparative Productivity in British and American Industry*, Occasional Paper 13, Cambridge, 1948.

effects which accompany (among other things and within limits) the growth of population: (i) the increase in the division of labor and specialization, (ii) the increase in the scale of economic organization and the economies consequent thereupon, and (iii) the improvement in inter-industry fit, the term industry being understood to embrace every form of public and private activity in which a nation's labor force engages. Each of these effects as well as their aggregate effect is susceptible of maximization. In category (2) may be placed the increase in the rate at which natural resources (land, mineral supplies, etc.) are exploited, together with the consequence that recourse must finally be had to lower-grade resources whose exploitation entails a greater input of productive agents (especially labor) per unit of output. In (3) is placed the increase in the rate at which sub-surface supplies of natural resources (e.g., fuels, minerals) are used up, together with the consequence that the long-run upward movement (if any) of imputed physical output per worker engaged in removing and extracting such resources tends to be decelerated and even reversed. For the present we shall ignore effect (3) except in so far as it manifests itself in the form of effect (2) and compels recourse to lower grade natural resources. At the same time we shall take into account the fact that the incidence of effect (3) may be cushioned at least temporarily through international trade.

Let us subdivide effect (1) into (i) the effects flowing from changes in the division of labor, specialization, and scale of economic organization, most of whose elements are interrelated, and (ii) the effects consequent upon changes in inter-industry fit. Let us suppose that the supply of first-grade raw materials is adequate and that (ii) may be ignored. Then, as population and the extent of the market expand, the influences included under (i) grow until they reach the attainable maximum. But the influences included under (ii) cannot be neglected. Aggregate effect (i) can be maximized only on condition that the extent of the market permits an inter-industry fit allowing the utilization in all lines of economic activity of optimum-size firms operating at the point of minimum costs; and such a fit is compatible with populations of various but by no means all sizes. Actually, however, even though only a fairly large population, or some multiple thereof, will permit the attainment of a perfect inter-industry fit, the supply and demand conditions obtaining in most industries will permit the attainment of an almost perfect inter-industry fit in the same economy even though the population is very much smaller.[12] It may be assumed, therefore, if effect (2) is neglected, that there exists a wide range of populations compatible with essentially the same level of net output per capita.

Let us turn now to effect (2). So long as unutilized first-grade natural resources are available, increments of population may be combined there-

12. See my paper cited in note 7 above.

with, with the result that output per worker engaged in their exploitation does not fall, it being assumed, of course, that the economies included in category (i) of (1) are maximized in the aggregate. But when nonutilized first-grade natural resources no longer are available, recourse must be had to those of inferior grade whose exploitation entails a greater input of productive agents (particularly direct and indirect labor) per unit of output than did that of the first-grade resources.

Let us now divide the industries of an economy into three classes, (1) representing industries especially subject (within limits) to effect (1), (2) representing industries subject to effect (2), and (3) representing industries comparatively insensitive to effects (1) and (2) and essentially independent of changes in the size of the population. Within class (1) will fall principally transportation, communication, and other public utilities, together with those branches of manufacturing and government in which economies of scale are particularly pronounced. Within class (2) will fall agriculture, forestry, fishing, and mining. Within class (3) will fall all branches of activity (e.g., services, distribution, small scale manufacturing, etc.) that belong neither in class (1) nor in class (2). Let L_1 represent, in index form, the base year average net output *imputable*[13] per employee engaged in class (1) industries, and ΔL_1, the change in percentage per year in this index. Let L_2 and ΔL_2 and L_3 and ΔL_3 represent corresponding values for industries (2) and (3). Finally let w_1, w_2, and w_3 represent the respective fractions of the labor force engaged in industry classes (1), (2), and (3), with the sum of these fractions being equal to unity when the entire labor force is employed.

Suppose that the population and labor force of a country increase by a small percentage per year, that the amount of capital invested in each class of industry increases by the same percentage, that w_1, w_2, and w_3 remain virtually unchanged, and that no improvements in technology are introduced. Then L_3 will remain virtually unchanged, L_1 may remain unchanged or increase somewhat, and L_2 will increase, decrease, or remain

13. Average net output imputable per employee engaged in class (1) industries is obtained as follows. From total net product of class (1) industries subtract the part of the net product imputable to the "capital" employed therein and divide the residuum by the number of full-time employees. For present purposes the amount of net product imputable to "capital" is to be obtained by multiplying the estimated amount of "capital" employed in class (1) industries by a rate of return on "capital" assumed to be representative of the economy as a whole. Average net output imputable per employee engaged in class (2) and class (3) industries, respectively, is computed in a similar manner. This rough method of computation, the validity of which turns principally upon whether the marginal yield of capital is the same in all three classes of industry, provides a fairly satisfactory measure of that part of the average output per employee (by class of industry) which is not imputable to the complementary nonhuman agents of production being used jointly with such employee. Even so this method of computation is only approximately accurate since it assumes that the rate of return i on "capital" does not change between year 0 and year 1 even though the ratio of nonhuman to human agents of production does change, thus underestimating or overestimating the imputed product of "capital"; but the margin of error probably is much the same for each of the three industry classes.

unchanged. Population maladjustment M may be said to have diminished if $w_1 \, \Delta L_1 > w_2 \, \Delta L_2$, and to have increased if $w_2 \, \Delta L_2 > w_1 \, \Delta L_1$.

This formulation of M is invalid if an economy is dynamic. Average net product per worker (i.e., total net product divided by the number of employees engaged in its production) may increase in consequence of improvements in technology and/or increases in the amount of capital employed per worker even though the population and the labor force remain unchanged. Our definition of L_1, L_2, and L_3 takes into account increases in net output imputable to increase in capital, but not increases imputable to improvements in technology. Accordingly, if we would isolate the influence of population growth, we must also sequester that portion of the change in average net product per worker which is attributable to improvements in technology. Presumably $\Delta L_3/L_3$ affords a rough measure of the relative contribution of improvements in technology; for since changes in L_3 are not attributable in significant measure to changes in the size of the population or in the amount of capital utilized in class (3) industry, they must be imputed predominantly to technological and related improvements. (Inasmuch as there may be relatively greater pressure upon entrepreneurs to improve technology in class (1) and (2) industries than in class (3) industry, $\Delta L_3/L_3$ may understate the effect of technological improvements; but we shall assume this is not the case). Accordingly, we may define population maladjustment (i.e., M) as follows.

$$M = w_1\left(\frac{L_1 + \Delta L_1}{L_3 + \Delta L_3} - 1\right) + w_2\left(\frac{L_2 + \Delta L_2}{L_3 + \Delta L_3} - 1\right)$$

If M has a value of zero, it may be assumed that the growth of population taking place concomitantly with the changes in the values of L_1, L_2, and L_3, has not altered the existing degree of population maladjustment (if there be such). If M has a positive value this maladjustment may be assumed to have been reduced, while if M has a negative value, maladjustment may be supposed to have been increased.

If a country imports a considerable fraction of its consumption of class (2) industry products, exchanging class (1) and/or class (3) industry products therefor, a given increase in the population magnitude will affect M differently than when class (2) products are largely produced at home. In general, when this is the case, ΔL_2 will tend to remain positive and approximate ΔL_3 in value. The effect exercised by foreign trade upon the level and the rate of growth of L_2 may, however, be taken into account. For, since estimates of the cost of exploiting inferior resources (assuming, of course, that these exist within the country under analysis) usually are to be had, one can estimate roughly how L_2 would behave in the absence of imports from abroad. A corresponding estimate is possible for a country that is exporting L_2 products. It is sometimes possible also to estimate very roughly the effect upon the cost of class (2) imports of an increase in a country's population and consumption. The fact that class (2) products are imported needs to be taken into account only if their inflow is subject to significant (monopolistic) price changes or to partial or complete interruption by hostile foreign governments.

The changes in M do not reveal the magnitude of m, the degree of population maladjustment (see Section I). These changes may indicate, however, whether or not m has been modified by the change in the population magnitude. The validity of this finding turns, of course, upon the correctness of the estimate of the respective contributions of capital and technological progress and upon the absence of any other significant output-affecting forces. The equation for M has the merit of directing attention to the categories of economic activity most sensitive to changes in the size of the population. Emphasis upon M rather than upon m has the additional merit of stressing that concerning which action may be taken; for while the magnitude of the population is not likely to subject to great change, it probably is possible for modern states to accelerate or decelerate the rate of population growth in light of the behavior of M.

There exist other indices of M which, while based also upon the existence of activities which are especially sensitive to population growth, appear to be inferior to the measure just developed. (i) An increase in the proportion of the national output definable as land-rent (since other agents of production are imperfectly substitutable for land), or an increase in ratio of the rent index to the index of wages or to an index of prices, tends to signify an increase in population maladjustment. (ii) A decline in the proportion of the national output imputable to labor has similar significance. (iii) A rise in the ratio of the price of food and/or raw materials to a general price index or to a representative wage index may have similar significance.

IV

While the growth of net output per capita is conditioned by many determinants other than the growth of capital equipment as such, the expansion of capital equipment per worker epitomizes in summary form, just as does that of livestock and energy utilization (see Section II), the influences of many more basic determinants. For this reason the relation obtaining between the growth of per capita income and that of the capital supply is significant for the analysis of population maladjustment.

Let W represent a country's physical assets, and let W be composed of W_1, assets directly used, and W_2, assets less directly used in the production of national income Y. Let S represent Y/W ; and let s represent $\Delta Y/\Delta W$, the ratio of the annual increment in income consequent upon the annual increment in physical assets. Let p represent population and r its annual rate of increase in per cent; y, per capita income and j its annual rate of increase; and i the annual rate of increase in Y. Let a represent the annual increment in W expressed as a percentage of Y. Accordingly, we may say that $i = sa$, and, if s remains constant and equal to S, that $i = Sa$. But, since s tends to decline as W/p increases, a corrective factor c, with a value less than unity, must be employed to reduce the value of S appropriately so that $i = Sac$, and $j = [(1 + Sac)/(1 + r)] - 1$. This equation indicates that so long as S is independent of the rate of population growth and c approximates 1, a 1 per cent increase in population costs approximately a 1 per cent increase in per capita income.

The values of S and s are not independent of the rate of population growth, being governed in the long run largely by the rate of technological progress, by the comparative availability of natural resources, and by r. Let $f(r)$ represent the amount by which s must be increased if $r > o$ and s supposedly is the product of circumstances other than population growth. Then the rate of increase in y may be expressed as

$$j = \frac{sa[1 + f(r)]}{1 + r}.$$

Under static conditions, judging by the values obtained for the Douglas-Cobb type of production function, $f(r)$ would commonly have a value in excess of $0.7r$, but under more dynamic conditions, judging by estimates such as Olson's, the value of $f(r)$ will lie closer to $0.5r$. Presumably, then, when a population is in excess of the optimum in size, a 1 per cent increase in population entails somewhat less than a 1 per cent increase in national income.[14]

14. Let $Y = f(O, W)$, where Y represents national income, P represents the employed population, and W physical assets, with all income-increasing forces other than P and W inoperative. Suppose that 100 units of P are combined with 100 units of W, with each unit of W equal in value terms to four units of Y, and that the combination yields 100 units of Y, the marginal yield of a unit of P being 0.75 and that of a unit of W being $0.25Y$. Under the circumstances S, or Y/W, would have a value of 100/400, or 0.25, and this value remains unchanged if P and W are each increased by 1 per cent. If, however, with P unchanged at 100, W is increased to 101, Y increases to approximately 100.25, s approximates 0.25/4, or .0625, the value of S declines from 100/400 to 100.25/404, and output per unit of P rises from 1 to $1.0025Y$. Accordingly, since if P had also increased by 1 per cent, output per unit of P would have remained at $1.0Y$, this 1 per cent increase in P would have cost a 0.25 per cent increase in per capita income (as represented by output per unit of P). This cost becomes 0.5 and 0.75 per cent, approximately, if the initial marginal products of P and W are, respectively, 0.5 each and 0.25 and 0.75. When conditions are dynamic, with increases in capital essential to the introduction of technological and related improvements, the latter pair of values will be more closely approximated than the former. This matter is treated and relevant bibliography is presented in my paper, *Economic Factors in the Development of Densely Populated Areas*, Proceedings of the American Philosophical Society, XCV, 1951, pp. 20–53. On the Douglas-Cobb production function on which the above example is based see Paul Douglas, *Are There Laws of Productivity?*, American Economic Review, XXXVIII, 1948, pp. 1–41, and Olson's paper, cited in note 8 above. Population growth also absorbs "capital", thereby substituting human for nonhuman productive power (see p. 256 of my paper cited in note 7 above).

The behavior of several of the elements in this equation may be indicative of changes in population maladjustment. If a backward and/or agricultural economy is undergoing economic development, its *s* value should be appreciably higher than that of developed countries, and its *j* should be higher, the value for *a* being given. If such marked superiority is not found and population is growing, it may be inferred that population maladjustment is increasing. It may be supposed that the value of *f*(*r*), whatever it happens to be, changes slowly. It may be inferred, accordingly, that if, *a* being given, *j* continues to decline, population maladjustment is increasing unless the decline can be attributed to a decline in the rate of technological progress. While a continual rise in *j* is compatible with a decrease in population maladjustment, such a rise is to be attributed to an increase in the progress of technology and nondemographic income-increasing forces unless the population of a country is quite sparse and/or all other relevant indicators suggest such a decrease.

V

The magnitude of a country's population optimum, given its size, turns principally on the kind of economic activities in which its labor force is engaged and upon the exchange relations obtaining between this country and others with which it trades; for a national optimum is a weighted average of regional optima. Furthermore, questions concerning a given country's population optimum sometimes tend to be confused with questions concerning the optimum spatial requirements of a sovereign politico-economic unit. In this section certain of these questions are considered.

Inasmuch as some kinds of economic activity entail a geographical concentration of the labor force whereas others involve a geographical scatter of this force, what constitutes optimum population density for a country turns on which (if either) of these two categories of economic activity predominates. If agriculture and/or mining are the dominant basic forms of occupation, optimum density will be relatively low, for these activities are resource-oriented. If, on the contrary, manufacturing predominates, optimum density will be high, for manufactures are labor-oriented. If, finally, a country is very large, comparatively self-contained, and free of dependence upon external trade, its optimum population density will be greater than that of countries engaged in primary production and lower than that of countries engaged largely in manufacturing. In consequence, population densities expressed in terms of persons per square kilometer are misleading.

A better measure of density is provided by the average amount of relevant equipment of all kinds (i.e., arable land, buildings, machinery, etc.) available per worker. If this average, accurately and appropriately computed, is the same for a number of countries, if their respective labor forces are qualitatively similar, and if their external trading relations do not differ appreciably, net output per worker should not vary greatly from country to country, since the *economic* density of the population is nearly the same in all the countries under consideration. It is, of course, virtually impossible to estimate in comparable terms and with accuracy the average amount of relevant equipment in use per worker, by country. Even so, Olson's estimates suggest that something like three-quarters of the variation in output per worker is immediately traceable to differences in equipment per worker.[15]

What constitutes a population optimum for any country, given its size, is governed by its trading relations and fixed by the optima of other countries.[16] Thus, if a country's labor force is engaged principally in manufacturing and if, therefore, its population optimum is relatively large, this country will be dependent upon foreign sources for much of its raw materials and/or foodstuffs, and this dependency will imply that the population optima of the countries engaged in supplying the manufacturing country with food and raw materials must be relatively low. As a result, on the assumption that international trade was unimpeded in any way and that the population of every country was of optimum size, actual population density would vary greatly, ranging from maxima in Eastern North America and Northwestern Europe to minima in Africa, Oceania, and South America.

This international interdependence of populations may be illustrated in the following manner. Let us divide the world into a given country C and the rest of the world W. Now suppose that the population of the rest of the world increases relative to that of C. The population of C is affected in two ways. (i) There is an aggregative effect in that the external demand for the goods and services of the population of C rises, with the result that the growth of C's population is stimulated. (ii) There is a substitutional effect, in that W's augmented population now competes more effectively than before with C's population in respect of both the supply of various goods and services and access to raw stuffs imported by C. Effect (ii) is unfavorable to the growth of C's population. How C is finally affected by the increase in W's population thus turns on whether effect (i) or (ii) is dominant, and this depends significantly upon the economic structure and the industrial composition of C vis-à-vis that of W. If C is a spatially large enough unit it can virtually insulate itself against the behavior of W, but it cannot do this if it is a small politico-economic unit situated within a circumscribed territory. It follows, therefore, that the capacity of a sovereign politico-economic unit to guard itself against population maladjustment is significantly conditioned by its size.

Because population optima vary with the industrial composition of coun-

15. See Olson's paper (note 8 above); also Clark, *The Economics of 1960*, pp. 73–74.
16. This dependence of the population of any one country upon that of other countries was clearly recognized by the mercantilists who, however, were interested in achieving not an optimum but a large population at the expense of their neighbors. E.g., see my *French Predecessors of Malthus*, Durham, 1942, pp. 361–363.

tries, disparity of interest[17] arises at the international level and this disparity is accentuated when, the conditions of exchange being what they are, the terms of international trade develop in a manner unfavorable to countries engaged principally in the production of primary products. For political and military as well as for economic reasons, therefore, countries engaged in primary production have sought to industrialize themselves and augment their populations while countries specializing in manufacturing have endeavored to increase their domestic supply of raw materials and/or foodstuffs. While the effects of these policies have sometimes been beneficial in terms of an economic optimum theory, they have served, on the whole, to expand the world's population unduly, and to cause the populations of most countries to exceed in size what is for each of them the optimum under present conditions as well as under the conditions that would have obtained had the population of the world been very much smaller and had trade and migration been unimpeded.

The disparity described in the preceding paragraph has arisen out of the fact that so long as agriculture and handicrafts everywhere constituted the dominant forms of activity, as land was the only important natural resource, and as transportation and communication were difficult and comparatively expensive, a country's spatial optimum was small and no important economic or political advantage was to be had (by the *vast majority* of the population) from further extension of the prevailing geographical limits. Moreover, for any such country the optimum population density was small. The advent of the Industrial Revolution changed all this. It gradually became necessary, in part because of restrictions upon trade but chiefly for military and political reasons, either to enlarge the spatial limits of the typical state or, since this usually was hard to accomplish, to pursue economic policies which served almost automatically to expand population so long as reproductive institutions and habits remained unchanged. Accordingly, population optima came to be exceeded in nearly all countries, only English-speaking North America, Russia, Australia, and parts of South America constituting exceptions because, having been settled late, they were sparsely populated as well as large. It is likely that, had Europe (exclusive of Russia) on the eve of the Industrial Revolution constituted one instead of many sovereign states, its course of development would have resembled more closely that of North America with the result that much of its present spatial and numerical maladjustment of population would have been avoided.

17. It has sometimes been suggested that a population tends to develop until it has assumed an optimum size. This argument is invalid on individual grounds since it assumes that the income-reducing or the income-increasing effects of population growth are incident almost wholly upon the individuals responsible for this growth. At most it may be said that, in a modern society that is capable of regulating its numbers, there is some tendency for the resistance to population growth to rise as the population departs from the optimum. This tendency is compatible in part with the logistic theory.

In view of what has been said it is probably more meaningful for most purposes to express population maladjustment in terms of large and comparatively self-contained areas than in terms of states so restricted in space as to be lacking in elements essential to political, military, and economic viability under circumstances such as obtain at present. For units that are so large as to be viable under these circumstances are more nearly alike in industrial composition, or can be made more nearly alike, than are the smaller and consequently more specialized states of today. At least five such units are identifiable and at least the first three are fairly comparable. These five are Europe exclusive of Russia but inclusive of North Africa and the Near East; the Soviet Union; the United States and Canada; India, Burma, and Ceylon; and Japan and Eastern and Southeastern Asia. Perhaps Malaysia should be included with Japan and Eastern and Southern Asia. While South America may possibly be treated as a sixth unit, Africa (exclusive of North Africa) is not convertible into a viable unit, nor is Latin America exclusive of South America. Australia, though marked by little or no population maladjustment, does not appear to be definable as a viable unit.

Were the many smaller national units replaced by a small number of large and comparatively self-sufficient politico-economic units much external trade would be converted into internal trade, the ratio of external trade to national income would decline, and the importance of the terms of trade and changes in regional population density would be diminished. Such redistribution of population as would result would indicate empirically the interdependence of both the actual populations and the theoretical population optima of most of the states composing the world economy.[18]

VI

In theory measures of population maladjustment may reveal three things, the degree of maladjustment, whether maladjustment is increasing, and whether it is decreasing. Actually, as has been shown, available measures are not well suited to disclose the degree of maladjustment, for they do not

18. Especially relevant to the discussion of this section are the many studies of the location of economic activities. E.g., see E. M. Hoover, *The Location of Economic Activity,* New York, 1948; and the many studies cited by Hoover; and G. K. Zipf, *Human Behavior and the Principle of Least Effort,* Cambridge, 1949, and the many studies cited by Zipf. In 1938 Europe exclusive of the Soviet Union absorbed 46.6 per cent of all imports, but had Europe been one unit it would have absorbed only 17.5 per cent, since 29.1 were of European origin. See *League of Nations,* "The Network of World Trade," Geneva, 1942, p. 40. While the replacement of small by large units would not dissolve the many institutional barriers which today stand between peoples needing resources and arable land, it might, by facilitating interunit exchange, afford greater access to these needs via the medium of trade than is to be had at present.

define the optimum with precision. As will be indicated, however, a comparative approach may provide a rough ordinal estimate.

Inasmuch as the meaning to be attached to the movement of any one of the indices discussed always is marked by ambiguity and uncertainty, joint use of all possible measures is indicated, since such use tends to reduce the amount of uncertainty. When several or more measures unite in indicating an increase in population maladjustment, it is highly probable that the direction of the change is correctly indicated, for it is much more likely in most instances that population growth will be attended by an increase than by a decrease in population maladjustment. When several or more measures indicate a decrease, the direction of the change may be correctly indicated, but it can be accepted as correct only if the change cannot be explained in a manner compatible with a finding of no diminution in maladjustment.

Comparison of states in terms of the various indicators discussed reveals much concerning the relative amount of population maladjustment prevailing. For example, income and related data suggest that there is less population maladjustment in the United States and Canada than in any of the remaining viable units identified at the close of Section V and that maladjustment is most pronounced in the two Asiatic regions. Since there is a strong presumption that per capita net output in the United States and Canada would be as high as it now is (if not higher) were the population of this unit somewhat smaller than at present, there is a presumption that population maladjustment already characterizes this unit. It follows that a much greater degree of maladjustment is to be found in Europe and the Soviet Union and a much greater degree still in the two Asiatic regions. It follows also, since there is no evidence that further population growth will improve economic conditions in these four regions, that such growth will accentuate population maladjustment in both the shorter and the longer run. In general, then, it is probable that, with the exception of Africa and South America, all the larger regions of the world are marked by population maladjustment and that it is being increased by population growth even though this growth is accompanied by increases in per capita income.

Conclusion: In this paper various measures of population maladjustment have been examined. None of these appears capable of indicating the prevailing degree of population maladjustment. International comparison may, however, disclose roughly the rank of countries in terms of population maladjustment. Furthermore, a number of indices may, if used properly and jointly, indicate whether population maladjustment is increasing, and they may be capable, if a country's population is not too dense, of disclosing whether maladjustment is decreasing. For lack of space and because the required data are not available for many countires, a detailed application of these measures has not been attempted.

Summary

It is shown that population maladjustment may have a number of meanings in addition to the economic which receives major attention in this paper. It is shown that the more commonly used measures of maladjustment are ambiguous and inadequate. While none of these measures can disclose the degree of population maladjustment, several of them may indicate if maladjustment is increasing or decreasing. It is then shown that the best type of index is one sensitive to changes in classes of economic activity sensitive to changes in the size of a country's population. Next it is shown how the relation between capital formation and progress in national income may be utilized to discover if population maladjustment is changing. Finally, it is reasoned that questions relating to the population optimum must be distinguished from questions relating to the spatial requirements of the modern state. In the concluding section it is suggested that while no measure or group of measures can reveal unequivocally the degree of population maladjustment obtaining, the use of a number of measures commonly will disclose whether population maladjustment is increasing or decreasing. It is also suggested that international comparisons may disclose ordinal differences between countries and regions in respect of degree of population maladjustment.

Addendum: C. Clark believes s (see p. 257 above) to be higher in developed than in under-developed countries (*Review of Economic Progress*, II, 1950, No. 1). In his *Forecasts of the Population of the United States, 1945–1975*, Washington, 1947, P. K. Whelpton proposes measuring population maladjustment somewhat after the manner suggested on pp. 254–255 above.

Welfare Economics and the Problem of Overpopulation*

> *"And there is nothing so naturally opposite to our taste, as satiety, which comes from ease and facility, nor nothing that so much sharpeneth it, as rareness and difficulty."* M. Montaigne, Essays, *Book II, chap. 15.*

In this essay the population question will be considered in terms of modern welfare economics. It will be suggested also that an approach to the population question in terms of modern welfare economics lies within the framework of the Malthusian tradition when this tradition is broadly conceived. The present essay is composed of seven parts: I, devoted to production theory; II, devoted to the Malthusian conception of the population-adjustment process; III, devoted to distinguishing the impact of population growth upon per capita income from its impact upon per capita welfare; IV, devoted to a restatement of the optimum theory in terms of the welfare theory developed in III; V, devoted to consideration of the variability of optimum magnitudes; VI, devoted to the fact that concomitants of dynamic change tend to obscure increases in population maladjustment; and VII, devoted to an inquiry respecting the existence of a tendency toward over-population in human societies.

I

Malthus did not contribute appreciably to the development of the theory of production, the formulation of the classical theory of production being attributable largely to Ricardo;[1] for Malthus's concern was primarily with the disposition of numbers to grow and only secondarily with the supposedly comparative incapacity of subsistence to be augmented. Malthus assumed the capacity of the environmental milieu accessible to any particular population to be finite. Accordingly, the amount of population-support that could be derived from this milieu was finite, tending, after a population had improved its technology and achieved a size essential to the use of such technology, to increase slowly and at a decreasing rate. Such at least seems to be the import both of Malthus's unhappy use of an arithmetic ratio to represent production potentialities and of his scattered observations respecting production possibilities.[2]

* I am indebted to my colleague, Dr. James Walter, for several suggestions.

1. See Victor Edelberg, *The Ricardian Theory of Profits*, Economica, XIII, 1933, pp. 51–74; also J. M. Cassels, *A Re-Interpretation of Ricardo on Value*, Quarterly Journal of Economics, XLIX, 1935, pp. 518–32.

2. For Malthus's views on production see *An Essay on the Principle of Population*, last edition, Everyman's Library, Vol. 1, Bk. I, chaps. 1–2, pp. 314–315, Vol. 2, pp. 117–118, 147–

Malthus's mode of argument was improved, as a result of much discussion and controversy, until it assumed the form given it by J. S. Mill in his treatment of the laws of growth of the determinants of production and of the tendency of the "state of wealth and population" to become "stationary" at a level compatible with the maintenance of some one of a number of initially attainable patterns of living.[3] The concern of Malthus and his followers respecting questions of population and mass poverty arose from their inference that, production potentialities being so very limited, the continuance for very long of any significant positive rate of population growth would press the pattern of living attainable by the masses appreciably below the level attainable if the population were smaller. These writers thus implied the existence of an optimum density of population; and Mill sought to define this optimum explicitly.[4]

With the gradual refinement of the laws of returns and the development of marginalistic economics, production theory improved even though it remained oriented to problems associated with functional distribution rather than to questions connected with economic development as such. For purposes of the present discussion we shall make use of a modified version of the Douglas-Cobb type of production function, even though other and more complicated formulations of production theory may be used for the analysis of economic development.[5] Accordingly, let

$$Y = A(L^m K^{1-m})R^t;$$

Y represents the index value of produced income; L, the index value of the employed labor force; and K the index value of income-producing wealth in use. The symbol R^t represents the effect of technical progress; its significance is discussed later. A and m are constants; the former, with a value of one or nearly one, will be ignored; the latter, which is related to the marginal productivities of labor and capital, will be considered presently.

Let it be assumed initially that returns are constant. This assumption implies that R^t has a value of one, and that the sum of the exponents of L and

148, 150; *Principles of Political Economy,* 2nd ed., pp. 327–328. On economic progress, see *ibid.,* Bk. II.

3. See J. S. Mill, *Principles of Political Economy,* W. J. Ashley, ed., Bks. I, IV.

4. *Ibid.,* Bk. I, chap. 13, sec. 2. The concern of the classical economists respecting questions of population and mass poverty is reflected in their emphasis upon production, "productive labor," etc., and in their lack of emphasis upon the allocation problem. E.g., see Hla Myint, *Theories of Welfare Economics,* Cambridge, 1948, Part I; also Lionel Robbins, *The Theory of Economic Policy,* London, 1952. Regarding the reactions of Malthus's critics see Kenneth Smith, *The Malthusian Controversy,* London, 1951, and *Some Observations on Modern Malthusianism,* Population Studies, VI, 1952, pp. 92–105.

5. E.g., see Trygve Haavelmo, *Contribution to the Theory of Economic Evolution with Particular Reference to the Problem of Backward Areas,* Memorandum fra Universitetets Socialøkonomiske Institut, Oslo, 1952; also Silvio Vianelli, *A General Dynamic Demographic Scheme and Its Application to Italy and the United States,* Econometrica, IV, 1936, pp. 269–283.

K is one. If returns are constant, a given relative increase i in L and K will be accompanied by a corresponding relative increase i in Y; an increase of i in L or K accompanied by a lesser relative increase in K or L will be accompanied by an increase of less than i in Y.

With returns constant, let the marginal productivity of labor, $\delta Y/\delta L$, be represented by M_1 and the marginal productivity of income-producing wealth, or capital, $\delta Y/\delta K$-, be represented by M_k. Then

$$
\begin{aligned}
M_1 &= m(Y/L) \\
&= Am(K/L)^{1-m} \\
M_k &= (1-m)(Y/K) \\
&= A(1-m)(L/K)^m.
\end{aligned}
$$

It is evident that, with returns and K constant, M_1 declines as L increases, and that average output per worker, y ($= Y/L$), falls accordingly; for

$$
\frac{\delta}{\delta L}\left[\frac{Y}{L}\right] = \frac{(m-1)Y}{L^2}.
$$

Of course, y would not fall with K constant and L increasing if returns, represented by R^t, were increasing sufficiently to offset the effect of the increase in L/K under conditions of constant returns as defined above.

Empirical studies suggest that m, the exponent of labor, commonly takes a value of between somewhat under 0.7 and slightly over 0.8. For the sake of expositive convenience we shall put this value at 0.75. If, under these circumstances, the ratio L/K of labor to capital increases one per cent, average output per worker will fall about one-fourth of one per cent. Only if both capital and labor increase at the same rate — 1 per cent in this instance — will the average output per worker remain unchanged. Increasing capital K one per cent per year entails a saving rate of 4–5 per cent, on the assumption that a nation's income-producing wealth K approximates in value to 4–5 times this nation's produced income. Under similar conditions, with population and the labor force stationary, increasing output per worker one per cent per year would entail a saving rate of about 16–20 per cent per year.

It may be that Malthus underestimated the rate at which per capita income was to increase because he assigned relatively low values to the forces of progress represented by R^t, and because he did not expect that the ratio K/L would continue to rise significantly. His underestimate may have arisen in part also from his conclusion that, the laws of production being what they were, the solution of the problem of mass poverty lay primarily in the control of numbers even in the event that production was susceptible of considerable increase.[6]

6. See *Essay*, Vol. 2, p. 150, where Malthus writes: "the allowing of the produce of the earth to be absolutely unlimited, scarcely removes the weight of a hair from the argument, which depends entirely upon the differently increasing ratios of population and food."

It is not empirically valid to assume the persistence of constant returns in advanced countries. Returns may increase as a result of improvements in technology, in division of labor, in economic organization, in the quality of the labor force, in the terms of trade, and in the quality of the natural resources in use. Returns may decrease as a result of deterioration in technology, in division of labor, in economic organization, in the quality of the labor force, in the terms of trade, and in the quality of the natural resources in use. In recent decades returns, as usually measured, have increased, with the result that R^t has assumed a value in excess of 1: according to Tinbergen,[7] this value lies in the neighborhood of 1.01 when t relates to a single year and thus assumes a value of 1. In other words, increasing returns have caused national income to grow about one per cent per year more rapidly than it would have grown, given constant returns and the recorded increments in labor and capital. Although estimates of this sort have been subjected to criticism, on both empirical and theoretical grounds, they probably suggest the orders of magnitude involved.

Should returns no longer increase in consequence of improvements in technology, division of labor, economic organization, and/or the terms of trade, it is probable that they would eventually diminish as a result of deterioration in the quality of natural resources in use. Population growth hastens such deterioration in so far as it makes recourse to inferior natural resources necessary either by making their exploitation economic or by accelerating the rate at which exhaustible resources are depleted. If, under these circumstances, population growth persists, average output and the level of real wages must fall, since the rate of saving and hence the rate of increase in K must fall until K, L, and Y/L become stationary. The path that will be followed depends primarily upon the level of wages workers insist upon when making decisions respecting family size, upon whether savings come only out of the imputed product of K, and upon what portion of this imputed product its recipients stand ready to save. Average income and wages may still increase, however, with returns diminishing, provided that K is augmented sufficiently through capital formation and that L remains virtually stationary.

In underdeveloped countries there may become operative for some time a force additional to those generative of increasing returns in the most advanced countries, namely, the introduction of improved methods orginated

7. See J. Tinbergen, *Zur Theorie der langfristigen Wirtschaftsentwicklung*, Weltwirtschaftliches Archiv., 55 Band, Heft 3, 1942, pp. 511–545; also Paul H. Douglas, *Are There Laws of Production?*, American Economic Review, XXXVIII, 1948, pp. 1–41; Colin Clark, *Conditions of Economic Progress*, London, 1951, chap. 11; G. Tintner, *Econometrics*, New York, 1952. While our formulation of the production function implies that the exponents of labor and capital are affected in the same proportion by R^t, it is possible that the two exponents may be affected in different degrees by the changes represented by R^t, since the incidence of such changes need not continue to be distributed in the proportion implied. For the sake of simplicity, however, it will be assumed that the exponents are affected in the same degree.

abroad. For this reason, it is possible that, for a time, R^t may assume higher values in underdeveloped than in developed countries. It is also possible that, as the age composition of a population improves, the fraction of this population in the labor force will increase and therewith elevate output and income *per capita*. Since this improvement, having been made, cannot be repeated after a population's age composition has become stable, possible increases in income issuing out of improvements in age composition are disregarded.

When returns are increasing, a smaller rate of capital formation is required to permit a given rate of increase in average output than when returns are constant. For example, if R^t takes a value of 1.01 – that is, if technical and related progress increases income one per cent per year – a saving rate of 16 per cent would permit per capita income to increase about 2 per cent. Empirical data suggest, however, that a saving rate of less than 16 per cent will enable per capita income to increase 2 per cent per year, by augmenting the stock of capital as has been suggested and by permitting the translation of input-economizing improvements into practice. If this be the case, then either the marginal product of capital is higher than we have been supposing, or the rate of technical progress has been exceeding one per cent, or both conditions have been present.

Increasingly higher rates of investment in income-producing wealth may, of course, be called for, given specific conditions and specific objectives. With returns constant – i.e., with the value of R^t continuing unchanged at unity – and K/L increasing, maintanance of a constant percentage rate of increase in Y/L requires the saving and investment of an increasing fraction of produced national income Y. Likewise, when R^t is falling, an increasingly higher fraction of Y must be invested in order that, other conditions remaining unchanged, a given percentage rate of increase in Y/L may be realized.

In general even though population and the labor force L were increasing, Y/L and per capita income could continue to increase so long as returns were increasing and/or capital was being formed at a sufficient rate. Conceivably, even if the labor force were growing as much as 2 per cent per year, average output per worker and per capita income might for a time grow annually one per cent or slightly more, given a saving rate approximating 8–12 per cent of the national income and given that these savings were offset by investment in income-producing wealth.[8] For this reason, among others, some writers are less concerned about actual and prospective population growth – even about such high rates as are now being occasioned by un-

8. See my *Economic Factors in the Development of Densely Populated Areas,* Proceedings of American Philosophical Society, XCV, 1951, pp. 20–53, *The Population Obstacle to Economic Betterment,* Proceedings of American Economic Association, XLI (2), May, 1951, pp. 342–354, and *Measures of Population Maladjustment,* Proceedings of the XIV International Congress of Sociology, III, Rome, 1951, pp. 336–364.

precedented declines in mortality—than are those who continue in the Malthusian tradition. Whether this lack of concern is warranted will be considered later.

II

The writings of Malthus and the classical economists suggest the existence in their schemes of two models, each of which was premised upon the finiteness of the relevant economic universe and consequently upon eventual and continuing declines in the returns to both labor and capital at the intensive and the extensive margins. Model (1) rested upon the assumption that the population insisted upon enjoying a structure or level of living which remained stationary in the longer run. Accordingly, given this level of living and the propensity to save therewith associated, the labor force L and the stock of capital K continued to increase until (a) incremental output per worker just sufficed to support the associated increment in population at the accepted level of living and under the conditions of income distribution prevailing, and (b) the concomitant return to capital K, though sufficient to maintain the stock of capital intact, was insufficient to induce further additions to K through net saving and investment.

Explicit attention was not given to the possibility that R^t might decline, make necessary a higher rate of saving, and thus accelerate the advent of a state of nongrowth, though this possibility could have been taken into account. Model (2) rested upon the assumption that per capita income would rise until falling incremental returns halted the growth of both population and capital, at which time model (2) became transformed into model (1). Per capita income would rise so long as K increased faster than L, and this rise would be intensified if R^t rose to levels in excess of unity. Eventually, of course, R^t would fall to or below unity, and the marginal productivity of capital K would decline until the return to capital merely sufficed to maintain its quantity intact. Population growth, which had lagged behind capital growth, would then come to a halt; and per capita income would settle to a stationary level that was below but usually not unduly below the peak value which had been attained whilst model (2) conditions obtained. Accordingly, though model (2) conditions had given place to model (1) conditions, much of the gain in per capita income achieved while model (2) conditions prevailed was retained. Such an outcome at least was possible and, many believed, probable. The classical economists thus may be said to have envisaged a world in which model (1) conditions, though commonly obtaining, occasionally gave place, in various parts and for shorter or longer periods, to model (2) conditions. Hereupon rested such optimism as is to be found in their writings.

The empirical conditions of a given model (1) equilibrium, with K and L stationary, depended upon the series of events that had marked a population's progress toward this stable state along one of the paths initially available to it. A model (1) equilibrium population having been established, however, numbers might oscillate about this level, or they might even move in ways remindful of the movements of agricultural production when it is subject to the cobweb principle,[9] but they could not permanently depart from this level in the absence of changes in certain conditions underlying the model (1) equilibrium. These conditions apparently included: (i) the price structure; (ii) the volume of income or means of support; (iii) the distribution of this income; and (iv) the conduct-determining tastes and values,[10] upon which depend in part the propensity to save, the composition of consumption, and decisions respecting marriage and family size. Under both model (1) and model (2) circumstances, a change in (iv) was necessarily of exogenous origin. Changes in (i), (ii), and (iii) were of exogenous origin under model (1) circumstances; they might be of either exogenous or endogenous origin under model (2) circumstances.

While Malthus seems to have been aware of the import of (i) price-structure changes, he did not clearly specify their origin, probably because he sometimes had model (2) equilibrium in mind, and because he did not attach much importance to the possible effect of such changes under model (1) conditions. Apparently he was aware that a substitution effect would be set

9. E.g., see A. T. Peacock, *Theory of Population and Modern Economic Analysis*, I, Population Studies, VI, 1952, pp. 114–122, esp. pp. 119–120; and Mordecai Ezekial, *The Cobweb Theorem*, Quarterly Journal of Economics, LII, 1937–1938, pp. 255–280; or William Baumol, *Economic Dynamics*, New York, 1951, pp. 108ff.

10. While we refer to both values and tastes, it was primarily through changes in tastes (presumably) that Malthus expected the magnitude of the equilibrium population to be modified. We use the expression tastes and values because, as Arrow indicates, the two are essentially distinguishable. "The objects of choice are social states. The most precise definition of a social state would be a complete description of the amount of each type of commodity in the hands of each individual, the amount of labor to be supplied by each individual, the amount of each productive resource invested in each type of productive activity, and the amounts of various types of collective activity." Arrow assumes, for purposes of his own analysis, that each individual "orders all social states" in terms "of their desirability to him" on the basis of "whatever standards he deems relevant." These standards therefore include more than "the commodity bundles which accrue to his lot under each," orderings on the sole basis of which would be orderings on the basis of reflected tastes; they also include "general standards of equity" which reflect "his values" and therefore take into account more than such economies and diseconomies of consumption as fail to receive expression through the market mechanism. See K. J. Arrow, *Social Choice and Individual Values*, New York, 1951, pp. 17–19, also pp. 71–73, and chap. 7. We may treat values as the root of both tastes and other criteria for ordering that which is to be ordered and then make variation in values, so defined, serve in the capacity in which we have made variation in tastes and values serve. See also I. D. M. Little, *Welfare Economics*, London, 1950, chaps. 10, 12, and *Social Choice and Individual Values*, Journal of Political Economy, LX, 1952, pp. 422–432, and Goran Nyblen, *The Problem of Summation in Economic Science*, Lund, 1951, esp. chap. 3; G. T. Guilbaud, *The Theory of Games*, reprinted in International Economic Papers, N. 1, 1951, esp. pp. 38–41, 47ff. See also works cited in note 17 below.

up against (in favor of) more children by a change in the price-structure embracing a relative increase (decrease) in the prices of elements entering into the cost of reproducing and rearing children and a relative decrease (increase) in other prices. For he described it as "desirable" that the "habitual food" of the common people "be dear" and that the prices of conveniences, decencies, and luxuries be sufficiently low to extend their custom through the population.[11] Presumably, having in mind model (2) conditions, he was supposing that the introduction of this kind of price structure would check natality, stimulate consumption, generate wants, cushion per capita income against population pressure, and retard the transformation of model (2) into model (1) conditions. Had he supposed model (1) conditions and a price structure change of exogenous origin, he would have had to suppose either an eventual diminution in K or the diversion of consumables from the wealthy.

While Malthus noted, as do modern writers, that a governmentally-induced reduction in income inequality would stimulate natural increase, he supposed that this effect would be shortlived. He inferred that some of the income transferred to the relatively poor would represent a diversion from gross capital formation. Accordingly, if model (1) equilibrium conditions obtained, this diversion would make the stock of capital K smaller than it otherwise would have been. If model (2) equilibrium conditions prevailed, the rate of capital growth would be diminished, with the result that the advent of model (1) conditions would be accelerated.[12]

Let population elasticity be defined as the ratio of the small relative rate of increase (say 0.5 per cent) in population to the small relative rate of increase (say 1 per cent) in income upon which the stipulated population increase is consequential; in this instance the elasticity is $0.5 \times 1 = 0.5$. It is now evident that the major distinction between population models (1) and (2) consists in the fact that the former is characterized by a population elasticity of unity and the latter by one of less than unity. While Malthus, who thought of income in terms of means of existence or support, favored a population elasticity of less than unity, he observed that it very frequently approximated unity and sometimes even exceeded unity for a short period.[13] Given model (1) equilibrium, income can rise only in consequence of an exogenous change such as the movement of R^t above unity. Then, in accordance with model (1) conditions, population and capital, the increase of each stimulating that of the other, grow until R^t moves back to or below unity, net saving falls to zero, and per capita income and the pattern of living

11. Cf. my essay *Malthus's Total Population Theory: A Restatement and Reappraisal,* Canadian Journal of Economics and Political Science, XI, 1945, pp. 108–110, 240–241; also Malthus, *Essay,* Bk. IV, chap. 11. See also my *Some Economic Aspects of the Subsidization by the State of the Formation of "Human Capital,"* Kyklos, IV, 1950, pp. 316–343.

12. *Essay,* Bk. III, chaps. 1–3, Bk. IV, chap. 13.

13. *Ibid.,* Vol. 1, Bk. 1, chaps. 1–2, pp. 304, 313–314, Vol. 2, pp. 137–140, 242, 254–255.

settle back to the initially given stationary level. Under model (2) conditions, given an increase in income, whether because of an increase in K or of an improvement in R^t or of both, and given a population elasticity of less than unity, population, capital K, and per capita income would increase until model (2) was again transformed into model (1); but the gain in per capita income would be retained.

Malthus attached most importance to the introduction of what he considered to be salutary changes in tastes and values, since only changes of this sort could produce significant and persisting changes in the conditions of demographic equilibrium and in the level of per capita welfare. Given a change of tastes and values in a population-growth-retarding direction, population elasticity and natural increase would fall, per capita consumption and/or capital formation would rise, and per capita output and income would increase. Malthus recognized, of course, that environmental and technological conditions set limits to the extent to which changes in tastes and values could elevate the level and the rate of increase of per capita income.[14]

III

In this section we shall examine the case of a country in which, though population has grown appreciably, the statistical magnitude, produced income Y, has increased in even greater proportion, with the result that Y/L and per capita income have risen. In circumstances such as these it usually is inferred that "welfare" per capita has increased, particularly when some possibly adverse concomitants[15] of changes in Y have been averted and others seemingly[16] are susceptible of being offset through use of the compensation principle. It tends also to be inferred that population growth has not operated, and is not likely to operate, to reduce "welfare" per capita. Are these inferences valid?

Let us therefore consider a country and its population at five sequential points in time t, . . . , t_5. With these successive temporal points are associated population magnitudes 1, 2, . . . 5, each larger than its predecessor, and each characterized by a higher Y/L ratio than its predecessor. The upward movement through time of the Y/L ratio may be conceived of as reflecting an upward movement in the population's income-producing capacity per capita; and this upward movement may in turn be thought of as reflecting the combined influence of an upward movement in the capital : labor ratio K/L and a sufficient persistence of an R^t value in excess of one.

14. *Ibid.*, Bk. III, chap. 14; Bk. IV, chaps. 2, 13–14.

15. E.g., see Jan Tinbergen, *The Influence of Productivity on Economic Welfare*, Economic Journal, LXII, 1952, pp. 68–86.

16. We say "seemingly" offset because compensation has been made, as Samuelson states, on the assumption "in some sense (of) the correctness of the *status quo ante* and/or the *status quo post.*" See P. A. Samuelson, *Evaluation of Real National Income*, Oxford Economic

Use of the expression income-producing capacity obscures the fact that any such capacity is but an aggregate of dissimilar output-producing capacities which are at best imperfectly substitutable one for another. Accordingly, in place of the expression income-producing capacity we shall use the term Production Possibility, and suppose that with populations 1, 2, . . . 5 are associated, respectively, production possibilities P_1, P_2, . . . , P_5. Each of these production possibilities refers to the *range* of alternative specific combinations of goods and services of whose production the population in question, together with its resource-equipment, technology, etc., is capable. For reasons noted below each of these production possibilities will differ from each other such possibility, in that each possibility will embrace some goods and services peculiar to itself and some, but not all, of the goods and services peculiar to other of the production possibilities. In our subsequent discussion we shall express the production possibility of each of our five populations in per capita terms, since it is in per capita comparisons that we are interested.

A production possibility necessarily embraces both combinations of goods and services produced when the available agents of production are ineffectively used and combinations produced when the best possible use is made of these agents. Since the latter set of combinations includes the former set, our discussion will relate only to such combinations or collections of goods and services as are produced when the productive agents are efficiently used. Let us call any such set of efficiently produced collections C; and let us label C_1, C_2, . . . , C_5 the five sets associated with production possibilities P_1, P_2, . . . , P_5, it being assumed that the collections are expressed in per capita terms. Each collection included within a given set will be represented by a superscript 1, . . . , n. For example, the term $C_1^{1,\cdots,n}$ represents the set of n collections embraced by C^1 and associated with production possibility P_1; the term C_1^3 represents specific collection 3 included in C_1 and associated with P_1; and so on. The number n of specific collections found in any set (say C_1) most likely will differ from that found in any other set (say C_5); and many of the particular collections included in any one set (say C_5) will differ from many of the particular collections embraced in some other set (say C_4). The total number of possible collections is bound to be very large; but the number of collections from among which the population of a community will be disposed to choose under probable conditions is likely to be only a fraction of the total possible number.

Suppose now that we sequester all the distinct and unique collections of goods and services, included within sets C_1, C_2, . . . , C_5 associated with

Papers, II, 1950, pp. 9-11; Also W. E. Armstrong, *Utility and the Theory of Welfare, ibid.,* III, 1951, pp. 259-271. Cp. also E. R. Rolph and G. R. Break, *The Welfare Aspects of Excise Taxes,* Journal of Political Economy, LVII, 1949. pp. 46-54.

production possibilities $P_1, P_2, \ldots, P_5$. These collections are susceptible of being ordered in various ways. Suppose, for example, that these collections are arrayed in terms of a community's preference scale as expressed through the medium of a rule that is founded upon particular criteria drawn from the field of welfare economics.[17] The array resulting will be but one of many available, with the number actually depending upon the number of unique collections under consideration, a number whose magnitude may be conditioned in part by the number of production possibilities relevant. What array will be chosen from among the available number of arrays will depend upon the distribution of tastes and values obtaining in the community and upon the kind of ordering system that is employed to reflect this distribution and arrange the collections accordingly. With each change in the number of collections, in the nature or the distribution of tastes and values, or in the ordering system, there probably will be associated choice of an array different from that previously chosen. Any particular collection will have as many positions in arrays as there are distinct ordering systems, the number of collections and the distribution of tastes and values being given and its position may vary greatly from ordering system to ordering system. As will be shown, the multiplicity of arrays available may make it difficult to determine whether an increase in Y/L, when accompanied by an increase in L, constitutes an increase in per capita economic welfare.

Among the significant causes of changes in production possibilities are changes in the size of the population and the labor force, in K and K/L, and in the value of R'. For example, increases in population can affect the K/L ratio adversely, either by reducing it (though this possibility has been ruled out), or by operating cumulatively to slow down the rate of capital formulation and thereby make K/L smaller than it otherwise would have been. In consequence of this effect, the production possibility would be less rich and its outer boundary would be less extended than otherwise. Again, even though the ratio K/L and the state of technology are unaffected by an increase in population, the composition of its income-producing wealth K may be affected, and with it the production possibility. For K represents the sum of many particular kinds of capital $K_1, K_2, \ldots, Kn$, each present in some specific amount, and no one particular kind perfectly substitutable for any

17. See P. A. Samuelson, *op. cit.*, pp. 12ff., and *Foundations of Economic Analysis*, Cambridge, 1947, chap. 8; A. C. Pigou, *Real Income and Economic Welfare*, Oxford Economic Papers, III, 1951, pp. 16–20, and *Some Aspects of Welfare Economics*, American Economic Review, XLI, 1951, pp. 287–302; Tibor Scitovsky, *The State of Welfare Economics, ibid.*, pp. 303–315; Little, *Welfare Economics, passim*, esp. pp. 272–275; and *Social Choices and Individual Values*, Journal of Political Economy, LX, 1952, pp. 422–432; Arrow, *op. cit.*; Simon Kuznets, *On the Valuation of Social Income*, Economica, XV, 1948, pp. 2ff.; William J. Baumol, *Welfare Economics and the Theory of the State*, Cambridge, 1952, chaps. 3–4, 10, and *The Neumann-Morgenstern Utility Index — an Ordinalist View*, Journal of Political Economy, LIX, 1951, pp. 61–66. The argument in the text is largely an application of the analyses employed in the works cited in this note.

other particular kind. As K increases concomitantly with the increase of L, some kinds of capital increase less rapidly than do others whose quantity is more readily augmented, and some productivity-affecting agencies which formerly were free (e.g., water) become relatively scarce and take on the guise of capital. Because of this change in the composition of K, the production possibility P changes even though K/L does not change; and it now becomes impossible to produce some collections of goods that formerly were producible, and it becomes possible to produce some collections that formerly were not producible. Only if, with K/L constant, either the composition of K remained unaffected, or enough particular kinds of capital were perfectly intersubstitutable, would the production possibility P be unaffected by population growth. Even if capital K increases faster than labor L and, returns not diminishing, average output rises, the composition of capital undergoes modification and with it the production possibility.

Our argument may be put otherwise. Because some forms of capital are relatively nonaugmentable and nonreplaceable, even given technological improvements, the aggregate output of some goods and services is absolutely or relatively nonaugmentable; and because some forms of capital are nonreplaceable and subject to diminution in supply, the aggregate output of some goods and services may decline in time. Accordingly, if population continues to grow, the amounts available per capita of some goods and services, certain representatives of which may even have been free when the population was sparser, are bound to diminish. Because many forms of capital are augmentable and intersubstitutable with one another and with labor, and because the effects of this capital growth are intensified by changes generating increasing returns, the rate of supply of many forms of goods and services is sufficiently augmentable to insure considerable increases in the amounts of these goods and services made available per capita. If tastes and values are such, or change in such a way, that the per capita increment in augmentable goods more than offsets the per capita decrement in relatively nonaugmentable goods, it may be said that the index of welfare has risen. If, however, tastes and values are such and remain such that the increment in augmentable goods does not serve to offset the decrement in non-augmentable goods, it may be said that the index or welfare has fallen. Later we shall inquire respecting the prospective course of tastes and values in an economy undergoing population growth and other changes.

For purposes of illustration let us contrast the production possibilities P_1, P_2, and P_3, associated with population magnitudes 1, 2, and 3. Suppose that Y/L is greater under P_3 conditions than under P_2 conditions, and greater under P_2 conditions than under P_1 conditions. It then would appear that per capita welfare had risen as the population magnitude had increased from 1 through 2 to 3. This appearance may, however, be misleading. Whether it is or is not so turns on the significance of the differences, if any, that distinguish the composition of the goods and services associated with any one production possibility from those associated with other production possibilities. Thus, a change in composition consequent upon population growth may signify that some goods and services can no longer be made available in so large a volume per capita as was formerly the case even though a sufficiently strong preference for these goods and services remains indicated. For example, population 3, with which production possibility P_3 is connected, might prefer to any collection included in set C_3 associated with P_3 some collection in set C_2 or C_1 (associated with P_2 or P_1, respectively) which is not to be found in set C_3. If such be the preference of the choosing population, in this case the population of magnitude 3, the advance of the population in magnitude from 1 or 2 to 3 may be said to have been accompanied by a reduction in welfare per capita, even though an increase in Y/L has accompanied the growth of the population. The preferred collection cannot be chosen, of course, because its production has been made impossible by the passage of the population from magnitude 1 or 2 to magnitude 3.

What has been said may be expressed, albeit imperfectly, in graphic form, as in Figure I. The possible per capita outputs of relatively augmentable goods are measured along the Y-axis, and the possible outputs of absolutely and-or relatively nonaugmentable goods, along the X-axis. Only collections lying on the curves (1), (2), and (3) associated with production possibilities P_1, P_2, and P_3 are included in sets C_1, C_2, and C_3; for all collections, which lie to the left of a relevant curve and thus represent an inefficient use of productive resources, are inferior to corresponding collections which lie on this curve. Of the defects present in this mode of representation several may be noted. The transformation curves probably suggest more substitutability between the two categories of goods than is realizable. Of greater importance is the fact that, since the categories measured, respectively, along the X and Y axes include a variety of goods, not all the particular alternative collections included in a production possibility are graphically disclosed. Nonetheless, since the essence of the argument is indicated, Figure I may be utilized despite its defects.

Curves (1), (2), and (3) are transformation curves representing production possibilities P_1, P_2, and P_3; curve (2′) represents still another such possibility which is considered in Part IV. Each of these curves indicates the various per capita combinations of X-goods and Y-goods that may be derived from the labor force and other agents of production on which the production possibility in question depends. For example, given curve (1), either Ob of Y-goods, or Oa' of X-goods, or any one of a large number of intermediate combinations of Y-goods and X-goods, is possible and available; while, given curve (3), either Ob'' of Y-goods, Oa of X-goods, or any one of many intermediate combinations of both types of goods, is

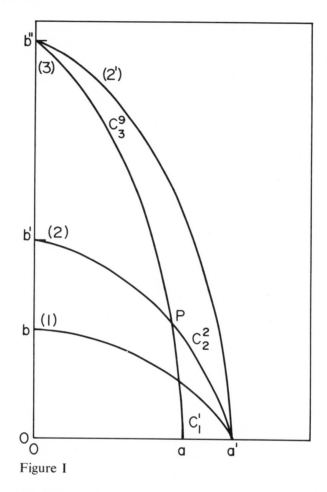

Figure I

possible and available. It is obvious that production possibility P_2 represented by curve (2) is superior to P_1 represented by curve (1), since with one exception every combination on (2) is superior to every corresponding combination on (1); that exception is combination Oa' of X, which is common to both curves. With this exception, it follows that, whatever be the distribution of tastes and values, per capita welfare is greater, given population (2) and production possibility P_2 than given population (1) and production possibility P_1. When, however, we pass to population (3) and production possibility P_3, we no longer find it possible to describe one production possibility as universally superior to another, or to select a point on one curve that is better than all points on another curve; for now possession of the property of being superior turns also on the distribution throughout the population of those tastes and values upon which depends the determination of what is the most preferred collection of goods. For example, if the preferred collection of goods is C_3^3, P_3 is superior; P_3 is superior, in fact, so long as the preferred collection lies on curve (3) above point p where curve (3) intersects curve (2). If the preferred collection — e.g., C_2^2 — is below and to the right of point p, it will be found on curve (2) associated with P_2, which, in this portion of the quadrant, lies above curve (3) associated with P_3. Even some collections on curve (1) — e.g., C_1^1, — are superior to some collections on curve (3). It is evident, therefore, that even though Y/L is higher under P_3 circumstances than under P_2 conditions, P_3 is superior to P_2 only on condition that the population's tastes and values dictate the selection of a collection lying on curve (3) above point p. If selection of a collection lying below p is indicated, growth of population from (2) to (3) may be said to have reduced per capita welfare, since this growth has eliminated curves (1) and (2) and therewith the opportunity to choose collections lying below and to the right of point p. (Malthus seems to have been partially aware of somewhat analogous possible ill effects of changes in the composition of output when he indicated that, even though "wealth" i.e., produced income per head, had increased, the welfare of the majority could only be described as having been adversely affected if at the same time the per capita amount of "funds for the maintenance of labour" had fallen.[18]

Let us consider more specifically the nature of such possible adverse effects of population growth as have just been described. As population grows, the per capita output of goods of the sort represented along the X-axis — e.g., room, space, sunlight, land-embodying products such as meat, and generally products made out of scarce and relatively non-augmentable and non-replaceable productive agents — must decline. For example, if population increased from 3 to 4 or 5, the intersection of the new per capita production possibility curve with the X-axis would lie to the left of point a. Even so, if under these circumstances Y/L rose in value, it would be inferred that per capita welfare had risen even. This inference might or might not be valid; it would not be valid if the collections of goods preferred by the population continued to lie roughly below and to the right of p, whereas it would be valid if the collections preferred were located roughly above and to the left of p.

Population growth may obscure declines in per capita welfare by removing alternatives that would have been indicated for selection had they remained in existence. For example, when population grows from 2 to 3 and P_3 and C_3 replace P_2 and C_2, respectively, segment pa' of curve (2) disappears, and therewith the opportunity to choose from among the collectons included within this portion of C_2. Accordingly, even though selection of some collection lying on pa' would have been indicated had it remained avail-

18. *Essay*, Bk. III, chap. 13; cp. 1st ed., chap. 16.

able, the opportunity to make such a selection has been eliminated by the growth of population from 2 to 3. Such elimination and the consequent confinement of choice within the set (i.e., C_3) associated with the current production possibility (i.e., P_3) reenforces the illusion that an increase in Y/L represents an increase in per capita welfare even though the most preferred collection (which in this instance lies on the eliminated segment pa') no longer remains available.

If the argument that has been presented is valid, it follows that some of the argument of antiMalthusian writers is invalid. For these writers, noting that a statistical magnitude called per capita income has increased despite population growth, draw the conclusion that per capita welfare has increased and tend to infer that welfare is not likely to be very adversely affected by the rate at which population is growing. The argument which I have presented is to the effect that, despite increases in per capita income that have accompanied increases in population, per capita welfare may have decreased; and that, if this be the case, further population growth would be likely to depress per capita welfare still further. When, as is done in the next section, this type of argument is translated into something like welfare optimum terms, population growth is found much more likely to affect welfare adversely.

IV

The kind of argument developed in the preceding section may be extended to questions relating to population optima. As usually defined, an optimum population magnitude is one, given which and given also various relevant circumstances that are independent of population size, some chosen index of per capita welfare assumes approximately a maximum value. What population magnitude is optimum for a country depends, of course, upon the state of that country's technology, upon its resource-equipment, upon its economic relations with other countries, upon divers other relevant circumstances, upon the distribution of prevailing values and tastes, and, under certain conditions, upon the relative number of unproductive persons that country is required to support.[19] If with H. Dalton we call the optimum magnitude O and the magnitude of the actual population A, population maladjustment M may be said to exist when the expression $M = (A/O)\text{-}1$ assumes a positive or a negative value, and to increase (decrease) when this value increases (decreases).

Changes in population maladjustment may be represented in terms of Figure I. Suppose that a population of magnitude 2 would be large enough

19. Cf. A. Sauvy, *Théorie générale de la population*, Paris, 1952, pp. 64ff., also chaps. 6–7, and various discussions of the optimum concept.

to develop and exploit the technological and other conditions underlying production possibility P_3 represented by curve (3). Under these circumstances, had the population remained of size 2 and at the same time had the other indicated and relevant production-increasing changes taken place, the resulting per capita production possibility curve would lie to the right of curve (3). We have, therefore, inscribed curve (2') in Figure I to represent this production possibility P_2. Since this curve, as drawn, lies to the right of all points other than a' and b'', it represents a set of collections superior to every collection other than the two associated with points a' and b'', and equal to these two. It could be said, therefore, that the growth of population from magnitude 2 to magnitude 3 had served to contract the per capita production possibility from (2') to (3) and had therefore increased population maladjustment. Suppose, however, that the upper portion of curve (2') intersects curve (3) and passes under it in the neighborhood of the point marking collection C_3^9. Under these circumstances population 2 may be described as nearer optimum size than population 3, given that the population prefers a collection lying below and to the right of point C_3^9; and population 3 may be described as nearer optimum size than population 2, given that the population prefers a collection lying above and to the left of point C_3^9.

V

Because what constitutes an optimum population is a function of many variable conditions, both the magnitude of the optimum and the degree of population maladjustment vary as these conditions vary. The degree of variability differs from country to country, being great or small according as a society's internal economy, pattern of tastes and values, external relations, and related circumstances are static or dynamic. Societies may, in some measure, therefore, be divided into those whose optimum magnitudes are changing and those whose optimum magnitudes are not changing, there falling into the latter category both relatively static societies and relatively dynamic societies wherein the various relevant changes experienced countervail one another.

Most if not all of the classical economists from Malthus on seem to have conceived of the world as composed largely if not wholly of societies ranging from the comparatively static to the low-level dynamic. In their analyses, therefore, they usually had in mind societies in which the supposedly ill effects of increases in population density tended to be apparent. And, having noted such supposed effects, they arrived at the empirical generalization that the populations of most if not all countries tended to exceed what they considered to be the optimum level of density. This generalization seems to have been implicit in the contention of a number of nineteenth-century economists (e.g., J. S. Mill, J. N. Keynes, J. B. Clark)[20] that a population was most likely to escape from its Malthusian trap if its economy were to experience a stimulus that would elevate the level of average income appreciably and for a time sufficiently long to permit the population to acquire habits, tastes, and values compatible with this income.

Late nineteenth and early twentieth century critics of the classical writers, having adopted the supposition that the optimum magnitude (as defined by them) tended to increase, sometimes implied that the optimum might increase more rapidly than the actual population and so eliminate "overpopulation," particularly now that the rate of population growth had descended to so low a level.[21] Some acceptance was won also by the view that the magnitude of a population composing a society does not, as a rule, tend to deviate greatly from the optimum, even under primitive conditions.[22]

The optimum population magnitude is subject to modification from many quarters, sources of variation being found both in conditions of supply characterizable as objective and in conditions of demand describable as subjective. It may vary, as has been noted, with variation in the circumstances governing the production of goods and services, increasing, decreasing, or remaining unaffected as these circumstances change. It is bound to vary as a result of variation in the subjective conditions affecting the structure of demand. The possible character and distributions of tastes and values—let us represent them as $d_1, d_2, \ldots, d_n$—that might be found in a society's population are many; and they may be subject to considerable modification even in the short run. So also there exist many possible bridges from any one given such distribution of individual tastes and values, say d_1, to what may be called the realm of single social values T, only some one of which may be selected at any one time for maximization in per capita terms. Each of these possible bridges rests upon one of a number of possible underlying rules, and each rule reflects and implies specific conditions. Accordingly, if there exist n such bridges and some given collection or

20. E.g., see Mill, *op. cit.*, pp. 348–349; J. N. Keynes, *The Scope and Method of Political Economy*, London, 1890, chap. 9, sec. 2; J. B. Clark, *Essentials of Economic Theory*, New York, 1907, chaps. 18–19; see also a forthcoming study by Harvey Leibenstein to be published by the Princeton Press (Harvey Leibenstein, *A Theory of Economic-Demographic Development*, Princeton, 1954).

21. E.g., see Edwin Cannan, *Economic Scares*, London, 1933, chap. 4; *A Review of Economic Theory*, London, 1930, chap. 4.

22. E.g., see A. M. Carr-Saunders, *The Population Problem*, Oxford, 1922, pp. 230, 270–271, 293, 476–477; cf. Henry George, *Progress and Poverty*, New York, 1880, pp. 149–150. See also A. B. Wolfe's criticism, "Superest Ager," *Quarterly Journal of Economics*, XL, 1925–1926, pp. 172ff.

distribution d_1 of tastes and values from which to run a bridge, there are available n single social values $T_1, T_2, \ldots, T_n$, from among which some one may be selected at any given time for maximization with respect to changes in size of population. Moreover, $T_1, T_2, \ldots, T_n$ change whenever a given

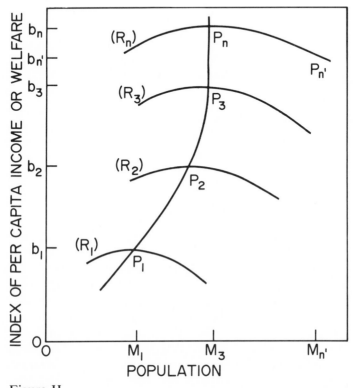

Figure II

distribution d_1 gives place to another d_2. In view of what has been said, it is difficult in practice both to determine upon an index of "welfare" suitable to a society and to discover how this index varies with respect to variations in the magnitude of that society's population. The amount of difficulty is much greater in a relatively dynamic society than in a relatively static society, since a dynamic society is characterized by greater and more frequent changes in the conditions affecting production, in the distribution of tastes and values symbolized by d, and in the rules regulating the construction of bridges between d and the relevant index of social value, T, than is a relatively static society.

VI

When a society is undergoing dynamic change, the ill effects, if any, of population growth tend to be masked. In these circumstances the statistical magnitude, per capita income, will be rising; life expectancy will be increasing; and the ratio of inputs to outputs will be falling in various sectors of the economy. Furthermore, as has been noted, adverse effects of population growth upon per capita welfare are hidden, since choices available when numbers were smaller have been eliminated by population growth, whilst knowledge of the former existence of these choices tends gradually to disappear. Finally, it is possible that increases in per capita income of nondemographic origin may mistakenly be attributed to increases in population density.

Figure II is designed to illustrate this last point. Along the X-axis is measured the size of a country's population; along the Y-axis, an index of per capita income or "welfare" which may be variously defined and accordingly represented in cardinal or in ordinal terms. The R's, of which only several of a large number are shown, refer to particular composite states of technology, capital supply, and related circumstances affecting productivity per worker; they are not production possibilities (which represent fixed quanta of productive power), but they do reflect conditions underlying production possibilities. The curve (R_1) traces the response of the welfare index to increments in population under R_1 conditions; the index moves to a maximum at p_1 which corresponds to a population of size Om_1, and with which is associated per capita welfare Ob_1; beyond population Om_1 the value of the index moves steadily below the maximum Ob_1. Each improvement in R is reflected in a movement to a higher R curve with which a higher welfare maximum is associated: e.g., Ob_2 with p_2 on R_2, Ob_3 with p_3 on R_3, and so on; but given any state R, the index value falls when population increases beyond the number associated with the maximum p-value connected with this given state R. Within limits, therefore, given any state R, the associated index value rises as population increases until the maximum p-value associated with that state is reached. But after the limit, represented by a point corresponding to p_3 and associated with a population corresponding to Om_3, has been reached, the index value no longer rises as population increases, even though ever more superior R-states come into being. The population Om_3 therefore represents a kind of optimum.

Suppose now that, with the population of size Om_3 and at welfare level Ob_3 corresponding to maximum p-value p_3 on curve (R_3), numbers continue to increase steadily whilst simultaneously ever more productive states R come into being. Suppose specifically that population moves to Om_n, and the index of welfare to Ob_n, on the curve (R_n) representing that state. The per capita welfare index will have risen by b_3b_n, whilst population has increased by $m_3m_{n'}$. It may be inferred, therefore, that the increase in the welfare index is attributable in some measure to the increase in population. Examination of Figure II discloses, however, that had the population remained at Om_3, the welfare index would have risen to Ob_n. The population increase $m_3m_{n'}$, therefore has produced a loss in per capita welfare corresponding to $b_nb_{n'}$.

Two observations may be made respecting the construction of Figure II. First, the locus of the p-points has been made perpendicular to the Ox axis beyond point p_3 on the assumption that thereafter the optimum magnitude is unaffected by further changes in the R-conditions. Conceivably, however, the locus of the p-points beyond point p_3 might have been drawn either to bend leftward or to continue in a rightward direction. In the former case the replacement of old by new R-conditions would have entailed an actual diminution in the optimum magnitude; in the latter case, an increase. Empirical information respecting the locus of the p-points is inadequate. It seems probable, however, that even if the locus of the p-points continues to the rightward for some distance beyond point p_3, it will proceed in this direction with increasing slowness: in other words, should the optimum magnitude continue for a time to increase as the R-conditions change, it will increase at a decreasing rate. It follows that changes in the R-conditions will operate only within limits to augment the optimum magnitude. Second, the course traced by the p-points as the R-conditions change depends upon the kind of index being used to represent a "welfare" along the Y-axis. For each definition and index of welfare, a different p-point locus will be described; with each index will be associated a particular optimum magnitude for the given sequence of R-condition changes, and a particular path leading to and beyond this magnitude.

VII

It has been established that it is difficult to determine upon an index in terms of which to define a population optimum and discover just how this index responds, especially in a dynamic world, to variations in population size. Even when these requirements have been met, there still remains the problem of creating a set of institutions which will bring the marginal social cost and the marginal social benefit—both satisfactorily defined in terms of the chosen index—of population growth into balance and thus insure the amount of population growth compatible with maximization of the value of the index in question. In this section, therefore, we shall consider whether population maladjustment M—previously defined as (A/O)-1 where A and O represent the sizes, respectively, of the actual and the optimum populations—is more likely to increase or to decrease, and whether this likelihood tends to be affected by variations in the degree of change which countries experience.

While available data do not permit a precise empirical resolution of this question—though gatherable data might—the nature of the answer might be inferrable. Presumably, if A could be shown to tend to increase faster than O, it might be said that M tends eventually to increase; and if this tendency could be shown to be greater in some types of societies than in others, the former category might be described as relatively more prone to population maladjustment. (1) Respecting the behavior of A, it may be said that the population growth process is asymmetrical; for one may infer from the past behavior of human populations, that they usually tend to grow and that they rarely tend to decrease, and that this process goes on until a population maximum G is reached. This maximum G itself is variable within wide limits, for it depends upon the resources accessible to a society, upon its skills, upon its aspirations, and upon behavioral constraints present in both groups and individuals. The growth tendency of A probably is accentuated by conditions such as the following: (a) the recurrence of wars which temporarily increase the magnitude of the economic optimum and therefore may stimulate growth; (b) the opportunity, when there is uncertainty and ambiguity respecting dimensions of the optimum magnitude and when (as is usually the case) favoritism of birth control lags behind favoritism of death control, for special interest groups to introduce new and reenforce old constraints favorable to the increase of A; (c) the fact that individual decisions respecting marriage and family size usually are made in disregard of their prospective external repercussions and in terms of a conspectus of alternatives which is much narrower than the conspectus that is relevant in the individual case; and so on.

Simple generalization concerning the comparative rates of growth of A in dynamic and nondynamic societies is not possible, since what takes place turns so largely upon a society's stage of evolution. The rate of increase of A depends upon the rate at which a society's produced income Y is increasing and upon its population elasticity. In a nondynamic society high population elasticity is offset by low growth of income; the converse may hold in a dynamic society if its population remains quite short of the maximum G. When, however, a nondynamic society becomes dynamic and its income begins to rise, A increases significantly since the reproduction-favoring character of the age structure initially retards the decline of population elasticity. Eventually, however, this elasticity tends to fall markedly, in which event the rate of growth of A declines unless Y somehow increases at a sufficiently increasing rate to counterbalance the fall in population elasticity. Even if Y should for a time increase in this manner, it could not long continue to do so, because of physical and institutional obstacles to the augmentation of production, there existing at any time a ceiling amount of produced income to be had from a society's income-producing equipment. This ceiling can be raised through time, of course, but not continuously, there always being some maximum that cannot be exceeded. As this ceiling is approached A must virtually cease to grow. In short, then, the comparative rates of growth of A in two types of societies depend significantly upon their respective stages of economic development.

(2) Respecting O, howsoever defined, it may be said that its magnitude does not continually keep pace with A when A continues to increase. An exception to this statement would exist if O were so defined as to place emphasis almost exclusively upon size of population; for then by definition O might increase at least as rapidly as A increased. This exception may be ruled out as empirically irrelevant. (i) There exists no evidence to show that the optimum magnitude, expressed in terms of per capita capacity to produce any stipulated bill of goods, continues to increase as the concrete conditions of production change in response to population or other changes; in terms of Figure II, it probably tends to behave much as does the locus of the p-points, it being here supposed that not population but the index of these production conditions is measured along the X-axis. (ii) There is no evidence, on the subjective side, to the effect that, given any acceptable definition of O, its magnitude increases in about the same degree as A increases, with the result that M is not increased by increases in A. It would be necessary, in order for O to behave in this fashion, that, as A increased and the production possibility changed in consequence, d underwent appropriate and sufficient modification. This would mean, in terms of Figure I, that as A increased, d would also have to change in such measure as to push upward adequately, if that were possible, the point on the relevant production possibility curve, say (3), marking the collection chosen. Presumably, there could not be enough such movement unless d also underwent sufficient and appropriate change, and the upper portion of curve (3) stood above the upper portion of curves (1), (2), and (2'). In the event that this were not the case, it would be necessary somehow to modify d in favor of populousness and to redefine production possibility to include populousness so that, as population grew, the Y-intercept of the relevant curve would rise and with it the locus of the now preferred collection. The probability that tastes and values would undergo such necessary modification is negligible. It is extremely unlikely, therefore, that, given a continually increasing A, O would also continually increase.

It has been argued that if A continues to increase, it will pull away from O, with the result that M increases. This is but another way of saying that under many though not necessarily under all empirical conditions, a tendency toward overpopulation exists in societies. While this is a different sort of overpopulation than Malthus envisaged, it resembles the latter's in that it is couched in terms of "welfare."

Proneness to population maladjustment is more pronounced, other conditions being given, in subjectively static than in subjectively dynamic societies. National patterns of consumption change in consequence of changes in the price structure and of changes in tastes and values which reenforce responses to changes in the price structure and which facilitate the replacement in living budgets of old goods and services by new goods and services. By a subjectively static society we mean one whose population is not disposed to modify its values and tastes or their distribution appreciably, or to readjust its pattern of consumption significantly in response to changes in the price structure. By a subjectively dynamic society we mean one which is disposed to make both types of adjustment in a marked degree. As population increases, and particularly when this increase is accompanied by great technological changes, the price structure undergoes modification, some products—among them products formerly favored—become relatively scarce, and other products—including both newly introduced products and products formerly relatively scarce—become relatively abundant. When a subjectively dynamic society experiences an increase in numbers, it readjusts its pattern of consumption in the light of the changes just described, and thereby tends to make its optimum population magnitude greater, under the new conditions, than this magnitude otherwise would have been. In like circumstances a much smaller readjustment tends to be made by a subjectively static society, with the result that its optimum magnitude changes very little. Accordingly, other conditions being given, the tendency to population maladjustment tends to be relatively greater in a subjectively static society than in a subjectively dynamic society. For like reasons changes in economic welfare tend to be less closely associated with changes in per capita income in the former than in the latter type of society.

VIII

In this paper questions centering about population optima have been reexamined in terms of modern welfare economics. It has been suggested that this approach lies within the Malthusian tradition, and it has been inferred, that even in modern welfare terms, there probably exists a bias toward overpopulation in many societies. It is likely that the kind of analysis employed in this essay can be extended to appraisal of the impact of changes in population distribution upon both objective conditions of production and subjective conditions reflecting tastes and values.

Limitational Factors in Population Theory: A Note*

"So poverty is obsolete and hunger is abolished." — W. S. Gilbert in *Utopia, Limited.*

In recent years there have appeared a variety of studies which, taken together, suggest that the supply of food potentially available to the world is much greater, much more elastic, than formerly was supposed. These studies, it is alleged, have finally laid the supposedly already many times laid ghost of Malthus. For example, the publishers of M. K. Bennett's excellent *The World's Food* describe it, in the words of a *New York Times*'s book-reviewer, as a "dissection of the ghost of Malthus, and of living revivalists of the Malthusian doctrine." This note is concerned with the validity of such interpretations.

I

The argument of the "dissectors" appears to run as follows. (1) Should the food supply become sufficiently elastic in response to inputs of labor and associated agents of production themselves in elastic supply, Malthus's principal line of argument would be deprived of virtually all such empirical validity as it once may have possessed. (2) From (1) it tends to be inferred that, supposing the food supply to be thus highly elastic, man need no longer be apprehensive lest continuing population growth affect his "welfare" adversely. Our counter-argument will run as follows. (*a*) On a narrow but somewhat questionable interpretation of Malthus's argument, implication (1) might be allowed. (*b*) But inference (2) is not allowable.

While our argument is based, for purposes of discussion, upon acceptance of the postulate that the food supply is highly elastic, we do not accept this postulate as a satisfactory empirical description of the state of the food supply in most parts of the present-day world. Even in countries where the supply of calories may be described as highly elastic (within limits), the supply of some food elements (e.g., meat) may not be so elastic. Furthermore, even though one accepted Jacob Rosin's forecast[1] of an eventual chemistic Eden wherein even preferred meats would be plentiful, one would also have to remain cognizant of present-day realities and of the many obstacles which must be surmounted before this Eden could become an actuality, even in advanced countries.

Our counter-argument takes into account the fact that the scale or structure[2] of living is made up of many elements, or components, of which the

* I have had the advantage of critical comments of my colleague, C. B. Hoover.
1. See *The Road to Abundance,* New York 1953.

genus food is but one. Even though food is in highly elastic supply, divers other components are bound to be in comparatively inelastic supply. The more important of these components operate, because of their comparative scarcity, to deter population growth. They may therefore be called limitational factors. The role played by these factors in population theory is somewhat analogous, therefore, it will be shown, to the role played in agricultural theory by the "minimum factor."

II

It is not absolutely clear to what extent nineteenth-century and early twentieth-century students of the population problem thought in terms of limitational factors, since they did not so express themselves explicitly. Malthus, of course, supposed the growth of population to be dependent upon that of the food supply, though how much weight he actually attached to this factor remains a subject of dispute. Moreover, until the 1920's the importance of the food supply continued to be emphasized by students of population. There is apparent in the analyses of these post-Malthusian writers, however, a diminution in the degree of importance attached to the role of subsistence; and it is inferrable that they saw the population-limiting role gradually passing, in some parts of the world, from food to other components of the structure of living. For these students observed that in the sphere of European civilization the structure of living was undergoing what they considered to be improvements in quality and increases in quantity with the result that the relative importance of food was declining. It not being our purpose to review the development of population theory in detail, the drift of nineteenth century British thought, which was fairly typical of thought elsewhere, can only be suggested by greatly abridged samples of the views of Malthus and three outstanding writers in the Malthusian tradition.

Because Malthus gave expression in his *Essay on the Principle of Population* only to a faulty and imperfectly formulated theory of population, and because he never reconciled all the propositional and empirical statements found in the *Essay,* it is possible to infer either that he put overwhelming emphasis upon the role of food, or that he attached considerable importance to non-food elements. In what must have been for him a more theoretical part of the *Essay,* he wrote as if the "means of subsistence"—an increase in which amounted to an increase in the capacity of "the mass of society to command more food"—constituted the factor by whose growth, to the exclusion of the growth of almost all other factors, the growth of population was regulated. For he said:

1. Population is necessarily limited by the means of subsistence.
2. Population invariably increases where the means of subsistence increase, unless prevented by some very powerful and obvious checks.

3. These checks, and the checks which repress the superior power of population, and keep its effects on a level with the means of subsistence, are all resolvable into moral restraint, vice, and misery.[3]

The first two of these propositions would have had the support of many who wrote on population in 1750–1798, since in that period, as C. E. Stangeland concluded, the "doctrine, that population tends to increase more rapidly than the food supply, found almost universal acceptance."[4] These views may be said to reflect in part the then prevailing pattern of consumption which was founded largely upon materials of organic origin.[5]

While Malthus sometimes observed – e.g., on the basis of F. M. Eden's studies – that not much more than two-thirds of the income of a laborer's family would be expended upon provisions, and while he anticipated that the proportion of this income going for provisions might or would decline, he usually looked upon food as the principal limitational factor. Accordingly, if we infer Malthus's meaning from his various statements wherein the importance of food is indicated to be overriding, we may suppose that he considered it the primary population-limiting factor. If however we infer his meaning from other statements, we must diminish somewhat the role allowed food in his theory; but even then it remains very important. He did not, however, express himself explicitly in terms of limitational factors.[6]

Less emphasis was placed upon the role of food by the distinguished late-classical economist, J. S. Mill, in the various editions of his *Principles of Political Economy* (1848–1871). He implied that subsistence would be the sole limiting factor, and that numbers would keep pace with subsistence, only if multiplication proceeded, as among animals, "from a blind instinct." Only "in a very backward state of society" (e.g., Medieval Europe, much of Asia), wherein merely a few enjoyed much more than "actual necessaries," was population "kept down by actual starvation." In "a more improved

2. We shall use the terms scale and structure interchangeably. Since inequality characterizes the distribution of income, consumables, etc., it is not very useful to conceive of the term scale as representing an amount received and enjoyed by each and all. It is more accurate to think of scale in a structural context, since then some value may be chosen as the parameter representative of the structure or the distribution of the divers individual scales of living characteristic of a population. On this matter see Harvey Leibenstein, *A Theory of Economic-Demographic Development*, Princeton 1954, pp. 12ff.

3. *Essay*, Everyman's Library edition, Bk. I, p. 18–19. Malthus expressed himself less carefully in the first edition; see pp. 37–38.

4. *Pre-Malthusian Doctrines of Population*, New York 1904, p. 353. Some eighteenth-century writers drew attention to limitational factors other than food.

5. "A hundred years ago, nearly 80 per cent of all the things men used were derived from the plant and animal kingdoms. . . . Today only about 30 per cent of the things used in industrialized countries come from things that grow." See K. F. Mather, *Enough and to Spare*, New York 1944, p. 55.

6. For references to various of Malthus's works wherein the role of food and other factors is treated see my "Malthus's Total Population Theory: A Restatement and Reappraisal," *Canadian Journal of Economics and Political Science*, XI, 1945, pp. 87–92, 108–110, 240–41; e.g., see *Essay*, Bk. IV, chap. 11.

state" this was not the case; for there the modal scale of living embraced more than "actual necessaries," and many inhabitants were actuated by "prudent or conscientious self-restraint" to limit births. In general, as the condition of mankind rose above that of beasts, population would be "restrained by fear of want rather than by want itself," and the growth of numbers would be conditioned by a number of circumstances, of which the growth of the food supply would be but one.[7] Mill's approach had been anticipated in part by those French writers who preferred the expression "means of existence" to the expression "means of subsistence."

The economic historian, William Cunningham, wrote in 1883 that "population has generally increased up to the relative limit set by the power of procuring subsistence at any given time and place"; but he added that "sometimes population does not increase so rapidly as the quantity of procurable subsistence is increased." It did not increase so rapidly because the "standard of comfort" characteristic of the population in question had improved qualitatively and increased quantitatively.[8]

Alfred Marshall, having reviewed the improvements that had taken place in the British standard of living in the nineteenth century, pointed out, in his discussion of the long-run supply of labor, that the elasticity of supply of labor (i.e., population) depended upon the composition of the standard of living, being greatest when the workers spent their income mainly on necessaries.

> Thus the question how closely the supply of labour responds to the demand for it, is in a great measure resolved into the question how great a part of the present consumption of the people at large consists of necessaries, strictly so called, for the life and efficiency of young and old; how much consists of conventional necessaries which theoretically could be dispensed with, but practically would be preferred by the majority of the people to some of those things that were really necessary for efficiency; and how much is really superfluous regarded as a means towards production, though of course part of it may be of supreme importance as an end in itself.[9]

Marshall's analysis implied that food was losing its population-limiting power to other components of the structure of living.

Generalizing, we may say that writers in the Malthusian tradition observed that, in the European sphere of civilization, the scale of life had expanded to include a non-food component appreciably larger than that insisted upon in Malthus's day, and that the habits of the people were be-

7. See *Principles* (Ashley edition), pp. 158–160, 348, 371–72.

8. See "On the Statement of the Malthusian Principle," *Macmillan's Magazine,* XLIX, 1883, pp. 81–86; *Modern Civilization in Some of Its Economic Aspects,* London 1896, p. 173. I am indebted to Professor Thornton Steele for these references.

9. *Principles of Economics,* 8th ed., London 1920, Bk. VI, chap. 2, par. 3, esp. p. 530; also Bk. IV, chaps. 4–5. In his preface, pp. xv–xvi, Marshall noted that importations from abroad had temporarily increased the elasticity of the supply of foodstuffs accessible to Britain.

coming adjusted to the maintenance if not to the further expansion of this scale and this component. Had these writers studied more carefully the changes that had taken place in the composition of the net national product, they might have stressed even more the increase in the relative and absolute importance of the non-food component. They did, however, attach less importance than had Malthus to the limitational role played by subsistence. Some writers in the tradition critical of Malthus stressed in even greater measure the decline in the limitational role assignable to food.

III

For the purpose of clarifying the argument to be employed, use will be made of a logistic model. Accordingly, let K represent the asymptotically limiting or maximum population of whose support a given finite environment is capable under prevailing cultural conditions whereunder are included the resident population's aspirations and its methods of production. Let N represent the size of the actual population; b, the maximum rate of increase of which this population is capable in the absence of any environmental resistance to population growth; and R, the realized annual percentage rate of population growth. The logistic model rests upon the supposition that environmental resistance to population growth increases as N approaches K; whence the extent of this resistance may be expressed by N/K. Since the incremental rate of growth is $bN(K-N)/K$, R becomes $b(K-N)/K$. The value of R thus declines as N approaches K.

If we are content to describe what happens very simply, we may say that, as N/K increases, the logistically-behaving population responds by reducing its rate of growth R. It may do this by increasing its age-specific mortality, or by decreasing its age-specific fertility, or by accomplishing both, so that the direct effects, together with the indirect effects attendant upon the resulting changes in age composition, produce the indicated decline in R. However, since it is not likely that a population capable of reducing its age-specific fertility would choose to respond by increasing its age-specific mortality, it may be supposed that the population in question would have recourse only to the former alternative. If, however, its fertility-limiting capacity were sufficiently small, it would experience some increase in age-specific mortality.

If a logistically-behaving population responds to a rising N/K by reducing its age-specific fertility, it may do so either because, its minimum acceptable scale of living being fixed, it encounters increasing difficulty providing this standard, or because, its desired scale of living being assumed to rise through time, it finds itself incapable of supplying this rising scale and at the same time maintaining its age-specific fertility intact.[10] The former situation cor-

10. Again the term scale is conceived of in a structural sense (see note 2 above). It is assumed, furthermore, that the desired scale is not beyond the reach of the population, given some

responds much more closely to that which Malthus usually had in mind than does the latter. For, while Malthus hoped that a rise in scale would take place and even drew attention to evidence suggesting such a rise, he often reasoned on the supposition of a comparatively fixed scale.

If a logistically-behaving population, whose minimum acceptable scale of living is fixed, responds to a rising N/K by diminishing its age-specific fertility and hence its R, the fall in R is traceable to the fact that, as N/K increases, it becomes increasingly difficult for the population in question to increase the output of the goods and services comprising its structure of living. For as labor and other inputs are increased, their yields at the margin decline and output becomes increasingly inelastic, until finally the yields at the margin are inadequate to permit further population growth and N approximates K. The stationary state of Malthus and the classical economists is then at hand, N having stopped growing because the output of goods and services stopped growing, and this output having stopped growing because (under the conditions given) N stopped growing.[11]

Let us designate as O the output of goods and services wherewith the growth of population N is associated in our logistic model. Let us suppose that O is perfectly homogeneous, any one of its components being perfectly substitutable for any other. Let us suppose further, for the sake of expositive convenience, that the structure of living remains unchanged. Then N will increase so long as O increases, subject to the condition that the structure of living remain undiminished by the increase in N. In turn output O will increase as N increases, though not proportionately, ceasing to grow when the growth of N comes to a standstill. Should we define O as food or subsistence, we should have a situation approximating that Malthus had in mind when he supposed the growth of population to be almost solely dependent upon the growth of a food supply which he believed to be subject to diminishing incremental return (*ceteris paribus*).[12]

Malthus's system is defective because the intervening variables have been specified imperfectly or not at all. Again let our logistic model be employed to illustrate the defect. In this model population N has been represented as

---

reduction in age-specific fertility. It is implied, finally, that the elements, the desire for which supposedly may be growing through time, are not offspring, and that the increasing introduction of these elements into the scale of living may operate to displace offspring and so bring about a reduction in age-specific fertility.

11. E.g., see William Baumol, *Economic Dynamics*, Princeton 1951, chap. 2; A. T. Peacock, "Theory of Population and Modern Economic Analysis, I," *Population Studies*, VI, 1952, pp. 114–122. The specific value assumed by N turns, in the short-run, on how the output is distributed. The value assignable to K also turns on how output is distributed and used because, *ceteris paribus*, the amount of capital at the disposal of the population depends upon the distribution of income, and the greater is this amount, the higher will be K.

12. Malthus's system permitted improvements in methods of production; but, given these and a corresponding redefinition of the content of *ceteris paribus*, the condition of diminishing incremental return reasserted itself.

an essentially linear function of O, and the falling rate of growth R of N has been supposed to reflect the falling rate of growth of O. It is not specified, however, why or how the diminution in the rate of growth of O causes N to behave as it does; nor are the factors which intervene between O and N and condition the response of N to variations in O identified. In the logistic model O has been represented as increasing, though not proportionately, as N increases, presumably because of what N does, directly and indirectly (e.g., work, form capital, etc.). But the variables which intervene between N and O and condition the response of O to increases in N have not been specified. Accordingly, if we give up the restrictions of the logistic model, but remain in ignorance of the roles of what we have called intervening variables, we cannot depict the growth paths of O and N, nor can we define population capacity K.

Our primary concern being with the role of limitational factors, it should be noted that, so long as O is homogeneous, O is the limitational factor, and N's growth is dependent solely upon that of O, the intervening variables remaining as given. Even if O were heterogeneous, but constant in composition, with all of its components growing at the same rate, O would be the limitational factor, or constant complex of limitational components.

IV

It is because O is neither homogeneous nor, if heterogeneous, of constant composition, that it becomes useful for population students to think in terms of limitational or bottle-neck factors, the character of which changes in consequence of changes in technology, structure of living and other cultural manifestations, discoveries, depletion of resources, population magnitudes, etc. Output O is made up of a number of components, $O_1, O_2, \ldots, O_n$, few if any of which are perfectly substitutable, one for another. Moreover, these components differ in respect of their elasticity of supply at any particular time, some being relatively augmentable and others relatively non-augmentable. It follows that at all times some components of O may be described as being in a state of potential plenty, whereas others may be described as being in a state of potential if not actual dearth. It is the latter to which the term limitational factor is applicable, for it is their scarcity that is experienced whilst other components remain in plentiful supply, and it is to the impact of their scarcity that population-regulating behavior is ultimately traceable in large measure, particularly since this scarcity tends to be intensified by population growth.

Ultimately, of course, the comparative scarcity and relative non-augmentability of some components of O are to be traced to the comparative scarcity and relative non-augmentability of some (if not all) of the productive agents (or inputs) by which the scarce components are produced and of which, in a sense, the scarce components may be said to be composed. The scarcity of the relatively non-augmentable and hence relatively scarce components of O is traceable, therefore, to the comparative dearth of those scarce productive inputs which enter into the composition of the scarce components of O. While it is possible, therefore, to speak of population-limiting factors at either the production or the use level, it is those at the latter level with which this discussion is concerned; for population-regulating behavior is more immediately traceable to relative scarcity at the use level than to relative scarcity at the production level. So our argument will continue in terms of relatively scarce components of O rather than in terms of the inputs of which these relatively scarce components are composed.

What we have called a limitational factor is somewhat analogous to the "minimum factor" of soil theory. Let us call its *optimum* the amount of each plant-food required if we are to obtain a maximum yield of some crop (say corn). Suppose further that each plant-food is present in the soil in an amount falling short of its optimum, with some falling more short than others. Suppose that nitrogen falls relatively most short of its optimum. Then a given small percentage increase in nitrogen will produce a larger percentage increase in yield of the designated crop (i.e., corn) than will a like increase of any other of the plant-foods. Lack of nitrogen may be said, under the circumstances, to be checking the output of corn in greater measure than is the lack of any other of the requisite plant-foods. In like manner, a limitational factor may be said to be deterring population growth in much greater measure than a factor not describable as a limitational factor.[13]

The extent to which relatively non-augmentable components of O constitute, or are likely to constitute, the population-limiting factor turns on two circumstances. (1) It tends to be greater in proportion as the agents of production (which make up a part of population N and of its environment and which produce O) are not substitutable, one for another, at the *production* level. (2) It tends to be greater in proportion as the components, or the possible components, of O are not substitutable, one for another, at the *consumption or use* level. If agents of production are highly substitutable at the production level, a relative decline in the availability of some is easily overcome by increasing the availability of others. If components of O are highly substitutable at the consumption level, a relative decline in the availability of some components of O occasions little more than a shift to other components which are (or can easily be made) more available. Given both forms of substitutability in a high degree, a population may continue to enjoy, despite persisting population growth, a structure of living which, though its composi-

13. See W. J. Spillman and Emil Lang, *The Law of Diminishing Returns*, New York 1924, pp. IX–XI, 89ff.; also A. J. Lotka, *Elements of Physical Biology*, Baltimore 1925, pp. 211–213, 222ff., 292.

tion may change somewhat, is deemed as preferable as the structure which formerly was enjoyed. If, on the contrary, with neither type of substitutability highly developed, continuing population growth entails increases in the input cost of producing important components of O (say O_1, O_2, and O_3), a larger fraction of the society's inputs must be devoted to maintaining the output of these components at something like a constant per capita level, with the result that the per capita output of other components must fall in the absence of technological and similar improvements. It is to this fall that the population responds by reducing R, given that its pattern of tastes and values remains essentially unchanged. The limitational factors prompting the response are components O_1, O_2, and O_3, even though the per capita rate of their consumption may remain substantially unchanged whereas that of some other components drops off.[14]

Should *ex hypothesi* population grow at the same rate as the more augmentable components of O, even though it was the relatively nonaugmentable components for which the population had preference, the structure of living would decline. For per capita consumption of the preferred, relatively non-augmentable components would decline, and this decline would not be offset by the fact that per capita consumption of the relatively augmentable components had remained constant or even had risen. To illustrate. Suppose that food was relatively augmentable and that non-food was not. If population kept pace with an increasing food supply, non-food consumption per head would fall, and the structure of living would be affected adversely. Of course, if the population adjusted its numbers to the environmental situation in which it found itself, its numbers would be governed by the movement of the non-food component rather than by that of the food component, with the result that the outcome, if adverse at all, would be much less adverse than on the preceding supposition.[15]

V

It is not easy, short of detailed study of changes in the price structure, in the composition of national product, and in the make-up of living budgets, to identify empirically, even under fairly static conditions, what currently are,

14. This argument is easily adapted to a dynamic situation in which methods of production continually improve and the structure of living rises in the sense that more and more units of input are consumed per capita. If, for example, we suppose that the desired scale of living increases in quantity though temporarily retaining its proportional composition, an increase in the comparative cost of O_1, O_2, and O_3 would produce a change in the proportional composition of the scale though not necessarily a diminution in the per capita rate of consumption. These comparatively costly components would therefore become limitational factors or (assuming aggregate output had increased sufficiently) potentially limitational factors.

15. Elsewhere I try to deal with the concept of an optimum population in terms of modern welfare economics, and to indicate that over the longer run human societies tend strongly toward overpopulation (in welfare terms). See "Welfare Economics and the Problem of Overpopulation," *Scientia*, 1954.

or are most likely to be, population-limiting factors. Identification is made more difficult by the fact that what may be the limitational factors for some of the distinct groups composing a population may not be limitational for other groups, and that, therefore, aggregation of findings for particular groups into one for an entire population may involve considerable arbitrary judgment. In general, the limitational factor should be found among those components of the set of living budgets, or of the gross or net national product, which are relatively important and whose costs and prices have been significantly rising relatively to the costs and prices of other components; for it is probably these components, the keeping of whose output abreast with population growth will prove relatively most difficult.

To illustrate what has been said (see Table I). Let us represent the real cost (i.e., cost in terms of input) and the price (which supposedly corresponds to real cost) of three important components of O, as of the base and three later years, together with the magnitude of the population N which supposedly is increasing. On the supposition that the indices of $O_4 - O_n$ behave approximately as O_1, which is not a limitational factor in the present context, the limitational factors are O_2 and O_3, with sometimes one and sometimes the other ascendant. If O_2 bulked less importantly in living budgets, or in national product, than did O_3, the scarcity of the latter might be a greater deterrent to population growth than that of the former.

Table I

Year	Population N	Index of real cost		
		O_1	O_2	O_3
0	100	100	100	100
5	105	100	102	104
10	108	100	105	105
15	110	100	110	106

It is to the movement of real costs and prices that one must turn for information rather than to the movement of outputs. It is conceivable, for example, that in year 15 consumption per capita of O_2 remains nearly where it was in year 0, whereas the per capita consumption of some other components has fallen. Given that tastes have remained substantially unchanged, it is evident that the growth of population, by making the production of O_2 more costly, has caused inputs to be diverted in such amount to the production of O_2 from the production of other components that the diminution in the structure of living is immediately reflected in the reduced per capita consumption of these components, though its origin is to be found in the rising cost of O_2.

While food (or components of the genus food) may be a limitational factor, it often is not. Food is the preponderating component of living budgets in many parts of the world, but it never is the sole component. According to C. C. Zimmerman it is seldom that "any important part of the masses of the population devote more than 75 per cent of its total economic energy to the satisfaction of food values." He puts the minimum fraction at 25 per cent, though it now seems possible that this fraction may fall as low as 10 per cent in technologically very advanced societies characterized by very high per capita incomes and very low population/wealth ratios. Most peoples fall within a range lying between 35 and 65 per cent.[16]

Although it does not appear necessarily to follow that the population-limiting character of food is highly and positively correlated with the proportion of a population's efforts devoted to the supply of food, this association commonly obtains empirically. As a rule, if not always, the supply of food currently consumed appears to be relatively elastic in countries whose populations devote relatively little effort to food production, and to be comparatively inelastic in countries whose populations devote relatively much effort to food production. While this difference in elasticity is traceable in part to differences in culture and technology, it is also traceable in considerable measure to differences in man/land and man/wealth ratios. It may be concluded, therefore, that food is very likely to be one of the components making up the complex of population-limiting components operative in countries wherein relatively much effort is given to food production.

This conclusion is also borne out by the fact that, even when inter-country differences in per capita food consumption by weight or calorie content are not great, intercountry differences in diet-composition may be great, with the diets found in countries devoting relatively little energy to the supply of food requiring (*ceteris paribus*) for their production two or three times as many units of input as are required in the production of the diets found in countries devoting relatively much energy to the supply of food. Accordingly, countries in the former category can greatly increase their supply of calories and nutrients by introducing diets more economical of inputs as well as by diverting more units of input into agriculture.[17]

It seems to be inferrable that food (considered generically) is not very likely to constitute the limitational factor in countries where per capita real income is relatively high, animal products furnish a considerable fraction

16. See C. C. Zimmerman, *Consumption and Standards of Living,* New York 1936, pp. 59–61; and on sources, Faith M. Williams and C. C. Zimmerman, *Studies of Family Living in the United States and other Countries: An Analysis of Material and Method,* U.S.D.A. Miscellaneous Publication No. 223, Washington 1935. On production possibilities see T. W. Schultz, *Economic Organization of Agriculture,* New York 1953, chaps. 7–8, and M. K. Bennett, *The World's Food,* New York 1954, *passim.* In the United States in 1950 agricultural raw materials comprised, in value terms, about 8.2 per cent of the gross national product, and about 9.8 per cent of the net national product. Distribution costs are not included in these figures.

17. See Schultz, *op. cit.,* Part I; also my "Aspects of the Economics of Population Growth," *Southern Economic Journal,* XIV, 1948, pp. 233ff.

of the calorie intake, and the non-food component of output and consumption per head is relatively high. In countries where an opposite set of conditions is met, food probably is one of the elements composing the complex of components by which population growth is limited. At the same time it is possible that an important preferred species (say meat) of the genus food may be operating as a limitational factor. This might be the case if the demand for the species in question were quite inelastic and quantitatively important whilst (as a result of the population growth) its supply price was moving upward relatively to the prices of other budgetary items.

It is not likely, and price movements do not suggest, that in the aggregate goods and services made up predominantly of labor inputs constitute limitational factors, assuming the scale of living to be given. For the capacity to produce such goods and services tends to keep pace with population growth, except in the instance of types which consist (in addition to labor inputs) of other kinds of input whose relative scarcity tends to increase appreciably as population grows.

It is probable that raw materials[18] — in particular, minerals, and possibly also some of those of agricultural as well as those of forestry origin — presently constitute limitational factors, and that they will increasingly constitute limitational factors if both population and per capita consumption of raw materials increase. For since some of these materials are derived from non-renewable sources whilst others are produced under conditions of rising costs, it is probable that their costs and prices will rise relatively to the costs and prices of other goods and services. If this be the case then, given the structure of living and methods of production, per capita consumption of various other goods and services will be reduced. If, though this be the case, the structure of living undergoes change and methods of production are improved, per capita consumption of goods and services in general will rise even in the face of population growth, but it will rise less than it would have had numbers not increased.

Summary

It is now sometimes being said that the food supply is becoming so elastic that men need no longer be apprehensive lest population growth affect their welfare adversely. This assertion respecting the elasticity of the food supply lacks empirical validity so far as most parts of the world are concerned. It is true, however, that in some countries food is no longer the operative population-limiting factor, and food may cease to be such in yet other countries. It does not follow, however, that population-limiting factors will

18. For comparative accounts of raw material situations see *Resources for Freedom*, A Report to the President by the President's Materials Policy Commission, Washington 1952; and E. A. Ackerman, *Japan's Natural Resources*, Chicago 1953.

cease to be operative. The dynamics of culture, production, and consumption serve to change the character of these factors, but they do not remove them. For if one factor ceases to be operative, its place is necessarily taken by others. Population growth may not affect adversely man's consumption of food or some other item of living supposedly in highly elastic supply; but then it is quite likely, in many empirical situations, to make his consumption of some other items of living lower than it otherwise would have been.

The Aesthetics of Population*

> *There is no sorer misfortune in all human destiny, than when the mighty of the earth are not also the first men. Then everything becometh false and distorted and monstrous.* — Friedrich Nietzsche, in *Thus Spake Zarathustra*, LXIII.

Under the title, the aesthetics of population, I shall attempt to deal with certain of the interrelations obtaining between population movements, on the one hand, and the content of the aesthetic component of our system of values, on the other. Inasmuch as these interrelations often manifest themselves in economic form, a considerable part of my address has to do with such economic manifestations. Moreover, as this is a presidential address and not a report of research findings, I shall allow myself the luxury of some population grumbles, since, in what men write of population, there is much to grumble about.

You may be asking yourself, What has aesthetics to do with population? I shall supply an answer as I go along. Again, if your overwhelming interest lies in mensuration, you may be saying, What is there to measure in aesthetics? I might, by way of reply, list works dealing with the quantitative aspects of aesthetic matter. I prefer, however, an answer given to a similar question by W. F. Lloyd a century and a quarter ago: "It does not follow that because a thing is incapable of measurement, therefore it has no real existence."[1]

I. Professionalization and Aesthetic Value

Aesthetics is concerned with aesthetic value, above all, with beauty, with the beautiful. Whether this value is autonomous, or whether it must somehow be harmonized with ethical and utilitarian considerations, is not my primary concern. It is to be noted, however, that the capacity of the beautiful to affect human conduct need not depend significantly upon its appeal to utilitarian self-interest. Aesthetic value is, nonetheless, a part of reality. In essentially materialist societies, however, it may tend, along with other values, to be subordinated to things as such. Even so, use and ornament may be combined; beauty and utility may flow from the same object.

My concern this evening is not with the beautiful as such, but with the disregard of beauty, in popular and technical writings about population — and they must be voluminous — into which beauty might properly enter as a subject of consideration. It may be true, as Whitehead has contended, that actualized beauty exists "even though no percipient organism fully

---

*Address by the author, as retiring President of the Population Association of America, at the Association's Annual Meeting in Philadelphia May 4–5, 1957.

1. In *A Lecture on the Notion of Value*, London, 1834, pp. 29–30.

appreciates it."[2] It is also true, however, that when the percipient organism, man, fails to appreciate beauty, the days of that in which it is actualized may be numbered, and there must follow other effects consequent upon the disregard of beauty.

Disregard of aesthetic value by those who write about population is easier to explain than to condone. It is not necessary to fall back upon complex explanations. This disregard is largely the outcome, as Whitehead has implied, of professionalization. Ours has become an age of high specialization and professionalization. On this has rested the progress of demography, as of other sciences. But progress consequent upon high specialization exacts its price; it grooves the science and it grooves the practitioner; it produces, in science as in business, "a celibacy of the intellect," an imperviousness to abstractions requisite "for the comprehension of human life." It results in a superficial treatment of all aspects of life except those which fall within the groove of the specialist's "science." It results also in a virtual abdication, by the scientific elite, to politicians, journalists, and mere data-manipulators, of the task of interpreting, coordinating, and applying the findings of science, be it demography or something else. A by-product of this grooving and perhaps also of the associated lenity of practitioners of demography toward its misinterpreters is the current neglect of aesthetic value in writings and policies having to do with population.[3]

This outcome might have been avoided had these same forces of specialization produced a really firm critical elite, capable of articulating a sensitivity to aesthetic values and of communicating this sensitivity to a significant fraction of our population. Of this elite, however, there is little sign, and there is even less sign of media through which their critical evaluations might be widely propagated. Most of the media formerly suitable have given place to periodicals of a sort better suited to accommodate contemporary tastes and the more modish efforts of today's hucksters. In consequence, few spokesmen exist outside the environs of demography to draw the attention of its practitioners to the significance and the role of aesthetic values.[4]

II. Adequacy of Measures of Impact of Population Growth

Having suggested why aesthetic value is currently assigned so little weight in literature and policies having to do with population movements, I shall

2. See A. H. Johnson, "'Truth, Beauty and Goodness' in the Philosophy of A. N. Whitehead," reprinted from *Philosophy of Science*, XI, 1944, p. 20. The above paragraphs have been influenced also by Whitehead's observations in *Science and the Modern World* (1925), New York, 1947, pp. 281–82, 287, 291; and by George Santayana's remarks in his *The Sense of Beauty*, New York, 1899, pp. 49ff., 161–67, 208–220. At one point later on I have followed E. Jordan's approach in *The Aesthetic Object*, Bloomington, 1937, chaps. 15–16.

3. I have drawn on A. N. Whitehead's comments on professionalization, in *Science and the Modern World*, chap. 13, esp. pp. 282ff. Cf. also José Ortega Y Gasset, *The Revolt of the Masses*, New York, 1932.

4. Cf. W. H. W., "The Art of the Presentation," in *Fortune*, March, 1957, pp. 130–31; Ortega Y Gasset, *op. cit.*, chaps. 7–8.

touch upon a statistico-economic aspect of my fundamental thesis, that undue population growth is currently tending to debase aesthetic values and to be fostered by such debasement. Our notions of what is taking place in the country and in the world at large are formed by the reports that we receive of what is happening. Of necessity these reports are not only quantitative but also summary in character; they tend therefore to illude the uncritical reader into believing them to be more concrete and more complete than in fact they are. What I have said is applicable to our notions of the movement of real income and to the impact of population growth upon income and welfare. Preference scales suitable to the task are not being used to evaluate effects consequent upon the growth and spread of population. Indices currently in use neglect aesthetic values and imperfectly represent the consequences and the concomitants of population growth. Presumably, the index-maker looks upon himself as equipped with at least a dipper; frequently, however, he is armed with little more than a sieve.

The growth and spread of population affect the magnitude and the composition of the average quantum of environment at the disposal of the individual. Population growth is a process involving the conversion of substances and services into the origination, development, repair, replacement, and increase of members of the human species. This process is accompanied, therefore, by transformation and dissipation: (*a*) by the transformation of a given population, together with its replaceable and its irreplaceable environment, into a successor population and environment; (*b*) by the permanent dissipation of at least that part of the environment which is not susceptible of replacement or increase, even in an effective surrogate sense. What this process precipitates may be translated into terms, either of the flow of goods and services, or of the stock of environment available; this flow or this stock may then be measured.

The flow of goods and services is measurable in a number of ways; but no widely used measure adequately reflects the impact of population growth upon this flow and hence upon man's material well-being. Even the measures usually employed by statisticians — many of whom seem to be more interested in counting what they can find than in discovering what is important — mask some of the adverse influences of population growth and concentration. By way of example we may consider gross and net national product. Each includes outlays that have passed the test of the market and outlays that have had the approval only of a governmental or other bureaucracy. Of especial concern to demographers, however, is the failure of this measure to allow for the fact that, with the growth and agglomeration of population, there are associated disadvantages which must be offset through the use of productive powers that might otherwise have been employed to increase the flow of final goods and services. Yet these uses are represented as eventuating in real product — in the sense of the stuff that a husbandman puts upon his customer's table — even though they do not do so any more than do outlays upon an exploded hydrogen bomb. These outlays might be even greater, e.g., if commuters were fully compensated for time spent in traveling to and from work.

How defective gross and net national product are on the ground indicated has not been determined. Careful estimates have not yet been made. We do not know to what extent these measures include offsetting outlays that are really costs, or in what degree such costs are imputable to population growth. Moreover, the cost-effects of urbanization and/or population growth have not been sharply distinguished from concomitant redistributive effects. Kuznets's findings suggest, however, that these costs and redistributive effects make up a considerable fraction of gross national product; they include sizeable outlays upon "extensive transportation and intensive handling in distribution, credit, and other service channels," together with excessive expenditures upon housing and other services by urban residents.[5] Conceivably, between five and ten per cent of our gross national product, of which perhaps half was imputable to past population growth, consisted of costs or offset-outlays already in the early 1930's. Whatever be the correct figures, they are average values. The corresponding marginal values would be higher, since both urbanization and its costs are increasing functions of size of population. Today's average values must be appreciably higher, therefore, than were those of the 1930's.

Having pointed to one flaw in gross and net national product, considered as measures of the impact of population growth, namely, its treatment of certain costs as if they represented income, we may note a second, to wit, disregard of effects consequent upon decline in the amount of free resources available per head. Well-being depends upon both free and scarce goods and services; yet only those which are scarce command a price and are counted. So long as a good or service is free and hence of zero price, its contribution to well-being is not included in gross and net national product; it enters the hallowed environ of the income calculator only by becoming scarce and hence of positive price. Or in H. J. Davenport's inimitable words, "the distribuendum does not include all of the values in life, but only those which, being adapted to the price denominator, are submitted to it and received under it."[6]

Consider a natural resource such as land, and suppose the average amount used per head does not exceed a. When population grows beyond the size at which each and all may have quantity a at zero price, the quantity obtainable per head will have to be cut down to what is available, (say) a' per capita, and this will have to be done by putting such price on the use of land as will reduce the average share from a to a' and impute corresponding

5. See Simon Kuznets, *Economic Change*, New York, 1953, pp. 159–65, 185–87.
6. *Economics of Enterprise*, New York, 1918, pp. 489–90.

prices and income-yields to land. We thus have two effects. First, there is a redistribution of product to the owners of land from the owners of other factors of production; thus a considerable fraction of what urban dwellers pay for services is made up of such redistributed rental income, of income, that is, which might otherwise have appeared in gross national product as wages, etc. The flaw we refer to, however, is not this redistributive effect; it is the fact that the reduction in the amount of land-service supplied per head, from a level of a to one of a', is not reflected in changes in gross or net national product.

Before turning to the suitability of asset-change as a measure, it is to be noted that the recent behavior of gross and net national product, together with related measures, reveals, despite their shortcomings, that current opinion regarding an economic breakthrough is somewhat myth-ridden. For, in the words of the Red Queen, we are not doing a great deal more than enough running "to keep in the same place." Between 1946 and 1955 our gross national product increased, in real terms, about 38 per cent. Expressed in per capita terms, this becomes only about 18 per cent, or just over 1.75 per cent per year. Net national product per head has increased at something like the same rate. If, however, we turn to what matters even more to most of us, namely, to real "personal disposable income," to what is left of personal income after taxes, we find that it has increased no more than 10 per cent, if that much. Whatever else this rate of increase of one per cent or less per year may mean, it can hardly be said to signify a breakthrough.[7]

One may argue, much as has Boulding,[8] that the movement of physical assets per head affords a better measure of the impact of population growth upon welfare than does the movement of net national product per head. This measure is not perfect, of course. It may not take adequately into account increases in assets which are analogous to the costs of urbanization discussed earlier. It is subject to the qualification that some mortality is essential, in the world of assets and ideas as in the world of men and values, if we are to have, not Struldbruggian stagnation, but Odyssean flux. The principle underlying this measure does, however, guard us against certain forms of error and confusion. It stresses the utilization and increase rather than the consumption of assets. It recognizes that consumption entails destruction. It does not endorse deliberate acceleration of obsolescence, or purposeful shortening of the life of consumer durables and housing, or asset-squandering under the guise of supposedly useful consumption, a guise more easily

7. Data on income, etc., are reported in the *Survey of Current Business*, July 1956. See also E. L. Rauber's "Population and Economic Growth," *Population Bulletin*, XIII, February 1957, pp. 2–9, and his "The Realm of the Red Queen," *Monthly Review* of the Federal Reserve Bank of Atlanta, January 31, 1956. Rauber puts the rate per year at about 0.5 per cent per year.
8. See K. E. Boulding, "Income or Welfare," *Review of Economic Studies*, XVII, 1949–50, pp. 77–86.

sembled in countries where pennies need not be watched. Above all, it reflects the tendency of the growth of assets per head to be retarded, usually by population growth under present-day circumstances, and always by high reproduction. Emphasis upon the movement of assets instead of upon that of national product is of peculiar interest to demographers; it implies that expenditure is a better index of an individual's tax-paying capacity than is income, and taxes based upon expenditures appear to be at least potentially less favorable to population growth than are taxes based upon income.

III. Current Assessment of Impact of Population Growth on Well-Being

Having argued that the measures of output which we employ do not adequately reflect the impact of population growth upon material well-being, I shall touch upon some of the assessments currently being made of the impact of population growth upon man's well-being. These assessments are of two sorts, those encountered in scientific literature and those appearing in popular and special-interest media. The content of these assessments arises in varying degree from disregard of aesthetic and related values, and from failure to utilize preference scales which are really suited to measure and assess the impact of the growth and the spread of population.

Disregard of aesthetic and related values, together with failure to develop and make use of suitable preference scales, is of multiple origin. It arises in part from a diversity of conditions: e.g., that population literature is shot through with radical empiricism; that the theory of economic growth has not been effectively integrated with that of population growth; and that minutiae too frequently are the subject of excessive concern. It arises also from a disposition, even on the part of Malthus's critics, to accept his main posing of the population question. For his way of putting the problem led many to infer, when food and/or other kinds of output continued to outstrip numbers in England and Western Europe, that Malthus's ghost had been laid. Subsequent commentators have reasoned similarly when they have indicated that production has been rising faster than population; or when they have urged that the earth could continue to support its inhabitants, almost irrespective of their rate of multiplication; or when they have asked, in the words of a recent title, *Must Man Starve?*, and have given the obvious answer, No! It is possible even that this way of putting the question has led to misinterpretation of such correlation as may at times seem to exist between the rate of population growth and the rate of increase of per capita income. For Kuznets's statistical findings bear out theoretical reasoning that, because of the divers relationships and intervening variables present, such correlations as exist are without much if any significance.[9]

More extreme by far is the population booster, now as ever extemporizing after the manner of Carver's fox, who recommended "large families to the rabbits." In the Middle Ages the population booster, then a lord, found in his serfs' goodly "litters," as they were then plainly designated, a source of "surplus value."[10] Today's population booster is a less rational fellow than his medieval forbear; often he is a politician, an unwitting businessman, a local chamber-of-commerce spokesman, or a journalist; sometimes he is a land or other speculator in search of a quick promoter's profit. He writes optimistically of the market expansion to which population growth supposedly gives rise, apparently oblivious to the fact that, since every recruit to a population is eventually a producer as well as a consumer, the amount of market available per producer is affected little if at all. The modern booster behaves as if he depended for sight entirely upon a monocle that gave sight only to the eye through which he looked at consumption and demand whilst leaving totally blind the other eye through which alone supply might be made visible. Our booster seems to be unaware that he is implicitly endorsing the very stagnation theory, which he found so unpalatable in the 1930's when it was being asserted that the entrepreneur had lost his élan, with the result that business prosperity was made to depend largely upon the behavior of the stork instead of upon the intelligence of man. Our businessman booster may also be unaware that, when he talks so optimistically of the empty spaces and the unused resources remaining to be exploited, he is but repeating remarks common among communist dialecticians. The population boosters of old — the nationalists and the imperialists — are no longer as vocal as in the past, having succumbed perhaps to the humanitarian sentiments of the day; and yet, in most countries, it is only on nationalist and imperialist grounds that a strong case can be made, it being given that the stork sometimes is the ultimate arbiter of national destiny.

To the arguments of the population boosters, as to those of writers who underestimate the adverse effects of population growth, various answers are possible. One may infer that humans no more thrive when crowded than do crappies. One may remark the unfavorableness of the age composition of a growing population. One may point out that a rate of population growth of one per cent per year offsets an annual savings rate of four to five per cent of national income, and thereby appreciably reduces the rate of growth of per capita income. Or one may observe that, even should Lil Abner's "schmoos" allay man's hunger for food, other of his hungers would not only remain but would be made more unsatisfiable by population growth; for, of

9. See "Quantitative Aspects of the Economic Growth of Nations," *Economic Development and Cultural Change*, V, 1956, pp. 28–31.

10. See G. C. Coulton, *Medieval Panorama*, New York, 1955, pp. 76–77, 82.

the elements present in man's environment and upon which his well-being depends, many are fixed or depletable in nature, with the result that the amount available per head must decline as population increases, thus imposing limitations upon the augmentability of various goods and services.

A better and more intelligent answer was given 33 years ago by A. B. Wolfe, when he was considering the question, whether America could support 500 million people on a diet substantially free of meat and waste. His answer was, *cui bono?* To what purpose? For whose good? Mill had expressed a somewhat similar view already in 1848; and so had Matthew Arnold in 1867, when he remarked, apropos authors who talked solemnly of large English families and looked upon them as meritorious *per se,* that these authors reasoned "as if the British Philistine would have only to present himself before the Great Judge with his twelve children, in order to be received among the sheep as a matter of right."[11]

Exponents of optimum-population theory are agreed that the amount of mundane "welfare" available per capita, howsoever defined, almost invariably depends upon the size and the rate of population growth. They disapprove of population growth which makes this welfare less than it otherwise would have been. As economists, they are bound to look upon children as prospective sources of satisfaction to their parents much as newly acquired durable goods are prospective sources of satisfaction to their owners. Accordingly, if economists set great store by consumer sovereignty and freedom of choice (and one can hardly fail to do so and yet remain in the Western liberal tradition), they cannot condone economic-institutional arrangements — arrangements apparently based upon the principle of need set forth in the Parable of the Vineyard rather than upon the principle of productivity endorsed in the Parable of the Talents — which interfere with consumer sovereignty and so bias the allocation of resources as to give undue stimulus to population growth. This bias has been introduced into almost all Western countries and is partly responsible for the post-war increase in the rate of population growth.

In the United States and elsewhere the rate of growth would not be so high were potential parents required to meet nearly all of the costs of procreating and rearing children, costs which at present are being shifted in considerable part to others. For, while it may be true that natality has been stimulated in America by the development of a quasi-matriarchate, whereunder the young male passes early from the suzerainty of "Mom" to that of a spouse bent upon establishing herself similarly, this stimulus would be appreciably weakened if the costs of such behavior were made incident upon the responsible parties instead of upon the forgotten taxpayer. So long as population policy is not based upon optimum theory and upon a predomi-

11. See *Culture and Anarchy* (1869), New York, 1925, p. 49. For Wolfe's remark see his essay in L. I. Dublin, ed., *Population Problems,* New York, 1925, p. 65.

nance of consumer sovereignty and freedom of choice, population growth is likely to be excessive, at least on economic and "welfare" grounds.

Whether the American people will remove economic stimuli making for excessive growth—say, by adopting an expenditures tax and doing away with hidden subsidies to natural increase and with tax exemptions for living children beyond the second (except perhaps for parents with high I.Q.'s)—remains to be seen. We live in an age of egalitarian sentiment, in an age in which the silk purse and the sow's ear are commonly rated of nearly equal importance, and in such an age it is hard to maintain consumer freedom, or to base rewards wholly upon economic productivity. It is of interest to note, however, that the *U.S. News & World Report,* which had been reporting approval of our high rate of population growth, recently reported Americans as asking, when they learned that there might be 300 million Americans by 1993, "How long can this go on? How many more people can this country handle without overcrowding?"[12] This concern would be all the greater if they realized that increase in population density beyond a critical level is likely to be unfavorable to economic and other forms of liberty to which Americans and others attach a high degree of importance.

IV. Interrelation of Aesthetic Value and Population Growth

I come now to aesthetic values proper. I shall touch upon the significance of variation in the importance of aesthetic values for variation in the rate of natural increase, and upon the significance of variation in the rate of natural increase for variation in the importance attached to aesthetic values. I take it for granted that the precise content of artistic expression of beauty tends to vary in time, and that artistic expression sometimes becomes decadent.[13] For the sake of expositive convenience, therefore, I shall mean by beauty, conformity with relevant aesthetic criteria, and by ugly, extreme deviation from such conformity. I shall argue, in general, that an overworked stork is the enemy of the beautiful, and that, when men no longer prize the beautiful highly, the stork is likely to be given too much rein.

The overworked stork is the enemy of the beautiful because satisfaction of the demands of the stork absorbs resources which might otherwise have been devoted to satisfying the criteria of beauty and to meeting the requirements of excellence. Population growth entails diversion of resources from the elevation of people above what has been the common level to mere multiplication of those at or near the common level. A people that worships the stork cannot escape paying the piper. Witness the average non-rural

12. See *U.S. News & World Report* for March 1, 1957, pp. 30–31.
13. See P. A. Sorokin, *Social and Cultural Dynamics,* New York, 1937, I, Part Two.

school child: viewed as an object of improvement, he often is worse off today than in the 1930's, in part because population growth is diluting the amount of resources we are willing and able to devote to the disciplined and skill-incorporating upbringing of the average child. More generally, agents of production required to support population growth might otherwise have been used to improve the health, education, and cultural attainment of the given self-replacing population. A probable outcome, I like to think, would then have been increase in the conformity of man's behavior and artifacts with aesthetic criteria.

Population growth not only absorbs resources; it also accelerates their dissipation and intensifies many kinds of scarcity. For, since aggregate demand depends upon per capita demand as well as upon the number of demanders, it grows both as population grows and as average requirements grow. Poverty, in the sense of particular forms of relative shortage, thus arises both because there are many demanders, as in India, and because every demander wants so much, as in America. Population growth, because it increases the rate at which gross national product expands, intensifies the rate at which depletable resources are used up. Illustrative of this class of resources are inorganic substances of use to man, but subject to reduction to a state of non-utilizability by the relentless march of economic entropy consequent upon use.[14]

Of perhaps greater significance is steady diminution in the amount available per head of factors essential to production and well-being, but in approximately fixed supply. Illustrative are water, land, and suitably situated space, the last itself largely dependent upon accessible landed area. Water, long the economist's stock example of a free good, has become scarce, a factor presently setting limits to economic growth in various parts of the United States. This shortage will be felt increasingly as population growth augments both water pollution and water requirements; it will be intensified if underground water-tables fall. Recourse to widespread use of purified saltwater would prove expensive at best, as would migration of the inhabitants of water-short areas to other lands.[15]

Turning to land, we shall soon find our population numbering 60 per square mile, and by the close of the century, perhaps around 100 per square mile, a figure not far below that of Indo-China, or that of Eire whence people have been emigrating for the past 125 years. By the close of the century per capita landed acreage, now about 11, may have fallen to 6 or less. The growing shortage of land will be increasingly felt as numbers increase, for

14. See my "Aspects of the Economics of Population Growth," *Southern Economic Journal*, XIV, 1948, pp. 238–39, 257.

15. For summary accounts of data relating to land and other natural resources see my "The Population Problem: Dimensions, Potentialities, Limitations," *American Economic Review*, XLVI (2), May 1956, pp. 337–351, and "The World's Hunger . . . Malthus, 1948," *Proceedings of the Academy of Political Science*, XXIII, January, 1949, pp. 53–72.

the consumption pattern of America is already the most space-oriented in the world. At present every year 1.1 million acres reportedly are taken permanently out of crop use by urban and suburban development, together with the expansion of industry, airports, military establishments, and new highways; and another 700,000 acres are lost annually through soil erosion, tree planting, waterlogging, salt deposits, and other contamination.[16] Much of this land is lost also to those uses which prompted John Ruskin to call land "the most precious 'property' that human beings can possess." He would probably have found operative a Gresham's law of aesthetics in the continuing replacement of Arcadian beauty by car-dominated, bill-boarded, neon-signed shabbiness.[17]

The figures I have given indicate that currently nearly 0.5 per cent of our limited crop land — 409 million acres in 1950 — is being lost to crop use every year, even as other land is being lost to uses that fail to take into account the intrinsic worth of natural environment. For these and related reasons Americans may expect increasingly to feel the lash of land famine. Eventually there will be too little land to provide the kind of diet we prefer. Our seashore, a priceless scenic and scientific resource, will be given over more and more to the often uglifying hands of profit-seeking subdividers, and therewith the fate of our wildlife, the future of our shoreline, and access to beaches, already a diminishing quantity at best.[18] Within the interior, along rivers and lakes, similar constrictive forces will operate, with water pollution also exacting an increasing toll. Replacement of ugly human rabbit warrens, common in many American metropolitan areas, by clusters of human habitations which better satisfy aesthetic criteria, will prove ever more costly. Access to playgrounds and parks, public and otherwise, will prove increasingly difficult, as a rule. In short, all the amenities — and they are many — into the satisfaction of which land and space enter, will become more and more scarce; and men will feel increasingly, as Longfellow would feel, were he to return to the present-day environs of the great university with which he once was associated. Nor will there be much opportunity to substitute under-ground or above-ground space for surface-space; suitably situated space of this sort is very limited in amount and costly of access. From the eventual threat of an approximation to standing room only there is thus but one effective means of escape, namely, limitation of numbers.

16. See Charles Grutzner's report, the first of a series, "Changes Ahead in City and Suburban Living," appearing in the *New York Times,* January 27 to February 3, 1957. See also J. F. Dewhurst et al., *America's Needs and Resources,* New York, 1955, chaps. 17, 22; U.S.D.A., Agricultural Research Service, *Major Uses of Land in the United States,* Bulletin No. 168, Washington, D.C., January, 1957.

17. See his *Essays on Political Economy,* in James Fuchs, ed., *Ruskin's Views of Social Justice,* New York, 1926, p. 48. See also Dan Jacobson, "Cars, Cars, Cars, Roads, Roads, Roads," *Reporter,* February 21, 1957, pp. 18ff.

18. *Our Vanishing Shoreline,* U.S. Department of Interior, Washington, D.C., 1956. One may consult also data relating to the use of our national parks.

One cannot get rid of excess numbers after they have come into being. Only if numbers are duly limited can men give effective expression to the beautiful and the excellent.

Having argued that an overworked stork is the enemy of the beautiful, I shall now argue that we have given so much rein to the stork because we do not prize the beautiful, because we may be afflicted with what Mencken called "the libido for the ugly"; for this attitude causes us to disregard the destructive impact of population growth upon beauty and excellence. Of this tendency to neglect beauty, excellence, and related values, there are various manifestations. For example, critics of manners in America are beginning to look upon the behavior of the American Leviathan as being under the empire of something like ancient Rome's Fortuna, which, in Voltaire's words, makes all "blindly play her terrible game," and which seemingly inspires many of Leviathan's leaders to behave as figurines in a ballet under the governance of a similar but not very foresightful élan. Moralists might assert that wealth is possessing its possessors, or that the chase is outweighing the quarry, or that men hold with Samuel Butler that progress has its origin in an "innate desire on the part of every organism to live beyond its income."[19] Whatever be the forces at work, ethical and aesthetic values play but a small part in ordering the behavior of many of those upon whom largely depends the aggregate growth, demographic as well as economic, of the American Leviathan. Our recent economic-demographic growth, for all its phenomenal character, has some of the quality of a megalomaniac's dream; it appears to be too much dominated by a kind of blind dinosaurism, and too little by the discipline of ethical and aesthetic values.

All this is well illustrated in Russell Lyne's acutely perceptive *A Surfeit of Honey*.[20] Herein the average American is represented as intent on being in fashion and yet shuddering "at the idea of being fashionable." Our servomechanistically minded executives are portrayed as having "built-in ulcers" and as buying "two-hundred-and-forty horsepower cars" fitted "with built-in safety belts." Our American society is described as equipped "with more built-in tranquilizers of more different sorts than any that has ever existed." Were Thomas Carlyle still alive he might be prompted to repeat his evaluation, exaggerated of course, made in 1843, of the impact of England's growing wealth. "No man of you shall be the better for it; this is enchanted fruit."[21] Mr. Lynes's portrait would hardly have occurred, even to a social critic, were aesthetic values in the saddle in American society. For then

19. This sentence has been partly inspired by Gelett Burgess's "A Prayer" and by Robert Burton, *Anatomy of Melancholy;* and the preceding, by Wyndham Lewis's *The Demon of Progress in the Arts,* London, 1954, p. 51.

20. Published by Harper and Brothers, New York, 1957. My quotations are from pp. 1, 84–85.

21. *Past and Present* (1843), Oxford, 1932, Bk. I. chap. 1.

premium would be attached to real excellence, to beauty, and behavior and production would generally be so oriented. Presumably, many would agree that, "in the wisdom of our choice of purposes to be achieved,"[22] we have hardly even marked time.

I should like to refer again to my earlier observation that increases in gross and net national product per head, especially when accompanied by population growth, are partly offset by the adverse effects of changes in the composition of this product. These effects, whilst expressible in economic terms, may also be reduced to terms of aesthetic debasement. Although some of these adverse effects accompany income growth, even in the absence of population growth, they are very greatly accentuated by population growth. Population growth entails both urban concentration and an essentially escapistic suburbanward dispersal of people, together with a usurpation of land for conversion into suburbs and highways, and for diversion to various analogous purposes. All of these uses chew up and uglify the countryside, and some of them intensify the spread of "urban blight" within metropolitan areas.

This dissipative process tends to be more powerful when gross national product per head is relatively high, as in the United States; and it is accelerated when product per head is rising. It is possible, of course, that the spread of urban blight may be prevented through heavy expenditure on urban renewal, as in parts of Manhattan; but a sufficiency of resources is seldom provided for this purpose, and when it is provided, it is made available through the nonsatisfaction of many other important wants, such as education, health, the preservation of natural beauty, and so on. It cannot be validly argued, therefore, that when population growth is accompanied by increases in product per head, these increases are improving the well-being of the average individual as much as they would have improved it in the absence of such population growth. For the countryside is necessarily much more chewed up than it would have been in the absence of population growth, and the amount of urban blight is almost invariably much greater. These dissipative effects, reflected in adverse changes in the composition of gross national product, thus offset, in part if not wholly, supposed increments in measured product per head.

If American production and behavior were oriented to real excellence and beauty, aesthetic quality would be stressed far more, and mere quantity far less, than it is in present-day American society. Moreover, if aesthetic and related values were given greater support than at present, resources would be diverted away from population growth—much of it blind and pointless—and to the service of beauty and excellence. In consequence,

22. A. J. Lotka used these words in a slightly different connection in his "Contact Points of Population Study with Related Branches of Science," *Proceedings of the American Philosophical Society,* LXXX, No. 4, 1939, pp. 625–26.

the rate of population growth, underpinned as it is in part by band-wagon attitudes, would fall, here as well as abroad, and now instead of in the future when growing scarcity of growth-limiting factors had finally made itself felt.

Were there greater emphasis upon questions stressed by exponents of optimum theory, and were their modes of thought more common, adequate attention might be given to the role of aesthetic values in economic-demographic development. It would then be recognized that the aesthetic component might be an important element in a system of values, in which event this element might be both an important determinant of population growth and a variable modifiable through population growth.[23]

Before I close I must indicate how the qualitative composition of a population tends to be affected when the tastes of its elite undergo proletarianization and their values become vulgarized. This vulgarizing process, to which Toynbee[24] has called attention, entails a decline in the importance that a people attaches to the creative and value-imposing role of the elite, and to excellence in general as distinguished from excellence in a restricted number of particulars. Such a pseudo-orthogenetic drift, once it gets under way, becomes cumulative, particularly in societies of the sort that Pareto has described as fox-dominated: lowered tastes permeate environments in which children are reared, and these environments in turn produce children with perhaps even lower tastes. When this state of affairs becomes widespread, it is not easy to give selective preference to excellence, whether of genetic or of euthenic origin. Eugenic programs are not likely to prove effective, therefore, in the face of a declension in popular emphasis upon excellence and aesthetic values. Jefferson's natural aristoi are not likely to flourish in a world of mass-men. Under the circumstances it is hardly to be expected that reproductive selection will be of a sort to favor the maintenance of excellence, or the strengthening of aesthetic values.

V. Conclusion

I have come to the end of my tale. You may respond to it as men reportedly responded to Cassandra's. Should you, however, require a tranquilizer, be assured that you are in a state in which most people will be thirty to forty years from now when we are 300 instead of only 170 million. But perhaps it is better to conclude in the words of Thomas Gray:

> . . . Why should they know their fate,
> Since sorrow never comes too late . . . ?

23. On the optimum see H. Leibenstein, *A Theory of Economic-Demographic Development*, Princeton, 1954, chap. 9; also my "Welfare Economics and the Problem of Overpopulation," *Scientia*, LXXXIX, 1954, pp. 128ff., 166ff.

24. See A. J. Toynbee, *A Study of History*, V, London, 1939, pp. 188ff., 445–79.

Population Change: Cause, Effect, Indicator

> *It is possible to study a given problem, in some degree of approximation, without first taking into account the infinity of factors that are needed for a perfectly precise prediction of any given result.* — David Bohm, in *Causality and Chance in Modern Physics*, p. 14.*

Population movements are of significance to the student of economic growth because population change and economic change interact. Population change may function as cause, as effect, and as equilibrating agent when economic growth is under way. It may serve also as an indicator of the behavior of phenomena connected with economic growth, provided that adequate allowance is made for the great changes that have taken place since (say) 1700 in demographic and output-producing processes and in the variables connecting or conditioning them.

*London, 1953.

Bibliographical Note:

I have made very great use of J. R. Russell, "Late Ancient and Medieval Population," *Transactions of the American Philosophical Society*, n.s., XLVIII, Part 2 (June, 1958): idem, *British Medieval Population* (Albuquerque, 1948); Roger Mols, S. J., *Introduction à la démographie historique des villes d'Europe du XIVe au XVIIIe siècle*, 3 vols. (Louvain, 1953–1956).

I have also made considerable use of the following works:

W. Abel, *Die Wüstungen des ausgehenden Mittelalters* (Jena, 1943), and "Bevölkerungsgang und Landwirtschaft im ausgehenden Mittelalter im Lichte der Preis- und Lohnbewegung," *Schmollers Jahrbuch*, LVIII 1 (1934), 33–62.

E. H. Phelps Brown and Sheila V. Hopkins, "Wage-rates and Prices: Evidence for Population Pressure in the Sixteenth Century," *Economica*, XXIV, No. 96 (1957), 289–306, and "Builders' Wage-rates, Prices and Population: Some Further Evidence," *ibid.*, XXVI, No. 101 (1959), 18–38.

Cambridge Economic History of Europe, I–II (Cambridge, 1941, 1952); F. de Dainville, "Grandeur et population des villes au XVIIIe siècle," *Population*, XIII, 3 (1958), 459–480.

L. I. Dublin et al., *Length of Life*, rev. ed. (New York, 1949); J. D. Durand, "The Population Statistics of China A.D. 2–1953," *Population Studies*, XIII, 3 (1960), 209–256.

P. M. Hauser and O. D. Duncan, eds., *The Study of Population* (Chicago, 1959); J. T. Krause, "Changes in English Fertility and Mortality," *Economic History Review*, XI, 1 (1958), 52–70.

Simon Kuznets, "Quantitative Aspects of the Economic Growth of Nations," *Economic Development and Cultural Change*, V, 1 (1956); Friedrich Lütge, "Das 14./15. Jahrhundert in der Sozial- und Wirtschaftsgeschichte," *Jahrbücher für Nationalökonomie und Statistik*, CLXII, Heft 3 (1950), 161–213; Richard Nelson, "Growth Models and the Escape from the Low-Level Equilibrium Trap: The Case of Japan," *Economic Development and Cultural Change*, VIII, 4 (1960), 378–388.

Ping-ti Ho, *Studies in the Population of China* 1368–1953 (Cambridge, 1959); J. J. Spengler and O. D. Duncan, eds., *Demographic Analysis* (Glencoe, 1956); Brinley Thomas, ed., *The Economics of International Migration* (London, 1958); United Nations, *Demographic Yearbook*.

I. Types of Population Change

Population movements assume three main forms.

Form (i), change in an area's population, results because births (deaths) exceed deaths (births), and this excess is not offset by net migration.

Form (ii), redistribution of population in space, results when persons immigrating into (emigrating from) an area exceed in number those emigrating from (immigrating into) it, and their arrival (departure) does not generate offsetting changes in fertility.

Form (iii), change in the proportions in which a population is distributed among social or demographic categories, may be affected or even dominated by migratory or reproductive selection. Disbalance in sex composition, generally under the empire of sexually selective migration, in the past was occasioned much more than now by sexual selection in survivorship. Change in genetical structure (i.e., changes in gene or genotypic frequencies) is dominated by reproduction selection, since a given genetically distinguishable fraction of a population (say, a cohort) may give rise to a disproportionate fraction of its successor population. The composition of a population's values and aspirations may be affected similarly, though never so completely. Changes in racial structure may result from both migratory and reproductive selection.

The change in composition of most concern in this essay, that in age structure, results in the long run from changes in mortality and/or fertility, though it can be produced in the short run by migratory selection. Change in age composition exemplifies, as probably does change in genetic structure, a type of demographic change that has become significant only in modern times. Before 1800 changes in fertility and mortality seldom were sufficiently marked and persistent to modify age composition greatly, though they might augment natural increase. Gross reproduction rates usually fell within the range 2.5–3. Life was typically short; "death was at the center of life, as the cemetery was at the center of the village." "Average durations of life in excess of 30–35 years were exceptional, and life expectancies of 20–30 years were the norm."[1] Not until the 1700s, if then, did this norm begin to be exceeded significantly. The ratio of persons aged 15–59 to all persons in a stable population would increase only about 5–6 percent in consequence of a decline in gross reproduction from 3 to 2.5; it

---

1. The quotations are from J. Fourastié, "De la vie traditionelle à la vie tertiaire," *Population,* XIV, 3 (1959), 418, and from A. J. Coale, "Increases in Expectation of Life and Population Growth," in Union internationale pour l'etude scientifique de la population, *International Population Conference* (Vienna, 1959), p. 36. See also J. D. Durand, "Mortality Estimates from Roman Tombstone Inscriptions," *American Journal of Sociology,* LXV, 4 (1960), 365–373; works of Mols and Russell.

would decline only about 5 percent as the result of an increase in life expectancy at birth from 20–25 years to 30–35 years.[2]

II. Population Change as Cause

The role of population change as a causal agency in economic growth may be dealt with in stimulus-response terms. The responding is done by three sets of decision-makers (households, firms, and agencies of the state) whose relevant responding behavior is dealt with in Sub-section II.B. The stimuli to which these decision-makers respond are changes in the macro-economic environment in which they carry on economic activity. The stimuli or changes of concern in Sub-section II.A (which follows) are those produced in this macro-economic environment by population movements. The significance attached by decision-makers to these changes, together with their responses thereto, is conditioned by variables or constraints which lie outside the stimulus-response circuit proper and which may be treated as exogenous elements. These intermediate variables tend to change in character and importance over time even as do components of the macro-economic environment and capacities of decision-makers.

A. Macro-Economic Environment

One may distinguish at least ten dimensions of a modern macro-economic environment which are sensitive to population change, and to modifications in which modern economic decision-makers are likely to be sensitive. Because population growth has been the rule in modern times, attention will be focused upon the effects of population increase instead of upon the effects of population decrease, even though the latter may differ from the former in more than mere change of sign.

Empirical treatment of interaction between changes in population and changes in various dimensions of a population's macro-economic environment is handicapped in two ways. First, the quantitative data available seldom fit nicely into the analytical categories or boxes employed by economists. Second, relations and findings are often space-bound or time-bound. Economies have changed greatly in organization, structure, technology, and resource base, and decision-makers have experienced great increases in the range of choice open to them. As a result the comparative importance of the ten dimensions discussed below has changed markedly over time. Only dimension 3 was more important formerly than now; dimensions 4, 9, and 10 were less significant formerly; dimensions 1–2, 5–8 were probably of little significance until modern times.

2. United Nations, *The Aging of Populations and Its Economic and Social Implications* (Population Studies, No. 26) (New York, 1956), pp. 26–27.

1. *Producer-population ratio.* The ratio of persons of productive age in a population to the whole of that population depends (*ceteris paribus*) solely upon its age composition. This ratio, representable (say) by the fraction of a population in the age group 15–59, is not often greatly affected by migration even in the short run, though it was so affected in nineteenth century America and other newly settled lands. It declines as mortality falls; e.g., about 6–7 percent when life expectancy at birth rises in a stable population from 35 to 60 years. It increases as fertility falls; e.g., about 10–12 percent when the gross reproduction rate declines from 2.5 to 1.5. It varies little from one stable population to another, the fraction aged 15–60 always approximating six-tenths.[3]

During the past 160 years increase in the average duration of life has largely counterbalanced such improvement in age composition as is attributable to decline in fertility. For example, given a gross reproduction rate of 2.5 and a life expectancy of 30 years as of 1800, and corresponding values of 1.25 and 70 as of 1960, the ratio would have increased only a percent or so. Had gross reproduction not declined as postulated, the relative number of persons aged 15–59 would have been about 11 percent lower. Should life-expectancy be extended appreciably beyond 70, with gross reproduction given, the relative number of persons aged 15–59 would decline accordingly. Average income would be adversely affected since, as Johansen found, the upper limit of productive ages needs to rise in order that increase in average lifetime may appreciably elevate average income.[4]

The economic significance of the ratio of persons aged 15–59 to the total population is affected by the correlation obtaining between age and labor-force participation and by that found between age and productivity among persons participating in the labor force. While these correlations depend largely upon a country's technology, educational composition, industrial structure, degree of urbanization, income levels, and social-security conventions, they are affected also by factors responsible for increase in life expectancy. These factors make for decline in morbidity, for increase in a population's general health, and, hence, for increase in its capacity to work hard and regularly. Increase in life expectancy, unlike increase in fertility, is thus accompanied, within limits, by a compensatory change in the working capacity of labor-force participants.

2. *Dependency ratio.* The ratio of persons of unproductive age to those of productive age (say, of persons aged under 15 and over 65 to those be-

3. *Ibid.*, pp. 26–27; see also Conseil National de Statistique du Brésil, "Sur la durée moyenne de la vie économiquement active," in United Nations, *Proceedings of the World Population Conference, 1954*, III (New York, 1955), 370–381.

4. Coale, *op. cit.*, pp. 38–41; Leif Johansen, "Death Rates, Age Distribution, and Average Income," *Population Studies*, XI, 1 (1957), 77; Spengler and Duncan, *op. cit.*, pp. 497–517.

tween 15–64) fell in most developed countries between 1800 and 1950 when it approximated 0.54. It was only about two-thirds as high as that found in the underdeveloped world (around 0.81 in 1950).[5] Eventually, of course, declining mortality counterbalances improvement occasioned by declining fertility; e.g., in a stable population with a gross reproduction rate of 1.5 and a life expectancy of 70.2, the ratio differs little from that found in a stable population with corresponding values of 2.5 and 30.

Difficulties attendant upon the supply of education in high-fertility countries may be represented by the ratio of persons aged 15–64 to those under 15. This ratio, in the neighborhood of 1.3 in such countries, is about half that found in low-fertility countries. It thus takes about twice as large a fraction of the labor force in a high-fertility as in a low-fertility country to supply comparable education (e.g., 4 percent of the labor force as compared with 2 percent, given a pupil-teacher ratio of 20 to 1). The advantage low-fertility countries enjoy in respect of teacher-supply is partly offset by the greater cost of supporting their aged; it could be wholly offset, given sufficiently high life expectancy.

3. *Man-land ratio.* Because population growth, together with net immigration, increases the ratio of population to land and to other raw-material sources, it may depress output per variable input in affected industries. Inasmuch as outlay upon raw materials other than products of land, though of increasing importance since the mid-nineteenth century, still remains small in relation to gross national product, the impact of population growth upon the availability of raw materials may be treated in terms of the man-land ratio, and agricultural land may be assigned the role played by limitational factors in demographic models.

Population growth elevates the demand curve for output into whose production the services of agricultural land enter. Accordingly, if unexploited sources of these services (similar to sources already in use) are not easily accessible, population growth tends to be followed by increase in the intensity with which land is utilized. In consequence variable inputs per unit of output increase at the margin and (*ceteris paribus*) output per worker in the economy as a whole falls; or, if technical progress is being realized, variable inputs per unit of output do not decline as much as they might otherwise have done.

This statement was applicable in Malthus' day and long before.[6] It remains applicable in various densely populated countries in which agricul-

5. United Nations, *The Aging of Populations,* pp. 8–9, 15; also V. G. Valaoras, "A Reconstruction of the Demographic History of Modern Greece," *Milbank Memorial Fund Quarterly,* XXXVIII, 2 (1960), 128.

6. See Colin Clark, *Conditions of Economic Progress,* 2nd ed. (London, 1951), pp. 225–226; W. R. Robinson, "Money, Population and Economic Change in Late Medieval Europe," and M. M. Postan's reply, *Economic History Review,* XII, 1 (1959), 63–82.

tural land has not diminished in importance and the agricultural labor force has not yet begun to decline appreciably.[7] It has proven of use in the analysis of income determination in agriculture (though at times movement of capital into low-wage areas can be more important than movement of labor out of these areas),[8] and it helps to explain migration from land-short to land-long regions and countries. It is pertinent to the utilization of non-agricultural land, though difficult to employ empirically because of imperfections in the urban property market, and because in many countries the land absorbed by urbanization, recreation, and transportation still forms only a small fraction (about 5 percent in the U.S.A.) of that used in the supply of forest and farm products. Comparison over time of the role played by urbanization in making for economy in the use of non-agricultural land is complicated by the fact that change in urban transport has greatly modified the urban population-land ratio (which is usually lower today than it was in ancient and medieval times, or in the eighteenth century when it often rose above earlier levels).

4. *Structure of demand.* The composition of demand reflects the incidence of many forces, among them rate of population growth and age composition of population. Under *ceteris paribus* conditions an increase in the requirement of some products (e.g., food) is associated with increase in population, and of others (e.g., dwelling units, furnishings), with increase in number of households. Population growth particularly stimulates the consumption of products, the elasticity of household demand for which is below unity, and the absorption of the services of lumpy products, the elasticity of whose supply is likely to be low periodically in a slowly expanding economy. Population growth may shape demand indirectly in so far as demand is a function of population concentration and such concentration is a function of size of population. Changes in age composition affect the structure of demand in two ways: by their impact upon man's age-connected needs, and by modifying the ratio of households to population. The incidence of population movements, both upon investment in population-sensitive capital and upon the structure of demand in general, tends to be reflected, albeit imperfectly, in the composition of gross national product so long as consumer sovereignty and freedom of choice prevail (as is unlikely in state-dominated economies).[9]

7. See B. F. Hoselitz, "Population Pressure, Industrialization and Social Mobility," *Population Studies*, XI, 1 (1957), 124–127.

8. Frank T. Bachmura, "Man-Land Equalization through Migration," *American Economic Review*, XLIX, 5 (1959), 1004–1017; G. H. Borts, "Returns Equalization and Regional Growth," *ibid.*, L, 2 (1960), 319–347.

9. Simon Kuznets, "Long Swings in the Growth of Population and Related Economic Variables," *Proceedings of the American Philosophical Society*, CII, 1 (1958), 33–35, 49; Clark, *Conditions*, p. 410.

Here structure of demand is described as mirroring the impact of population change. This structure also mirrors the impact of technological, income, and related changes. These in turn may modify the response of population movements to changes in per capita income.

5. *Time horizon of decision-makers.* When a population is growing, the time horizons of decision-makers tend to be longer than when it is not growing. This is true of entrepreneurial and governmental decision-makers and it may be true of household decision-makers. For a prospectively positive rate of population growth projects the impact of currently utilized resources farther into the future than does a prospectively zero rate of population growth. On balance, the prospect of population growth probably diminishes the development-retarding influence of uncertainty respecting the future, since it tends to swell entrepreneurial estimates of future demand more than entrepreneurial estimates of future supply.

6. *Ratio of ex-ante investment to ex-ante saving.* Population growth tends to increase this ratio. Equipping increments to a population with industrial, consumers', and public capital requires investment; a 1 percent rate of population growth will absorb savings supplied by a 3–5 percent rate of saving. At the same time the addition of children to a household, income being given, tends to reduce its capacity to save and its actual rate of saving.

7. *Labor-supply-demand relations.* When a population is growing appreciably (instead of remaining approximately stationary), its dependency ratio is comparatively high and its relative number of persons of productive age is comparatively low. On the assumption that the size of a country's labor force corresponds closely to the size of its population, one would therefore expect the ratio of a country's labor force to its population to be inversely associated with its rate of natural increase. Labor-force participation, together with the supply of labor, is not entirely under the governance of age composition, however, although in a number of advanced countries the ratio of the labor force to the population of working age seems not to vary greatly.[10] Labor force data reveal much international disparity in the labor-force-population ratio which cannot be attributed to disparity in age composition; but these data, together with the economies to which they relate, are too heterogeneous to permit precise isolation of the demographic and economic influences at work.

An increase in the dependency ratio may give rise to a certain amount of compensatory change and it tends to do so. In most countries employed workers can easily supply additional man-hours, since they work far fewer

10. C. D. Long, *The Labor Force under Changing Income and Employment* (Princeton, 1958), Chs. 1, 5–7, 12–13.

hours than they are capable of working (e.g., in 1950 the work-week averaged 40 and 48 hours, respectively, in the U.S.A. and Europe; in 1850–90, 62–70 and 69–84 hours); much larger numbers of women can participate in the labor force than do; and entry into the labor force can be accelerated and withdrawal delayed. There is, in short, a reserve of labor power that may be tapped.

A rise in the dependency ratio may be interpreted as a rightward shift in the potential demand curve for labor that will not be met by the existing labor force should its demand for income in terms of effort not be such as to generate a fairly elastic supply of man-hours. Then additional man-hours must be sought elsewhere, either through the employment of additional women, or, as happens in underdeveloped agricultural countries, by deferring retirement and reducing the age of entry into the labor force.[11] Undoubtedly, if increase in the number of dependents per household reduces per capita income therein, or greatly slows down its advance, many households will be disposed to supply more man-hours even at current wage-rates, by working longer hours or by setting more of their members to work. This disposition operates to slow down the tendency of the average number of man-hours worked per adult to fall, and it could even increase it.

The increasing entry of women into the labor force appears to be dominated by forces other than changes in age-composition and in number of dependents per family. It has accompanied decline in the participation of males in the labor force as well as decline in both fertility and the length of the standard work-week. It has been governed, above all, by the spread of industrialization, modernization, and urbanization.[12]

8. *Flexibility.* Population growth makes for greater flexibility in an economy so long as overall population density remains below levels at which constraints on freedom of choice are deemed increasingly necessary, given prevailing technology. Underlying this greater flexibility is the fact that, when population is growing, additions to demand and supply are more important, in comparison with replacements (of products no longer considered serviceable), than when a population is stationary. For then gross national product, capital and wealth, and the labor force are growing faster, with the result that adjustments to technical progress, style and fashion change, purposeful obsolescence, etc., are easier to accomplish. Moreover, since entrepreneurs seemingly assume population growth to augment demand more than supply, they are more inclined to make adjustments, to undertake

11. *Ibid.,* pp. 72–82; J. D. Durand, "Population Structure as a Factor in Manpower and Dependency Problems of Under-developed Countries," *Population Bulletin of the United Nations,* No. 3 (1953), pp. 1–16, esp. 6–8, 13.

12. United Nations, *The Determinants and Consequences of Population Trends* (Population Studies, No. 17) (New York, 1953), pp. 200–203; Long, *op. cit.,* Ch. 1; C. E. V. Leser, "Trends in Woman's Work Participation," *Population Studies,* XII, 2 (1958), 100–110.

new and relatively untried ventures, and to count on population growth to correct overestimates of future demand.

(i) Suppose that the average life of gross national product is 5 years and that per capita income is increasing 2 percent per year. Then, if population is stationary, the ratio of additions (i.e., increment in total realized demand or output) to replacements will approximate 10 percent. This ratio becomes 15 percent if population and the labor force are growing 1 percent per year. Now suppose a two-percent-per-year decline in the per capita demand for a given product, or for the labor incorporated into it. The 1 percent increase in population will offset half this decline and thus make the required adjustment to the decline slower and, hence, somewhat easier.

(ii) Suppose a stationary male population with a life expectancy of 70. Each year approximately 2 percent of the labor force withdraw from it for reasons of death, retirement, and disability, and their places are taken by an equal number of males newly entering the labor force. Accordingly, in the absence of recruits, the set of individuals attached to a given employment would diminish 2 percent in the first year and at progressively higher rates in subsequent years. The males newly entering the labor force (but not shrinking employments) constitute a mobile reserve whose members enter expanding employments and enable these to grow even though the aggregate male labor force remains unchanged. This reserve would be appreciably larger, however, if the labor force were growing 1 percent per year, and it would accordingly be somewhat easier to keep workers distributed optimally among employments. How important this advantage is turns on the extent to which the younger members of the labor force are interoccupationally mobile when its total membership remains constant.

(iii) When a population is growing, its aggregate stock of capital and durable wealth grows faster than when its numbers are stationary, though probably not enough faster to make capital and wealth per head grow faster. This tendency is associated with the fact that income growth is positively correlated with population growth, and that capital needs to be provided for increments in the population as well as for improvement of the capital-population ratio; and it is somewhat reenforced by the fact that the ratio of capital-replacement to depreciation varies inversely with the rate of growth of gross national product.[13] The average age of equipment in use will be somewhat lower, therefore, and a larger fraction of the stock of equipment will incorporate recent "know-how," given that the economy is technically progressive. Moreover, since a larger fraction of the stock of capital equipment will have been installed recently, its composition will be better adapted to current demands. In consequence of the seemingly greater opportunity to install new equipment, the rate of innovation may be somewhat higher, and, as a result, the rate of invention would tend to be higher.

13. E. D. Domar, *Essays in the Theory of Economic Growth* (New York, 1957), Ch. 7.

An economy tends (*ceteris paribus*) to be technologically more progressive if its population is growing instead of non-growing. The pattern of invention will not be quite the same, however, since invention is more likely to be capital-saving when the rate of population growth is relatively high than when it is relatively low. Furthermore, in so far as economic fluctuation is associated with fluctuation in the output of durable assets, increase of the latter in relative importance could intensify economic fluctuation.

9. *Size of population versus size of country.* It is essential to distinguish between size of population and size of country. Within limits increase in size of a country's population permits release of economies associated with increase in scale, division of labor, and so on. Moreover, it is accompanied by increase in the ratio of the size of relevant regional or national markets to the capacity of firms of optimum size in various industries. In consequence, elasticity of demand and (probably) industrial elasticity of supply increase, with the result that the economy becomes more competitive and inputs are utilized under more nearly optimal conditions. Population growth tends to accentuate this tendency.

In contrast, with overall population density given, increase in size of a country is accompanied, within limits, by increase in the size and diversity of its economy. It is accompanied by increase in the size of the stream of inputs that may be made subject to a single and essentially sovereign set of market and political mechanisms which, acting in combination, are capable of optimally transforming these inputs into output. For, as a rule, under otherwise similar conditions, mobility of factors is greater within than between countries; moreover, competition is more intense, and entrepreneurial estimates of profit-prospects tend to be more favorable in larger than in smaller economies. Presumably a point might be reached when further increase in the size of a country and its economy would no longer be a source of economic advantage, though it might not yet be a source of disadvantage.[14]

10. *Population concentration.* The forces which make for population growth also make for population concentration and, hence, for such economic changes as are associated therewith. Two processes are involved. (i) Expansion of the agricultural sector is limited (in the absence of exportation) by the inelasticity of domestic demand for agricultural produce. Accordingly, the (surplus) agricultural population beyond what is required (given current technology) to supply a community's demand for produce must seek employment outside agriculture. Much of this surplus, which functions as an industrial reserve army, tends to emigrate to the economy's non-rural communities, or abroad where it may increase demand for the

14. Austin Robinson, ed., *The Consequences of the Size of Nations* (London, 1960).

output of these communities. So long as the rural population is much larger than the non-rural and rural natural increase is relatively high, the rural industrial reserve army declines very slowly and the flow of rural migrants into the non-rural sector serves to hold down non-rural wages and to augment non-rural profits; this circumstance has been largely responsible for the slowness with which wages have risen in the early stages of industrialization. This flow may also intensify and protract urban boom conditions, thereby making for greater contraction and, hence, for greater amplitude of fluctuation.[15]

(ii) The migrating surplus, together with such population growth as it subsequently generates, tends to become concentrated in relatively large urban centers, though not in a regular enough way to permit simple formulation of the association between the size of population and summary indices of the concentration of non-rural population.[16]

B. *Micro-Economic Response*

We now inquire into the probable responses of strategically situated decision-makers to the dimensional changes, or stimuli, just described. These decision-makers are of three sorts: (1) family households; (2) business firms whose primary concern is the profitable transformation of inputs into output; and (3) governmental agencies empowered to determine how certain inputs are used. We are here concerned only with responses affecting the supply and/or the use of inputs over which the decision-makers exercise control in the shorter run.

1. *Household.* Changes in a population's rate of growth and age composition affect the disposition of households to supply labor-service in two ways. (i) An increase in the number of children, or dependent members, of a household, tends to increase its aggregate outlay upon consumption, to diminish its current rate of saving, and to affect the uses to which its savings are put.[17] Such increase is roughly equivalent, in analytical terms, to a decrease in family income. It often animates a household's non-dependent members (other than mother) to supply more labor-service at given prices than they

15. Dorothy S. Thomas, *Social and Economic Aspects of Swedish Population Movements* (New York, 1941), Chs. 8–9, 12; D. Mazumdar, "Under-employment in Agriculture and the Industrial Wage Rate," *Economica*, XXVI, 4 (1959) 328–340; N. Georgescu-Roegen, "Economic Theory and Agrarian Economics," *Oxford Economic Papers*, XII, 1 (1960), 11–29; Nicholas Kaldor, *Essays on Economic Stability and Growth* (London, 1960), pp. 288–297.

16. Otis Dudley Duncan et al., *Metropolis and Region* (Baltimore, 1960).

17. E.g., see R. W. Goldsmith, Dorothy S. Brady, and Horst Mendershausen, *A Study of Saving in the United States*, III (Princeton, 1956), 202–223; A. M. Henderson, "The Cost of a Family," *Review of Economic Studies*, XVII, 2 (1949–50), 127–148; *idem* (with J. Hajnal), "The Economic Position of the Family," in Royal Commission on Population, *Papers*, V (London, 1950), 9–19; Janet A. Fisher, "Postwar Changes in Income and Savings among Consumers in Different Age Groups," *Econometrica*, XX, 1 (1952), 47–70.

would otherwise have been ready to supply. It may even affect the labor-service supply curve of the mother similarly, though in lesser measure and usually after the children have advanced in age sufficiently to diminish the mother's double burden of caring for them and working outside the household. Unfortunately, empirical data bearing upon the shifts of household labor-service supply curves are not abundant, particularly those relating to women. For researchers have been largely concerned with the correlation between membership of wives in the labor force and their relative infertility, and with that between number of children and freedom of wives to participate in the labor force.[18]

(ii) Change in the dependency ratio tends to affect fullness of employment under *ceteris paribus* conditions. Thus, a rise in this ratio tends to accompany an increase in the rate of natural increase and to be accompanied by an upswing in the potential demand for labor-service. This upswing serves to offset the upswing in supply discussed under (i), particularly since the latter has been partly counterbalanced already by the tendency of motherhood to remove women temporarily from the labor force. The negative income effect of the increase in dependents reduces the chance that the labor supply curve will be backward bending in the relevant range.

2. *Business-firm.* Whether the effects described eventuate in greater employment depends upon the response business firms make to increases in potential demand for labor-service associated with increases in the dependency ratio and in the need for additional durable assets. For the business firm will be responding to all the changes in the economy's macroeconomic dimensions described under (A), together with its estimate of the probable response of competing and complementary business firms to these same changes. In the absence of a temporary downswing in overall economic activity, movement to a higher level of fertility is more likely than movement to a lower level of fertility to actualize potential demand for labor, at least in developed countries. After population growth has become stable and an economy has become adjusted thereto, however, the significance of the rate of population growth diminishes, though not enough to offset entirely (under *ceteris paribus* conditions) the tendency of a higher rate of growth to be more favorable than a lower rate to full employment (given a sufficiency of capital).

3. *State-agencies.* The responses described under (1) and (2) are condi-

18. E.g., see Jeanne Ridley, "Number of Children Expected in Relation to Non-Familial Activities of the Wife," *Milbank Memorial Fund Quarterly,* XXXVII, 3 (1959), 277–296; R. K. Kelsall and Sheila Mitchell, "Married Women and Employment in England and Wales," *Population Studies,* XIII, 1 (1959), 23, 30–31; Alain Girard, "Le budget-temps de la femme mariee dans les agglomerations urbaines," *Population,* XIII, 4 (1958), 590–618; Durand, "Population Structure as a Factor . . . ," *loc. cit.,* p. 7; Long, *op. cit.,* pp. 114–116, 123–133.

tioned by the responses made by agencies of the state, which in the aggregate enjoy considerable autonomy. Let C, G, and I represent, in aggregate terms, private demand for consumer goods and services, governmental absorption of goods and services, and private investment (or offsets to "savings"); and let these aggregates be expressed in terms of average hours of labor-service, of which L would normally be forthcoming under conditions of full employment. Accordingly, if L should exceed $C + G + I$, it would be necessary only to manipulate the magnitude and the content of G to eliminate the disparity. Of course, the impact of such manipulation upon the capacity of the economy to produce in the future would depend largely, as would its impact upon population growth, upon the content of the change made in the magnitude of G. Similarly, the capacity of the state to manipulate G would depend *ceteris paribus* upon the nature of the state's institutional and agency structure. A state's agencies thus may constitute an effective lever wherewith to supplement or counterbalance the response-mechanisms discussed under (1) and (2). Our discussion has run in terms of sustaining full employment. It could also run in terms of preventing inflation, since population growth might generate increases in I in excess of the amount of savings the economy stood ready to supply; in this event C or G might be reduced, or L could be augmented.

III. Population Change as Effect

Migration, mortality, and fertility are sensitive to economic change. Regarding migration it need only be said, that in the absence of restraints, a person will move from his current situation in space to some other if he expects his economic welfare to be increased thereby in sufficient measure more than to offset the costs of movement and the uncertainties involved. Before 1800, legal and other restraints, costs of movement, and uncertainties respecting what a migrant might achieve probably operated, together with the fact that income disparity was much smaller than in modern times, to limit individual and very small-scale migration. As these conditions changed, largely because of changes in the macro-economic environment, the disposition to migrate was affected accordingly.

The relationship between economic conditions and mortality is not a simple one. First, this relationship may change as a result of changes in the socio-economic composition of a population, since mortality usually is higher among the relatively less well rewarded or housed elements of the population. Second, mortality may eventually prove sensitive to a cumulation of minor economic changes, though not to any one such change. Third, mortality may be sensitive to a major economic change (e.g., famine), but not to minor changes; this sort of relationship is likely when economic conditions are hard and mortality already is very high (e.g., life expectancy in the low 20s). Fourth, mortality may no longer be very sensitive to minor economic changes if economic conditions are very good (as in some modern societies), or if highly effective methods of death control have been introduced (e.g., in post-1930 Ceylon). Finally, a great deal of mortality has been attributable to catastrophes (war, famine, pestilence, etc.) which, while they produced adverse economic effects, were only partly if at all of economic origin. Most important of these catastrophes was epidemic pestilence and the pronounced upsurges in abnormal mortality which accompanied it. Such mortality greatly reduced Europe's population several times (e.g., A.D. 200–600, and again in the fourteenth century); in fact, Europe's population did not begin to grow at a sustained and accelerated rate until in the eighteenth century when pestilential mortality greatly declined. Such mortality continued, however, to interrupt growth in large non-European countries (e.g., India, China).[19]

Even though the relationship between economic conditions and mortality is not a simple or linear one, a portion of mortality has been quite sensitive to economic change. So long as population remained largely at the mercy of the elements, as was true even in eighteenth century Europe, a turn for the worse in weather and other economically-oriented conditions would be accompanied by marked upturns in mortality. In the course of this century, however, at least in England, mortality began to fall significantly as a result of improvement in economic conditions, and this double improvement continued, though not without interruption, throughout the nineteenth century.[20]

Gross reproduction has always been somewhat subject to social control, but, prior to the contraceptive revolution of the nineteenth century, it could not be modified greatly or rapidly. The maximum gross reproduction rate may be put at 4; this implies crude birth rates of roughly 60–64 and 56–57, respectively, in stable populations with life expectancies of 20–30 and 40–50 years.[21] Given a gross reproduction rate of 4 and an average effective reproductive life of 22–23 years, a representative woman completing this period would average a birth every 2.8–2.9 years. Even though a married woman

19. Karl F. Helleiner, "The Vital Revolution Reconsidered," *Canadian Journal of Economics and Political Science,* XXIII, 1 (1957), 1–9; *idem,* "Population Movements and Agrarian Depression in the Later Middle Ages," *ibid.,* XVII, 4, 368–377; *idem, Readings in Economic History* (Toronto, 1946), Introduction; G. Utterström, "Some Population Problems in Pre-Industrial Sweden," *Scandinavian Historical Review,* II, 2 (1954), 103–165; works of Mols and Russell.

20. E.g., see Helleiner, "The Vital Revolution Reconsidered," *loc. cit.,* pp. 1–2; M. M. Postan and J. Titow, "Heriots and Prices on Winchester Manors," *Economic History Review,* XI, 3 (1959), 399–410; J. Titow, "Evidence of Weather in the Account Rolls of the Bishopric of Winchester, 1209–1350," *ibid.,* XII, 3, 362–365.

21. Joseph W. Eaton and Albert J. Mayer, *Man's Capacity to Reproduce* (Glencoe, 1954), pp. 38–42; George Sabagh, "The Fertility of the French-Canadian Women during the Seventeenth Century," *American Journal of Sociology,* XLVII, 2 (1942), 683–687; F. Lorimer, *Culture and Human Fertility,* UNESCO (Paris, 1954), Ch. 1.

survived to complete her reproductive period, however, she might have produced less than 8 births. For her period of exposure to reproduction commonly was reduced by deferment of her initial marriage, or by its premature termination (e.g., because of death of spouse, etc.), together with her failure to remarry promptly. How much her production of children would be reduced thereby would depend upon whether or not reduction of exposure at earlier ages diminished fertility more than did reduction at higher ages and on whether this reduction came early (e.g., because of deferment of marriage) or later in her reproductive period (e.g., because of the death of her spouse).[22]

Because of these and other restraints, gross reproduction rates have seldom approximated 4. Prior to the 1800s (when new methods of fertility control became available in medically advanced parts of the world) these rates usually remained within the range 2.5–3.0, yielding birth rates in the 40s. Even so, a rate of population growth of 0.5 to 1.0 percent per year could easily be attained, at least for a short time; a birth rate in the 40s would suffice, given a death rate in the middle or high 30s. Russell's observation that medieval society could produce "more than enough children to maintain its numbers except under the most severe circumstances" seems applicable to the Roman and to many oriental societies.[23]

Of the eleven intermediate variables which, according to Davis and Blake, govern fertility by conditioning exposure to intercourse and conception, together with gestation and successful parturition, only some are *both* significantly sensitive to economic changes and quantitatively important.[24] Involuntary abstinence, voluntary control over fecundity (e.g., by castration), involuntary sterility (apparently somewhat sensitive to economic conditions), coital frequency, and voluntary abstinence within unions (which is greater in preindustrial than in industrial societies) are not of this sort. The adverse effect of unfavorable economic conditions upon foetal viability is partly offset by the resulting reduction in interval between pregnancies. Voluntary control over foetal mortality through recourse to abortion, while sensitive to economic change (among other factors), was prohibited, though not with complete success, in the Christian world as was its functional equivalent, infanticide (a form of mortality). The amount of time spent outside a sexual union by a member of a terminated union depends upon mortality, upon the frequency of separation and divorce, and upon the opportunity of

22. W. Brass, "The Distribution of Births in Human Populations," *Population Studies*, XII, 1 (1958), 56–58, 61–63, 67–68; Chi-Hsien Tuan, "Reproductive Histories of Chinese Women in Rural Taiwan," *ibid.*, pp. 40–50; H. Hyrenius, "Fertility and Reproduction in a Swedish Population Group without Family Limitation," *ibid.*, XII, 2, 121–130; Louis Henry, *Fécondité des mariages* (Paris, 1953), Chs. 7–8; Christopher Tietze, "Reproductive Span and Rate of Reproduction among Hutterite Women," *Fertility and Sterility*, VIII, 1 (1957), 89–97.

23. *Late Ancient and Medieval Population*, p. 22.

24. See Kingsley Davis and Judith Blake, "Social Structure and Fertility: An Analytic Framework," *Economic Development and Cultural Change*, IV, 3 (1956), 211–235.

victims of broken unions to remarry; of these factors the first and the last are somewhat sensitive to economic change.

Three variables, each sensitive to economic affairs and aspirations, have been primarily responsible, along with abortion, for the fact that gross reproduction has usually fallen short of its theoretical maximum. They are contraceptive practice, age of entry into marriage, or other sexual unions, and permanent celibacy. The first of these, while it played a role of some importance before the nineteenth century when folk methods predominated, became quite important only in the later 1800s.[25] Until then deferment of marriage and (in lesser measure) non-marriage constituted the main curbs on fertility. In a society little subject to contraception, postponement of a woman's marriage until in the middle or late 20s might reduce by 1.5–2 or more the number of children she would bear. This curb was primarily operative in those parts of the world (especially Europe) in which the nuclear family predominated and young people could not, as a rule, marry until the prospective spouse had access to support for a family in the form of cultivable land or employment; it sometimes was found, however, even in familistic societies (e.g., Japan). Deferment of marriage was much less common, as was non-marriage, in areas (e.g., much of Asia and Africa) in which the joint family system prevailed and acquisition of economic independence was not a precondition to marriage.[26] In these parts, therefore, fertility usually was higher than in Western Europe, as apparently was mortality.

The fertility-affecting variables which serve, together with mortality, to condition a household's size and composition are interrelated, constituting an equilibrium system that is subject to exogenous constraints and influences. Within a household, therefore, a change in any one of these variables may substitute for a change in another. Similarly, within the world at large one sort of change sometimes offsets another, as when the sometimes greater ease of marriage in cities was offset by the fact that urban mortality commonly exceeded urban natality. In general, the disposition of a household to modify any one fertility- or mortality-affecting variable has been affected by what has taken place in the external economic world, as well as by changes in other variables internal to the household viewed as a system.

Changes in a household's aspirations may greatly modify its disposition to control fertility. Such change is much more characteristic, however, of modern than of traditional or other pre-1800 societies in which very few

25. *Ibid.*, pp. 223–225; works of Russell; United Nations, *The Determinants and Consequences*, pp. 75–77; A. Sauvy, "La prévention des naissances dans la famille," *Population*, XV, 1 (1960), 115–120; Irene B. Taeuber, *The Population of Japan* (Princeton, 1958), pp. 29–31.
26. K. Davis, *The Population of India and Pakistan* (Princeton, 1951), p. 108; Taeuber, *op. cit.*, pp. 30–31, 169; Davis and Blake, *op. cit.*, pp. 214–223; T. H. Hollingsworth, "A Demographic Study of the British Ducal Families," *Population Studies*, XI, 1 (1957), 13–14, 25–26; works of Mols and Russell.

people were optimistic respecting their futures. Before the late eighteenth century the dynamic components of most societies were comparatively small. It was not anticipated that the real income of more than a small fraction of the population would improve appreciably. Not many individuals were likely to be animated by high and rising aspirations, in the light of which their reproductive conduct ought to be determined. Moreover, the likelihood that high aspirations might give rise to "fertility planning" was much reduced by the high mortality prevailing and the consequential inference that mere replacement of a household would probably prove difficult.

Inasmuch as some of the determinants of mortality and the main determinants of fertility are sensitive to changes in economic and related conditions, natural increase will be sensitive thereto. Prior to the nineteenth century, however, mortality was both more volatile than natality and more immediately sensitive to changes in economic conditions. Some mortality (other than infanticide) responded almost tropismatically to economic change, whereas fertility usually responded only in so far as individuals of reproductive age were disposed to modify it through variation in age at marriage or recourse to abortion or contraception. Natural increase, of course, fluctuated more than either fertility or mortality which tended to move in opposite directions as economic conditions changed.

If, for expository convenience, we use the concept population elasticity e (where $e = dp \cdot Y / dY \cdot P$, P denotes aggregate population, and Y denotes some index of aggregate economic conditions such as total output or income), it may be said that prior to the nineteenth century e was positive and probably close to unity except when the movement of population was dominated by abnormal mortality. In the course of this century, however, the value of e fell. For the forces making for increase in Y also made for change in the socio-economic composition of populations, for increasing knowledge of contraception, and for supersession of traditional modes of life by a highly rational one. Within some components of the population, furthermore, materially-oriented aspirations rose faster than income and intensified the pressure households already were under (e.g., because of diminution in infant and child mortality, increase in the number of dependents per household, child labor and related legislation, etc.) to regulate family size.

Decline in e signifies that a population may be escaping from a Malthusian trap in which high fertility keeps household incomes depressed. Escape entails three steps. (i) Income must be made to increase faster than population, by increasing the work-week, by making fuller and more efficient use of available agents of production, and by augmenting savings and importing capital. (ii) This upward movement of income must be sustained by increasing the rate of innovation, the marginal propensity to save, and the capital-labor ratio. (iii) In time fertility must be reduced, since otherwise limitational factors may slow down the increase of income and permit *e* to rise. Step (iii) may prove easier to realize today than formerly because methods of fertility control are much more effective now than formerly, and men are as indisposed as ever to relinquish a scale of living once attained, or even one intensely desired.

Steps (i) and (ii) may prove more difficult to take, however. Today the populations of underdeveloped countries may be increasing 2–3 percent per year, whereas 175 years ago they were increasing 1 percent or less.[27] Today, therefore, increasing per capita income 1 percent per year may call for savings of 9–16 percent of income, whereas before 1800 the bulk of savings (perhaps 3–5 percent) often could be used to increase per capita income. The presence of limitational factors may even operate, especially in densely populated lands, as they often did in less densely peopled pre-1800 economies, to make realization of the required annual increase in output (at least 3–4 percent) difficult. Escape may prove possible, however, through the introduction of tested innovations, through orienting investment to the supply of producer goods, and through the avoidance of unproductive use of those inputs which are not required to satisfy current minimal needs. Even then income may not rise rapidly enough to transform a society's social structure and aspirations and thereby set in motion a pronounced and rapid decline in gross reproduction. Yet it is upon such decline as well as upon initially successful efforts to increase per capita income that escape from a Malthusian trap ultimately depends.

IV. Population Movements as Indicators

Because before 1800 population growth implied income growth and income growth usually signified population growth, certain inferences may be drawn from pre-1800 population movements.

1. Continuing "pull" migration (i.e., movement *toward* centers of attraction) signified rising aggregate and per capita real income, since "free" migrants usually seek higher income and since urban expansion improves the demand for rural produce.

2. Persisting rural population growth in a traditional society (in contradistinction to one capitalistically and rationally organized) has been compatible with overall economic retardation when this growth absorbed the surplus produce that would otherwise have been available to a more dynamic non-rural population.[28]

3. Long-run swings in population have signified swings in the affected economy, though these usually have been partly of demographic origin.

4. In the past when the rate of innovation was much lower than today,

27. Colin Clark, "World Population," *Nature*, CLXXXI (May, 1958), 1235–1236.

population growth, together with its spread, was the main absorber of newly formed capital; it thus tended to stiffen both profits and real interest rates (though the movement of monetary rates was sometimes cushioned by the associated tendency of money prices to fall, as noted in [10] below).

5. A continuing and fairly stable increase in population signified continuing increase in total output and at least the maintenance of per capita income.

6. The gradual slowing down of population growth (e.g., in the late 1200s and early 1300s) signified the increasing operation of formerly quite powerful limitational factors (e.g., diminishing returns in agriculture, deceleration in growth of strategic markets) and approach to a population ceiling fixed largely by the prevailing technology, mode of agricultural organization, and socio-economic structure of society.

7. Inasmuch as the "normal" tendency, in the absence of catastrophe or of economic collapse, was for numbers to grow until the ceiling noted in (6) had been reached, a sharp but non-persisting decline in population, though associated with economic contraction, merely signified the incidence of catastrophes, whereas an initially marked and subsequently persisting decline signified collapse of the existing politico-economic organization.

8. Prior to the nineteenth century persistently falling real wages must usually have signified a rising man-land ratio in agriculture and a turning of the terms of trade against the non-agricultural sector. Of course, as implied in (6), growth of population might long persist before limitational factors became effective and began to depress the marginal productivity of labor and (eventually) real wages.

9. Persisting population growth, particularly when not associated with extension of settlement, signified increase in the real agricultural rental share.

10. Since the movement of aggregate output almost always was positively associated with population growth, such growth tended to make for falling money prices in the absence of sufficient accessions to the stock of hard money. For while increase in the exchange value of the monetary unit usually makes for increasing economy in its use, the resulting increase in velocity could have offset only partially the increasing pressure of the volume of activity upon that of available hard money.

Decline in population and total output produced opposite effects. Rising (falling) prices did not necessarily reflect population growth (decline) since the supply of hard money of standard quality sometimes changed markedly for reasons not closely associated with population movement.[29]

28. N. Keyfitz, "Développement économique et accroissement de population: Un exemple actuel en Indonesie," *Population*, XIII, 3 (1958), 407–433.

29. For an excellent account of price movements see E. J. Hamilton, "The History of Prices before 1750," *XIe Congres Internationale des Sciences Historiques* (Stockholm, 1960), pp. 144–164.

11. While the economic implications of pre-1800 population growth seem clear, interpretation of the impact of population decline is not always easy, since the conditions responsible for this decline may also affect directly the economic variables responding to population decline (e.g., business confidence, money supply, gross interest rates, economic organization).

Even given that these inferences are generally tenable and that demographic indicators may be employed to help determine the current state of economic development of backward economies,[30] it does not follow that inferences may be similarly drawn today, or that quite rigid growth models incorporating population movements are nearly so applicable in today's advanced economies as in yesterday's relatively primitive and static societies. Today the range of choice open to men is much wider than it was before 1800, and the functional connections between population and economic movements are much more variable. Thus, since population growth is now dominated by fertility which is both volatile and relatively unpredictable, the response of population growth to output growth is susceptible of wide variation. Moreover, because technological change plays so large and increasing though somewhat variable a role in the formation of output, and because both the volume and the composition of capital formation may vary greatly, the response of output to population growth is also susceptible of wide variation.

---

30. P. M. Hauser, "Demographic Indicators of Economic Development," *Economic Development and Cultural Change*, VII, 2 (1959) 98–116; E. G. Stockwell, "The Measurements of Economic Development," *ibid.*, VIII, 4 (1960) 419–432.

The Economist and the Population Question*

> *No quantity can increase by compound interest and remain within finite limits.* — Lawrence Dennis
>
> *Man's industrial activities are merely a highly specialized and greatly developed form of the general biological struggle for existence.* — A. J. Lotka
>
> *In Megalopolis the sentiment of friendship wastes away.* — R. M. Weaver

My concern is to put the population question in temporal and statistical perspective. I pass over classical concern lest numbers become excessive and Asian and Roman concern lest they not become extensive enough. I pass over the upward shift of the military and nonmilitary demand for manpower in the Age of Mercantilism and the emergence of a populationist philosophy. I pass over those who after 1750 rejected populationism. I begin with Malthus, at the time of whose birth the world's population numbered just over 750 million, perhaps treble what it was at the start of the Christian era, though growing faster than ever before, now that pestilence had been partially tamed and the supply of the means of existence had become more elastic and more stable.

I. The Malthusian Age: 1800–1930

Malthus may well serve as eponym to the period 1800–1930, since it was he who conceptualized and put into *paradigm* the demographic issues which dominated it. At its start Malthus was warning that an unfettered stork could visit poverty upon most and prevent realization of the aspirations of the Age of Enlightenment. At the period's close the world's rate of population growth was double what it had been in 1800, and its annual increment roughly 22 instead of 4 millions. Meanwhile the world's population had risen from less than a billion to just over 2 billion; that of Europe and the Soviet Union to over a half billion, nearly triple the 1800 figure. Of Europe's population nearly three persons in ten lived in 248 cities of 100,000 and over, compared with only about one in thirty in 18 such cities in 1800. Meanwhile the world's cities of 100,000 and over had risen in number eighteenfold to nearly 700 and their relative population eightfold to 11 per cent of the world total. It is not entirely surprising, therefore, that Alfred Marshall could write in 1920 (*Principles*, preface):

* Presidential address delivered at the Seventy-eighth Annual Meeting of the American Economic Association, New York, December 29, 1965. The author is indebted for suggestions to his colleagues, Ralph Braibanti, F. T. de Vyver, C. B. Hoover, and William Yohe.

In the present age, the opening out of new countries aided by low transport charges on land and sea, has almost suspended the tendency to Diminishing Return . . . and yet, if the growth of population should continue for very long even at a quarter of its present rate, the aggregate rental value of land for all uses . . . may again exceed the aggregate of incomes derived from all other forms of material property.

Nor is it surprising that Malthus's Geometrical Ratio should be rediscovered in the 1920's (39), and that J. M. Keynes could warn that the Malthusian Devil had broken his chains in a world ridden by diminishing returns.** Overpopulated Europe in particular was threatened, he believed. The inequality essential to adequate capital formation was unlikely to be tolerated, and Europe's terms of trade were destined to turn against her, dependent as she was upon produce imported from a New World now become subject to diminishing returns. It was questionable, therefore, if her precarious economy any longer enjoyed a margin of safety against dislocation, a probable sequel to the treaty of Versailles (23). At least four aspects of economists' response to Malthus's *Essay* in this period merit attention.

1. Malthus's *Essay* directed attention to the critical role of limitational factors and to the impact of adverse externalities associated with population growth. His ultimate limitational factor was land or "room." He implied, however, that it could be some other source of man's living budget, should man practice moral restraint. While England's marginal per acre wheat yield was only 8 bushels in 1812, the average having fallen from 24 in 1771 to 22 in 1812 (8, 2nd ed., pp. 225–26), Malthus did not draw upon this sort of evidence. Instead he seems to have reasoned from the limitedness of arable land and its yields to his expositive theorem that the food supply could grow only $1/n$ per quarter-century where n denotes the existing food supply. This model gives a falling average but not finally a falling incremental rate of food and population growth as did P. F. Verhulst's logistic curve, designed in 1838 to reflect the increasing resistance population growth encountered from increasing density and its concomitants.

Malthus's model stressed the services of land. This interpretation is in keeping with K. F. Mather's account of the changes both in man's demands upon his environment and in the nature of his resource limitations. "A hundred years ago, nearly 80 per cent of all the things men used were derived from the plant and animal kingdoms, with only about 20 per cent from the mineral kingdom. Today only about 30 per cent of the things used in industrialized countries come from things that grow; about 70 per cent have their sources in mines and quarries" (25, pp. 55–56). Some present-day economists, of course, take into account all or nearly all services, the demand for which derives significantly from demand for population. They view economic growth as a process of accumulating capital in all its manifold

** Numbers in parentheses indicate references given at conclusion of this essay.

forms (20, Ch. 14), and population growth as a process of transforming population, physical environment, and capital of all sorts, as of given time periods, into population of subsequent time periods. "Life," as A. N. Whitehead (38, p. 160) observed, thus becomes "robbery," with human societies living on other societies and (as A. J. Lotka noted), having triumphed over their subhuman foes, finding themselves pressed by increasing numbers to struggle with one another. Malthus may thus be looked upon as an inspirer of post-Darwinian as well as of Darwinian theories of struggle. Moreover, Malthus, in his rationalization of essential agricultural self-sufficiency, a doctrine that later helped inspire German agricultural protectionism, reveals himself a defender of bastions of strength against both leveling forces and hordes. "When degree is shak'd," he might have said with Shakespeare, "the enterprise is sick."

Malthus's emphasis upon limitations to the augmentability of the food supply was not reasserted again until the close of the century. For, although natality did not begin generally to decline in Europe until in or after the 1870's, and then not enough to affect the rate of population growth significantly, per capita food consumption improved, both because yield per acre had gradually increased and because food, mainly cereal, was imported in large quantity from land-rich Eastern Europe and Europe Overseas as well as from some heavily peopled parts of Asia (14) (8, 3rd ed., pp. 296–301). Toward the end of the nineteenth century, one and one-third centuries after England began to import cereals on balance, Sir William Crookes (1832–1919) warned that the question of the food supply "is of urgent importance today, and it is a life and death question for generations to come. . . . England and all civilized nations stand in deadly peril of not having enough to eat." He pointed to the importance of wheat, the lowness of yields, and the limited additional acreage suited to sowing—conditions that would permit world population to overtake world wheat supplies by 1931. Augmentation of yields and acreage prevented the materialization of Sir William's forecast. J. S. Davis, having reviewed its basis and nonmaterialization, declared in 1932 that "the specter of coming dearth of food is a ghost that deserves to be laid" (13).

The shift in the bias of the resource base from organic to inorganic facilitated a higher rate of development and some economy in transport already near the beginning of the nineteenth century, if not earlier. It did not become pronounced until later in the century, however. Thus, between 1880 and 1937, while world population was growing about two-thirds and its industrial production was almost sextupling, world metal and fuel production increased 606 and 652 per cent, respectively (14) (31, pp. 248–50). The shift, however, added to the fear of classical diminishing returns, the additional fear of mineral depletion, analogue of soil-fertility depletion. Already in 1865 W. S. Jevons forecasted that rising costs of coal attendant upon the working out of the superior seams would depress British industry and trade (19). A quarter-century later, there arose even in the United States concern respecting both soil depletion and unduly rapid mineral exhaustion. This concern contributed to the development of the conservation movement later popularized by anti-Malthusian Theodore Roosevelt.

2. Malthus as well as subsequent writers drew attention to the externalities associated with population growth, many of them adverse. A clear-cut distinction was not initially made, however, between externalities produced directly and externalities produced indirectly through urban concentration. Malthus and his successors hoped to control aggregate growth and thus minimize the impact of adverse externalities—through institutional and related controls of private origin, that channeled costs and benefits to responsible and discretionary individuals and households. He had little confidence in Leviathan. In fact J. S. Mill was almost alone in believing that under communism—albeit small-scale communism rather than present-day bureaucratic socialistic or mixed-economy collectivisms—the feedback system generative of population-control would be much more effective than it was under noncommunism (*Principles*, II, i, 3). Concern regarding externalities associated with urban growth became both more intense and more research-oriented toward the close of the century. Even Marshall manifested such concern (24).

3. In the wake of this growing awareness of externalities there developed interest in improvement of the quality of populations. While few economists had the faith of a Helvetius or a Bentham in the capacity of education to eliminate inequality, not many attached to reproductive selection the importance assigned it by F. Galton's followers or by some exponents of Social Darwinism. After all, it was economic environment with which economists worked, and it was their usual view as well as Marshall's that A. C. Pigou (29, pp. 113–14, 121) expressed when, despite his awareness of the importance of genetic selection, he said, "The environment of one generation *can* produce a lasting result, because it can affect the environment of future generations. Environments, in short, as well as people, have children." He inferred, furthermore, that "improvement in the distribution of the dividend may be expected actually to diminish the proportion of the children born from inferior stocks" whose untrammeled propagation remained "notorious." Pigou seems to have been less alert than Ricardo (*Principles*, Ch. 31), however, to the possible depression of the demand for labor, especially among the inferior members of society, by accumulating capital. Otherwise he might have put more stress upon eugenics as well as upon adverse effects of life in large, input-short families.

4. Corollary to Malthus's thesis is the notion that there exists, under given conditions in a given state, an optimum population size and an optimum population growth rate. J. S. Mill was the first to give some precision to the

former notion. "After a degree of density has been attained, sufficient to allow the principal benefits of combination of labour," wrote Mill in 1848, "all further increase tends in itself to mischief, as regards the average condition of the people." Such density had been attained in England. Mechanical inventions could, of course, increase average income, but they would increase it even more were numbers not to grow (*Principles,* I, xiii, 2–3; IV, vi, 2). Unlike present-day technicians with their dehumanizingly exclusive emphasis upon *know-how,* Mill was concerned also with *know-why* – he was not prepared to trade natural grandeur, solitude, "the spontaneous activity of nature," and other free goods for the junkyards and carscapes and deteriorating landscapes so characteristic of unaesthetic twentieth-century societies seemingly bent upon frustrating Henry Ford's desire that his car give even the man of little means easy access to "God's great open spaces." Mill would probably have endorsed B. A. Weisbrod's suggestion that account be taken of the willingness of nonusers of facilities (e.g., a park) to pay for the option of using them in the future, given that total revenue from users falls short of costs (37).

Mill's view was endorsed 78 years later by A. B. Wolfe, foremost economic demographer, who declared that "economically, the desideratum is . . . to obtain, in return for whatever expenditure of effort the people may regard as normal and proper, the largest permanently practicable, *per capita* product" (15, p. 68). The population permitting this would be of optimum size. Wolfe did not accept, any more than had J. S. Mill, the inference of A. M. Carr-Saunders (6) (and earlier Henry George) that a population normally assumed optimum size. Mill emphasized, as had Jeremy Bentham and others, the need for contraception, a need increasingly stressed during the Malthusian period (18). Only a tremendous stimulus resulting in an improvement of "signal character," such as had been produced in France by the Revolution, could change men's habits, elevate their standards, and reduce their natality, Mill observed (*Principles,* II, xi, 2); and J. B. Clark (*Essentials,* Ch. 19) 59 years later expressed a somewhat modified version of this view. Not until the 1950's, however, did H. Leibenstein and R. Nelson incorporate a Mill-like view into growth models entailing the displacement of populations from the Malthusian equilibria in which they had been trapped.

The Malthusian period witnessed many improvements in both the art of population projection and the quantity and quality of statistical data, together with the instruments employed to analyze them. A major objective was to eliminate distortions occasioned in crude measures of fertility or mortality by differences or abnormalities in age, sex, and marital composition. Gross and net reproduction rates came into use toward the close of the period, some years after they had been anticipated; they made it possible to determine the rate of increase per generation in a population of stable age distribution, a model developed by A. J. Lotka as early as 1911. The demographer could then cope with changes in age composition associated with adjustment to constant age-specific fertility and mortality rates, though not with unpredictable variations in mortality, fertility, or sex composition (16, Ch. 12). Population forecasters therefore resorted to projections of present populations based upon various sets of assumed age-specific fertility and mortality rates. Recourse was had also to logistic curves fitted to past populations, a method originated by Verhulst and rediscovered by Raymond Pearl and L. J. Reed, who forecast a maximum world population of about 2,646 million and a maximum American population of about 197 million as of around A.D. 2100 (10).

II. A Time of Reconsideration: 1930–65

Opinion on population issues was homogeneous during the period 1800–1930. All but Marxian opinion, whether critical or affirmative of Malthus's views, took his model as a point of departure. Not so in the period 1930–65, or perhaps better, the period 1925–65. Voices were many and discordant, and divers earlier views were rejected. Honored in the breach was Jacob Viner's advice to this body (in 1939), that the economic theorist "is the special custodian for society of the long view in economic matters" (*Am. Econ. Rev.*, March 1940, p. 9) as well as the discoverer of hidden costs; or Winston Churchill's observation that "a hopeful disposition is not the sole qualification to be a prophet"; or Walter Bagehot's reflection that "it is a question whether the benevolence of mankind does most good or harm" (*Physics and Politics*, Ch. 5).

First of the earlier views to be reversed was that imbedded in the population forecasts (or projections as they now are more cautiously labeled) of the 1930's. Already in 1895 Edwin Cannan forecast a virtual cessation of population growth in England and Wales by 1950. In the late 1920's and 1930's it was inferred that the populations of most Western countries would soon become stationary, the American at a level below 200 million. Even eventual decline was anticipated. Net reproduction rates were near unity, and sometimes still falling. Economists began exploring economic life in hypothetically stationary or declining populations. Publicists and reformers, some of whom may have recognized an opportunity to clothe welfare-state philosophy in demographic terms, refurbished old arguments for a family wage as well as diverse subsidies to parents, with the result that family allowance systems won widespread approval. Inadequately explored in a still-Kiplingesque West, however, were implications of the fact that while the rate of population growth in a politically fissured Western world was falling, that of underdeveloped lands, containing about two-thirds of the world's people, was incipiently high and potentially rising.

By the late 1940's, however, changes in both fertility and population prospects were evident. Not only was death control augmenting natural increase in the underdeveloped world, natality and natural increase had risen in the developed world, in part as a response to rising employment and the emergence of the welfare state. Although fertility later moved somewhat below its postwar peak, population projections were revised upward, sometimes by a factor of 2 or more. Thus the population anticipated for the United States in 2000 was set above 300 million instead of below 200 million (10). Still, should age-specific fertility move downward, as it now seems to be doing, postulated growth rates will be reduced. Real cohort analysis, designed in the 1940's to replace use of synthetic cross-sectional cohorts, should presently confirm whether current fertility declines reflect a decline in desired family size and signal the advent of a growth rate of only about 1 per cent. In the 1930–70 interval, of course, population will have increased more than anticipated in the 1930's, about 283 million, or 42 per cent, in the developed world, and 1,271 million, or 91 per cent, in the underdeveloped world.

A second reversal of interpretation relates to population growth and capital formation. G. Cassel (7, pp. 134–35, 149) had implied that a 1 per cent rate of population growth absorbs annual savings approximating 5 per cent of national income, but he did not anticipate excessive saving. Such confidence gave way, however, to fear of the advent of a stationary population, despite Mill's earlier description of its advantages. "Investment" (or savings-offsetting expenditure) had been freed meanwhile of its moralistic trappings, and made *a,* and after the appearance of Keynes's *General Theory* in 1936, *the* strategic variable in employment theory and policy. Given little population growth, investment would be inadequate because provision would no longer have to be made for large population increments, and at the same time there would be too little inclination to invest in improving the environment, quality, and productivity of those already here or replacing those here. This concern reflected an excessive estimate of the difficulties supposedly attendant upon adjustment from a higher to a lower rate of population growth, in an economy made sensitive to the contractile impact of the acceleration principle by a high ratio of reproductive wealth to population. In fact, J. R. Hicks, in his review of the *General Theory* (*Econ. Jour.,* June 1936, p. 252), declared population to be Keynes's "strongest card," and three years later added (*Value and Capital,* Ch. 24) that the "whole Industrial Revolution of the last two hundred years" had been "such a disappointing episode in human history" because (perhaps) it had been "nothing else but a vast secular boom, largely induced by the unparalleled rise in population." Alvin Hansen clearly posed the problems in his address to this body in 1938 (*Am. Econ. Rev.,* March 1939, pp. 1–15), at a time when economists were not yet writing about compensatory public investment in an affluent society. There were critical responses to exponents of stagnation theory, of course, especially G. W. Terborgh's respecting the favorable behavior of investment in a past marked by falling population growth (34), and those of economists who believed that small adjustments in a flexible economy could easily bring annual savings and offsets thereto into balance and assure "full" employment in an economy whether population was growing appreciably or not. Man need not be slave to the stork in the twentieth century any more than he was in the late nineteenth. Ansley Coale (12, p. 371) aptly capped this theme in 1960 when he pointed to implications of current American fertility levels:

> Thus a continued secular economic boom could gain partial support from a continued baby boom. But after a century this trend would produce about a billion Americans, and after two centuries some six billion. There must be a better way to stimulate employment.

After all, it should be quite easy to adjust saving and/or offsets thereto, along with other significant variables, to changes in population size and age composition, both of which are quite predictable in the short run. Until recently, the inverse of the stagnation argument, the thesis that excessive population growth generates inflation, especially in underdeveloped countries, received little attention.

Perhaps the greatest reversal of opinion in the period 1930–65 is that relating to the role played by land and other natural resources in economic development and the disenthralling of populations from Malthusian traps. The importance of this role has been played down for a variety of reasons. First, investment in scientific discovery, applied technology, and education has been found to account for a major fraction of the increase in output per head in advanced countries, although recently the need to complement this type of investment with physical capital has again begun to be emphasized. Second, input of the services of land and natural resources per unit of GNP has greatly decreased in advanced countries. The composition of an individual's consumption changes as his income rises and becomes more biased toward products with relatively small resource content. This is reflected in a below-unity income elasticity of demand for most organic and inorganic raw materials. Furthermore, considerable economy has been achieved in the use of raw materials, with the result that resource-service input per unit of output of many specific types of products has fallen. For example, the input of cropland service per unit of output of agricultural products declined by nearly half in the United States between 1930–32 and 1960–62. In short, changes in the character of both demand and technology have slowed down the growth of various material requirements, sometimes to the pace of population growth and sometimes even below it. Third, discovery and technological change, together with substitution at producer and consumer levels, have greatly augmented both the visible and the immediately potential stock of fuel, mineral, and related sources of natural-resource services. Man, it is supposed, is confronted by chains of natural-resource substitutes which modern molecular engineering and alchemy can subvert to his purposes, replacing links that weaken and elevating inferior sources (e.g., taconite rock) as well as substituting less expensive for more expensive sources of particular natural-resource service needs (1) (33). For example, energy should prove producible in large amounts through fission assisted by breeder reactors, and in almost unlimited amounts should fusion prove technologically and economically feasible.

A measure of parochialism permeates this optimistic account. It neglects the Apostle Matthew's dictum that "for whosoever hath to him shall be given, and he shall have abundance," and the observation in Deuteronomy "that man doth not live by bread only." Skill and capital, so essential to overcoming mineral and agricultural shortages, are generally least abundant where needs are greatest. Should income grow as expected in the under-developed world, natural-resource shortages will be intensified, probably in greater measure than technical capacity to countervail them. Similarly, diets reportedly are quantitatively and/or qualitatively most deficient in Asia, Africa, and parts of Latin America—in areas commonly short of skill and capital, even when not also of land. There one finds not even a basis for the inverted Malthusianism of Western optimists which equates solution of the population problem with a full stomach. One also finds neglected two income-depressing effects of population growth: (*a*) absorption of nonagricultural land which might better have supplied man with amenities; (*b*) steady diminution of the amount available per capita of suitably situated space and goods and services formerly *free*.

Neglected above all is man's conversion of such "parameters of state" as atmosphere, topography, and climate into variables with the result that conditions of life and interspecies equilibrium—never very stable—are changing. Lotka anticipated this possibility in his remarkable *Elements of Physical Biology* (1925). Malthus had treated physical environment as a constant even though man had for many centuries been modifying this environment (35). But then Malthus lived before the goat had been replaced by bulldozer, dragline, and nuclear explosives, and man had become the most destructive of biotypes. After all, even the physicist, R. A. Millikan, could write as late as 1928: "The energy available . . . through the *disintegration* of radioactive, or any other, atoms may perhaps be sufficient to keep the corner peanut and popcorn man going, on a few street corners in our larger towns," but no more (*Science,* Sept. 28, 1928, p. 284). Today, man is confronted not only by denudation and erosion of soil as well as possible mineral shortages but also by the threat that accumulating filth will convert his promised great society into a merely gray society. Witness here in America endless dumping of trash (four pounds per person per day), lead contamination in excess of that experienced in ancient Rome, and water and air pollution soon destined to cost above $7 billion yearly. Merely cleaning up the nation's polluted waters could cost over $50 billion. Indeed, some hold, J. K. Galbraith had better labeled ours an effluent society than an affluent one, perhaps so effluent that many of its members have lost their sensitivity to effluvia. Possibly more threatening still are the changes man is producing "in the geochemical cycles of the elements," thereby "disturbing their natural balance in the uppermost geospheres." Thus since 1900 the carbon dioxide content of the air has risen about 10 per cent and is still rising (30, pp. 365–66, 546–47). In short, multiplying man, forced by population pressure to cope with emerging shortages in his micro-environment, may be worsening his macro-environment and constraining the adaptive potentialities which have gotten him where he is.

Optimum theory has been elaborated and clarified in recent decades. While account has been taken of the content of the welfare index being maximized, it has been noted that output per man-hour may constitute a quite satisfactory index, insofar as deviations from any other index can be resolved through exchange supplemented by taxes. It has been observed also that, while population size may condition a society's capacity for reducing income inequality, it is size of economy much more than size of population which facilitates economies of scale, competitiveness, flexibility, etc. The circumstances governing the response of welfare indicators to variation in population size have been found to include extent of economies of scale, interindustry fit, external economic relations, tastes, technology, length of time horizon, burden of defense or tribute and foreign aid, and so on. Deviation of actual population size from optimum size does not tend to induce a decline in fertility unless this deviation reduces the rate of growth of income below the expected level; this rarely happens in the neighborhood of the optimum, and is not very likely when other income-increasing forces are ascendant. It is possible, of course, that as man's time horizon is extended through prolongation of life and institutionalization of expectations, sensitivity to possible deceleration of income growth increases. Little attention has been given to the stability conditions surrounding an optimum; yet failure to act in conformity with these undermines some of the conditions defining this optimum.

Today emphasis is placed less on the optimum as such than on the broader question: Is additional population growth advantageous? Will it elevate or reduce the rate of growth of per capita income with which other indicators of welfare are highly correlated? Will it contract or extend the range of choice? After all, in much of the world average population density exceeds the optimum level; moreover, many states are too small to accommodate a modern economy, even given a great deal of external exchange. In those countries, moreover, where a larger population would be advantageous, it is highly desirable that increments be added slowly, since a high growth rate sacrifices population quality and equipment to sheer quantity (e.g., in Latin America and Africa). Major issues tend to be examined when inquiry is directed toward assessment of the effects of further growth. Such inquiry led Richard Stone to ascertain how population growth retarded a society's approach to F. P. Ramsey's state of Bliss. It directs attention to the adverse input-absorbing externalities generated by population growth in general and through increasing megalopolitan concentration – usually in greater measure than associated external economies (if any). It prompts examination not merely of effects associated with short-run allocation and partially offsetting responses to disadvantages of population growth, but also of the longer-run consequences of alternative uses of inputs transformable into population. It reveals how population growth and megalopolitan concentration tend to bureaucratize society and dissipate individual autonomy (32).

The optimum concept has been applied to cities as well as to national populations, though with even less success, because of the heterogeneity of cities. Some attention is also being directed to the advantages and disadvantages of city growth. Much of the work currently done on cities amounts to little more than empiricist inquiry, insensitive to the manner in which distortion of exchange in the urban realm, especially distortion of key exchanges, may distort the urban structure and impose suboptimal conditions of existence upon the passive majority.

Turning from optima to change in population composition, we find two dimensions of increasing concern. The first is age structure. France's population was the first to shed the child-ridden Oriental age structure common to populations in Malthus's day. Modern age structures, together with increases in the proportion of the population over 60–65 years, are concomitants of relatively low fertility; prolongation of life, unless beyond 70, affects this proportion very little. Of course, should it be forgotten that death is essential to progress and should man become immortal, a really Struldbruggian society could develop. For then, given a Gross Reproduction Rate of 1.5, the proportion over 60 would approach 41.4 per cent (11, p. 40). There would still be a way of escape, however; for, by raising the GRR to 3.0, the proportion aged 60 and over could be held to 9.1 per cent. Man would thus be faced with a choice – between life in a nursing home and life in a sardine can. Fortunately, the bad as well as the good still die, though perhaps in suboptimal proportion. There is need for hardheaded socioeconomic gerontological inquiry into the allocation, employment, income, and related implications of a doubling or more of the fraction of the population over 60 or 65 years since (say) 1870 when only about 5 per cent of the males were 65 or older and many of these lived in nonurban areas.

Perhaps the central economic task flowing from this aging is that of optimizing, over the life span of the representative individual, his work-time and his discretionary time. Presumably, this arrangement would result in greater vacation time than now – say six weeks per year – and deferment of retirement until age 70. Such arrangement is currently threatened by corporate, trade union, and governmental bureaucrats who, abhorring discriminating decision as the devil abhors holy water, would fix the age of retirement at or below 60 when one still looks forward to 17–21 years of life. Such a policy would produce an army of endowed, if not particularly happy, loafers. Even in the absence of continuing inflation, decrease in the ratio of work life to retired life by four-sevenths since 1900 entails an off-setting increase in saving for retirement which has not usually been achieved. And even then, as a rule, the retiree does not share appreciably in the fruits of technical progress. Solution consists in part in the re-establishment of flexible, discriminatory wages, periodic worker retraining, possible job reassignment, portable retirement provisions, price stability, and an evolution of work scheduling. The alternative could be a variant of Townsendism.

The second problem-ridden structural change accompanying population growth is not mere urbanization (which within 30 years, according to K. Davis, will gather over half the world's population into cities of above 100,000), but the concentration of so large a proportion of the population in megalopolitan centers which appear to be uneconomic devourers of time and capital as in the past they were devourers of population. This concentration appears to be the product of an indeterminate mechanism, made up in the part of random variables and fostered by disparities between social costs and social benefits as well as by neglect of adverse externalities associated with concentration. In short, the urban growth pattern may be stochastically determined, with chance working on the side of the largest centers and in keeping with Zipf's generalized Paretian, or rank-size, "the-higher-the-fewer rule." Here we may not have a causal mechanism operative, since, as M. G. Kendall (21) notes, "chance can mimic choice," nor do we have simple, unlagged cause-effect relationships (22). There could, of course, be something like G. Myrdal's cumulative causation at work, or perhaps a cumulative process somewhat analogous to that described by W. J. Baumol in his "theory of cumulative deterioration" (2).

What is of immediate concern, however, is whether the mechanism at work produces an optimum distribution of activities in space and of population among cities. The outcome, whether good or bad, is almost irreversible, underpinned as it is by fixed capital, special interests, inertia, subsidies, and so on. That the outcome is optimal is to be doubted despite the clamor of hyperurbanists. They forget that vulnerability to attack by missile and from the air is positively associated with population concentration. It is essential that one take into account *all* costs as well as *all* benefits associated with large-city expansion, so remindful of the growth of polyp colonies; only then is the marginal net effect ascertainable. Excessive concentration of population in large cities not only tends to dissipate *gemein-schaftliche* ties, and generate alienation; it is also inimical to individual political and consumer sovereignty. Mathematically, the larger the city, the smaller is the relative size of the resolute minority that could rule it (28). Politically and psychologically, the larger the city, the weaker tends to be the belief of the voter that he can do anything to influence the ruling camarilla and improve his community. Finally, as political power is channeled into the hands of city-ruling minorities, the taxing power of the central government tends to be placed increasingly at the disposal of these minorities and perhaps in keeping with what one may call the Augustus Caesar principle of public finance. (You will recall Seutonius's account. Caesar once considered discontinuing the practice of distributing free grain, but he decided against it even though it was injuring Italian agriculture. "I did not carry out my purpose," he said, "because I felt sure that the practice would one day be renewed by someone ambitious of popular favor.")

While notable contributions have been made to the economic analysis of fertility (3, 12), the explanation of its short-run behavior has not yet been made as economic as possible, nor have the actual and the potential feedback connections of household with economy been adequately identified and explored. If one allows for random variables and treats certain fertility-affecting elements (religious and other values, rural-urban and educational differences) as short-run constants, one should be able to explain changes in gross reproduction in terms of changes in price structure and opportunity costs and of movements along curves of demand for children and of shifts of both these curves and curves representing costs of children. For a change in fertility reflects the response, usually lagged, of actual and potential households to changes in (*a*) the prices and character of alternatives to children, and (*b*) the benefits anticipated to be derivable from children and/or changes in the input costs of children, together with additions (subtractions) in costs associated with changes in family economic status. It must be assumed, of course, that fertility is easily controlled. This assumption is quite tenable in advanced countries, now that earlier contraceptive methods, including the unreliable "safe-period" – in Spain children who owe their existence to failure of this method are eponymously described as *Oginitos* after the method's discoverer (*New Leader*, Sept. 13, 1965, p. 7) – have been supplemented by contraceptive pills and cheap, effective intrauterine devices. It is essential also that the analyst view the child as the partial analogue of both a consumer's and a producer's durable good. Then the analytical as well as the empirical problem becomes one of isolating the determinants that affect the demand for, and the supply of, children at household levels, and thus give rise, along with household interdependence, to aggregate demand and supply functions.

The demand for children is not quite parallel, however, to that for ordinary durable goods. The relevant time interval is too long to permit a household to test *ex ante* expectations respecting children by *ex post* experience. No one can foresee what the genetic grab bag will bring forth, probably a useful citizen, possibly a genius, perhaps a hooligan or a cretin, but by then corrective response may no longer be possible. There is less uncertainty, of course, on the supply side. Most direct costs are fairly predictable, and optional additional costs need not be incurred unless they fall short of the prospective benefits. Less predictable is the impact of trade and longer cycles, or of increases in unemployment consequent upon upswings in the relative number of young job-seekers, cobweb-like sequels to earlier upsurges of births (12). Less predictable also, especially in a modern demand-oriented economy, is the response over time of a household to its increasing access to durable goods and imperfectly foreseen complements thereto. For in this sector of consumption the income elasticity of demand can easily rise above unity and, if this rise is widespread enough, divert income from support of procreation to purchase of durable products and complements. The full significance of the emergence of durable goods for reproductive and other activities has yet to be analyzed adequately. Indeed, the Ford Foundation might fund a project permitting a corporate body of social scientists to follow through life a representative cohort, or better still a sequence of cohorts chosen at (say) 10-year intervals, and ascertain how and why patterns of expenditure change and with it fertility and related behavior.

Underdeveloped countries, United Nations demographers find, differ from developed in respect of both fertility and indices of modernization. Gross reproduction is below 2 in all developed countries, and above 2 in the underdeveloped world which includes nearly all African, Asian, and Latin American countries. Within the modern world there is no correlation between variation in indicators of modernization and variation in fertility; and within the underdeveloped world there is only slight correlation. The data do suggest, however, that there exists a threshold, or a set of thresholds, movement beyond which by indicators of modernization is quite likely to be accompanied by a perceptible downward movement of fertility, though not by one immediately adequate to offset falling mortality.

Convincing evidence of a widespread, imminent, and pronounced decline of fertility and natural increase remains to be uncovered. The United Nations reports: "the launching of new countries upon the transition from high to low fertility seems to have been temporarily halted." The evidence reveals no continuing inverse relation between population density and fertility in keeping with the logistic theory; only a mildly inverse relation is found in both the developed and the underdeveloped world. The pressure of numbers upon family resources generated by the decline of infant and child mortality has not yet widely reduced births per mother. Governments not only show little awareness of the urgency of the population problem;

they even cushion the incidence of child-rearing costs on responsible parents. The Economic and Social Council of the United Nations, together with individual countries, has sanctioned making contraceptive assistance internationally available, but governments have provided little incentive thereto (36).

The economic implications of United Nations studies of fertility and population growth are at least fourfold. First, for a number of decades population growth will absorb large amounts of physical and personal capital that might otherwise have been used to elevate per capita income. For example, *ceteris paribus,* per capita income can grow at least one percentage point more per year, given a zero instead of a two-per-cent-per-year rate of population growth. Second, little explanatory insight is provided by economic models which merely suggest that income will permanently outstrip numbers, but which are unequipped with feedback mechanisms that produce at least limited downward movements of fertility. It is necessary to show that movements of income generate even greater relative demands for present and future goods, services, and leisure; that elasticity of consumption expectations exceeds elasticity of income expectations. Then, if the standard of life rose ratchet-like, but always guarded against decline by pawl-like acquired tastes, one might count upon the retention of internalized standards. Third, the apparent existence of a set of interrelated thresholds suggests that international differences in shorter-run fertility-affecting constants are dissipatable through subjection to socioeconomic solvents. Fourth, even though these parametrical differences exist, it is certain that fertility can be greatly reduced, given availability of contraceptives, if having more than a stipulated number of children, say three, is economically penalized instead of subsidized as at present. That it would pay the governments of underdeveloped countries to reward those who curb their fertility has been demonstrated by Stephen Enke who estimates one dollar thus spent to be worth about $100 of other forms of aid (17).

III. The Future

Technology, prudence, and reason could generate a bright future. That it will be bright, however, is questionable, given an unfettered stork, together with continuing escalation of submarginal man in a world of Freudian irresponsibility and distribution according to alleged need rather than demonstrated performance. Just as relative immunity of an organ's cells to division and mutation causes that organ to age, so does the relative immunity of a society to rigorous selection tend to bring about its deterioration. It may be well, however, for one interpreting these portentous trends to recall what Samuel Johnson wrote in the preface to his dictionary about the prophecies he had made earlier in his launching prospectus: "I . . . now begin to fear that I have indulged expectation which neither reason nor experience justify." Yet, mankind does appear to be at a demographic crossroads, along which weak homeostatic response under current conditions may not properly direct man. Population growth still resembles too closely Newton's "uniform motion in a straight line," unrelieved by the prospective emergence of fertility-controlling "impressed forces."

Consider India. Down one of the crossroads could lie a sanguine future. For, as S. J. Patel suggests, the economic distance between India and present-day America might be bridged, though hardly in a half-century; the difference between Indian and American real agricultural output per capita could be removed in some 50 years; that in other sectors, in a longer period. Yet, as Coale and Hoover have shown, there can be little improvement in the average Indian's lot if India persists down the road of population growth (26).

More generally, to paraphrase President Kennedy's warning against war: Unless man halts population growth, population growth will halt man. As matters stand, two demographic processes are bound to bedevil man increasingly and, if they are not soon resolved, will greatly diminish whatever prospect he has of establishing a society both peaceful and great, both moral and aesthetic. These two processes are continuing population growth in a finite world and increasing concentration of people in progressively larger megalopolitan centers. Progeny and space will have to be rationed much more effectively in the future than in the past.

The more remote prospect is bleak while the immediate prospect, blurred by current income growth, is misleadingly hopeful. Population growth — demographic entropy — is dissipating man's capacity for maneuver much as economic entropy is dissipating the utility locked up in depletable natural resources. After all, increase in number is an essentially irreversible process; men usually multiply, but they seldom dwindle as did avian, mammalian, and other species now extinct. Even in the United States should natural increase plus a prospective annual immigration of 350,000 long continue to increase population 1.0–1.5 per cent per year, our population, 325–350 million in 2010, would number 0.8–1.33 billion by 2100, and 1.5–2.8 billion (with perhaps one-fourth nonwhite) two centuries hence. Acres of land of all sorts per capita, probably still close to 5.5 in 2010, would continue to decline until there would hardly be space even for our national flower, the concrete cloverleaf. Aesthetic considerations of all sorts would be swamped by masses instead of by costs masquerading as pseudo-utility as at present. Even in the absence of strepitous poverty-mongers many would be conscious of being poor.

An even worse prospect obtains in the world at large. Between 1960 and 2000, according to United Nations estimates, world population will grow nearly twice as fast as in 1920–60—around 113 per cent to between 6 and 7 billion. The proportion in the developed world will fall to around 22 per cent, since its numbers will grow only 61 per cent, or but two-fifths as fast as the population of the underdeveloped world which is expected to increase about 151 per cent. Should world population continue to grow about 2 per cent per year it would number 16–18 billion by 2050 and 43–50 billion by 2100. Even if it should proceed only 1.5 per cent per year it would number 13–15 billion by 2050 and 26–31 billion by 2100. Acres of all sorts per capita, still about 4.7 to 5.5 in 2000, will then have fallen to 0.6–1.25 by 2100, and close to one-half of this amount will be unfit for habitation except by Lower Slobbovians. Man will have become essentially spaceless in a space age, unless competition for living space should accidentally transform the "ultimate deterrent" into the "ultimate detergent" and, as D. M. Heer estimates (in his *After Nuclear Attack*), destroy perhaps 30 per cent of the population, mostly in heavily urbanized areas.

Given growth of the order suggested as likely in the absence of concerted efforts to limit numbers, food shortages would eventually develop despite schemes for deriving protein from coal and petroleum as well as subsistence from algae and other crude organic matter, or for supporting a man on 20 well-cultivated square meters of soil. First, cultivable land is limited, though only about 7 per cent is used for nonfood crops, mainly fibers. In 1964 arable and permanent-crop land totaled about 3.6 billion acres; land in permanent meadows and pasture, about 6.2 billion acres; and land in forest, about 10 billion acres. Just how much land in the two latter categories is convertible into crop land is indeterminate, though subject to exaggeration. It depends upon technology, upon mastery of cultivation in the tropics and in droughty and cold regions, upon land clearing and development, often a costly process, and upon adequacy of the water supply. From the gross amount of land so converted must be subtracted land blotted out of agriculture by creeping concrete, construction, city growth, etc., which in the United States has amounted to one-half acre or more per inhabitant added to the urban population.

Second, though average yield per acre could prove capable of 300 or more per cent increase, crop yield per acre is limited. Yield increases are promising, of course. After all, "over a large part of the world today agricultural productivity is now the same as, or even inferior to, what it was in the leading civilized communities 2,000 years ago" (9, p. 78). Yields per acre vary widely; thus Japan produces roughly 3–4 times as much rice per acre as do South and Southeast Asian lands. This variation is associated mainly with variation in input of fertilizer, addition of a kilogram of which may increase grain output about 10 kilograms, given suitable methods of cultivation. Developed countries use 5 times as much fertilizer per acre as do the underdeveloped; Europe uses about 20 times as much as do Africa and Asia and 9 times as much as does Latin America; Japan uses over 100 times as much as do India and Pakistan.

In many if not most underdeveloped countries pre-takeoff conditions essential to the great upsurges in yields experienced in the United States, Britain, and Japan have not yet been established (5). Nor are they soon likely to be established, given excessive population growth and heightened barriers to the detraditionalizing of agriculture. Yet, as James Bonner shows, even if a takeoff is experienced, it cannot carry average production per acre above the limits "determined by the factors that regulate photosynthetic efficiency" and "being approached today . . . in parts of Japan, of Western Europe, and of the United States" (4, p. 14) (5). Within limits, of course, the amount of nutrient supplied per acre can be augmented through recourse to higher-yield crops (e.g., soya beans).

The future of the food problem may be stated simply. Suppose we increase world output 700 per cent by doubling crop acreage and quadrupling yields. World population would catch up with this increase in about 107 years, given an annual growth rate of 2 per cent, and in about 140 years, given a 1.5 per cent rate. Trebling crop acreage would add perhaps a quarter to the above output, but only about one-tenth to the years of grace. Rationalization of fisheries would not change the data significantly. Augmentation of the food supply in the measure indicated is unlikely. This is not *one* world; requisite knowledge and its necessary complements are not likely to be imported and assimilated rapidly in backward lands; nor will progressive lands have incentive to export food, mainly cereal (of which about 5 per cent net is redistributed by international commerce) to exchange-short countries.

Turning from land, the principal source of man's food and the sole source of his living space, to water and minerals, the other primary ingredients of man's material well-being, one encounters limitations parallel to those of land. A precise measure of these limitations is not available. It depends on rates of consumption which are rising, upon actual and exploitable reserves which remain underinventoried, and upon man's ability to develop substitutes for current sources. Even so, the outlook is not as promising as our Indian Summer natural-resource experts would have it. Consider water, long the economist's standard exemplar of a free good. We Americans use in all forms over 370 billion gallons of water per day and by 2000 we shall require 900 billion gallons, which probably can be provided out of the 700 billion available of the 1,200 billion that daily flow to the sea (40). This amount, together with what is otherwise required and used of an average daily rainfall of about 5 trillion gallons, will not suffice beyond the present century. Then we shall have to reduce our average consumption, so imbedded in our mode of living, since it is improbable that desalination of sea water can add greatly to our supply of appropriately situated water.

The long-run availability of large-volume materials (e.g., steel, aluminum, concrete, ceramics, glass), together with our ability to cope with shortages of special small-volume materials, depends, as F. G. Tryon (15, pp. 136–38) suggested 40 years ago, upon man's ability to produce and appropriately distribute cheap energy. Under present conditions and at prospective use rates, the world's exploitable reserves of a number of minerals will last less than a century. Aluminum and iron would last 4 centuries at recent use rates, and the key fertilizers, potassium and phosphorus, much longer. The World Power Conference of 1962 put economically exploitable coal reserves at 3.5 trillion tons, enough for 800 years at current annual world consumption rates (about 4.4 billion tons in 1960) and 100 years at American rates. Other fossil fuels will last only into the next century. Water power could supply the equivalent of 2.5 billion tons of coal per year, or less than half current world energy consumption. Given breeder reactors, usable uranium might come close to supplying as much energy as current mineral or fossil fuel reserves; and low grade thorium could supply 10–20 times as much. Fusion, when it becomes manageable, could make the supply of energy virtually inexhaustible, even in the absence of tidal, solar, geothermic, and related sources (27) (33, pp. 74–97). In short, given the cheap energy likely to be available, shortage of space, land, and water rather than of minerals would check the growth of population and living standards. Limits will be imposed also, of course, by unavoidable shortages of skilled personnel. Even given requisite natural talents, we cannot long increase skilled manpower faster than population; otherwise the whole of the labor force will be transformed into economists, engineers, physicians, and other categories of skilled manpower, and none will be left to minister to other wants.

I have just been concentrating upon what exponential growth can do in a finite environment, upon a growth process which, as Coale reports (11, p. 36), within 65 centuries and in the absence of environmental limits, could generate "a solid sphere of live bodies expanding with a radial velocity that, neglecting relativity, would equal the velocity of light." Let me now recall that second process operative in our world of shrinking space, a process to which man must respond even as the ratio of suitably situated space to population declines. I refer to that seemingly stochastic process which is concentrating an ever larger fraction of the world's population within the confines of a small number of megalopolises or human rabbit warrens. This process accentuates the adverse externalities associated with population growth and, as has been suggested, may produce unfavorable political effects as well as frustrate the demand for living space which tends to rise with income. But let me turn to solutions.

Curbing population growth could prove easy in modern nations, given current contraceptive methods and knowledge thereof. It is necessary only to alter the terms of trade between gross increments to the population and alternative uses of the inputs involved. In essence, this might entail holding each couple responsible for all or most costs, visible and invisible, direct and indirect, of reproducing and rearing children, in keeping with at least minimal standards prescribed by the state. Should the number of births still be too large, excise taxes could be imposed upon higher-order children and upon child-oriented products and services, while if births were too few, these products and services could be cheapened through use of subsidies.

Control of megalopolitanization and the redirection of urban growth are achievable through use of taxation, penalties, and constraints. Initially, however, much more study needs to be made of longitudinal and cross-sectional relations between variation in city size and marginal cost-benefit ratios under essentially comparable conditions.

As matters stand, the longer-run prospect is definitely Malthusian, with man sitting on a demographic time bomb into which legislators, and others, here and abroad, continue to shovel combustibles. Yet there may be grounds for conditional optimism. Not only can economists devote to the population question more attention than they gave it in the past 80 years when they devoted only about 1–1.5 per cent of their articles to population,[1] but there are many more economists to do the job. Today more economists are practicing than lived and died in the past four thousand years, and their number is growing even faster than the world's population.

References*

1. H. J. Barnett and C. Morse, *Scarcity and Growth*, Baltimore 1963; T. W. Schultz, *Economic Organization of Agriculture*, New York 1953.
2. W. J. Baumol, in H. G. Schaller, ed., *Public Expenditure Decisions in the Urban Community*, Resources for the Future, Washington, D.C. 1963.
3. G. S. Becker, "A Theory of the Allocation of Time," *Econ. Jour.*, Sept. 1965, *75*, 493–517; B. Okun, *Trends in Birth Rates in the United States since 1870*, Baltimore 1958.
4. James Bonner, "The Upper Limit of Crop Yield," *Science*, July 6, 1962, *137*, 11–15.
5. L. R. Brown (U.S. Department of Agriculture), *Increasing World Food Output*, Washington, D.C., and *Man, Land and Food*, Washington, D.C. 1963; T. W. Schultz, *Transforming Traditional Agriculture*, New Haven 1964.
6. *The Population Problem*. London 1922.

1. This estimate is based upon entries in the *Index of Economic Journals*, sponsored by the American Economic Association.

* Bibliographical note: For statistical and background information I have drawn on W. S. and E. S. Woytinsky, *World Population and Production*, New York 1953; United Nations, *Population Bulletin*, Nos. 6–7, and *Provisional Report on World Population Prospects . . . in 1963*, New York 1964; D. V. Glass and D. E. C. Eversley, eds., *Population in History*, Chicago 1965.

7. *On Quantative Thinking in Economics.* Oxford 1935.
8. Colin Clark, *Conditions of Economic Progress,* 2nd ed., London 1951, 3rd ed., 1957.
9. Colin Clark and M. R. Haswell, *The Economics of Subsistence Agriculture.* London 1964.
10. M. Clawson *et al., Land for the Future,* Baltimore 1960; Irene B. Taeuber, "The Development of Population Predictions in Europe and the Americas," *Estadistica,* Sept. 1944, No. 7, 323–46; J. J. Spengler and O. D. Duncan, eds., *Demographic Analysis,* Glencoe 1956; J. S. Davis, *The Population Upsurge in the United States* (Food Research Institute War-Peace Pamphlet 12), Stanford 1949.
11. A. J. Coale, "Increases in Expectation of Life and Population Growth," in Louis Henry and Wilhelm Winkler, eds., *International Population Conference,* Vienna 1959.
12. ———, ed., *Demographic and Economic Change in Developed Countries.* Princeton 1960.
13. J. S. Davis, "The Specter of Dearth of Food: History's Answer to Sir William Crookes," in *Facts and Factors in Economic History,* Cambridge 1932, pp. 732–54.
14. J. F. Dewhurst *et al., Europe's Needs and Resources,* New York 1961; S. N. Prokopovicz, *L'Industrialisation des pays agricoles et la structure de l'économie mondiale après la guerre,* Neuchatel 1946.
15. L. I. Dublin, ed., *Population Problems in the United States and Canada.* New York 1926.
16. ——— *et al., Length of Life,* rev. ed., New York 1949; R. R. Kuczynski, *The Balance of Births and Deaths,* New York 1928, and *The Measurement of Population Growth,* New York 1936.
17. S. Enke, *Economics for Development,* New York 1963; "Economic Programs to Prevent Births," presented at World Population Conference, Belgrade, Sept. 1965; and "The Economic Aspects of Slowing Population Growth," *Econ. Jour.,* March 1966, 76, 44–56.
18. N. E. Himes, *Medical History of Contraception,* Baltimore 1936; R. O. Greep, *Human Fertility and Population Problems,* Cambridge 1963.
19. *The Coal Question,* London 1865; H. W. Singer, "The Coal Question Reconsidered: Effects of Economy and Substitution," *Rev. Econ. Stud.,* June 1941, 8, 166–77.
20. H. G. Johnson, *The Canadian Quandary.* Toronto 1963.
21. M. G. Kendall, "Natural Law in the Social Sciences," *Jour. Royal Stat. Society,* Ser. A, Part 1, 1961, *124,* 1–18; H. A. Simon, *Models of Man,* New York 1957, Ch. 9.
22. ———, *New Prospects in Economic Analyses* (Stamp Memorial Lecture 1960). London 1960.
23. *The Economic Consequences of the Peace.* New York 1920.
24. *Memorials of Alfred Marshall,* edited by A. C. Pigou, London 1925; A. F. Weber, *The Growth of Cities,* New York 1899; Don Martindale's introduction to Max Weber, *The City* (1921), Glencoe 1958; P. A.

Sorokin and C. C. Zimmerman, *Principles of Rural-Urban Sociology*, New York 1929.

25. *Enough and to Spare*. New York 1944.

26. S. J. Patel, "The Economic Distance between Nations: Its Origin, Measurement and Outlook," *Econ. Jour.*, March 1964, *74*, 126–30 and Sept. 1965, *75*, 632–36; A. J. Coale and E. M. Hoover, *Population Growth and Economic Development in Low-Income Countries*, Princeton 1958.

27. E. W. Pehrson, "Mineral Resources-Hydrosphere vs. Lithosphere," unpublished; D. F. Frasché, *Mineral Resources*, Washington, D.C. 1962; K. Hubbert, *Energy Resources*, Washington, D.C. 1962; *Index*, no. 6, 1965, 1–2.

28. L. S. Penrose, "Elementary Statistics of Majority Voting," *Jour. Royal Stat. Society*, 1946, *109*, 53–57.

29. *Economics of Welfare*. London 1932.

30. K. Rankama and T. G. Sahama, *Geochemistry*. Chicago 1950.

31. J. J. Spengler, "Aspects of the Economics of Population Growth," *So. Econ. Jour.*, Jan. 1948, *14*, 233–65; E. A. Wrigley, "The Supply of Raw Materials in the Industrial Revolution," *Econ. History Rev.*, Aug. 1962, *15*, 1–16.

32. ———, "Population and Freedom," *Population Review*, June 1962, *6*, 74–82; also Colin Clark's counterargument, "Do Population and Freedom Grow Together?" *Fortune*, Dec. 1960, 136ff.

33. ———, ed., *Natural Resources and Economic Growth*, Resources for the Future, Washington, D.C. 1961.

34. *The Bogey of Economic Maturity*. Chicago 1945.

35. W. L. Thomas, *Man's Role in Changing the Face of the Earth*. Chicago 1962.

36. United Nations, *Report of the Secretary General* (E/3895, May 18, 1964) to the Economic and Social Council, 37th Session, Agenda item 21.

37. "Collective-Consumption Services of Individual Consumption Goods," *Quart. Jour. Econ.*, Aug. 1964, *78*, 471–77.

38. A. N. Whitehead, *Process and Reality*, New York 1929; A. J. Lotka, *Elements of Physical Biology*, Baltimore 1925.

39. A. B. Wolfe, "The Population Problem since the World War," *Jour. Pol. Econ.*, in 3 parts, 1928–29, *36–37*.

40. Abel Wolman, "The Metabolism of Cities," *Scientific Amer.*, Sept. 1965, *213*, 178–93; Roger Revelle, "Water," *ibid.*, Sept., 1963, *209*, 92–109; C. C. Bradley, "Human Water Needs and Water Use in America, *Science*, Oct. 26, 1962, *138*, 489–91.

Was Malthus Right?

"If I had confined myself merely to general views, I could have intrenched myself in an impregnable fortress." — Malthus, *Essay,* 2nd edition, preface

The title of this paper embraces two sets of questions, one pertaining to Malthus' theoretical structure, the other to its empirical plausibility. This paper is more concerned with the latter than with the former set of questions. For expositive convenience we may say that Malthus' *Essay* was dominated by two propositions: (*a*) that population elasticity commonly though not necessarily approximated unity;[1] and (*b*) that the augmentability of the supply of product or income was limited and subject to diminution at the margin.

This paper is concerned mainly with the second proposition. After discussing Malthus' conception of the problem and the roles of limitational factors and checks, I review the present status of food-supply prospects, the primary limiting factor in Malthus' scheme. The first proposition, as I have stated it, may misrepresent Malthus' view somewhat, since his basic proposition was that man has a great capacity to multiply in the absence of checks. His model of the determinants of fertility was incomplete, however, and overestimated population elasticity in some circumstances, in part perhaps because he underestimated so markedly the prospective increase in aggregate output and the changes in the economic environment to which man must adjust. While some of his statistical analysis was defective, in part because such analysis was not his primary interest, his basic arguments were unaffected thereby.[2]

Much of the criticism directed against Malthus' theory is, as Antony Flew shows, misleading or beside the point. Correction of his modes of statement makes inapplicable a number of the criticisms to which Malthus' presentation is subject. He is asking about population, much as Newton asked about the motion of bodies, why and how it happens that population grows less rapidly than it could if unchecked, given its enormous power of increase. It followed, of course, as Flew points out, that it is "preposterous to assert or assume that every (married) couple has a right to produce as many children as they wish, regardless of what others may be doing or want to do, and that

---

1. That is, dPO/dOP approximates unity where P denotes population and O national income or net product. Population growth oscillated about subsistence, rising when income exceeded subsistence, and becoming negative when income fell below subsistence. See Malthus, *Essay on the Principle of Population* (London: Ward, Lock, and Co., 1890), Bk. I, chap. 2, p. 11.

2. See Kingsley Davis, "Malthus and the Theory of Population," in P. F. Lazarsfeld and Morris Rosenberg, eds., *The Language of Social Research* (Glencoe: Free Press, 1955), pp. 540–53; and (with Judith Blake), "Social Structure and Fertility: An Analytical Framework," *Economic Development and Cultural Change,* April 1956, pp. 211–235; R. R. Kuczynski, *The Measurement of Population Growth* (New York: Oxford University Press, 1936); also Kingsley Davis, "The Theory of Change and Response in Modern Demographic History," *Population Index,* October 1963, pp. 345–366.

all these children will have a right to support in childhood and as adults to earn a living, to marry and to have a similarly unrestricted right to produce children with similar rights in their turn."[3] It does not follow, however, that Malthus gave an adequate explanation of the behavior of fertility.

I. Outline of Malthus' Conception of the Problem

Recognizing that the "power of increase in plants and animals" was "prodigious"[4] and that man's biotic potential,[5] now at about 5 per cent, was in the neighborhood of 3 per cent, he believed this rate needed to be greatly reduced; otherwise mortality would rise until the rate of natural increase was brought down to the level of increase in the food supply, or, better still, the means of existence. Presumably, he wanted to see established a set of institutional commitments which, together with the set of expectations inculcated in the individual would function as a kind of homeostat, prompting the individual to limit his family size sufficiently to bring his standard of

3. See Flew, "The Structure of Malthus' Population Theory," *Australasian Journal of Philosophy*, May 1957, pp. 1–20, esp. 16–19; on fertility see Section III below. Attention may be called to three essays which translate Malthus' theory into economic theory: A. T. Peacock, "Theory of Population and Modern Economic Analysis," *Population Studies*, November 1952, pp. 114–122; J. E. Moes, "A Dynamic Interpretation of Malthus' Principle of Population," *Kyklos*, XI, Fasc. 1, 1958, pp. 58–80; Ryoshin Minami, "An Analysis of Malthus' Theory," *Journal of Economic Behavior*, April 1961, pp. 53–63. See also P. A. Samuelson, *Foundations of Economic Analysis* (Cambridge: Harvard University Press, 1948), p. 296.

4. Malthus' argument is stated tersely in his contribution to the Supplement of the Encyclopedia, also published separately in 1830 as *A Summary View of the Principle of Population* and reprinted in D. V. Glass, ed., *Introduction to Malthus* (London: Watts and Co., 1953). See *ibid.*, pp. 121–122; Malthus, *Essay on the Principle of Population*, Bk. I, chaps. 1–2, Bk. III, chap. 14. The extent of the power of unimpeded increase has often been stressed. Thus "the progeny of a single spherical cell, 1 μ in diameter, would produce a mass of the radius of the Earth in 3 or 4 days provided that all survived." K. Rankama and T. G. Sahama, *Geochemistry* (Chicago: University of Chicago Press, 1950), p. 338. See also W. I. Vernadsky, "Problems of Biogeochemistry" in *Transactions of the Connecticut Academy of Arts and Sciences* XXXV, 1944, p. 498, where it is estimated that elephants, whose "speed of colonization is less than 10^{-7} times that for the bacterium," could people the earth in 1000–1100 years. See also A. J. Coale's observation that "in about 6,500 years, if current growth continues, the descendants of the present world would form a solid sphere of live bodies expanding with a radial velocity that, neglecting relativity, would equal the velocity of light." See "Increase in Expectation of Life and Population Growth," in L. Henry and W. Winkler, eds., *International Population Congress* (Vienna: Christopher Reisser's Sohne, 1959), p. 36.

5. By biotic potential is meant the inherent rate of growth of a population in a logistic model at $t = 0$. E.g., see R. Pearl, *Medical Biometry and Statistics* (Philadelphia: Saunders, 1941), p. 461. J. Bourgeois-Pichat's calculations suggest a maximum of about 5 per cent. See United Nations, *The Aging of Populations and Its Economic and Social Implications*, Population Studies No. 26 (New York: United Nations, 1956), p. 27. The so-called law of Malthus is sometimes written as if the rate of growth v is constant and the size of a population N at time t is $N(O)e^{vt}$. But if v is inversely related to the size of the population, $v = v_0(1 - N/a)$ where v_0 and a are constants, and the solution to the corresponding differential equation $dN/dt = v_0 N(1 - N/a)$ is the "logistic" law of Verhulst and Pearl and Reed. See M. G. Kendall, "Stochastic Processes and Population Growth," *Journal of the Royal Statistical Society*, Series B, XI, 1949, pp. 230–264, esp. pp. 231–232, also 244–245. See note 12 below.

life to a suitable level and thereafter at least maintain this level. Action along these lines, he believed, could reduce population elasticity below unity.[6]

Malthus opposed recourse to contraception, however. Indeed, he believed that if man's fertility could be easily controlled, indolence and underpopulation would result.[7] Malthus therefore recommended that marriage be deferred until the ages of 27 or 28. This arrangement is theoretically capable of reducing fertility notably. J. W. Leasure estimates that in Bolivia raising the singulate age at marriage from 22.5 to 27.2 years, with the proportion single at age 50 unchanged at 11.1 per cent, would reduce the Net Reproduction Rate (NRR) by 25 per cent and the birth rate from 41 to 30. In Turkey raising the singulate age at marriage from 19.7 to 27.2 years would reduce the NRR by 35 per cent and the birth rate from 50 to 33. It is doubtful if Malthus' recommendation could have been made both effective and entirely uncompensated by a rise in illegitimate natality. In Western Europe in 1900–1950 changes in marriage patterns "accounted for only an estimated 12–15 per cent of the total decline in fertility." Today in Turkey, even if marriage were deferred as assumed, natural increase would still be 2 per cent per year, about double the rate in Malthus' day and a serious hindrance to development.[8]

Malthus' emphasis upon the need to establish or strengthen what I called a homeostatic set of arrangements and expectations flowed from: (a) his apparent belief that only if fertility could be easily controlled would it be held down in the absence of such arrangements;[9] and (b) his hypothesis that produce tended to grow at a decreasing rate — $1/n$ where n denoted the aggregate of produce, and the period to which $1/n$ referred was typically 20–25 years, or the period in which a population could double in the absence of checks. His mode of expression, however, obscured the conduct-determining significance of the indicator of subsistence to which a population adjusted.

We may illustrate the problem by dividing the population P of a crowded closed economy based on land and labor into P_x and P_y, and the labor force L, a fixed percentage of P, into L_x and L_y, where the subscripts x and y signify agricultural and non-agricultural. Let Y_x and Y_y designate the incomes of P_x and P_y, with their sum Y corresponding in value terms to net output O. If $f(x)$ denotes the output of agricultural labor L_x, cultivation will be carried to the point where its marginal product $f'(x)$ coincides with the minimal required "subsistence" income s. The income, in produce, of

6. *Essay*, pp. 529–531, 540–544.

7. *Essay*, Bk. IV, chap. 1; Glass, *op. cit.*, pp. 25–54.

8. This paragraph summarizes Leasure's findings in "Malthus, Marriage and Multiplication," *Milbank Memorial Fund Quarterly*, Part I, October 1963, pp. 419–435.

9. *Essay*, Bk. III, chap. 14. While he pointed to the operation of the preventive check in some countries (e.g., Norway), he commonly associated a cessation of population growth, or a decline in numbers, with a decline in the flow of subsistence (e.g., American Indians, South Sea Islands) rather than with checks immediately operative.

agricultural labor $= L_x f'(x)$ while the residuum R imputable to land $= L_x (f[(x)/x - f'(x)]$. All of R passes into the hands of P_y which includes landowners, and so does a small fraction of $L_x f'(x)$ which is exchanged for a portion of the output $f(y)$ of the non-agricultural labor force L_y. Upon completion of the transactions the average incomes of P_x and P_y are Y_x/P_x and Y_y/P_y, with the former approximating s and falling below Y_y/P_y. We thus have an income structure consisting of two sets of incomes, with one set at the subsistence level, by definition, and the other embracing incomes at various levels ranging upward from s, only some of which are high enough to permit population growth in addition to population replacements. If this structure,[10] as just described, is represented by a single value v, this value remains high enough to permit some population growth. If, however, v declines enough, population growth will cease, either because each socio-economic group just replaces itself, or because the positive growth of some groups is offset by negative growth in others. Malthus did not employ the concept of income structure, though he envisaged a kind of pyramid of incomes, only some of which permitted population growth in then well-settled countries.

It may be noted parenthetically that if population grew at the same rate $1/n$ as the food supply n in his arithmetical ratio model, it would grow at a decreasing rate as in a logistic model. The growth patterns of the two models differ, however; in Malthus's model the increments are of constant absolute magnitude whereas in the logistic the increments increase in magnitude to a peak and then decline, tracing out a bell-shaped incremental curve. Adjustment of voluntary control of numbers to Malthus' arithmetical-ratio model would require, so he believed, a diffusion of "middle class" values.[11] He did not, however, suggest a model summarizing the probable path of diffusion of these values, a path implicit in the logistic model to which his work gave rise.[12]

II. Elasticity of Output

Were all inputs so abundant that the price of each was null or zero there would be no economic problem. It is only as the prices of inputs become positive that the economic problem becomes manifest and with it, in respect of resources quite inelastic in supply, declines in outputs of variable agents

10. H. Leibenstein uses the term "income structure" to denote a range of incomes, by socio-economic income groups, which may just suffice for population replacement by each group. See his *A Theory of Economic-Demographic Development* (Princeton: Princeton University Press, 1954), pp. 12–13.

11. *Essay*, Bk. IV, chap. 13, pp. 535–37, also chap. 14, pp. 543–544.

12. Let C denote the fraction of the population with middle-class values who regulate family size and N the fraction which do not; then $C + N = 1$. These values are communicated from members of C to some members of N. Suppose the members of the entire population $C + N$ interact at random: then some members of C will interact with some members of N and com-

and the emergence of economic rents. Were there few or no inputs of very low or even zero elasticity of supply—that is, were there no limitational factors—there would be no population problem in the sense Malthus envisaged it but instead constant returns. While there might, of course, be no manifestation of this problem at time t, and yet, given population growth, a manifestation scheduled to emerge at time t_n, Malthus found much evidence of it already in his day (i.e., t,). The demand for the services of limitational factors being mainly a derived demand, we may consider the operation of limitational factors at the consumer as well as the producer level.

The components of a household budget consist in part (as do components of somewhat parallel activities not included in household budgets)[13] of inputs of very scarce factors. Suppose a household budget embraces six components, or categories of goods serving given wants, A, B, C, D, E, F, embodying, respectively, significant quantities of a, b, c, d, e, f.[14] If the demand curve for A rises and the supply of a is inelastic, the price of A will rise relatively to the prices of B-F. A substitution effect will be set up against A. Moreover, cheaper forms of A will tend to displace dearer forms. For example, if A assumes two forms, A_1 and A_2, and a unit of A_2 embodies less a than does a unit of A_1, the latter will be partially displaced by the former and a will be less scarce than it otherwise would have been. This type of substitution is evident in national diets; thus when land is abundant (scarce) diets include much (little) meat.[15] Consumers of A, however, may resist a heavy substitution of A_2 and A_1 even though A_2 is comparably

---

municate the values in question. No change in value composition is produced by members of C or N who communicate only with their own kind. The increment to C is represented by the middle term in $C^2 + 2CN + N^2$. Then the proportion that C will bear to $C + N$ at any time t is $C_o/(C_o + N_o e^{-Kt})$ where the subscript o denotes the starting time and e and K are constants. It is here supposed, of course, that increments to C are proportional to communication between C and N. This model is that of Stuart C. Dodd, "Sociomatrices and Levels of Interaction," *Sociometry*, May–August 1951, pp. 237–248, esp. pp. 244–46. Minami has indicated, however, how one may proceed to deduce a logistic curve from Malthus' abstract reasoning, *op. cit.*, pp. 57–60. See also note 5 above.

13. E.g., see H. B. Chenery and P. G. Clark, *Interindustry Economics* (New York: Wiley, 1959), chaps. 2, 8.

14. This illustration is unduly simple, of course, since many goods embody a number of quite scarce inputs. For example, the proportion of certain kinds of inputs absorbed by the automotive industry ranges from 12.8 per cent of the U.S. output of copper to 75 per cent of that of plate glass. *Fortune*, June 1965, p. 137.

15. E.g., the pounds of protein produced per acre range from 500 for soybeans through 200 for corn and wheat to 45 for beef. See Paul Weiss, *Renewable Resources* (Washington, D.C.: National Academy of Sciences, Publication 1000-A, 1962), p. 116. Presumably the levels can be raised, but the proportions cannot be greatly altered. Nevertheless, consumers may still prefer beef or even corn to soybeans. For a full account of the two-level substitution process see my "Aspects of the Economy of Population Growth," *Southern Economic Journal*, October 1947, pp. 124–137.

nutritious.[16] Or they may resist substitutions within *B-F* and between *A* and *B-F*. If the budget of purchasing power is limited in the case of most or all households, and the prices of the components rise, exhaustion of the known and acceptable substitution possibilities imposes on younger households the need to limit family size. Enlargement of the budget produces an opposite effect; new components are added and there is some shift to new components of better quality.[17] Any one, or a set, of these new components can become a reproduction-limiting factor if it should become scarce, expensive, and hard to replace.

It is at the production level, the level where *a-f* are used, that the restrictive influence of limitational factors first becomes manifest. For, in proportion as *a* or *b* is limited in supply, so are A and B limited in availability. Indeed, the pace of growth of any output is set by that "needed component" of this output which is itself "of slowest growth."[18] This needed component can be anything essential to growth for which a substitute cannot be found;[19] while it normally exists in the environment external to that which is growing, it may be a product of the growth process itself.[20] This limitational factor can be time itself; thus the utility or serviceability which the consumer derives from consumables is a function of leisure time which, as a complement to consumables in final consumption processes, absorbs time that

16. Around 1800 an Irishman's daily diet consisted only of 10 pounds of potatoes and a pint of milk; yet this supplied an adequacy, by modern standards, of all he needed but Vitamin A which fell short by two thirds. See T. W. Schultz, *Economic Organization of Agriculture* (New York: McGraw-Hill, 1953), pp. 89–90. Great economies are achievable in diets, sometimes with the assistance of computers. See *ibid.,* chap. 6; also Robert Dorfman *et al., Linear Programming and Economic Analysis* (New York: McGraw-Hill, 1958), pp. 9–31. Even so, only the pressure of want wins many adherents to cheap diets.

17. E.g., U.S. Department of Labor, *How American Buying Habits Change* (Washington, D.C.: U.S. Government Printing Office, n.d., c. 1959); Ruth Mack, "Trends in American Consumption and Aspiration to Consume," *American Economic Review,* May 1956, pp. 55–68.

18. Dorfman *et al., op. cit.,* p. 281. Justus von Liebig in 1855 restated the law of the minimum, originally suggested by Carl Springle in 1839, in terms of a static conception of soils: "The productivity of a field is in direct relation to the necessary constituent contained in the soil in the smallest amount." See W. J. Spillman and Emil Lang, *The Law of Diminishing Returns* (New York: World Book Co., 1924), p. 89, and critique at pp. 119ff. See also A. J. Lotka, *Elements of Physical Biology* (Baltimore: Williams and Wilkins, 1925), pp. 97, 212–213; Schultz, *op. cit.,* pp. 142–143, U.S.D.A., *Yearbook of Agriculture* (Washington, D.C.: U.S.D.A., 1957), pp. 165–171, on soils and soil fertility.

19. Cf. A. Guha, "Scarcity of Resources as a Limit to Output," *Review of Economic Studies,* February 1963, pp. 37–42.

20. E.g., "the increasing 'self-shadowing'" that accompanies plant growth. Spillman and Lang, *op. cit.,* p. 121. The "yield of algae per unit area increases directly with the loading of organic matter per unit area until light becomes limiting." See H. B. Gotaas *et al.,* "Photosynthetic Reclamation of Organic Wastes," *Scientific Monthly,* December 1954, p. 376. Somewhat parallel is the shrinkage in prey and perhaps in predator population consequent upon prior over-predation, overfishing, overfarming, etc. See also on the impact of man-made environmental change, René Dubos, "Logic and Choices in Science," *Proceedings of the American Philosophical Society,* October 1963, pp. 365–374, esp. 371ff.

might have been devoted to production as such and thus sets limits to production. The limitational factor may be types of skill,[21] key links in food chains,[22] types of organic raw materials (e.g., wood), types of inorganic materials, energy sources, agricultural land, suitably situated non-agricultural land, utilizable water, utilizable air, space as such, channels and channel capacity for radio, television, and other modes of communication, ceilings upon realizable speeds, acceleration of processes, and so on.[23]

With every limitational or bottleneck factor a time dimension may be associated. For some obstacles are absolute, and some may be overcome, at least until absolute barriers are reached, or, more likely, barriers deemed too expensive to warrant surmounting. Some may be overcome at constant or increasing rates, at least within limits, and some, as Hornell Hart's many studies suggest, at decreasing rates of the sort implicit in S-shaped growth curves. In many instances, the overcoming process is marked by rising costs in the short-run, though technical progress continually lowers the rising cost function and thus prevents much change in recorded real cost over periods of several or more decades.[24]

Bottleneck factors operate in two ways. They set limits to rates of flow achievable in activities (e.g., hydro-power, agriculture, fisheries, utilizable wild life) susceptible of *continuous* flow; and they condition the life pattern of the flow achievable in activities based upon depletable raw-material sources. The "limiting factor in the productivity of plants is the photosynthetic efficiency with which the plant converts light energy to energy stored in plant material."[25] The "upper limit of crop yield corresponds to conservation in plant material of the order of 2 to 5 per cent of the energy of the incident visible light, the exact figure depending upon the average intensity of the incident light." These limits are roughly approached only in parts of Japan, Western Europe, and the United States. They probably could be raised somewhat if increased conductivity of CO_2 could be bred into plants.[26] As in agriculture, so in the fields of hydro-power, fisheries,

21. See Norbert Wiener, *Cybernetics* (New York: Wiley, 1948), pp. 8–9. "If the difficulty of a physiological problem is mathematical in essence, ten physiologists ignorant of mathematics will get precisely as far as one physiologist ignorant of mathematics, and no further." *Ibid.*, p. 9.

22. Lotka, *op. cit.*, pp. 176–84: *idem.*, Théorie analytique des associations biologiques, Part I (Paris: Hermann et cie., 1934), pp. 35–45.

23. For examples see Lotka, *Elements*, pp. 96–97, 179ff., 211–212, 222ff., 225, 276–279, 292ff., 334; John R. Platt, "The Step to Man," *Science*, August 6, 1965, pp. 607–613.

24. See H. J. Barnett and C. Morse, *Scarcity and Growth* (Baltimore: Johns Hopkins Press, 1963).

25. James Bonner, "The Upper Limit of Crop Yield," *Science*, CXXXVII, July 6, 1962, p. 11; also Harrison Brown *et al., The Next Hundred Years* (New York: Viking Press, 1957).

26. Bonner, *op. cit.*, p. 14. O. W. Wilcox related the upper yield limit to the nitrogen content of the dry substance of the plant species cultivated. He estimated that no plant species could utilize more than 318 pounds of nitrogen per acre. He reported yields as high as 20.9 per unit of the theoretical maximum had been attained only for sugar beets. *ABC of Agrobiology* (New

and utilizable wild life, upper limits are being attained only in certain areas. Continuation and augmentation of current use of depletable resources will exhaust current reserves of most of these in not many decades. It is quite possible, however, that fusion and fission, assisted by breeder reactors, can provide inexhaustible energy sources, and that these in turn may make available substitutes for all or most scarce resources.[27]

Changes in what Lotka called parameters of state—topography, climate, oxygen and carbon dioxide content of the atmosphere, and so on—can shift the locus of limitational factors much as a change in technology can shift supply functions, or as an alteration of parameters changes the values of the coefficients which fix equilibrium.[28] Changes of this sort have taken place in the distant past and account for great changes in the abundance of life in the biosphere,[29] though the "mass of living matter" in the biosphere "has remained fairly constant."[30] It is possible, for example, that continuation of the post-1900 increase in the carbon dioxide content of the biosphere can materially alter man's habitat.[31] It is also possible that changes in the parameters which define the character of various species, especially man, can modify the locus of limitational factors.[32]

Malthus reasoned in terms of limitational factors though his reasoning was obscured by his use of an arithmetical ratio to represent plausibly the

York: Norton, 1937), chaps. 13–15: *idem.,* "Sugar Can Win the Race against World Hunger," reprinted from *Sugar,* April 1949, and "Why Some Crop Plants Yield More Than Others," *Science,* July 9, 1948, pp. 38–39. Food yields could therefore be greatly increased by substituting plants low in nitrogen content for those relatively high in nitrogen content. For criticism see Schultz, *op. cit.,* pp. 142–143.

27. Paul McGann, "Technological Progress and Minerals," in Joseph J. Spengler, ed., *Natural Resources and Economic Growth* (Washington: Resources for the Future, 1961), pp. 74–97, also my comments, pp. 294–303. See M. K. Hubbert, *Energy Resources* (Washington, D. C.: National Academy of Sciences, 1962); Weiss, *op. cit.:* D. F. Frasché, *Mineral Resources* (Washington, D.C.: National Academy of Sciences, 1962); J. T. Madell, "Breeder Reactors," *Industrial Research,* July 1965, pp. 58–63.

28. Lotka, *Elements,* pp. 43–44, 300ff., 319ff.

29. E.g., see L. V. Berkner and L. C. Marshall, "The History of Oxygenic Concentration in the Earth's Atmosphere," in *Chemical Reactions in the Atmosphere, Discussions of the Faraday Society,* No. 37, 1964, pp. 122–141, esp. pp. 130–131, 133–39; M. N. Bramlette, "Massive Extinctions in Biota at the End of Mesozoic Time," *Science,* June 25, 1965, pp. 1696–1699; N. D. Newell, "Crises in the History of Life," *Scientific American,* February 1963, pp. 77–92.

30. Vernadsky, "The Biosphere and the Noösphere," *loc. cit.,* p. 3. The mass is still increasing "towards a limit." *Ibid.*

31. Rankama and Sahama, *op. cit.,* pp. 545–548; Lotka, *Elements,* chap. 17; F. H. Day considers it "unlikely that human contributions" of CO_2 will "have much permanent geochemical significance." *The Chemical Elements in Nature* (London: George W. Harrap & Co., 1963), chap. 13, esp. pp. 215–216.

32. On the impact of parameter change, see Lotka, *Elements,* pp. 44–46. L. C. Eiseley points out that man's capacity to survive, barring nuclear destruction, probably turns upon his avoiding excessive specialization, since it is always the unspecialized who become ascendant. "Is Man Here to Stay?" *Scientific American,* November 1950, pp. 52–55.

decrease in the marginal productivity of inputs. It is land, or shortage of land, that constituted Malthus' fundamental limitational factor. Man's power to increase "the means of his support" is "obviously limited by the scarcity of land—by the great natural barrenness of a very large part of the surface of the earth—and by its decreasing proportion of produce which must necessarily be obtained from the continued additions of capital to land already in cultivation." Malthus mentions also the "diminishing and limited power of increasing the produce of the soil" and "the want of room and nourishment" which is "the great check to the increase of plants and animals," but he does not note that overfarming and overgrazing could produce erosion and deplete soil fertility. The ultimate check, "want of food,"[33] the main component of most household budgets, is traceable to want of land and the low elasticity of the productivity of land. He did not, however, take into account the high rate of use of land for non-agricultural purposes.

That other wants than food might limit population is compatible with Malthus' argument though not stressed by him. It was desirable that the budgets of workers include some conveniences and comforts, the elasticity of supply of which was greater than that of food.[34] Such addition could stimulate moral restraint, and in some instances, could cushion the impact of a crop shortage.[35]

Malthus' stress upon the low elasticity of the food supply probably was based upon general observation rather than upon the rising food costs and rent which must have influenced Ricardo.[36] Of course, had Malthus been fully aware of the general lowness of yields and the very limited improvement achieved, his pessimism would have been fortified.[37]

In Malthus' day a notable change was taking place in the relative importance of the sources upon which Englishmen drew for raw materials. A

33. *A Summary View*, in Glass, *op. cit.*, p. 122; also *Essay*, pp. 4–5, 7, 436–38. On limitational factors in general see my "Limitational Factors in Population Theory," *Kyklos*, Vol. VII, Fasc. 3, 1954, pp. 227–243. On Malthus's neglect of soil depletion, see *Essay*, Bk. I, chap. 8, on Africa; there is no reference to the adverse effect overcropping and overgrazing exercise upon the soil and its fertility.

34. *Essay*, pp. 419–420.

35. The use of "grain in making spirits" operated as a cushion because in times of crop failure grain could be diverted from this use to use as food. *Ibid.*, pp. 125–126; see also *ibid.*, pp. 435–436.

36. In England wheat yield per acre fell from 24 to 22 bushels between 1771 and 1812, with marginal land yielding only 8 bushels, or little more than the average of 9 for France in 1789. See Colin Clark, *The Conditions of Economic Progress*, 2nd ed. (London: Macmillan, 1951), pp. 225–27, and (with M. R. Haswell) *The Economics of Subsistence Agriculture* (London: Macmillan, 1964), pp. 95, 99. The rise in grain prices between the 1790's and 1812 elevated agricultural rents and strengthened the impression that only high prices could evoke an adequate domestic supply of grain. See Kenneth Smith, *The Malthusian Controversy* (London: Routledge & Kegan Paul, 1951), pp. 82–85.

37. "Over a large part of the world today, agricultural productivity is now the same as, or even inferior to, what it was in the leading civilized communities 2,000 years ago." Clark and Haswell, *op. cit.*, p. 78, also pp. 91–92, 105–107, 146–53 on income elasticity of demand for food.

shift was taking place from organic flow resources to inorganic stock resources, especially from wood to coal and iron and brick. Whence the dependence of industry upon agriculture, so much stressed by Quesnay and
Smith, was somewhat relaxed. It was becoming possible to increase some
sectors of the economy much more rapidly than ever before, by drawing on
long accumulated inorganic reserves instead of on current organic flows
of produce and wood in a land-short country with declining forests. The
shift from organic to inorganic raw materials, together with the resulting
greater concentration of activity, also reduced the relative input of transport, usually heavy in an agricultural economy.[38] If Malthus recognized the
partial easing of the agricultural constraint upon industrial expansion and
the possible release of landed resources to food production, he ignored it.
After all, the elasticity of the food supply had not really been increased,
nor had that of population fallen significantly enough. He did not even suggest, as Jevons would less than a half century later, that English industry
was living on borrowed time, that a day would come when easily accessible
mineral reserves would be exhausted. Malthus' great concern remained
the food supply: it stifled other concerns that might have risen within the
context of the "population question." We shall therefore disregard the role of
natural resources other than food and examine the validity of Malthus'
view respecting the degree of adequacy of the prospective food supply.
After all, as Simon Kuznets and others have shown, the present economic
state of many underdeveloped countries remains inferior to England and
Western Europe in Malthus' day.[39]

III. Operation of Checks

Much of Malthus' *Essay* dealt with the operation of checks since checks
constituted the response whereby the growth of population was kept in
line with the growth of output. While the positive checks, other than infanticide and abortion, of which Malthus strongly disapproved, were essentially automatic, the preventive checks, together with abortion and infanticide, were essentially conscious and behavioral. They were responses to
man's numbers/habitat situation, or to his perception of the current and
prospective status of this situation. He did not count upon overcrowding,

38. E. A. Wrigley, "The Supply of Raw Materials in the Industrial Revolution," *Economic
History Review*, XV, No. 1, 1962, pp. 1–16, esp. 1–4. On transport in agricultural economies,
see Clark and Haswell, *op. cit.*, chap. 9; on changes in the composition of the labor force,
Phyllis Deane and W. A. Cole, *British Economic Growth 1688–1959* (Cambridge: University
Press, 1962), chap. 4.
39. *Economic Growth and Structure* (New York: Norton, 1965), pp. 176–193, and Kuznets'
essay in A. N. Agarwala and S. P. Singh, eds., *The Economics of Underdevelopment* (New
York: Oxford University Press, 1963), pp. 137–153. See also Clark and Haswell, *op. cit.*

even in the animal world, to reduce fecundity.[40] Deliberate action was indicated. He supposed the advantages of family limitation to be so great that, once fully apprehended by the individual, they were likely to prompt him to defer marriage until he could support a family in keeping with the household head's station in life. Malthus thus reinvigorated a rule of perhaps medieval origin. Others seem to have believed that the benefits and the costs of excessive fertility were too widely diffused to insure appropriate action at the individual level. Such could have been J. S. Mill's view when he indicated that Utopian "Communism" was well-suited to curb population growth.[41]

Two misunderstandings have led to criticism of Malthus' reasoning. Checks emerge because the rate of population growth R_p exceeds or threatens to exceed the rate of growth of income R_y. It makes no difference whether R_y is very low and/or falling so long as it is likely to fall short of R_p in some measure. Malthus, as we saw, believed R_y would usually be very low; whence even a low R_p might generate check-exercising behavior which was directed to preserving a level of per capita income rather than a desired rate of increase of income. The rate of growth R_y that was developed in much of Europe and Europe overseas and later in Japan appreciably exceeded R_p, however, and permitted a continuing rise in average income y and hence in the "objective" and the "subjective" standards of life and the spread between them.[42] Individuals in the populations of these countries were interested, therefore, not merely in preserving y but in preserving some rate of increase $\Delta y/y$. Accordingly, they resorted to abortion, deferment of marriage, contraceptive practices, celibacy, and occasionally even infanticide to keep R_p sufficiently behind R_y, especially when mortality began to fall and increase R_p.[43] Malthus' theory of the emergence of voluntary or preventive checks when R_p threatens to outstrip R_y and reduce $(R_y - R_p)R_y$ to a negligible magnitude belongs to the same set of theories as the modern

40. See E. D. LeCren and M. W. Holdgate, eds., *The Exploitation of Natural Populations* (Oxford: Blackwell, 1962).

41. "Any augmentation of numbers which diminished the comfort or increased the toil of the mass, would then cause (which now it does not) immediate and unmistakable inconvenience to every individual in the association; inconvenience which could not then be imputed to the avarice of employers, or the unjust privileges of the rich." Opinion could reprobate and, if necessary, repress "this or any other culpable self-indulgence at the expense of the community. The Communistic scheme, instead of being peculiarly open to the objection drawn from the danger of overpopulation, has the recommendation of tending in an especial degree to the prevention of that evil." *Principles of Political Economy* (1848), W. J. Ashley, ed. (New York, 1909), pp. 206–207.

42. Here the term "objective" refers to actual patterns of consumption or want-satisfaction whereas the term "subjective" refers to the "objective" standard *plus* unsatisfied but actively desired latent wants which border on those satisfied and are or easily could become conduct determining. An increase in the spread between the two standards may produce a change in the composition of the objective standard, reduce fertility, increase the supply of effort, etc.

43. Davis, "The Theory –," *loc. cit.,* pp. 345–366; see also A. Landry, *La révolution demographique* (Paris: Librairie du Receuil Sirey, 1934), pp. 169–204.

one which stresses prevention of the decline of $(R_y - R_p)/R_y$ below a minimally acceptable positive level. This is the first misunderstanding.

The second misunderstanding is a sequel to the first. Malthus pointed to the possibility of both a decline in incomes in some countries, among them the United States, and an increase in others, especially England.[44] This increase was limited, of course, by limiting factors in a finite universe which limited the realizable upward shifts of returns functions.[45] Of primary concern here, however, is Malthus' failure to develop a social mechanism that would insure a population's continuing to grow less rapidly than income, provided income began for a time to grow more rapidly than population. He was not equipped with such concepts as rising expectations, expanding aspirations, demonstration effects, rising subjective standard of living, etc. Not only were the means of communication and social mobility limited in his day. The marked absence of durable goods from budgets in which outlay upon food, clothing, and housing bulked large also militated against the easy extension of expenditures to complexes of goods whose consumption was likely to entail outlays growing faster than disposable income. Should this category of complexes of goods and services come to bulk sufficiently large in budgets, its further growth would entail diminution in expenditure upon some other components in living budgets.[46] Even today economists and demographers neglect this task with which Malthus was inadequately equipped to deal. For, since income cannot be made to grow as fast as population can grow if unimpeded, it becomes necessary to explain how increase in per capita income and income-use operates to increase the subjective and objective standards of life and thus divert all or nearly all of the continuing increment in income from the support of increase in population to increase in per capita consumption, savings, and leisure, all components of the standard of life. Here is not the place to describe this mechanism. It cannot properly be assumed to be part of a model, as economists often do; it must be shown to be an integral part of the processes underlying income growth.[47]

---

44. *Essay*, pp. 294–95, 360, 461–62.

45. See "My Aspects . . . ," *loc. cit.*, Secs. IV–V; Minami, *op. cit.*, pp. 60–62.

46. Let y denote an individual's disposable income, N the category of goods and services newly introduced into the individual's living budget, and O the category of old goods, or goods and services consumed prior to the addition of N. If the income elasticity of demand for $N > 1$, the proportion of y spent upon O must decline, and if expenditure upon N continues to grow, in keeping with this elasticity, expenditure upon some components of O must decline. We thus have a situation in which components of the *subjective* standard of living for which demand had been *latent* are introduced into niches formed in the objective standard by rising income y, but from which they spread (after the manner of some plants when introduced into favorable ecological settings) until the relative and finally the absolute importance of some components of the *objective* standard is reduced. See note 42 above.

47. I have touched upon the process in "Values and Fertility Analysis," to appear in *Demography*. R. A. Easterlin dealt with this process in "On the Relation of Economic Factors to Re-

IV. Malthusian vs. Non-Malthusian Countries

The countries of the world may be assembled into three pairs of sets, based, respectively, on stage of economic development, on adequacy of the food supply, and on level of fertility. Since these three pairs roughly coincide, it may be inferred that a quite similar set of causes is responsible for each dichotomization. For example, if we classify as developed economies, Europe, Northern America, the Soviet Union, and Oceania, we include, as of 1960, about 29 per cent of the world's population and 45 and 46 per cent, respectively, of its arable land and its permanent meadows and pastures, on which are produced about 56 per cent of the world's food. Moreover, the land susceptible of cultivation is subject to appreciable increase, at least outside Europe. This convenient classification is open to objection, however, in that Japan, Israel, and South Africa ought to be included, on the basis of level of income attained and the progressiveness of their industry and agriculture. Then the remainder of the world's countries with perhaps several exceptions in Latin America is describable as economically underdeveloped.

Again, countries may be classified on the basis of the quantitative and the qualitative adequacy of their food supply. Let requirements of calories be put at 2600 per day in the developed world and at 2300–2400 elsewhere. Then undernutrition is pronounced only in Asia where average consumption is about 10 per cent below the required level, though it is quite manifest also in Africa and Latin America where the realized average level of calorie intake is so near the required level that the intake for many individuals must fall below this level.[48] If, in addition, average protein requirements per day are put at 70 g., of which half are to be of animal origin, there is also much malnutrition in Africa and Latin America as well as in Asia.[49] Thus estimates of degree of diet-deficiency turn on the definition of adequacy. For example, Sukhatme observes that only 10–15 per cent "of the world's population are undernourished"; but he adds that if one uses

---

cent and Projected Fertility Changes," presented at the 1965 meeting of the Population Association of America. He accounted in particular for the fall *in fertility* in younger age groups. During the past 10–15 years a number of papers, among them essays by Richard Nelson, H. Leibenstein, Everett Hagen, and others, have dealt with escape from the Malthusian equilibrium trap, though in a different way than J. S. Mill whose main stress was upon fertility control rather than upon increase of output. E.g., see Ryoshin Minami, "A Model of Economic and Demographic Development," *Hitotsubashi Journal of Economics*, February 1964, pp. 51–61.

48. Food and Agricultural Organization (hereafter FAO), *Third World Food Survey* (Rome: FAO, 1964), pp. 36–44; R. Passmore, "Estimation of Food Requirements," in M. G. Kendall, ed., *Food Supplies and Population Growth* (Edinburgh: Oliver and Boyd, 1963), pp. 22–33; P. V. Sukhatme, "The World's Hunger and Future Needs in Food Supplies," *Journal of Royal Statistical Society*, CCXXIV, Part 4, 1961, pp. 463–525, esp. 471–82; U.S.D.A., *World Food Budget, 1970* (Washington, D.C.: U.S.D.A., 1964), pp. 23–27, 45.

49. Passmore, *op. cit.*, pp. 30–31; FAO, *op. cit.*, pp. 88–93.

British, French, or FAO, nutritional standards, "one-third to one-half of the world's people suffer from undernutrition or malnutrition."[50] A U.S. Dept. of Agriculture (hereinafter U.S.D.A.) study, using age- and weight-based calorific reference standards of 2300–2700 calories, together with 39–46 grams of fat, found diets generally adequate in Europe, the U.S.S.R., Northern America, Oceania, Southern Africa, Mexico, Brazil, Uruguay, Argentina, and Japan, but inadequate elsewhere.[51] The population of these diet-adequate regions, 36.2 per cent of the world's population in 1959–61 and averaging 17 persons per 100 acres, is growing about 1.3 per cent per year. That in the diet-deficit areas, 63.8 per cent of the world's population and averaging 53 persons per 100 acres, is growing 2.1 per cent or more per year.[52]

Finally, the countries of the world fall nicely into two quite distinct fertility groups, those with Gross Reproduction Rates (GRR) above 2 and those with rates below 2.[53] Rates of less than 2 are found only in Northern America, Europe (exclusive of Albania), the Soviet Union, Australia, New Zealand, Zanzibar, White South Africa, Cyprus, Israel, Japan, the Ryuku Islands, Argentina, and Uruguay. These countries include only about 32 per cent of the world's population. Comparison of the unweighted averages for these countries with those characterized by a GRR above 2 indicates fertility to be less than half as high; average income is over four times as high, energy consumption per head is over six times as high, and urbanization and nonagricultural activities are about twice as high. In short, important differences in cultural, economic, and social conditions set the high-fertility countries apart from the low-fertility countries. The data suggest that fertility is not likely to begin to fall until the values of social and economic indicators pass into certain threshold zones such as $230–339 or higher for average income, 16–33 per cent for urbanization, 62–75 per cent for female literacy, 45–61 per cent for non-agricultural activities, etc.[54] At present, however, the annual rate of population growth ranges in the underdeveloped world from 1.5 or less per cent in parts of Asia to around

50. *Op. cit.*, pp. 493–494. He rejects the views of M. K. Bennett and Helen Farnsworth who, among others, believe that the extent of undernutrition and malnutrition is over-estimated. *Ibid.*, pp. 473, 488ff.; also Farnsworth, "Defects, Uses, and Abuses of National Consumption Data," *Food Research Institute Studies*, November 1961, pp. 179–202; and C. Clark's inference that current reference standards may be too high, in "Future Sources of Food Supply: Economic Problems," in Kendall, ed., *op. cit.*, pp. 53–57. See also Hefford, note 57 below.

51. *The World Food Budget, 1970*, pp. 27–31; also L. R. Brown, *Food Consumption Expenditures: India, Japan, United States* (Washington, D.C.: U.S.D.A., 1962). While diets in some groups and areas are adequate even in diet-deficit regions, their relative number tends to fall as the average consumption level falls.

52. U.S.D.A., *World Food Budget, 1970*, p. 31.

53. A rate in excess of 2 signifies a crude birth rate in excess of 31 and, in most places, a rate of natural increase of 15 and over per 1000.

54. This paragraph is based upon chap. 9, *Population Bulletin of the United Nations*, No. 7, 1963, published in 1965.

3 in Africa and Latin America; in the developed world, the rate ranges from close to 0.5 per cent in Europe to close to 2 per cent in Oceania.[55]

The three classifications of countries suggest that conditions unfavorable to control of fertility are associated with conditions unfavorable to augmentation of output per acre and per agriculturalist. It is mainly in the developed countries that high output per acre and per agriculturalist has been achieved, and yet it is in the underdeveloped countries that the need to increase yields per acre is generally greatest.

V. Land Shortage: Achilles Heel

A high rate of increase in the per capita food supply is essential, in underdeveloped countries, both to the facilitation of economic development[56] and to escape from the Malthusian trap in which many such countries are caught. The food supply must annually increase approximately $R_p + iR_y$ where R_p denotes the rate of population growth, R_y signifies the rate of growth of per capita income, and i indicates the income elasticity of demand for food. Since R_p lies between two and 3 per cent, R_y often approximates 2 per cent, and i usually lies between 0.9 and 0.4 (probably between 0.8 and 0.6 in countries with per capita incomes of \$50 to \$1000), the food supply must increase 3.5 to 5 per cent or more per year in underdeveloped countries. Changes in the price structure probably do not affect this rate much; but changes in the kinds of commodities available may increase or sustain the value of i, since as income rises calories are derived from more expensive sources.[57] How difficult it is to achieve an annual increase of 3.5–5.0 per cent in required food output depends upon the form in which it

55. United Nations, *Provisional Report in World Population Prospects* (New York: United Nations, 1964), pp. 41–42.

56. B. F. Johnston and J. W. Mellor, "The Role of Agriculture in Economic Development," *American Economic Review*, September 1961, pp. 566–593; T. W. Schultz, *Transforming Traditional Agriculture* (New Haven: Yale University Press, 1964); United Nations (ECAFE), *Economic Survey of Asia and the Far East, 1964* (Bangkok: United Nations, 1965), Part I, esp. pp. 117–36.

57. R. D. Stevens, *Elasticity of Food Consumption Associated with Changes in Income in Developing Countries*, Foreign Agriculture Economic Report No. 23 (Washington, D.C.: U.S.D.A., 1965), esp. pp. iii–iv, chap. 11. See also T. W. Schultz, *Economic Organization of Agriculture*, chap. 5, and *Transforming Traditional Agriculture*, pp. 12–15 and references; National Council of Applied Economic Research, *Long Term Projections of Demand for and Supply of Selected Agricultural Commodities, 1960–61 to 1975–76* (New Delhi: National Council of Applied Economic Research, 1962), pp. 60–66, 209–14; Clark and Haswell, *op. cit.*, pp. 139–156. On the response of elasticity of inter-commodity and locational differences and on the positive association of caloric cost and income see Clark, in Kendall, ed., *op. cit.*, pp. 58–60; H. Kaneda and B. F. Johnston, "Urban Food Expenditure Patterns in Tropical Africa," *Food Research Institute Studies*, November 1961, pp. 229–275, esp. pp. 256–60; R. K. Hefford, "Asian Food Requirements—A Review," *Australian Journal of Agricultural Economics*, December 1963, pp. 151, 156–57.

is sought, since this conditions both the weight of yields per acre of food-stuffs and the number of calories and nutrients yielded per pound of food.[58] Augmenting the food supply sufficiently need present no problem to developed countries for a few decades; R_p will exceed 1 per cent only in those with excess[59] cultivable land, while in some i may already be near 0.1 or even close to falling below it.[60] Some of these countries can enlarge the area under cultivation and all can still increase yields per acre of major crops; indeed since 1935–39 per capita food production has risen in most of these countries, usually by around 10–20 per cent though in Japan by about 40 per cent.[61]

International trade transfers foodstuffs and agricultural raw materials to Europe and Asia (mainly Japan) from the other continents. Northern and Central America and Africa exported food, agricultural raw materials, and forest products on the balance, while South America and Oceania were net exporters of food and agricultural raw materials but not of forest products.[62] The situation is somewhat different in respect of grain which occupies about 71.2 per cent of world harvested crop area and yields 53 per cent of the world's calories. While only about 7.7 per cent of the world grain output was exported in 1960–61, 13.5 and 54.1 per cent, respectively, of the outputs of Northern America and Oceania were exported net. Net imports of grain approximated 28.8 per cent of Western Europe's output, 5.4 per cent of Africa's, and 4.4 per cent of Asia's.[63] If we consider only food that yields calories (i.e., food exclusive of tea and coffee and seeds not used for food) we find that in the late 1950's Europe was importing *net* about 13 per cent of its food supply (exclusive of tea and coffee) and a comparable amount of agricultural raw materials; Japan was importing *net* about 11 per cent of her

58. One cannot get 2000–3000 calories a day from "less than 500 g. (dry weight) of food and it is more likely to weigh 800 g." See N. W. Pirie, "Future Sources of Food Supply: Scientific Problems," in Kendall, ed., *op. cit.*, pp. 34–52, esp. pp. 47–48.

59. I use the term "excess" to indicate that land remains to be diverted to cultivation, but not to suggest that population growth is advantageous.

60. Colin Clark estimates that man's consumption in wheat equivalent terms cannot, compatibly with health, exceed 2½ tons or fall below ¼ ton. See Kendall, ed., *op. cit.*, p. 61. The land-saving effect of decrease in i is partly offset by the associated tendency of consumption to shift toward meat and other land-oriented foods as y rises.

61. U.S.D.A., *World Food Budget*, p. 41; also U.S.D.A., *The World Agricultural Situation* (Washington, D.C.: U.S.D.A., 1965), p. 4, together with regional supplements, ERS 113–115. See also Lester R. Brown, *Man, Land & Food* (Washington, D.C.: U.S.D.A., 1963), and *Increasing World Food Output* (Washington, D.C.: U.S.D.A., 1965), chaps. 8–10; W. H. Pawley, *Possibilities of Increasing World Food Production* (Rome: FAO, 1963), chaps. 2–4, p. 230; United Nations, *Some Factors in Economic Growth in Europe during the 1950's* (Geneva: United Nations, 1964), pp. 27–30.

62. FAO *Trade Yearbook 1962* (Rome: FAO, 1963), Table 1.

63. Brown, *Man, Land & Food*, pp. 22, 50, 58, 70. Grain formed 17.3 per cent of all agricultural trade and nearly one-third of trade in food. Fibers, natural rubber, and other non-food crops occupied less than 7 per cent of the crop area but accounted for about two-fifths of all trade in crops. Coffee, tea, and cocoa made up 12 per cent of trade but only 1.0 per cent of harvest crop area. *Ibid.*, pp. 22, 60, 70.

food supply and a larger amount of agricultural raw materials.[64] It is not expected that Japan, which currently imports about one-fifth of the agricultural products she uses, will increase this proportion in the next decade, though the composition of these imports will change.[65] Europe and Japan, unlike low-income food-short countries, are presently able to earn the foreign exchange wherewith to purchase their required agricultural products; so they continue to add to the aggregate demand for landed products in regions with surpluses for export. It should be noted that because only a small fraction of the world's food supply is available for export and because most food-short countries are short of exchange, not much relief is to be had from food imports.[66]

The diet-deficit world, which includes all of the underdeveloped world except Mexico, Brazil, Argentina, and Uruguay, presents a quite different situation than does the developed world. In the diet-deficit world, exclusive of Communist Asia, food production per capita has increased only 0.32 per cent per year since the late 1930's and this rate is not expected to be exceeded, at least before 1970 if then. If Communist Asia is included, the rate is reduced to 0.12 per cent for the early period, while the prospective post-1960 rate is unlikely to attain the 1.03 per cent level originally anticipated.[67] In Asia, Africa, and Latin America food production thus has done little (if any) more than keep pace with population since the 1930's, and each continent has become something of a net importer of calories instead of an exporter as formerly.[68] Given the generally high income elasticity of demand in low-income countries for food together with urbanization and rising incomes, the upward pressure on food prices must often have been severe, making for inflation and retarding economic development.

Increase in agricultural output in much of the world is conditioned by increase in output per acre rather than by increase in acreage. Even if our world were "one world," as peace-loving men wish, acreage would be limited. Land that is arable or in tree crops is usually estimated at 3.5–

64. U.S.D.A. *World Food Budget 1970*, pp. 11, 51, 52, and the four studies on *Food Balances* (E.R.S. 86, 88, 119, 124 Washington, D.C.: U.S.D.A., 1964–65); J. F. Dewhurst et al., *Europe's Needs and Resources* (New York: Twentieth Century Fund, 1961), pp. 500, 640–641, 646, 649; United Nations, *Economic Survey of Europe 1960* (Geneva: United Nations, 1961), pp. III–35, IV–44–45.

65. Institute for Agricultural Economic Research, *Japanese Import Requirement: Projections of Agricultural Supply and Demand for 1965, 1970, and 1975* (Tokyo: University of Tokyo, 1964), pp. 2, 14–17; also H. H. Spurlock, *Trends and Developments in Japan's Economy Affecting the Market for U.S. Farm Products, 1950–62* (Washington, D.C.: U.S. D.A., 1964).

66. About 9 per cent of the world's food output enters international trade, of which about four-fifths is imported by diet-adequate, developed countries. See *World Food Budget*, pp. 45, 52.

67. *World Food Budget*, p. 41. See my Table I.

68. U.S.D.A., *World Agricultural Situation 1965* and supplements on Asia, Africa, and Latin America; Brown, *Man, Land & Food*, pp. 75–79.

4.0 billion acres of which hardly 2.5 billion are annually harvested. Here and there this acreage can be swelled by converting into crop land some permanent meadow and pasture land, of which there are about 6.3 billion acres, nearly 3.5 being located in Africa, Asia, and Latin America. It has also been suggested that one billion acres in the tropics and 300 million acres in the north temperate zone could be made cultivable, though at considerable developmental expense,[69] and even larger estimates of potentially arable land have been put forward. Of the harvested area, 71.2, 7.2, and 5 per cent, respectively, were devoted to grains, oilseeds, and roots and tubers around 1960; only 5.5 per cent were devoted to fibers, rubber, and tobacco.[70] There continues to be increase in harvested grain acreage; that in underdeveloped regions rose 32 per cent between 1934–38 and 1960–61 while that in developed regions as a whole rose not at all, declines in some countries offsetting increases in others. But this increase was more than offset by population growth, acres in grain per capita declining from 0.48 to 0.43 in the underdeveloped world and from 1.02 to 0.85 in the developed world.[71] Moreover, grain yield per harvested acre rose only 8 per cent in the underdeveloped world, in contrast with 51 per cent in the developed world. Furthermore, per capita grain output declined 3 per cent in the underdeveloped world whilst rising 26 per cent in the developed.[72]

India, Pakistan, and Mainland China where live about 70 per cent of Asia's population, and about 40 per cent of the world's, epitomize land- and food-shortage problems. Population is dense and increasing around 2 per cent or more per year, per capita income and food consumption are very low, arable land per capita is low and yields per acre are appreciably below those in advanced countries and increasing much less rapidly, and there is little uncultivated arable land.[73] The past performance of agriculture has not been good. Thus in British India agricultural output increased very little between 1900 and independence (1947).[74] While agricultural output has roughly kept pace with population since then, even though crop acreage is becoming relatively fixed, there has been little improvement in agricultural

69. Pawley, *op. cit.*, chap. 2; Brown, *Man, Land & Food*, chap. 3. Most optimistic is Colin Clark's estimate that, by weighting different grades of land and allowing for double cropping, one can put at the equivalent of about 19 billion standard temperate zone acres the cultivable land of the earth. Of these 65 per cent are in Asia, Africa, and Latin America. See *Conditions of Economic Progress*, 3rd. ed. (London: Macmillan, 1957), pp. 308ff.

70. Brown, *Man, Land & Food*, pp. 22.

71. *Ibid.*, pp. 50, 53, 55.

72. *Ibid.*, pp. 52, 56.

73. See *ibid.*, p. 56; Brown, *Increasing World Food Output*, pp. 5–6; and *An Economic Analysis of Far Eastern Agriculture* (Washington, D.C.: U.S.D.A., 1961), pp. 3, 5, 7, 10, 12, 25, 26, 43, 47; data relating to Asia in my Table I. In Pakistan additions of new land are offset by losses of farm land "due to waterlogging and salinity." Brown, *Man, Land & Food*, pp. 100–101.

74. Clark, *Conditions*, Table III, facing p. 257, and Table XXVIII, pp. 296–300; also Clark and Haswell, *op. cit.*, pp. 78–79; United Nations, *Economic Survey of Asia and the Far East 1964*, pp. 117–18, 131.

conditions and yields and both India and Pakistan have had to import considerable grain.[75] These imports will rise, at least in India, if, as now seems likely, the food supply does not keep pace with population in the coming decade.[76] The food situation of Communist China seems to be worse than that of India. Since the mid-1950's agricultural production has increased only negligibly, and since 1960 about half China's exchange earnings have been used to purchase foreign grain.[77] In the future China, along with India and Pakistan, will have to rely almost entirely upon activities that increase output per acre, that is, on multiple cropping, fallowing, greater fertilization, irrigation, pesticides, improved varieties, mechanization which saves land and permits better allocation of time and superior crop combinations, other yield-increasing cultural practices, and sufficient price incentive.[78]

Conditions of the sort found in India, Pakistan, and Mainland China are encountered in other regions as well, albeit in not so severe a form. In Table I are summarized data for representative diet-adequate countries and for diet-deficit regions. The food deficit is about one-sixth in China, 5–6 per cent in South and East Asia, somewhat lower in Central America, and 1–3 per cent elsewhere. Average income and food consumption are much lower in the diet-deficit countries than elsewhere and their populations may grow nearly twice as fast. Yield per acre is much lower than in the diet-adequate countries. The prospects of West Asia and most of Latin America and Africa appear superior to that of other food-deficit areas; their populations are much less dense and their area under cultivation is more susceptible of increase than is that of South and East Asia. Modernization of the cultivation of African soils may, however, be hindered by lack of knowledge of their behavior.[79]

Exemplars of what can be done to cope with land- and food-shortage are the United States and Japan. In 1870–1920 increase in inputs, mainly land

75. Brown, *Increasing World Food Output*, pp. 27–28, and *Man, Land & Food*, pp. 101–102; W. F. Hall, *Agriculture in India* (Washington, D.C.: U.S.D.A., 1964), pp. 7, 34–36, and *Agriculture in Pakistan* (Washington, D.C.: U.S.D.A., 1965), pp. 5, 7, 10–11; also U.S.D.A., *The Far East, Communist China, Oceania Agricultural Situation 1965* (Washington, D.C.: U.S.D.A., 1965), pp. 32–36, 46; United Nations, *Economic Survey of Asia and the Far East 1964*, pp. 117–128, 131–133. Net cereal imports in 1960–63 averaged 6.2 per cent of India's cereal production and 7.5 per cent of Pakistan's. *Ibid.*, pp. 120, 132.

76. C. E. Pike, *India-Projections to 1975–76 of Supply and Demand for Selected Agricultural Products* (Washington, D.C.: U.S.D.A., no date, probably 1964). The projections criticized are in National Council of Applied Economic Research, *op. cit.*

77. U.S.D.A., *The 1965 Far East, Communist China, Oceania Agricultural Situation*, pp. 37–39; see note 68 above. See also J. R. Wenmohs, "Mainland China's Agriculture Showing Some Improvement," *Foreign Agriculture*, May 31, 1965, pp. 6–7.

78. Brown, *Man, Land & Food*, pp. 103–115, and *Increasing World Food Output*, chap. 9; Pawley, *op. cit.*; O. Nervik and E. Haghjoo, "Mechanization in Underdeveloped Countries," *Journal of Farm Economics*, August 1961, pp. 663–666.

79. FAO, *State of Food and Agriculture* (Rome: FAO, 1958), pp. 93, 128–129, 131; D. L. Linton, "Population and Food in the Tropical World," *Advancement of Science*, November 1961, pp. 392–401; W. O. Jones, "Food and Agricultural Economies of Tropical Africa," *Food Research Institute Studies*, February 1961, pp. 3–20.

Table I. Food Production, Productivity, and Consumption Relative to Population, 1959–61.*

Subregion	Share of world's		Population per 100 acres	Grain yield per acre	Per capita food consumption	Income per capita
	Agricultural land %	Population %				
Diet adequate						
United States	11.3	6.0	16	972	$109.20	$2,342
Northern Europe	2.5	7.0	88	1145	93.20	1,093
U.S.S.R.	15.3	7.1	15	355	64.50	–
Japan	0.2	3.1	527	1646	51.20	395
Mexico	2.4	1.2	15	369	43.70	281
Total**	62.7	36.2	17	638	77.00	1,074
Diet deficit						
Central America, Caribbean	0.6	1.1	61	456	47.50	227
Part of South America	2.1	1.7	25	217	49.40	263
North Africa	4.7	2.8	19	418	35.40	112
West Central Africa	6.6	3.6	17	465	31.30	81
East Africa	5.0	1.6	10	696	40.90	86
West Asia	5.1	2.7	16	328	42.40	193
India	4.4	14.3	100	372	29.80	69
Other South Asia	1.2	4.2	108	503	35.30	69
Communist Asia	7.4	23.7	100	–	23.50	–
Other East Asia	1.6	8.2	154	492	35.80	82
Total	37.3	63.8	53	411	31.00	97
World	100.0	100.0	31	544	47.40	–

* Based upon U.S.D.A., *World Food Budget 1970*, pp. 11, 14, 18, 31, 48.
** Includes several areas otherwise omitted.

and labor, accounted for about 77 per cent of the 2.2 per cent per year increase in agricultural output in the United States. Since the late 1930's, however, increased fertilizer has accounted for over half the continuing 2.2 per cent per year increase, with irrigation, new varieties, and better practices mainly responsible for the rest.[80] Japan, though "essentially a fixed-land agricultural economy," has been able to increase its productivity per acre and its output 1.0 to 1.5 per cent per year, or almost enough to match its population growth.[81] Today rice production per acre in Japan is nearly four times as high as in India and about three-tenths higher than in the United States. Japan uses 118.7, 52.03, and 75.62 pounds per acre, respectively, of nitrogen, phosphate, and potassium fertilizers; the corresponding figures for India are 1.1, 0.18, and 0.11, and for the United States 12.96, 12.32, and 10.45.[82]

80. R. P. Christenson, *et al.*, *How the United States Improved Its Agriculture* (Washington, D.C.: U.S.D.A., 1964), pp. 3, 8–9, 19–21, 25–27.
81. Brown, *Increasing World Food Output*, pp. 68–73.
82. Brown, *An Economic Analysis*, pp. 14, 26, also p. 25 where the dollar value of crops per acre in Japan is reported as 3.6 times that in the United States and 8.3 times that in India. See also Clark, *Conditions*, p. 280, on fertilizer inputs.

How much average yield can be raised is problematical. It is probable that in many areas fertilizer inputs can increase output 100–300 per cent.[83] Within a range the addition of a kilogram of chemical fertilizer plant nutrients tends to be accompanied by an increase of 10 kilograms in the output of grain. In fact, some Japanese rice farmers average about 11,000 pounds of paddy rice per acre or "nearly two-and-one-half times the high national average rice yield of Japan" much as some corn farmers get 150 bushels or more per acre instead of 80 to 85.[84] The response of output to fertilizer increments varies, however, from region to region and from country to country. It is affected by conditions of the soil, cultivation, and so on, tending to be higher in advanced countries than in relatively backward areas.[85] It may be affected by the tendency of the cost of grain production to rise as arable land per capita falls and agricultural intensity rates rise; it will probably be affected by severe limits to the extension of irrigation as well as by the rising costs of an inelastic supply of water.[86] There is, of course, an upper limit to yields per acre,[87] even when a country can produce the required fertilizer, or the foreign exchange wherewith to purchase it. If we assume that current yields can shortly be quadrupled, the limit to population will still be reached in about 57 years, should population grow 2.5 per cent per year. If the diet shifts somewhat toward more land-embodying products (e.g., animal products), the limit will be reached even earlier. Whether the upper limit to yields will be reached is doubtful, however, given the many changes besides increased fertilization that must be made in agriculture if yields are to be raised to the maximum levels economically attainable. It should be noted also that non-modern, underdeveloped, land-short, food-short countries are the ones least capable of substituting chemistic Edens for land-based agriculture.[88]

Malthus, it will be recalled, made land or "room" the overriding limitational factor. Whether it is, depends upon the composition of the content of living budgets. If food is the predominant component of the living budget, land will probably turn out to be the limitational factor. If dearth of food

83. H. L. Richardson, "What Fertilizers Could Do to Increase World Food Production," *The Advancement of Science*, January 1961, pp. 472–80.

84. Brown, *Increasing World Food Output*, pp. 102–103, and *Man, Land & Food*, pp. 127–28. Colin Clark estimates that in time 20 square meters could be made to supply the annual food requirements of one man, or one acre could, if laboratory conditions were met, feed about 200 men. Clark, in Kendall, ed., *op. cit.*, p. 64. Clark also calls attention to F. Daniels's estimate that the cultivation of algae might yield 50 tons of organic matter, dry weight, per hectare per year. *Conditions of Economic Progress*, 3rd ed., p. 306, note.

85. J. W. Mellor and R. W. Herdt, "Contrasting Response of Rice to Nitrogen," *Journal of Farm Economics*, February 1964, pp. 150–160; Brown, *Increasing World Food Output*, pp. 94–96, and *Man, Land & Food*, pp. 127–28.

86. *Ibid.*, pp. 94–97, 110–11, 127–28; Brown, *Increasing World Food Output*, pp. 90–93.

87. See Bonner, footnote 25 above. Incremental yields decline as fertilizer input per acre rises. See U.S.D.A., *Yearbook of Agriculture 1957* (Washington, D.C.: U.S. Government Printing Office, 1957), pp. 269–276; C. J. Pratt, "Chemical Fertilizers," *Scientific American*, June, 1965, pp. 70–72.

88. Jacob Rosen, *The Road to Abundance* (New York: McGraw-Hill, 1953).

operates indirectly to check economic development and transformation, land may prove the limitational factor. If the standard of life rises, however, other components may replace food as the fundamental limitational factor. It is quite likely, however, that limitation of food due to limitation of land will become the limitational factor in parts of Asia, Africa, and Latin America. Elsewhere land in the sense of living space is likely to become the limitational factor. Thus Malthus will have been proven right in stressing the role of limitational factor, above all agricultural land.

Having put a pessimistic face upon my discussion I may, emulating Malthus, put a conditionally optimistic mien upon the prospect. First, since food consumption per capita is quite limited, as the dwindling elasticity of demand for food shows, the immediate halting of population growth could enable even a poor people to satisfy most of their basic food requirements at the close of a few decades of economic progress. Thus, as S. J. Patel suggests, since agricultural output per head is only 2.2 times as high in the United States as in India, an increase of 2 per cent per year for about four decades would put India's output on the present American level. It would take 70 years for India to attain the present American industrial level, even were industrial output per capita to rise 5 per cent per year, assisted by the flow into industry of labor released from agriculture by progress there.[89] One might assent to Patel's inference that an adult lifetime could suffice to bridge the present day gap between India's and our own levels of living, but one would have to stipulate a virtual cessation of population growth. Still bridging the gap could prove very difficult. For, as Brown shows, the preconditions to a rapid rise in agricultural output include widespread literacy, the yield-raising capability suggested by a fairly high per capita income, a market-oriented agriculture, and a nonagricultural sector advanced enough to supply the goods and services essential to high yields. Even then, a rapid rise in yields would result only if agricultural prices were favorable and the conditions of landownership, taxation, and marketing linked reward for yield-increasing effort closely with that effort.[90]

In sum, while it is possible to demonstrate that Malthus' expectation was not well founded, it will not be easy to do so. The road to affluence remains hard. Unless the wings of the stork are clipped in the short Indian summer that lies ahead, at least one of the four horsemen, Hunger, will ride within the lifetime of our children.[91]

89. "The Economic Distance between Nations: Its Origin, Measurement and Outlook," *Economic Journal*, March 1964, pp. 127–130.

90. Brown, *Increasing World Food Output*, chaps. 5–6; also Schultz, *Traditional Agriculture*.

91. See M. K. Bennett's thoughtful, "Longer and Shorter Views of the Malthusian Prospect," *Food Research Institute Studies*, IV, No. 1, 1963, pp. 1–11. A century from now, given the current world rate of population growth, world population could number 30 billions, or about one person per acre of land of all sorts.

DEVELOPMENT

Economic Factors in the Development of Densely Populated Areas

Without frugality none can be rich, and with it very few would be poor.[1]

Industrialization, as defined in this paper, comprehends the sum total of the factors that have made and will continue to make for increase in net output per worker and/or per capita.[2] Because of limitations of space, however, and because our predominant concern is with the economic determinants of industrialization, we shall deal fully only with some of the circumstances governing industrial progress. Our treatment has been organized under seven heads, to each of which a section is devoted: I, the determinants of industrialization; II, strategy in the industrializing of under-developed countries; III, the role of material equipment in industrialization; IV, industrial development and industrial composition; V, the evolution of the labor force; VI, exchange relations and international disparities in income; VII, historical illustrations and future prospects.

While this paper treats of the industrialization of under-developed countries, it is concerned primarily with that of countries marked by pressure of population, lowness of average income, and concentration of the labor force in agriculture and forestry. For purposes of comparison and completeness of presentation, however, considerable attention will be given to under-developed countries where, though income is low and agriculture predominates, population pressure is not so marked. In this latter category fall most countries of Latin America, Africa exclusive of parts of North Africa, and Oceania. In the former category fall most countries of Asia and North Africa, together with the principal islands situated in the Caribbean area. We shall touch only cursorily upon the remaining relatively under-developed parts of the world, namely, Southern and Eastern Europe and Soviet Russia. Accordingly, while we shall not deal with all the world's under-developed economies (which embrace close to four-fifths of the world's population but get somewhat less than three-tenths of the world's output of goods and services), we shall treat of most of those within which reside that part of the world's population—more than one-half—which is still living in the neighborhood of the bare subsistence level.[3]

1. Johnson, Samuel, *The Rambler*, No. 57.

2. Our approach to industrialization emphasizes not so much its cultural and economic consequences as its nature, viz., a complex of interrelated processes governing the level and movement of output. On the definition of industrialization see Kuznets, S., An outline of a comparative study of industrialization, in *Problems in the study of growth*, N.Y., National Bureau of Economic Research, 1949; also Chang, P. K., *Agriculture and industrialization*, chap. 3, Cambridge, Harvard Press, 1949.

3. Two decades ago more than half the world's population was producing an income insufficient for subsistence, while in 1947 the per capita income of more than half the world's popula-

While the cultures of the peoples living in densely populated under-developed countries usually are more ancient and more imbedded in the social structure than are the cultures of the less densely populated under-developed countries, both sets of countries share many conditions in common. Evidence for this is provided in Tables I–III, presented at the close of this paper. Agriculture is the predominant occupation. Both within and outside agriculture workers are poorly supplied with relevant forms of productive equipment such as cultivatable land, machinery, and other forms of fixed and working capital. Education and industrial training are lacking, with something like three-fourths of the population illiterate and with technological knowledge restricted in quantity and confined to a few. Fiscal, financial, and related institutions and practices are primitive and defective, in terms of Western standards. Nutrition is quantitatively and qualitatively inadequate. Disease is widespread, mortality is high in most age brackets, and expectation of life at birth is low. Natality, together with potential natural increase, is high with the result that improvements in mortality normally are accompanied by corresponding increments in the rate of population growth. In consequence of these and other circumstances, per capita incomes are very low.

I. Determinants of Industrialization and Net Output Per Capita

Progress in industrialization, however defined, is intimately associated with that of per capita net output (= net income).[4] If industrialization is broadly defined, its determinants tend to coincide with those governing the movement of per capita income. If industrialization is more narrowly defined, its progress both conditions and is conditioned by that of per capita income. Finally and irrespective of the manner in which industrialization is defined, what constitutes its most appropriate tempo is determinable only in the context of the conception of income assumed to rule, involving, as it does, questions of income distribution and use, consumer sovereignty, and consumer freedom of choice.

---

tion was below, often appreciably below, $100. See Clark, Colin, *The conditions of economic progress*, 53, London, Macmillan, 1940, and *The economics of 1960*, appendix, London, Macmillan, 1942; United Nations, *Technical assistance for economic development*, 4, Lake Success, United Nations, 1949. For corroborating evidence see Tables I and II at the close of this paper; also Tables III–IV which indicate how lowness of money income is translated into lowness of consumption in respect of food, textiles, transportation, steel, and other significant items.

4. In this paper the terms net output and income are used interchangeably as measures of productive effectiveness. On the technical aspects of national income measurement see Shoup, Carl S., *Principles of national income analysis*, New York, Houghton Mifflin, 1947; and League of Nations, *Measurement of national income and the construction of social accounts*, Geneva, United Nations, 1947.

It should be noted that some of the aggregates used in this paper, together with the averages based thereon, are subject to various limitations. First of all, data relating to income production and use and to capital equipment in most of the under-developed countries are quantitatively and qualitatively defective and ridden with conjecture. Second, the aggregates and averages employed are subject to those limitations to which all aggregates of incommensurable elements are subject. These limitations are intensified when the aggregates are compared in time and space, for the introduction of the cultural differences associated with differences in space and time accentuates the difficulties arising out of incommensurability as such. Finally and even more difficult is the assessment of the meaning of these diverse and changing aggregates when expressed in terms of subjective, or psycho-physiological, welfare. Fortunately, the validity of most of our findings appears to be largely independent of the difficulties mentioned.[5]

The movement of net output per capita has many determinants, most of which directly govern the progress of industrialization even when this process is narrowly defined. Few if any of these determinants are completely independent, each being connected, as a rule, with one or more of the others. In fact, each of the societies of which we treat may be looked upon as a loosely integrated but essentially distinct cultural whole that is required, upon being exposed to the forces of industrialization, to accommodate itself, to these forces and absorb their effects. For this reason the progress of industrialization, while in large measure the same in all societies, varies from society to society. Even so, the determinants of industrialization, though physically inseparable, are analytically and empirically distinguishable from one another.

We present below a list of twenty determinants of the progress of industrialization, sixteen of which govern its movement directly and four of which affect its movement indirectly through the medium of income and related changes. Some of these determinants are described at this point. Others are merely listed, since they are treated below. While all of these determinants affect the course of industrialization in a closed or a world-wide economy, some lose much of their significance when the economy to which they relate is an open component of the world-wide economy, for under these circumstances the economy in question can draw upon other economies in respect of the determinant under consideration. The sixteen determinants that directly affect the course of industrialization follow:

1. Material equipment (i.e., productive machinery, utilizable land, natural

5. Some of the difficulties referred to have been treated by Samuelson, Paul A., Evaluation of Real National Income, *Oxford Econ. Papers* 2: 1–29, 1950; Little, I. M. D., The foundation of welfare economics, *ibid.*, 1: 227–246, 1949; Arrow, Kenneth J., *Social choice and individual values*, Chicago, Cowles Commission Discussion Paper (Economics: No. 258), 1949; Bergson, A., Socialist economics, in Ellis, H. S., ed., *A survey of contemporary economic theory*, 412–418, Phila., Blakiston, 1948.

resources, and other forms of "capital") per worker. This determinant is conditioned by the rates of saving, capital formation, and population growth.

2. The state of health of the population.

3. The exchange relations obtaining between the economy under analysis and other economies.

4. State of the industrial arts. Hereunder may be included the level of applied technological and related knowledge and practice, together with the extent to which this knowledge is diffused throughout the population. The occupational composition of a country's labor force reflects, as do other rough indices, the level of applied and applicable knowledge. In general, the more varied and the more differentiated the nonprofessional component of the labor force, the more advanced is the state of a country's industrial arts. This being the case, questions relating to the occupational composition of a country's labor force are in essence questions relating more fundamentally to the state of that country's industrial arts.

5. The educational, the scientific, and the related cultural equipment of the population. Hereunder should be included all basic and facilitating information (i.e., knowledge that resembles "seed corn" rather than mere engineering "knowhow" which is included under [4]), together with the elements that govern the accumulation and dissemination of such information. Inasmuch as institutional and other circumstances invariably cause the level of *applied* knowledge to fall short of the level of *available* knowledge, the state of the industrial arts almost always may be improved somewhat even though determinant (5) remains unchanged. Ultimately, however, the progress of (4) is restricted by that of (5).

6. Dominant character of the politico-economic system. Such a system may be free-enterprise, mixed or dual, social-democratic, or "totalitarian" in character, with the result that the role of the state in economic affairs may vary greatly. Presumably, since these systems differ in the effects they exercise upon consumer sovereignty, capital formation, "incentive," and the accumulation and diffusion of technological and related knowledge, they must differ in their aggregate effects upon the rate of industrialization.

7. The relative magnitude of that part of the population which is adept at making entrepreneurial and innovational decisions, together with the location and the distribution of the power to make and execute such decisions. For industrial progress is markedly dependent upon (a) the relative number of imaginative and energetic innovators and entrepreneurs present in the population, (b) the extent to which these qualified persons are empowered to make and execute relevant decisions, and (c) the degree to which these individuals are free of hampering legal and institutional arrangements. In the past this distribution has been most favorable in countries possessing a comparatively strong "middle class" that enjoyed sufficient support at the hands of the state; while countries lacking a sufficiently strong middle class

have had to depend upon the state to provide entreprenuerial leadership in so far as possible.

8. The distribution of workers among occupations and the relative amount of unemployment (complete, partial, or disguised) present in the economy. An individual is completely unemployed if he is an unengaged job-seeker, or if, given accepted standards, he ought to be enrolled in the labor force. An individual is partially unemployed if he is engaged for less than the normal work period. An individual is describable as disguisedly unemployed if he is so engaged that he produces less than he could produce in other employments which he is able and disposed to enter. As will be noted later, agriculture is the main repository of the disguisedly unemployed. It may be said that, other things equal, the presence of unemployed workers facilitates industrialization, while their employment augments output.

9. Make-up of the prevailing value-system. Most important of the elements of such a value system for our analysis are: (*a*) the values which animate economic, political, and social leaders; and (*b*) the values which significantly affect economic creativity and the disposition of man to put forth economically productive effort. The values included under (*a*) are unfavorable to material progress in proportion as they stress immaterial instruments and ends, or as they sanction the attainment of income and wealth through exploitation as distinguished from the organization and management of resources in a manner suited to serve mass demands. The values included under (*b*) relate to the content of the aspiration levels of representative individuals. If these levels include material objectives which, though not achievable with ease, may be won through the exercise of appreciable effort, representative individuals will be disposed to be industrious and creative.

10. Effectiveness and stability of the rules, institutions, and legal arrangements designed to preserve economic, political, and civil order. Stability and order are prerequisite to progress in both industrialization and income. Where these conditions are not met, the time horizon is necessarily short, capital formation is retarded, and the disposition to undertake ventures is greatly reduced. Industrialization is bound to proceed slowly at best, therefore, so long as stability and order are lacking in fact and in prospect.

11. Degree of cooperation and amity obtaining between the groups and classes composing the population. So long as such cooperation and amity are not sufficiently present, and their lack is not made up by a strong government capable of exercising compensatory force, determinants (10) and possibly (9) will be adversely affected, and progress in industrialization and income will be influenced accordingly. Determinant (11) appears to be of considerable significance, therefore, in many of the countries here under consideration.

12. Flexibility of the institutional structure and the physical apparatus of the economy. Flexibility permits an economy to adapt to changes that are

unforeseen and thereby operates both to accelerate the rate of change and to increase the effectiveness with which income-increasing changes are taken advantage of.[6] In proportion as an economy is inflexible, these fruitful accommodations are not attainable. Accordingly, since income and industrial progress entail change that is both saltatory and in part unpredictable, flexibility is essential to industrialization. In some of the countries here under analysis, inflexibility appears to offer great resistance to industrialization in its early stages.

13. Relative amount of vertical and horizontal mobility characteristic of a population. Per capita net output is at a maximum in a population when, ceteris paribus, it is making optimum use of the productive resources at its disposal; and a population is making such use of its resources when, with the marginal social benefit of every product equal to its marginal social cost, the value of the marginal product of each factor of production is equal to its price in all uses. Furthermore, as circumstances affecting production change, per capita output will move to the new maximum consistent with such changes, so long as the conditions of optimum resource use are met. These conditions can be met only if a population is sufficiently mobile, and able and disposed to modify its geographical, occupational, and related distributions. For industrialization and other sources of income-affecting change entail a continual redistribution of human productive agents in space and among employments, old and new. Determinant (13), therefore, resembles (12) in that the former reflects the flexibility of the population as such, whereas the latter reflects the flexibility of the population's institutional and physical equipment. Mobility, like flexibility, appears to be much less characteristic of non-industrialized than of industrial populations.

14. Degree to which a population's pattern of consumption is adjusted to its pattern of resource-equipment. Some adjustment along these lines is always found, since that which is relatively abundant commands relatively low prices, and that which commands relatively low prices tends to be substituted in some part for that which commands relatively high prices. Even so, however, adjustment is never complete, and progress in income and capital formation is less than it might be. This proposition appears to hold in some measure for the countries with which we are concerned.

15. Internal geographical distribution of economic activities. Other con-

6. Because of man's inability to eliminate economic and other relevant forms of uncertainty, and his associated incapacity to predict the relevant course of events, it is essential that he give great weight to the retention of flexibility. This proposition holds in respect of matters ranging from the construction of plants and cities to the formulation of general policies at the economic and the political levels. What is the appropriate amount of flexibility is, of course, a matter of judgment and therefore itself permeated by uncertainty, particularly since increments in flexibility usually entail short-run decrements in output, etc. When A. J. Toynbee implies that caste and specialization are responsible in large measure for the arrest of civilizations, he is arguing, in effect, that failure to retain flexibility has been primarily responsible for the interruption of the progress of diverse societies. See his A study of history 3: 79–111, London, Oxford Press, 1935.

ditions remaining the same, per capita net output will be greater or less in proportion as economic activities are well or badly distributed in space. The distribution of economic activities in space is highly significant also for an economy's progress in industrialization: (*a*), indirectly, because the progress of industrialization is positively associated with the already existing level of per capita output; and (*b*), directly, because the better situated a new industry-increasing venture is in space, the more likely it is to succeed and thus further the industrialization process.

16. The structure of that part of the institutional framework which touches immediately upon economic activities, together with the manner in which this structure functions. Among the institutions of most relevance here are those having to do with money, banking, taxation, etc., and those bearing upon primary, secondary, and technical education.

The sixteen determinants just enumerated and/or described condition industrialization directly. A number of factors, themselves concomitants of industrialization, affect its course indirectly in consequence of their direct influence upon the movement of per capita income. The most important of these factors are the following.

A. Degree of specialization and division of labor in effect. If industrialization does not proceed compatibly with specialization and division of labor, the extent of the market being given, it affects the level of output less favorably than it otherwise might.

B. Scale of economic organization and activity prevalent. Hereunder are included those sources of economy in operation consequent upon increase in scale which do not properly fall under (A).

C. Age composition of the population. Per capita output is governed, *ceteris paribus*, by the ratio of persons of productive age (say 15–64, 20–69, etc.) to the total population. This ratio rises when gross reproduction begins to fall and when expectation of life at birth increases (provided that enough of the increment of increase is situated within the productive age range). Changes in age composition in England and Wales between 1875 and 1935 increased potential productivity per male about 22 per cent. Substitution of the age composition of the United States and Canada for that of the populations of Africa, Asia, and Latin America would increase potential per capita productivity in these regions by about one-sixth.[7] Improvements in age composition make necessary a somewhat higher increment in capital than would otherwise be required.

7. These estimates are based upon United Nations, *World population trends*, 14–17, Lake Success, United Nations, 1949. See Table I, line 3, at the close of this paper. The effect of changes in age composition is conditioned, of course, by occupation, year of entry into and withdrawal from labor force, etc. See on age composition and output New York State Joint Legislative Committee on Problems of the Aging, *Birthdays don't count* (Legislative Document No. 61), Newburgh, 1948; Durand, John D., *The labor force in the United States 1890–1960*, N.Y., Social Science Research Council, 1948.

D. Biological composition of the population. Any change in the genetical composition of a population that increases (decreases) the relative frequency of individuals with supra-average potentialities operates to increase (decrease) per capita productive capacity. This determinant operates more slowly than most and may, therefore, be disregarded if the time span under analysis is short. Several inferences may be made in respect of changes in biological composition, however. (a) With the progress of a society in industrialization, its relative requirement of superior individuals increases and its relative capacity for making use of inferior individuals decreases. Industrialization may be said, therefore, to call for improvement in a population's biological composition. (b) An increase in the relative number of superior persons produces two effects analogous to substitution and income effects: (i) the relative rate of imputed productivity of the superior persons tends to fall; (ii) aggregate national income rises, usually enough to permit an increase in the absolute amount of income imputable to superior persons despite the kind of adverse substitution effect described under (i).

Industrialization tends to be accompanied by improvements in (A) and (B). Industrialization may be accompanied in the longer run by income-increasing improvements in the age composition of the population, provided that both the birth rate and the death rate move downward as a result of industrialization. If only mortality in the lowest age groups responds significantly to industrialization, the relative number of persons of working age may be reduced somewhat. In the past industrialization has been accompanied, but only gradually, by a decline in gross and net reproduction and by improvement in age composition.

Should the preceding list of determinants of industrialization and per capita income be deemed incomplete, a residual category may be added to comprehend factors that at present appear to be insignificant.

II. The Strategy of Industrialization in Under-Developed Countries

Contemporary interest in the industrialization of under-developed countries is premised upon the supposition that the process of industrialization can be accelerated through appropriate intervention at strategic points in comparatively non-industrialized economies. Intervention, it is assumed, may flow from two sources, from powerful interest groups and from the apparatus of state in the non-industrialized country, and from other countries already industrialized. It is inferred that the rate of industrialization in non-industrialized countries may be elevated above that observed in the past in countries presently industrialized because: (a) the retarded countries may draw upon the experience, knowledge, and material and human resources of industrialized countries; and (*b*) the state may assume a much larger and more effective role in industrialization than it assumed in Northern and Western Europe and the English-speaking world prior to World War I. Let us therefore consider the strategic aspects of industrialization.

The progress of industrialization is most likely to be maximized if action is exerted simultaneously upon many of the determinants of industrialization, and not merely upon one at a time. For while industrialization is a cumulative process, an improvement in any one determinant being propagated to others and becoming the occasion of their improvement, the fundamental relation obtaining among the determinants is one of complementarity, with the effects consequent upon the improvement of any one determinant being definitely limited by what is independently taking place in respect of other determinants. It should be added that industrialization, while always susceptible of cyclical retrogression, does not appear subject to secular decumulation subsequently to its having obtained an effective foothold in an economy, presumably because the determinants of industrialization become immune to adverse change beyond a limited amount.

Strategy requires that action be exerted upon those determinants of industrialization which are relatively most responsive to action, since it is assumed that the remaining determinants will in time undergo appropriate modification in consequence of the changes that have been produced in the more responsive of these determinants. The determinants may be classified, therefore, into those which are likely to be responsive to action from abroad and those which are likely to be amenable to action from within.

In the category of determinants responsive to external action fall (1)–(5) and (16). For a non-industrialized country can draw, but only within quite circumscribed limits, upon industrialized countries for equipment, for assistance in respect of public health, industrial "know-how," and scientific information, and for guidance regarding the establishment of a salutary institutional structure. These six determinants, together with (10), also appear to be the ones most susceptible to action from within, a matter of importance in view of the fact that the amount of assistance obtainable from abroad is limited both by the shortage of foreign personnel and material equipment and by the fact that the annual capacity of a non-industrialized country to absorb such personnel and equipment is restricted. Determinants (6), (9), (C), and (D) appear to be comparatively immune to direct action from within or without. The remaining determinants, while susceptible of little or no direct influence from abroad, appear to be somewhat subject to such influence from within. In this category fall determinants (7) and (8), (11)–(15), and (A) and (B), with (7) and (8) perhaps the most susceptible.

If the preceding analysis is correct, it follows that action from abroad should be concentrated upon determinants (1)–(5) and (16) and that action from within should be taken principally in respect of (1)–(5), (10), and (16).

Some action may be exerted upon (7) and (8) and a lesser amount upon (11)–(15) and (A) and (B). No action is indicated in respect of (6), (9), (C), and (D). It may be assumed that the determinants which are largely or wholly unresponsive to direct action from within and/or without will of necessity undergo modification in consequence of the changes that are produced in the determinants responsive to action from without and/or within.

III. Material Equipment Per Capita: Its Effects and Its Sources

The most important of the tangible factors that govern the level of per capita output and condition the rate of industrial progress is the availability of material equipment in its various guises. Most inventions and innovations, even though they be capital-saving on the balance and in the longer run, must be incorporated materially before they can enlarge man's productive powers. Furthermore, it is largely in virtue of the average amount of appropriate equipment at the disposal of workers that average output per worker is high in an economy, since then (within limits) more equipment can be used per worker in given industries and relatively more workers can engage in industries in which both equipment and output per worker are high. Finally, of the relatively mutable determinants of industrialization, none is potentially more responsive to concrete and salutary action from within and without an economy than is the stock of equipment, for its amount is significantly augmentable while the number of its users may be restricted through the employment of effective means of birth and immigration control. In this section we shall (a) present in summary form information relating to the income-producing effects of material equipment and (b) indicate how rapidly per capita income may be raised through the augmentation of the stock of material equipment.

Data relating to material equipment per worker by country are quantitatively and qualitatively unsatisfactory in respect of most parts of the world, and above all in respect of the under-industrialized parts of the world. The attainment of satisfactory international comparisons is rendered difficult, moreover, by the fact that information may be available only for some forms of material and not for all. For example, information may be available for "arable land" but not for such non-landed capital (working capital and fixed capital) as is employed in agriculture along with land. It may be assumed, however, that although the composition of fixed capital and the ratio of working capital to fixed capital vary by country and industry, the dominant relation obtaining among the major forms of capital is complementary rather than competitive in character. For example, the amount of non-landed and working capital utilized per worker in agriculture tends to vary in the same direction, although not in the same measure, as does the amount of land cultivated per worker.[8] It may be inferred, therefore, that, if we have data relating to a significant amount of the equipment used per worker by country, we have a fairly representative sample of the international differences in equipment per worker that actually obtain.

(*a*) We present data relating to equipment and output per worker in Tables I–II and IV. These data suggest that lack of equipment is a dominant characteristic of non-industrialized countries and that the principal immediate cause of mass poverty in most parts of the world is the lack of an adequate supply of effective and productive equipment.

Output per worker in agriculture is closely associated with the various forms of equipment, such as land and energy, at his disposal. Clark finds production per farm worker to vary inversely with the square root of the number of male workers per 1,000 hectares of farm land. Essentially the same relationship is found when farm land has been converted into more standard units. Output responds significantly also to nonhuman energy inputs.[9] As we have indicated, while other forms of capital may be substituted for land, the relationship obtaining between land and the various forms of agriculture capital usually is complementary rather than substitutive. Hence it is aggregate investment per agricultural worker that is important. In the United States in 1929, for example, net output per farm worker appears to have increased somewhat more than $100 for each increment of $1,000 in the amount of agricultural property being used per farm worker. In the late 1930's a somewhat similar relationship obtained.[10]

Outside agriculture and in economies as wholes, relationships similar to those just described also obtain. The role of land, of course, is much less important, since land forms a much smaller fraction of a worker's equipment outside agriculture and in economies as wholes than in agriculture. The role of non-human energy is extremely important outside as well as inside agriculture, an increment in the amount of energy available per worker

8. See Black, J. D., Agricultural population in relation to agricultural resources, *Annals Amer. Acad. Polit. and Soc. Sci.* 188: 211, table 3, 1936; Mandelbaum, K., *The industrialization of backward areas*, 95, Oxford, Blackwell, 1945.

9. On the relation of farm land to output per worker in agriculture see Clark, *Economics of 1960*, 34–36, and The productivity of primary industry, *Rev. Econ. Progress* 1: 5–6, 1949. A Spearman rank correlation of 0.95 obtains, for 8 countries, between output per male farm worker (as estimated by Clark in *ibid.*) and crop land per member of the farm population (as estimated by the FAO *Mission for Greece*, 155, Washington, FAO, 1947). Between output per male farm worker (as estimated by Clark) and energy consumption per person engaged in agriculture (as reported in N. B. Guyol, *Energy resources of the world*, 7, Washington, U.S. Dept. of State, 1949) a Spearman rank correlation of 0.87 obtains. Line 8 of Table IV indicates that in the non-industrialized parts of the world the tractorization of agriculture has made only insignificant progress.

10. These estimates are based upon Black, *op. cit.*, 211–212. On the late 1930's see Johnson, D. G., *Forward prices for agriculture*, chap. 7, Chicago, Univ. of Chicago Press, 1947.

tending to add a sizeable increment to his output. Comparison of line 10 with lines 4–6 in Table I reveals the importance of energy; so also does comparison of column 8 with columns 4–6 in Table II. The role of energy may be illustrated even more strikingly through the use of production functions designed to disclose the quantitative relationship obtaining between increments in energy and increments in income.[11] It is because the role of energy in current productive operations is so great that it may be said that whether or not an economy has a real industrial future turns largely on whether it has abundant reserves of energy-containing resources (e.g., see column 9 in Table II and line 11 in Table IV).

The importance of capital equipment is on a par with that of energy. Among the reasons for this is the fact that in large measure equipment per worker is an index of energy available per worker, since the inventions, etc., incorporated in the capital equipment put energy at the worker's disposal. The importance of capital is suggested by the correlation obtaining in Tables I and II between indices of income and indices of equipment and by the fact that the best-equipped regions (see Table IV) are also the regions where income per worker is highest, and conversely. International data centered around 1913 suggest roughly that at that time a \$100 increment in non-landed capital per worker was accompanied by something like a \$20 increment in his output.[12] Clark estimates the relationship between income $(= y)$ and non-landed capital $(= x)$ per worker to be parabolic, with $\log y = 2.884 - 1.108x + 0.323 (\log x)^2$.[13]

11. While international differences in output per farm worker are significantly associated with international differences in arable land per farm worker, international differences in land per worker are not significantly associated with output per worker, in part because land varies in quality but principally because the relative importance of land in the productive equipment of nations varies greatly. The comparative lack of association between land and output is suggested by a comparison of column 10 with columns 4–5 in Table II and confirmed by E. C. Olson's studies. Let Y represent national income; E, total energy excluding human energy; P, employed population; L, head of livestock expressed in livestock units; and A, area of cultivated land. If, after the manner of the Douglas-Cobb production function (see note 17 below), $Y = f(P,E,L)$, the following approximate percentage change in Y accompanies a 1 per cent change in the designated variable, given that the other two variables remain unchanged: E, about 0.5 per cent; L, about 0.28; and P, about 0.23. When A is introduced into the income equation, the corresponding percentages become: E, 0.48; L, 0.41; P, 0.35; and A, −0.18. Olson suggests that, since national economies differ in structure and since countries may be grouped into two or three relatively homogeneous categories, the income-estimating equation appropriate for any one of these groups will tend to differ from that most appropriate for the other groups. See Olson, Factors affecting international differences in production, *Amer. Econ. Rev. Proc.* 28 (2): 502–522, 1948. It may strike the reader that Olson's findings run counter to the argument advanced in sections I and II of this paper. This is not the case. The magnitudes of the variables E and L, together with the quality of P and the effectiveness of all three, are functionally related to most of the determinants we have listed and reflect their aggregate influence in a summary manner.

12. Estimated from Clark, *Conditions*, 389.

13. *Economics of 1960*, 74. I have discussed the matters treated in the preceding paragraphs in my Aspects of the Economics of Population Growth, *Southern Econ. Jour.* 14: 123–147, 233–265, esp. 246–265, 1948.

Having examined the relations obtaining in particular branches of industry between equipment per worker and output per worker, let us discover if a definite relation obtains between the aggregate income produced within a nation and either all its physical assets or those of its physical assets which are immediately employed to bring this income into being. While our quantitative information relating to this relationship is inadequate for the purposes of our analysis, it may nonetheless be employed to explore the role of capital formation in industrialization.

Let W represent all of a nation's physical assets, and let these be divided into two categories, W_1 and W_2. Within W_1 may be placed all assets which, under prevailing institutional and other relevant conditions, are viewed as yielding income in a significant degree; while within W_2 are included all remaining physical assets, namely, those which, under the given conditions, are yielding no income or significantly little income. Under W_2, therefore, may be included physical assets of the following types: those employed for defense; those utilized for other public purposes (e.g., streets and highways, public schools and buildings and cognate equipment); those in the form of excess reserves (e.g., subsoil wealth and other forms of wealth not in use; excessive inventories at consumer and other levels); consumer durables; and so on. There are also forms of W_1 which, in the early stage of a country's development, closely resemble W_2 and may even be included with it (e.g., railroads).

Let us now call the ratio of income to wealth S, with S equal either to Y/W or to Y/W_1; and let s represent the ratio of the annual increment of income to the annual increment of wealth upon which it is consequent, namely, $\Delta Y/\Delta W$ or $\Delta Y/\Delta W_1$. The value of S, as well as that of s, turns on whether we define it in terms of Y/W or Y/W_1, and, given the latter definition, what assets are included under W_1. In the United States S defined as Y/W had a value of 0.21–0.24 in 1923 and 0.20–0.25 in 1929.[14] The value of S, defined as Y/W_1, has a much higher value, since in a country like the United States W_2 may form 30–45 or more per cent of W. Available estimates suggest that S defined as Y/W_1 has a value lying within or around 0.3–0.35. For example Fellner, upon defining W_1 to include assets other than monetary metals and land and goods in the hands of consumers, found the ratio s of yearly real output to real capital stock (i.e., $\Delta Y/\Delta W_1$) to range between 0.39 and 0.30 in 1879–1938, with 1919–1938, a period marked by

14. Physical assets in the United States were evaluated at $321–353 billion in 1922 and $428 billion in 1930. National wealth was evaluated at $309 and $354 billion, respectively, as of 1923 and 1929, by the National Industrial Conference Board. National income approximated $87.4 billion in 1929 and $70–73 billion in 1923. See Doane, R. R., *The anatomy of American wealth*, 35, 37, 120–121, N.Y., Harper, 1940, and U.S. Bureau of the Census, *Historical statistics of the United States, 1789–1945*, 9–11, Washington, D.C., 1949. Of the $32 billion difference in the 1922 estimates, $22 billion are attributable to the inclusion of streets, roads, and highways.

relatively full employment, represented by a value of 0.35.[15] E. H. Stern,[16] having defined W_1 much as Fellner has and having established a regression equation between Y and W_1, discovered the value of $s\,(= \Delta Y / \Delta W_1)$ to approximate 0.3 in both the United States in 1879–1938 and the United Kingdom in 1924–1938. For comparatively under-developed South Africa in the 1930's Stern found a corresponding value of around 0.5.

Progress in industrialization and income will be at a maximum only if, the rate of investment being given, the annual increment of investment is appropriately distributed between W_1 and W_2 and among the various forms of W_1 and W_2 according to their relative significance at the time. For since all forms of W_1 and W_2 absorb some savings, the increase of any one form is always at the expense of others, the volume of savings being given. What constitutes the optimum distribution of savings between W_1 and W_2 turns on a country's stage of industrial development, the degree of complementarity then obtaining between W_1 and W_2, and the degree of sovereignty and choice being allowed consumers. In the earlier stages of industrialization relatively heavy increases of immediately less productive forms of W_1 and of forms of W_2 oriented to collective purposes frequently tend to be indicated. Furthermore, savings sufficient for the forms of investment indicated will not be forthcoming if the rate of saving is too low, or if savings are diverted into non-indicated forms of W_2. While industrial progress tends to be accompanied over the long run by a rise in the ratio of W_2 to W, the rate at which this ratio advances may be curbed through the introduction of appropriate restrictions upon consumer sovereignty and the uses to which savings may be put. Nonetheless, a considerable fraction of the annual savings is bound at all times to be absorbed by W_2 investment. Even so, in view of what has been said, a strong case may be made for appropriate restrictions upon both consumer sovereignty and the disposition of savings in countries undergoing industrial development.

The value of S may fluctuate or undergo non-secular changes for a number of reasons. (*a*) In view of what has just been said, Y/W will rise if the W_1/W ratio, having deviated from the optimum level, is brought back to it through appropriate investment; it will fall as W_1/W departs from the optimum. (*b*) Y/W will fall if less productive forms of W_2 are increased at the expense of more productive forms even though W_2/W_1 remains constant. (*c*) The

15. Fellner, W., *Monetary policies and full employment*, 78–83, Berkeley, Univ. of Calif. Press, 1946. Of the $353 billion of national wealth as of the end of 1922 (according to the Federal Trade Commission), only $183.7 billion is made up of real capital stock, according to Fellner. Kuznets's data on real capita formation are employed to extend the 1922 estimate backwards and forwards.

16. Stern, E. H., Capital requirements in progressive economies, *Economica* 12: 163–171, 1945. Stern gives values only for what we have called $1/s$. Comparison of Douglas's figures on capital growth in the United Kingdom with Clark's income estimates suggests that in the period 1875–1909 the value of s was close to 0.3. See Douglas, P. H., *The theory of wages*, 464, N.Y., Macmillan, 1934, and Clark, *Conditions . . .* , 397.

value of S falls as the level of employment falls and rises as the level of employment rises. (d) The value of S will change, moreover, in response to changes in the number of shifts of workers used per day. For example, if the number of shifts is increased from one to two, W_1 will be used more intensively, with the result that Y/W will rise. Whether an increase in the number of shifts from two to three will further increase Y/W is less certain and must be determined empirically. In general it is advisable that under-developed countries which are short of W_1 operate at least two shifts of workers per day and thereby increase Y/W and improve the prospects for further industrialization. (e) The shift of workers from agriculture and forestry into industries in which output per worker is higher tends to hold the value of Y/W at a higher level than would otherwise be sustained. This movement loses force, of course, as the relative number of persons engaged in agriculture and forestry declines.

The value of S is subject to two secular influences which, other conditions being given, cause the value of s to differ from that of S. These influences are population growth and technological and related forms of change. Let us therefore consider the former, under the assumption that technological and related circumstances remain constant. Y progresses in consequence of increases in the labor force (which we shall call L) and its equipment (i.e., W) and as the result of significant changes in other income-affecting forces (e.g., the relative amount of *free* output-affecting agencies; the *quality* of the labor force; the *quality* of equipment; etc.) which we shall call R and for the present suppose to be without effect. If, under these conditions, W increases more rapidly than L, Y will increase less rapidly than W and Y/W will fall, for the value of $s(=\Delta Y/\Delta W)$ will be less than that of $S(= Y + \Delta Y/W \pm \Delta W)$ after the change. A similar result is obtained if S and s are defined in terms of Y and W_1.

What has just been said may be illustrated with a numerical example based upon the original Douglas-Cobb[17] production function. Suppose we

---

17. See Douglas, *op. cit.*, and Are there laws of production? *Amer. Econ. Rev.* 38: 1–41, 1948. Let aggregate net output be represented by O; the labor force and its marginal productivity, by L and l; and the marginal productivities of W_1 and W_2 by w_1 and w_2, respectively. Then, in accordance with the usual assumptions, $O = Ll + W_1w_1 + W_2w_2$. It is usually assumed, moreover, that the ratio of l to w_1 or to w_2, varies inversely with the ratio of L to W_1, or to W_2; if L, W_1, and W_2 each increases by a certain fraction f, O will increase by f since, under the circumstances, l, w_1, and w_2 remain unchanged. Under these conditions the value of $s = \Delta O/(\Delta W_1 + \Delta W_2)$ remains the same as $S = O/(W_1 + W_2)$. If, however, W_1 and W_2 increase by f whereas L remains unchanged in quantity, O will increase by less than f, and the value of s will fall below that of S. This decline would not take place, of course, if some other residual force R were operating either to increase the value of w_1 and w_2 sufficiently, or to contribute enough to the increase of O to offset the decrease in w_1 and w_2. It is because such a force as R is operating through time that the value of s has fallen no more than it has despite the decline in the ratio of L to W, it being assumed that the ratio of W_1 to W_2 remains substantially unchanged. The residual force R is made up of elements not included when O is represented as a function only of L, W_1, and W_2. Representative of these elements are changes in the quality of L, W_1,

combine 100 units of L with 100 units of W, with each unit of W equal in value terms to 4 units of Y, so that the combination produces 100 units of Y, the marginal product of a unit of L being $\frac{3}{4}$ of a unit of Y and the marginal product of a unit of W being $\frac{1}{4}$ of a unit of Y. Under the circumstances S has a value of 100/400, or 0.25, and the average output per unit of L is 1 unit of Y. These values will remain unchanged if we increase L and W by one per cent each. But suppose we hold L constant at 100, and increase W to 101, it being assumed that 4 per cent of the preceding year's income of 100 units of Y has been saved and invested in W. The aggregate income will now approximate 100.25 units of income; the average output per unit of L will be 1.0025; the value of s will be, in terms of Y, approximately 0.25/4, or .0625; and the value of S will have fallen, in terms of Y, from 0.25 to 100.25/404. Since, if L had also increased 1 per cent, the average output of L would have continued at the level of 1 instead of rising to 1.0025, we may say that a 1 per cent increase in L (i.e., population) costs the population a $\frac{1}{4}$ of one per cent increase in per capita income. If the respective marginal productivities of W and L were not $\frac{1}{4}$ and $\frac{3}{4}$, respectively, but $\frac{1}{2}$ each, the value of s would be 0.5/4, or 0.125, and the cost of a 1 per cent increase in L would be the prevention of a $\frac{1}{2}$ of one per cent increase in per capita income. Under static conditions, therefore, an increase in W unaccompanied by a corresponding increase in L, operates to reduce s and S. In consequence the income-opportunity cost of population growth is *relatively* lower than when conditions are dynamic and S manifests a lesser tendency to fall.

Let us now hold L relatively constant and suppose that dynamic changes represented by changes in the value of R accompany the increase in W. Changes of this sort presuppose an increase in W since most of them must find embodiment in material equipment before they can become effective. In consequence of changes of this sort, therefore, the combined marginal productivities of L and W may rise sufficiently to cause Y to increase

and W_2, changes in the influence of "free" resources, changes in organization, invention, innovation, and so on.

Let us, in keeping with what has been said, change the form of our production function from $O = f(L, W_1, W_2)$ to $O = f(L, W_1, W_2, R)$, with R subject to variation whether or no all the other variables vary. Accordingly, even though W_1 and W_2 increase by f while L increases by less than f, O still will increase by f if R varies enough in an output-increasing direction to offset the failure of L to increase by f. It is because production functions are not usually defined to include a variable such as R and take its influence into account that economists find difficulty in accounting for the fact that O sometimes increases by more or less than f in the world of reality even when L, W_1, and W_2 each increases by f, or in explaining the fact that O may sometimes increase by f even when, with W_1 and W_2 (say) increasing by f, L increases by less than f. The accounts of Stigler and Allen indicate that the role of a residual force similar to R is not customarily made use of to cope with the problem of "increasing" and "decreasing" returns. See Stigler, G. J., *Production and distribution theories*, chap. 12, N.Y., Macmillan, 1941; Allen, R. G. D., *Mathematical analysis for economists*, 264–265, 317–319, London, Macmillan, 1938; also note 11 above.

nearly as rapidly as W and conceivably more rapidly, for the production function itself is modified. Dynamic changes of the sort we have lumped together under the residual R thus operate, if they are favorable on the balance, to cushion the tendency of S to fall as the ratio W/L rises. Changes of this sort thus increase the opportunity cost, in terms of per capita income, of population growth. Thus if, even though L is constant, dynamic change prevents a decline in S, a 1 per cent increase in population will cost a 1 per cent increase in per capita income whereas, if S falls in value, this cost, as we have seen, will be somewhat lower. Under all circumstances, however, so long as a nation's population is in excess of the optimum in size, an increase in population must entail some cost in terms of per capita income.

Both population growth and technological and similar improvements have operated in industrialized countries to prevent greater declines in S and s than otherwise would have been experienced. In the United States, for example, although W_1 increased more than twice as fast as L between the 1880's and the 1920's, the value of s defined as $\Delta Y / \Delta W_1$ declined only about one-tenth.[18] Had L not grown at all, the value of s thus defined would have fallen about one-half. The decline in the value of s (similarly defined) in the United Kingdom since the 1860's appears to have been greater, perhaps around one-fifth[19]; but it would have been greater still had L not grown. In both countries continuing improvements in technology called for and absorbed savings, elevated the marginal productivity of labor, at least weakened the tendency for the marginal productivity of capital to fall, and thus operated, together with increases in L, to prevent much greater declines in S than would otherwise have been experienced. In the future in underdeveloped countries both technological and demographic change will serve to sustain the value of S; in industrialized countries technological change will be the principal source of support for S.

Analysis of the part played by savings and capital formation in industrialization entails two choices. First, one must define S either as Y/W or as Y/W_1. In view of the fact that the industrialization of under-developed countries involves heavy and continuing outlays for many forms of capital included under W_2, the Y/W definition appears to be the more useful. Second, we must determine upon a value for Y/W representative of underdeveloped countries. In the United States Y/W has a value in the neighbor-

18. In the United States, between a period centered around 1883 and one centered around 1928, the following increases per year took place: aggregate real output, 3.5 per cent; real capital stock, just under 4; the labor force, about 1.75; and real output per capita, about 2. The rates are based upon Fellner's estimates. See *op. cit.*, 80. Carl Snyder estimated that, between 1850 and 1930, the ratio of capital to annual value of product nearly doubled. See *Capitalism the creator*, 126, N.Y., Macmillan, 1940. On the ratio of wealth to income see also Cassel, G., *On quantitative thinking in economics*, chap. 6, Oxford, Clarendon Press, 1935.

19. This statement is based upon data presented by Stern, Douglas, and Clark, whose works are cited in notes 16–17 above.

hood of one-fifth. This value must be much higher in non-industrialized countries where capital is scarce and S has not yet fallen in consequence of progress in industrialization. A value of 0.4 or higher is probably indicated. For example, since the value of Y/W_1 (as noted earlier) has been about 1.67 times as high in South Africa as in the United States, and since the ratio W_1/W must be somewhat higher in South Africa than in the United States, it is likely that Y/W has a value in the neighborhood of 0.4 in South Africa. Comparison of annual savings and investment rates with the rate of growth of income suggests that in Japan in 1908–1925 S, or $\Delta Y/W$, probably had a value close to 0.4.[20] In less developed countries than South Africa and Japan the value of both Y/W and $\Delta Y/\Delta W$ probably exceeds 0.4. For purposes of analysis we shall assume that in under-developed countries $S(=Y/W)$ has a value in the neighborhood of 0.4 and that the combined influence of population growth and technological progress will keep the value of both S and $s\ (=\Delta Y/\Delta W)$ in this neighborhood. If our estimate is too low, we shall underestimate the influence of industrialization whereas, if it is too high, we shall overestimate it.

In absence of an aggressive, state-supported, and state-implemented program for birth control and planned parenthood in the non-industrialized countries, it is likely that their populations will increase 1–1.5 per cent per year. For these populations are coiled or Oriental in character, being marked by high mortality, low life expectancy, high natality, and high potential rates of increase which will tend to be actualized under the impact of such improvements in economic conditions as accompany industrialization. As we have already indicated, an increase of 1 per cent in population may cost an 0.5–1 per cent increase in per capita income. It is advisable, therefore, that programs for industrialization also include plans for the diffusion of cheap and practical means of contraception and the stimulation of their use.

(b) Let us turn now to estimating the capital and savings requirements of under-developed countries, in especial those with per capita incomes in the neighborhood of $100 and with 60 or more per cent of the labor force

---

20. According to Clark (see *Conditions . . . ,*116ff., 406) between 1897 and 1928 the national income of Japan advanced about 4.75 per cent per year while savings approximated one-fifth of the national income, suggesting that $\Delta Y/\Delta W$ had a value of only about 0.24. However, Staley's figures on the progress of the national income between 1900–1909 and 1920–1929 and the annual rate of investment suggest that $\Delta Y/\Delta W$ probably had a value in excess of 0.4. This estimate appears to be too high in consequence of exaggeration of the rate of income growth. Between 1908 and 1925, according to Clark's estimates, national income advanced nearly 5.5 per cent per year, while investment, accordingly to Staley's figures when made comparable with Clark's, absorbed about 14 per cent of the national income. Accordingly, $\Delta Y/\Delta W$ must have been around 0.4. See Staley, E., *World economic development,* appendix to chap. 4, Montreal, International Labor Office, 1944. According to estimates reported by H. G. Moulton for 1928 Japan's national income approximated only 10.7 per cent of her estimated wealth. This ratio is obviously much too low. See Moulton, *Japan,* 248, 614, Washington, Brookings Instn., 1931.

engaged in agriculture and forestry. We shall first have recourse to a hypothetical, though representative, case. Subsequently we shall formulate the problem in more general terms.

Suppose a country with a population of 1,000,000; a labor force of 350,000, 80 per cent of whom are engaged in agriculture and forestry; per capita and aggregate equipment (i.e., W) of \$250 and \$250 million, respectively, with equipment per worker averaging \$714 and other wealth averaging \$50 per capita.[21] Suppose that S defined as Y/W remains constant at its initial value of 0.4. Suppose further that we plan, over a 25-year period, to transfer 140,000 workers out of agriculture, and reduce the agricultural fraction of the labor force to 31 per cent, given a 1 per cent annual increase in population, and to 24 per cent, given a 2 per cent annual increase. Suppose, finally, that we equip all new and transferring workers at \$1,500 per head; that over the 25-year period we gradually raise equipment per worker of all other workers from \$714 to \$1,500; and that we increase non-business equipment per inhabitant 1 per cent per year.

The plan outlined will absorb about 13.8 per cent per year of the national income for 25 years if the population continues to increase 1 per cent per year, and about 19.5 per cent if the population grows 2 per cent per year.[22] Since S is assumed to remain constant at 0.4 and since about 8 per cent of the annual income is devoted to increasing equipment per worker and per capita, per capita income will increase about 3.2 per cent per year, rising, in the course of the 25-year period, from the initial \$100 to nearly \$220. It is quite unlikely that, short of considerable foreign investment, the 13.8 per cent investment rate, required when population grows 1 per cent per year, can be realized. The 19.5 per cent investment rate, required if population grows 2 per cent per year, seems impossible of attainment short of very considerable foreign assistance.

Proponents of industrialization usually emphasize the increase in aggregate and per capita income to be obtained from a shift of the excess labor force out of agriculture, in which there usually is much disguised unemployment, and into appropriate non-agricultural occupations. Suppose 80 per cent of the labor force is engaged in agriculture where output

21. Our assumption that one-fifth of the hypothetical country's wealth is devoted to purposes other than equipping the labor force is suppositional and may be too low. In the United States in the last half of the nineteenth century, dwellings, household equipment, clothing, personal ornaments, theatres, churches, etc. comprised 20–25 per cent of the estimated tangible wealth. See Doane, *op. cit.,* 263.

22. Equipment of the transferring and the non-transferring workers will cost about \$7.5 million, or 7.5 per cent of the national income in the first year, and a like percentage in subsequent years as the absolute outlay is stepped up with the rise in income. Equipping a 1 per cent increase in the labor force will cost \$5.25 million, or 5.25 per cent of the national income, in the first year, and double this amount if the labor force increases 2 per cent per year. The absolute outlay will rise in later years, but the percentage figure will remain around the first-year level. Non-business capital formation will absorb 1 and 1.5 per cent per year of the national income, given population growth rates of 1 and 2 per cent, respectively.

per worker is 1 in contrast with 2–3 in non-agricultural occupations. Then the transfer of $\frac{1}{80}$ of the agricultural labor to non-agricultural employments will, under essentially static conditions and on condition that agricultural output remains unchanged, permit an increase of between $\frac{1}{60}$ and $\frac{3}{140}$ in total output. Given the dynamic conditions which accompany industrialization, however, the increase may be greater. It has been estimated, for example, that a 1 per cent decrease in the number of persons engaged in primary occupations tends to be accompanied by a 3.94 per cent increase in per capita income.[23] In our discussion we do not take this transfer problem explicitly into account, since it is automatically taken care of when the capital stock is increased and employed where it is most effective, and since its direct influence virtually ends in most countries when the relative number of persons engaged in agriculture falls significantly below one-fifth. The comparative lowness of output in agriculture appears to be attributable to the relatively small amount and poor quality of the equipment employed therein, to the lesser education of agricultural workers, to the presence of much disguised unemployment, and, when agriculturalists are exploited, to the unfavorable terms of trade. Accordingly, given an adequate supply of capital and an appropriate redistribution of workers among occupations, the differences between agricultural and non-agricultural productivity per worker tend to be eliminated.

We may now formulate in more general terms the relation obtaining between capital formation and progress in industrialization and income. We have already defined Y, W, W_1, and W_2. For present purposes we shall define S as Y/W and s as $\Delta Y/\Delta W$. Let p represent population and r its annual rate of increase in per cent; y, per capita income and j its annual rate of increase in per cent; and i, the annual rate of increase in Y in per cent. Let a represent the annual increment in W expressed as a percentage of Y. Furthermore, let a be broken up into its two components, each expressed as a percentage of Y, with a_1 representing the increment in W originating in domestic saving and a_2 the increment originating in net investment flowing in from abroad. We may now express the annual rate of increase in Y as

$$i = s(a_1 + a_2).$$

If the value of S is constant and equal to that of s, we may substitute S for s. However, since s tends to differ from S and to decline as W/p increases, a

23. Suppose 80 per cent of the labor force is engaged in agriculture where output per worker is 1 and that average (= marginal) output per worker in non-agricultural employments is 3. Then a transfer of 1/80 of the agricultural labor force to non-agricultural occupations will increase aggregate income 2–3/140, or 1.4–2.14 per cent. Under dynamic conditions the effect may be larger. Thus S. Raushenbush estimates that a 1 per cent decrease in the relative number in primary occupations tends to be accompanied by a 3.94 per cent increase in per capita income. See *People, food, machines*, 79, Washington, Public Affairs Inst., 1950. See also L. Bean's estimates in *Studies in income and wealth*, Part Five, N. Y., National Bureau of Economic Research, 1946; and Ezekial, M., *Towards world prosperity*, 14–29, N.Y., Harper, 1947. See column 11 in Table II and line 8 in Table I on the relative number engaged in agriculture by country.

corrective factor c, with a value less than unity, must be employed to reduce the value of S appropriately so that

$$i = S(a_1 + a_2)c.$$

Then the annual rate of increase in y may be expressed as

$$j = \frac{1 + S(a_1 + a_2)c}{1 + r} - 1.$$

This last equation indicates that so long as s remains constant or as c has a value of unity, a 1 per cent increase in population costs approximately a 1 per cent increase in per capita income; but that, if c has a value less than unity, the cost in terms of j is less than 1 per cent.[24]

Let us now assign values to the elements composing the equation for j. We have already assigned a value of 0.4 to S and we shall assume it to remain constant for 50 years. To r we may assign a value of 1 per cent. For reasons to be indicated we may assign to a_1 a value of 0.03–0.12 Y, and to a_2 a value not in excess of $0.33a_1$. Accordingly, a tends to have a value ranging between 0.04 and 0.16 Y. These values suggest that i will assume a value ranging between 0.016 and 0.064 Y, while j will assume a value lying between 0.006 and 0.053 Y. Judging by past experience the value of j is not likely long to exceed 4 per cent per year unless the countries undergoing industrialization experience much more foreign assistance than did Japan, the non-Western under-developed country whose industrial progress has been the most remarkable.

Let us now examine the values we have assigned to a_1 and a_2. In the nineteenth and early twentieth centuries the average annual propensity to save (let us call it q) ranged between 0 and 20 per cent.[25] But not all of q is likely to assume the form of W, there being a fractional wastage w of q, such that $a_1 = (1 - w)q$. If w normally has a value lying between 0.1 and 0.2,

24. The statement of the income : capital problem in this paragraph resembles that developed by Domar in his attempt to estimate the amount of income growth needed to absorb the amount of savings provided when income is at the full employment level. His emphasis is upon the maintenance of full employment whereas ours is upon the supply of enough savings (= investment) to sustain a high rate of income growth. Furthermore, his definition of s approximates our $\Delta Y / \Delta W_1$. On the income : capital relationship see Harrod, R. F., *Towards a dynamic economics*, chap. 3, London, Macmillan, 1948; Domar, E. D., Capital expansion, rate of growth, and employment, *Economica* 14: 137–147, 1946, Expansion and employment, *Amer. Econ. Rev.*, 37: 34–55, 1947, and The problem of capital accumulation, *ibid.* 38: 777–794, 1948; Schelling, T. C., Capital growth and equilibrium, *ibid.* 37: 864–876, 1947; Stern, E. H., The problem of capital accumulation, *ibid.* 39:1160–1169, 1949; and Robinson, Joan, Mr. Harrod's dynamics, *Econ. Jour.*, 59: 68–85, 1949.

25. In the late nineteenth and the early twentieth centuries the ratio of savings to national income normally ranged between 5 and 20 per cent, with an intermediate range of 8–14 representative of most countries. Per capita income has rarely grown more than 2 per cent per year over a period of 40–50 years, Japan affording the only instance in which it long progressed at a rate close to 4 per cent. See Clark, *Conditions*, 148, 406, and *Economics of 1960*, chap. 6; Domar, E. D., The "burden of the debt" and the National Income, *Amer. Econ. Rev.* 36: 826, 1944; Goldenberg, L., Saving in a state with a stationary population, *Quart. Jour. Econ.* 59: 50, 65, 1946. In the countries of Western Europe in 1938, gross domestic investment

we may suppose that a_1 will approximate $0.8-0.9q$. If this is the case, a_1 may conceivably attain a value as high as $0.16\ Y$ provided that conditions extremely favorable to saving are maintained and that the value of w is held down. In practice, however, it is doubtful, given the lowness of per capita income in the under-developed countries, whether q will be high enough and w low enough to permit a_1 to assume a value in excess of $0.12\ Y$, if that much. For reasons that we develop later, it does not appear feasible long to elevate a_2 above $0.33\ a_1$, since when a value of this order is exceeded foreign investment is not likely to be effectively absorbed and/or serviced. As a rule, over long periods the value of a_2 lies below one-third of a_1. It should be noted that, because of waste of foreign exchange, the absolute amount of foreign investment in a country tends to fall short of the amount of exchange that appears to be available for such use.

Growth of per capita income in under-developed countries at a rate of 3–4 per cent per year—i.e., at a rate double that in prospect in industrialized countries—presupposes that at least two conditions will be met by non-industrialized countries. First, these countries must step up q, minimize w, compel most savings to assume the form either of W_1 or of the comparatively essential types of W_2, attract foreign capital, and utilize virtually all of their foreign exchange for the servicing of foreign debt and the procurement of relatively productive kinds of equipment and services not obtainable at home. Among the complementary courses of action suited to accomplish this first condition are the following: (*a*) establishment of foreign exchange controls which are designed to divert foreign exchange to uses that directly or indirectly increase output; (*b*) creation of financial and related insitutions which will assemble the savings of large and small income-receivers and shunt them into appropriate lines of activity; (*c*) employment of the apparatus of state to compel most of the income received by wealthy though unenterprising individuals to assume the form of W_1 and of essential types of W_2.

Second, it is essential that S and s not decline appreciably in value. Attainment of this objective turns on there being available either a sufficient supply of arable land and other essential natural resources, or means by which shortages of these factors can be made up. While there will probably be enough land in most of Latin America and Africa, there will be far too little in Asia and the Caribbean area (see Table II, column 10, and Table IV, lines 4–7).[26] It is essential, therefore, that steps be taken to alleviate the

---

expressed as a percentage of gross national product, ranged between 6 in Czechoslovakia and 25 in Sweden, in contrast with 8 in the United States. Net foreign investment ranged from plus 2 to minus 2 per cent of gross national product. In 1947 both gross domestic and net foreign investment were appreciably higher, see United Nations, *Selected world economic indices,* 50, Lake Success, United Nations, 1948.

26. Data relating to crop land per capita (see Table II, column 10, and Table IV, line 4) indicate that the amount of crop land in use per inhabitant is hazardously low in regions other

shortage of arable land in these land-lacking regions (e.g.: increased investment per acre; control of plant and animal diseases; substitution of more
productive for less productive plant and animal types; and development of a
diet which, though predominantly vegetable in character as at present
[see columns 7–9 in Table III and lines 23–26 in Table I] is adequate).

Data presented in column 9 of Table II and line 11 of Table IV indicate
that energy resources (other than atomic)[27] are probably in too short supply
to permit great industrial development in much of Latin America, in much of
the Near East and Southern Asia, and in many parts of Africa, particularly
since this shortage of energy reserves is accentuated in many of the energy-
lacking regions by an associated shortage of iron ore and other crucial
minerals.[28] It appears, therefore, that even though these shortages may be
somewhat counterbalanced by economy in resource use and by the tendency
of returns to increase with industrialization,[29] they probably cannot be
wholly compensated. It follows, if this be the case, that S and s will be under

---

than the Western Hemisphere, Oceania, and Russia. Data relating to the amount of land which,
though now in forest, is both accessible and susceptible of being used for agriculture (see
Table IV, line 7) indicate the per capita amounts to be smallest in the regions where the shortage of arable land is already most pronounced. The importance of this point is accentuated by
the fact that several acres of forest land are required per capita to supply minimal timber and
related requirements. It may be said, in general, that there exists in the world a sufficiency of
arable land, if it be brought into use and used effectively, to supply the food requirements of
an expanding world population. The practical significance of this potential supply of arable
land is greatly reduced, however, by the fact that its location and ownership, together with
institutional and economic obstacles in the way of its use, make this land relatively inaccessible
to the land-short peoples. (In geological time, of course, the rise in world temperature initially
will add to the supply of cultivatable land. This trend is not relevant to the present argument,
however, since the rate of change per time period is so much greater for population than for
the supply of cultivatable land.) On the above issues see Brown, A. J., *Industrialization and
trade*, 18–25, London, Oxford Press, 1943, and my The World's Hunger—Malthus, 1948,
Annals Acad. Polit. Sci. Columbia Univ., 53–71, 1949. It appears, therefore, that efforts to
increase yields per acre offer a more practical solution to the food problem in the land-short
countries of the world than do efforts to augment the area under cultivation. For it has been
estimated that plant and animal yields may be increased as much as 50 per cent or more in a few
years through the introduction of better methods of cultivation, improved plant and animal
varieties and breeds, modern animal breeding and feeding methods, and effective disease, pest,
and fungi controls. See United Nations, *Technical assistance for economic development*,
22–24, 138, 143–145, 152–156, 182, Lake Success, United Nations, 1949.

27. Commercially exploitable deposits of uranium ore reportedly are to be found principally
in the Belgian Congo, Canada, Czechoslovakia, and the United States.

28. Data on energy resources are given in Guyol, *op. cit.;* Brown, *op. cit.,* 18–24: and Usher,
A. P., The resource requirements of an industrial economy, *Jour. Econ. Hist.* 7: Supp. 7:
35–46, 1947. Brown reports iron ore supplies in terms of millions of tons of metal content as
follows: Western Europe 8,485; Eastern Europe, 472; United States, Canada, Cuba, and
Newfoundland, 9,000; Australia and New Zealand, 200; South Africa, 3,000; Argentina,
Uruguay, and Chile, 250; U.S.S.R., 16,000; India, 2,330; China, 650; Japan, 30. Considerable
iron ore is to be found also in Brazil, Rhodesia, and Egypt. See Table IV, line 12, on supplies
by continent. Venezuela's newly discovered deposits are extraordinarily rich.

29. See Jones, G. T., *Increasing return*, Cambridge, Cambridge Univ. Press, 1933; Clark,
Conditions, 306–317, and The productivity of manufacturing industry, *Rev. Econ. Progress*
1 (8–10), 1949.

strong pressure to fall, and that advancing per capita income 3–4 per cent per year for many years will not be easy even if it should prove possible.

IV. Industrial Composition and Industrial Development

Maximization of the rate of industrialization, other conditions being given, requires that both investment and the labor force be appropriately distributed among the industries that compose or may compose a developing economy. Such distribution presupposes both recognition of each of the following sometimes antithetical principles and the assignment of appropriate weight to each. These principles are: (1) full account must be taken of the implications of the fact that much capital equipment is immobile, and that a considerable fraction of this immobile equipment is not very productive directly and/or immediately; (2) due weight must be given to the establishment of industries which ease the pressure for foreign exchange; (3) it is essential that, in so far as possible, industries suited to satisfy the more urgent consumer wants be given the highest priority; (4) capital should initially be directed, in so far as possible, into industries (i) characterized by low capital-intensity and (ii) capable of utilizing most effectively the kinds of labor available and/or in relatively immediate prospective supply; (5) industrial development should proceed along lines suited to exploit the relatively more accessible land and natural-resource equipment of a country; (6) a workable balance must be maintained among the industries composing an economy so that, given prospective foreign trade relations and the fact that some industries must initially be developed ahead of the market, inter-industry complementarities may be taken advantage of and uneconomic and excess capacity may be averted.

(1) Inasmuch as a major fraction of the physical assets used for productive purposes—two-thirds or more when land, roads, and highways are included in the total and one-half or more when they are excluded[30]—is immobile, account must be taken of the restrictions imposed by this immobility. (a) A country must produce more than half of its capital equipment and probably cannot with safety long attempt to secure more than one-fourth of its

30. According to Doane's estimates about 70 per cent of the physical assets used for production in 1922 and about 65 per cent of all physical assets were essentially immobile. If investment in roads and highways is included these percentages become 75 and 70. If investment in land, roads, and highways is excluded the percentages are 52 and 47. These estimates are rough approximations. See Doane, *op. cit.,* 35, 37, 116, 120–121. See also Buchanan, N. S., *International investment and domestic welfare,* chaps. 2, 6–7, N.Y., Holt, 1945; Buchanan, N. S. and Lutz, F. A., *Foreign economic relations of the United States,* chap. 8, N.Y., Twentieth Century Fund, 1946. It has recently been estimated that of the agricultural investment feasible in under-developed countries in the next decade, about 71 per cent is composed of equipment and services that will have to be imported. See United Nations, *Methods of financing economic development in under-developed countries,* 55–56, Lake Success, United Nations, 1949.

annual increment through foreign borrowing. (*b*) While, other conditions being equal, the ratio of some forms of immobile equipment (e.g., highways, railroads, communications, etc.) to the population tends to be higher in sparsely than in densely peopled countries,[31] any advantage derivable therefrom by the latter countries tends to be more than offset by the associated low ratio of cultivatable land to the population. (*c*) Since under-developed economies tend to be ridden with various kinds of unemployment, these countries may easily utilize their unemployed and ineffectively employed workers to build immobile capital (buildings, highways, railroads, communications, etc.) and thus obtain it at relatively small net cost to the economy. (*d*) When a country embarks upon an industrialization program, it tends initially to encounter a sub-normal value of *s*, since the ration of immobile to mobile equipment is abnormally high at first, and the immobile capital, being *directly* less productive on the average than are other forms of investment, contributes in a relatively smaller measure to the embarking country's income. As industrialization proceeds, however, mobile and more productive equipment tends (at least within limits and for a time) to increase relatively more rapidly than assets that are immobile and directly less productive. This trend tends to push up the values of *s* and *S* to the high levels seemingly normal for under-developed countries.[32] Illustrative of immobile and immediately less productive investments indicated for under-developed countries are canals, railroads, highways, land-clearing,

31. In Japan the ratio of population-oriented to space-oriented investment rose from 1.67/1 in 1900–09 to 3.4–4.1/1 in 1919–36. See Staley, *op. cit.,* chap. 4 appendix.

32. Data suited to demonstrate the points made above in the text are not readily available. Some circumstances tend to increase the productive effectiveness of *W* while others tend to diminish it. Industrialization initially entails two types of investment on the part of under-developed countries which, since they are not directly productive, must be financed from government funds: (*a*) the execution of "projects which are essential to organic development" and (*b*) the provision of expanded social services. (See United Nations, *The effects of taxation on foreign trade and investment,* 4, Lake Success, United Nations, 1950.) Since these investments cannot be nicely adjusted to the size, income, and needs of the population, they sometimes tend to be too large initially, with the result that their effectiveness increases with time. Data presented in Table I, line 13, and Table III, column 2b, reveal that only after economies have progressed appreciably are railroad facilities adequately used and indicate that initially subsidies out of tax revenues tend to be required. If data were available they would permit similar inferences in respect of highways and related facilities. Doane's data (*op. cit.,* chap. 7 and appendix D) suggest that after industrialization had made some progress in the United States, directly productive mobile assets tended to increase faster than mobile assets. In short, for reasons such as have been illustrated, the effectiveness of *W* probably tends to increase because W_2 or closely related forms of wealth come to be more fully used. In time, however, as income rises, the ratio of W_2 to W_1 tends to rise, with the result that Y/W falls. Data on the ratio of capital (exclusive of farm land and natural wealth) to income, by industry, in the United States in 1929, suggest that Y/W may vary in response to the composition of the industrial component of *W*, for these ratios vary: agriculture, 3.1; mining, 3.3; transport and communications, 4.8; electric light, power, and gas, 12.2; all manufacturing, 3.5; trade, banking and insurance, 2.6; all the groups covered, 3.9. (These intergroup differences are attributable in much larger measure to differences in the capital-labor ratio than to differences in the productivity of capital as such.) See Hilgerdt, F., *Industrialization and foreign trade,* 47–48, Geneva, League of Nations, 1945.

buildings for needed industries and essential public activities, and irrigation, drainage, and flood-control projects suited to improve agriculture, provide hydroelectric power, and facilitate the control of disease (e.g., malaria).[33]

(2) Because of the composition of an economy's physical assets (noted under [1]) and because of the difficulties that an industrializing country encounters in its efforts to secure an adequate supply of foreign exchange, it is advisable, other things being equal, that investment be canalized into industries which can ease this pressure of the demand for foreign exchange against its necessarily limited supply. These industries are of two sorts: (a) those producing goods that were previously imported; and (b) those producing goods for export. Class (a) industries comprise principally firms that produce cheap and relatively labor-embodying manufactures (e.g., food products, textiles, simple house furnishings, etc.) while class (b) industries comprise firms that produce raw materials and partly manufactured products.[34] In the past foreign investment in under-developed countries has tended to flow into transportation, water-power, power, and other utility developments, into mineral raw-material producing industries, and into branches of agriculture that supply food-stuffs and agricultural raw materials required in advanced countries.[35]

(3) In view of the lowness of the scale of living prevailing in most non-industrialized countries, and in light of the manner in which the composition of economic output has evolved in the past, it is essential that primary emphasis long be placed upon increasing the supply of consumer goods and services in most of the countries here under consideration.

33. See United Nations, *Methods of financing economic development in under-developed countries,* 44–50, Lake Success, United Nations, 1949; FAO, *Mission for Greece,* 160–162, Washington, FAO, 1947.

34. See Buchanan, *op. cit.,* 102–106. In the 1920's and 1930's the non-industrialized countries imported manufactured articles and exported raw materials predominantly. See League of Nations, *The network of world trade,* 23–24, Geneva, League of Nations, 1942.

35. While agriculture, as a whole, has not attracted foreign capital, forms of agriculture adapted to foreign control have; e.g., bananas, sugar, vegetable oils, rubber, tea, coffee, spices, cinchona bark, sisal, abacá, chicle, cacao, kapok, tobacco, cotton, timber, and grazing and related industries. A number of mineral resources have attracted foreign capital: e.g., petroleum, iron ore and ferro-alloys, non-ferrous metals, fertilizer raw materials and other non-metals. Coal production has not drawn foreign capital. Some foreign capital has flowed into water-power developments in under-developed countries and more may do so. Transportation, telecommunications, and other public utilities have drawn foreign capital into under-developed countries. There has been very little foreign investment in manufacturing in under-developed areas. See Lewis, C., *The United States and foreign investment problems,* chap. 5, Washington, Brookings Instn., 1948. Of the $11.4 billion private American direct investments abroad in 1948 4.2 were in petroleum, mining, and smelting; 1.3 in public utilities; 3.6 in manufacturing; and 0.6 in agriculture. See Abelson, M., Private United States direct investments abroad, *Survey of Current Business* 29: 20, 1949. The nature of these investments supports the conclusion of one study "that foreign capital is in the main confined to preparing the way for . . . industrialization [in the form of manufacturing for the home market], and that, when it has done so, the growth of manufacturing for the domestic market will in the main have to rely on domestic capital formation." See United Nations, *International capital movements during the inter-war period,* 33–34, Lake Success, United Nations, 1949.

This inference is supported by revelations concerning the dietary and health deficiencies found in these countries and by the principles of consumptive evolution implicit in family budgets when classified according to level of disposable family income. On the assumption that individual and corporate savings constitute an effective demand for capital goods, analyses of budgets in a given country, classified according to income, may serve to disclose roughly how the composition of private expenditure will evolve as industrialization progresses and familial income rises. If we combine with this projection one of public expenditure based upon the past response of the composition of governmental outlay to increases in per capita income and another of the prospective composition of exports and imports, we have a composite projection of the composition of prospective economic output and an indication how capital and man-power should be disposed in the future. Analysis along these lines indicates that for years to come the non-industrialized countries must concentrate upon increasing their output of consumer goods.[36] Typical of the consumer industries initially indicated for under-developed countries are those suited to preserve, process, and distribute food; to produce cheaper textiles and simple types of farm equipment; and to manufacture inexpensive home furnishings and equipment. Typical of the more durable industries indicated are housing, building, and simple health-improving ventures.

Historical analysis bears out this inference, for it reveals that industrialization is attended by complementary changes in the composition of employment and output. (*a*) The absolute and the relative number of persons engaged in agriculture, forestry, and fishing tends to decline until, assuming that a country in effect just supplies its requirement of the products of these industries, the relative number engaged therein reaches a level of 8–20 per cent of the labor force. The relative number engaged in manufacturing, mining, and building begins to rise only to be surpassed, after some decades, by the relative number engaged in the supply of ever more diverse services. (*b*) Within the industrial sector proper, as a rule, consumption-goods industries remain paramount for many decades, but in a decreasing measure. The rapidity with which the capital-goods industries overtake consumption-goods industries in relative importance is greater in proportion as (i) the necessary raw materials are available at home or readily obtainable abroad and as (ii) the state restricts consumer sovereignty and choice and takes steps forcibly to accelerate the development of capital-goods industries. For example, the capital-goods industries progressed more rapidly in the

36. On family-budget behavior see Zimmerman, C. C., *Consumption and standards of living,* N.Y., Van Nostrand, 1936; Allen, R. G. D., and Bowley, A. L., *Family expenditure,* London, P. S. King, 1935; Williams, F. M., and Zimmerman, C. C., *Studies of family living in the United States and other countries,* Washington, U.S. Dept. of Agriculture, 1935. For an estimate of structure of evolving wants from budgetary studies see *The structure of the American economy,* chap. 2, Washington, Nat. Resources Comm., 1939.

resource-rich United States and in totalitarian Russia than in Western Europe where the resource equipment was poorer than in the United States and the consumers were much freer than in Soviet Russia. Capital-goods industries have tended to develop more rapidly, furthermore, in countries which, because they undertook industrialization more recently, were able to profit by the experiences of countries that underwent this process earlier. Industrial history thus reveals, in considerable measure, the operation of a principle analogous to the biological principle embodied in the dictum that ontogeny recapitulates phylogeny; for the development of any particular country lately undergoing industrialization recapitulates in a significant degree the course of events experienced by countries that have preceded it in industrialization.[37]

(4) Inasmuch as non-industrialized countries are relatively short of both capital and skilled labor they must, in so far as possible, economize in the use of each of these agents. This means that they must emphasize industries in which the ratio of capital to labor is low and/or in which the ratio of skilled to relatively unskilled workers is low. Accordingly, if as theory leads us to expect, both capital and diverse kinds of labor are distributed among employments so that each such agent receives essentially the same remuneration in all employments, the ratio of wages to average output will be lower in the capital-intensive than in the labor-intensive industries while the wage structure will be essentially the same from industry to industry. Actually, this situation tends only to be approximated. Even so, in the absence of strong governmental intervention, the pressure of internal and/or external competition will cause the under-developed countries initially to specialize in industries that make relatively little use of capital and skilled labor. These countries cannot, of course, develop only industries of this sort, for embarkation upon an industrialization program calls for considerable investment in capital-intensive branches of the economy[38] and for the employment of an adequate number of skilled workers and technically competent people. In general, industrial development can proceed successfully only if it progresses upward from the bottom, and no steps are taken in the absence of the necessary preliminary preparation.[39]

37. On these points see Clark, *Conditions*, chaps. 5–6, and *Economics of 1960*, chap. 5; Chang, *op. cit.*, chap. 3; Hoffmann, W., *Stadien und Typen der Industrialisierung: Eine Beitrag zur quantitativen Analyse historischer Wirtschaftssprozesse*, Jena, Fischer, 1931, and The growth of industrial production in Great Britain: A quantitative study: *Econ. Hist. Rev.* 2: 162–180, 1949. Great Britain, which began to industrialize much earlier than did Japan, and which allowed its population far more consumer sovereignty and choice than did Soviet Russia, passed from the first through the second and into the third stage of industrialization much less rapidly than did Japan or Russia, the studies of Hoffmann and Chang show.

38. For example, in Palestine in 1937 and 1946, respectively, 34 and 26 per cent of all industrial capital was invested in power stations and electrical appliances, with a capital investment of $10,000 per worker in 1942 compared with a capital investment of $1,900 per worker for all Jewish industry. See *Investing in Israel*, 14, N.Y., Jewish Agency for Palestine, 1949.

39. In the *Report on seven year development plan for the plan organization of the imperial government of Iran* 1: 8–12, N.Y., Overseas Consultants, Inc., 1949, three principles are

(i) While the amount of investment required per job usually may be varied somewhat, given the production functions technologically practicable, and while production functions for given industries vary from country to country, it remains true that capital investment per job varies widely from industry to industry and, in a lesser degree, from one branch of a given industry to another. What is more important, such variation characterizes both investment in land and buildings (which must be produced at home) and investment in plant and machinery (much of which has to be imported in the case of countries that have made little progress in industrialization). Investment per job is comparatively low in terms of both domestically-produced and foreign-produced capital in furniture and house furnishings, clothing, textile, leather and related industries. It is relatively small also in light metals, electrical products, semimanufactured metals, engineering, and some building materials. While it is relatively large in food, drink and tobacco products as a whole, it is relatively small also in some branches of industry. In short, investment per worker is relatively low in most of the industries that rate high priority under (3), only the importation of equipment, steel, motors, and the like being necessary in the early and intermediate stages of industrialization. While investment per job is necessarily very high in electric light and power and other utilities and likely to be high in industries oriented to raw materials, foreign capital is likely to be obtainable for these purposes, and particularly for the development of raw materials marketable abroad.[40]

(ii) Since industries vary widely in the amount of skill required of their workers, and since the industrialization of non-industrialized countries requires the importation of "know-how" and skilled technicians and the gradual development of a skilled labor force, it is essential that emphasis be placed initially upon industries requiring relatively little skill. The skill-factor is low in a number of industries that make relatively little use of capital (e.g., textiles, footwear, rubber manufacture, glass, etc.) and supply consumer wants of high priority. This factor is low also in a number of industries in which investment per worker is around or above average and which either make use of local raw materials (e.g., fertilizers, butter-making, soap,

---

emphasized: (1) "national development effort must first be applied near the bottom"; (2) "capital is not a substitute for skill or experience"; and (3) "co-ordination is an essential ingredient of the plan." This is a very detailed and illuminating study of the problems of an under-developed country.

40. For estimates of the amount of investment required per worker or job in various industries and countries see Mandelbaum, *op. cit.,* 35, 36, 95; Brown, *op. cit.,* 30–31; Buchanan, *op. cit.,* 25ff.; Hilgerdt, *op. cit.,* 47–55; Ezekial, *op. cit.,* 24–26; p. 14 of the study cited in note 38; Perloff, H. S., *Puerto Rico's economic future,* 361–366, Chicago, Univ. of Chicago Press, 1950; Clark, *Conditions,* 71, 80; Bliss, C. A., *The structure of manufacturing production,* chap. 3, N.Y., Natl. Bureau of Econ. Research, 1939; Spiegel, H. W., *The Brazilian economy,* 231, Phila., Blakiston, 1949; Rosenstein-Rodan, P. N., Problems of industrialization of eastern and southwestern Europe, *Econ. Jour.* 53: 210, 1943; Guyol, N. B., *op. cit.,* 6–10; Chang, *op. cit.,* 216; United Nations, *Economic survey of Latin America,* 1948, 16, Lake Success, United Nations, 1949.

cement, sugar-refining) or provide products of great significance for industrialization (e.g., steel production). The lowness of the skill-factor in this second group of industries may enable relatively backward countries to develop them early inasmuch as the relatively low wage that may initally be paid to the less skilled workers offsets the relatively high cost of capital and skilled and technical labor.[41] In short, therefore, while it is not possible to substitute capital for training and experience, it is possible already to use considerable capital even when the number of skilled workers is relatively small.

(5) Just as industrial progress initially calls for the economical use of such scarce agents as capital and skilled labor so also does it call for the exploitation of relative abundant natural resources. This means that in countries in which population is sparse landed products must be duly emphasized, while, in countries in which land is scarce, raw material resources must be exploited, particularly since these are the most likely sources of the foreign exchange needed for the importation of equipment and know-how and the maintenance of foreign debt service. In general, this emphasis, which one would expect competitive forces to bring about, has characterized both foreign investment in under-developed countries and the progress of domestically financed industry.[42]

(6) Because of the linkages that obtain between various industries, it is essential that each be developed in proper proportion to the others, given prevailing external trading relations. For if this is not done, either some industries will be characterized by excess capacity, or inter-industry complementarities will not be fully exploited. This rule cannot be fully carried out, however, since certain industries such as public utilities and certain forms of investment such as highways and transportation, not being nicely adaptable to current requirements, often must be built up ahead of demand.

41. On labor requirements by representative types of industry see Brown, *op. cit.*, 30–33. On time required to learn job in the United States see War Manpower Commission Bureau of Manpower Utilization, *Training grades for selected occupations*, Washington, 1943, and National Resources Planning Board, *Industrial location and national resources*, chap. 11, Washington, Natl. Resources Planning Board, 1943. While wage structures appear to be somewhat affected by the amount of equipment used per worker, they also appear to reflect differences in the degree of skill, etc., required, by industry. In so far as this is the case types of industry that are low on the wage structure scale probably are well suited to newly industrializing countries unless they require materials not readily accessible. On the wage structure see, for example, Lebergott, S., Wage structures, *Rev. Econ. Statistics* 29: 274ff., 1947.

42. See note 28 above. Hoffmann found that whereas labor-oriented consumer-goods industries predominated in countries in which labor was relatively plentiful, material-oriented necessity producing industries developed in a number of countries producing the necessary raw materials. Iron and machine industries predominated where the raw materials were to be had. See *op. cit.*, 134ff., 164. In Latin America 78 per cent of the raw materials used in manufactures are of local origin. See United Nations, *Economic survey of Latin America*, 23–24, Lake Success, United Nations, 1949. As industrialization progresses in a country, its industries and output become relatively more capital intensive. See Bonné, A., *State and economics in the Middle East*, 222, London, Kegan Paul, Trench, Trubner and Co., 1948.

Leontief's methods appear well suited to disclose the complementarities referred to and the course of their development.[43]

V. The Development of the Labor Force

Industrial progress presupposes a healthy, adequately trained, and sufficiently motivated labor force. Industrial development programs therefore require action on the health, the training, and the motivation fronts.

(*a*) Health. In most of the under-developed countries diets are quantitatively and qualitatively inadequate, and preventable forms of infectious and contagious disease afflict unduly large fractions of the population and reduce both their capacity and their desire to engage effectively in economic activities. Accordingly, steps must be taken both to correct dietary deficiencies and to bring preventable diseases under control before industrialization can progress far in any country, in part because the spread of disease (whether of man, animal, or plant) is greatly accelerated by the intensification of communication consequent upon industrialization and economic development. The steps indicated as necessary involve quantitative and qualitative improvements in food supply and diet, the importation of necessary medicines, the training of an initially sufficient number of medical technicians and workers, the organization of effective public health programs, and so on.[44]

43. E.g., see Leontief, W. W., Exports, imports, domestic output, and employment, *Quart. Jour. Econ.* 60: 171–193, 1946. On inter-industry linkages see National Resources Planning Board, *Industrial location and national resources*, chap. 5.

44. Data presented in Table I, lines 19–21 and 23–26, and Table III, columns 7–11, indicate that in the under-developed countries life expectancy is quite low, t.b. mortality is high, the number of physicians is far from adequate, and diets are so defective, quantitatively and qualitatively, as to impair the productive effectiveness of the labor force and reduce its resistance to disease. Illustrative of the incapacitating effects of ill health in the under-developed parts of the world are these: malaria affects 300 million persons per year, killing 3 million and causing a loss of 20–40 days per person afflicted per year; schistosomiasis, a debilitating rural disease like malaria, afflicts 20–30 million people in the Near East alone and millions more in Africa, Asia, and Latin America; filiarsis cases number about 189 million per year in under-developed countries; yaws, widespread in tropical countries, afflicts over one million in Haiti alone; hookworm and other intestinal parasites debilitate millions; cases of syphilis number 20–100 millions and those of gonorrhea 2–3 times as many. There is high incidence also in many under-developed countries of diseases accompanied by high mortality (e.g., smallpox, typhus, cholera, plague, kala-azar, some fevers) or by disability (e.g., trachoma, leishmaniasis). Finally, in many under-developed countries infant mortality is very high (e.g., over 500 per 1,000 births in Iran). Yet, every one of the diseases mentioned can be virtually eliminated at relatively small cost through a three-fold attack: (*a*) insect control, general sanitation, and reduction of contact between infected and non-infected persons; (*b*) use of vaccines, etc., to prevent infection; and (*c*) use of drugs and medicines to cure victims and remove reservoirs of infection. It appears that, of the various conditions prerequisite to industrialization, the one that can be attained with most speed and economy is a relatively satisfactory state of health. For an excellent and detailed account of the existing state of health and the means of improving it in a representative under-developed country see volume 2 of the work on Iran cited in note 39 above. On the incidence

(*b*) Education and industrial training. Illiteracy and lack of industrial training characterize most of the non-industrial populations. Yet a certain amount of education and industrial training is essential to the initiation of an industrialization program. Adequate provision must therefore be made for such education and training.[45]

(*c*) Motivation. Industrial progress is impossible in the absence of a well-organized system of motives, incentives, and social pressures that impels men to work hard and effectively. Moreover, such a system must be elastic, so that, as output per worker rises, the system's compulsion increases, with the result that the representative member of the labor force remains disposed to work almost as many hours per year as he did prior to the enlargement of his output and income. Such a system is not easily introduced into a culture that is not already shot through with at least potentially appropriate motives and incentives. Furthermore, a diversity of means must be employed to introduce suitable systems of motives, incentives, and other social pressures, since the cultures of under-developed countries are heterogeneous, ranging from the complex cultures of essentially independent Oriental and Latin-American countries through the somewhat dualistic cultures of societies long under colonial rule (even though recently "liberated") to the less complex cultures of some of the African and Oceanic peoples. In fact, if only some Western methods are introduced into a non-industrialized area, and jointly with conditions of the sort long associated with "colonialism," the outcome may resemble proletarianization much more closely than incentive-impregnated industrial development.

Following Moore we may classify under four heads the courses of action essential to the development of an adequate motivational system. (i) Barriers to industrial employment must be removed. These include besides sheer ignorance of the industrial way of life, attachment to pre-industrial forms of social and economic security and a lack of interest in the attributes of status and prestige characteristic of industrial societies. (ii) Propellants toward industrialization must be supplied. Agricultural overpopulation is such a propellant as is the destruction, by external competition, of the mar-

---

of disease and methods for its control see United Nations, *Technical assistance for economic development*, 25–26, 243–308; U.S. State Department, *Point four*, 150–156. Concerning the influence of industrial development upon the diffusion of disease see Furnivall, J. S., *Colonial policy and practice*, chap. 10, Cambridge, Univ. Press, 1948. It may be noted, for purposes of comparison, that in the United States in the winter of 1935–1936, 2–3 per cent of the population of working age were disabled on a given day. See Dublin, L. I., and Lotka, A. J., *The money value of a man*, 113–114, N.Y., Ronald Press, 1946.

45. On the high incidence of illiteracy, together with the comparative lack of means of communication and diffusion, in the under-developed countries see Table III, columns 3–6, and Table I, lines 14–17. An effective educational program entails more than the elimination of most illiteracy; it requires also the development of technical schools and the gradual formation of a technically competent labor force. See volume 2 of work on Iran (cited in note 39 above) for practical ways of solving the educational problems of an under-developed country.

kets hitherto existing for the skills of pre-industrial craftsmen. Political and economic coercion and the imposition of taxes and other burdens that must be paid in cash, together with the discriminatory impact of local customs, operate individually and in combination to press adversely affected individuals to engage in industry. (iii) The attractions of industrial employment must be magnified. Of paramount importance is the introduction of a money economy, together with the corollary condition that money serve both as the primary symbol of prestige and as the principal means by which men can obtain the things which they prize. Opportunity to increase and use industrial skill is quite important also. Industrialization is more likely to progress rapidly in a society with a well developed state apparatus than in one without a well-organized state, since industrial progress is essential to a state's realizing its political and its military aspirations. Industrial employment may prove attractive to individuals also if it is conducive to individual social achievement, or if it promises a greater amount of individual freedom than is possible in a non-industrial society.

(iv) After the individual has been drawn into an industrial system it is essential both to keep him there and to impel him to be active. This calls for an appropriately advancing wage-level, for the inculcation in the individual of aspirations which material rewards can effectively and uniquely satisfy, and for appropriate recognition of those job-oriented incentives which non-material rewards are best suited to satisfy. Other steps are also in order: encouragement of the individual worker to acquire skill; effective imposition of industrial discipline; avoidance of ostensible inter-individual or inter-group inequities and discrimination; replacement of pre-industrial by adequate industrial forms of economic and social security; and integration of the individual into a system of culture that makes the enhancement of his satisfaction dependent upon industrial progress.[46]

Of the various courses of action that must be pursued if an under-developed country is to be industrialized, none is more amenable to assistance from abroad and to action by the state than are (a) and (b) under V. The state, moreover, may contribute in considerable measure to the creation of a system of motives, incentives, and pressures suited to adapt individuals to an industrial mode of life and enable them to function effectively thereunder. While such action on the part of the state necessarily entails an initial reduction of consumer and worker sovereignty and choice, it probably is much more defensible than the very marked restriction of consumer sovereignty that appears to be necessary if densely populated countries are to supply enough capital internally to industrialize themselves at comparatively high rates.

46. These two paragraphs are largely summaries of W. E. Moore's two studies: Primitives and peasants in industry, *Social Research* 15: 44–81, 1948, and Theoretical aspects of industrialization, *ibid.*, 277–303. On the effects of cultural pluralism see Furnivall, J. S., *Netherlands India*, chap. 13, Cambridge, Univ. Press, 1939.

VI. Exchange Relations, Industrialization, and International Income Disparity

At present international disparity in income per capita is very marked, with per capita income in the United States 15–30 times as high as that in non-industrialized countries. In this section, therefore, we shall inquire whether international income disparity is likely to be reduced in the future.

Empirical data suggest that income disparity has increased both at the national and at the international level in the past hundred years. In the United States in 1945, for example, the level of farm living in the highest Iowa counties was 12–39 times that in the lowest Kentucky counties. It is unlikely that so great a discrepancy between two long-settled agricultural counties prevailed a century ago. Per capita output apparently has increased more rapidly in the United States and other advanced countries in the course of the past century than in under-developed countries. For example, during comparable periods output per man-hour has risen more rapidly in indus-trialized than in non-industrialized countries, and in the United States than in continental Europe and Asia, with only newly-developing South Africa, Japan, and parts of South America and Europe (i.e., Belgium, Czechoslo-vakia, and Latvia) temporarily experiencing higher rates of growth. Thus, whereas the American level was 11–13 times the Indian level and 30–40 times the Chinese level in the 1940's it was only about 9 times the Indian and Chinese levels in 1860.[47]

International isolation makes for disparity whereas international inter-course makes for its reduction. For in the absence of relatively free inter-national economic and cultural intercourse, the income-increasing forces manifest relatively more momentum in countries already developed and industrialized than in countries in which industrialization has made little or no headway.

Given a persistingly satisfactory combination of the following circum-stances, international income disparity would be greatly reduced: (*a*) an appropriate international distribution of land, (*b*) unrestricted international trade in productive agents, goods, and services; and (*c*) freedom on part of the population to move internationally and maintain a suitable distribution of population. It is not likely, however, that within the calculable future (*a*) and (*c*) will prevail in sufficient measure to permit freedom of international trade to correct most of the remaining disparity.[48] Migration will be less

47. The data used in this paragraph are from Clark, *Rev. of Econ. Progress* 1 (4): 2, 1949; Hagood, M. J., *Farm operator family level of living indexes for counties of the United States 1940 and 1945*, Washington, U.S. Dept. of Agriculture, 1947. On the causes of the persistence of poverty within agriculture and on their similarity to the causes of the persistence of inter-national poverty see Schultz, T. W., Poverty within agriculture, *Jour. Polit. Econ.* 58: 1–15, 1950.

48. P. A. Samuelson has recently shown that international trade not only reduces interna-tional differences in factor prices (as economists have long held) but, under certain conditions,

free than in the past. Only technological knowledge will become more evenly distributed. Restrictions upon competition and freedom of trade, while they probably will be less marked than in the 1930's, are not likely to be reduced to their pre-1914 dimensions.

Despite these difficulties, it is possible that the spread of industrialization will appreciably reduce international income disparity. Judging by past tendencies per capita income may advance about 1.5 per cent per year in countries presently industrialized. In 50 years such a rate will elevate current incomes of $500, $1,000, and $1,500, respectively, to $1,053, $2,105, and $3,158. Now suppose that S and s remain fairly constant for 50 years in countries presently under-developed and that per capita income there rises 2.5–4 per cent. Given a 2.5 per cent rate, incomes of $75, $100, and $150 will rise, in 50 years, to $258, $344, and $516. Given a 3 per cent rate and the corresponding figures are $329, $438, and $658; and given a 4 per cent rate, $533, $711, and $1,066. In short, if per capita income advances 2.5 per cent per year for 50 years in under-developed countries, given a 1.5 per cent rate of increase in industrialized countries, the disparity between the two types of countries will be reduced about four-tenths; if 3 per cent, about one-half; and if 4 per cent, about seven-tenths.

Realization of such a reduction in international income disparity presupposes a considerable increase in the volume of exports moving out of countries undergoing industrialization. For this there are two reasons. First, since a country undergoing industrialization must long import scarce technical services, equipment, and other needed physical assets from abroad, it must convert a part of its domestic savings into foreign exchange wherewith to purchase equipment in industrial countries. Second, eventually, when such a non-industrialized country's foreign borrowing falls short of its service charges on past foreign borrowings, it must meet the difference through net exportation.

For purposes of illustration let us suppose a country of 1,000,000 inhabitants who increase 1 per cent per year and produce an annual income of $100 million in the base year. Assume further that s has a value of 0.4; that national income increases 4 per cent per year, and per capita income 3 per cent per year; that imports of physical equipment aggregate 5 per cent of national income each year, of which half are paid for through foreign borrowing and half through the conversion of domestic savings into foreign exchange; that the service charge on each increment of foreign investment

can eliminate them. These conditions not being realizable in reality, it follows only that international trade may in some measure reduce international differences in factor prices consequent upon international differences in factor equipment. See International factor-price equalization once again, *Econ. Jour.* 59: 181–197, 1949, and International trade and the equalisation of factor prices, *ibid.* 58: 163–184, 1948. The removal of tariffs and the establishment of larger free-trade areas will not benefit, and probably will injure, the less-developed components of such area in the event that essentially free competition does not obtain *within* the area. See Rothschild, K. W., The small nation and world trade, *ibid.* 54: 26–40, 1944.

amounts to 8 per cent per year for 20 years, upon the expiry of which the loan may be considered amortized; and that consumer imports which do not directly or indirectly augment the capital stock remain fixed at $10 million per year. Under the conditions given annual investment must aggregate 10 per cent of the national income, of which 7.5 per cent is provided out of domestic sources and 2.5 out of foreign. Since, with s equaling 0.4, an annual increment of investment amounting to 10 per cent of the national income increases national income by 4 per cent, 0.25–0.35 of which probably is imputable to capital, such increment produces and earns more than enough income to cover service charges of 8 per cent. For, whereas the income produced and earned by the assumed annual increment of investment ranges between 1 and 1.4 per cent of the national income, the service charges amount to but 0.8 per cent of the national income. The principal problem, therefore, is that of transforming one-half of the service charges on the annual increment in wealth into foreign exchange. It is assumed throughout, of course, that all investment expenditures labeled as such, whether domestic or foreign, are actually income-increasing investment, with every increment of 2.5 units of investment being accompanied by an increment of 1 unit of income. It is also assumed, despite some of the contrary facts presented, that scarcity of land and/or natural resources will not operate as a limitational factor.

In the first year, with national income equal to $100 million, we require $12,706,000 of foreign exchange: $10 million for consumer imports, $5 million for capital imports; and $200,000 for foreign debt service, against which may be set $2.5 million foreign borrowings. While the absolute amount of foreign exchange required increases as the years pass, it increases less rapidly than the national income under the conditions given, falling from 12.7 per cent of the national income in the first year to about 9.1 per cent in the twenty-fifth year. This percentage approximates 10.4 in the sixteenth year when for the first time aggregate service on the foreign debt approximates annual foreign borrowings, thereafter to exceed them. If we hold consumer imports constant at $5 million instead of $10 million, the amount of foreign exchange required, expressed as a percentage of the national income, remains in the neighborhood of 7.7 until the twentieth year (when the last payment is being made on the first foreign loan) and thereafter declines slightly. If, consumer sovereignty being assumed, consumer imports rise (say) half as fast as the national income, the amount of foreign exchange required, expressed as a percentage of the national income, remains in the neighborhood of 12.7 until the twentieth year when it begins to decline slightly. These figures rest, of course, upon the assumption that all foreign exchange except that used for debt service and the stipulated consumer imports is utilized to purchase income-producing agents, with s remaining constant at 0.4.

In view of what has been said, the industrialization of the under-developed countries can proceed as has been assumed only if they can obtain enough foreign exchange to meet their expanding needs for equipment and for rising aggregate foreign debt-service. Yet, for reasons to be indicated, it is likely that, in the absence of outright gifts from the industrial to the non-industrial countries, a sufficiency of foreign exchange will not be forthcoming. If this be the case, the borrowing countries will not be able to service their foreign debt,[49] foreign sources of loan funds will contract, and the rate of progress of the non-industrial countries in industrialization and income will fall to a level not much above that obtaining in the countries already industrialized. This tendency will be accentuated if, as has been suggested, a shortage of crucial natural resources operates to reduce the value of s below the level of 0.4 assumed.

The availability of foreign exchange (against the industrialized equipment-supplying countries) to the non-industrialized equipment-purchasing countries will be governed principally by two circumstances: (*a*) the ratio of income growth in the former to that of output-growth in the latter; and (*b*) the terms of trade obtaining between the two sets of countries. Condition (*a*) tends to be unfavorable to exchange availability, while condition (*b*) may be rendered favorable, but probably not enough so to offset (*a*).

(*a*) By assumption, aggregate income will grow only about half as fast in the industrialized countries as will aggregate output and income in the non-industrialized countries. Accordingly, in the absence of significant changes in the relation of the price structures of non-industrialized countries to those of industrialized countries, the aggregate monetary demand of the latter countries for the products of the non-industrialized countries will not grow as fast as will the aggregate demand of the latter countries for the products of the former. In consequence, an increasing shortage of foreign exchange will develop in the non-industrialized countries; and this shortage, while reducible, will not be eliminatable through the development of tourism, inasmuch as tourists favor the more industrialized countries. (*b*) Since the demand of industrial countries for the products (principally raw materials and labor-embodying fabricated goods) of non-industrialized countries tends to be inelastic in terms of price, advances in the export prices and conse-

---

49. When, under circumstances such as are described above, default takes place, its cause is, not the nature of the foreign investment, but the inability of the borrowing country to sell enough goods and services. On why defaults tend to occur see Buchanan, *op. cit.*, 115–116. Difficulties attendant upon an under-developed country's obtaining a sufficiency of foreign exchange may be accentuated also by the fact that the spread of industrialization may undermine such international division of labor as has been inherited from the past without replacing it by a new international division of labor that is adapted to the new circumstances. For example, see Rahmer, B. A., Note on the industrialization of backward areas, *Econ. Jour.* 56: 657–662. On the purported and the actual structure of international trade see Hirschman, A. O., *National power and the structure of international trade*, chap. 6, Berkeley, Univ. of Calif. Press, 1945. See also next note.

quently improvements in the terms of trade of non-industrialized countries may operate to increase the income and improve the exchange position of such countries. The future may bring such improvement,[50] and it may be accentuated, as we indicate below, by state action.

In our discussion so far we have assumed a somewhat higher amount of foreign investment and foreign importation than appears warranted. Earlier it was inferred that, since considerably more than one-half of a nation's income-producing wealth is immobile, it ought to limit its annual foreign borrowing to something like one-fourth of its total annual investment. It would appear advisable also that a country draw less than half of its actual annual increment of capital from foreign sources if this be possible. In our earlier example we assumed that foreign-produced equipment and foreign borrowing amounted to 5 and 2.5 per cent, respectively, of the national income each year, with foreign borrowing supplying a rising proportion (16.4 per cent in the first year and 21.3 in the twenty-fifth year) of the gross foreign exchange requirement. If foreign borrowing and foreign equipment purchases are cut to 1.25 and 3.75 per cent of national income, respectively, net foreign exchange requirements grow less rapidly even though foreign borrowing now supplies only about two-thirds (9 instead of 16 per cent the first year, and 14 instead of 21 the twenty-fifth year) as large a fraction of the gross foreign exchange requirement as formerly. The ratio of foreign exchange requirements to income, virtually the same under both conditions in the initial year (i.e., 12.7 and 12.6 per cent), falls somewhat more rapidly under the new assumptions (approximating 7.8 instead of 9.2 in the twenty-fifth year). It is open to question, of course, whether in its early developmental stages a non-industrialized country investing the equivalent of 10 per cent of its income annually can produce 6.25 tenths of this increment locally and rely upon foreign sources for but 3.75 tenths, as our new assumptions require.

In view of what has been said, several inferences may be drawn in respect of exchange relations. (a) Foreign borrowing and foreign equipment purchases probably should supply somewhat less, respectively, than one-fourth and one-half of the annual increment of capital. (b) Since the demand for their products tends to be inelastic, non-industrialized countries may employ

50. On the past and the prospective course of the terms of trade, see Clark, *Conditions*, chap. 14, and *Economics of 1960*, chaps. 4, 7. For some 50 years prior to 1939 the terms of trade were turning against the suppliers of primary goods and in favor of countries exporting manufactures, the purchasing power of primary goods falling about two-fifths in the course of this period. This trend adversely affected under-developed countries, the bulk of whose exports necessarily consist of primary commodities. Since the late 1930's the exchange value of primary exports has risen, in terms of manufactured imports, about one-tenth. Whether this trend will continue, however, is not certain, particularly in view of the fact that considerable new foreign investment may flow, as in the past, into the production of primary commodities. See United Nations, *Relative prices of exports and imports of under-developed countries*, 7-8, 127, Lake Success, United Nations, 1949.

appropriate measures (e.g., tariffs, export taxes) to improve their terms of trade with industrialized countries. For such action, while it may operate directly, by reducing import prices relative to export prices, to retard the development of some domestic manufactures,[51] will also operate indirectly to stimulate industrialization by making available a larger amount of foreign exchange than otherwise would be on hand for the purchase of equipment abroad. (*c*) It is essential that non-industrial countries restrict consumer sovereignty by installing foreign-exchange and related controls, curbing the importation of foreign-produced non-essentials, and appropriating virtually all available foreign exchange for the purchase of foreign equipment and the payment of foreign debt service. (*d*) In the event that foreign funds and equipment are to be had more cheaply if the government of an under-developed country acts as principal, or as agent for its private entrepreneurs, then such action is indicated (provided that, of course, there are not generated other costs which more than offset the gains attendant upon such governmental action).

VII. Illustrations and Prospects

In this section we shall do two things. (i) We shall illustrate by example how industrialization has progressed in some countries and how it has been retarded in others. (ii) We shall show that present plans for industrialization usually assign a much larger role to the state than was the case in the nineteenth century.

(1) *Japan.*[52] The uniquely remarkable industrial progress of Japan is illustrative both of the extent of accomplishment possible and of the comparative unsurmountability of the obstacles to be overcome when a nation's internal resource equipment is poor. Japan's industrialization program may be said really to have begun in 1868, at which time the nation was still essentially feudal, internationally isolated, overpopulated, and lacking much of

51. On this point see Metzler, L. A., Tariffs, the terms of trade, and the distribution of national income, *Jour. Polit. Econ.* 57: 17–25, 1949.

52. On output per man-hour in Japan and other countries discussed in this section see Clark, C., Levels of real national product per man-hour, *Rev. Econ. Progress* 1 (4): 2, 1949. On Japan's income see Schumpeter, E. B., ed., *The industrialization of Japan and Manchukuo, 1930–1940,* 16, N.Y., Macmillan, 1940, and Clark, *Conditions,* 116, 124–125. On savings see *ibid.,* 406. On investment see Staley, *op. cit.,* chap. 4 and appendix. On Japan's foreign investment, economic development, etc., see Moulton, *Japan,* and Reubens, E. P., Foreign capital in economic development: A case-study of Japan, *Milbank Memorial Fund Quart.* 28: 173–190, 1950. (In 1872 Japan's population already numbered about 730 per square mile and about 1,500 per square mile of productive land.) By way of contrast with pre-1940 Japan the Philippine economy has wasted much of the approximately $2 billion poured into it since the close of the war, with waste characteristic of both the private and the public sectors of the economy. In view of the experience of the Philippine economy, it is questionable whether, in the absence of a strong and prudent government, foreign aid can contribute much to industrial development. See *The Banker's Magazine,* 246–247, March, 1950.

the institutional equipment essential to industrialization. The potential strength of the national government rapidly materialized, however; inter-class relations were kept stable; and the population manifested a striking disposition to learn, work, save, and otherwise carry out the government's industrialization program. The government, moreover, offset the lack of an adequate entrepreneurial class by performing many of the functions of this class and facilitating the accomplishment of others through the use of ap-propriate monetary, fiscal, and related policies. By 1930 the relative number of workers engaged in agriculture and fishing had fallen to about 50 per cent from an estimated 85 as of 1873. Even so output per man-hour apparently did not begin to rise above the Oriental level of 3 cents an hour until the close of the nineteenth century, when it began to climb 4.5 to 5 per cent per year to a level of 19–20 cents in the early 1940's. During this 40-year period output per worker rose slightly more than 4 per cent per year, while the population increased about $1\frac{1}{4}$ per cent per year (in contrast with an annual increase of about $\frac{7}{8}$ per cent in 1872–1900). Despite its high rate of growth Japan's output per man-hour in the early 1940's still only approxi-mated that attained in the United States by 1825, in Britain by 1850, and in Germany by 1870.

Japan had relatively little assistance from foreign investment. In the early 1870's net foreign investment approximating a little over one per cent of the then national income was contracted, but this was liquidated by 1896. Be-tween 1896 and 1913 net foreign investment increased, the average annual increment approximating something like 2–2.5 per cent of the average an-nual income during that period. By 1929, largely as a result of the favorable effects of World War I, net foreign investment was reduced one-third below the 1913 level. By 1938 Japan had become a net creditor nation to the extent of $534 million (i.e., about 8 per cent of the 1938 national income).

Apparently Japan was able to develop industrially, despite its small and dwindling net influx of foreign capital and its lack of natural resources, be-cause it sold, saved, invested, and spent wisely. And it was able to do these things because it had economical access to foreign markets for its products and to foreign sources of supply for the things its industries lacked. Clark estimates Japanese savings in 1900–1940 at about one-fifth of the national income while Staley estimates investment to have varied between 10 and 17 per cent of the national income. Judging from the rate at which income progressed, the rate of investment probably lies between these two esti-mates. In any event it was high, given the lowness of per capita income. (Even so, investment per capita per year rose in 1936 dollars from only about 1.67 in 1900–1909 to about 5.25 after 1920, which is but a fraction of the $800–1,300 required in the middle 1930's to equip a worker in manu-factures.) The foreign exchange provided by foreign loans initially was multiplied a number of times and subsequently was replaced by the expanding sale of Japan's predominantly labor-embodying products. This exchange was used, moreover, almost exclusively for the purchase of foodstuffs for the working population and for the procurement of raw materials, semi-finished products, and equipment essential to industry. Even in the absence of war Japan could not have continued to progress so rapidly had her government become weak, her inter-class relations instable, her working population less industrious, and her income-receivers less disposed to save.

(2) *India*.[53] The industrial history of India is probably more typical than that of Japan of development in an Asiatic country marked by a non-primitive and ancient culture. Although nearly three-fourths of the occupied population remains in agriculture, its aggregate output is very low and inadequate for the nation's needs. Energy consumption per capita is less than 1.5 per cent of the American average. Although gross reproduction has always been high, the population has grown sporadically and at an average annual rate (about $5/8$ per cent per year) only about half that observed in Japan. While India's resource equipment appears to be somewhat superior to that of Japan, its output and its wealth have grown less rapidly. Between 1860 and the early 1930's output per man-hour increased about $1\frac{3}{8}$ per cent per year from 3 cents to 8–9 cents, while output per occupied person increased just over 0.75 per cent per year between 1866 and 1944. Even so, output per man-hour remains near or below the level attained in Britain in the late eighteenth century while the wage level appears to be appreciably below that realized around 1600 when India's population was only one-fourth as large as at present.

While capital is essential to India's industrialization, it is not evident at present that it will be formed at a sufficiently high rate. In the light of our earlier analysis and of the fact that India's population will probably grow at least 1 per cent per year, a 3 per cent per year increase in per capita income calls for investment at an annual rate of around 11 per cent of the national income. Staley estimates that should India develop during the next four decades as Japan did, it will require an investment of about 81 billion 1936 dollars, which would probably entail annual savings in excess of 10 per cent of the national income. These funds are not to be had from foreign sources, judging by the fact that outstanding foreign investment aggregated only about $7 per capita in 1938 and that, abstracting from India's acquisition during the war period of a sterling balance in excess of one billion, not much

53. On India's income see Clark, *Rev. Econ. Progress* 1 (5): 1–3, 1949. On past investment see Lewis, *op. cit.*, 335. On India's supposed capital requirements (which are generally put too low) see Staley, *op. cit.*, chap. 4; Harris, S. E., *Economic Planning,* chap. 11, N.Y., Knopf, 1949; Iyengar, S. K., Industrialization and agriculture in India, *Econ. Jour.* 54: 189–205, 1944. Annual saving is put at 2–3 per cent of the national income in United Nations, *Methods of financing economic development in under-developed countries,* 73. At the close of 1949 India owned one-third of Britain's overseas debts, or about one billion sterling (*Fortune* 72, April, 1950).

foreign capital is flowing into India. Neither is there evidence that domestic savings in India, recently estimated at 2–3 per cent of national income, will approach 10 per cent of the national income.

(3) *China*.[54] While China is as well equipped with natural resources as is India and better equipped than Japan, her industrial progress has been negligible, and her output per man-hour still remains at the 3-cent level attained in Germany before 1800. At present many obstacles stand in the way of China's industrialization. China has long lacked a strong government, good politico-economic institutions, political order, and social stability. Her population is dense, exceeding 100 persons per square mile in settled areas, with arable land per person averaging about 0.55 acres. If her population is not increasing at present, it still could easily begin to increase 1 per cent per year. Three-fourths of the population is engaged in agriculture where crop yields are so low as probably to be susceptible of a 50 per cent increase. Most important of all the obstacles to industrial progress is China's lack of equipment and her seeming inability to form capital at a high rate. In the late 1930's, at which time outstanding foreign investment in China approximated $6 per capita, *modern* industrial investment was estimated at about $2.50 per capita, while energy consumption per capita was but $1\frac{1}{4}$ per cent as high as in the United States and only about 7 per cent as high as in Japan. Data relating to 1930–1936 confirm the impression that capital formation is proceeding at a very low rate. For, during this period, foreign investment approximated 1.8 per cent of income; net investment, 1.3 per cent; and domestic investment, −0.5 per cent. The corresponding rates for 1936, the best year in the six, were 3.9, 5.5, and 1.6. According to Staley, should China develop in the next four decades as Japan did in 1900–1940, she will require, in 1936 dollars, 133 billions of capital, with the annual requirement rising from 1.36 billion in the first decade to $5.2 billion in the fourth. These figures must be increased at least one-half to allow for increases in the price level. If we put China's national income at $22.5 billion and assume that consumers' capital formation will absorb 2 per cent of the national income, we get a required saving rate of about 12 per cent per year. This rate, which might permit per capita income to rise close to 3 per cent per year is far above any recently observed sustained rate of investment.

(4) *Puerto Rico*.[55] The industrialization of Puerto Rico represents that of a very densely populated country (about 645 persons per sq. mi.) poorly endowed with nonhuman resources and characterized by a high rate of population growth (2 or more per cent per year). Individual savings are

54. On foreign investments in China see Remer, C. F., *Foreign investments in China*, N.Y., 1933; Lewis, *op. cit.*, p. 334. The estimates of *modern* capital and capital needs are from Staley, *op. cit.*, chap. 4. Income data for 1931–1936 are reported in Ou, Pao-San, A new estimate of China's national income, *Jour. Polit. Econ.* 54: 547–554, 1946, and United Nations, *National income statistics* 1938–47, 46–47, Lake Success, United Nations, 1948.

55. On Puerto Rico, see Perloff, *op. cit.*, 162, 179, 186, 365–366.

small, representing about 2 per cent of income payments to individuals in 1940–1944, while net additions to the island's capital stock are small. Whence it is not likely that per capita income ($271 in current prices in 1946), which, under the impact of war, increased 42 per cent in real terms in 1940–1946, will continue to grow appreciably, unless population growth is effectively controlled, investment is greatly increased, and labor-oriented manufactures are developed.

(5) *Israel and the Middle East.*[56] Contrast of conditions in Israel with those in surrounding lands illustrates admirably what can be done, given capital, entrepreneurship, and a technically trained labor force. Israel's investment has more than kept pace with its population growth — some 160 per cent in 1938–1949 — investment representing 40 per cent of the national income in 1949. There is an adequate supply of entrepreneurial ability, while the labor force resembles the American in composition. Income distribution is comparatively equal by Western standards, and the welfare of the working population is held paramount. The apparatus of state is well-developed and effective. In the remainder of the Middle East an opposite set of conditions prevails: most of the population, nine-tenths of whom live at the margin of existence, remain ineffectively engaged in agriculture; there are relatively few resourceful entrepreneurs and the apparatus of state remains primitive; and there is little saving and investment, the favored few squandering most of the foreign exchange that the export of raw materials and other products brings in. In consequence, while investment (about $2,500) and output per worker are appreciably below the American level, per capita income is 3–10 times as high in Israel as elsewhere in the Middle East, and it is rising.

(5) *Brazil.*[57] The industrialization of Brazil represents that of a country with a comparatively sparse though growing population, a West-European culture, limited resources other than land, a predominantly agricultural (i.e., 68 per cent) labor force, and a very low though apparently growing per capita income ($57 in 1944) and output per man-hour (7 and 11 cents, respectively, in 1940 and 1946). Capital formation is progressing at a very rapid rate if estimates are to be accepted as valid, investment forming 24–29 per cent of income payments to individuals in 1944, and a somewhat smaller fraction of the national income. Even so, capital per industrial worker is low, averaging around $500 in São Paulo. These investment estimates appear to be much too high. Moreover, should they approximate reality, it

56. On Israel see *Investing in Israel* (cited in note 38 above) and *Economic Horizons,* monthly publication of the Jewish Agency for Palestine. On Israel and the Middle East see United Nations, *Final report of the United Nations Mission for the Middle East,* Part I, 34–41, Lake Success, United Nations, 1949.

57. On Brazil see Spiegel, *op. cit.,* chaps. 2, 5, 14. On the standing of Brazil relative to that of other Latin American countries see United Nations, *Economic survey of Latin America, 1948.*

is not likely that Brazilian workers will long tolerate a situation permitting so high a rate of capital formation, howsoever salutary are its longer run effects.

(ii) Modern plans for industrialization almost invariably assign a large role to the state. In fact, contemporary emphasis upon "national planning" is in considerable measure an outcome of the failure of nations, given essentially *laissez faire* conditions, to form capital rapidly enough and do the other things that comparatively speedy industrialization requires. Needless to say, of course, the apparatus of state often has served to check industrialization, usually by perpetuating anti-industrial minorities in power and diverting potential savings from capital formation.

Under-developed and non-industrialized countries today encounter a hazard that was not so conspicuous prior to World War I, a hazard consequent upon the increase in the political power of the common man. The working populations of under-developed countries, having before them inklings of the high material standards and the degree of power attained by workers in industrialized Western countries, today are demanding a larger share of after-tax national income than was commanded by their nineteenth-century prototypes, and they are insisting upon spending most of this relatively heightened income for consumer goods and services. In consequence, saving and capital formation have been affected adversely.

The rise of this hazard, therefore, is imposing a new duty upon the state, that of compelling the population to form adequate amounts of capital. It has become evident that, so long as the masses enjoy both consumer sovereignty and consumer freedom of choice, under-developed countries undergoing industrialization probably will not be able to find at home enough capital to complete the process. It follows, that, so long as individuals refuse to supply enough capital, consumer sovereignty must be curbed. The state must appropriate a considerable proportion of the national income (say one-fifth) and divert it into capital-forming activities, allowing the consumers freedom of choice only in respect of how they spend their after-tax income. The state can accomplish this objective through an appropriate combination of measures, ranging from taxation and exchange-control to differential pricing and the imposition of obligations to contribute in kind to the formation of collective forms of capital (e.g., highways).

Given that the government is strong enough and the apparatus of state is sufficiently developed to facilitate capital formation, an under-developed state still must make important choices. (*a*) It must not attempt to force the relative rate of capital formation so high that the aggregate supply of effort is diminished, for the diminution of this aggregate consequent upon attempts to elevate unduly the percentage of the aggregate diverted to capital formation may bring about a reduction in the absolute amount of capital formed per year. (*b*) Since capital formation entails the substitution of future want-satisfaction for present want-satisfaction, care must be taken lest social and economic welfare are significantly reduced through the adoption of oppressive policies that are intended to accelerate industrialization and capital formation. The methods employed by Soviet Russia in this respect, together with the experiences of the Russian people, highlight the issue here under consideration. While modern welfare economics cannot supply precise answers to the questions involved, it can indicate the kinds of arbitrary standards that must be employed if a workable balance between current and future requirements is to be maintained.[58] (c) State-dominated approaches to capital formation must not become so rigid that they operate to decelerate the dynamic forces which, together with capital formation, make for industrial progress in the long run.

The various plans that have been proposed and/or introduced in nations intent upon accelerating their industrialization almost invariably call for higher rates of investment than voluntary savings are likely to permit. The under-developed countries, in which live about four-fifths of the world's population, have estimated their annual investment needs, over a four year period, at $17 billion, of which about one-fourth is expected from foreign sources. This figure approximates 11 per cent of aggregate income of the under-developed countries, estimated at about $150 billion. Of the $17 billion, only about 7, of which 3 are expected from foreign sources, are reported for Africa, Asia, and Latin America. By contrast, the annual investment needs of the developed regions outside of North America have been estimated at $27 billion, or 18 per cent of an estimated income of $150 billion, with about $6 billion to be supplied by foreign sources. The United States and Canada, with an annual income of some $240 billion, are destined to supply the $9 billion required by but not obtainable in the remainder of the world.[59]

Inasmuch as these capital requirements, though less than the industrialization of the under-developed countries entails, are in excess of voluntary domestic savings, state action designed to increase savings will prove necessary. That such action will prove necessary is suggested also by the fact that the world, including North America, is not likely to supply the $8-9 billion required from foreign sources. Prior to World War II the amount of foreign investment supplied by *all* investing countries never exceeded $2 billion per year. Outstanding foreign investment approximated only $53 billion in 1938, or about $25 per capita, and only $9 billions more

---

58. On welfare economics and its degree of relevance to decisions concerning what is the most appropriate rate of industrialization for a country see the works of Bergson and Arrow, cited in note 5 above. In Russia in the late 1920's opinion differed greatly respecting how fast and in what manner Russia should industrialize. See Erlich, A., Probrazhenski and the economics of Soviet industrialization, *Quart. Jour. Econ.* 64: 57–88, 1950.

59. The figures given in this paragraph are based upon United Nations, *Methods of financing economic development in underdeveloped countries*, 44–45, 52–56, 64, 73–77, 84–85, Lake Success, United Nations, 1949.

than in 1913–1914. In 1938 as in 1913 about 56 per cent of all foreign investment was situated in Europe, Oceania, Canada, Soviet Russia, and the United States, the per capita figure approximating $42 in 1938. American gross investment abroad totaled only $11.5 billion in 1938.[60] During and after World War II, however, American foreign "investment" increased greatly, averaging about $7.5 billion per year in 1946–1949, of which the United States government furnished (in the form of grants, credits, and capital equipment) about $6.7 and private investors about $0.8 billion.[61] It is questionable whether, even in the not too likely event that political stability and creditor security are assured, so high a rate of American investment can be maintained and, assuming repayment of most investment made after 1952, serviced. For the dollar requirements of industrializing under-developed countries will be intensified by their high internal rates of investment; and their ability to obtain dollars will be made difficult by the fact that the demand of non-industrial countries for the products of industrial countries will tend to grow much more rapidly than will the supply of foreign exchange wherewith to purchase these products.

Data relating to foreign investment in Asia, Africa, and Latin America indicate that these regions are not likely to receive significantly large amounts of investment from investing countries in general or from America in particular. In 1938 outstanding foreign investment approximated $9 billion, or $72 per capita in Latin America; $4 billion, or $24 per capita, in Africa; and $10 billion, or $9 per capita, in Asia. In 1913–1914 roughly comparable figures were, in billions: Latin America, 8.5; Africa, 4.7; and Asia, 6. Of the $11,491 million of American foreign investments outstanding in 1938, $4,154 million were in Latin America and $1,155 million in Asia and Africa.[62] Since 1945 only a negligible amount of American government credits have been extended to these areas; and, while appreciable private investment has flowed into Latin America, not much has gone into Asia and Africa.[63] Of the estimated aggregate investment needs indicated by various plans, etc., only about one-sixth was destined for Asia, Africa, and Latin America.[64]

60. Staley, *op. cit.*, 80; Lewis, *op. cit.*, 49–50, 296, 334, 338; United Nations, *International capital movements during the inter-war period*, 2, Lake Success, United Nations, 1949.
61. Kerber, E. S., Foreign transactions of the U.S. Government in fiscal 1949, *Survey of Current Business* 29: 9, 1949, and Abelson, M., Private United States direct investments abroad, *ibid.*, 20. In 1941–47 the United States furnished loans, grants, etc. in excess of repayments to the extent of $63.3 billion, at an average annual rate of $9 billion. The Marshall Plan will have raised this figure above $70 billion by 1952, a figure in excess of the $53 billion of world foreign investment outstanding in 1938. On the factors competing for American savings see my Prospective population and income growth and fiscal policy, *Natl. Tax Jour.* 3: 36–63, 1950.
62. Lewis, *op. cit.*, 49–50, 296, 322–323; United Nations, *International capital movements*, 2.
63. See references cited in note 61 above.
64. See p. 52 of reference cited in note 59 above.

It is evident, in view of what has been said, that neither prospective foreign investment, nor, given great consumer sovereignty, domestic savings will be of the magnitude required if industrialization is to progress in under-developed countries at a rate allowing per capita income to advance in the neighborhood of 3 per cent per year. This objective can be realized pre-sumably only if state action is employed to step up the rate of saving and insure that savings and foreign exchange are utilized in a manner suited, given their volume, to maximize the rate at which needed capital is formed.

Conclusion

The contents of this paper are not easily summarized. They suggest cer-tain conclusions, however, both for nations undergoing industrialization and for countries — particularly the United States — whence much of the re-quired foreign capital, equipment, personnel, and know-how must be drawn. From the standpoint of the countries undergoing industrialization the following conclusions are indicated. Because of the many difficulties attendant upon industrialization and because of the limitedness of the re-sources available for this purpose, it is essential that an industrializing country pursue only those courses of action which are of strategic impor-tance, given that country's stage of development, resource-equipment, and other relevant conditions. Because a country's industrial development of necessity depends largely upon its internal resources, industrializing countries must do everything possible to render their internal conditions favorable to industrialization. Because capital and know-how are in such short supply, each must at all times be used with economy, and every effort must be made to augment the supply of both. Initially great improvements must be made in conditions relating to health and motivation, and popula-tion growth must be brought under control.

For various reasons already discussed the state will have to assume a far greater role than it filled in respect of the industrialization of the Western world.[65] In addition, the state must provide a favorable environment for industrialization, insure continuity of the industrialization program, provide diverse forms of leadership, and, through cooperation with other govern-ments and with the various international bodies such as the United Nations, bring to its people the benefit of foreign planning, guidance, and assistance.[66]

65. On nineteenth-century instances of deliberate industrialization see Aubrey, H. G., Delib-erate Industrialization. *Social Research* 16: 158–182, 1949; also Hirschman, *op. cit.*

66. Concerning what may be done see United Nations, *Technical assistance for economic development*, Lake Success, United Nations, 1949; also the work cited in note 59; also the reports of the International Bank for Reconstruction and Development. Illustrative of the kinds of change industrial development calls for are those indicated for the states characteristic of the Middle East and Islamic society. On this question and on the broader sociological implica-tions of industrialization for the Middle East see Bonné, *op. cit.*

All this means that the apparatus of state of most of the under-developed countries will have to be greatly improved and adapted to the performance of new functions. And even then, the best that can be hoped for, supposing that the world remains at peace, is a significant reduction in international economic disparity.[67]

From the standpoint of the United States and the Western world in general, the most important conclusion is the following. We live in a world extremely short of resources, capital, and know-how. The amount of capital that the United States and other Western investing countries can supply, given present and prospective defense needs and rising social security requirements, is very limited, both absolutely and in relation to the real needs of the under-developed countries. The Western world is engaged in what promises to be for many years an intense and unremitting struggle with anti-Western forms of totalitarianism. It follows that the Western world, and the United States in particular, should invest its quite limited resources predominantly in regions which, because of their friendliness to Western values, their geographical situation, and other relevant strategic considerations, represent good investment risks. The Western world cannot afford to squander its limited resources either on its actual and/or potential enemies, or upon countries which, though essentially friendly, fail to make good use of these resources.

Tabular Appendix

Tables I–IV summarize the main reported and measurable economic and cultural differences between the relatively industrialized and the non-industrialized countries. In Table I information is given for three categories of countries, classified on the basis of per capita income in 1939: (a) Upper, over $200; (b) Middle, $101–200; (c) Lower, $100 and below. Data are given for only 1,836 of the world's 2,170 millions of population as of 1939. Presumably, however, nearly all of the 336 millions for whom data were lacking in 1939 fell in category (c). On the assumption that this was the case, the world's population was distributed as follows in 1939: (a) 361 millions; (b) 304 millions; and (c) 1,505 millions.

In Tables II and III information is reported by country, and particularly for class (c) countries for which data are available. The United States

67. It is of interest, in the light of current discussion of the Point Four program, that the need for a somewhat similar program was suggested by Col. E. M. House in a letter (June 26, 1914) to President Wilson. (My colleague, Professor E. M. Carroll, called this to my attention.) See Seymour, C., *Intimate papers of Colonel House* 1:264–269, Boston, Houghton Mifflin, 1926. In essence House proposed that the capital-exporting nations agree on a plan to develop the undeveloped parts of the world, supply needed capital at "reasonable rates," and establish conditions making such loans "reasonably safe." Implementation was prevented by the Sarajevo assassination and its aftermath.

Table I. Economic and Social Indicators, by Countries Grouped According to Industrialization.*

Item	Country group		
	Upper	Middle	Lower
1. Per cent of world's population in 1939	17	14	69
2. Population per sq. km. in 1947 (range)	1–285	7–151	2–204
3. Per cent of population aged 15–59 years	[62–64]	[59]	[54–55]
4. Income per capita in 1939 (dollars)	461	154	41
5. Income per capita in 1939 (range in dollars)	201–554	101–200	22–100
6. Index of per worker income in 1925–34	[100]	[34]	[13]
7. Index of per capita income of farm population	100	39	8
8. Per cent of occupied populations in agriculture	[22]	[57]	[75]
9. Index of industrial equipment per worker	[100]	[39]	[11]
10. Energy consumed per capita per day (H.P.H.)	26.6	6.4	1.2
11. Miles of railroad per 1,000 sq. mi. of area	40	29	13
12. Annual freight carried per capita (ton miles)	1517	927	58
13. Line 12 ÷ line 11	37.9	32	4.5
14. Motor vehicles per 1,000 population	111	7	1
15. Telephones per 1,000 population	90	7	2
16. Per cent illiterate (population age 10 and over)	Below 5	20	78
17. Elementary school teachers per 1,000 population	3.98	3.42	1.76
18. State of population growth	Controlled	Controlled or transitional	Uncontrolled
19. Physicians per 1,000 population	1.06	0.78	0.17
20. Expectation of life at birth (years)	63	52	30–40
21. T. B. death rate per 100,000 population	64	143	333
22. Net annual textile consumption per capita (lbs.)	18.63	7.52	4.8
23. All foods: calories per capita per day	3040	2760	2150
24. Animal proteins, oz. per capita per day	1.6	0.9	0.3
25. Fats, oz. per capita per day	4.0	2.3	1.3
26. Typical per cent of calories of animal origin	[20–40]	[10–15]	[under 10]
27. Steel consumption per capita (kilos)	[100–500]	[25–80]	[10–20]

* Figures in brackets are for roughly comparable group of countries, or are estimates.

Sources: Lines 4–5, 7, 10–12, and 14–25 are from U.S. Department of State Publication 3719, *Point Four*, 103–113 (mean values), Washington, 1950. Lines 1–3 are based upon United Nations publications. Lines 6, 8, 9, and 26 are from my Some Aspects. *loc. cit.*, 261–265. Line 27 is roughly estimated from United Nations, *European Steel Trends*, 120–123, 132–136.

Table II. Economic Indicators, by Country.

| (1) Country | Population (1947) | | Income | | | (7) Miles railroad (per sq. mi. of area) | (8) Energy consumed per day (H.P. hrs. per capita) | (9) Energy reserves in tons of bit. coal per sq. km. | (10) Arable land per capita (hectares) | (11) Per cent of labor force in agriculture[e] |
	(2) Total (millions)	(3) Density per sq. km.	(4) Per worker 1925-34	(5) Per capita 1939[d]	(6) Product per man-hour (highest yr.)					
United States	144.0	18	$1,381	$554	$1.19	80	37.6	320.665	1.55	22
United Kingdom	49.5	203	1,069	468	.62	222	27.1	565.647	.11	7
Argentina	16.1	6	1,000	218	.44	23	5.0	5,750	1.68	(36)
Union of So. Africa	11.6	10	276	188	.15	30	10.1	172.152	[.46]	26 [75][f]
Chile	5.5	7	550	174	—	20	10.7	12.724	.26	(36)
U.S.S.R.	200.0	9	320	158	.18	14	6.8	62.034	—	67
Cuba	5.1	44	—	98	.20	70	2.6	—	0.39	(41)
Yugoslavia	14.8	58	330	96	.14	72	2.1	45.802	—	79
Poland	23.8	76	352	95	.19	89	5.6	250.981	.54	65
Japan	78.0	204	353	93	.20	102	6.6	109.052	0.07	52
Venezuela	4.4	5	—	92	.21	2	5.1	14.375	—	(51)
Egypt	19.2	20	325	85	—	9	1.7	1.881	0.31-	67
Palestine	1.9	72	360	81	.19	30	1.0	—	—	31
Algiers	8.5	4	300	—	—	—	2.2	267	—	—
Turkey[a]	24.1	25	200+	(100-125)	.11	—	1.1	[3,720]	.51	82
Morocco[b]	11.5	20	200+	—	—	—	0.8	1.700	—	—
Costa Rica	0.8	15	—	76	—	22	1.4	—	—	—
Colombia	10.5	9	—	76	.08	5	1.5	10.521	0.26	(74)

Peru	7.9	6	—	72	—	4	1.1	11,569	0.25	(62)
Panama	0.7	10	—	71	—	17	12.3	—	—	(52)
Ceylon	6.9	104	—	63 (91)	—	38	1.4	Negligible	0.20	(62)
Mexico	23.4	12	360	61	—	19	2.2	9,221	0.28	(65)
Uruguay	2.3	12	650	56	—	26	3.2	4,701	0.43	—
Iran	17.0	10	—	(85)	—	—	0.8	5,929	—	76
Dom. Republic	2.2	43	—	51	—	8	0.5	—	—	High
Haiti	3.6	127	—	50 (36)	—	14	0.4	—	—	High
Nicaragua	1.1	8	—	50	—	4	0.7 ⎫	} 26,259	—	—
Guatemala	3.6	33	—	48	—	17	0.6 ⎬		—	(73)
Bolivia	3.9	4	—	47	—	5	0.3	—	—	—
Honduras	1.2	8	—	45	—	17	1.4	—	—	—
El Salvador	2.0	60	—	45	—	30	0.6	8,607	0.33	(67)
Brazil	47.6	6	435	46	.11	6	1.9	9,694	—	—
Ecuador	3.4	12	—	44	.11	7	1.0	12,795	—	—
Paraguay	1.2	3	—	39	—	4	0.6	2,254	—	—
Afghanistan	12.0	18	—	(50)	—	—	0.2	13,022	—	—
Ethiopia	15.0	17	—	(40)	—	—	0.2	—	—	—
Saudi Arabia	6.0	2	—	(40)	—	—	0.1—	365	—	—
India	411.0	101	200	34 (43)	.09	26	0.5	21,297	0.31	(67)
Philippines	19.5	66	375	32 (88)	—	8	0.6	14,848	0.20	(69)
China	463.0	48	110ᶜ	29 (23)	.03	3	0.5	246,584	0.24	70–75
Indonesia	76.4	40	200—	22 (35)	—	21	0.4	16,231	0.18	(69)
Rest of Asia	—	—	200—	—	—	—	[1.0]	—	—	—
Rest of Africa	—	—	200—	—	—	—	—	—	—	—
Rest of America	—	—	350	—	—	—	—	—	—	—

ᵃIncludes Syria and Lebanon. ᵇIncludes Tunisia. ᶜIncludes Korea. ᵈFigures in parentheses are United Nations estimates for 1946 or 1948. ᵉFigures in parentheses are for agriculture only. ᶠFigure in brackets for colored population.

Sources: See under table I for sources of cols. 2–5 and 7–8. Col. 6 is from Clark, *Review of Economic Progress*, I, No. 4. 2. 1949. Col. 8 is taken in part from Guyol, *op. cit.* Col. 9 is from Usher, *op. cit.*, 40–43; it represents major energy reserves converted into terms of tons of bituminous coal. Col. 10 is from FAO, *State of Food and Agriculture*, 1948, 51, 72, and *Mission For Greece*, 155. Col. 11 is from United Nations, *Economic Survey of Asia and the Far East*, 1948, 110, and *Economic Survey of Latin America*, 1948, 87, and Hilgerdt, *op. cit.*, 26–27.

Table III. Cultural and Developmental Indicators, by Country.

Country	Annual freight carried in ton miles		Motors vehicles (per 1,000 population)	Telephones (per 1,000 population)	Newsprint consumed per capita (kgs.)	Per cent of population age 10 and over illiterate	Daily per capita food supply			Physicians per 1,000 population	T.B. death rates per 100,000 population
	Per capita	Per capita per 1,000 sq. miles					All foods (calories)	Animal proteins (ounces)	Fats (ounces)		
(1)	(2a)	(2b)	(3)	(4)	(5)	(6)	(7)	(8)	(9)	(10)	(11)
United States	2,977	37.2	250	148	31.8	Below 5	3,098	1.8	4.3	1.37	47
United Kingdom	424	19.1	53	59	26.1	Below 5	3,095	1.6	4.3	1.13	62
Argentina	671	29.2	21	27	7.9	17	2,777	2.2	3.3	1.05	103
Union of So. Africa	777	25.9	30	15	3.7	60	2,354	1.2	1.8	.41	Low
Chile	324	16.2	20	13	3.7	24	2,322	0.8	1.5	.63	264
U.S.S.R.	1,134	9.6	5	3	—	19	2,827	—	—	.76	160
Cuba	119	1.7	11	11	4.8	35	2,626	0.8	1.7	.63	76
Yugoslavia	43	0.6	1	3	0.8	45	3,013	0.7	2.1	.31	234
Poland	432	4.8	1	8	1.5	27	2,710	0.8	2.2	.32	195
Japan	138	1.3	3	16	5.5	Below 10	2,230	0.4	0.9	.87	207
Venezuela	—	—	10	5	2.0	63	—	—	—	.41	233
Egypt	69	7.7	2	3	0.8	86	2,469	0.4	1.5	.21	52
Palestine	77	2.6	10	12	—	69	—	—	—	1.38	56
Costa Rica	43	2.0	6	5	—	35	2,014	—	—	.25	172
Colombia	12	2.4	4	4	—	44	2,004	0.7	1.5	.29	Low
Peru	45	11.3	3	3	1.1	90	1,835	0.5	1.4	.19	High
Panama	26	1.5	23	11	—	47	—	—	—	.21	119

Ceylon	—	—	5	0.3	—	60	2,059	0.3	1.6	.15	62
Mexico	182	9.6	5	7	2.4	62	1,855	0.7	1.5	.51	56
Uruguay	514	19.8	31	16	7.6	30	2,426	1.0	3.3	.71	101
Dom. Republic	1	0.1	2	2	0.3	71	2,130	—	—	.20	Medium
Haiti	—	—	0.8	0.8	0.1	90	—	—	—	.09	High
Nicaragua	10	2.5	0.7	1.5	—	57	—	—	—	.28	Medium
Guatemala	13	0.8	1	0.7	—	72	—	—	—	.11	Medium
Bolivia	—	—	0.6	0.9	0.4	92	—	—	—	.15	Medium
Honduras	19	1.1	1	3	0.3	68	2,079	—	—	.11	Low
El Salvador	9	0.3	2	2	—	73	1,944	1.1	—	.16	High
Brazil	94	15.7	4	5	1.3	62	2,173	—	1.8	.31	250
Ecuador	18	2.6	1	3	1.1	80	—	—	—	.24	High
Paraguay	23	5.8	2	3	0.4	65	2,813	—	—	.28	102
India	60	2.3	0.3	0.2	0.1	91	1,976	0.3	1.0	.12	283
Philippines	—	—	3	1.9	0.9	51	1,855	0.7	1.2	.26	298
China	17	5.7	0.2	0.5	0.2	85	2,234	0.2	1.4	.04	400–500
Indonesia	9	0.4	1	0.6	—	92	—	—	—	.02	High

Source: See under table I for sources of col. 2a, 3–4, and 6–11. Col. 5 is from the United Nations. *Statistical Yearbook*, 1948 (the figures are the higher of the 1935–39 and 1948 averages). Col. 2b is obtained by dividing col. 2a by col. 7 from table II.

Table IV. Economic and Cultural Indicators, by Region.

Item	Region North America	Oceania	Europe excl. U.S.S.R.	U.S.S.R.	Latin America	Africa	Eastern Asia	South Central Asia	Near East	World
1. Population growth, 1920–1947 (per cent)	36.5	33.3	17.7[a]	23.3[b]	62.8	41.5	24.8	37.0	29.8	31.1
2. Population in millions	157	12	384	195	153	191	738	426	74	2.330
3. Population per square km.	8.0	1.4	71.2	9.2	7.4	6.3	45.0	98.0	17	7.6
4. Acres crop land per capita	3.95	4.03	0.88	[2.00]	1.48	–	0.52	0.84	1.01	1.04
5. Acres crop land per head farm population	17.10	11.27	2.64	–	3.95	–	0.74	1.16	1.31	1.90
6. Productive forested area per capita (hectares)	3.0	4.2	0.3	3.2	4.7	2.0	0.3	–	0.2	1.1
7. Accessible productive forested area per capita (hectares)	1.96	2.2	0.3	1.6	2.2	0.95	0.15	–	0.07	0.6
8. % of world tractors ÷ % of world crop land	3.568	1.188	1.261	0.05	0.206	0.056	0.009	–	0.036	1.0
9. Steel consumption per capita (kilos)	371[c]	–	139	110	20	11	12	–	10	63
10. Energy consumed per capita (K.W. hrs.)	10.074	3.543	3.117	1.873	741	686		286		1.676
11. Energy resources (in tons of bituminous coal per sq. km.)	155.503	17.783	147.382	62.034	9.592	25.560	142.562	21.001	2.721	65.503
12. Known and probable iron ore reserves (million tons)[a]	58.000	600	8.000	100.000	12.500	1.400		12.000		192.500
13. Textile consumption per capita (kgs.)	18.3	7.7	6.3	3.7	3.7	1.5		2.3		3.9

[a] Non-eastern Europe only.

[b] Eastern Europe and Asiatic U.S.S.R.

[c] United States only.

[d] Central America and Mexico are included with North America; Latin America includes only South America; Oceania includes only Australia. World *known* reserves total 24,050 million tons.

Sources: Lines 1–3 are based on United Nations publications. Lines 4 and 5 are from United Nations, *Mission for Greece*, 155 (orchards and vineyards excluded). Lines 6–7 are from FAO, *State of Food and Agriculture, 1948*, 28. Lines 8 and 13 are taken or computed from FAO, *State of Food and Agriculture, 1949*, 134, 140. Lines 9 and 12 from United Nations, *European Steel Trends*, 132–136 (data for 1937 and 1939, whichever is higher) and 41. Line 10 from Guyol, *op. cit.*, 90ff. Line 11 from Usher, *op. cit.*, 40–43.

stands at the top of class (*a*) and Argentina at the bottom. The Union of South Africa, Chile, and the USSR represent class (*b*). The remaining countries, beginning with Cuba, are in class (*c*). It should be noted that population growth is essentially uncontrolled in class (*c*) countries, whose potential rate of growth is high. It is controlled in class (*a*) countries, whose potential rate of growth is very low. It is either controlled or rapidly passing under control in class (*b*) countries.

In Table IV information is given by continent and subcontinent. While no per capita income data are reported by continent, fairly good measures of relative standing in respect of income are provided in lines 9, 10, and 13.

The Population Obstacle to Economic Betterment

*"The sire of gods and men, with hard decrees,
Forbids our plenty to be bought with ease . . ."* — *Virgil,* Georgics I

*"When goods increase, they are increased that
eat them; . . ."* — *Ecclesiastes,* 5:11

The population factor is only one of the many by which the course of human betterment is affected; but it is one of the most important. Of this we have evidence in man's frequent manifestation of concern lest population grow too much or too little to maximize some variable in which he is interested.

If we would discuss economic betterment meaningfully, we must choose an index suitable to reflect its course. Of the indices available, the most satisfactory appears to be net output per capita per time period, for this index is both a summary measure of many elements after which man aspires and an end result of that process of technological and industrial change which has transformed the economies of at least a quarter of the world's population and raised its levels of living far above the Oriental plane found almost everywhere two centuries ago. We shall make use of this index, therefore, though without implying that it is, of necessity, highly correlated with that inner state known as physiopsychic well-being.

This paper consist of four parts. The first treats of the determinants of economic betterment; the second, of prevailing population trends; and the third, of the nature of the improvement-retarding effects of population growth. In the fourth part, a quantitative estimate of some of these effects is attempted.

I

The determinants of economic betterment, as represented by the movement of per capita real income, may be variously classified. For the purposes of this paper they are categorized on the basis of their sensitivity to changes in the population factor (i.e., to changes in population density, composition, or total), most sensitive being those included under A and least sensitive those listed under C:

$A.1$ Ratio of a nation's labor force to its population.

$A.2$ Productive assets *in use* per employed worker.

$A.3$ The effectiveness with which economic activities are organized.

$A.4$ Genetic composition of the population.

$B.1$ International exchange relations.

$B.2$ Ratio of the employed portion of the labor force to the total labor force.

B.3 Extent to which occupational and spatial distribution of employed human and nonhuman agents of production is optimal in character.

B.4 Skill and efficiency of labor force, properties which reflect (i) the state of the industrial arts and (ii) the educational, scientific, and cultural attainments of a population.

C.1 Social structure.

C.2 Culture.

D.1 Residual determinant.

Since the information available does not permit us to show with precision how per capita real income responds to changes in each of these determinants and how they in turn respond to changes in population, we shall merely indicate how population change affects per capita income through the medium of some of the more sensitive of these determinants. We shall ignore *A*.4 and determinants listed under *C* and *D* and treat only incidentally some listed under *B*.

A.1 – the ratio of a nation's labor force to its population – tends to be most favorable when this population has become stationary under Western mortality conditions. For this ratio is conditioned by (*a*) the age composition of the population and (*b*) its state of health. This ratio is most unfavorable to per capita output, therefore, in the underdeveloped countries where the age composition may be something like one-sixth less favorable than in the United States, and where, largely because of poverty due in considerable part to population pressure, the incidence of illness and disease is much higher than in advanced countries. If conditions "*a*" and "*b*" were westernized, per capita income in underdeveloped countries might rise 20 to 30 or more per cent above current levels, other circumstances remaining unchanged.

Determinants *A*.2 and *A*.3, while of significance for all countries whose population has passed the income optimum (in which category fall most countries),[1] are of greatest importance for countries which are both overpopulated and characterized by a high population growth potential. Respecting *A*.2 and *A*.3 this may be said. (1) Output per worker is highly correlated with the amount of productive assets in use per worker. (2) For this reason, and because the consumption of raw materials is highly correlated with national income, population growth eventually tends to make necessary

[1]. See my "Measures of Population Maladjustment," *Proceedings* of the Fourteenth International Sociological Conference, Rome, 1950–51. As is shown in this paper, the population optimum tends to be confused with the spatial optimum. There is no evidence to suggest that the population optimum has increased in recent decades; but there is, as the analyses of A. Toynbee and others suggest, evidence to indicate that the magnitude of what constitutes a viable politico-economic system has been increasing for some decades. If this inference be valid, consolidation of the many nonviable small systems into a small number of large viable systems would be accompanied by some alleviation of both consciousness of population pressure and concern lest numbers be growing too slowly. Presumably, as A. Sauvy suggests (in *Population et Richesse*, Paris, 1949, pp. 34–35), consolidation of smaller units tends to alter their individual optima.

recourse to natural resources which, because they are inferior or less accessible, cost more to exploit. (3) Population growth is accompanied, within limits, by economies of organization which operate to increase output per worker. (4) An increase in numbers makes for an increase in output per capita so long as (*ceteris paribus*) the increment in output per capita due to the increase in economies of organization consequent upon an increment in population more than offsets the associated decrement (if any) in output per capita due to cost-increases in the extractive industries. (5) The population of a country may be said to be of optimum size when, given the cost of supporting the economically unproductive part of the population,[2] the aggregate population is of the minimum size required to maximize per capita income in a manner compatible with the relevant rate of interest and the assumption that other conditions remain constant.[3]

2. By unproductive population is meant that part of a population which, though it produces no income, must be or is supported by the productive population at some aggregate, variable cost C. The best example of an unproductive population is that sequesterable part of a population which is continually required to provide a nation's military forces and which, therefore, includes women, children, and both retired and active military personnel. Since the determinants of the magnitude of this "unproductive" population are not describable with precision in a few words, we shall represent it by p' and the cost of supporting it by $C = f(p')$. Then the total population P may be defined as made up of p' and p, with p representing the "productive" population. Let Y represent the national income which, by definition, is produced by p; y, the per capita income retained by p, which equals Y/P when p' and C have zero values and $(Y - C)/p$ when p' and C have positive values; and y', per capita production of income at the margin; namely $\Delta Y/\Delta p$. If p' and C have zero values and therefore p is identical with P, the population of optimum size is the smallest population associated with the condition of that $y = y'$. (The stipulation that the optimum be the smallest population compatible with this condition must be made if the maximization of income through time is the desideratum since, other conditions being given, the smaller the optimum population, the smaller the drain on nonrenewable resources.) If, however, p' and C assume positive values, the income retained per capita by p will no longer by Y/p but $(Y - C)/p$ which is less than Y/p. It will therefore be to the advantage of the productive population p to increase its magnitude; for, although in the original position y and y' were equal, in the new position y', whose value as yet remains at the original level, exceeds y whose value has been reduced from Y/p to $(Y - C)/p$. The optimum size for p is attained when y' and $(Y - C)/p$ again become equal. Whence, given the magnitude of p', the optimum size for P may be defined as p' *plus* the optimum size for p given by the fact that p is required to support p' to the extent of outlay C. Of course, it being given that p' may feasibly be reduced to zero, the preferred optimum is $p(= P)$, with $y = y'$. If, however, for reasons of security or otherwise, p' cannot be reduced to zero, it is to the advantage of p that its size be increased so long as such increase augments p's retained income y. While this note has been suggested by A. Sauvy's analysis (see *op. cit.*, p. 27), the concept of the cost of supporting the economically unproductive population component, if any, has been substituted for his concept of "general expenses."

3. That the optimum is affected by the relevant rate of interest i may be illustrated as follows, it being assumed that C and p' as defined in the preceding note have zero values. Let W represent productive assets in use; Y, national income; P, population; and y, per capita income Y/P. Now suppose an increase ΔP in population requiring an increase ΔW in W such that the assets/population ratio is unchanged from its initial W/P value. Suppose further that increment ΔP in population is accompanied by Δy_0, an increment in y due to increased economy of organization and Δy_r, a decrement in y due to increased costs in the extraction of raw materials. So long as W and i may be ignored, whether increment ΔP is economically advantageous turns on whether Δy_0 is greater or less than Δy_r. But W and i may not be ignored. The increment $P\Delta y$ in the income of the initial population P, which accompanies the increment ΔP in population, entails an increment ΔW in the nation's stock of capital for the equipping of the increment ΔP

It follows that the attainment by a country's population of a magnitude in excess of the optimum is an important deterrent to that population's economic betterment. This conclusion is reinforced by the fact that nations whose populations have passed the optimum seldom are again presented with an opportunity to halt their population growth when their numbers have moved into the neighborhood of the optimum. For it is difficult to reduce an actual population in magnitude until it has attained optimum size; and it is rare that circumstances so change as to increase the magnitude of the optimum beyond that already attained by the actual population. The task confronting overpopulated nations, therefore, is not that of striving after an unattainable optimum but that of doing whatever is necessary to increase their per capita income levels even though their numbers are too great. This task includes the prevention of further population growth, however, for reasons to be indicated and because such stimulus as population growth sometimes gives to invention, innovation, and progress, is at a minimum in countries where density of numbers and lowness of per capita income occur jointly.

Let us turn now to determinants $B.2$–$B.4$. While one may, under given circumstances, accept the thesis of the stagnationists, it is nonetheless apparent that only under certain institutional conditions does a low or a negative population growth rate make for unemployment. Presumably, an analogous argument may be made in respect of countries where great population density, together with continuing population growth, appears to be producing unemployment. Regional and occupational differences in the rate of natural increase may operate to prevent a country's employed population from becoming optimally distributed in space and among occupations when these differences are not offset by social arrangements designed to secure an optimal distribution. Underutilization of labor of demographic origin appears to be most pronounced in underdeveloped countries where there is considerable agricultural overpopulation. Of importance also is the absorption of capital by population growth. For, as will be shown, such absorption reduces the rate at which the labor force can improve its health, skill, efficiency, and material equipment.

II

It is growth rather than nongrowth of population that is a major obstacle to man's economic betterment in all but a few countries. The stagnationist's

---

in population. This increment ΔW entails an annual interest cost $i\Delta W$. Accordingly, the initial population P will find advantage in the increment Δy in its per capita income (an increment supposedly associated with increment ΔP in population) only if $(P\Delta y/\Delta W) > i$. Of course, if the initial population P derives from ΔP some noneconomic advantage such as a feeling of greater security, it will deem ΔP advantageous even though $(P\Delta y/\Delta W) < i$. Should p' and C have positive values (see note 2) these may be taken into account.

explanation of unemployment, insofar as it can be formulated in valid terms, is relevant at present only to about a fifth of the world's population; and this fifth has attained a relatively high income level and is capable of making effective unemployment-preventing adjustments to the nongrowth of its numbers. Most of the remainder of the world's inhabitants are found in countries where population growth is already retarding the improvement of man's living standards. It is of these countries, therefore, that the rest of my paper treats.

That population pressure is a major obstacle to economic betterment in most of the world is readily suggested, though not always demonstrable with precision. Data indicate that per capita income tends to be low where crude population density is relatively great and to be high where it is relatively low. This relationship would be even more marked were the influence of differences in transfer and trading relations taken into account, since these are relatively favorable in most if not all of the densely populated countries where per capita income is relatively high.

That population growth will continue to be a major obstacle to the betterment of man's material lot is apparent. Only about one-fifth of the world's population appears to be approaching a stationary state, and this fifth is composed principally of peoples already enjoying relatively high per capita incomes. Something like another fifth, though describable as proto-stationary, may experience an increase of 50 or more per cent in a half-century. Yet, many of the peoples composing this fifth already have difficulty extracting more than mediocre incomes from their limited equipment of land and resources. The balance of the world's population, close to 60 per cent, is expanding, even though most of its members already receive very low incomes and are badly equipped with land and resources essential to the comfortable support of expanding numbers.[4] Evidently, a major fraction of the population growth in prospect will take place among peoples not well equipped to supply even their present wants.

How much population growth will take place in high-growth-potential countries is not empirically determinable with certainty at present. However, judging by past experience and abstracting from the possibility that a cheap contraceptive could be widely and rapidly diffused, the 1.5 billions concerned and living in Asia,[5] Africa, and Latin America may, in the ab-

---

4. For supporting data see my "Aspects of the Economics of Population Growth," *Southern Economic Journal*, 1948, and my "Economic Factors in the Development of Densely Populated Areas," *Proceedings* of the American Philosophical Society, Philadelphia, February, 1951.

5. In 1947 that 20 per cent of the world's population which lived in noneastern Europe, North America, and Oceania enjoyed a mean expectation of life at birth of 50 to 60 or more years; the 15 per cent living in Eastern Europe and Japan, 40 to 50; the 6.6 per cent in Latin America, 35 to 40; and the 58 per cent in Asia and Africa, close to 30, as a rule. See *World Population Trends*, United Nations, pp. 10–13. Let e represent life expectancy at birth and k the annual number of births. Then, on the assumption that k remains unchanged, the population of a coun-

sence of pronounced obstacles, increase by 100 to 200 or more per cent before they acquire Western fertility patterns and develop a Western age structure; for life expectancy at birth is only about half as high in most of these regions as in the Western World. The order of magnitude of the growth in prospect is suggested by the fact that, should the populations of these regions treble, the population of the world, now close to 2.4 billions, would exceed 5.5 billions a century from now. It is evident, therefore, that, unless a cheap, easily-used contraceptive is developed and widely diffused, population growth is likely to eat up much of those fruits of technical progress which escape the maws of war.

III

Improvement of the economic condition of the some 60 per cent of the world's population whose incomes are very low, often miserably low by Western standards, is possible only on condition that the economies of these peoples are completely transformed. The outstanding characteristic of these economies is their dominance by nonmechanized agriculture, something like three-fourths of their working population being engaged in agriculture pursued in an archaic manner. Accordingly, economic progress presupposes a considerable mechanization and transformation of the agriculture of these countries together with the transference out of agriculture of such "excess" labor as is engaged therein and the creation of a labor force that, in both its agricultural and its nonagricultural branches, has acquired the attitudes, values, and occupational aptitudes essential in rational, mechanized economies.

The development of branches of industry and commerce suited to absorb both the growing nonagricultural labor force and the workers flowing in from agricultural areas involves a number of coinciding steps. (1) There must be brought into being a sufficient supply of persons capable of performing "entrepreneurial" functions. (2) A system of incentives suited to an industrial society must be created. (3) Appropriate facilitating economic, educational, and governmental institutions must be formed. (4) Adequate support

---

try will approach and finally reach ek, increasing as e increases. If, as has always been the case in the past, fertility fails to fall fast enough to offset increases in e, k will increase for a time, with the result that the final population becomes not ek but $e(k + \Delta k)$. Thus, if e doubles and k increases by one-half before it levels off, the population will treble. For example, by the time Japan's population has completed the growth cycle begun in the mid-nineteenth century, its population will have attained a magnitude three or more times that obtaining in 1850. Having indicated that "at least a threefold multiplication is implicit in the processes by which peoples hitherto have achieved low birth and death rates," M. C. Balfour, R. F. Evans, F. W. Notestein, and I. B. Taeuber conclude that "in the Far East . . . we have no reason to expect a smaller multiplier." See *Public Health and Demography in the Far East* (Rockefeller Foundation, 1950), pp. 6–7. What is said here is applicable to other parts of Asia and to much of Africa and Latin America.

must be given to the development of public utilities in appropriate amount and to the establishment of industries which, for one or several reasons, are highly advantageous to economies in the stage of development characteristic of most of the countries under consideration; i.e., industries capable of utilizing available resources and labor, or of satisfying the more urgent wants, or of easing the pressure for foreign exchange, or (because they are complementary to other industries in existence or being established) of reinforcing the industrial development under way.

Industrial evolution along these lines involves two further conditions, the capacity to meet which tends often to be greatly reduced by population growth: (*a*) the availability of a sufficiency of land and/or natural resources, (*b*) the formation and/or acquisition of capital at a rate commensurate with the rate of industrial development projected.

Further population growth will accentuate such shortages of land and/or resources as exist in countries where a condition of population pressure already obtains. In North America and Oceania, most of whose population is approaching a stationary state, both resources and land are relatively abundant. In Europe both land and resources are relatively scarce, but much of the population is approaching a stationary state. In Africa, where the population growth potential is high, resources and in some measure land are relatively abundant; but their distribution in space relative to that of population is not such as to afford relief to more than a portion of the inhabitants. Further growth, therefore, will retard the improvement of the economic state of those African populations which lack ready access to lands and resources unexploited or ineffectively exploited at present. In South America, where the population growth potential remains high, both land and ore resources are relatively plentiful; notwithstanding, industrial development promises to be greatly restricted by the shortage of coal, water power constituting the principal widespread potential source of energy. Land and energy resources appear to be relatively plentiful in the Soviet Union; still, according to some estimates, iron ore resources are both relatively scarce and not too well located in space. The most acute actual and/or potential shortages, however, are found in Asia, where live over half the world's population and where numbers may well treble in a century. For already Asia's population is short of land, hardly as well equipped with power resources relative to population as are the peoples of Europe, and only about one-fifth as well supplied with iron ore reserves as is the rest of the world. Furthermore, the spatial factor is unfavorable, the bulk of the iron resources of Asia being situated in India, and the bulk of the power resources in China. Presumably, then, only in parts of Africa and South America will further population growth prove economically advantageous. Redistribution of population will serve to correct such localized shortages of numbers as are to be found on other continents.

When a country is short of land and/or raw materials and this shortage is being aggravated by continuing population growth, it may resort to several complementary remedies. First, it may attempt to step up its rate of capital formation, since capital is needed to exploit such natural resources as are at hand, to provide substitutes for critical resources in relatively short supply, to facilitate technical progress, to create good health, and to implant productive skills and attitudes in the labor force. Yet, it is difficult to establish a very high absolute or relative rate of capital formation, when, as is the case in most lands where population pressure and high growth potentials are found, per capita income ranges between $25 and $150 and the relatively wealthy minority devotes most of its income to consumption instead of to capital formation. Second, relief may be sought in foreign lending and foreign trade. However, foreign loans can relieve in but limited measure a shortage of capital imputable to a low rate of domestic capital formation, how much foreign capital an economy can effectively absorb being governed, for technical and economic reasons, by its rate of domestic capital formation. Furthermore, international trade can significantly (but by no means completely) counterbalance a domestic shortage of natural resources only after the domestic economy has been appropriately developed and other relevant conditions have been met. The capacity of a people to find relief for poverty in capital accumulation will be less, in all cases in which the population is of supra-optimum size and land and/or resources are relatively lacking, when a population is growing than when it is stationary.

In sum, population growth operates in four ways to retard the betterment of man's material condition. First, it increases the pressure of numbers upon a nation's land and resource equipment as of any given time. Second, it tends to accentuate this pressure through time by accelerating the rate at which the store of exhaustible and nonreplaceable natural resources is used up and the costs of their use are increased. Third, it diminishes the rate at which capital can be accumulated, and this diminution is greatly accentuated when, as is the case in most overpopulated countries, much potential capital is utilized in maintaining for a few years children who eventually die before they reach a productive age.[6] Fourth, given the rate of capital formation, the rate at which the equipment of the labor force can be increased is reduced. Only in the small number of countries where the population is of infra-optimum size will an increase in numbers, through its salutary influence upon economic organization, more than offset the adverse effects enumerated.

6. D. Ghosh estimates at something like 22.5 per cent of the Indian national income the cost of maintaining those who die before they reach the age of 15. The corresponding figure for England is put at 6.5 per cent. See *Pressure of Population and Economic Efficiency in India* (New Delhi, 1946), p. 22. In 1934–38, according to C. Clark, capital formation approximated only 6 per cent of India's national income. Analogous conditions are found in many other parts of Asia.

IV

Both the problem being posed and the consequences of population growth may be translated into terms of per capita real income. Consider first the problem itself. Per capita income in many lands is only a minor fraction of per capita income in Oceania, North America, and Northwest Europe. Furthermore, judging by the past, we may assume that for some time to come per capita real income will increase 1 to 2 percent per year in these parts. It follows that, if the material condition of peoples living in very low-income areas is to improve both absolutely and relative to that of high-income populations, these peoples must advance their per capita incomes appreciably more than 2 per cent per year for many years to come. While such an advance may tend to be restrained by the relatively slower rate of growth of the high-income countries,[7] it will be facilitated by the higher rate of technical progress of which the low-income countries are susceptible in virtue of the fact that their economies remain founded upon technically primitive methods of production.

Since an increase in a nation's capital equipment per worker tends to be accompanied by an increase in output per worker, population growth may be looked upon as a deterrent to the increase of per capita income whenever a nation's population is of supra-optimum size. For population growth, together with excessive mortality among those of infra-working age, diverts resources from the formation of capital to the formation of population, whilst the necessity of equipping increments in population makes the magnitude of the increment in per capita equipment lower than it would have been had the population not grown.

Let us first suppose that both the rate of saving and the income-producing power of capital are independent of the rate of population growth. Then a 1 per cent increase in population will be purchased at the cost of something like a 1 per cent increase in per capita income. Given the validity of these assumptions, the 1 per cent per year increase in population roughly characteristic of many densely populated low-income countries operates to prevent

7. Suppose we divide the countries of the world into two categories, the rapidly growing, G, and the slowly growing, S, with their rates of growth represented by R_g and R_s. Then $R_g = f(R_s)$, the specific relation between the two rates turning on whether G and S are primarily substitutes for each other, complements to each other, or independent systems. If, as appears likely, the dominant form of relationship will be a complementary one in the early stages of the development of G, R_s will exercise a restrictive influence upon R_g. This influence will diminish in time, however, as the complementary type of relationship gives place to one that is substitutive or independent. Presumably, an economy that is large (e.g., the Russian or the Chinese) can more easily free its rate of expansion of the conditioning influence of expansion elsewhere than can an economy that is small and relatively short of elements requisite for economic expansion. That the less developed countries are significantly dependent upon the more developed countries is suggested by data presented in F. Hilgerdt, *The Network of World Trade* (Geneva, 1942), especially pp. 37ff., and Tse Chun Chang, "A Statistical Note on World Demand for Exports," *Review of Economic Statistics*, 1948, pp. 106ff.

an increase of about 1 per cent per year in per capita income. Thus, if per capita income would grow 3 per cent per year in the absence of population growth, it will grow only about 2 per cent per year when the population is increasing 1 per cent per year.[8]

The assumptions just made must be modified, however. First, the income-producing power of capital is not independent of changes in the size of the labor force. On the basis of past experience, when a 1 per cent increase in both the employed labor force and the stock of capital or wealth in use is accompanied by a 2 per cent increase in income, this 2 per cent may be imputed to the forces generating it somewhat as follows: technical progress, 1; labor, 0.7; other productive agents, 0.3. Accordingly, given a 12 per cent saving rate, a 1 per cent increase in the labor force, and technical progress as indicated, about $\frac{7}{26}$ of the 2.6 per cent increase in national income would be attributable to the 1 per cent increase in the employed labor force. In general, it is probably safe to say that 25 to 35 per cent of the annual increase in output consequent upon increases of 1 and 1 to 3 per cent, respectively, in labor and capital is attributable to the increment in labor.[9] Secondly, account must be taken of the absorption, by population growth and relevant

8. Let Y represent national income; W, the wealth or capital used to produce that income; ΔY and ΔW, the annual increment in Y and W, respectively; r, the annual rate of growth of population P; y, the per capita income Y/P; j, the annual rate of increase in per capita income, $\Delta y/y$; a, the annual rate of capital or wealth formation expressed as a percentage of Y, namely $\Delta W/Y$; and s, the increment in Y consequent upon an increment in W, namely $\Delta Y/\Delta W$. Let us assume for the sake of simplicity, furthermore, that s remains constant for the period under consideration. It follows that

$$j = \frac{1 + as}{1 + r} - 1.$$

If population is not growing and r has a zero value, $j = as$. Accordingly, if the value of s were independent of that of r, the value of j would be reduced by approximately r. Thus if a has a value of 0.1, the annual rate of saving approximating 10 per cent of the national income and s has a value of 0.25 (on the assumption that W/Y has a persisting value of about 4), j will have a value of 0.025 so long as population is not growing and r has a zero value. If, however, r has a value of .01, the value of j will approximate 0.015 instead of 0.025. If a has a lower value when r has a value of .01 than when r has a zero value, the value of j will be further reduced. See note 10 below.

This formulation does not take net capital imports into account. If these are represented by A, then as in the above equation becomes $(a + A)s$. There is a practicable upper limit to A/a. In the paper cited in note 4 above it is suggested that the average upper limit to A/a may be in the neighborhood of one-third. If it be true that the poorest half of the world's population produces only one-tenth of the world's income, and if it should save and invest 0.3 of this, it still could use (on the supposition that A/a cannot long exceed one-third) only about one-fifth of the savings which the richest tenth can supply if they save and invest 10 per cent of the 55 per cent of the world's income which they supposedly receive.

9. See J. Tinbergen, "Zür Theorie der langfristigen Wirtschaftsentwicklung," *Weltwirtschaftliches Archiv*, 55 Band, Heft 3, 1942, pp. 511–547. See also E. C. Olson, "Factors Affecting International Differences in Production," *American Economic Review*, May, 1948, pp. 502–522. In the four largest industrial nations in 1870–1913, at the time when about 10–15 per cent of the national income was saved, population was growing about 1 per cent per year, and national income was increasing 2.1–2.5 per cent per year, this increment was dis-

premature mortality, of resources that would otherwise have been transmuted into wealth or capital. When these two conditions are taken into account, a 1 per cent increase in population is usually found to be purchased at a cost of between somewhat less and somewhat more than a 1 per cent increase in per capita income.[10] It should be noted finally that the productivity of reproducible capital will be higher *ceteris paribus* when the land and natural resources with which this capital can be combined are relatively plentiful. The absence of this condition from many low-income economies makes more difficult their counterbalancing population growth by capital formation.[11]

By way of summary it may be said that population growth is a major obstacle to economic betterment in most parts of the world. It is retarding capital formation, accelerating the rate of depletion of the world's limited store of nonreplaceable resources, augmenting the rise of costs in increasing-cost industries, and decelerating the rate of increase of per capita income. Whether a cheap contraceptive, together with a set of motives conducing to its widespread use in the overpopulated parts of the world, can be developed

---

tributable somewhat as follows: population, 0.7; capital accumulation, 0.4–0.8; technical improvement, 1.0. Cp. Tinbergen and J. J. Polak, *The Dynamics of Business Cycles* (Chicago, 1950), p. 128.

10. Let s, as defined in note 8 above, be divided into s_r and s_n where s_r is due to population growth r and s_n is due to other circumstances. Further, let $a = a_n - a_r$ where a_n represents the annual rate of saving or capital formation when $r = O$, and a_r represents the reduction in a_n due to r's having a positive value. Then the annual rate of increase in per capita income

$$j = \frac{1 + a_n s_n + a_n s_r - a_r s_n}{1 + r} - 1.$$

When r has a value of zero, the value of j becomes as_n. It follows that j will have a greater value when r has a zero instead of a positive value so long as $(r + a_r s_n) > (a_n s_r)$. The values to be assigned to these variables vary with situation. Suppose we make $a_n = 0.2$, and $a_r = 0.1$. Let the elasticity of productivity for capital be 0.3 and that for population be 0.7. Finally let technical progress increase Y one per cent per year. (Actually the capacity of technical progress to increase income is itself a function of a, but here it is treated as a constant fraction of Y.) If $r = O$, j becomes .025; but if $r = .01$, j approximates .0094. Under the assumed conditions, therefore, r's having a value of .01 instead of zero reduces the annual rate of increase in per capita income by about three-fifths. The value to be assigned to a_r in any particular case depends both upon the magnitude of r and upon the amount of resources absorbed by premature mortality associated with r and destined, in the absence of such mortality, to be saved and invested.

The income optimum population may be defined in terms similar to those used above in this note. Let $s = s_n[1 + f(r)]$ where s and s_n are defined as above and $f(r)$ replaces s_r. Then

$$j = \frac{as_n[1 + f(r)]}{1 + r}.$$

When r has a zero value j becomes as_n. When r has a positive value j is higher than when r has a zero value only on condition that $f(r) > r$. Accordingly, population maladjustment may be said to increase whenever, as is usually the case, $r > f(r)$.

11. Colin Clark concludes that the value of s, when only reproducible capital is taken into account, rises as reproducible capital per worker and output per worker per hour increase. With income and reproducible capital per worker represented by y and c, the ratio y/c rises

in good time remains to be seen. It is evident, however, in view of the limited-ness of the fund of nonreplaceable resources at the disposal of mankind and in view of the dangers to the security of the relatively stationary peoples implicit in the continued growth of peoples living in overpopulated lands, that the former should not give impetus to the multiplication of unfriendly components of the latter.

---

from about 0.22 when real income in I.U. per man-hour approximates 0.10 (the figure for India in 1944 is put at .09) to about 0.28 when hourly real income is 1.0 (as in the United States in 1945). (See *Review of Economic Progress,* II, 1950, No. 1.) Since this increase in y/c, granted the accuracy of the data on which it is based, is not attributable to an increase in nonrepro-ducible capital or labor, it must be attributed to technical progress and similar output-increasing forces. While Clark's data relate more largely to time than to space, they lend support to the view that, insofar as space may be equated to time, the spread of Western methods in space will be accompanied for a while by an increasing rate of technical progress in the underdeveloped countries.

The Population Problem: Dimensions, Potentialities, Limitations

"A hopeful disposition is not the sole qualification to be a prophet." — Winston S. Churchill (in Speech, April 30, 1927).

In accordance with my assignment, I shall undertake to do four things: define the population problem and the role of limitational factors; touch upon strategic courses of action available for easing their impact; distinguish the major problem areas; and indicate limitational factors operative in these areas. I shall hypothesize that world population will continue to grow for a century or more at between 1 and 1.5 per cent per year. This implies a world population of 4–5 billion by the year 2000 and 6.5–10.5 billion by the year 2050.

I. Limitational Factors and the Population Problem

The population problem of any collectivity (e.g., a nation) has its origin in imbalance between numbers, output, and desired level of consumption. It resembles in part the general economic problem — for this problem also has its origin in imbalance — that between a collectivity's aggregate of conduct-determining material wants and its capacity to satisfy these wants. But the collectivity can cut the coat of satisfiable wants to the cloth of supply through recourse to price and rationing systems that are re-enforced by a system of police and suitable institutional arrangements. The collectivity cannot, however, through use of these instruments bring the demand for population into balance with the supply of population at a level of consumption deemed satisfactory.

We may think of a collectivity as being confronted by two curves which may or may not be optimally tangent to one another. (See Figure I and the appendix at the close of this paper. One might, of course, use some other index than per capita income.) The one depicts the response of per capita income (or output) to increases (decreases[1]) in the collectivity's population. The other joins various combinations of per capita income and population magnitudes which the collectivity finds equally attractive; it is the relevant member of the collectivity's indifference map.[2] If the relevant indifference curve is tangent to the income curve at a point which coincides with the

1. It is most unlikely that, were the population of a collectivity to diminish, the response of per capita income to this diminution would retrace the very path which it pursued as population increased.

2. Our discussion above and in the appendix does not take account of the objections to which the concept of community indifference is subject. E. g., see R. W. Pfouts, "Some Difficulties in a Certain Concept of Community Indifference," *Metroeconomica*, 1955, pp. 16–26.

locus of actual population and actual per capita income, a population problem does not exist. If, as is usual, however, population is so great and per capita income is so low that their point of coincidence lies to the right of the point at which the indifference curve is tangent to the income curve, demographic imbalance exists. But this imbalance can rarely if ever be rectified by an enforced or voluntary diminution in numbers, since prevailing institutions and values rarely if ever conduce to a diminution of numbers. Nineteenth-century Ireland constitutes a partial exception to this statement, since it greatly reduced its population through emigration. Correction of imbalance must be sought rather through measures (e.g., capital formation, technological improvements, economic reorganization, etc.) suited to increase per capita income, population being given. Yet the effectuation of such measures tends to be made difficult when it is not prevented altogether by the magnitude of the existing population, coupled with its tendency to increase even though numbers already are pressing hard upon resources. Herein lies the population problem. It exists whenever the aggregate of wants presses beyond the aggregate supply, whether because numbers are great, as in India, or because per capita consumption is great, as in America, or because both numbers and consumption are great, as in England.

The population problem usually arises because labor is not the only economic factor of production and therefore not all output is imputable to labor. If labor were the sole factor of production and there were no economies of scale, the population problem would not manifest itself until the amount of space available per head had begun to prove inadequate. Even given economies and diseconomies of labor organization, per capita output would tend to increase until the labor force had reached a size commensurate with full realization of the net economies of labor organization; beyond this point diseconomies would outweigh economies of organization and per capita income would decline until it had descended below the level deemed desirable, given the size of the population. Not all output is imputable to labor, however. Only in the neighborhood of 80 per cent of net output is attributable to labor in its various forms, the balance being imputable to the nonhuman productive agents utilized jointly with labor. The population problem comes into being, therefore, because the stock of these agents available for use with labor becomes too small. (Of course, if per capita requirements exceeded what could be produced with an optimum stock of these agents, the population problem would continue to exist until per capita requirements had declined sufficiently.)

Inasmuch as embodied labor forms a part of capital (inclusive of land), the agent to which nonlabor income usually is imputed, attention will here be focused, not upon the agents used jointly with labor, but upon categories of goods, the longer run comparative nonaugmentability of which operates to decelerate the rate of growth of both per capita income and population and eventually to halt income and population growth. These categories, four in number, may be looked upon as limitational factors, or, in more accurate phrase, as species of the genus limitational factor.[3] They are food, energy, other mineral and nonmineral raw materials, and water. They become limitational factors because their ultimate sources of supply are fixed in quantity, or subject to depletion.

Respecting the quantitative significance of these factors, three observations may be made. (1) While the value of the amount of them consumed has increased more rapidly than population, only that of some (minerals and mineral fuels and water) has increased more rapidly than gross national product. Such at least is the implication of American data. For in the United States, while population was doubling between 1900 and 1950 and gross national product was increasing 372 per cent, the value of the consumption of raw materials other than gold increased about 1.5 times; that of agricultural products, about 1.3 times; that of minerals and mineral fuel, about 4.9 times; that of water, 7 times; and that of all raw materials except gold and food, about 1.9 times. Only the consumption of forest products continued unchanged in value. Expressed as a percentage of gross national product, the value of raw materials consumed declined as follows between 1900 and 1950: all raw materials but gold, 23.9 to 12.8 per cent; all raw materials except gold and foodstuffs, 10.1 to 6.2; foodstuffs, 13.8 to 6.7; agricultural raw materials other than food, together with forest products, 6.8 to 2.2. Meanwhile the value of mineral fuel consumed rose from 2 to 2.5 per cent of gross national product, and that of minerals other than gold and fuel, from 1 to 1.2. (2) While minerals and raw materials play an important role in the world economy, we have less information concerning this role, since we lack a world Paley Report. Around 1949–50, however, the value of primary production (of which nearly one-fifth represented minerals and about one-eighth represented mineral fuel) amounted to something like three-tenths of world income. Even outside the United States mineral fuel made up about seven-twelfths of all mineral consumption.[4] (3) The impact of significant increases in the input-cost of agricultural and/or other raw materials may be felt less in an advanced than in an underdeveloped country, since a relatively larger fraction of the latter's productive resources are engaged in raw-material production.

3. See my "Limitational Factors in Population Theory: A Note," *Kyklos*, 1955, pp. 227–244, and "Aspects of the Economics of Population Growth," *Southern Economic Journal*, 1947–48, pp. 123–147, 233–265.

4. The world data are quite rough; they are based upon W. S. and E. S. Woytinsky, *World Population and Production* (1953), pp. 315, 394, 455. The American data are derived from *Resources for Freedom*, a report by the President's Materials Policy Commission, 1952, I, pp. 6–7, II, p. 180. In the United States the ratio of BTU input to national income has fallen appreciably since World War I.

The first of these limitational factors — agricultural raw materials — has several sources, the significance of which for partial solution of the population problem varies. First, increases in the efficiency with which existing land is used, deemed capable of increasing average yield per acre by more than one-fifth, presuppose greater education, modification of institutions, and significant increases in working and other capital inputs per acre; but they do not entail a surmounting of barriers to trade, transportation, and migration. It is increases in output from this source, therefore, that seem most likely of realization at present. In the same category, perhaps, fall increases achievable through irrigation of land presently cultivated or susceptible of cultivation if irrigated — increases that reportedly might double prewar output. Second, cultivation of 1.3 billion acres not now used (900 million in South America and Africa; 100 million in Sumatra, Borneo, New Guinea, and Madagascar; and 300 million in northern portions of North America and Eurasia) might add at least the equivalent of prewar food production to the total amount of food available to the world. It is not likely that much of this land will soon be cultivated, however, unless obstacles to its settlement are removed, enough capital is made available for its exploitation, and the prospect is good that its exportable surplus can be profitably marketed.

Should the potentialities just described (corrected for the diversion of land to the production of inedible raw materials and to use as building sites) be realized, world food production might rise to 3–4 times its prewar volume. There would then be nutrition that was adequate, though far below American standards, for a population 2.5–3.0 times that of 1950, a number that could be reached sixty to seventy-five years from now. Beyond, except for additional and possibly significant improvements, lie algae, not perhaps a food that would tempt the palate of Lucullus, but nonetheless a promising source of nutriment.[5] Although the food-production potentialities described above appear to be great, they cannot be realized unless many difficult obstacles are overcome. For this reason some students anticipate but low rates of progress in world food production, little improvement in the relative position of low-income peoples, and continuation of the pressure of numbers upon food resources (particularly if present rates of increase continue). Presumably a 50 per cent increase in the real cost of a country's agricultural production (*ceteris paribus*) would approximate a 5–20 per cent reduction of per capita income.[6]

5. On these points see Harrison Brown, *The Challenge of Man's Future* (1954), Chap. 4; Sir George Thompson, *The Foreseeable Future* (London, 1955); J. S. Burlew, *Algae Culture* (Carnegie Institution Publication 600, 1953); Robert Brittain, *Let There Be Bread* (1952); F. G. W. Smith and H. Chapin, *The Sun, the Sea, and Tomorrow* (1954); F. J. Weiss, *Agricultural and Food Chemistry* (1953); L. D. Stamp, *Land for Tomorrow* (1952); E. Taschdjian, "The Hunger Problem," *Scientia*, 1949, pp. 208–219, 244–251; M. K. Bennett, *The World's Food* (1954).

6. The late O. E. Baker put at 6–7 million square miles the amount of land cultivatable, at 50 per cent the average increase in yield per acre attainable over the level of the thirties, but

Whereas thirty years ago some looked upon a shortage of lumber, paper, and fibers as a major prospective manifestation of population pressure, F. G. Tryon apprehended that shortage of energy and rising fuel costs would check population growth and the advance of living standards—unless man learned to tap inexhaustible sources of power (water, wind, sun, photosynthesis, the atom).[7] His conclusion is supported by recent estimates which suggest that cumulative American and world energy requirements over the next seventy-five years could exceed the net energy recoverable from quite economically accessible fossil fuels. Tryon's apprehension has been somewhat alleviated, however, by the fact that nuclear fuels, of which there is an abundant supply, may be made eventually to furnish as much as 60 per cent of all energy requirements, with nonexhaustible sources providing another 15 or more per cent. Tryon was sensible of the high correlation existing between input of energy and output of income and of the importance of energy for the utilization of ores, water, etc.;[8] but he probably underestimated the disposition of energy-users to economize in its use as its price rose; and he did not allow adequately for the fact that *ceteris paribus* a doubling of real energy costs might reduce per capita income only several per cent.

While components of the third limitational factor—minerals other than fuel—give rise to scrap, this factor too is subject to the law of increasing economic entropy. Accordingly, even though iron, nickel, magnesium, manganese, bauxite, fertilizer ingredients, etc., remain relatively abundant, for the time being, other mineral reserves (e.g., copper, lead, zinc, tin, chromite) already have become very small, and their exhaustion is being accelerated, as is that of all nonrenewable minerals, by increases in population and its incremental rate of growth. It is to be expected, therefore, that deep mining and exploitation of the ocean, together with improvements in the use of metals and of other minerals, will presently become necessary, and that increasing attention will be given to economizing in the use of minerals.[9] Inasmuch as mineral costs are relatively small, an increase in

---

at only 75 per cent above the prewar level, potential world crop production. His figures suggest, therefore, that adequate nutriment can be provided for a population of only 3.5 to 4.0 billion people. See his pamphlet, *The Population Prospect in Relation to the World's Agricultural Resources* (1947), pp. 4–5. See also J. H. Richter, "Population and Food Supply," *Social Research*, 1953, pp. 253–266; R. Barlowe, "Population Pressure and Food Production Potentialities," *Land Economics*, 1949, pp. 227–238; H. H. Villard, "Some Notes on Population and Living Levels," *Review of Economics and Statistics*, 1935, pp. 189–195; Sir John Russell, *World Population and World Food Supplies* (London, 1954); *The Determinants and Consequences of Population Trends* (United Nations, 1953), Chap. 10.

7. See L. I. Dublin, ed., *Population Problems in the United States and Canada* (1926), pp. 109–110, 136–138.

8. See P. C. Putnam, *Energy in the Future* (1953), pp. 231–254, 449–453; E. C. Olson, "Factors Affecting International Differences in Production," AEA *Papers and Proceedings*, May, 1948, pp. 502–522; J. F. Dewhurst, *America's Needs and Resources* (1955), pp. 903–909, 1099–1116; Thomson, *op. cit.*

9. On minerals, see *Resources for Freedom;* Woytinsky, *op. cit.*, Chaps. 10, 22; Smith and Chapin, *op. cit.*

their magnitude may not depress per capita income greatly, though a decline in their availability may produce changes in industrial patterns.

Water—frequently described as a free good by nineteenth-century economists—has become a limitational factor in some regions and may become one in others. In several or more American states water consumption is close to the maximum attainable, and in others it will become so should population and per capita consumption continue to grow. In still other parts of the world, water shortages may be encountered, and they will increase in number as population and industrialization progress. Whence increasing efforts to economize in the use of water and to utilize salt water are to be expected.[10]

It is not always easy to assess with precision the significance of a marked increase, or decrease, in the availability of agricultural or other raw materials. Comparative costs and real income levels are affected, to be sure; and yet, as has been shown, these effects may not be very great. Often what is of more significance is whether, because certain materials are or are not available or accessible, particular activities may or may not be carried on, since industrial patterns are conditioned by the kinds of activities pursuable. Even then it is essential that the country's labor force be suitably skilled and equipped to work up the available raw materials.

II. Strategic Courses of Action

Only some of the strategic courses of action open to overpopulated countries can be considered here: technological improvements; technical and related education; capital formation; reorganization of economic life; international migration, trade, lending.

The importance of technological improvements, together with technical and related education, can hardly be overstressed. It is to technological improvements that a large part of the increase in per capita output experienced in the Western world must be imputed—perhaps half, perhaps more. Increasingly, as the experience of the Soviet Union appears to be demonstrating, both the introduction and the extension of technological improvements presuppose availability of a skilled labor force and easy accessibility to technical and related education. Furthermore, since the economies of nearly all, if not all, of the countries suffering from population pressure are technologically laggard, the mere introduction and adaptation of technologies already in use in advanced countries will greatly augment output; for a long time to come it will not be necessary for these countries to create new and unique methods.

10. *Resources for Freedom*, I, Chap. 10, IV, Chap. 9, V, pp. 83–98; Colin Clark, "Afterthoughts on Paley," *Review of Economics and Statistics*, 1954, pp. 267–273, and E. S. Mason, "Comment," *ibid.*, pp. 273–278; Brown, *op. cit.*, pp. 211–215; C. B. Ellis, *Fresh Water from the Ocean* (1954); *Water, Yearbook of Agriculture, 1955* (U.S.D.A., 1955).

Capital formation is of great importance, because of the direct income increasing effect of capital increments, because of the dependence of technological progress upon the availability of a sufficiency of capital, and because capital may be indirectly substitutable (within limits) for some of the factors which we have described as limitational. In advanced countries a 4–5 per cent saving rate often is essential to keep the wealth-population ratio constant when population is growing 1 per cent per year; and a like saving rate may permit an increase of close to 1 per cent per year in per capita income when population is constant, provided that the rate of technological progress is sufficiently high. Whence it may be said that a 1 per cent per year rate of population growth usually entails the sacrifice of an increase of something like 0.5–1.0 per cent per year in per capita income, with the magnitude of the sacrifice positively associated with the rate of technological progress. Population growth itself absorbs or neutralizes capital in various ways, thereby limiting the rate at which a collectivity can increase its stock of wealth per head. (For a detailed statement, see my "The Population Obstacle to Economic Betterment," *AEA Papers and Proceedings,* May, 1951, pages 342–354.) The supply of savings must be much higher, therefore, when numbers are growing than when they are not, given that a collectivity seeks to achieve a specific rate of increase in per capita income; but the supply is not likely to exceed 10–15 per cent, an amount that might permit the stock of wealth to increase 2–3.75 per cent per year.

Reorganization of the economic life of overpopulated countries usually is indicated for a variety of reasons. Thus mere formation of assets does not of itself insure continuing growth of per capita income; otherwise in many countries per capita incomes would tend to be higher than they are, since man's disposition to increase assets (productive and unproductive) usually is strong even though his disposition to form productive capital may not be. Again, reorganization may make possible a much higher rate of capital formation than might otherwise be achieved, by strengthening a population's disposition and capacity to save, and by drawing into the orbit of productive activity a great deal of the underemployed labor found in underdeveloped economies. (E.g., see W. A. Lewis, "Economic Development with Unlimited Supplies of Labor," *The Manchester School of Economic and Social Studies,* 1954, pages 139–191.)

International migration, trade, and capital flow could contribute significantly to the alleviation of population pressure were they not subject to important constraints. Migration could carry numbers from places where the population-wealth ratio was relatively high to places where it was relatively low. Trade could increase international division of labor and thereby augment world production and cushion the impact of limitational factors. International capital flow could reduce international disparities in equipment per worker and might strengthen forces making for the international diffusion of the technologies developed in advanced countries. Individual countries troubled by the population problem might, it would appear, derive great relief from emigration, capital imports, and the export of products, particularly those that were labor-oriented. Yet, because of barriers to migration and because of costs attendant upon the transplanting of migrants, it is unlikely that emigration will significantly ease population pressure. It is unlikely, moreover, that capital imports will contribute greatly to aggregate capital supply in densely populated underdeveloped countries; these countries will have to provide most of the capital they use. Not only do inauspicious politico-economic conditions in underdeveloped countries, together with prospects of good earnings in developed countries, check the outflow of capital from high-income countries. The capacity of under-developed countries to obtain and utilize capital imports effectively is limited also by the lowness of their rates of domestic capital formation, by fiscal, financial, and technological circumstances, and by shortages of appropriately skilled personnel. Even in the nineteenth century, in countries then under-going development, domestic savings greatly outweighed capital imports in importance.

The capacity of international trade to provide relief for population pressure, though great under possible conditions, is not likely to be great under probable conditions. Trade cannot overcome water shortages. It may not prevent hunger. In the past only about 7 per cent of world agricultural production has entered into foreign trade, with Oceania, Latin America, Africa, and even Asia helping to make up Europe's 10 per cent deficit. Of the three major underdeveloped areas, only Asia may be described as exporting little raw produce on the balance; Africa and Latin America remain important net exporters. Trade cannot wholly offset mineral short-ages. Although mineral production is geographically highly concentrated and most countries have to import some minerals, only about one-fifth of the world output of minerals has been entering international trade, with fossil fuels, copper, iron, tin, and lead predominating.[11] It is not likely, therefore, that many countries could make up great deficits of raw materials by ex-changing for them both labor-oriented products and selected but relatively abundant raw materials. A fortiori, sheer size may be a source of advantage to a country, for when it is relatively large, it is relatively free of man-made barriers to the pursuit of comparative advantage and relatively capable of utilizing wide-scale governmental intervention to modify the impact of the price system upon the use of resources and the formation of capital and skill.

11. Woytinsky, *op. cit.,* pp. 320–324, 595–597, 769–780; *Resources for Freedom, passim;* J. Humlum, *Atlas of Economic Geography* (1955); U.S. Department of State (Publication 3428), *Energy Resources of the World* (1949), pp. 22–26.

III. The Problem Areas

I define as a problem area any area in which the per capita output of goods and services is very low, in large part because numbers are great and becoming greater. I do not so define the Soviet Union, English-speaking North America, or countries situated in Europe and Oceania, even though population pressure is present in some of these parts. Although per capita income remains low in many of these excluded countries, it still is a number of times as high as that reported for the overpopulated, low-income continents. In most of these non-problem-area countries, population density appears to exceed the income-optimum level. In fact, population density is three-fourths as high in Europe and Western Russia as in Eastern China and Southern India and nearly two-thirds as high in the Northeastern United States as in Europe. In these excluded countries, however, population growth is under effective control, or can shortly be brought under effective control.

Incomes are absolutely and relatively low in Asia, Africa, and Latin America (Woytinsky, *op. cit.*, Chapters 12–13). In Asia and Africa, according to 1938 and 1948 estimates, per capita income was only about one-third as high as that reported for the world as a whole; in Latin America it was 0.65–0.70 as high. Moreover, while per capita incomes vary considerably from country to country, they are absolutely and relatively low in most of the countries situated in Asia, Africa, and Latin America. According to 1948 estimates, per capita incomes above $200 were found only in Israel, the Union of South Africa, Cuba, Puerto Rico, Argentina, Uruguay, and Venezuela. At this time world per capita income approximated $230. In most Asiatic countries and in some African and Latin-American countries per capita incomes were below $100.

The low-income countries may be assembled into two classes: those marked by high density of population and those marked by low density. In the former class fall most of the countries in Asia and some of the countries in Africa and Middle America; in the latter class fall principally countries of South America and Africa. In 1950 the number of persons per square mile in Asia (126), while below the number found in Europe (207), was six times the number reported for North America (20) and three times that estimated for the world as a whole (42). By contrast, the numbers reported for South America (16) and Africa (17) were below that found in North America (20) and less than half that estimated for the world as a whole. Even in Middle America the number (44) was only about one-third of that found in Asia. These figures are reflected in the amounts of arable land available per capita, even though reportedly the percentage of land suitable for agriculture ranges from 37 per cent in Europe to around 3–6 in Oceania,

Asia, Africa, and South America. The number of acres per head varies from 0.64 in Asia and 1.02 in Middle America to 1.47 in South America and 2.22 in Africa; corresponding figures for Europe, the world, and North America are 0.94, 1.28, and 3.4.

Whereas nearly all the countries situated in Asia are densely populated, only some of those located in Africa and Latin America are heavily peopled. Of the countries in Asia only a few have less than 40 persons per square kilometer: e.g., Burma and Cambodia, 28; Laos, 5; Iran, 12; Iraq, 11; Jordan, 14; Syria, 19; Turkey, 29. Population density, though relatively heavy in coastal areas, does not exceed 40 per square kilometer in any of the countries of South America; it is in excess of 40 in but three of the countries of Africa (Egypt, Nigeria, and Ruandi-Urundi), and in six regions of Middle America (Cuba, Dominican Republic, El Salvador, Puerto Rico, and the British West Indies).

For purposes of discussion, we include among our densely populated problem areas Middle America, all of Asia, and that portion of Africa which is part of the Middle East. We exclude the rest of Africa and South America because, while the countries situated therein are economically underdeveloped, they are not yet heavily peopled, though eventually they will be if current growth rates persist. Within these two regions, moreover, are found nine-tenths of the as yet unutilized but cultivable tropical soil, a great deal of water power, rich iron reserves, and deposits of uranium and thorium. For lack of suitable coal, however, industrialization has made relatively little progress in South America and has been retarded in Africa. Even so, because the resource equipment of these two areas remains under-exploited, it is still possible for their inhabitants to bring mortality and natality into balance at low levels before population pressure becomes oppressive.

IV. Limitational Factors in the Problem Areas

In 1950, of the world's 2.4 billion people, there lived in problem areas nearly 1,400 millions, 1,272 in Asia (excluding the USSR), 51 in Middle America, and about 66 in northern and northeastern Africa. Of this number, 1,057 millions lived in five countries: China, India and Pakistan, Indonesia, and Japan—the first two of which, and in some measure the others, enjoy advantages of sheer size. While something like $\frac{5}{14}$ of the inhabitants of the problem areas may be thought of as in the labor force, many are under-employed and hence available for use in the construction of capital and in related activities. In most of the problem areas, it is proving difficult to form productive capital at a rate much in excess of that sufficient to counterbalance the rate at which population is growing. Thus India is not considered likely to get its saving rate above 8–9 per cent, of which perhaps half is required to equip new increments of population.

Except for the presence of building materials which are to be found in most parts of the world and for some bauxite deposits, Middle America, other than Cuba and Mexico, is poorly endowed with natural resources. Considerable unutilized productive land is available only in Mexico. Cuba, while short of coking coal, contains iron and several lesser minerals (e.g., chromium, nickel, manganese). Mexico has, besides oil and reserves of iron and coking coal, significant deposits of a number of other minerals (e.g., gold, silver, lead, zinc, antimony, beryllium, salt, mercury, copper, cadmium, graphite, fluorspar). Although propinquity to the United States is a source of commercial and technological advantage to most of the countries situated in Middle America, they are too small (except for Mexico) ever to be other than economic satellites to larger meta-states (e.g., North America, sterling bloc).

The countries composing the Middle East and contiguous parts of Africa are generally poor in resources, and too small to make good use of what they have. Here, as in the rest of Asia, the population, in the course of centuries of settlement, has carefully selected out the land cultivable under the technologies known to it, and there is little additional land available for cultivation in the absence of great technological change. Of potentially productive land there is considerable only in Iran and Ethiopia, and small quantities in but several additional countries (e.g., Syria). While petroleum is present in abundance in some Middle Eastern countries, the region is short of longer run energy reserves. It is very short also of iron and, except for the minerals found in Turkey (e.g., chromite, mercury, salt) and North Africa (e.g., antimony, beryllium, sulfur, phosphate, salt, cobalt, manganese, lead, gypsum), of other minerals. In these parts, therefore, as in much of Middle America, industrial opportunities are limited.

Elsewhere in Asia there may be opportunity to develop two 20-million-ton-a-year steel industries, one in India and possibly one in China, which, while relatively short of iron, is long on coal. Much of the additional mineral wealth (including uranium) of Asia is also located in these two countries. Some iron is to be had in Indonesia, the Philippines, and Korea, but only Korea has sufficient coal. Some minerals are to be found in still other countries (e.g., Malaya, Burma), but their industrial prospects appear quite limited. With the possible exception of India, Pakistan, and Burma, there is little unused potentially productive land other than that to be had in Borneo, Sumatra, and New Guinea.

The situation of Japan—the most advanced country in Asia—exemplifies what may eventually be in store even for South America and lower Africa. While Japan proceeded to industrialize, its population trebled because mortality fell and natality was not controlled, and numbers are likely to increase another 30–35 per cent despite the rapid progress family limitation is making. Japan must presently import at least one-fifth of its food consumption, given only a minimum adequate diet; more than half its wood and fiber requirements; over nine-tenths of its petroleum and some high quality coal; "nearly half of its phosphate, more than one-quarter of its potash, half of its iron, four-fifths of its lead, a substantial portion of its salt, all its aluminum, and nearly all the tin, antimony, and many other minor items." Her pressure to import is likely to grow, if she increases her national income 3–3.5 per cent per year, but probably not enough to carry the ratio of exports to national income greatly above the prewar level of 10–11 per cent.[12]

Conclusion

At the outset, it was hypothesized that world population would increase 1–1.5 per cent per year for many decades to come. But thereafter stress was placed upon the comparative nonaugmentability of final product, since science cannot transcend boundaries set by the "principles of impotence" and since some of the stuff entering into final product is limited in quantity and even subject to the contractile force of entropy. Is it reasonable to assume, therefore, that mortality will be sufficiently reduced relative to natality to permit continuation of a 1–1.5 rate of population growth? A negative answer is indicated.

The reasons why a negative answer is indicated are several in number. First, a decrease in infant mortality greatly increases pressure upon family income; thereby compelling re-examination of the economic implications of family augmentation. Given improvement in the political and social status of women, consciousness of this pressure will be intensified. Second, income and consumption expectations are likely to rise more rapidly than the capacity of developing backward economies to satisfy them, with the result that the disposition to substitute goods for offspring will be strengthened. Third, if governments find much of the resources they sequester for economic development absorbed by population growth instead of by income increasing investment, the governments themselves will be compelled to intervene and take steps to reduce the rate of population growth. Even communist problem-area satellites will find it very difficult to live with the communist principle: "The more, the merrier." Industrial development and modernization of economic life, as Veblen long ago observed, make for the

12. On Japan, see E. A. Ackerman, *Japan's Natural Resources and Their Relations to Japan's Economic Future* (1953), Chaps. 20–21; S. Kuznets, W. E. Moore, and J. J. Spengler, eds., *Economic Growth: Brazil, India, Japan* (1955). Other data used in this section are from Woytinsky, *op. cit.,* Chaps. 10, 15, 21–25; *World Iron Resources and Their Utilization* (United Nations, 1950), and *Coal and Iron Ore Resources of Asia and the Far East* (United Nations, 1952); *Energy Resources of the World,* cited in note 11 above; and Russell, *op. cit.*

rationalization of behavior, reproductive behavior included. Rationalization increasingly implies, when the augmentation of output is difficult, that men ask not, "How many more people can be accommodated?" but "Of what use is further population growth?" It is to be anticipated, therefore, that men will not want their efforts at modernization to be little more successful than were the activities of Sisyphus. Whence it is quite possible, but by no means certain, that age-specific fertility and natality will fall sufficiently to permit a considerable fraction of the prospective increase in the productive capacity of underdeveloped countries to be devoted to improvement of the material scale of living. But this implies a much more rapid decline in natality than took place in Japan or countries of Europe; and so rapid a decline may call for considerable state intervention.

Appendix

Three curves appear in Figure I. Curve π depicts the response of per capita income (= output per capita) to increases in population, with the highest point O representing the level of average income associated with what is usually called the income-optimum population (which lies on the Ox axis, at the point where a perpendicular dropped from O intersects the abscissa). Curves I and II are indifference curves joining combinations of per capita income and population which the population of the collectivity under analysis finds equally attractive; each may be said to belong to a different family of curves. If curve I rules, equilibrium exists at O which may be called the "Wolfe point" after A. B. Wolfe's definition of the optimum (in Dublin, *op. cit.*, page 68). If, however, relatively more importance is attached to population, and curve II rules, equilibrium exists at P. Should changes in population magnitude be under the empire of the collectivity's indifference map, technology and resources being given, numbers would tend toward the population magnitude associated with O if the map represented by curve I ruled, or to that associated with P if the map represented by curve II ruled. Then, given improvement in technology or in available resources and a corresponding upward shift of curve π, new equilibria would be established. Given the map represented by curve I, the new equilibrium point would probably lie directly above O; all or nearly all the improvement would be devoted to increasing per capita income. If, however, the map represented by curve II ruled, the new equilibrium point would lie northeast of P; the improvement would be devoted to increasing both per capita income and population. Should the available stock of resources shrink greatly and curve π shift downward in consequence, a converse movement would result; given the curve-I map, only per capita income would decline significantly, while, given curve-II map, both population and per capita income would decline.

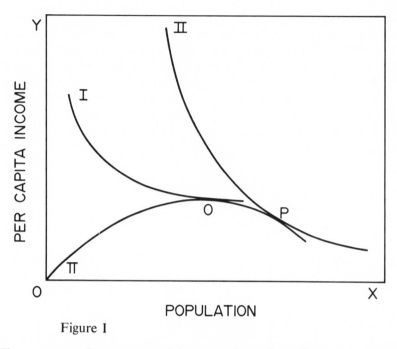

Figure I

The argument just presented is somewhat misleading on at least two counts. First, changes in population magnitude are not under the empire of the collectivity's indifference map, even given that such map exists. Changes in population magnitude reflect individual preferences which may or may not be adequately represented in this map, together with other circumstances even less adequately represented. Second, the argument presented implies greater fluidity and greater capacity on the part of the collectivity to introduce demographic change than is realizable in reality. Population tends to change markedly only in one direction; it tends to increase, particularly when aggregate income rises, but it does not tend to decrease, even when aggregate and per capita income fall significantly. Per capita income being much more mobile, it is the level of per capita income that tends to change when population changes, or when curve π shifts. Accordingly, if the collectivity is overpopulated (as it would be, e.g., if population exceeded the number associated with point P and average income were below the level associated with P), a downward adjustment in numbers does not take place; at most, Malthusian and other checks operate to diminish the rate of natural increase. Relief must be sought through an upward shift of curve π, and yet such an upward shift may be prevented by the existing magnitude of population, together with the fact that this magnitude may be increasing. When such a situation obtains, population and productive power are in a state of persisting imbalance. Escape from this state is hardly to be accomplished through a diminution of numbers, since prevailing values and institutions do not conduce to diminution. Escape is likely, therefore, only if somehow per capita income can be increased sufficiently. For a fuller account of the subject of this appendix, see my "Welfare Economics and the Problem of Overpopulation," *Scientia*, 1954, pages 128–138, 166–175, and "Some Economic Aspects of the Subsidization by the State of the Formation of 'Human Capital,'" *Kyklos*, 1950, pages 316–343.

Capital Requirements and Population Growth in Underdeveloped Countries: Their Interrelations*

> *"No branch of industry can be carried on . . . without . . . capital."* —Jeremy Bentham

This paper has to do with certain interrelations between capital growth and population growth. In Section I wealth classification is treated; in II, the substitutability of reproducible capital for natural resources; in III, the shortage, use, and formation of capital; in IV, the impact of population and income growth upon capital requirements; in V, the impact of income growth upon population growth.

I. The Composition of a Society's Wealth or Capital

By wealth is meant the economically scarce tangible or material objects (exclusive of human beings) at the disposal of men (as individuals or as members of groups) for use in the production of goods and services.[1] We shall sometimes use the term capital as a synonym for wealth, or for a category of wealth, though we recognize that the term usually is used to denote the discounted or present value of expected income flowing to the owners of wealth or to the beneficiaries of particular contractual arrangements. Whilst human beings are excluded from the category of wealth (since under normal accounting conventions a value is not set upon them), cognizance must be taken of the fact that goods and services may be diverted to capital formation, or utilized to improve the health and education, and hence the productive power, of individuals. For the decline in the rate at which physical capital is formed may be offset in part by an increase in the rate of investment in the improvement of human beings. For example, in the United States in 1950 when national income approximated $241 billion, savings approximated $31 billion, and expenditures on civilian health and education,

---

* This paper is an expansion of one presented at the World Population Conference, Rome, 1954.

1. It is somewhat misleading to include in the category of wealth only economically scarce material objects. This practice is not objectionable when the time interval under consideration is very short, but it may be objectionable when the time interval is long. For as population grows, and even as Net National Product grows, material objects which have heretofore been economically free become economically scarce and therewith become classifiable as wealth. Yet production may have been contingent upon the presence of these elements even before they became scarce and had imputed to them a portion of the output. In other instances, of course, it is the extension of exploitation to inferior grades of resources that makes wealth of them. In view of what has been said, therefore, distinction may, on occasion, have to be made between increments in wealth attributable to productive effort and increments having their origin in newly generated scarcity. On some implications of "unpaid factors" see Meade (1952).

12.7 and 10.5 (of which 2.1 went for higher education). Since expenditures for health, education, etc., are relatively greater in developed than in underdeveloped countries, the rate at which capital is really formed in the former must be appreciably in excess of three times the corresponding rate obtaining in the latter, even though the rates at which nonhuman capital is formed in advanced countries have often been about three times those found in many underdeveloped countries.

For purposes of the present discussion three methods of classifying a society's wealth are considered.

(i) The tangible wealth wherewith men work (Table I contains a summary of the classifications of wealth which are laid out in [i], [ii], and [iii]), or whence they derive income, is distinguishable into that which is (I.A) reproducible (i.e., Reproducible Wealth, hereinafter called RW) and that which is (I.B) not directly reproducible (i.e., Nonreproducible Wealth,

Table I. Summary of Classifications of Wealth.

I. Reproducibility.
    A. Reproducible wealth (RW)—i.e., wealth which may be increased by investment, e.g., any manufactured item of capital, fertility of soils, etc.
    B. Nonreproducible wealth (NRW)—i.e., wealth which may not be increased by the investment process, e.g., mineral deposits.
II. Contribution to the production of net national product (NNP).
    A. Wealth forms which contribute significantly to the production of NNP (productive assets).
        1. Overhead capital.
            a. Directly productive overhead capital—structures and equipment utilized directly by persons who are engaged in extractive activities, industry, and manufacturing or in the supply of certain services.
            b. Economic overhead capital—elements (e.g., transportation, communication, power, irrigation, drainage, soil conservation, etc.) which are utilized indirectly to make possible productive activities of the sort included under (II.A.1.a).
            c. Social overhead capital—elements (e.g., sanitation, educational, housing, social welfare, etc., facilities) which, while serving to improve the quality of the population and the milieu within which it resides, both create income and augment the capacities of individuals to produce income.
        2. Working capital—inventories of real and monetary assets which are used to facilitate the process of production in its ongoing state, e.g., inventories of raw and semi-processed materials, spare parts for output and for capital equipment items, balances of cash or liquid assets which facilitate purchase and sale of inputs and outputs, gold reserve in a monetary system.
    B. Wealth forms which do not contribute significantly to the production of NNP (unproductive assets).
        1. Hoarded wealth which does not perform a reserve or inventory function, plus a large fraction of precious stones and metals, ecclesiastical edifices, patriotic monuments, etc.
        2. Standby wealth, e.g., standby plants, subsoil wealth not yet exploited, which, though capable of contributing to the production of NNP, is not currently being so utilized. Resources employed in the production of (II.B.2) are also included in (II.B.2).

---

hereinafter called NRW).[2] Within the latter category belong accessible minerals, favorableness of terrain and transfer conditions, landed surface and (in large measure) utilizable land, etc.[3]

It has been estimated that in Western Europe and the United States at any moment in time since 1870 something like 0.2–0.35 of the net national product (hereinafter called NNP) has been imputable to the tangible wealth that is employed jointly with labor; the balance, 0.65–0.8, has been imputable to human services. If, however, one views productive experience in the long run, one infers that improvements in technique, organization, etc., may have been responsible for 0.25–0.5 of the average annual increment in NNP (Tinbergen 1942; Clark 1951, ch. 11; Douglas 1948).[4] The fruits of these improvements are distributed among the cooperant agents of production by the price system, with the result that they appear to be products of these agents as such.[5]

Inasmuch as NRW is nonaugmentable whereas RW is augmentable, population growth tends eventually to be accompanied by several effects, given probable conditions. (1) Let it be assumed that a society is technologically progressive, that its favorably-situated members are adequately disposed to form capital, and that RW is sufficiently substitutable for NRW. (a) Then, as population grows, the ratio of the value of NRW to population tends eventually to fall whilst that of RW to population tends to rise; and *pari passu,* as NNP rises, the ratio of the value of NRW to NNP falls whilst that of RW to NNP rises. (b) Furthermore, as per capita income rises (i.e., as the ratio of NNP to population rises), the proportion of a society's NNP

2. The stock of NRW is not absolutely fixed in amount. It is advisable, on the one hand, that elements susceptible of only slight increase be included. On the other hand, there are included elements which are exhaustible through use and nonrestorable after exhaustion (e.g., "capital energy," or "economically recoverable reserves of energy in the fossil fuels"). Thus, the fossil fuels recoverable at near present costs amount to not more than three times the cumulative amount of energy that will (according to estimates) be consumed in the world in 1950–2000 (Putnam 1953, pp. 77ff., 115, 136, 145, 231–40).

3. Some but not all of these elements may have values placed upon them (e.g., land, minerals) whereas others may have their cost-saving effects reflected in the value of other agents whose income yield is higher in consequence (e.g., land with good transfer conditions will be worth more than similar land with poor transfer conditions because less of its gross yield will be absorbed by transportation costs).

4. S. Valavanis-Vail (1955, p. 217) estimated the contribution of technology to American income growth at about 8 per cent per decade. In the United States, between 1869 and 1928, Jacob Schmookler (1952) estimates, the increase in gross national product "reflected in roughly equal parts an increase in resources and an increase in resource efficiency." (Here the term resource stands for input.) He found "little or no evidence . . . to support the common belief that technical progress grows at an ever increasing rate." The annual rate of increase (in per cent) in output per unit of input was 1.09 for the economy as a whole; 1.11 in agriculture; 1.41 in manufacturing; and 2.49 in mining. Cp. also Bruton (1955), which came to my attention after I had finished this paper.

5. The quality of many of these agents has, of course, improved. Much reproducible wealth is superior to that which it has replaced, and much of a modern labor force is superior to that which went before. These improvements in quality, however, reflect improvements in applied knowledge which has been embodied in the agents of production.

imputable to NRW tends to decline, even though population continues to increase; and so eventually does the ratio of the cost of raw materials to that of finished goods and services. Tendencies (a) and (b) run counter to the expectations of some early nineteenth century writers who expected that, as population grew, land would become ever more scarce, with output per head falling and the proportion of output going to the landlord increasing.[6] These writers supposed, of course, that technology would improve very little, and that land-lacking societies would not be able to overcome shortage of land by importing the products of land, or by developing substitutes for these products.

The experience of the late nineteenth and/or the present century lends some support to what has been said. In the United States while RW per head (expressed in constant dollars) continued to increase about 2 per cent per year, the value of land per head (here used to represent NRW) by 1950 had descended below the 1900 level after having risen between 1805 and the early twentieth century. The ratio of NRW to NNP eventually fell, but apparently not until after the 1920's. That of RW to NNP rose between 1879 and 1934, but thereafter descended to an early twentieth century level (Goldsmith 1952, pp. 30, 78, 82, 86; Kuznets 1952, pp. 269, 272, 278, 307; Goldsmith 1951).** In a number of West-European countries and even in Japan the relative importance of land and/or of agriculture as a source of NNP has declined markedly, but this trend has not been pronounced in countries that are underdeveloped or suffering from great population pressure (Clark 1951, esp. ch. 10; Schultz 1953, ch. 8; Gilbert 1953, ch. 2–3; and unpublished estimates prepared for the International Association for Research in Wealth and Income, 1951 and 1953). It is the decline in the relative importance of agriculture, traceable to low elasticities of demand for agricultural products, that is primarily responsible for the decline in the ratio of the value of all raw materials consumed to the value of finished goods when such a decline has occurred. Thus in the United States this ratio fell from 24.3 to 12.7 per cent between 1900 and 1950, though meanwhile the ratio of the value of minerals (except gold) to Gross National Product (hereinafter called GNP) rose slightly from about 3.0 per cent to about 3.7 per cent. The amount of energy required per unit of real income, but not its relative value, has fallen appreciably in the United States; elsewhere it has shown a tendency to level off for the time being.

The empirical trends noted reflect the fact that the elasticity of substitution of RW for NRW has been sufficiently great to reduce the relative im-

6. H. J. Davenport (1918, p. 180) later put it this way: "With an increasing population, and an increasing relative scarcity of the products especially derived from land . . . there falls out, per capita, a smaller product in society to be divided, there goes to the landlords a larger and larger proportion of this more and more tragically inadequate total. The landlords gain by the general ill-fortune. Those classes disinherited of land are doomed to a double and compounded pressure of adversity. The land famine smites them with both edges of its sword."
** See list of references at end of this article.

portance of the latter. It has been so great because of the combined influence of international trade, technological changes, discoveries, and changes in the composition of consumer demand as consumption per head has risen. Should some of these substitution-favoring forces lose strength, and should the elasticity of substitution of RW for NRW in a nation's economy as a whole fall below unity, the share of income imputable to NRW will rise even as some of the early classical writers anticipated. It is to be expected that initially, as underdeveloped countries advance, NRW will decline in relative importance, but that in time the progress of population and industrialization may again increase the relative importance of NRW.

(2) An increasing relative scarcity of NRW, consequent from a society's continuing population growth, must, in time, operate to decelerate (if not to prevent) the growth of its NNP per capita unless somehow steps can be taken by a society to counterbalance the failure of its NRW to grow in physical amount. One cannot dig the same ton of ore twice. Among the countervailing steps available the following are of greatest importance to given countries: importation of NRW, or of its products, from abroad on satisfactory terms; reductions in the input of NRW per unit of output (e.g., by increasing the efficiency with which energy, crop land, etc., are utilized); development of essentially man-made substitutes (i.e., forms of RW) for NRW; and the discovery of relatively plentiful forms of NRW and their substitution for relatively scarce forms of NRW (e.g., substitution of coal for wood when woodland was limited).[7] The first of these courses is not open to the world as a whole; and the last is of limited effectiveness, the discoverable being limited, unless there take place remarkable advances in service and applied technology.

(3) When NNP is growing (because the labor force and/or output per worker is growing), both the extensiveness and the intensiveness with which a society utilizes its NRW increases, since increasingly inferior grades of NRW are brought into use and the grades already in use are utilized more intensively.[8] By contrast, it is principally the extensiveness with which RW is utilized that increases. For, since RW is comparatively augmentable by definition, its quantity is continually augmented in anticipation of increases in requirements occasioned by the progress of NNP or GNP; there does not exist so much pressure to economize in its use as in that of NRW.

(ii) While there always exists a continuum of investment opportunities

7. Because, as was noted earlier, some of the elements included under NRW are exhaustible, it is often suggested that the use of these should be guided by a rate of discount which is lower than that obtaining in the market place and which therefore serves to slow down the current rate of consumption of these elements (Scott 1954).

8. In reality, of course, NRW often is less effectively used by countries characterized by population pressure and low incomes than by countries with higher income levels. E.g., see U.S.D.S. (1949, pp. 32–34); UN (1952); Putnam (1953, pp. 88, 101–102, 114, 227).

ranging from those giving promise of negligible yields to those offering high yields, we shall simply classify elements of wealth and investment opportunities into (II.A) those which contribute significantly to the production of NNP and (II.B) those which contribute little or not at all thereto. Under class (II.A) fall most of the elements described under (iii) below. Into class (II.B) fall unproductive assets: (II.B.1) hoarded wealth which does not perform a reserve or inventory function (e.g., gold reserve in a monetary system), together with a considerable fraction of a society's precious stones and metals, ecclesiastical edifices, patriotic monuments, etc.; and (II.B.2) standby wealth (e.g., standby plants, subsoil wealth not yet exploited) which, though capable of contributing to the production of NNP, is not currently being so utilized. When resources are employed in the production of (II.B.1), they cannot be employed in the production of NNP and the formation of productive wealth.[9] The diversion of resources from the production of class (II.B.1) wealth to that of class (II.A) wealth therefore serves to accelerate the growth of NNP and to counterbalance somewhat the income-depressing effects of population growth. Not much can be done, however, in respect of class (II.B.2) wealth. For, while such forms as standby plants can be held to a necessary minimum, it does not pay to increase the rate of use of subsoil wealth (most of which is depletable) above the optimal level.

(iii) Wealth which contributes to the increase of NNP – i.e., elements falling in class (II.A) described under (ii) above – may be distributed into three categories: (II.A.1.a) directly productive capital; (II.A.1.b) economic overhead capital; (II.A.1.c) social overhead capital. Within (II.A.1.a) fall elements (e.g., structures, equipment, etc.) which are utilized directly by persons who are engaged in extractive activities, in industry and manufacturing, or in the supply of certain services. Under (II.A.1.b) may be placed elements (e.g., transportation, communication, power, irrigation, drainage, soil conservation, and similar facilities) which are utilized indirectly to make possible productive activities of the sort included under (II.A.1.a). (II.A.1.c) embraces elements (e.g., sanitation, educational, housing, social welfare, etc., facilities) which, whilst serving to improve the quality of the population

9. It is not here denied that societies may prefer to utilize some of their resources in the production of elements falling into class (II.B.1). In fact, when welfare is defined in certain ways, such resource use is indicated. However, that which class (II.B.1) wealth produced is not usually treated as part of NNP. Furthermore, even if it were so classified, it could not continuously contribute to NNP in the degree that class (II.A) wealth does. Social and economic factors, ranging from a "lack of familiarity with modern banking and financial institutions and habits" to various forms of insecurity, are responsible for some of the importance attached to class (II.B.1) forms of wealth. "Complicated social factors have encouraged the holding of assets and savings in the form of hoarded wealth, gold, silver, paper currency, etc." See UN (ECAFE) (1951, p. 7). As R. Solo (1955, pp. 156–159) shows, although the bidding up of land values does not, as does the hoarding of precious metals, divert resources from the formation of productive wealth, the complex of conditions underlying the overvaluation of land is unfavorable to capital formation.

and the milieu within which it resides, both create income and augment the capacities of individuals to produce income.[10] Presumably, as an economy progresses, the relative amount of investment placed in social overhead capital (II.A.1.c) tends to rise.

Several observations may be made respecting each of these categories. Elements of direct overhead capital (II.A.1.a) contribute more immediately and directly to the augmentation of NNP and/or the increase of a nation's productive power than do most elements of social overhead capital (II.A.1.c) and many elements of economic overhead capital (II.A.1.b). Furthermore, direct overhead capital elements tend to be less lumpy than are some elements of economic and social overhead capital; hence the stock of direct overhead capital can be kept somewhat more nicely adjusted to the growth of NNP than can that of economic and social overhead capital, these often being built in advance of the time when they can be fully used (though their construction sometimes does not keep pace with NNP). Accordingly, when, in low-income countries, capital is scarce and the rate of discount is high, investment in direct overhead capital tends to be given preference over that in economic overhead capital, and investment in these may be given preference over investment in social overhead capital. Within a considerable range apparently the marginal efficiency of capital invested in direct overhead capital is considered to be higher than that of capital invested in economic and/or social overhead capital. Insofar as this is the case it probably has its origin in the fact that both the minimum required scale of investment and the minimum required degree of anticipation of the future are greater with respect to economic and social overhead capital than with respect to direct overhead capital, when each is treated as a whole.

Because of the conditions just noted, investment may tend to be carried less far, under private auspices, in elements in economic and social overhead capital than in elements in direct overhead capital. This tendency is further accentuated insofar as the marginal private benefits attendant upon investment in economic and social overhead capital tend to fall short of their marginal social benefits. This discrepancy has its origin in the fact that some elements included under economic and social overhead capital must be constructed long in advance of the time when they will be fully used, and that many elements in both categories produce beneficial effects for which investors in these elements are not remunerated. The discrepancy may be accentuated furthermore by the fact that investment in any one category of elements tends to increase the demand for, and the return to, elements included in the other two categories, since each category is essentially com-

10. As noted above some would be disposed to argue that investment in personal capital (e.g., education, health), so important in modern societies, might well be included in (II.A.1.b) since it affects output similarly. IBRD missions have fixed at between one-sixth and one-third investment in social overhead as compared with investment in economic overhead capital (Spengler 1954, p. 591).

plementary to the other two. Because of this discrepancy optimum resource use often requires that investment in some economic and social overhead capital elements be subsidized by the state or carried out directly by the state, since when this is not done investment in these categories tends to fall even more short of the optimum than does investment in direct overhead capital under conditions of the sort obtaining in advanced countries. In underdeveloped countries, as has been implied, the discrepancy between marginal private and marginal social benefit tends to be greater than in advanced countries, because of the comparative indivisibility of various forms of investment, because it is harder to achieve balanced growth, and because the international flow of goods and services consequent upon foreign investment in underdeveloped countries may not optimize welfare and capital-allocation therein.[11]

The state may intervene (e.g., the Russian state's favoritism of scientific and engineering education over other forms) to induce greater investment in the relatively more productive forms of wealth included in economic and social overhead capital, or otherwise plan investment. It is quite possible, however, that such investment will then be carried beyond the optimum level, particularly when the government in control of the apparatus of state is dependent upon the masses for political support. For central planners are not always likely to be better informed, or less immune to error, than are private investors. In practice discrepancy between marginal private and marginal social benefit, given suitable definition of the latter, can be reduced in some instances and in some degree, but it can rarely ever be removed entirely.

Implications of the preceding discussion may now be noted. (1) The tendency for the rate of growth of NNP per head to diminish, particularly if population continues to grow, is largely attributable to the fact that RW is imperfectly substitutable for NRW. This tendency will increase insofar as the substitutability of RW for NRW diminishes. (2) While the rate of growth of NNP per head may be augmented by converting into productive wealth resources that have been assuming unproductive form, the resulting gain is not likely to exceed that realizable from a 3-5 per cent capital formation rate. (3) The distinction of investment into that which is more immediately productive and that which, being in the form of economic or social overhead capital, is less immediately productive serves to direct attention to difficulties attendant upon securing an efficient allocation of capital resources among uses; but it envisages the allocation problem in essentially static

11. See Scitovsky (1954); Lerner (1953); Meade (1952). On the limitations to which the principle of balanced growth is subject, see Fleming (1955); and on weaknesses in Scitovsky's favorable assessment of centralized investment planning, see Stockfisch (1955). That the marginal rate of return on investment in the human agent appreciably exceeds that realized on nonhuman capital is suggested by Procter Thomson in his forthcoming *Educational Finance,* Ch. 2. That imbalance retards growth was noted already by Burns (1934, pp. 244ff.).

terms, thereby neglecting the population effect of investment. (4) What is really wanted, as will be seen, is investment that is revolutionary and culture-changing in effect — investment that operates to substitute modern for old social patterns and to dissipate the complex of institutions and values that make for high age-specific fertility; for only such investment is well suited to raise per capita income in underdeveloped countries.

II. Capital Requirements and the Extent of Natural-Resource Exploitation

Countries differ in respect of the pressure they are under to exploit their stock of natural resources or NRW. This pressure arises immediately from the increase of NNP, since the requirement of NRW tends to rise (though not necessarily in proportion) as NNP rises, and ultimately from the fact that the growth of NNP depends upon the increase of both population and output per head. Near one pole we encounter a somewhat developed country like Japan, overpopulated and with a considerable growth of population still in prospect, and suffering from extreme deficiencies in the domestic supply of food, fibers, wood, minerals for chemical manufacturing, metals, coking coal, and liquid fuels. Near the other pole we encounter a country like the United States, with an abundance of resources, with imports amounting to only 4–5 per cent of GNP, and with most of its raw materials of domestic provenience.[12] In Japan pressure upon resources arises principally from the comparative magnitude of the population; in the United States, where per capita consumption of raw materials exceeds 10 times that of the rest of the free world, pressure upon resources arises primarily from the comparative magnitude of per capita consumption. Even so the United States is not under nearly so great compulsion to exploit its domestic resources intensively as is Japan, whose situation fore-shadows that awaiting underdeveloped but heavily peopled countries when they become industrialized.

The full significance of pressure of numbers upon resources, or NRW, is not easy to gauge. Consider the United States. In 1950 the value of all raw materials consumed, exclusive of gold, approximated 12.8 per cent of GNP. The corresponding figures for agricultural raw materials were: foods, 6.7; nonfoods, 1.4; all, 8.1. Those for minerals, exclusive of gold, were 3.7, with mineral fuels approximating 2.5. Comparison of these proportions with those

12. See *Resources for Freedom* (PMPC 1952, I, pp. 59–62; II, pp. 176–84); Ackerman (1953). The United States, of course, is dependent upon foreign sources even for some strategically important materials. Recently the Economic Counsel Board of Japan (*The Mainichi*, 1954) estimated that by 1965 that country would have to increase its exports at least 100 per cent above the 1952 level. Even so Japanese exports might not run much above one-tenth of national income.

obtaining in 1900 indicate that, as a society progresses, aggregate raw-material consumption increases more rapidly than population but less rapidly than GNP, consumption per head having increased only about one-fifth in this 50-year interval. The input-cost of raw materials will rise more rapidly than the consumption of raw materials, of course, if, as is probable, the production and extraction of raw materials become relatively more difficult as time passes, depletion proceeds, and other limitational forces become operative.

Evidently a considerable increase in the input-cost of raw materials would affect GNP per head in much lesser measure. For example, with other conditions given, a 50 per cent increase in the cost of these materials would diminish per capita GNP only about 6 per cent; while, if the cost increase were confined to nonagricultural raw materials, GNP per head would decline only about 2 per cent. Of course, in economies in which a larger fraction of inputs was required to supply the requirement of agricultural and other raw materials, the impact upon GNP per head of a 50 per cent increase in raw-material costs would be greater; but it would still be relatively small. Presumably, therefore, and as a rule, it is not so much the comparative scarcity and costliness of raw materials that presently is of primary significance. It is rather the fact that, unless the requisite raw materials are to be had, it is not possible to establish and maintain certain industries and to bring into being the various industries ancillary to those in which availability of raw materials plays an important role.[13] In time, however, if the input-cost of raw materials continued to rise, further increases in their cost would increasingly retard income growth.

A country undergoing continuous population growth may respond by utilizing its equipment of natural resources more intensively, or, if it finds itself short of various resources, by having recourse to international trade and/or the development of domestic substitutes. The impact of continuing population growth tends to be obscured, however, when it is accompanied by changes in both industrial structure and degree of industrial progress. If a country, be its population resource ratio high or low, is relatively underdeveloped, it tends to be a net exporter of foodstuffs and/or raw materials and a net importer of manufactures, whereas, if it is developed, it tends to be a net importer of foodstuffs and raw materials and a net exporter of manufactures. As an underdeveloped country advances, and generally as a country's industrial structure changes, its import requirements change quantitatively and qualitatively, usually with the amount per head increasing. It may be said, therefore, that, given the stage of economic development of

13. The figures given here are derived from (PMPC 1952, II, p. 180). Data presented by W. S. and E. S. Woytinsky (1953, pp. 315, 394, 455, 756) suggest that the value of primary production approximates at least three-tenths of that of world output. The value of minerals approximates about one-fifth of all primary production; that of mineral fuel, about two-thirds of all mineral production.

countries under analysis, international differences in the composition and relative importance of their imports are attributable primarily to inequalities in the international distribution of resources. At the same time, given GNP per head, countries experiencing increases in population density find themselves more dependent than formerly upon external sources for foodstuffs and/or raw materials in short domestic supply (Hanson 1952; E. A. G. Robinson 1954; Schlote 1952, pp. 51–78; Woytinsky 1955, ch. 1, 3–4).

If a country is long on land and natural resources, it will be under less pressure to form capital (though perhaps more capable of doing so) than if it is short of land and natural resources (as, e.g., is Japan). When land and natural resources remain available for exploitation, there should be less need for capital (*ceteris paribus*), in that relatively large amounts of labor can be set to work in activities using much land and natural resources, and relatively little capital. The activities in question apparently include agriculture, mining, and certain other industries.[14] Insofar as the domestic market for the agricultural, mineral, etc., products of these activities is limited, the products may be exported. When, however, the domestic supply of these products is limited, there is less of them to exchange for capital and other imports. The magnitude of the volume of these imports (*ceteris paribus*) depends, of course, on the terms on which the exporting country supplies the produce, minerals, etc., and these terms will depend significantly upon the alternative-use value of its labor when devoted to the direct supply of goods and services for the home market (Lewis 1954, pp. 181–189; Scitovsky 1954; Kindleberger 1935; Myint 1954; G. M. Meier 1952).

The burden of our argument is that plentitude of land and natural resources eases the task of capital formation for a country, be it relatively developed or not, particularly when population is growing rapidly. Either the land and natural resources may be partly substituted for capital; or agricultural, mineral, and related products may be exchanged for capital and other essential imports. But there is a limit to this way of proceeding. Land and natural resources are substitutable for capital only within limits, and some forms of capital are complementary to land and/or natural resources. Accordingly, since substitutability is limited and since, in the absence of sufficient complementary capital, labor is not continuously combinable with land and natural resources, the labor force can be fully

14. In agriculture, real-estate improvements and equipment, expressed as a percentage of the value of land, approximated just over 30 in the United States in 1880 and 1922. The corresponding percentages in mining in 1880 and 1922 were 64 and 93; in manufacturing, 323 and 571; in steam railroads, 428 and 566; in a variety of industries 174 and 152 (Kuznets 1946, pp. 201–202, 213; 1952, pp. 118, 120, 122). According to Black (1936, p. 209), in the United States in 1930 the value of agricultural property other than land approximated seven-tenths of the value of agricultural land. D. G. Johnson (1948, p. 734) estimates the percentage of agricultural income imputable to land in 1910–46 at between 31.9 and 35.4; the share of capital at 7.5 per cent; and the share of labor at between 57.1 and 60.6 per cent.

employed only if there is a sufficiency of capital both to complement land and natural resources and to make possible in addition the employment of all workers not engaged in the exploitation of land and natural resources.[15] Accordingly, even when land and natural resources are abundant, considerable capital formation is needed. In terms of our earlier formulation, RW complementary to NRW and/or labor must be formed if unexploited land and natural resources and underemployed (or unemployed) labor are to be brought into use. But such capital formation is likely to be difficult in a country with low incomes, a low average propensity to form production assets, and comparative scarcity of land and natural resources.

III. Capital Shortage, Capital Use, and Capital Formation

When, because NRW per head is low and the stock of RW has not been augmented sufficiently to offset the shortage of NRW, the ratio of a society's wealth to its population is low, this situation may be ameliorated by increasing the rate of capital formation, by avoiding the transformation of productive agents into unproductive assets, and by using with economy the stock of productive assets and the increments thereto.

In 1949 estimated savings rates in underdeveloped countries are said to have ranged, when calculated for large areas, between 3 and 6 per cent of national income in Asia (exclusive of Japan) and Africa, and to have averaged about 8 per cent in Latin America.[16] The reports on savings rates in many of these countries agree in stating these rates to be appreciably below 10 per cent of national income.[17] While recent reports for Asia do not indicate substantial improvement in savings rates, those for Latin America (which, with the partial exception of Middle America, is free of the population pressure characteristic of Asia and the Middle East) indicate considerable saving and a 2.5 per cent per year growth of GNP per capita in various countries in 1935–51. Unfortunately, information is not supplied respecting the capacity of these underdeveloped countries to form both productive and unproductive assets, and so it is not determinable if, as many believe, their asset-forming power is nearly as high, when compared with income,

15. This amounts to a partial denial of the nineteenth-century version of Say's Law, the validity of which depended in part upon there being in an economy a sufficient degree of substitutability between any one category of productive agents and some other category (Fukuoka 1955; Eckaus 1955; cp. Fellner 1951).

16. See UN (1951, pp. 35, 76). In his review of this work Bauer (1953, esp. pp. 217–219) implies that the above estimates may somewhat understate actual savings rates.

17. See UN (ECAFE) (1951, pp. 9–11); Clark (1952, pp. 5–6). But see note 18 below, on Latin America; and also *The Eastern Economist,* where investment in India in 1953–54 is put at somewhat above 7 per cent of national income, or below an estimated maximum of 8–9 per cent (*New York Times*).

as that found in developed countries (UN [ECAFE] 1954; UN [ECLA] 1954, pp. 31–32).[18]

The task confronting many underdeveloped countries is that of pushing up the rate at which productive wealth is formed from around 5 to 10–15 per cent of national income. This task confronted present-day developed countries when they were underdeveloped, and they apparently accomplished it as a result of a number of changes (e.g., the disposition to save became stronger; a rising rate of growth may have re-enforced itself; income became more unevenly distributed, particularly as a result of the profit-increasing post-1500 price revolution; the recipients of "surplus value" devoted an increasing fraction of it to capital formation; resources were diverted from forming unproductive to forming productive assets; with the rise of the national state at least some members of the ruling classes came increasingly to look upon capital formation as advantageous) which were not offset by increases in population growth.[19] For, as is shown later, a savings rate of 4–5 per cent is too low to permit much if any economic growth per head when population is growing appreciably.[20] If, however, the required increase in saving can temporarily be achieved, and if there is

18. According to UN (ECLA) (1953, pp. 24–28), gross investment (exclusive of working capital) in 1946–52 was 16.5 per cent of GNP, with 11.1 of the 16.5 representing net investment. Accordingly, the rate of capital formation exceeded 11 (and even 12) per cent of national income. Gross investment expressed as a percentage of GNP exceeded 20 in Venezuela and Peru in 1945–52; the corresponding rate for Argentina approximated 17; that for Brazil, 15; those for other countries, 10–14. In 1952–53 what amount to similar rates (but adjusted for foreign-trade balance) approximated 17 and 21 in the United States and Canada, and 26, 23, and 15 in the Soviet Union, Poland, and East Germany; they ranged between 2 and 30 in Free Europe, with a median value of 20 (JCER 1955, p. 16). In the United States, Net Capital Formation/GNP was 0.6 of Gross Capital Formation/GNP in 1869–98, 0.68 in 1894–1923, and 0.38 in 1919–48 (Kuznets 1952, p. 155).

19. Phyllis Deane (1955, pp. 8–10) believes that gross capital formation somewhat exceeded the 4–5 per cent of gross domestic product suggested by Gregory King's figures for England and Wales in 1688. Domestic Net Capital Formation expressed as a percentage of NNP approximated 13.7 in the United States in 1869–1908; just over 8 in the United Kingdom in 1870–1913; under 3.5 in Sweden in 1861–70 and just under 7 in 1871–90; just over 10 in Denmark in 1870–1909; 8.3, 4.6, and 5.6 in France in 1853–78, 1878–1903, 1903–11; about 14 (exclusive of inventory change) in Canada in 1901–30. Thus only in Sweden do we find a rate below 5 (Kuznets 1955; Hoselitz 1955). On effects of price revolution, see Hamilton (1952). In a forthcoming study of the consumption function Milton Friedman questions the unqualified proposition that increases in inequality tend to augment the average propensity of a people to save. He speculates that this effect is associated, not with increases in inequality that are permanent, but with increases that, having their origin in transitory factors, are likely to be impermanent. It is increases of the latter sort that may issue out of economic development and associated increases in interclass mobility.

20. There must, of course, be a sufficient supply of finance to facilitate the distribution of savings since, irrespective of actual and potential savings rates, savings or resources cannot be effectively utilized by entrepreneurs unless they can obtain sufficient credit (Robinson 1952, pp. 80–87). Finance appears to be in much shorter supply, other conditions being given, in underdeveloped than in developed countries, with the result that the national asset structures of the former are less liquid than those of the latter. The ratio of bank assets to GNP is much higher in developed than in underdeveloped countries (Spengler 1954, note, p. 593). Furthermore, as Goldsmith (1955a) finds, the ratio of intangible to tangible assets tends to rise with

a sufficiency of natural resources (or ready access thereto), it is quite possible for a self-sustaining growth process to get under way and in time perhaps bring about a reduction in natality and natural increase. This process would be re-enforced if real depreciation and obsolescence absorbed a diminished fraction of gross capital formation, in consequence of an increase (within limits) in the life of durable goods, or of a movement (occasioned perhaps by an increase in the rate of growth of the labor force) of the rate of growth of NNP to a higher level; for then the ratio of net to gross capital formation would rise.[21]

Many of the densely populated underdeveloped countries of today must carry on capital formation under less favorable conditions than prevailed in the developing countries of the late eighteenth and early nineteenth centuries. First, in many contemporary underdeveloped countries, population, though already pressing much harder upon cultivable land and natural resources than it did in England and Western Europe 100–200 years ago, is growing much more rapidly today as a result of modern death control, and per capita incomes are much lower.[22] Second, in democracies the influence of the masses is much greater today than it was in the early nineteenth century, with the result that consumption is more stressed than formerly, that wages are often too high to permit as much employment as might be had, that capital formation is retarded, that relatively large fractions of capital increments consist of residential construction and overhead capital, and that in general the influence of interest rates upon the allocation of capital among uses is diminished.[23]

---

economic development. Accordingly, "liquidity preference" must be satisfied in part in underdeveloped countries by investment in readily saleable tangible assets such as jewelry.

21. The converse holds true also (Kuznets 1955; Domar 1953, pp. 1–32). Kuznets remarks that the ratio of net to gross capital formation may be lower in underdeveloped than in advanced countries because durable capital constitutes a smaller fraction of all capital in the former. Clark (1952, Nos. 2–3, pp. 2, 8, Nos. 4–6, pp. 4–6) suggests "that a country must be able to accumulate a capital stock of over 1,000 O.U. (i.e., Oriental Units) per head of population before it can begin to industrialise, but beyond that point its progress may be fairly steady per head." This figure implies a per capita income of perhaps 250 O.U. per year. Output per head approximated 191 O.U. in India in 1948–49, 322 in Japan in 1919, and 513 in Italy in 1914. Clark's figure is merely an indication of order of magnitude. See Section V in text.

22. According to Deane (1955) per capita income increased by something like one per cent per annum between 1688 and 1770 in England and Wales at which time population was increasing only about ¼ per cent per year (population increased just over 1 per cent per year in 1760–1860). Kuznets (1954b) estimates that per capita incomes in many underdeveloped countries of today are "from about one-sixth to one-third of the per capita incomes of the developed countries a century ago."

23. How great are the ill effects of basing capital allocation upon interest rates (actual or implied) which do not reflect the marginal rate of substitution between capital and other factors of production depends upon the circumstances surrounding the use of capital. The effects are greater on capital-use than on capital-supply, however, since the interest rate is much more important as an index of capital scarcity than as a determinant of the amount of saving. On the Russian experience see Grossman (1953). On the wage question see Rottenberg (1953); Bauer (1953, pp. 211–212). On forces supposedly making for an increase in the propensity to con-

Because of difficulties attendant upon increasing the domestic rate of capital formation in underdeveloped countries, several methods have been suggested for increasing it. (1) So long as there exists a large industrial reserve army of unemployed and underemployed persons in the agricultural and other sectors, labor will be available under conditions of high elasticity of supply, with the result that "surplus value" may for a time increase nearly as rapidly as the nonagricultural labor force and that much of this increase can be appropriated and added to the nation's stock of wealth (Lewis 1954, pp. 140–160, 171–176; Nurkse 1953, pp. 36–47; cp. Rao 1952; Navarrette 1952). (2) Resources may be forcibly diverted to developmental investment from the formation of unproductive assets, from the consumption of those whose consumption can be diminished, and from output that might otherwise be transferred abroad.[24] (3) Recourse to forced-savings-generating inflation has been recommended by some.[25]

Respecting foreign lending there is controversy concerning the amount that can be utilized. It is argued that, since an underdeveloped country may require more economic-overhead and other forms of capital to get off dead center than it can supply out of domestic savings, it must fall back upon foreign loans, sometimes to such an extent that foreign investment approximates and even exceeds domestic investment (Singer 1952, esp. pp. 10–18; Derksen 1952, pp. 108ff.; UN 1951, pp. 76, 79–80). But it is also pointed out that the amount of foreign capital available is relatively small, that internal limits may exist to the volume that can be gotten and effectively utilized, and that external conditions may set a ceiling to the net influx of foreign capital. Two sets of internal circumstances (among others) may limit how much foreign capital is to be had and used effectively: (a) the extent to which political and social conditions are favorable (unfavorable) to foreign investment, given a country's economic potential; and (b) the degree to which domestic productive factors (e.g., domestic capital, labor of appropriate skill, land, natural resources) are available for combination with foreign capital in enterprises involving the joint use of imported and domestically

---

sume (forces which are intensified in low-income countries by international media of communication) see Duesenberry (1949, pp. 25–28); Nurkse (1953, Ch. 3); Jewkes (1951, pp. 11–13). Milton Friedman (see note 19 above) casts doubt upon the "demonstration effect" thesis, that the low propensities to save supposedly found in underdeveloped countries have their origin in the examples of absolutely high levels of consumption provided by high-income countries. See also Bruton (1955, pp. 329–330). For an example of a high propensity to consume that was not even reduced by a redistribution of income in favor of profits and against wages see Sturmthal (1955).

24. See Bronfenbrenner (1955), and on rates of capital formation found in Eastern and Western Europe respectively, UN (1953, pp. 24, 47–48, 68–69).

25. Inflation has often accompanied sustained development. On the possible effects of inflation see Lewis (1954, pp. 160–167); Axilrod (1954, pp. 334–338); Rao (1953); Bronfenbrenner (1953, pp. 209–218); Pazos (1953); Wallich (1951, esp. pp. 26–30); Nurkse (1953, pp. 111–114, 117, 144–145). On the effect of inflation on real depreciation and capital formation, see Domar (1953, pp. 10, 23).

supplied agents of production. An external limit arises from the fact that the annual increment of gross foreign investment in a country must exceed the sum which that country is required to pay abroad each year in the form of interest and amortization charges on cumulated foreign investment. This limit is roughly set, therefore, by the rate at which foreign gross investment can grow, which depends in turn on the changing composition of GNP and on the rate of growth of GNP in the countries whence the foreign investment flows. Conditions (a) and (b) are susceptible of improvement by capital-seeking underdeveloped countries, particularly when these countries are assisted by foreign investors bent on increasing the supply of complementary domestic agents of production (e.g., skills of the labor force, complementary entrepreneurship, the flow of utilizable domestic resources, etc.). Improvement of these conditions may even raise somewhat the financial limit arising from the growth of loan-service charges, since, given the rate of growth of GNP found in foreign-lending countries, these countries will be more disposed to increase their foreign lending when conditions (a) and (b) are favorable than when they are unfavorable. In the past, however, with few and transitory exceptions, foreign countries have furnished but a small fraction of total investment in underdeveloped countries, though they have provided considerable "human capital" in the form of immigrants. Moreover, of the foreign investments made outside of Europe, nearly all have been made in lands where population was relatively sparse and relatively skilled immigrants were disposed to settle, and where exploitable natural resources were relatively abundant. Furthermore, a new difficulty may be encountered: the course of technical progress in a capital-exporting country like the United States may so affect the composition of its GNP as to slow down the growth of its demand for foreign exports and therewith reduce its disposition to invest abroad.[26]

Having found that wealth per head is low in underdeveloped countries, and not easily augmentable out of domestic savings and foreign borrowings, we turn to the problem that is intensified, namely, optimizing the distribution of a nation's wealth and its increment among the actual and potential uses

26. See on this last point Balogh (1954, pp. 243–84, esp. pp. 268ff.); Leontief (1953a, pp. 332–349). Hicks (1953, pp. 128ff.) implies that foreign investment is strongly attracted to export-biased economies, of which Canada was an example in 1900–1913 when it attracted nearly as much investment from abroad as it provided from savings at home (Cairncross 1953, Ch. 3, pp. 41–42). When an economy is export-biased, of course, its structure is somewhat complementary to the structures of economies importing its products. Data on foreign investment are given by Kuznets (1955). Data presented by Clark (1951, pp. 512–513) indicate that foreign investment per head of occupied population is generally very much lower in densely populated countries with resources available for exploitation. See also Buchanan and Ellis (1955, Ch. 14–17); Nurkse (1955, Ch. 4, 6; and 1954, pp. 744–758). The balance-of-payments problem of an underdeveloped country is the inverse of that of a developed, capital-exporting country (Domar 1950, pp. 805–826). Bruton (1955, pp. 330–335) shows, among other things, how an underdeveloped country must alter its technology and its consumption pattern in order to free itself eventually of dependence on foreign capital.

to which wealth may be put. Capital, being scarce, must be rationed by price or other systems in both developed and underdeveloped economies. But since capital is relatively more scarce, compared with other productive agents, in underdeveloped than in developed economies, mistakes in capital rationing in underdeveloped economies are more likely to be serious, or to be difficult to remedy, than are mistakes in capital rationing in developed economies.

Two aspects of capital rationing are of especial relevance for economic growth. (1) As was noted in (ii) in Part I above, growth may be fostered by diverting to economic development the maximum possible fraction of a nation's stock of unproductively used wealth, or at least as much as is compatible with acceptable and maintainable criteria of welfare.[27] (2) Growth is fostered also when optimum use is made of the wealth available for economic development. This involves curtailing the relative amount utilized as social overhead capital (see [iii] in Part I above) and carefully allocating the balance among directly productive and economic-overhead activities. It may also entail so locating new industry and wage jobs as to minimize outlays upon social overhead capital whilst avoiding consequent increases in outlays upon directly productive and economic overhead capital. As A. Lowe (1955) indicates, however, the physical-technical structure of economic systems is often such as to limit greatly investment in low-capital-output activities at the expense of high-capital-output activities.[28]

When, as in nineteenth-century Western countries and in some contemporary totalitarian societies, the influence of the masses is less powerful than in present-day democracies, investment in social overhead capital tends to lag behind both that in directly productive capital and that in economic overhead capital which gives great promise of facilitating economic development. In time, however, as wealth per head increases and consumer sovereignty and freedom of choice become more powerful, investment in social overhead capital tends to rise. In the United States the fraction of all RW invested in business and agriculture declined from somewhat in excess of seven-tenths in 1850 and 1890 to just over two-fifths in 1939 and 1948. Meanwhile the fraction invested in consumer durables, government wealth, and non-farm residences increased about one-third. Industrial investment

27. What is possible depends on technological, economic, political, and social conditions, and on the nature and flexibility of a country's economic structure. What is compatible with welfare criteria depends upon the indices of welfare by which developmental policy is guided and by the willingness of the population (voluntarily or under such duress as the ruling elite can exercise) to sustain the austerity of living conditions, the hardships, and the costs which continuance of a high rate of development necessarily imposes on most of the population of an underdeveloped country. Cp. Bronfenbrenner (1953, Part I, pp. 93–104).

28. See papers by Lowe (1955) and Grossman (1955). In the United States in 1920–45, urban development absorbed 23.6 per cent of capital goods expenditures, and in the 1920's over 30 per cent, nearly all of this being for housing and social overhead capital (Hartley 1950, pp. 12–15).

seems to have bulked large in early nineteenth-century Britain, with outlays upon transportation, town-building, and foreign investment subsequently becoming dominant; in 1870–1914 expenditure upon housing approximated when it did not exceed that upon railways and machinery, averaging about one-fifth of home investment and (in 1907) about three-fifths of all building. By contrast, during Mexico's income-increasing boom, 1939–1950, building of all kinds comprised but 20.4 per cent of gross domestic investment.[29]

When the ratio of productive wealth to the labor force is low, as in underdeveloped countries, it is arithmetically necessary that this wealth be concentrated in industries in which the capital-labor ratio is low. If we represent by R the ratio of a country's stock of capital (or productive wealth) to its labor force, and by $r_1, r_2, \ldots, r_n$ the capital-labor ratios found in the n industries composing that country's economy, it follows that the weighted average of these r's must approximate the value of R, the latter value imposing a restraint upon a country's industrial mix. It is inescapable, accordingly, that the bulk of an underdeveloped country's labor force be engaged in activities in which the typical r-value is low, given the production coefficients in effect in that country. Accordingly, when lists are compiled of industries supposedly well-suited for introduction and/or expansion in underdeveloped countries, one finds on these lists, beside industries which require relatively little skilled labor, which are small scale, and which (when they are not oriented to raw materials) are scattered rather than concentrated in space, industries in which fixed capital per worker and machinery and equipment per worker are relatively low. When these characteristics are intercorrelated, as happens within limits, choice is easy, but when some characteristics of an industry make it suitable for establishment in an underdeveloped country whereas other characteristics do not, choice is less easy.[30]

It does not follow, of course, that all r-values must be kept in the neighborhood of R, even though the selection of some r-values in excess of R necessitates the selection of other r-values below R. Considerable investment in transportation and public utilities is necessary even though in these industries the capital-labor ratio is high and the ratio of fixed capital to output may be three or more times that obtaining in the economy as a whole (Kuznets

29. See Goldsmith's (1952, pp. 306–307) estimates and Kuznets' (1952, p. 118) estimate that residential fixed capital in the United States comprised close to one-fourth of all fixed capital in 1880–1922. Concerning Britain see Cairncross (1953, pp. 5–6, 123, 167, 169, 203). See also Bank (1953, p. 190); Gayer (1953); Clark (1951, pp. 486–494). Nearly half the funds made available to British colonial governments for financing development in 1955–60 are for social overhead capital and related expenditures (*The Times*).

30. For lists of industries suitable for establishment in underdeveloped countries see Lewis (1950). See also Bhatt (1954a, pp. 1251ff.); Bohr (1954, pp. 157–166); Bhatt (1954b); Grosse (1955, p. 305); Leontief (1953b). In the United States in 1949 capital invested per production worker in manufacturing ranged between $83,286 in petroleum and coal products and $3,149 in apparel and products made from fabrics; the average for manufacturing was $9,429 (NICB 1954, p. 316; also Bliss 1939, Ch. 3).

1952, p. 122).[31] If resource conditions warrant, investment in mining is indicated even when the capital-product ratio is relatively high.[32] Of greater importance is the fact that investment usually is indicated in the most advanced technologies and in modes of industrialization entailing the use of fully or almost fully automatic facilities instead of in traditional combinations of capital, skilled operators, and semi-skilled laborers. For then, even though capital investment per worker is high, the ratio of workers and capital to output is relatively low, and there is brought into being a much greater surplus above costs out of which additions can be made to the nation's stock of capital. Sometimes, too, if automation can be carried on outside large cities, heavy investment in urban development can be avoided or postponed and the formation of industrial capital can be further facilitated in consequence. For the time being, until modernization and capital accumulation have proceeded far enough, those who cannot find employment in the technologically advanced sectors of the economy must find it in sectors where the capital-labor ratio is low, or through recourse to more intensive use of advanced forms of capital (e.g., several shifts a day). In the past countries undergoing industrialization have usually introduced the most advanced technologies, in part perhaps because a country just embarking upon industrialization is relatively free of the obsolescence and other costs incident to technological change in advanced countries (Gerschenkron 1952, pp. 5–9; Frankel 1955; R. L. Meier 1954).

Respecting the allocation of capital in capital-poor underdeveloped countries, the following conclusions appear valid. (1) Since economic overhead capital often is of strategic importance, investment therein frequently cannot be greatly restricted even though a nation's stock of capital and current savings are small. (2) The influence of the masses, when not held in check, intensifies the demand for social overhead capital, and this demand is reenforced by the fact that it is usually supplied under governmental auspices. (3) When foreign exchange is in short supply, the formation of low-import-content capital (e.g., building) tends to be favored, and exchange tends to be used to purchase imports important for economic development. (4) It is essential, though not always easy, to emphasize types of investment which make for increasing returns. (5) A capital-short society is compelled to favor many activities marked by relatively low capital-labor and capital-product ratios. (6) High capital-product-ratio investments are indicated, however, when shortages of strategically necessary economic overhead capital must be made up, or when technologically advanced methods entailing relatively

31. In the United States about three-tenths of fixed capital has been invested in transportation and public utilities (Kuznets 1952, p. 118).

32. Actually, Kuznets found in 1879–1928 the ratio in mining averaged higher than that in manufacturing, but lower than that in the other main industrial categories. See his unpublished paper, "Capital-Product Ratio and Technological Change."

high ratios are superior, from the standpoint of the whole economy, to less advanced methods. (7) Given that acceleration of the rate of growth of NNP is sought, investment in directly productive capital and in strategical forms of economic overhead capital should be emphasized whilst that in social overhead capital should be carefully rationed.

IV. Population Growth, Income Growth, and Capital Growth

Having considered problems associated with the supply and allocation of capital or productive wealth, we shall examine the effects of population growth upon the aggregate of capital requirements.[33] A nation's capital requirements may be estimated in two ways: (1) by determining how much capital is required to equip a representative worker, newly added to the non-rural labor force by natural growth or by urbanward migration, and how much additional wealth is required for residential and other purposes and for rural improvement;[34] (2) by making use of the relationship obtaining between wealth and income. It is this relationship, together with the effects of population growth upon it, that will now be considered.

Let us call the average propensity to form capital a; the ratio of a nation's national income (or NNP) to its wealth, s; the annual percentage rate of population growth, p; per capita income, y; and the average annual rate of growth of y, y'. Let us assume, furthermore, that a and s are constant, and that their values are independent of p. Then $g = as$; or, to illustrate, if a approximates 0.1 in value and s approximates 0.2 in value, g will approximate 0.02, or 2 per cent per year. The value of y', under these circumstances, will be $(1 + g)/(1 + p)$; or, if p approximates 1 per cent per year when g has a value of 2 per cent, y' will approximate 1 per cent per year. Furthermore, if we are given a value for s, we can easily determine the value a must assume, if a given rate p of population growth is not to result in a fall in per

33. It is not our purpose to examine the incidence of particular manifestations of population growth (e.g., increments in labor force, in total population, or in number of households; changes in age composition; shifts in population from rural to urban situations) upon the demand for particular kinds of wealth, or to note what kinds of wealth tend to be formed in advance of population growth, and what kinds after growth has taken place. Empirical data confirm the expectation that, since the volume of savings is augmentable at any time only up to a point, when an increase in the incremental rate of population growth takes place, and with it an increase in population-sensitive capital requirements (e.g., residential construction, transport capital), there is relatively less capital formed to serve other needs. See forthcoming study by Simon Kuznets and Dorothy S. Thomas (Hope T. Eldridge and Dorothy Swain Thomas, with introduction by Kuznets, *Population Redistribution and Economic Growth: United States 1870–1950.* American Philosophical Society, Philadelphia, 1964).

34. In the United States in recent decades about three-tenths of the nation's RW has been required for residential purposes; the fraction invested in agriculture and nonagricultural business was close to five-tenths in 1890 and to four-tenths in 1939. See Goldsmith's (1952, p. 307) estimate. For estimates of capital requirements based on requirements per worker see UN (1951, pp. 77ff.).

capita income y, for the value of a must approximate $p(1/s)$. Thus if population grows at an annual rate of $p = 2$ per cent per year, and s has a value of 0.2, a must approximate 10 per cent, since otherwise per capita income y would decline. If it is desired, furthermore, that per capita income grow at a rate y' per year, the value of a must approximate $(1/s)\,(p + y')$.[35] Thus, if population is growing 1 per cent per year, and it is desired that per capita income increase 1.5 per cent per year, the proportion of the annual income that must be saved and invested is 12.5 per cent when the value of s is 0.2.

The figures we have presented throw some light on why per capita income could rise in pre-industrial European countries such as England even though the rate of capital formation was low. We noted earlier that in England between 1688 and 1770 per capita income may have increased by something like one per cent per year even though the gross saving rate probably was not much above 5 per cent of GNP. Had s a value of 0.2 in England at that time, a 5 per cent saving rate might have been adequate to permit an annual increase of 1 per cent per capita income in the absence of any population growth. During this period, however, population was growing very slowly, only about $\frac{1}{4}$ per cent per year. The then low rate of saving permitted an increase in per capita income only because the rate of population growth was so low and nearly all the capital formed could be used to increase per capita income. Had population grown one per cent per year as in the century succeeding 1760, the then low rate of capital formation could have permitted very little increase in per capita income.

On the assumptions we have been making, it will be difficult for the more densely populated underdeveloped countries to increase per capita income rapidly. For, because of the spread of Western methods of death control to underdeveloped countries, some densely populated and some not so densely populated, mortality has fallen remarkably while natality has remained very high; as a result natural increase often equals 3 per cent per year, a rate higher than prevailed in the United States in 1800–1860. If we put their typical rate of population growth at 2–3 per cent per year and assume s has a value of 0.2, a saving rate of something like 10–15 per cent per year is required if per capita income is not to decline. If it be desired that y (per capita income) is not to decline, but rather to increase 1.5 per cent per year, with population growing 2 per cent per year, a saving rate or a value of something like 22.5 per cent is indicated. When the value of a is so low as barely to prevent a decline in per capita income, given the prevailing rate of population growth, and when in addition there is much pressure upon the central authorities to take steps to increase per capita income, the adoption of inflationary policies is likely. Such policies eventuate when, intentionally or otherwise, the central authorities, lacking access to a suffi-

35. Expressed more accurately, the required value of a is $(1/s)\,[(1+p)\,(1+y) - 1]$. For refined accounts see Domar (1946); Koo (1955, pp. 47–62); also Spengler (1951).

ciency of voluntary savings, have recourse to the credit- or money-creating powers of the banking system.

Let us consider now what values a and s have assumed in various countries. The value of a appears to have ranged between zero and perhaps as high as one-fifth, with rates usually falling within a 10-15 per cent range in late-nineteenth-century Western Europe and the United States. Population growth tends to reduce the value of a, since it absorbs resources, a portion of which might otherwise have assumed the form of capital; but the effect of such growth is diminished when a large proportion of a nation's savings is supplied by high-income receivers and collective bodies (especially corporations).[36] The value of s depends upon what is included under "wealth," being much higher when only RW and NRW are included, and higher still when only fixed capital is included. Presumably, all wealth should be included, since when consumers are sovereign and free, a nation does not devote all of its RW and NRW to activities whence flows income as defined in income estimates. In the past half century or more s has taken a value of around 0.2 in the United States when all wealth is included, and a value of 0.17 to 0.25 in other countries (Goldsmith 1951; and 1952, pp. 298-302).[37] Other conditions being given, the value of s should be higher if only RW is included in the category of wealth compared with the category of income, and income imputable to NRW is not excluded from this category. This expectation is borne out in that the value of s in Australia, Canada, and the United States—usually within the range 0.3 to 0.33—has been higher than that found in Britain, France, Germany, and the Netherlands—usually 0.15 to 0.22; it is also borne out in that the ratio fell in Britain and France in the 60 years preceding 1913 (Clark 1951, ch. 11; Kuznets 1952, p. 82; Kuznets 1954a).

The average value of s is not constant, its marginal value sometimes rising above and sometimes falling below its average value. It rises (falls) in consequence of forces which increase (decrease) income more than wealth. Among the forces (other than population growth) which increase s are the following: increase in the number of hours per year capital equipment is

36. A very detailed account of the sources of savings in the United States, together with annual estimates for 1897-1949, is given by Goldsmith (1955b). The impact of increase in family size upon family savings is discussed by Brady (1955) and by Henderson (1950, pp. 267-298).

37. Kuznets (1952, p. 82) gives s a value of slightly below 0.18 for the United States, 1879-1944; and the Royal Commission on Population (1950, par. 182), one of 0.24 for pre-war Great Britain. At the 1951 meeting of the International Association for Research in Income and Wealth, F. Coppola d'Anna's estimates for Italy, 1860-1938, give values ranging between 0.2 and 0.17 for the ratio of national income to all private wealth; and P. Jostock's estimates indicate that national income in Germany and wealth in Saxony grew at the same rate in 1886-1911. Clark's (1940, p. 389) figures for 1913 indicate ratios of capital (exclusive of land and national debt) to national income, ranging from 3.5 in Austria to 5.85 in Argentina. Clark (1951, p. 503) also estimates the capital-income ratio to range from 4.73 in moderately low-income countries to 3.0 in high-income countries.

worked; increase in the intensity with which NRW and economic and social overhead capital (built in advance of its full use) are employed;[38] increase in output attributable to increase in the rate of technological progress and the operation of the law of increasing return; increase in the relative importance of industries with low capital-output ratios;[39] decrease in the average life of the goods and services composing GNP (Goldsmith 1952, pp. 293, 298–99, 302–303); and decrease in the rate of capital formation. Also included among these forces are increases in the proportion of wealth that is used to produce income—increases, that is, in the ratio of productive to unproductive assets, and (probably) in the ratio of directly productive and economic overhead capital to social overhead capital (see Section I, iii). Forces of a sort opposite to those enumerated make for a decrease in s.

The level of population growth was not included among the forces treated in the preceding paragraph, nor was it indicated whether s-increasing or s-decreasing forces tend to be dominant. An increase (decrease) in the rate of growth of the labor force serves to increase (decrease) s. To illustrate: suppose that, given constant returns and the current capital-labor ratio, the ratio of capital to income is 4 to 1, and the marginal productivities of the incremental units of capital and labor are 0.3 and 0.7, respectively. Then, if both the stock of capital and the labor force increase 1 per cent, income will increase 1 per cent, income per worker will be unaffected, and the capital-labor ratio will be unchanged at 4 : 1, with the value of s continuing at 0.25. If the labor force grew more than 1 per cent, the value of s would rise above 0.25. Now suppose that population remains constant, while capital is increased 1 per cent by the 4 per cent saving rate. The 1 per cent increase in capital is accompanied by a 0.3 per cent increase in income; but no increase in income is traceable to an increment in the labor force, since this force has remained constant. The resulting capital-income ratio then becomes 4.04 : 1.003, and the value of s becomes 0.248. In sum, with population constant, the value of s will remain constant only if other income-increasing forces become powerful enough to offset the failure of the labor force to increase (e.g., if the rate of capital formation approximated 13 in-

38. The ratio of fixed capital to output fell by more than half in transportation and public utilities in the United States in 1880–1938. In Surinam a drop of about one-sixth in the capital-output ratio was forecast while in Mexico in 1940–50 the ratio reportedly approximated 2.11 : 1 (IBRD 1953, p. 204; 1952, pp. 28–29; Bhatt 1954a, pp. 317–319). A spurious rise in s may be noted when, as a country undergoes development, an increasing amount of its economic activities becomes commercialized. For income gotten from such activities is better recorded than income gotten from noncommercialized or subsistence activities, with the result that the progress of commercialization introduces an upward bias in income estimates.

39. Kuznets (1952, pp. 127–128) estimates that inter-industry shifts accounted almost wholly for the rise in the ratio of fixed capital to NNP between the 1870–80's and the end of the 1910's in the United States. The "rise in the intra-industry ratios in agriculture and the mining-manufacturing sectors was largely offset by the decline in the ratio in the transportation and the public utility sector." Cp. also Goldsmith's (1952, pp. 296ff.) data. Concerning the possible role of innovation see Weber (1954, esp. pp. 112–116).

stead of 4 per cent). It is to be expected, therefore, that (*ceteris paribus*) as a country developed and the relative importance of land (NRW) declined, the ratio of income to RW would fall.[40]

Let us suppose, in view of what has been said, that savings in the amount of 4–5 per cent per year of national income are necessary to counterbalance a 1 per cent per year rate of population growth, or to make possible a 1 per cent per year rate of income growth. Then a saving rate of 8–10 per cent is required to enable a population to grow 1 per cent per year and at the same time experience an increase of 1 per cent per year in per capita income. If each of these growth rates is doubled, the required saving rate becomes 16–20 per cent per year. These required rates — essentially rough orders of magnitude — might prove too high, given a rapid introduction into an under-developed country of advanced methods used abroad, given that capital-output ratios in industries using the new methods are not unduly high, and given that countervailing forces (e.g., rising rate of capital formation; pro-longation of average life of output) are not operative. If, however, NRW is in full and intensive use, or if much of the annual increment in assets is used unproductively, the required rate of saving may have to be higher than those given above.

V. Capital Formation, Income Growth, and Population Growth

While an increase in the rate at which a society forms capital may tem-porarily divert resources from the formation of population, it will increase that society's population capacity in the longer run, *ceteris paribus,* and it may cause that society's population to be larger than it would have been in the absence of the supposed increase in its rate of capital formation.

An increase in a society's rate of capital formation will augment its popu-lation capacity, since population growth depends (*ceteris paribus*) upon the growth of NNP, and NNP is greater, other things equal, when a society's stock of income-producing wealth is greater. But the extent to which an increase in a society's population capacity is accompanied by an increase in population turns on the manner in which other things cease to be equal. For the aspirations of the bulk of the population tend to change, particularly when heavy investment transforms the socio-economic system; when many individuals find themselves shifted into new social milieux, some of which at least are relatively unfavorable to procreation; and when still others find

40. Clark (1951, p. 503) suggests, however, that the ratio of RW to national income tends to rise, in the early stage of a country's development, from 4.27 to 4.73, and thereafter to decline to and below 3. Concerning the technological and other factors that have tended to make for the constancy of *s* see Bruton (1955, pp. 325–328).

themselves within the grasp of new consumption patterns that may or may not conduce to reproduction.

Given an increase in a society's rate of capital formation and in its population capacity, the demographic response of its members will turn principally on whether the quantity and the quality of their aspirations change, on how they change, and on their expectations respecting their capacity to realize old and newly acquired aspirations. Aspirations being given, whatever increases the expectation that these will be more fully realized must operate temporarily to augment the longer-run rate of population growth; for, population being temporarily elastic to an increase in income consequent upon an increase in a society's capital stock, such increase must elicit some population growth. Capacity and expectations being given, whatever increases (decreases) the overall quantity of these aspirations, their composition remaining unchanged, operates to reduce (increase) the long-run rate of population growth; and whatever decreases (increases) the relative importance of procreation-favoring aspirations, the quantity of aspirations remaining unchanged, operates to decrease (increase) the long-run rate of population growth. Finally, capacity and expectations being given, the rate of population growth varies with the quality or composition of prevailing aspirations, since these may be more or less favorable to fertility and life expectancy. Should the shock attendant on the maintenance, for a few years, of a very heavy rate of investment sufficiently increase the quantity and/or appropriately modify the quality of a people's aspirations, their number would not increase as much as it would have increased given a lower rate of investment and a smaller increase in economic capacity.

Expectations respecting capacity to realize aspirations may affect, as well as be affected by, aspirations. Improved expectations tend to generate (especially when realized) increases in aspirations, particularly when the increment in capacity is of a form (e.g., some consumers' durables) with which imperfectly anticipated complementary wants are associated, or of a kind with which an increase in security against old age is correlated. With an increment in aspirations favorable to procreation, an increment or a decrement in the favorableness of expectations respecting capacity may be associated, though a decrement is likely to be encountered when incomes are very low. With an increment in aspirations neutral or unfavorable to procreation, an increment in the favorableness of expectations respecting capacity is likely to be correlated. The interrelations that actually obtain vary with culture; they must be determined empirically before quantitatively meaningful statements may be made concerning them. In sum, an increase in a society's productive capacity, associated with an increase in its capital stock originating in fuller employment, technological improvements, lessened discounting of the future, etc., must operate, until an offsetting adjustment in aspirations takes place, to reduce mortality, especially if high initially, (possibly) to increase natality, and to extend the period during which a given rate of population growth can be accommodated. Since empirical data indicate that both high and low rates of capital (population) growth have been associated with high (low) rates of population (capital) growth, they can tell us little until the relevant intervening variables have been isolated and assessed.

It has been implied that, so long as aspirations remain unchanged, a society will increase its numbers in consequence of changes making for increases in income per head. It has been further implied that these changes may operate independently of their effects upon income to produce a milieu in which aspirations become less favorable to natality. If these effects are powerful enough, they can produce a decline in the rate of population growth even though the income-increasing changes have increased population capacity; then the negative population effects of these changes may be said to outweigh such positive effects as were associated with income growth. But, as has also been implied, these changes may, under certain circumstances, even operate to reduce natality through the medium of income increase. Moreover, this negative population effect may be intensified by acceleration of the rate of income growth.

In the shorter-run the aggregate effect of an income increase would depend upon the relative amount of influence exercised by those population elements which responded positively, negatively, or not at all to the income increase. The upper range of income-receivers, together with those no longer of reproductive age, could hardly be expected to respond reproductively; their aggregate propensity to save would rise therefore. A second group of income-receivers, situated at various income levels, finding themselves temporarily indisposed to increase their consumption at the same rate as their incomes were increasing, would respond by stepping up their average propensities to save and/or their natality levels. A third group of income-receivers, situated at various income levels above those supplying only "necessities," would reduce their average propensities to save and/or their natality levels. This group, which might be relatively large or relatively small, would include all individuals who, because their income-increments were sufficiently large to generate modification of their consumption patterns and make available the fruits of consumer-goods complementarity and quality-improvement, would experience what amounted to an increase in the marginal utility of their money (cp. Norris 1952, ch. 11) and (hence) an uncompensated substitution effect in favor of commodities and services and against offspring. If there are enough individuals in this third category, and if, in time, their newly acquired patterns of living are propagated to individuals in the second group, the level of natality will fall despite the increase in income.

What has just been said may be put this way. Families and/or individuals have relatively stable consumption patterns, ordinarily subject only to changes in the small as family income increases or decreases. But there may exist certain goods (e.g., important members of the durable-goods category), the use of which entails a great deal of complementary spending, much of it not foreseen at the time of purchase. These goods might act, within the pattern of consumption, as metastasizing agents which, by the time they had run their course, would have significantly modified the consumption pattern and augmented the cost of this pattern. Since consumer income would not keep pace with the resulting increase in propensity to spend, something would have to give, and this something would be savings and/or procreation, and it would tend to be procreation in greater degree if the family's gross savings plan had already been institutionalized (e.g., insurance, annuity plans, etc.).

In sum, increases in national income, consequent upon increases in the rate of investment and/or effectiveness of resource use, will be favorable, other conditions remaining equal, to increase in natural increase. But other conditions do not remain equal. With income increases are associated changes in socio-economic structure, in the distribution of the population among socio-economic groups, in aspirations, and in consumption patterns; and these changes almost certainly tend to be unfavorable in the aggregate to fertility and they may be unfavorable to natural increase. If, as seems probable, the second set of changes is more powerful than the first, circumstances making for an increase in income are likely in time to make for a reduction of the rate of natural increase, especially if the increases are large. If this be the case, a supra-Malthusian population equilibrium must result, with a relatively low natality balancing a relatively low mortality, and with per capita income rising, though possibly at a low rate.

It usually is assumed that the objective of investment is the augmentation of income (or "welfare") per head, but it appears to be taken for granted that this increment in income is to be achieved through augmenting the stock of wealth and facilitating innovation. However, since (within limits) the progress of per capita income is inversely associated with the level of natural increase, the goodness of an investment must be judged both in terms of its capacity to increase NNP and in terms of its capacity to reduce natality and natural increase. More specifically those investments are best which contribute, or which may be enabled to contribute, most effectively to the increase of per capita income in the longer run. This means, as a rule, therefore, that (*ceteris paribus*) those forms of investment which tend in time to depress natality are superior to those which do not. It is in order, therefore, to discover what forms of investment are unfavorable to natality, or can be made unfavorable through the introduction of side conditions.

Let us abstract from the output-increasing effect of investment and note only the population effects of investment. As has been remarked, the influence of investment upon population growth is exercised through two channels, through the income-increasing effect of investment, and through modifications produced by investment in a population's cultural milieu. While effects exercised through the income-channel may or may not be unfavorable to population growth, effects exercised through the second channel tend to reduce the rate of natural increase. Inasmuch as investment is rarely an isolated series of events, its net effect will usually be conditioned by the measures that are made to accompany the process of investing in a line of activity.

It is not possible as yet to indicate with any degree of precision or certainty what forms of investment are relatively unfavorable to natality and what forms are relatively favorable. There follows, however, a speculative indication of the probable population effects of a number of forms of investment. (1) Investment that increases the prices of goods and services entering into the reproduction and rearing of children relative to the prices at which competing goods and services are to be had sets up a not wholly compensated substitution effect against children. Such a change in price structure may be brought about by investment which diminishes the prices of goods and services competitive with children, or by investment which increases the prices of goods and services complementary to children. In the latter category falls investment which accentuates the long-run tendency of the value of units of NRW, expressed in terms of units of RW, to rise. (2) Investment that tends to redistribute population in geographical and social space in a manner calculated to increase the level of aspirations will tend to depress natality. (3) Investment that favors the increase of goods and services the demand for which is relatively elastic is likely to be less favorable to natality than is investment which favors the increase of goods and services the demand for which is relatively inelastic. Agricultural products usually are illustrative of the latter category, though such products may at times encounter an elastic demand in foreign markets. (4) Investment that long continues to swell the monetary purchasing power of the bulk of the labor force faster than it makes available to them consumer goods and services is likely to affect natality adversely. Representative is investment in economic overhead capital and in some forms of social overhead capital. (5) Investment that increases the output of durable and other goods which are well suited to metastasize otherwise relatively stable consumption patterns affects natality adversely as was shown earlier. (6) Investment which dissipates the tradition-ridden culture patterns of underdeveloped countries and establishes in their places modern, western patterns serves to reduce natality. Most effective of investments of this sort are those which cannot easily be fitted into a society's culture unless many and widely spread patterns of this culture must be changed to accommodate the investment. Illustrative perhaps is extensive electrification or the extension and modernization of transport. (7) Investment which is continued on a large scale and for a long time, particularly if it is strategically distributed in time, is almost certain to augment income sufficiently to compel modernization of living patterns, generate new aspirations, produce widespread cultural change, and set in motion a decline in natality. Small investment for short periods, on the contrary, can do little except increase numbers and make more difficult than ever the escape of a people from a Malthusian trap.[41] (8) Investment which is more rather than less productive of income is the more favorable, in the longer run, to a decline in natality. (9) While investment which reduces infant mortality immediately augments the rate of population growth, it may so increase pressure upon family income as to produce modification of reproductive behavior, but whether it tends to decrease natality sufficiently more than to offset the decrease in infant mortality is doubtful.

VI. Conclusion

Of the conclusions indicated in this paper the most important are those respecting the importance of capital formation, the difficulties that beset efforts to increase capital per head and thereby increase the rate of technological change, and the need to judge the net efficacy of investment in the light of *both* its income-producing *and* its natality-reducing effects.

References

Ackerman, E. A.
  1953 *Japan's Natural Resources,* Chicago.
Axilrod, S. H.
  1954 "Inflation and the Development of Underdeveloped Areas," *Review of Economics and Statistics,* XXXVI.
Balogh, T.
  1954 "The Dollar Crisis Revisited," *Oxford Economic Papers,* VI.
Bauer, P. T.
  1953 "Review of *Measures for the Economic Development of Underdeveloped Countries* [see UN 1951]," *Economic Journal,* LXIII.
Bhatt, V. V.
  1954a "Capital-Output Ratios of Certain Industries," *Review of Economics and Statistics,* XXXVI, pp. 308–19.
  1954b "Employment and Capital Intensity," *The Economic Weekly,* November 6.

41. See Leibenstein (1954, esp. Ch. 4–5; and 1955, pp. 343–370). Only in these two works (which deal also with several of the points treated above) have population and capital growth received attention along the lines considered above.

Black, J. D.
1936   "Agricultural Population in Relation to Agricultural Resources,"
        Annals of the American Academy of Political and Social Science,
        CLXXXVIII.
Bliss, C. A.
1939   *The Structure of Manufacturing Production,* New York.
Bohr, K. A.
1954   "Investment Criteria for Manufacturing Industries in Under-
        developed Countries," *Review of Economics and Statistics,*
        XXXVI.
Brady, Dorothy
1955   in *A Study of Saving in the United States,* Princeton, Vol. III.
Bronfenbrenner, M.
1953   "II—The High Cost of Economic Development," *Land Eco-
        nomics,* XXIX.
1955   "The Appeal of Confiscation in Economic Development," *Eco-
        nomic Development and Cultural Change,* III, pp. 201–218.
Bruton, H. J.
1955   "Growth Models and Underdeveloped Economies," *Journal of
        Political Economy,* LXIII, pp. 322–336.
Buchanan, N. S., and H. S. Ellis
1955   *Approaches to Economic Development,* New York.
Burns, A. F.
1934   *Production Trends in the United States since 1870,* New York.
Cairncross, A. K.
1953   *Home and Foreign Investment, 1870–1913,* Cambridge.
Clark, Colin
1940   *Conditions of Economic Progress,* London, 1st ed.
1951   *Conditions of Economic Progress,* London, 2nd ed.
1952   "The Economy of the Under-developed Countries," *Review of
        Economic Progress,* IV.
Davenport, H. J.
1918   *The Economics of Enterprise,* New York.
Deane, Phyllis
1955   "The Implications of Early National Income Estimates for the
        Measurement of Long-Term Economic Growth in the United
        Kingdom," *Economic Development and Cultural Change,* IV,
        No. 1.
Derksen, J. D. B., and S. S. J. Kagan
1952   "Comments on . . . [Singer 1952]," *Indian Economic Review,* I.
Dewhurst, J. F.
1955   *America's Needs and Resources,* New York.
Domar, E. D.
1946   "Capital Expansion, Rate of Growth, and Employment," *Eco-
        nometrica,* XIV, pp. 137–147.
1950   "The Effect of Foreign Investment on the Balance of Payments,"
        American Economic Review, XL.

1953 "Depreciation, Replacement and Growth," *Economic Journal,* LXIII.

Douglas, P. H.
1948 "Are There Laws of Production?" *American Economic Review,* XXXVIII, pp. 1–41.

Duesenberry, J. S.
1949 *Income, Saving and the Theory of Consumer Behavior,* Cambridge.

The Eastern Economist, March 5, 1955, pp. 353–354.

Eckaus, R. S.
1955 "Factor Proportions in Underdeveloped Areas," *American Economic Review,* LXV, pp. 539–565.

Fellner, William
1951 "The Capital-Output Ratio in Dynamic Economics," in *Money, Trade, and Economic Growth,* New York.

Fleming, M.
1955 "External Economies and the Doctrine of Balanced Growth," *Economic Journal,* LXV, pp. 241–256.

Frankel, M.
1955 "Obsolescence and Technological Change," *American Economic Review,* XLV, pp. 296–319.

Fukuoka, M.
1955 "Full Employment and Constant Coefficients of Production," *Quarterly Journal of Economics,* LXIX, pp. 23–44.

Gayer, A. D., et al.
1953 *The Growth and Fluctuation of the British Economy, 1790–1850,* Oxford.

Gerschenkron, A.
1952 "Economic Backwardness in Historical Perspective," in *The Progress of Underdeveloped Areas* [Bert F. Hoselitz, ed.], Chicago.

Gilbert, Milton
1953 [ed.] *Income and Wealth,* Series III, London.

Goldsmith, R.
1951 "A Perpetual Inventory of National Wealth," *Studies in Income and Wealth,* XIV, New York.
1952 in *Income and Wealth of the United States* [S. Kuznets, ed.], London.
1955a in *Capital Formation and Economic Growth* [M. Abramovitz, ed.], Princeton.
1955b *A Study of Saving in the United States,* Princeton, 3 vols.

Grosse, R. N.
1955 "A Note on Capital-Output Ratios," *Review of Economics and Statistics,* XXXVII.

Grossman, Gregory
1953 "Scarce Capital and Soviet Doctrine," *Quarterly Journal of Economics,* XXXV, pp. 311–343.

1955 in *Capital Formation and Economic Growth* [M. Abramovitz, ed.], Princeton.

Hamilton, E. J.

1952 "Prices as a Factor in Business Growth," *Journal of Economic History*, XII (4), pp. 325–349.

Hansson, K. E.

1952 "A General Theory of the System of Multilateral Trade," *American Economic Review*, XLII, pp. 59–68.

Hartley, R. W.

1950 *America's Capital Requirements*, New York.

Henderson, A. M.

1950 "The Cost of Children, Parts II and III," *Population Studies*, IV.

Hicks, J. R.

1953 "An Inaugural Lecture," *Oxford Economic Papers*, V.

Hoselitz, B. F.

1955 in *Capital Formation and Economic Growth* [M. Abramovitz, ed.], Princeton.

International Bank for Reconstruction and Development (IBRD)

1952 *Surinam*, Baltimore.

1953 *The Economic Development of Mexico*, Baltimore.

Jewkes, J.

1951 "The Growth of World Industry," *Oxford Economic Papers*, III.

Johnson, D. G.

1948 "Allocation of Agricultural Income," *Journal of Farm Economics*, XXX.

Joint Committee on the Economic Report (JCER)

1955 *Trends in Economic Growth*, Washington.

Kindleberger, C. P.

1955 "Industrial Europe's Terms of Trade on Current Account, 1870–1913," *Economic Journal*, LXV, pp. 19–35.

Koo, A. Y. C.

1955 "Per Capita Rate of Economic Growth," *Weltwirtschaftliches Archiv*, LXXIV, pp. 47–62.

Kuznets, S.

1946 *National Product since 1869*, New York.

1952 [ed.] *Income and Wealth of the United States*, London.

1954a "Toward a Theory of Economic Growth," presented at the Columbia Bicentennial Conference, New York, May.

1954b "Underdeveloped Countries and the Pre-Industrial Phase in the Advanced Countries: An Attempt at Comparison," presented at the World Population Conference, Rome, September.

1955 in *Capital Formation and Economic Growth* [M. Abramovitz, ed.], Princeton.

Leibenstein, H.

1954 *A Theory of Economic-Demographic Development*, Princeton.

1955 (―――― and W. Galenson), "Investment Criteria, Productivity, and Economic Development," *Quarterly Journal of Economics,* LXIX.

Leontief, W.

1953a "Domestic Production and Foreign Trade: The American Capital Position Re-examined," *Proceedings of the American Philosophical Society,* XCVII.

1953b *Studies in the Structure of the American Economy,* Cambridge.

Lerner, A. P.

1953 "On the Marginal Product of Capital and the Marginal Efficiency of Investment," *Journal of Political Economy,* LXI, pp. 1–14.

Lewis, W. A.

1950 "The Industrialisation of the British West Indies," *Caribbean Economic Review,* II (1), pp. 1–61.

1954 "Economic Development with Unlimited Supplies of Labour," *The Manchester School of Economic and Social Studies,* XXII.

Lowe, A.

1955 in *Capital Formation and Economic Growth* [M. Abramovitz, ed.], Princeton.

The Mainichi, Overseas Edition, December 15, 1954, pp. 10–11.

Meade, J. E.

1952 "External Economies and Diseconomies in a Competitive Situation," *Economic Journal,* LXII, pp. 54–67.

Meier, G. M.

1952 "Long Period Determinants of Britain's Terms of Trade, 1880–1913," *Review of Economic Studies,* XX (1952–53), pp. 115–130.

Meier, R. L.

1954 in *Bulletin of the Atomic Scientists,* X.

Myint, H.

1954 "The Gains from International Trade and the Backward Countries," *Review of Economic Studies,* XXII (1954–55), pp. 129–142.

National Industrial Conference Board (NICB)

1954 *The Economic Almanac,* 1953–1954, New York.

Navarrette, A., and I. M. de Navarrette

1952 "Underemployment in Underdeveloped Economies," *International Economic Papers,* III, London.

The New York Times, November 18, 1955, p. 6.

Norris, Ruby T.

1952 *The Theory of Consumer's Demand,* New Haven, 2nd ed.

Nurkse, R.

1953 *Problems of Capital Formation in Underdeveloped Countries,* Oxford.

1954 "The Problem of International Investment Today in the Light of Nineteenth-Century Experience," *Economic Journal,* LXIV.

Pazos, F.
1953   "Economic Development and Financial Stability," *International Monetary Fund Staff Papers*, III, pp. 228–253.
President's Materials Policy Commission (PMPC)
1952   *Resources for Freedom*, Washington.
Putnam, Palmer C.
1953   *Energy in the Future*, New York.
Rao, V. K. R.
1952   "Full Employment and Economic Development," *Indian Economic Review*, I, pp. 43–57.
1953   *Deficit Financing, Capital Formation, etc.*, Eastern Economist Pamphlets No. 20, New Delhi.
Robinson, E. A. G.
1954   "The Changing Structure of the British Economy," *Economic Journal*, LXIV, pp. 443–461.
Robinson, Joan
1952   *The Rate of Interest and Other Essays*, London.
Rottenberg, S.
1953   "Note on 'Economic Progress and Occupational Distribution,'" *Review of Economics and Statistics*, XXXV, pp. 168–170.
Royal Commission on Population (RCP)
1950   . . . *Papers*, III, London.
Schlote, Werner
1952   *British Overseas Trade from 1700 to the 1930's*, Oxford.
Schmookler, Jacob
1952   "The Changing Efficiency of the American Economy," *Review of Economics and Statistics*, XXXIV, pp. 214–231.
Schultz, T. W.
1953   *Economic Organization of Agriculture*, New York.
Scitovsky, T.
1954   "Two Concepts of External Economies," *Journal of Political Economy*, LXII, pp. 143–151.
Scott, Anthony
1954   "Conservation Policy and Capital Theory," *Canadian Journal of Economics and Political Science*, XX, pp. 504–513.
Singer, H. W.
1952   "The Mechanics of Economic Development," *Indian Economic Review*, I.
Solo, R.
1955   "The Accumulation of Wealth in the Form of Land-Ownership in the Underdeveloped Areas," *Land Economics*, XXXI.
Spengler, J. J.
1951   "The Population Obstacle to Human Development," *American Economic Review*, XLI (2).
1954   "IBRD Mission Economic Growth Theory," *American Economic Review*, XLIV (2), pp. 343–354.

Stockfisch, J. A.

1955 "External Economies, Investment, and Foresight," *Journal of Political Economy*, LXIII, pp. 445–449.

Sturmthal, A.

1955 "Economic Development, Income Distribution, and Capital Formation in Mexico," *Journal of Political Economy*, LXIII, pp. 187–199.

The Times, London, February 1, 1955, p. 7.

Tinbergen, J.

1942 "Zur Theorie der langfristigen Wirtschaftsentwicklung," *Weltwirtschaftliches Archiv*, LV, pp. 511–547.

United Nations (UN)

1951 *Measures for the Economic Development of Underdeveloped Countries*, New York.

1952 *World Energy Supplies*, New York.

1953 *Economic Survey of Europe since the War*, Geneva.

UN (ECAFE)

1951 *Mobilization of Domestic Capital in Certain Countries of Asia and the Far East*, Bangkok.

1954 *Economic Survey of Asia and the Far East, 1953*, Bangkok.

UN (ECLA)

1953 *Preliminary Study of the Technique of Programming Economic Development*, prepared by the Economic Commission for Latin America for fifth session, Rio de Janeiro, Brazil, 9 April.

1954 *Economic Survey of Latin America*, New York.

United States Department of State (USDS)

1949 *Energy Resources of the World*, Publication 3248, Washington, D.C.

Valavanis-Vail, S.

1955 "An Econometric Model of Growth: U.S.A. 1869–1953," *American Economic Review*, Proceedings, XLV (2).

Wallich, Henry C.

1951 "Underdeveloped Countries and the International Monetary Mechanism," in *Money, Trade, and Economic Growth*, New York.

Weber, B., and S. J. Handfield-Jones

1954 "Variations in the Rate of Economic Growth in the U.S.A., 1869–1939," *Oxford Economic Papers*, VI.

Woytinsky, W. S., and E. S. Woytinsky

1953 *World Population and World Production*, New York.

1955 *World Commerce and Governments*, New York.

Population and World Economic Development

"In the long run, the lack of adequate space and resources is logically certain — unless fertility is reduced — to impose a ceiling on rising consumption, then to lower the availability of food per consumer, and ultimately to cause a rise in death rates. These conclusions all follow from the mathematics of geometric increase. . . . At current growth rates, the population of the United States would outweigh the earth in 2500 years" (1, pp. 330–31).

The economic development of any particular society is envisaged as entailing changes both in its aggregative economic magnitudes and in its economic composition. Of these changes there are various indicators, not all of which move in wholly parallel paths. For the sake of convenience in exposition, however, use may be made primarily of a single indicator, per capita real income, since the movement of this indicator is highly correlated with the movement of other welfare-oriented indicators, and since changes in it provide a great deal of information respecting the extent to which a community of people has become better or worse off. It is assumed, therefore, that economic development is reflected in the movement of per capita income, and that the role played by population growth in economic development is ultimately expressible in terms of its incidence upon the movement of per capita income.

This article is composed of two main parts: in the first the underlying theory is set down and in the second the prospective incidence of population growth upon the movement of per capita income is examined for each of the main demographic regions of the world. Analysis is restricted to quantitative aspects of the subject under discussion; genetical and most euthenic issues are disregarded. In a final section some implications of the population question are touched upon.

Economico-Demographic Theory

A complete economico-demographic theory would have to account adequately both for the response of aggregate income to population growth and for the response of population to income growth. In this article, however, major attention is devoted to the former response. The latter response is examined only in so far as it bears on one question: Does population growth respond to slight output changes in the same manner as it responds to large output changes? Relevant theory may therefore be expressed in terms of four principles: (i) changing age composition: (ii) changing factor complementarity; (iii) changing economic homosphere; and (iv) critical minimum economico-demographic stimulus. These principles are described below.

The per capita income in terms of which the course of economic development is plotted is a collection of goods and services, the enjoyment of many of which is contingent upon the availability of sufficient leisure. Increases in the size of this collection tend to be accompanied by increases in its variety and its quality, presumably because the eudemonic property of income depends upon variety as well as upon quantity. This fact is overlooked in much of the popular literature relating to population, in which it is suggested that so long as the food supply, irrespective of its composition, can be made to keep pace with numbers, there is no population problem. Unfortunately, man has taste buds and hence is not disposed to live on algae, or on a 21-cent daily mess of lard, beef liver, orange juice, and soybean meal, or on similar unpalatable minimum-cost diets (2). Nor is he content to live on minimum-cost, nonfood allowances. It is not very relevant, therefore, to ask how many people a given country can support. It is more relevant to ask why population continues to increase in a country after population growth has ceased to confer a *net* advantage upon the country's inhabitants.

Changing Age Composition

Potential productivity per capita depends, *ceteris paribus,* upon the size of the fraction of a country's population that is in the labor force. The size of this fraction, though subject to the influence of socioeconomic conditions, depends upon the age composition of a country's population. Furthermore, though this fraction may be only some 5 to 10 percent higher in developed than in underdeveloped countries, the margin of productivity enjoyed by developed countries will be greater; for around 10 or more percent of the labor force of underdeveloped countries is made up of children under 15, whereas the labor force of advanced countries includes almost no children (3).

When a population is growing, its age composition is less favorable than when it is stationary, and when a population's natural rate of growth increases (or decreases), its age composition becomes less (or more) favorable, within limits. More generally, under *ceteris paribus* conditions, the proportion of the population of working age (say 15 to 59 or 20 to 64 years) increases greatly as the gross reproduction rate falls and declines somewhat as life expectancy at birth increases. Model stable populations serve to illustrate this tendency (see Table I). Suppose we postulate a set of age-specific fertility rates which give us a gross reproduction rate of 3, or a crude birth rate of 43 to 46; then the percentage of the population falling within the age group 15 to 59 will range, in the associated stable populations, between 48.4, if life expectancy at birth is 70.2 years, and 52.5, if life expectancy is only 40 years. Should this set of age-specific fertility rates be replaced by another set yielding a gross reproduction rate of 1.5 and a crude

Table I. Gross Reproduction and Percentage of Population Aged 15 to 59 in Model Stable Populations (23).

Gross repro-duction rate	Life expectancy at birth (yr)					
	40		60.4		70.2	
	Percent aged 15–59	Birth rate (No./1000)	Percent aged 15–59	Birth rate (No./1000)	Percent aged 15–59	Birth rate (No./1000)
3.0	52.5	46.0	49.6	43.8	48.4	42.9
2.0	58.8	31.7	55.8	30.6	54.7	30.1
1.5	61.6	23.1	58.7	22.5	57.7	22.3
1.0	62.6	13.6	59.4	13.3	58.6	13.3

birth rate of 22 to 23, the percentage of persons aged 15 to 59 would rise one-sixth or more, to between 58 and 62. In short, if fertility declined from levels such as are found in much of Asia, Africa, and Latin America to those found in Europe, the fraction of the population of working age would be something like one-sixth higher under stable-population conditions. This amounts to an increase of one-sixth or more in potential productivity per capita. This theoretical finding is borne out, of course, in the real world; for example, 66.28 percent of the Swedish population but only 56.69 percent of the Brazilian population is aged 15 to 64 years.

High-fertility, underdeveloped countries would derive two advantages from the improvement in age composition that would result if fertility should decline until their populations had become approximately stationary. First, their potential per capita productivity would rise 10 to 15 or more percent; some of this potential productivity would assume the form of income and some the form of leisure. Second, the disposition of parents to put children to work and deny them education would be greatly reduced, and the capacity of the population to educate the children and so make them much more productive would be greatly augmented. Of this we have some evidence in the fact that in the slowly growing populations of developed European countries the ratio of children under, say, 15 to persons of an age (say 15 to 64) to be teachers is only about half as high as in the rapidly growing populations of underdeveloped countries.

Changing Factor Complementarity

Population growth would not affect productivity per capita adversely if output were entirely the product of labor and hence imputable solely to labor. Productivity partly depends, however, upon the number of complementary agents or factors of production (4) at the disposal of a population. This number governs the amount of equipment the average worker has to assist him in his occupational assignments. It also governs the rapidity with which technological advances can be given concrete form and the degree to which individuals can be trained and enabled to carry on that basic and applied research which underlies technological progress. Such progress is very important; it seems to have been responsible for some four-fifths of the increase in output per man-hour recently experienced in the United States (5). It is because population growth reduces when it does not altogether prevent increase in the number of productive factors available per capita that it tends to depress the rate at which output per capita increases. Population growth has this effect because it entails transformation of a given population, together with its replaceable and irreplaceable environment, into a successor population and environment, with the double result that increases in numbers are achieved at the expense of physical environment and that a portion of this physical environment is permanently dissipated (6).

These factors or agents of production are of two sorts: (i) those which are reproducible and augmentable and (ii) those which are nonaugmentable because their aggregate stock is either roughly fixed (for example, potential supply of water power) or depletable (for example, proved and potential oil reserves) and hence subject to the relentless march of economic entropy consequent upon their use (7). While the rate at which the stock of agents (i) is increased depends immediately upon the level of income and the average propensity of the community to save, it is affected, as may be the marginal productivity of this stock of capital, by the scarcity of agents (ii). For in so far as agents (ii) are in short supply, this shortage must be made up by agents (i), with the result that average income is somewhat lower than it otherwise would be.

Population growth slows down the rate at which the number of agents (i) available per capita can be increased. Inasmuch as a nation's stock of utilized wealth usually amounts to something like five times its national income (8), saving rates of 5 and 10 percent, respectively, are required to keep the wealth-population ratio constant when the population is growing 1 or 2 percent per year. Close association of this ratio and per capita income is prevented by various circumstances, however, among them variation in the composition of wealth, in the wealth-income ratio, in the extent to which increase in wealth is accompanied by technical progress, and in the manner in which wealth and income are measured (9). The wealth-income ratio does, however, provide a rough, internationally comparable index of the extent to which population growth absorbs output which might otherwise have been consumed or utilized to increase wealth or capital per head. It may be inferred that, even though the capital output ratio in industry or agriculture is sometimes as low as 3 : 1 or lower, savings of 8 to 10 or more percent are required in the longer run to offset the population growth rates of 2 or more percent found in many underdeveloped countries. For assets are normally accumulated not only to equip and house people but also for various other reasons which in the longer run bring the ratio of total physical assets to income up to 4 or 5 to 1.

Up to now the nonaugmentable factors have not seriously retarded the growth of output per head, because unused reserves remained, because substitutes were available, because technical progress has reduced the input of these factors per unit of output, and because the use of materials other than minerals and water has grown little more rapidly than population. Furthermore, technical improvements have increased the output of minerals per composite unit input of labor and capital. It is shortage of water and space that bids to restrict expansion here and there. In time, however, population growth, together with rising per capita consumption, will greatly increase the overall use of minerals and water and may even increase the marginal cost of produce, particularly if considerable amounts of cultivable land are diverted to nonagricultural purposes. Consumption of materials originating in nonaugmentable sources has been increasing markedly only since the late 19th century; this increase may not make itself felt in terms of rising costs for some decades, however, and even then the initial impact of such cost increases will be minor. Dearth of suitably situated space is likely to make itself felt, however (*10*).

Changing Homosphere

Man's earthly habitat, or homosphere, is a component of the comparatively invariant biosphere in which living matter flourishes (*11*). The capacity of this homosphere to sustain human life at a given level is conditioned in some measure by the growth process as such, independently of the operation of the principle of changing complementarity touched upon in the preceding section. The effects of growth may be adverse or favorable. They are adverse when growth permanently dissipates a portion of the environment capable of subserving human life without at the same time replacing it with a suitable substitute.

Illustrative perhaps is erosion consequent upon population pressure, or the dissipation of potential utility associated with increase in economic entropy, noted above. Illustrative also would be the covering of much land by water should continuing population growth so step up man's production of carbon dioxide that the oceans failed to absorb all of it, with the result that the carbon-dioxide content, and hence the temperature, of the atmosphere rose sufficiently to melt the polar icecaps.

Illustrative of the favorable effects are reductions in composite inputs per unit of output made possible, within limits, by economies consequent upon increase in the size of a population and in the apparatus of production. Of minor importance is the resulting fuller use of such indivisible agents as a railroad bed. Of major importance is the increase in organizational and other specialization made possible by population growth, together with the tendency of large economies to be more competitive and hence more inclined to make optimum use of factors than are small economies. Much of the restraint to which specialization and competition are subject is attributable, of course, not to smallness of population but to smallness of country or economy. This condition, usually inherited from the 18th century or from earlier centuries, when the optimum-size state was smaller than today, is now being partially rectified through the creation of metastates (12).

Population growth, when accompanied by corresponding growth in employment and income, may stimulate both the growth of firms which have not yet expanded to the greatest extent that seems economically desirable and the introduction of equipment and methods superior to those in use. For, so long as an economy is growing and expected to grow, stimulus is given to the disposition to plan and invest for the morrow and to suppose that enhanced output will find market outlets as satisfactory as those currently relied upon. Under these circumstances, also, it is relatively easy for labor and other factors, whether newly employed or situated in nonexpanding industries, to move into expanding industrial sectors. These various potential advantages of population growth, though realizable in a developed country, are not likely to be realized in a heavily populated, underdeveloped country where divers other preconditions for development are lacking. Their role in a developed country may be exaggerated, since in such a country, even if the population is stationary, death and retirement alone permit considerable and rapid readjustment of the labor force, while depreciation and obsolescence permit rapid modification of the composition of capital. Such flexibility is particularly marked when, as in advanced societies, governments are economically powerful enough to support aggregate demand at a level favorable to needed readjustment.

Critical Minimum Economico-Demographic Stimulus

Much of Asia, Africa, and Latin America—perhaps two-thirds of the world's population—is caught in a Malthusian trap, in "a quasi-stable equilibrium system" in which forces making for increase in income evoke counterbalancing income-depressing forces, among them a high rate of population growth.

Escape from this trap or system presupposes a stimulus, or set of continuing stimuli, sufficient to make the income-increasing and the population-growth-retarding effects dominant. This stimulus must operate both to increase income faster than population and to reduce the rate of population growth so that per capita income and expectations respecting the future course of per capita income rise sufficiently. What is called for is heavy investment over a sustained period of time — investment that is oriented not so much toward providing traditional support for a growing population as toward augmenting the stock of income-producing equipment, toward educating and urbanizing the population and rendering it productive and forward-looking, and toward replacing wants that foster population growth by different aspirations (*13*).

What alone is in dispute is the extent to which a people, even when its government is strong and well entrenched, can be induced to extend its time horizon, sacrifice today's simple material pleasures for tomorrow's uncertain returns, and substitute ideals of the sort found among advanced European peoples for those regnant in tradition-bound societies. Puerto Rico's experience demonstrates how very difficult it is to introduce effective family planning.

The significance of the above argument, subscribed to in part already by J. S. Mill, derives from the fact that population growth has been revolutionized in underdeveloped countries by the introduction of modern health measures that increase life expectancy. As a result, numbers increase, or soon will increase, two or three or more times as fast in these countries as they increased in Western Europe when that part of the world was undergoing modernization. The low rate of population growth characteristic of Western Europe (it was generally near or below 1 per cent per year) permitted initially low rates of saving to set self-sustaining economic development in motion. Similarly, in Japan, the only non-European country to undergo substantial modernization in the late 19th century, the rate of natural increase long remained close to 1 percent, and savings were relatively high and were put to good use. Even so the agricultural population has remained at the Meiji-era level; moreover, despite considerable modernization and the early adoption of family-limitation practices, Japan's birth rate did not fall sharply until after legal barriers to such limitation were relaxed, in and after 1949 (*14*). The demographic history of Japan suggests that, without strong governmental efforts to augment the rate of capital formation markedly and to stimulate effective control of fertility, underdeveloped countries, especially those which are already heavily populated and less productive of income than was early 19th-century England, are unlikely to escape their Malthusian trap, low incomes and excessive fertility.

Empirical Findings

Having noted ways in which population growth may affect the movement of per capita income and (if we may ignore Pope's dictum: "Fixed to no spot is happiness sincere") "welfare," we may turn to the current demographic situation, a conspectus of which is presented in Table II. Prospective rates of growth for Asia (exclusive of Japan), Africa, Middle America, and South America (exclusive of its temperate-zone countries) are much higher than for other areas. In these four areas fertility is uncontrolled, natality is high, and the diffusion of effective family limitation practices is retarded by a predominance of rural conditions, often accompanied by a high degree of illiteracy, elimination of which is difficult. While age composition is unfavorable to productivity in all these rapidly growing regions and per capita incomes are generally much lower than in the remainder of the world (that is, in Europe, northern North America, the Soviet Union, Japan, and most of Oceania), where fertility is subject to quite effective control (though this is not always exercised), population density appears to be a powerful depressant of income only in the Far East (where about half the world's population lives) and in Middle America. The low level of income in most of Africa and much of South America is primarily attributable, as are low income levels to some extent in the Far East, to conditions associated with economic underdevelopment as such rather than with population density, a considerable amount of which is compatible with relatively high per capita incomes (for example, population density is approximately 200 individuals per square mile in the northeastern United States and exceeds 300 in much of Europe and 500 in Japan).

Lowness of income is almost invariably associated with a heavy concentration of the labor force in agriculture, a condition found in Asia and Africa and in much of Middle and South America. There results a heavy pressure of agricultural population on the land under cultivation, especially when arable land per head of agricultural population amounts to less than 1 acre, as in Asia, or to about 2, as in Middle America, instead of more than 3, as in Europe and much of Africa and Latin America, or about 20, as in North America (15, pp. 474–477). Hence, agricultural income is very low in Asia and is augmentable principally through the reduction of the agricultural population by half or more and the augmentation of the frequently low yields per acre and per man; for, as the data in Table III indicate, pasture land is scarce and there is little utilizable forest or potentially productive land to bring into use. In the Near East, to some degree in Middle America, and in South America and much of Africa, the amount of land under cultivation apparently is still significantly augmentable. In all these areas, moreover, as in much of the Far East, output per acre could be greatly increased, given scientific methods of cultivation and a sufficiency of plant nutrients and moisture (15, p. 531; 16). There is little prospect, however, with current population trends, that the peoples of Asia, the Middle East, or Middle America can greatly reduce their excessive dependence on cereals and tubers (15, chap. 9).

While the easing of population pressure in agriculture depends in part

Table II. Demographic and Economic Characteristics, by Region, about 1950–55 (see 24). The Density and Population Estimates for A.D. 2000 Are Based on United Nations "Medium" Forecasts.

Region	Demographic and economic characteristics											
	Population (in millions)		Persons per km²		Birth rate (No./1000) in 1950	Per capita income (dollars) about 1955	Labor force (%)		Population (%)			
	In 1955	In 2000	In 1955	In 2000			In agri- culture	In in- dustry	Aged 15–59	In cities over 100,000		
World	2690	6267	20	46	39	50–1864	59	18	56	13		
Asia	1490	3870	55	143	46	50–487	73	10	55	8		
Africa	216	517	7	17	47	50–284	75	11	54	5		
South America	125	394	7	22	25–45	107–391	55	18	54	18		
Central America and Caribbean	58	198	21	72	35–50	80–426	62	16	53	12		
Rest of world	801	1288	14	23	20–26	150–1864	13–45	30–37	59–62	18–41		

Table III. Amount of Land, per Capita and by Use, 1955 (*25*).

Region	Agricultural area				Forest land (millions of hectares)	Unused but potentially productive land (millions of hectares)
	Arable land and land under tree crops		Permanent meadows and pastures			
	Total (millions of hectares)	Per capita (hectares)	Total (millions of hectares)	Per capita (hectares)		
U.S.S.R.	220	1.10	267	1.33	743	161
Europe	150	0.37	85	0.21	136	8
Northern North America*	228	1.26	278	1.54	668	79
Rest of North America†	27	0.47	78	1.34	71	17
South America	69	0.56	313	2.52	887	53
Oceania	24	1.71	376	24.00	87	6
Far East	355	0.25	271	0.19	475	60
Near East	78	0.56	295	2.11	145	116
Africa	219	1.29	502	2.95	652	76

*"Northern North America" includes Alaska, Canada, and the U.S.; † "Rest of North America" includes the balance of North and Central America.

upon greatly increased investment in agriculture, together with modernization of techniques, it depends largely upon the provision of relatively productive nonagricultural employment for both the excess agricultural population and additions to the labor force resulting from natural increase. Such provision requires not only considerable investment in suitable forms of education but also the formation of capital and the availability of the requisite mineral and other natural resources. Let us consider investment in education and capital formation first. In most underdeveloped countries investment in suitable facilities for education at the secondary and advanced levels is too low, and in many not even a full primary education is provided. In many, savings are barely adequate (if that) to offset population growth, probably averaging less than 10 percent of the national income in the whole of the semi- and nonindustrialized world (*17*). In Asia, with the exception of China, Israel, Japan, and possibly one or two small communities, the rate of capital formation is around 10 percent or less of income, and even in thrifty Japan gross fixed capital formation per capita is only one-ninth of that in the United States and one-third of that in Western Europe (*18*). In Latin America gross investment in fixed capital (some of foreign origin) has been in the neighborhood of 17 percent of the gross national product, and net investment, around 11 percent of the net national product (*19*). In Africa capital formation has varied greatly, ranging from levels of below 10 percent of national income, through perhaps close to 10 percent in Egypt, to much higher rates in Rhodesia, the Union of South Africa, and other countries *(20)*. Much higher rates of savings are required in most of the under-developed world, given current population growth, than are presently manifest.

While a number of underdeveloped countries are equipped with the natural resources requisite for economic development, in others the amounts of such resources are small or are offset by heavy population. China's iron-ore reserves (6.7 tons per capita), comparable to Mexico's, are greatly inferior to India's (54.2 tons per capita), which are superior to those of the United States; but India's coal reserves, roughly comparable in per capita terms to those of France, are greatly inferior to China's. Japan, with some coal, lacks iron ore as well as many other minerals. With the exception of these three countries and the partial exception of Korea, no Asian country is able to develop a considerable iron and steel industry and related industries; nor is a comparable industrial base now being provided by other minerals, or, in the long run, by petroleum (most heavily produced in the Near East). In South and Middle America, Brazil, Venezuela, and Cuba are well equipped with iron ore but are short of coal. Most of the coal and iron ore in Africa is in Southern Rhodesia and the Union of South Africa. In sum, a shortage of minerals in relation to population is likely to limit industrial development and the increase of per capita income in Asia, even in the absence of further population growth, and analogous limitation is likely eventually to become operative in much of Latin America and in parts of subsaharan Africa. Only a detailed inventory and study of available resources could disclose when and to what degree such limitation would become evident. Were such a study undertaken now and something like an optimum population determined for subsaharan Africa and South America, policy might be oriented toward reducing the actual and the potential rate of growth *(21)*.

Implications

It was suggested above that if a population were stationary instead of growing 2 or 3 percent per year it would have at its disposal, for improving the state of the existing population, current productive power and income amounting, in per capita income terms, to something like 20 to 25 percent of national income under *ceteris paribus* conditions. The precise magnitude of this figure depends upon the economic significance of differences in age composition and upon the relevant wealth-population ratio. It affords a rough measure of the current cost of a 2 to 3 percent yearly rate of population growth. The magnitude of this cost, together with the disadvantages, from the standpoint of education, of an unfavorable age composition, suggests that countries like Brazil which require larger populations for the optimum exploitation of their resources can progress more rapidly if they reduce their annual rates of population growth from the present 2 or 3 percent to, say, 1 percent.

The adverse effects of population growth in heavily populated underdeveloped countries have been well summarized by Coale and Hoover in their study of India. Assuming two postulates, that expectation of life at birth would rise from 32 years in 1951 to 52 years in 1986 and that fertility might either remain unchanged or decline 50 percent by 1986, the decline beginning in 1956 or not until 1966, they examined the economic implications of the population changes that would take place. They found that, if fertility began to decline at once, to be halved by 1986, income per consumer by the 1980's would be rising nearly four times as fast as would have been the case had fertility not declined at all. Moreover, the population, though still increasing 0.9 percent per year, would be approaching a stationary state, whereas, if fertility had not declined, the population would be increasing 2.6 percent per year and escape from the Malthusian trap would be even more difficult than it had been 30 years earlier (1, pp. 38, 273, 280). Analogous results were yielded by a similar inquiry in Mexico, where population has been growing faster than in India and where per capita income is two or three times that in India. Given a 50-percent decline in fertility, income per consumer would, as in India, be about 41 percent higher at the end of 30 years than it would have been in the absence of any decline in fertility (1, pp. 280, 305–306). Reduction in fertility, in short, makes possible higher and much more rapidly growing average incomes.

Because of the geometrical character of population growth and the fact that numbers rarely decline, the problem now confronting India or Mexico may eventually confront Europe or the United States or any other region where population is not yet so dense as it is in Europe, or where it is growing less rapidly than in, say, Latin America. It is sometimes supposed that maintenance (as in the United States) of two- to four-child families — that is, of a three-child-family average — would constitute a sufficient degree of control. Yet, under the conditions that exist in the United States, maintenance of a level of three children per family would result in an increase of population of about 1.3 percent per year, and this rate could easily be raised to 1.5 percent, approximately the rate at which the American population has been growing since 1950 (22). With an annual rate of increase of 1.5 percent, a population doubles every 47 years. In a mere 200 years, therefore, at this rate of increase the population of the United States would rise from a current 179 million to about 3.5 billion, or nearly 1200 persons per square mile, a density roughly double that presently found in Massachusetts and New Jersey.

In most of the world, persisting population growth constitutes the most serious of the long-run threats to the continuing improvement of man's material lot. Because of the existence of limitational factors, if only that of suitably situated space, there is a limit to the extent to which populations can grow, in any country or in the world as a whole. It is sometimes argued that fertility will never endanger man's standards of life, since men, having acquired a standard, are unwilling to surrender it, whether to population growth or to other income depressants. This argument overlooks a more fundamental ethical and eudemonic issue posed by population growth, however. It ignores the fact that resources currently used to support the costs of population growth might otherwise serve to augment welfare per capita. It fails to ask to what degree maximum welfare per capita would be more nearly realized if those preferring population growth, whether in the United States or elsewhere, were required to support more of its costs than at present. It neglects the fact that in much of the world living standards already are desperately low and will prove hard to raise even if the stork's wings are clipped.

References and Notes

1. A. J. Coale and E. M. Hoover, *Population Growth and Economic Development in Low-Income Countries* (Princeton Univ. Press, Princeton, N. J., 1958).
2. See *Time* 74, 84 (7 Dec. 1959). The mess described, reportedly the cheapest capable of supplying man with his minimum daily requirement of nutrients, was rejected even by the laboratory dog. Linear programming and related methods have indicated, however, ways in which the housewife can provide an adequate and reasonably palatable diet at minimum cost. See R. Dorfman, P. A. Samuelson, R. M. Solow, *Linear Programming and Economic Analysis* (McGraw-Hill, New York, 1958), p. 9ff.
3. *The World's Working Population* (International Labour Office, Geneva, Switzerland, 1956); J. D. Durand, "Population Structure as a Factor in Manpower and Dependency Problems of Under-Developed Countries," *Population Bull. of the United Nations No. 3* (Oct. 1953), pp. 1–16.
4. P. A. Samuelson has urged that the expression "factor of production" be avoided entirely. I have, however, retained it, in part because the discussion does not call for a precise, empirical, quantitative definition of the term. See *Foundations of Economic Analysis* (Harvard Univ. Press, Cambridge, Mass., 1947), pp. 84–85.
5. For example, see R. M. Solow, *Rev. Economics and Statistics* 39, 320 (1957), where seven-eighths of the increase in gross output per man-hour in 1909–49 is attributed to "technical change."
6. I have ignored the waste in resources resulting from high child mortality, since it does not, at worst, much exceed 2 percent of national income. See T. K. Ruprecht, "The cost of child mortality in developed and underdeveloped countries," *Proc. Conf. Western Economic Assoc. 33rd Conf.* (1958), pp. 21–25.

7. See J. J. Spengler, *Southern Econ. J.* 14, 238 (1948); *Kyklos* 7, 227 (1954).

8. See S. Kuznets, *Econ. Develop. and Cultural Change* 7, No. 3, pt. 2, app. B (1959).

9. See ———, *ibid.* 7, No. 3, pt. 2, 63, 65, 68 (1959).

10. For data on resources, see President's Materials Policy Commission, *Resources for Freedom* (Government Printing Office, Washington, D.C., 1952); *Univ. Maryland Studies in Business and Economics 12, No. 1* (June 1958); E. A. Ackerman, *Water Resources in the United States* (Resources for the Future, Washington, D.C., 1958).

11. See W. I. Vernadsky, *Am. Scientist* 33, 1 (1945). Living matter, some complementary and some antagonistic to man, constitutes an insignificant (about 0.0025 percent) and essentially unchanging fraction of the biosphere.

12. For example, see S. Kuznets, "Economic Growth of Small Nations," in A. Bonne, Ed., *The Challenge of Development* (Hebrew Univ., Jerusalem, 1958); F. Gehrels and B. F. Johnston, *J. Polit. Econ.* 63, 275 (1955).

13. The argument set forth in this paragraph has been admirably developed by H. Leibenstein in *Economic Backwardness and Economic Growth* (Wiley, New York, 1957). See also R. R. Nelson, *Am. Econ. Rev.* 46, 894 (1956) and J. J. Spengler, *Econ. Develop. and Cultural Change* 4, 321 (1956). For a critique of the above argument, see H. S. Ellis, *Quart. J. Econ.* 72, 485 (1958).

14. See I. B. Taeuber, *The Population of Japan* (Princeton Univ. Press, Princeton, N.J., 1958). Compare R. Hill *et al., The Family and Population Control: A Puerto Rican Experiment in Social Change* (Univ. of North Carolina Press, Chapel Hill, 1959).

15. See W. S. Woytinsky and E. S. Woytinsky, *World Population and Production* (Twentieth Century Fund, New York, 1953).

16. In Europe and America, yields per acre are more than double those reported for Africa and are higher by a fifth or more than those reported for Asia; see W. S. Woytinsky and E. S. Woytinsky, *World Population and Production,* p. 531, and also yield figures for most crops reported periodically in *U. S. Dept. Agr. Foreign Crops and Markets.* Output per capita of agricultural population is only about one-fourth as high in Asia as in Europe; it is only about half as high in Africa as in Asia.

17. The Netherlands Economic Institute estimates at about 5 and 7 percent, respectively, the over-all domestic rates of saving in non-industrialized and semi-industrialized countries (cited in *Bull. from the European Community No. 37* [Aug.–Sept. 1959], p. 2). These rates seem to be too low.

18. *Economic Survey of Asia and the Far East, 1958* (United Nations, Bangkok, Thailand, 1959), pp. 91–93, and *Econ. Bull. for Asia and the Far East* 9, No. 3, 19, 25 (1958). That gross investment has formed 22 to 23 percent of the gross national product in mainland China and only 13 to 14 percent in India is indicated by W. Malenbaum's estimates in

Am. Econ. Rev. 49, 285 (1959). Investment in China is more efficient also (*ibid.* 49, 299 [1959]). In 1955, 986 million of Asia's population of 1490 million were in China and India.

19. For example, see *Economic Survey of Latin America, 1956* (United Nations, New York, 1957), pp. 6–7, and *Analyses and Projections of Economic Development* (United Nations, New York, 1955), p. 11. In 1956 about 9 percent of gross investment in Latin America was of foreign origin.

20. See F. Harbison and I. A. Ibrahim, *Human Resources for Egyptian Enterprise* (McGraw-Hill, New York, 1958), p. 33; *Structure and Growth of Selected African Economies* (United Nations, New York, 1958), pp. 32–34, 121–122, 149.

21. On resources in Asia see *Econ. Bull. for Asia and the Far East* 9, 38 (1958); also the following UN surveys. *World Iron Ore Resources and Their Utilization* (1950); *Survey of World Iron Ore Resources* (1955); *Nonferrous Metals in Under-developed Countries* (1955); *New Sources of Energy and Economic Development* (1957); *La Energia en America Latina* (1957). See also W. S. Woytinsky and E. S. Woytinsky, *World Population and Production,* chaps. 21–25, and E. A. Ackerman, *Japan's Natural Resources and Their Relations to Japan's Economic Future* (Univ. of Chicago Press, Chicago, 1953).

22. See R. Freedman, P. K. Whelpton, A. A. Campbell, *Family Planning, Sterility and Population Growth* (McGraw-Hill, New York, 1959), pp. 372, 376–385.

23. Data given in Table I are based on *The Aging of Populations and Its Economic and Social Implications* (United Nations, New York, 1956), Table 16, p. 27.

24. This conspectus is based upon the following publications: *The Future Growth of World Population* (United Nations, New York, 1958); *The World's Working Population* (International Labour Office, Geneva, Switzerland), p. 503; K. Davis and H. Hertz, "The World Distribution of Urbanization," reprinted in J. J. Spengler and O. D. Duncan, *Demographic Analysis: Selected Readings* (Free Press, Glencoe, Ill., 1956), pp. 325–326; *Demographic Yearbook, 1956* (United Nations, New York, 1956), chap. 1; P. Studenski, *The Income of Nations* (New York Univ. Press, New York, 1958), pp. 228–233.

25. Data given in Table III are from *Food and Agr. Organization UN Yearbook of Food and Agr. Statistics* (1957), vol. 10, pt. 1, pp. 3–9, 15. Estimates of the amount of cultivable land in the world range from 2.6 to around 5 billion acres. The FAO reported, for 1956, 1.37 billion hectares in land and tree crops; 2.466 billion in permanent meadow and pasture; 2.864 billion in forest; and about 0.6 billion unused but potentially productive. According to R. M. Salter, of the 1.3 billion acres that might still be developed, only 100 million in islands south of Asia lie near areas of population concentration on that continent; 300 million are in northern North America and Eurasia; and 900 million are in Africa and South America. The yield of these acres, Salter estimates, might double pre-1939 world food production.

Publications of Joseph J. Spengler

1929

"The Merits and Demerits of the National Origins Provisions for Selecting Immigrants." *Southwestern Political and Social Science Quarterly* 10: 149–170.

1930

The Fecundity of Native and Foreign-Born Women in New England, p. 63. Washington, D.C.: Brookings Institution.
"Has the Native Population of New England Been Dying Out?" *Quarterly Journal of Economics* 44: 639–662.
"Is the Present American Immigration Policy Sound?" *Scientific Monthly* 30: 232–239.
"Social Science Becomes Exact." *American Mercury* 20: 202–205.
"When Population Ceases to Grow." *New Republic* 44: 61–63.

1931

"Comments on Institutionalism: What It Is and What It Hopes to Become." *American Economic Review* 21: 135–137.
"The Comparative Fertility of the Native and Foreign-Born Women in New York, Indiana, and Michigan." *Quarterly Journal of Economics* 45: 460–483.
"The Decline in the Birth-rate of the Foreign Born." *Scientific Monthly* 32: 54–59.
"Is America Slowing Up?" *Scribner's Magazine* 89: 367–376.

1932

"Babbit Looks at the Depression." *New Republic* 71: 64–66.
"The Declining Birth Rate Potential Dynamite." *Scribner's Magazine* 92: 6–12.
"Fertility in Providence, Rhode Island, 1856–1929." *American Journal of Sociology* 38: 377–397.
"John Graunt." *Encyclopedia of Social Sciences* 5: 158. New York: Macmillan.
"The New England Puritans: An Obituary." *Journal of Heredity* 28: 71–76.
"The Social and the Economic Consequences of Cessation in Population Growth." *Congresso Internazionale Per Gli Studi Sulla Populazione*, 1932, (Institute Poligrafico Dello Stato). *Proceedings* 9: 33–60. Rome, 1933.

1933

"Giammaria Ortes." *Encyclopedia of Social Sciences* 11: 498–499. New York: Macmillan.

"Note on Early Recommendation Relative to Contraception in America."
New England Medical Journal 209: 309–310.
"Population Doctrines in the United States: I. Anti-Malthusianism; II.
Malthusianism." *Journal of Political Economy* 41: 433–467, 639–722.

1934

"Have Values a Place in Economics?" *International Journal of Ethics*
44: 313–331.
"Population Growth, Consumer Demand and Business Profits." *Harvard
Business Review* 12: 204–221.

1935

"Malthusianism and the Debate on Slavery." *South Atlantic Quarterly*
24: 170–189.
"Malthusianism in Eighteenth Century America." *American Economic
Review* 25: 691–707.
"Notes on Abortion, Birth Control, and Medical and Sociological Inter-
pretations of the Decline of the Birth Rate in Nineteenth Century
America." *Marriage Hygiene* 2: 43–53, 158–169, 288–300.
"Der Rückgang der Antimalthusianismus in Amerika des Neunzehnten
Jahrhunderts." *Weltwirtschaftliches Archiv* 42: 484–503.

1936

"Alexander Hill Everett: Early American Opponent of Malthus." *New
England Quarterly* 9: 97–118.
"Birth Prevention in France." *Marriage Hygiene* 2, 3: 422–437, 67–77.
"Economic Opinion and the Future of the Interest Rate." *Southern Eco-
nomic Journal* 3: 7–28.
"Forecasting the Growth of Rural Population." In *Research in Rural Popu-
lation,* edited by J. C. Black, pp. 125–133. Social Science Research
Council, Bulletin 4 (May 1932).
"French Population Theory Since 1800." *Journal of Political Economy*
44: 577–611, 734–764.
"Migration Within the United States." *Journal of Heredity* 27: 2–20.
"Population Prediction in Nineteenth Century America." *American Socio-
logical Review* 1: 905–921.
"Population Theory in the Antebellum South." *Journal of Southern His-
tory* 2: 1–30.

1937

"The Economic Limitations to Certain Uses of Interstate Compacts."
American Political Science Review 31: 41–51.
"Population Problems in the South." *Southern Economic Journal* 3, 4:
393–410, 1–27, 131–153.

1938

France Faces Depopulation. Durham, N.C.: Duke University Press.
"Population Movements, Employment, and Income." *Southern Economic Journal* 5: 129–157.
"Seed Beds of America." *Journal of Heredity* 29: 475–488.
"Significance of Marxian Economics." Discussion. *American Economic Review* 38: 20–22.

1939

"Migration and Economic Change." *Proceedings of Fifth Annual Southern Social Science Research Conference,* pp. 1–12.
"Moheau: Prophet of Depopulation." *Journal of Political Economy* 47: 648–677.
"Population Trends and Prosperity." *Proceedings of the 1939 Ohio Conference of Statisticians on Business Research,* pp. 12–27.

1940

"Messance: Founder of French Demography." *Human Biology* 12: 77–94.
"The Political Economy of Jefferson, Madison, and Adams." In *American Studies in Honor of William Kenneth Boyd,* edited by David Kelly Jackson, pp. 3–59. Durham, N.C.: Duke University Press.
"Population Movements and Economic Equilibrium in the United States." *Journal of Political Economy* 48: 153–182.
"Sociological Presuppositions in Economic Theory." *Southern Economic Journal* 7: 131–157.

1941

"Population Policy in the United States: The Larger Crisis in American Culture." *Vital Speeches* 7: 177–180.
"Population Trends and the Future Demand for Teachers." *Social Forces* 19: 465–476.
"Regional Differences and the Future of Manufacturing in America." *Southern Economic Journal* 7: 475–493.
"Some Effects of Changes in the Age Composition of the Labor Force," *Southern Economic Journal* 8: 157–175.

1942

French Predecessors of Malthus. Durham, N.C.: Duke University Press.

1944

"Maintenance of Postwar Full Employment." With Dorothy K. Spengler. In *The Winning Plans in the Pabst Postwar Employment Awards,* pp. 79–83.

"The OPA, Price Control, and Inflation." *South Atlantic Quarterly* 43: 111–130.
"Pareto on Population." *Quarterly Journal of Economics* 58, 59: 571–601, 107–133.
"Some Criteria of Social Economy." Discussion. *American Economic Review* 34: 9–12.

1945

"Consumption Economics." Discussion. *American Economic Review* 35: 59–61.
"Malthus's Total Population Theory: A Restatement and Reappraisal." *Canadian Journal of Economics and Political Science* 11: 83–110, 234–264.
"The Physiocrats and Say's Law of Markets." *Journal of Political Economy* 53: 193–211, 317–347.
"Population and Per Capita Income." *Annals of the American Academy of Political and Social Science* 237: 182–192.
Review F. A. Hayek's *The Road to Serfdom. Southern Economic Journal* 12: 48–55.

1946

"Final Report of the Committee on Development of Economic Thinking and Information." Co-author. *American Economic Review* 36: 922–933.
"The Future of Prices." *Southern Economic Journal* 13: 1–35.
"Monopolistic Competition and the Price and Use of Urban Land." *Journal of Political Economy* 54: 385–412.
"The Teaching of Economics." Discussion. *American Economic Review* 26: 860–863.

1947

"Aspects of the Economics of Population Growth." *Southern Economic Journal* 14: 123–147, 233–265.
"The Role of the State in Shaping Things Economic." In *The Tasks of Economic History*, supplement, *Journal of Economic History* 7: 123–143.

1948

"Economic Effects of the Aging of the American Population." In *Birthdays Don't Count*, pp. 102–122. A report prepared for and published by the New York State Joint Legislative Committee on Problems of Aging. Newburgh, New York.
"The Problem of Order in Economic Affairs." *Southern Economic Journal* 15: 1–29.

1949

"How Should Our Population Problems Be Reviewed Now?," in McMaster University: Abstracts of Papers Discussed At an Invitation Symposium on Population Growth and Immigration Into Canada, April 1949, pp. 38–41.

"Laissez Faire and Intervention: A Potential Source of Historical Error." *Journal of Political Economy* 57: 438–441.

"A Realistic Theory of Entrepreneurship." Discussion. *American Economic Review* 39: 352–355.

"Round Table on Economic Research." Discussion. *American Economic Review* 39: 464–466.

"Theories of Socio-Economic Growth." In *Problems in the Study of Economic Growth*, edited by S. Kuznets, pp. 47–116. National Bureau of Economic Research.

"The World's Hunger—Malthus, 1948." In *Food, Proceedings of the Academy of Political Science* (January 1949), edited by John A. Krout, 23: 53–72.

1950

"Anthropologie et demographie: Generalities." In *IXᵉ congres international des sciences historiques, rapports* 1: 9–37. Paris: Librairie Armand Colin.

"Evolutionism in American Economics, 1800–1946." In *Evolutionary Thought in America*, edited by Stow Persons, pp. 202–267. New Haven: Yale University Press.

"Generalists versus Specialists in Social Science: An Economist's View." *American Political Science Review* 44: 358–379.

"Power Blocks and the Formation and Content of Economic Decisions." *American Economic Review* 40: 413–430.

"Prospective Population And Income Growth And Fiscal Policy." *National Tax Journal* 3: 36–63.

"Some Economic Aspects of the Subsidization by the State of the Formation of 'Human Capital.'" *Kyklos* 4: 316–343.

"Vertical Integration and Antitrust Policy." *Journal of Political Economy* 58: 347–352.

1951

"Economic Factors In The Development Of Densely Populated Areas." *Proceedings of the American Philosophical Society* 95: 20–53.

"Measures of Population Maladjustment." In *Proceedings of the XIVth International Congress of Sociology*, pp. 336–364. Rome.

"Notes on France's Response to Her Declining Rate of Demographic Growth." *Journal of Economic History* 11: 403–416.

"The Population Obstacle to Economic Betterment." *American Economic Review* 41: 343–354.

"Population Trends and Investment." *Commercial and Financial Chronicle* 174 (July 19, July 26, August 9): 11ff., 11ff., 11ff.

1952

"Cantillon, l'economiste et le demographe." In Richard Cantillon, *Essai sur la nature du commerce en general,* texte de l'edition originale de 1775, avec des etudes et commentaires par Alfred Sauvy, Amintore Fanfani, Joseph J. Spengler, Louis Salleron, pp. xliii–lviv. Paris: Institut National D'Etudes Demographiques.

"Population Movements and Investment," *Journal of Finance,* VI, VII (December 1951, March 1952), pp. 10–27.

"Population Prospects in Areas of Advanced Industrialization." In *World Population and Future Resources,* edited by Paul K. Hatt, pp. 39–54. Cincinnati: American Book Co.

"Population Theory." In *A Survey of Contemporary Economics,* edited by B. F. Haley, 2: 83–128. Homewood, Ill.: Richard D. Irwin Co.

1953

"Changes in Income Distribution and Social Stratification." *American Journal of Sociology* 59: 247–259.

"Development of Economic Thought." Discussion. *American Economic Review* 43: 269–271.

"Discussion of Migration and Mobility Studies." In "Notes on the Ninth Annual Industrial Relations Research Conference," pp. 1–5. Mimeographed. Duluth: University of Minnesota, May 14–15.

"Sociological Value Theory, Economic Analyses, and Economic Policy." *American Economic Review* 43: 340–349.

1954

"Demographic Patterns." In *Economic Development: Principles and Practices,* edited by H. F. Williamson and John A. Buttrick, pp. 63–103. New York: Prentice-Hall.

The Determinants and Consequences of Population Trends. Contributor. New York: United Nations.

Économie et population. Les doctrines francaises avant 1800. De Bude à Condorcet. Paris: Presses Universitaires De France. This is a translation, by Georges Lecarpentier and Anita Page, of *French Predecessors of Malthus,* Durham, 1942, and contains an introduction and an appendix by Professor Alfred Sauvy.

"IBRD Mission Economic Growth Theory." *American Economic Review* 44: 538–599.

"Limitational Factors in Population Theory: A Note." *Kyklos* 7: 227–243.

"Research Needs and Suggested Projects." Comment. In *The Interrelations of Demographic, Economic, and Social Problems in Selected Underdeveloped Areas,* pp. 159–163. New York: Milbank Memorial Fund.

"Richard Cantillon: First of the Moderns." *Journal of Political Economy* 62: 281–295, 406–424.
"Welfare Economics and the Problem of Overpopulation." *Scientia* 89: 1–21.

1955

"Aristotle on Economic Imputation and Related Matters." *Southern Economic Journal* 21: 371–389.
"Capital Requirements and Population Growth in Under-developed Countries." *Proceedings of the World Population Conference* (Rome, 1954) 5: 765–788. New York: United Nations.
Economic Growth: Brazil, India, Japan. Co-author and co-editor with Simon Kuznets and Wilbert Moore. Durham, N.C.: Duke University Press.
"An Economist Views Collegiate Business Education." *Collegiate News and Views* 8: 1–3, 8.
"Herodotus on the Subject Matter of Economics." *Scientific Monthly* 81: 276–285.
"The Influence of Enterprise and Business Organization in Underdeveloped Countries." Comment. In *Capital Formation and Economic Growth*, edited by M. Abramovitz, pp. 505–511. Princeton: National Bureau of Economic Research.
"Socioeconomic Theory and Population Policy." *American Journal of Sociology* 51: 129–133.
"From Theory to Public Policy." In *Economics and Public Policy*, edited by Robert Calkins, pp. 23–48. Washington, D.C.: Brookings Institution.

1956

"Basic Interrelations in Regional Development: Discussion." *Papers and Proceedings of Regional Science Association* 2: 95–97.
"Capital Requirements and Population Growth in Underdeveloped Countries: Their Interrelations." *Economic Development and Cultural Change* 4: 305–334.
Demographic Analysis: Selected Readings. Co-editor with Otis Dudley Duncan. Glencoe, Ill.: Free Press.
"The Population Problem: Dimensions, Potentialities, Limitations." *American Economic Review* 46: 337–351.
Population Theory and Policy: Selected Readings. Co-editor with Otis Dudley Duncan. Glencoe, Ill.: Free Press.
"Population Threatens Prosperity." *Harvard Business Review* 34: 85–94.
"Some Economic Aspects of Immigration into the United States." *Law and Contemporary Problems* 21: 236–255.
"Wage-Price Movements and Old-Age Security." In *Aging, A Current Appraisal*, edited by Irving L. Webber, pp. 105–119. Gainesville, Fla.: University of Florida Press.

1957

"The Aesthetics of Population." *Population Bulletin* 13: 61–75.
"Cottage Industries: A Comment." *Economic Development and Cultural Change* 5: 371–373.
"Economic Factors in Economic Development." *American Economic Review* 47: 42-56.
"Malthus the Malthusian *versus* Malthus the Economist." *Southern Economic Journal* 24: 1–11.
"Product-Adding versus Product-Replacing Innovations." *Kyklos* 10: 249–280.

1958

"The Commonwealth: Demographic Dimensions; Implications." In *Commonwealth Perspectives*, edited by N. Mansergh, et al., pp. 86–124. Durham, N.C.: Duke University Press.
"Desarrollo ecónomico y demográfico." *El Trimestre Economico* 25: 669–716.
"The Economic Effects of Migration." In *Selected Studies of Migration since World War II*, edited by Frank D. Boudreau and Clyde V. Kiser, pp. 172–192. New York: Milbank Memorial Fund.
"Effects Produced by Receiving Countries by Pre–1939 Immigration." In *The Economics of International Migration*, edited by Brinley Thomas, pp. 17–51. London: Macmillan and Co., Ltd.
"Issues and Interests in American Imigration Policy." In *A Crowding Hemisphere: Population Change in the Americas*, edited by Kingsley Davis. Appeared as *The Annals of the American Academy of Political and Social Science* 316: 43–51.
"Malthus Again." *Challenge* 7: 8–12.
"Population as a Factor in Economic Development." In *Population and World Politics*, edited by Philip M. Hauser, pp. 162–189. Glencoe, Ill.: Free Press.
"Public Bureaucracy, Resource Structure, and Economic Development: A Note." *Kyklos* 11: 459–487.
"Quesnay in America." In L'Association francaise de science économique, *Bi-Centenaire du "tableau économique" de Francois Quesnay (1758–1958)*, pp. 41–43. Paris.
"Quesnay philosophe, empiriste, économiste." In *Francois Quesnay & La Physiocratie*, edited by Alfred Sauvy, pp. 55–74. Paris: Institut national d'études démographiques.

1959

"Adam Smith's Theory of Economic Growth." *Southern Economic Journal* 25, 26: 397–415, 1–12.
"Economics and Demography." In *The Study of Population*, edited by Philip M. Hauser and Otis Dudley Duncan, pp. 791–831. Chicago: University of Chicago Press.

"Introduction." "The State and Economic Growth: Summary and Inter-
pretation." In *The State and Economic Growth*, edited by Hugh G. J.
Aitken, pp. 1–3, 353–382. New York: Social Science Research Council.
"John Rae on Economic Development: A Note." *Quarterly Journal of
Economics* 73: 393–406.
"Some Notes on Research Possibilities." In *The Comparative Study of
Economic Growth and Structure*, edited by Solomon Fabricant, pp.
185–192. New York: National Bureau of Economic Research.
"Veblen and Mandeville Contrasted." *Weltwirtschaftliches Archiv* 72:
35–67.

1960

"Economic Development: Political Preconditions and Political Conse-
quences." *Journal of Politics* 22: 387–416.
Essays in the History of Economic Thought. Co-author and co-editor with
William R. Allen. Chicago: Rand McNally.
"Mercantilist and Physiocratic Growth Theory." "John Stuart Mill on
Economic Development." In *Theories of Economic Growth*, edited
by Bert F. Hoselitz. Glencoe Ill.: Free Press.
"Population Changes, 1900–1950: Socio-Economic Implications." *Journal
of World History* 5: 929–953.
"Population and World Economic Development." *Science* 131: 1497–1502.
"Relations between Economic Theory and Economic Policy." Discussion.
American Economic Review 50: 52–54.

1961

"The Economy and Polity of Israel." *Southern Economic Journal* 28:
70–78.
"National Goals, Growth, and the Principle of Economy." In The Third
Duke American Assembly, *Goals for Americans*, pp. 7–24. Durham,
N.C.
"Population Change: Cause, Effect, Indicator." In *Essays in the Quantita-
tive Study of Economic Growth*, edited by B. F. Hoselitz. Special issue
of *Economic Development and Cultural Change*, 9: 249–266.
"The Population Problem: Yesterday, Today, Tomorrow." *Southern
Economic Journal* 27: 194–208.
"On the Progress of Quantification in Economics." *Isis*, 52: 258–276.
"Public Economic Policy in a Dynamic Society." In *Major Problems of
the American Economy*, edited by Edward S. Shaw, et al., pp. 12–18.
Washington, D.C.: Special Publication Series, National Academy of
Economics and Political Science, American University, No. 16.
"Quantification in Economics: Its History." In *Quantity and Quality*, edited
by Daniel Lerner, pp. 129–211. Glencoe, Ill.: Free Press.
"Summary, Synthesis, Interpretation." In *Natural Resources and Eco-
nomic Growth*, edited by Joseph J. Spengler, pp. 275–303. Washington,
D.C.: Resources for the Future, Inc.
"Theory, Ideology, Non-Economic Values, and Politico-Economic De-

velopment." In *Traditions, Values, and Socio-Economic Development,* edited by Ralph Braibanti and Joseph J. Spengler, pp. 1–56. Durham, N.C.: Duke University Press.

1962

"Aging Populations: Mechanics, Historical Emergence, Impact." *Law and Contemporary Problems* 27: 2–21.

"Food for an Exploding World Population." In *Food for World Peace,* edited by Roy M. Kottman, pp. 67–76. Columbus: Ohio State University Press.

"Population and Freedom." *Population Review* 6: 74–82.

"Population Movements and Economic Development in Nigeria." In *The Nigerian Political Scene,* edited by Robert O. Tilman and R. Taylor Cole, pp. 147–197. Durham, N.C.: Duke University Press.

"Role of Competition and Monopoly in Economic Development." In *Competition, Cartels and Their Regulation,* edited by J. P. Miller, pp. 7–58. Amsterdam: North-Holland Publishing Co.

"Some Society-Wide Research and Development Institutions: Comment." In National Bureau of Economic Research, *The Rate and Direction of Inventive Activity: Economic and Social Factors,* pp. 434–440. Princeton: Princeton University Press.

1963

"African Economic Prospects." *The High School Journal* 47: 71–88.

"Aging Populations." In *Employment, Income, and Retirement Problems of the Aged,* edited by Juanita M. Kreps, pp. 25–50. Durham, N.C.: Duke University Press.

"Arthasastra Economics." In *Administration and Economic Development in India,* edited by Ralph Braibanti and Joseph J. Spengler, pp. 224–259. Durham, N.C.: Duke University Press.

"Bureaucracy and Economic Development." In *Bureaucracy and Political Development,* edited by Joseph LaPalombara, pp. 199–232. Princeton: Princeton University Press.

"Demographic and Economic Change in the South, 1940–1960." In *Change in the Contemporary South,* edited by Allan P. Sindler, pp. 26–63. Durham, N.C.: Duke University Press.

"Equity and Social Credit for the Retired." With Juanita M. Kreps. In ibid., pp. 198–229.

"Machine-Made Justice: Some Implications." *Law and Contemporary Problems* 28: 36–52.

1964

"Comment on 'Usury in Medieval India.' " *Comparative Studies in Society and History* 6: 420–423.

"Creativity Versus Cultural Drift." *South Atlantic Quarterly* 63: 275–294.
"Economic Prospects in Asia." *The High School Journal* 47: 353–368.
"Economic Thought of Islam: Ibn Khaldun." *Comparative Studies in Society and History* 6: 268–306.
"The Economics of Population Growth." In *The Population Crisis and the Use of World Resources,* edited by Stuart Mudd, pp. 73–93. The Hague: W. Junk, Publishers.
"Population and Economic Growth." In *Population: The Vital Revolution,* edited by Ronald Freedman, pp. 59–69. New York: Doubleday & Co.
"Population Movements and Problems in Sub-Saharan Africa." In *Economic Development for Africa South of the Sahara* (proceedings of a conference held by the International Economic Association), edited by E. A. G. Robinson, pp. 281–304. London: Macmillan and Co., Ltd.
"Ssu-ma Ch'ien, Unsuccessful Exponent of Laissez Faire." *Southern Economic Journal* 30: 223–243.

1965

"El ambiente físico y el crecimiento de las economías en la América del Sur." *Revista de economía Latinoamericana* (1965): 135–194.
"Coin Shortage: Modern and Premodern." *National Banking Review* 3: 201–216.
"Kinked Demand Curves: By Whom First Used?" *Southern Economic Journal* 32: 81–84.
"Social Evolution and the Theory of Economic Development." In *Social Change in Developing Areas,* edited by H. R. Barringer, G. I. Blanksten, and R. W. Mack, pp. 243–272. Cambridge, Mass.: Schenkman.
"The Social Security and Pension Fund Systems – Their Place in the American Value Structure: Comment." With Juanita M. Kreps. *Journal of Risk and Insurance* 32: 621–628.
"Southern Economic Trends and Prospects." In *Continuity and Change in Sociological Perspective,* edited by J. C. McKinney and E. T. Thompson, pp. 107–131. Durham, N.C.: Duke University Press.
"Today's Circumstances and Yesterday's Theories: Malthus on 'Services.'" *Kyklos* 18: 601–614.

1966

"The Aging of Individuals and Populations: Its Macroeconomic Aspects." In *Aging and Social Policy,* edited by John C. McKinney and Frank T. de Vyver, pp. 42–77. New York: Appleton-Century-Crofts.
"Breakdowns in Modernization." In *Modernization,* edited by Myron Weiner, pp. 321–333. New York: Basic Books.
"The Economist and the Population Question." *American Economic Review* 56: 1–24.
"An Economist's Challenge: The Elastic Dollar." *Arizona Review* 15 (October): 6, 10–11, 15.

"The Implications of Population Change for Business." *Commercial and Financial Chronicle* 204 (August 11): 3, 26–27.

"The International Diffusion of Economic Ideas Within the Commonwealth." In *A Decade of the Commonwealth, 1955–1964*, edited by W. B. Hamilton, Kenneth Robinson, and C. D. W. Goodwin, pp. 211–235. Durham, N.C.: Duke University Press.

"Introduction." In *Economic Systems and Public Policy: Essays in Honor of Calvin Bryce Hoover*, edited by Robert S. Smith and Frank T. de Vyver, pp. ix–xix. Durham, N.C.: Duke University Press.

"The Leisure Component of Economic Growth." With Juanita M. Kreps. In National Commission on Technology, Automation, and Economic Progress, *The Employment Impact of Technological Change* 2 (appendix): 348–397. Washington, D.C.

"Malthus After Two Centuries." The *Jefferson Standard Economics Lectures for 1966*, pp. 3–20. Given at Guilford College, Greensboro, N.C., March 30.

"Nicholas Biddle." "Henry Charles Carey." "Karl Menger." "Vilfredo Pareto." "David Ricardo." In *Encyclopedia Britannica*. Chicago.

"Some Economic and Related Determinants Affecting the Older Worker's Occupational Role." In *Social Aspects of Aging*, edited by Ida H. Simpson and John C. McKinney, pp. 3–44. Durham N.C.: Duke University Press.

"Les Théories économiques de Boisguilbert comparées à celles des réformateurs de son temps." In *Pierre de Boisguilbert ou la naissance de l'economie politique*, edited by Alfred Sauvy, 1: 1–26. Paris: L'Institute national d'etudes démographiques.

"Values and Fertility Analysis." *Demography* 3: 109–130.

"Was Malthus Right?" *The Southern Economic Journal* 33: 17–34.

1967

"Africa and the Theory of Optimum City Size." In *The City in Modern Africa*, edited by Horace Miner, pp. 55–89. London: Pall Mall Press.

"The Costs of Population Growth." *Alma College Perspective* (Special Issue) 3: 32–38.

"Megalopolis: Resource Conserver or Resource Waster?" *Natural Resources Journal* 7: 376–395.

"Now That The Birth Rate Has Slowed . . . ." *Challenge* 15: 10–11, 39.

"Points of Contact Between the Growth of Population and the Growth of National Product." In *Proceedings of the World Population Conference* (Belgrade, 1965) 4: 108–111. New York: United Nations.

"Population Optima." In *The 99th Hour; The Population Crisis in The United States*, edited by Daniel O. Price, pp. 29–52. Chapel Hill: University of North Carolina Press.

"Services and The Future of the American Economy." *South Atlantic Quarterly* 66: 105–115.

1968

"Agricultural Development Is Not Enough." In *World Population: The View Ahead*, edited by Richard Farmer et al., pp. 104–126. Bloomington, Ind.: Bureau of Business Research, University of Indiana.

"Drift to the City: Way Out?" *South Atlantic Quarterly* 68: 611–626.

"Economics: Its History, Themes, Approaches." *Journal of Economic Issues* 2: 5–30.

"The Economics of Safety." *Law and Contemporary Problems* 33: 619–638.

"Exogeneous and Endogeneous Influences in the Formation of Post-1870 Economic Thought: A Sociology of Knowledge Approach." In *Events, Ideology and Economic Theory: The Determinants of Progress in the Development of Economic Analysis*, edited by Robert V. Eagly, pp. 159–187, 191–204. Detroit: Wayne State University Press.

"Hierarchy vs. Equality: Persisting Conflict." *Kyklos* 21: 217–238.

"Richard Cantillon." "Etienne Bonnot de Condillac." "Economic Thought." "Physiocratic Thought." "Alfred J. Lotka." "Population." "Optimum Population Theory." "John Rae." In *International Encyclopedia of the Social Sciences*. New York: Macmillan.

"Right to Work: A Backward Glance." *Journal of Economic History* 28: 171–196.

"South Asia: Demography, Implications." In *Southern Asia*, edited by Robert I. Crane, pp. 1–27. Atlanta: Southern Regional Education Board.

"World Hunger: Past, Present, Prospective." *World Review of Nutrition and Dietetics* 9: 1–31.

1969

"The Aged and Public Policy." In *Behavior and Adaptation in Later Life*, edited by E. W. Busse and E. Pfeiffer, pp. 367–383. Boston: Little, Brown.

"Allocation and Development, Economic and Political." In *Political and Administrative Development*, edited by Ralph Braibanti, pp. 588–637. Durham, N.C.: Duke University Press.

"Capital-Output Ratios: 'Caveat Emptor.'" *The Pakistan Times*, 9 September 1969, pp. 6–7.

"Cassel on Population." *History of Political Economy* 1: 150–172.

"Evolution of Public-Utility Industry Regulation: Economists and Other Determinants." *The South African Journal of Economics* 37: 3–31.

"India's Prospects According to Jean-Baptiste Say, 1824." *Journal of Asian Studies* 28: 595–600.

"Is Social Science Ready?" *Social Science Quarterly* 50: 6–7.

"Kautilya, Plato, Lord Shang: Comparative Political Economy." *Proceedings of the American Philosophical Society* 113: 450–457.

"Population Problem: In Search of a Solution." *Science* 166: 1234–1238.

"Return to Hobbes?" *South Atlantic Quarterly* 68: 443–453.

"Social Sciences and the Encyclopedia: Trends and a Forecast." *Social Science Quarterly* 50: 213–221.

"Will There Be Too Many People to Feed?" *Duke Alumni Register* (September): 8–13.

1970

"Adam Smith on Population." *Population Studies* 24: 377–388.

"Complementary Approaches to Societal Analysis: The Economic Versus the Sociological." In *Theoretical Sociology*, edited by J. C. McKinney and E. A. Tiryakian, pp. 467–497. New York: Appleton-Century-Crofts.

"Cost of Specialization in a Service Economy." *Social Science Quarterly* 51: 237–262.

"An Economically and Eudaemonically Progressive South." *The High School Journal* 54: 1–13.

"Notes on the International Transmission of Economic Ideas." *History of Political Economy* 2: 133–151.

"The Role of Agriculture in the Solution of the Population Problem." In *Studies in Demography*, compiled by Ashish Bose, P. B. Desai, and S. P. Jain, pp. 53–70. London: George Allen and Unwin, Ltd.

1971

"Alberuni: Eleventh-Century Iranian Malthusian?" *History of Political Economy* 3: 92–104.

Declining Population Growth Revisited. Chapel Hill, N.C.: University of North Carolina, The Population Center.

"Homosphere, Seen and Unseen: Retreat from Atomism." *Proceedings, Nineteenth Southern Water Resources and Pollution Control Conference*, April 1970, pp. 7–16.

Indian Economic Thought: Preface to its History. Durham, N.C.: Duke University Press.

"Malthus on Godwin's 'Of Population.'" *Demography* 8: 1–12.

"Population Control; Multidimensional Task." *Vanderbilt Law Review* 24: 525–542.

"Population Optima: Overview." In *Is There an Optimum Level of Population*, edited by J. Fred Singer. New York: McGraw-Hill.

"Small Island Economies: Some Limitations." *South Atlantic Quarterly* 70: 48–61.

Index of Names

DATE DUE